CONNECT TO YOUR COURSEWORK ONLINE.
ANYWHERE, ANY TIME.

McGraw-Hill ConnectPlus™ lets you engage with your course work efficiently through learning personalized for you. Receive an online eBook. Get immediate feedback on online assignments, quizzes, and practice tests. Even access your instructor's class lecture online. Connect to learning and to what you need for future success!

Access Card to accompany

Sociology, 13e
Prince George's Community College
Richard T. Schaefer

To register for and activate your ConnectPlus™ account, simply follow these easy steps.

1. Go to the Connect Plus course web address provided by your instructor.
2. Click on the link to register.
3. When prompted, enter the registration code listed below. Complete the brief registration form that follows online.

Questions? Need help? Visit **mhhe.com/support**

This code is unique and is not related to any other registration number or ID you may have. The registration code is good for one-time use only.

REGISTRATION CODE	

(CAREFULLY SCRATCH GRAY COVERING TO REVEAL ACCESS CODE.)

ONLINE ACCESS CARD FOR CONNECT PLUS
Students: Do not throw away. This is your personalized registration card for online access to eBook and assignment material.

 Learning Solutions

ISBN-13: 978-0-07-765555-6
ISBN-10: 0-07-765555-9

The McGraw-Hill Companies

Student Quick Tips

Use this Student Quick Tips guide for a quick and easy start with McGraw-Hill Connect. You'll get valuable tips on registering, doing assignments, and accessing resources, as well as information about the support center hours.

Getting Started

TIP: To get started in Connect, you will need the following:

- Your instructor's Connect Web Address

  Sample of Connect Web Address:

  http://www.mcgrawhillconnect.com/class/instructorname_section_name

- Connect Access Code

TIP: If you do not have an access code or have not yet secured your tuition funds, you can click "Free Trial" during registration. This trial will provide temporary Connect access (typically three weeks) and will remind you to purchase online access before the end of your trial.

Registration and Sign In

1. Go to the Connect Web Address provided by your instructor
2. Click on **Register Now**
3. Enter your email address

TIP: If you already have a McGraw-Hill account, you will be asked for your password and will not be required to create a new account.

4. Enter a registration code or choose **Buy Online** to purchase access online

5. Follow the on-screen directions

TIP: Please choose your Security Question and Answer carefully. We will ask you for this information if you forget your password.

6. When registration is complete, click on **Go to Connect Now**

7. You are now ready to use **Connect**

Trouble Logging In?

- Ensure you are using the same email address you used during registration

- If you have forgotten your password, click on the "Forgot Password?" link at your Instructor's Connect Course Web Address

- When logged into Connect, you can update your account information (e.g. email address, password, and security question/answer) by clicking on the *"My Account"* link located at the top-right corner

Home (Assignments)

TIP: If you are unable to begin an assignment, verify the following:

- The assignment is available (start and due dates)

- That you have not exceeded the maximum number of attempts

- That you have not achieved a score of 100%

- If your assignment contains questions that require manual grading, you will not be able to begin your next attempt until your instructor has graded those questions

TIP: Based on the assignment policy settings established by your Instructor, you may encounter the following limitations when working on your assignment(s):

- Ability to Print Assignment

- Timed assignments – once you begin a "*timed assignment*," the timer will not stop by design

TIP: "*Save & Exit*" vs. "*Submit*" button

- If you are unable to complete your assignment in one sitting, utilize the "*Save & Exit*" button to save your work and complete it at a later time

- Once you have completed your assignment, utilize the "*Submit*" button in order for your assignment to be graded

Library

TIP: The *Library* section of your Connect account provides shortcuts to various resources.

- If you purchased ConnectPlus, you will see an *eBook* link, which can also be accessed from the section information widget of the *Home* tab

- *Recorded Lectures* can be accessed if your instructor is using *Tegrity Campus* to capture lectures. You may also access recorded lectures when taking an assignment by clicking on the projector icon in the navigation bar

- Many McGraw-Hill textbooks offer additional resources such as narrated slides and additional problems, which are accessible through the *Student Resources* link

Reports

TIP: Once you submit your assignment, you can view your available results in the *Reports* tab.

- If you see a dash (-) as your score, your instructor has either delayed or restricted your ability to see the assignment feedback

- Your instructor has the ability to limit the amount of information (e.g. questions, answers, scores) you can view for each submitted assignment

Need More Help?

CONTACT US ONLINE

Visit us at:

www.mcgrawhillconnect.com/support

Browse our support materials including tutorial videos and our searchable Connect knowledge base. If you cannot find an answer to your question, click on "Contact Us" button to send us an email.

GIVE US A CALL

Call us at:

1-800-331-5094

Our live support is available:

Mon-Thurs: 9 am – 12 pm ET

Friday: 9 am – 7 pm ET

Sunday: 7 pm – 12 pm ET

Sociology's Global View

Sociology explores key sociological issues from the viewpoints of many cultures.
This map serves as a quick guide to a *sample* of passages related to globalization.

Africa

1 Cell phones and economic development (South Africa, Uganda) p. 494

2 Trade facilitated by transnational migrants (Africa, Southeast Asia) p. 495

3 Women in politics (Rwanda/USA) p. 378

4 Apartheid (South Africa) p. 248

Asia/Oceania

5 Population control (China, Japan) pp. 442, 443, 445

6 Transmitting culture through curricula (China) pp. 351–352

7 Hidden curriculum (Japan) p. 355

8 Divorce (South Korea) p. 319

9 Infant mortality (Japan) p. 413

10 Internet censorship (China) p. 493

11 Capitalism (China) pp. 397–398

12 Aboriginal people (Australia) p. 251

13 Solar cookers (Nepal) pp. 482–483

14 Working women (Nepal) p. 396

Central Asia

15 Vietnamese Americans return (Vietnam) pp. 253–254

16 Households without television (Bangladesh, India) pp. 151–152

17 Infant mortality (Afghanistan) p. 413

18 Population growth (Afghanistan, India) pp. 442–443, 444

19 Subcultures of call centers (India) p. 59

20 Treatment of cows (India) pp. 13–14

21 Caste system (India) pp. 188–189

22 Religion (India) pp. 342–343

23 Education of girls (Afghanistan) p. 358

24 McDonalds overseas (India) p. 58

25 Median age at first marriage (India) p. 313

26 Tolerance of cloning and stem cell research (India) p. 342

27 Microfinancing (Bangladesh, India) pp. 403–404

28 Women and new social improvements (India) p. 474

Europe

29 Fair trade movement (United Kingdom) p. 392

30 Adult children living with parents (Italy) p. 316

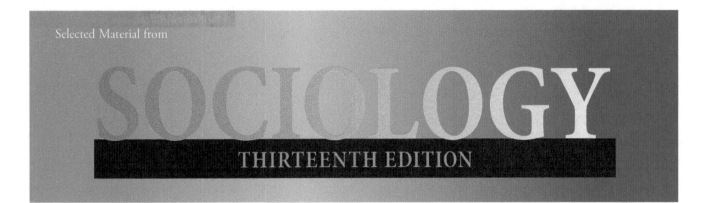

Selected Material from

SOCIOLOGY

THIRTEENTH EDITION

Richard T. Schaefer

DePaul University

PRINCE GEORGE'S COMMUNITY COLLEGE

 Learning Solutions

Boston   Burr Ridge, IL   Dubuque, IA   New York   San Francisco   St. Louis
Bangkok   Bogotá   Caracas   Lisbon   London   Madrid
Mexico City   Milan   New Delhi   Seoul   Singapore   Sydney   Taipei   Toronto

The McGraw·Hill Companies

Selected Material from
SOCIOLOGY, Thirteenth Edition
PRINCE GEORGE'S COMMUNITY COLLEGE

1 2 3 4 5 6 7 8 9 0 BOM BOM 14 13 12

ISBN-13: 978-0-07-765554-9
ISBN-10: 0-07-765554-0

Part of

ISBN-13: 978-0-07-765556-3
ISBN-10: 0-07-765556-7

Learning Solutions Consultant: Dave Fleming
Production Editor: Nina Meyer
Cover Design: Fairfax Hutter
Printer/Binder: BookMasters, Inc.

about the author

Richard T. Schaefer: Professor, DePaul University
B.A. Northwestern University
M.A., Ph.D. University of Chicago

Growing up in Chicago at a time when neighborhoods were going through transitions in ethnic and racial composition, Richard T. Schaefer found himself increasingly intrigued by what was happening, how people were reacting, and how these changes were affecting neighborhoods and people's jobs. His interest in social issues caused him to gravitate to sociology courses at Northwestern University, where he eventually received a BA in sociology.

"Originally as an undergraduate I thought I would go on to law school and become a lawyer. But after taking a few sociology courses, I found myself wanting to learn more about what sociologists studied, and fascinated by the kinds of questions they raised." This fascination led him to obtain his MA and PhD in sociology from the University of Chicago. Dr. Schaefer's continuing interest in race relations led him to write his master's thesis on the membership of the Ku Klux Klan and his doctoral thesis on racial prejudice and race relations in Great Britain.

Dr. Schaefer went on to become a professor of sociology, and now teaches at DePaul University in Chicago. In 2004 he was named to the Vincent DePaul professorship in recognition of his undergraduate teaching and scholarship. He has taught introductory sociology for over 35 years to students in colleges, adult education programs, nursing programs, and even a maximum-security prison. Dr. Schaefer's love of teaching is apparent in his interaction with his students. "I find myself constantly learning from the students who are in my classes and from reading what they write. Their insights into the material we read or current events that we discuss often become part of future course material and sometimes even find their way into my writing."

Dr. Schaefer is the author of the ninth edition of *Sociology: A Brief Introduction* (McGraw-Hill, 2011), *Sociology in Modules* (McGraw-Hill, 2011), and of the fifth edition of *Sociology Matters* (McGraw-Hill, 2012). He is also the author of *Racial and Ethnic Groups,* now in its thirteenth edition (2012), and *Race and Ethnicity in the United States,* seventh edition, both published by Pearson. Together with William Zellner, he coauthored the ninth edition of *Extraordinary Groups,* published by Worth in 2011. Dr. Schaefer served as the general editor of the three-volume *Encyclopedia of Race, Ethnicity, and Society,* published by Sage in 2008. His articles and book reviews have appeared in many journals, including *American Journal of Sociology; Phylon: A Review of Race and Culture; Contemporary Sociology; Sociology and Social Research; Sociological Quarterly;* and *Teaching Sociology.* He served as president of the Midwest Sociological Society in 1994–1995.

Dr. Schaefer's advice to students is to "look at the material and make connections to your own life and experiences. Sociology will make you a more attentive observer of how people in groups interact and function. It will also make you more aware of people's different needs and interests—and perhaps more ready to work for the common good, while still recognizing the individuality of each person."

brief contents

contents

PART 1
The Sociological Perspective

PART 2
Organizing Social Life

PART 3
Social Inequality

PART *4*
Social Institutions

chapter opening excerpts

Every chapter in this textbook begins with an excerpt from one of the works listed here. These excerpts convey the excitement and relevance of sociological inquiry and draw readers into the subject matter from each chapter.

boxed features

RESEARCH TODAY

SOCIOLOGY IN THE GLOBAL COMMUNITY

SOCIOLOGY ON CAMPUS

TAKING SOCIOLOGY TO WORK

TREND**SPOTTING**

social policy sections

maps

summing UP tables

preface

Sociology leads students to move beyond their intuitive understanding of the social world and to instead examine society by applying a sociological perspective to contemporary issues, events, and everyday life. Combining balanced coverage of theory with current research findings, examples that students can easily relate to, and abundant learning aids, the new edition continues to encourage the development of a sociological imagination that students can use in class and take with them on campus, in their careers, and into their communities.

Introducing . . .

This edition of *Sociology* is available to instructors and students in traditional print format, as well as online with an integrated e-Book, interactive activities, videos, and an adaptive learning system that generates a study plan specifically designed to address each student's strengths and weaknesses. These online tools and resources, collectively called *Connect Sociology,* make managing assignments easier for instructors and learning and studying more engaging and efficient for students.

LESS MANAGING.
MORE TEACHING.
GREATER LEARNING.

PREPARING STUDENTS FOR SUCCESS

McGraw-Hill Connect™ is a web-based assignment and assessment platform that helps you connect your students to their coursework and to success beyond the course.

1 2 3 ▶

WATCH INTRO VIDEO ▶
VIEW FULL PRODUCT TOUR ▶
GET STARTED ▶

GET TO KNOW CONNECT ▶

connect
ASSIGN | ASSESS ONLINE

Taking Sociology with You
in College

NEW!

Thinking Critically: These questions, appearing at the end of each section, prompt students to review and reflect on the content.

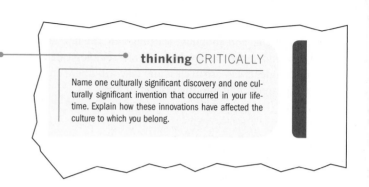

thinking CRITICALLY

Name one culturally significant discovery and one culturally significant invention that occurred in your lifetime. Explain how these innovations have affected the culture to which you belong.

Do you know the answer? (Be honest.)

| Easy! | Think I've got it | Unsure... | No Idea | Skip |

| Hmm, did know it | Almost had it... | No, had no idea | Skip |

NEW!

LearnSmart: An adaptive learning system designed to help students learn faster, study more efficiently, and retain more knowledge for greater success.

Chapter-Opening Excerpts: Each chapter opens with a lively excerpt from the writing of sociologists and others working in related fields, clearly conveying the excitement and relevance of sociological inquiry.

❝ I was made in America. My *Jingle These* Christmas boxers were made in Bangladesh.

I had an all-American childhood in rural Ohio. My all-American blue jeans were made in Cambodia.

I wore flip-flops every day for a year when I worked as a SCUBA diving instructor in Key West. They were made in China.

One day while staring at a pile of clothes on the floor, I noticed the tag of my favorite T-shirt: "Made in Honduras."

I read the tag. My mind wandered. A quest was born. Where am I wearing? It seems like a simple question with a simple answer. It's not.

The question inspired the quest that took me around the globe. It cost me a lot of things, not the least of which was my consumer innocence. Before the quest, I could put on a piece of clothing without reading its tag and thinking about Arifa in Bangladesh or Dewan in China, about their children, their hopes and dreams, and the challenges they face.

Where am I wearing? This isn't so much a question related to geography and clothes, but about the people who make our clothes and the texture of their lives. This quest is about the way *we* live and the way *they* live; because when it comes to clothing, others make it, and we have it made. And there's a big, big difference. . . .

Where am I wearing? This isn't so much a question related to geography and clothes, but about the people who make our clothes and the texture of their lives.

Workers flood the narrow alley beside the Delta Apparel Factory in San Pedro Sula, Honduras. They rush to catch one of the many waiting buses at the highway. Merchants hoping to part them from a portion of their daily earnings—$4 to $5—fight for their attention. Vehicles push through the crowd. A minivan knocks over a girl in her midtwenties and then runs over her foot. She curses, is helped to her feet, and limps onto a waiting bus.

The buildings behind the fence are shaded in Bahamian pastels and very well kept. The shrubs have been recently shaped, and the grass trimmed. In the bright Honduran sun, they seem as pleasant as a factory can get.

The lady at Delta Apparel, based in Georgia, giggled at me on the phone when I told her my plans. She was happy to tell me that their Honduran factory was located in the city of Villanueva just south of San Pedro Sula. She even wished me good luck.

Now that I'm in Honduras, the company doesn't think it's very funny.

I stand among the chaos overwhelmed. A thousand sets of eyes stare at me; perhaps they recognize my T-shirt. The irony that this is Tattoo's tropical paradise wore off long ago—somewhere between the confrontation with the big-bellied guards at the factory gate who had guns shoved down their pants like little boys playing cowboy and the conversation with the tight-lipped company representative who failed to reveal much of anything about my T-shirt or the people who assembled it. There was no way I was getting onto the factory floor. All I learned was that eight humans of indiscriminate age and sex stitched my shirt together in less than five minutes—not exactly information that required traveling all the way to Honduras to obtain. ❞

(Timmerman 2009:xiii–xiv, 14) Additional information about this excerpt can be found on the Online Learning Center at www.mhhe.com/schaefer13e.

SOCIOLOGY ON CAMPUS

3-4 A Culture of Cheating?

On November 21, 2002, after issuing several warnings, officials at the U.S. Naval Academy seized the computers of almost 100 midshipmen suspected of downloading movies and music illegally from the Internet. Officers at the school may have taken the unusually strong action to avoid liability on the part of the U.S. government, which owns the computers students were using. But across the nation, college administrators have been trying to restrain students from downloading pirated entertainment for free. The practice is so widespread, it has been slowing down the high-powered computer networks colleges and universities depend on for research and admissions.

Illegal downloading is just one aspect of the growing problem of copyright violation, both on campus and off. Now that college students can use personal computers to surf the Internet, most do their research online. Apparently, the temptation to cut and paste passages from website postings and pass them off as one's own is irresistible to many.

Surveys done by the Center for Academic Integrity show that from 1999 to 2005, the percentage of students who approved of this type of plagiarism rose from 10 percent to 41 percent. At the same time, the percentage who considered cutting and pasting from the Internet to be a serious form of cheating fell from 68 percent to 23 percent. Perhaps the worst form of Internet plagiarism is the purchase of entire papers from other writers. Increasingly, the websites that sell essays to

students are based in other countries, including India, Ukraine, Nigeria, and the Philippines.

The Center for Academic Integrity estimates that at most schools, more than 75 percent of the students engage in some form of cheating.

The Center for Academic Integrity estimates that at most schools, more than 75 percent of the students engage in some form of cheating. Students not only cut passages from the Internet and paste them into their papers without citing the source; they share questions and answers on

exams, collaborate on assignments they are supposed to do independently, and even falsify the results of their laboratory experiments.

To address what they consider an alarming trend, many schools are rewriting or adopting new academic honor codes. Observers contend that the increase in student cheating reflects widely publicized instances of cheating in public life, which have served to create an alternative set of values in which the end justifies the means. When young people see sports heroes, authors, entertainers, and corporate executives exposed for cheating in one form or another, the message seems to be "Cheating is okay, as long as you don't get caught."

LET'S DISCUSS

1. Do you know anyone who has engaged in Internet plagiarism? What about cheating on tests or falsifying laboratory results? If so, how did the person justify these forms of dishonesty?
2. Even if cheaters aren't caught, what negative effects does their academic dishonesty have on them? What effects does it have on students who are honest? Could an entire college or university suffer from students' dishonesty?

Sources: Argetsinger and Krim 2002; Bartlett 2009; Center for Academic Integrity 2006; R. Thomas 2003; Toppo 2011; Zernike 2002.

---

orientation. Soon, however, it took on a global meaning—especially after 9/11, as Americans wondered, "Why do they hate us?" Through 2000, global studies of public opinion had reported favorable views of the United States in countries as diverse as Morocco and Germany. But by 2003, in the wake of the U.S. invasion of Iraq, foreign opinion of the United States had become quite negative (J. Hunter 1991; Kohut ...

occupations of the early 21st century as a "clash of civilizations." According to this thesis, cultural and religious identities, rather than national or political loyalties, are becoming the prime source of international conflict. Critics of this thesis point out that conflict over values is nothing new; only our ability to create havoc and violence has grown. Furthermore, ... of a clash of "civilizations" disguises the sharp ...

THINKING ABOUT **MOVIES**

Brokeback Mountain

In the rural West, two men struggle to reconcile their social roles with their personal identities.

Frozen River

Two working-class women overcome racial prejudice to form an unlikely friendship.

When the Levees Broke

Spike Lee directs this documentary about the devastating social costs of Hurricane Katrina.

25

Taking Sociology with You

in Your Career

NEW!

Taking Sociology with You: These critical thinking questions and reflection prompts at the end of each chapter encourage students to apply the material that they have just read to their daily lives.

Taking Sociology to Work: These boxes underscore the value of an undergraduate or community college degree in sociology by profiling individuals who majored in sociology and now use its principles in their work.

Use Your Sociological Imagination: These short, thought-provoking sections encourage students to apply the sociological concepts they have learned to the world around them.

RESEARCH TODAY

1-1 Looking at the Gulf Coast Oil Spill from Four Sociological Perspectives

The Gulf Coast oil spill, which began on April 20, 2010, dominated the national news in the United States for much of that year. Like other disasters, the huge spill had social effects that can be analyzed from the four major sociological perspectives.

SWIMMING WATER QUALITY STATUS

HEALTH ADVISORY:

THE PUBLIC IS ADVISED NOT TO SWIM IN THESE WATERS DUE TO THE PRESENCE OF OIL-RELATED CHEMICALS

Functionalist View

In evaluating the effects of the Gulf Coast oil spill, functionalists would stress society's supportive function. For example:

- Functionalists might expect a revitalization of the environmental movement, as happened in the early 1900s after the damming of the Hetch Hetchy Valley just outside Yosemite, and later in the 1990s, after massive wildfires swept through the Everglades.

- Functionalists might note full employment in selected occupations, such as the manufacture of containment booms, even when jobs in other industries were scarce.

- Functionalists would observe that churches and other charities along the Gulf Coast provided both spiritual and material support to households affected by the spill.

- Functionalists would not be surprised that because offshore oil drilling is an integral part of the Gulf Coast economy, the governor of Louisiana strongly opposed a moratorium on deep-sea drilling, despite questions about its safety.

Conflict View

Because conflict theorists see the social order in terms of conflict or tension between competing groups, they would emphasize the coercion and exploitation that underlies relations between the oil companies and Gulf Coast communities:

- The oil industry, conflict theorists would note, is a form of big business, in which profits are more important than workers' health and safety.

- Conflict theorists would emphasize the often-overlooked effect of the spill on minority groups living in inland communities, including Vietnamese Americans, Native American tribal groups, and African Americans. These groups, which were living a marginal existence before the spill, endured particularly significant economic setbacks after the spill.

- Conflict theorists would note that although news outlets tend to focus on oil spills that affect wealthy industrial countries, often the worst spills afflict communities in disadvantaged developing nations, such as Nigeria.

Feminists would note that during times of economic upheaval and dislocation, women bear a disproportionate share of the burden in their role as caregivers.

Feminist View

Feminists would note that during times of economic upheaval and dislocation, such as the Gulf Coast oil crisis, women bear a disproportionate share of the burden in their role as caregivers:

- As family wage earners leave home to seek work elsewhere, women with children or elderly dependents are left to cope as best they can.

- With time, the physical separation these families experience may turn into marital separation.

Interactionist View

Interactionists would examine the Gulf Coast oil spill on the micro level, by focusing on how it shaped personal relations and day-to-day social behavior:

- Interactionists would note that difficult times often strengthen ties among neighbors and family members.

- At the same time, stressful events can contribute to social breakdowns, including divorce or even suicide—a pattern researchers observed in the aftermath of the Exxon *Valdez* oil spill in 1989.

Despite their differences, functionalists, conflict theorists, feminists, and interactionists would all agree that disasters like the Gulf Coast oil spill are a worthy subject for sociological study.

LET'S DISCUSS

1. Which of the four sociological perspectives seems most useful to you in analyzing the Gulf Coast oil crisis? Why?

2. For many people, the worldwide economic crisis that began in 2008 had disastrous personal consequences. Use the four sociological perspectives to analyze what happened to you, your family, and your community during the Great Recession.

Sources: Capriccioso 2010; Freudenburg and Gramling 2010; Greenemeier 2010; Jopling and Morse 2010; Liptak 2010; Molotch 1970; Samuels 2010; N. Wallace 2010.

APPENDIX Careers in Sociology

For the past two decades the number of U.S. college students who have graduated with a degree in sociology has risen steadily (Figure 1-2, page 22). In this appendix we'll consider some of the options these students have after completing their undergraduate education.

How do students first learn about the sociological perspective on society? Some may take a sociology course in high school. Others may study sociology at community college, where 40 percent of all college students in the United States are enrolled. Indeed, many future sociology majors first develop their sociological imaginations at a community college.

An undergraduate degree in sociology doesn't just serve as excellent preparation for future graduate work in sociology. It also provides a strong liberal arts background for entry-level positions in business, social services, foundations, community organizations, not-for-profit groups, law enforcement, and many government jobs. A number of fields—among them marketing, public relations, and broadcasting—now require investigative skills and an understanding of the diverse groups found in today's multiethnic and multinational environment. Moreover, a sociology degree requires accomplishment in oral and written communication, interpersonal skills, problem solving, and critical thinking—all job-related skills that may give sociology graduates an advantage over those who pursue more technical degrees.

Consequently, while few occupations specifically require an undergraduate degree in sociology, such academic training can be an important asset in entering a wide range of occupations. To emphasize this point, a number of chapters in this book highlight a real-life professional who describes how the study of sociology has helped in his or her career. For example, in Chapter 6 a Taking Sociology to Work box explains how a college graduate uses her training

in sociology in managing a small business that she started. And in Chapter 17, another Taking Sociology to Work box shows how a recent graduate uses the skill set he acquired as a sociology major in his role as a government analyst.

Figure 1-3 on page 22 summarizes the sources of employment for those with BA or BS degrees in sociology. It shows that the areas of nonprofit organizations, education, business, and government offer major career opportunities for sociology graduates. Undergraduates who know where their career interests lie are well advised to enroll in sociology courses and specialties best suited to those interests. For example, students hoping to become health planners would take a class in medical sociology; students seeking employment as social science research assistants would focus on courses in statistics and methods. Internships, such as placements at city planning agencies and survey research organizations, afford another way for sociology students to prepare for careers. Studies show that students who choose an internship placement have less trouble finding jobs, obtain better jobs, and enjoy greater job satisfaction than students without internship placements. Finally, students should expect to change fields during their first five years of employment after graduation—for example, from sales and marketing to management (American Sociological Association 2009; Salem and Grabarek 1986; Spalter-Roth and Van Vooren 2010).

Many college students view social work as the field most closely associated with sociology. Traditionally, social workers received their undergraduate training in sociology and allied fields such as psychology and counseling. After some practical experience, social workers would generally seek a master's degree in social work (MSW) to be considered for supervisory or administrative positions. Today, however, some students choose (where it is available) to pursue a bachelor's degree in social work (BSW). This degree prepares graduates for direct ser-

- Trendspotting box, "Working Mothers"
- Research Today box, "Give Me a Male Boss, Please"
- Updated Social Policy section, "The Battle over Abortion from a Global Perspective," with discussion of the controversy over "womb lynchings"

Chapter 13: Stratification by Age

- Chapter-opening excerpt from *Shock of Gray* by Ted C. Fishman
- Two Thinking Critically exercises
- Discussion of the projected rise in the median age of the world's population
- Research Today box, "Native Americans and Death"
- Figure, "Percentage of U.S. Population in Selected Age Groups, 1970–2050"
- Trendspotting box, "Job Wanted—Over 65"

Chapter 14: The Family and Intimate Relationships

- Chapter-opening excerpt from *The Marriage-Go-Round: The State of Marriage and the Family in America Today,* by Andrew J. Cherlin
- Trendspotting box, "Cougars on the Rise"
- Updated discussion of Internet romance
- Statistics on interracial and interethnic marriages in the United States
- Discussion of the impact of new media technologies, including the Internet, on the practice of polygyny in Turkey and Morocco
- Sociology in the Global Community box, "Family Life, Italian Style: Thirty-Something and Living with Mom"
- Discussion of the foreign perspective on international adoption
- Updated discussion of state law regarding adoption by unmarried and gay and lesbian couples
- Use Your Sociological Imagination exercise
- Updated Research Today box, "Divorce and Military Deployment," with photo
- Updated discussion of the cost of raising children as a consideration in marriage without children
- Updated discussion of public opinion of gay marriage, with Mapping Life Nationwide map, "Gay Marriage by State"

Chapter 15: Religion

- Chapter-opening excerpt from *Toying with God: The World of Religious Games and Dolls,* by Niki Bado-Fralick and Rebecca Sachs Norris
- Trendspotting box, "None of the Above:

The Nonreligious"
- Figure, "Test Your Religious Knowledge"
- Discussion of the socialization function of religion
- Use Your Sociological Imagination exercise
- Research Today box, "Wicca: Religion or Quasi-Religion?"

Chapter 16: Education

- Chapter-opening excerpt from *The Death and Life of the Great American School System,* by Diane Ravitch
- Figure, "Annual Median Earnings by Educational Level"
- Trendspotting box, "Rising College Enrollment among Racial and Ethnic Minorities, Women"
- Figure, "Tuition Costs, 1976–2009"
- Taking Sociology to Work box, "Diane Belcher, Assistant Director of Volunteer Services, New River Community College"
- Discussion of the immigration to the United States of families from countries where homeschooling is prohibited by law
- Social Policy section on charter schools, with Mapping Life Nationwide map, "Charter Schools"

Chapter 17: Government and Politics

- Chapter-opening excerpt from *Is Voting for Young People?* By Martin P. Wattenberg
- Sociology in the Global Community box, "Sovereignty in the Aloha State"
- Trendspotting box, "Democracy on the Rise?"
- Discussion of the nation-state perspective on the supposed socioeconomic benefits of war
- Taking Sociology to Work box, "Joseph W. Drummond, Management Analyst, U.S. Army Space and Missile Defense Command"

- Updated and expanded coverage of terrorism, including (a) factors that facilitate its development and (b) cyberattacks
- Updated discussion of the role of the Internet in politics, including social media sites
- Updated Social Policy section on campaign financing, including discussion of the 2010 Supreme Court decision in *Citizens United v. Federal Election Commission*

Chapter 18: The Economy and Work

- Chapter-opening excerpt from *The Fair Trade Revolution,* edited by John Bowes, with key term treatment of *fair trade*
- Trendspotting box, "Occupational Growth and Decline"
- Expanded coverage of the informal economy, including a cross-national comparison
- Dedicated section on the U.S. economy, with subsection on offshoring
- Social Policy section, "Microfinancing," including (a) research on the sophisticated use of financial tools by poor families in developing nations and (b) criticisms of microfinancing

Chapter 19: Health and the Environment

- Chapter-opening excerpt from *Shopping Our Way to Safety: How We Changed from Protecting the Environment to Protecting Ourselves,* by Andrew Szasz
- Mapping Life Nationwide map, "Percentage of Children without Health Insurance"
- Discussion of the Patient Protection and Affordable Care Act (2010)
- Trendsetting box, "Medical Technology and Telemedicine"
- Research Today box, "Health Care, Retail Style"
- Discussion of the Tea Party movement's objection to health care reform
- Subsection on ecological modernization, with key term treatment
- Coverage of the globalization of the environmental justice movement
- Coverage of the BP Gulf oil spill of 2010
- Discussion of the problem of water scarcity and its role in promoting armed conflict
- Figure, "Are U.S. Teens Green Enough?"

Chapter 20: Population, Communities, and Urbanization

- Chapter-opening excerpt from *Aerotropolis: The Way We'll Live Next,* by John Kasarda and Greg Lindsay

- Figure, "Population Growth Rate in Selected Countries"
- Trendspotting box, "Urbanization and Its Costs"
- Discussion of the *decoupling* of agriculture and small rural communities
- Figure, "Change in Population by County, 2000–2010"

Chapter 21: Collective Behavior and Social Movements

- Chapter-opening excerpt from *The Global Grapevine: Why Rumors of Terrorism, Immigration, and Trade Matter,* by Gary Alan Fine and Bill Ellis
- Trendspotting box, "Gun Control: The Public Speaks"
- Discussion of the mobilization of social movements by institutional insiders

Chapter 22: Social Change in the Global Community

- Chapter-opening excerpt from *I Live in the Future and Here's How It Works: Why Your World, Work, and Brain Are Being Creatively Disrupted,* by Nick Bilton
- Discussion of the vested interests that opposed cancellation of NASA's Constellation project
- Trendspotting box, "Longer Life Spans, More Social Change"
- Case study, "Social Change in Dubai"
- Discussion of the use of cell phones to improve agriculture in developing countries, as an alternative to biotechnology
- Discussion of the role of migrants in facilitating global trade and development in the Social Policy section on transnationals

Teaching and Learning with *Sociology*

The complete content of *Sociology* is available to instructors and students in traditional print format, as well as online with integrated and time-saving tools that involve students personally, critically, and actively.

The online tools, collectively called *Connect Sociology*, make managing assignments easier for instructors, and make learning and studying more motivating and efficient for students.

- **LearnSmart.** An adaptive learning system designed to help students learn faster, study more efficiently, and retain more knowledge for greater success.

- **Real-time Reports.** These printable, exportable reports show how well each student (or section) is performing on each course segment. Instructors can use this feature to spot problem areas *before* they crop up on an exam.

- **Learning Objectives.** Every assignment and every course resource can be sorted by learning objective, with point-and-click flexibility. Instructors can use this feature to customize the content and course materials to meet the particular needs of their syllabus.

- **Assignable and assessable activities.** Instructors can deliver assignments and tests easily online, and students can practice skills that fulfill learning objectives at their own pace and on their own schedule.

- **Instructor's Manual.** The Instructor's Manual provides sociology instructors with detailed chapter outlines and summaries, learning objectives, additional lecture ideas, class discussion topics, essay questions, topics for student research, critical thinking questions, video resources, and additional readings. The Instructor's Manual also features a special section on service learning resources and suggestions.

- **PowerPoint Slides.** These slides include bulleted lecture points, figures, and maps. They can be used as is or modified to meet the needs of individual instructors.

- **Student Study Guide.** This resource includes a detailed list of key points, key terms and their definitions, true or false self-quizzes, multiple-choice quizzes, fill-in-the-blank questions, and social policy questions.

- **Test Bank.** This collection includes multiple-choice, true or false, and essay questions for every chapter. Questions test recall of important factual information, application of theoretical perspectives, and understanding of key sociological concepts. McGraw-Hill's computerized EZ Test allows the instructor to create customized exams using the publisher's supplied test items or the instructor's own questions.

ⓣegrity campus

Tegrity Campus is a service that makes class time available all the time by automatically capturing every lecture in a searchable format for students to review when they study and complete assignments.

With a simple one-click start-and-stop process, you capture all computer screens and corresponding audio. Students replay any part of any class with easy-to-use browser-based viewing on a PC or Mac.

With Tegrity Campus, students quickly recall key moments by using Tegrity Campus's unique search feature. This search helps students efficiently find what they need, when they need it across an entire semester of class recordings.

Help turn all your students' study time into learning moments immediately supported by your lecture. To learn more about Tegrity, watch a two-minute Flash demo at http://tegritycampus.mhhe.com

CourseSmart
Learn Smart. Choose Smart.

Visit coursesmart.com to purchase registration codes for this exciting new product.

CourseSmart offers thousands of the most commonly adopted textbooks across hundreds of courses from a wide variety of higher education publishers. It is the only place for faculty to review and compare the full text of a textbook online, providing immediate access without the environmental impact of requesting a printed exam copy. At CourseSmart, students can save up to 50% off the cost of a printed book, reduce their impact on the environment, and gain access to powerful Web tools for learning, including full text search, notes and highlighting, and e-mail tools for sharing notes among classmates. Learn more at www.coursesmart.com

Acknowledgments
Author Acknowledgments

Since 1999, Elizabeth Morgan has played a most significant role in the development of my introductory sociology books. Fortunately for me, in the 13th edition, Betty has once again been responsible for the smooth integration of all changes and updates.

I deeply appreciate the contributions to this book made by my editors. Development editor Meghan Campbell assisted me to make this edition even better than its predecessors. Dawn Groundwater served as director of development.

I have received strong support and encouragement from Gina Boedeker, executive editor, and Holly Paulsen, production editor. Additional guidance and support were provided by Patrick Brown, marketing manager; Brittany Pogue-Mohammed, editorial coordinator; Andrei Pasternak and Allister Fein, design managers; Nora Agbayani, photo research coordinator; Toni Michaels, photo researcher; Judy Brody, text permissions editor; and Margaret Moore, copyeditor. At DePaul University, assistance has been provided by student workers Jessica Chiarella and Kathleen Tallmadge.

This edition continues to reflect many insightful suggestions made by reviewers of the twelve hardcover editions and the nine paperback brief editions. I have also benefited in earlier editions from the creative ideas of Rhona Robbin, Thom Holmes, and Jinny Joyner.

Finally, I would like to thank Peter D. Schaefer, Marymount Manhattan College, for developing the end-of-chapter sections, "Thinking about Movies."

As is evident from these acknowledgments, the preparation of a textbook is truly a team effort. The most valuable member of this effort continues to be my wife, Sandy. She provides the support so necessary in my creative and scholarly activities.

I have had the good fortune to introduce students to sociology for many years. These students have been enormously helpful in spurring on my sociological imagination. In ways I can fully appreciate but cannot fully acknowledge, their questions in class and queries in the hallway have found their way into this textbook.

Richard T. Schaefer
www.schaefersociology.net
schaeferrt@aol.com

Academic Reviewers

This current edition has benefited from constructive and thorough evaluations provided by sociologists from both two-year and four-year institutions.

Dennis Anderson, *Butler Community College*
Felecia Cantwell, *New Mexico State University*
Heather Griffiths, *Fayetteville State University*
Craig R. Humphrey, *Pennsylvania State University*
Love Mills-Byrd, *Cincinnati State Technical and Community College*
Dan Muhwezi, *Butler Community College*
Hence Parson, *Hutchinson Community College*
Shanta Sharma, *Henderson State University*
Robert Shirilla, *Cuyahoga Community College*
Tomecia Sobers, *Fayetteville Technical Community College*
Brandy Trainor, *Rowan University*
Deidre Tyler, *Salt Lake Community College*
Sally Vyain, *Ivy Technical Community College*

Connect Consultants

The creation of *Connect Sociology* has been a highly collaborative effort. Thank you to the following for their guidance, insight, and innovative suggestions.

James Bazan, *Central Piedmont Community College*
Scott Brooks, *University of California, Riverside*
Susan Cody-Rydzewski, *Georgia Perimeter College*
Russell Davis, *University of West Alabama*
Shelly Dutchin, *Western Technical College*
Isaac Eberstein, *Florida State University*
Tammie Foltz, *Des Moines Area Community College*
John Gannon, *College of Southern Nevada*
Thomas Kersen, *Jackson State University*
Melinda Messineo, *Ball State University*
Tommy Sadler, *Union University*
Theresa Schrantz, *Tarrant County College*
Sharon Wettengel, *Tarrant County College*

Connect Contributors

These instructors contributed their time, thought, and creativity to make our vision for *Connect Sociology* a reality. Thank you to the following content authors.

Heather Griffiths, *Fayetteville State University*
Linda Lombard, *Embry-Riddle Aeronautical University*
Cheryl North, *Tarrant County College*
Denise Shuster, *Owens Community College*
Rachel Stehle, *Cuyahoga Community College*
Brandy Trainor, *Rowan University*
Sally Vyain, *Ivy Tech Community College*
Marie Wallace, *Pima Community College*

Symposia Attendees

Every year McGraw-Hill conducts several Introductory Sociology symposia for instructors from across the country. These events offer a forum for instructors to exchange ideas and experiences with colleagues they might not have the chance to meet otherwise. They also provide an opportunity for members of the McGraw-Hill team to learn about the needs and challenges of the Introductory Sociology course for both instructors and students. The feedback we have received has been invaluable and contributed—directly and indirectly—to this edition of *Sociology:*

Douglas Adams, *University of Arkansas*
Isaac Addai, *Lansing Community College*
Robert Aponte, *Purdue University*
David Arizmendi, *South Texas College*
Sergio Banda, *Fullerton College*
John Batsie, *Parkland College*
James Bazan, *Central Piedmont Community College*
Janice Bending, *University of Cincinnati*
Scott Brooks, *University of California, Riverside*
Elaine Cannon, *El Camino College*
Nina Chapman, *Golden West College*
Margaret Choka, *Pellissippi State Tech College*
Rodney Clayton, *Central Community College*
Susan Cody-Rydzewski, *Georgia Perimeter College*
Charles Combs, *Sinclair Community College*
Lisa Coole, *Bridgewater College*
Carolyn Corrado, *University of Albany*
Larry Curiel, *Cypress College*
Scott Davis, *Treasure Valley Community College*
Aimee Dickinson, *Lorain County Community College*
Joe Donnermeyer, *Ohio State University*
Brian Donovan, *University of Kansas*
Gianna Durso-Finley, *Mercer County Community College*
Shelly Dutchin, *Western Technical College*
Ike Eberstein, *Florida State University*
Samuel Echevarria-Cruz, *Austin Community College*
John Ehle, *Northern Virginia Community College*
David Embrick, *Loyola University*
Kathryn Feltey, *University of Akron*
Tammie Foltz, *Des Moines Area Community College*
John Gannon, *College of Southern Nevada*
Sergio Gomez, *Chaffey College*

Kyra Greene, *San Diego State University*
Mike Greenhouse, *Middlesex County College*
Bram Hamovitch, *Lakeland Community College*
Carl Hand, *Valdosta State University*
Garrison Henderson, *Tarrant County College*
Peter Iadicola, *Indiana University–Purdue University Indianapolis*
Laura Jamison, *Parkland College*
Paul Ketchum, *University of Oklahoma*
Steve Keto, *Kent State University*
Brian Klocke, *State University of New York Plattsburgh*
Jodie Lawston, *DePaul University*
Jason Leiker, *Utah State University*
Joe Lengermann, *University of Maryland*
David Liu, *Harrisburg Area Community College*
David Locher, *Missouri Southern State University*
Michael Loukine, *Northern Michigan University*
Jean Lynch-Brandon, *Lansing Community College*
Lori Maida, *Westchester Community College*
Farshad Malek-Ahmadi, *Naugatuck Valley Community College*
Karen McCue, *Central New Mexico Community College*
Messineo Melinda, *Ball State University*
Kelly Mosel-Talavera, *Texas State University–San Marcos*
Frank Mossadeghi, *Palm Beach Community College*
Cheryl North, *Tarrant County College*
Pat O'Brien, *Elgin Community College*
Jacob Oni, *Cape Cod Community College*

Robert Orrange, *Eastern Michigan University*
Diane Owsley, *Elizabeth Community College*
Kevin Payne, *Park University*
Lisa Pellerin, *Ball State University*
Paul C. Price, *Pasadena City College*
Richard Rosell, *Westchester Community College*
Alan Rudy, *Central Michigan University*
Terri Schrantz, *Tarrant County Community College–Southeast*
Barbara Seiter, *Raritan Valley Community College*
Michelle Smith, *Lakeland Community College*
Rachael Stehle, *Cuyahoga Community College*
Lawrence Stern, *Collin College*
Rose Suggett, *Southeast Community College*
Richard Sweeny, *Modesto Junior College*
Margaret Taylor, *Greenville Technical College*
Baishakhi Banerjee Taylor, *Duke University*
Michelle Stewart Thomas, *Mt. San Antonio College*
Ruth Thompson-Miller, *Texas A&M University*
Ronald Thrasher, *Oklahoma State University*
Vu-Duc Vuong, *DeAnza College*
Marie L. Wallace, *Pima Community College*
Sharon Wettengel, *Tarrant County College*
Amanda White, *St. Louis Community College*
Susan Williams, *Kansas State University*
John Zipp, *University of Akron*

sociology

No matter where you're going—
to work, to study abroad,
or just on vacation—
you can take sociology
and its insights with you.

Understanding Sociology 1

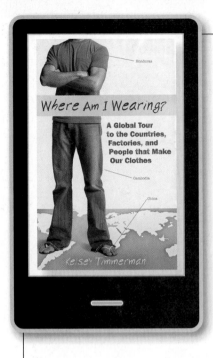

❝ I was made in America. My *Jingle These* Christmas boxers were made in Bangladesh.

I had an all-American childhood in rural Ohio. My all-American blue jeans were made in Cambodia.

I wore flip-flops every day for a year when I worked as a SCUBA diving instructor in Key West. They were made in China.

One day while staring at a pile of clothes on the floor, I noticed the tag of my favorite T-shirt: "Made in Honduras."

I read the tag. My mind wandered. A quest was born.

Where am I wearing? It seems like a simple question with a simple answer. It's not.

The question inspired the quest that took me around the globe. It cost me a lot of things, not the least of which was my consumer innocence. Before the quest, I could put on a piece of clothing without reading its tag and thinking about Arifa in Bangladesh or Dewan in China, about their children, their hopes and dreams, and the challenges they face.

Where am I wearing? This isn't so much a question related to geography and clothes, but about the people who make our clothes and the texture of their lives. This quest is about the way *we* live and the way *they* live; because when it comes to clothing, others make it, and we have it made. And there's a big, big difference. . . .

Workers flood the narrow alley beside the Delta Apparel Factory in San Pedro Sula, Honduras. They rush to catch one of the many waiting buses at the highway. Merchants hoping to part them from a portion of their daily earnings—$4 to $5—fight for their attention. Vehicles push through the crowd. A minivan knocks over a girl in her midtwenties and then runs over her foot. She curses, is helped to her feet, and limps onto a waiting bus.

The buildings behind the fence are shaded in Bahamian pastels and very well kept. The shrubs have been recently shaped, and the grass trimmed. In the bright Honduran sun, they seem as pleasant as a factory can get.

The lady at Delta Apparel, based in Georgia, giggled at me on the phone when I told her my plans. She was happy to tell me that their Honduran factory was located in the city of Villanueva just south of San Pedro Sula. She even wished me good luck.

Now that I'm in Honduras, the company doesn't think it's very funny.

I stand among the chaos overwhelmed. A thousand sets of eyes stare at me; perhaps they recognize my T-shirt. The irony that this is Tattoo's tropical paradise wore off long ago—somewhere between the confrontation with the big-bellied guards at the factory gate who had guns shoved down their pants like little boys playing cowboy and the conversation with the tight-lipped company representative who failed to reveal much of anything about my T-shirt or the people who assembled it. There was no way I was getting onto the factory floor. All I learned was that eight humans of indiscriminate age and sex stitched my shirt together in less than five minutes—not exactly information that required traveling all the way to Honduras to obtain. **❞**

Where am I wearing? This isn't so much a question related to geography and clothes, but about the people who make our clothes and the texture of their lives.

(Timmerman 2009:xiii–xiv, 14) Additional information about this excerpt can be found on the Online Learning Center at www.mhhe.com/schaefer13e.

In his book *Where Am I Wearing? A Global Tour to the Countries, Factories, and People that Make Our Clothes,* journalist Kelsey Timmerman recounts his travels to the countries where his jeans, T-shirts, and flip-flops—the uniform of today's young adult—were made. From Honduras to Bangladesh, from Cambodia to the United States, he tracked down the factories and befriended the seamstresses who labored there. Though owners were reluctant to allow him on the factory floor, they couldn't prevent him from visiting workers' homes and families. Timmerman found that both inside and outside the factory, garment workers lived in what would be considered substandard conditions in the United States. He argues that global apparel companies should take responsibility for conditions at their suppliers' factories, even if those factories are located halfway around the world (Fairtrade Foundation 2010).

Timmerman's book focuses on an unequal global economy, which is a central topic in sociology. His investigative work, like the work of many other journalists, is informed by sociological research that documents the existence and extent of inequality around the world. Social inequality has a pervasive influence on human interactions and institutions. Certain groups of people control scarce resources, wield power, and receive special treatment.

Although it might be interesting to know how one individual, like Kelsey Timmerman or a foreign factory worker, is affected by social inequality, sociologists consider how entire groups of people are affected by such factors, and how society itself might be altered by them. Sociologists, then, are not concerned with what one individual does or does not do, but with what people do as members of a group or in interaction with one another, and what that means for individuals and for society as a whole. For example, sociologists have considered how, together, college students have taken sociology with them, organizing to confront the sportswear companies that underpay the overseas workers who create their team uniforms and T-shirts proclaiming their school pride (Esbenshade 2008; Silverstein 2010).

As a field of study, sociology is extremely broad in scope. You will see throughout this book the range of topics sociologists investigate—from suicide to TV viewing habits, from Amish society to global economic patterns, from peer pressure to genetic engineering. Sociology looks at how others influence our behavior; how major social institutions like the government, religion, and the economy affect us; and how we ourselves affect other individuals, groups, and even organizations.

How did sociology develop? In what ways does it differ from other social sciences? This chapter will explore the nature of sociology as both a field of inquiry and an exercise of the "sociological imagination." We'll look at the discipline as a science and consider its relationship to other social sciences. We'll meet four pioneering thinkers—Émile Durkheim, Max Weber, Karl Marx, and W. E. B. DuBois—and examine the theoretical perspectives that grew out of their work. We'll note some of the practical applications for sociological theory and research. Finally, we'll see how sociology helps us to develop a sociological imagination. For those students interested in exploring career opportunities in sociology, the chapter closes with a special appendix.

What Is Sociology?

"What has sociology got to do with me or with my life?" As a student, you might well have asked this question when you signed up for your introductory sociology course. To answer it, consider these points: Are you influenced by what you see on television? Do you use the Internet? Did you vote in the last election? Are you familiar with binge drinking on campus? Do you use alternative medicine? These are just a few of the everyday life situations described in this book that sociology can shed light on. But as the opening excerpt indicates, sociology also looks at large social issues. We use sociology to investigate why thousands of jobs have moved from the United States to developing nations, what social forces promote prejudice, what leads someone to join a social movement and work for social change, how access to computer technology can reduce social inequality, and why relationships between men and women in Seattle differ from those in Singapore.

Sociology is, simply, the scientific study of social behavior and human groups. It focuses on social relationships; how those relationships influence people's behavior; and how societies, the sum total of those relationships, develop and change.

The Sociological Imagination

In attempting to understand social behavior, sociologists rely on a particular type of critical thinking. A leading sociologist, C. Wright Mills, described such thinking as the **sociological imagination**—an awareness of the relationship between an individual and the wider society, both today and in the past (Mills [1959] 2000a). This awareness allows all of us (not just sociologists) to comprehend the links between our immediate, personal social settings and the remote, impersonal social world that surrounds and helps to shape us. Kelsey Timmerman certainly used a sociological imagination when he studied foreign garment workers.

A key element in the sociological imagination is the ability to view one's own society as an outsider would, rather than only from the perspective of personal experiences and cultural biases. Consider something as simple as sporting events. On college campuses in the United States, thousands of students cheer well-trained football players. In Bali, Indonesia, dozens of spectators gather around a ring to cheer on roosters trained in cockfighting. In both instances, the spectators debate the merits of their favorites and bet on the outcome of the events. Yet what is considered a normal sporting event in one part of the world is considered unusual in another part.

The sociological imagination allows us to go beyond personal experiences and observations to understand broader public issues. Divorce, for example, is unquestionably a personal hardship for a husband and wife who split apart. However, C. Wright Mills advocated using the sociological imagination to view divorce not as simply an individual's personal problem but rather as a societal concern. Using this perspective, we can see that an increase in the divorce rate actually redefines a major social institution—the family. Today's households frequently include stepparents and half-siblings whose parents have divorced and remarried. Through the complexities of the blended family, this private concern becomes a public issue that affects schools, government agencies, businesses, and religious institutions.

The sociological imagination is an empowering tool. It allows us to look beyond a limited understanding of human behavior to see the world and its people in a new way and through a broader lens than we might otherwise use. It may be as simple as understanding why a roommate prefers country music to hip-hop, or it may open up a whole different way of understanding other populations in the world. For example, in the aftermath of the terrorist attacks on the United States on September 11, 2001, many citizens wanted to understand how Muslims throughout the world perceived their country, and why. From time to time this textbook will offer you the chance to exercise your sociological imagination in a variety of situations.

use your sociological *imagination*

You are walking down the street in your city or hometown. In looking around you, you can't help noticing that half or more of the people you see are overweight. How do you explain your observation? If you were C. Wright Mills, how do you think you would explain it?

Sociology and the Social Sciences

Is sociology a science? The term **science** refers to the body of knowledge obtained by methods based on systematic observation. Just like other scientific disciplines, sociology involves the organized, systematic study of phenomena (in this case, human behavior) in order to enhance understanding. All scientists, whether studying mushrooms or murderers, attempt to collect

Sociology is the scientific study of social behavior and human groups.

on? They study the influence that society has on people's attitudes and behavior and the ways in which people interact and shape society. Because humans are social animals, sociologists examine our social relationships with others scientifically. The range of the relationships they investigate is vast, as the current list of sections in the American Sociological Association suggests (Table 1-1).

Let's consider how different social scientists would study the impact of the earthquake that hit Port-au-Prince, the capital of Haiti, in 2010. Historians would stress Haiti's past economic exploitation as a colony of France and its resulting poverty today. Economists would discuss ways to rebuild Haiti's economy, perhaps by diversifying it. Environmental ecologists would treat Haiti and its neighbor, the Dominican Republic, as a single ecosystem—the island of Hispaniola. Psychologists would study individual cases of emotional stress caused by the traumatic event. And political scientists would study the short-term prospects for the nation's governance, which might include trustee status under the United Nations.

What approach would sociologists take? They might consider the possibility of reversing Haitians' generation-long migration from the countryside to the capital city, by making life in rural areas more sustainable. They might study the use of new media, such as Twitter, to funnel donations to charities. They might conduct short- and long-term research on the adoption of

precise information through methods of study that are as objective as possible. They rely on careful recording of observations and accumulation of data.

Of course, there is a great difference between sociology and physics, between psychology and astronomy. For this reason, the sciences are commonly divided into natural and social sciences. **Natural science** is the study of the physical features of nature and the ways in which they interact and change. Astronomy, biology, chemistry, geology, and physics are all natural sciences. **Social science** is the study of the social features of humans and the ways in which they interact and change. The social sciences include sociology, anthropology, economics, history, psychology, and political science.

These social science disciplines have a common focus on the social behavior of people, yet each has a particular orientation. Anthropologists usually study past cultures and preindustrial societies that continue today, as well as the origins of humans. Economists explore the ways in which people produce and exchange goods and services, along with money and other resources. Historians are concerned with the peoples and events of the past and their significance for us today. Political scientists study international relations, the workings of government, and the exercise of power and authority. Psychologists investigate personality and individual behavior. So what do *sociologists* focus

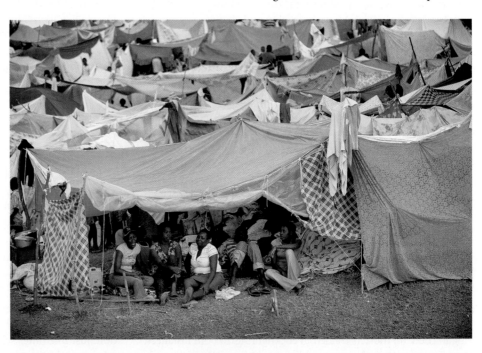

The earthquake that hit Haiti in January 2010 may have lasted only a few minutes, but the social impact on the small, impoverished island nation will last many years. This "temporary" tent city shelters 375,000 people whose homes were destroyed, and for whom there is still no permanent housing, as of June 2011.

Aging and the Life Course	Environment and Technology	Peace, War, and Social Conflict
Alcohol, Drugs, and Tobacco	Ethnomethodology and Conversation Analysis	Political Economy of the World-System
Altruism, Morality, and Sociology	Evolution, Biology, and Sociology	Political Sociology
Animals and Society	Family	Population
Asia and Asian America	Global and Transnational Sociology	Race, Gender, and Class
Body and Embodiment	History of Sociology	Racial and Ethnic Minorities
Children and Youth	Human Rights	Rationality and Society
Collective Behavior and Social Movements	International Migration	Religion
Communication and Information Technologies	Labor and Labor Movements	Science, Knowledge, and Technology
Community and Urban Sociology	Latino/a Sociology	Sex and Gender
Comparative and Historical Sociology	Law	Sexualities
Crime, Law, and Deviance	Marxist Sociology	Social Psychology
Culture	Mathematical Sociology	Sociological Practice and Public Sociology
Disability and Society	Medical Sociology	Teaching and Learning
Economic Sociology	Mental Health	Theory
Education	Methodology	
Emotions	Organizations, Occupations, and Work	

The range of sociological issues is very broad. For example, sociologists who belong to the Animals and Society section of the ASA may study the animal rights movement; those who belong to the Sexualities section may study global sex workers or the gay, bisexual, and transgendered movements. Economic sociologists may investigate globalization or consumerism, among many other topics.
Source: American Sociological Association 2011.

Think about It
Which of these topics do you think would interest you the most? Why?

Haitian orphans by U.S. families, many of them White. Or they might evaluate current and potential U.S. policy toward Haitian immigrants, refugees, and deportees.

Sociologists would take a similar approach to studying episodes of extreme violence. In April 2007, just as college students were beginning to focus on the impending end of the semester, tragedy struck on the campus of Virginia Tech. In a two-hour shooting spree, a mentally disturbed senior armed with semi-automatic weapons killed a total of 32 students and faculty at Virginia's largest university. Observers struggled to describe the events and place them in some social context. For sociologists in particular, the event raised numerous issues and topics for study, including the media's role in describing the attacks, the presence of violence in our educational institutions, the gun control debate, the inadequacy of the nation's mental health care system, and the stereotyping and stigmatization of people who suffer from mental illness.

Besides doing research, sociologists have a long history of advising government agencies on how to respond to disasters. Certainly the poverty of the Gulf Coast region complicated the huge challenge of evacuation in 2005. With Katrina bearing down on the Gulf Coast, thousands of poor inner-city residents had no automobiles or other available means of escaping the storm. Added to that difficulty was the high incidence of disability in the area. New Orleans ranked second among the nation's 70 largest cities in the proportion of people over age 65 who are disabled—56 percent. Moving wheelchair-bound residents to safety requires specially equipped vehicles, to say nothing of handicap-accessible accommodations in public shelters. Clearly, officials must consider these factors in developing evacuation plans (Bureau of the Census 2005b).

Sociological analysis of the disaster did not end when the floodwaters receded. Long before residents of New Orleans staged a massive anticrime rally at City Hall in 2007, researchers were analyzing resettlement patterns in the city. They noted that returning residents often faced bleak job prospects. Yet families who had stayed away for that reason often had trouble enrolling their children in schools unprepared for an influx of evacuees. Faced with a choice between the need to work and the need to return their children to school, some displaced families risked sending their older children home alone. Meanwhile, opportunists had arrived to victimize unsuspecting homeowners. And the city's overtaxed judicial and criminal justice systems, which had been understaffed before Katrina struck, had been only partially restored. All these social factors led sociologists and others to anticipate the unparalleled rise in reported crime the city experienced in 2006 and 2007 (Jervis 2008; Kaufman 2006).

Throughout this textbook, you will see how sociologists develop theories and conduct research to study and better understand societies. And hyou will be encouraged to use your sociological imagination to examine the United States (and other societies) from the viewpoint of a respectful but questioning outsider.

Sociology focuses on the study of human behavior. Yet we all have experience with human behavior and at least some knowledge of it. All of us might well have theories about why people become homeless, for example. Our theories and opinions typically come from common sense—that is, from our experiences and conversations, from what we read, from what we see on television, and so forth.

In our daily lives, we rely on common sense to get us through many unfamiliar situations. However, this commonsense knowledge, while sometimes accurate, is not always reliable, because it rests on commonly held beliefs rather than on systematic analysis of facts. It was once considered common sense to accept that the earth was flat—a view rightly questioned by Pythagoras and Aristotle. Incorrect commonsense notions are not just a part of the distant past; they remain with us today.

Contrary to the common notion that women tend to be chatty compared to men, for instance, researchers have found little difference between the sexes in terms of their talkativeness. Over a five-year period they placed unobtrusive microphones on 396 college students in various fields, at campuses in Mexico as well as the United States. They found that both men and women spoke about 16,000 words per day (Mehl et al. 2007).

Similarly, common sense tells us that in the United States today, military marriages are more likely to end in separation or divorce than in the past due to the strain of long deployments in Iraq and Afghanistan. Yet a study released in 2007 shows no significant increase in the divorce rate among U.S. soldiers over the past decade. In fact, the rate of marital dissolution among members of the military is comparable to that of nonmilitary families. Interestingly, this is not the first study to disprove the widely held notion that military service strains the marital bond. Two generations earlier, during the Vietnam era, researchers came to the same conclusion (Call and Teachman 1991; Karney and Crown 2007).

Like other social scientists, sociologists do not accept something as a fact because "everyone knows it." Instead, each piece of information must be tested and recorded, then analyzed in relation to other data. Sociologists rely on scientific studies in order to describe and understand a social environment. At times, the findings of sociologists may seem like common sense, because they deal with familiar facets of everyday life. The difference is that such findings have been *tested* by researchers. Common sense now tells us that the earth is round, but this particular commonsense notion is based on centuries of scientific work that began with the breakthroughs made by Pythagoras and Aristotle.

thinking CRITICALLY

What aspects of the social and work environment in a fast-food restaurant would be of particular interest to a sociologist? How would the sociological imagination help in analyzing the topic?

What Is Sociological Theory?

Why do people commit suicide? One traditional commonsense answer is that people inherit the desire to kill themselves. Another view is that sunspots drive people to take their lives. These explanations may not seem especially convincing to contemporary researchers, but they represent beliefs widely held as recently as 1900.

Sociologists are not particularly interested in why any one individual commits suicide; they are more concerned with identifying the social forces that systematically cause some people to take their own lives. In order to undertake this research, sociologists develop a theory that offers a general explanation of suicidal behavior.

We can think of theories as attempts to explain events, forces, materials, ideas, or behavior in a comprehensive manner. In sociology, a **theory** is a set of statements that seeks to explain problems, actions, or behavior. An effective theory may have both explanatory and predictive power. That is, it can help us to see the relationships among seemingly isolated phenomena, as well as to understand how one type of change in an environment leads to other changes.

The World Health Organization (2010) estimates that almost a million people die from suicide every year. More than a hundred years ago, a sociologist tried to look at suicide data scientifically. Émile Durkheim ([1897] 1951) developed a highly original theory about the relationship between suicide and social factors. Durkheim was primarily concerned not with the personalities of individual suicide victims, but rather with suicide rates and how they varied from country to country. As a result, when he looked at the number of reported suicides in France, England, and Denmark in 1869, he also noted the total population of each country in order to determine the rate of suicide in each nation. He found that whereas England had only 67 reported suicides per million inhabitants, France had 135 per million and Denmark had 277 per million. The question then became "Why did Denmark have a comparatively high rate of reported suicide?"

Durkheim went much deeper into his investigation of suicide rates. The result was his landmark work *Suicide,* published in 1897. Durkheim refused to accept unproved explanations regarding suicide, including the beliefs that inherited tendencies or cosmic forces caused such deaths. Instead, he focused on social factors, such as the cohesiveness or lack of cohesiveness of religious, social, and occupational groups.

Durkheim's research suggested that suicide, although it is a solitary act, is related to group life. He found that people without religious affiliations had a higher suicide rate than those who were affiliated; the unmarried had much higher rates than married people; and soldiers had a higher rate than civilians. In addition, there seemed to be higher rates of suicide in times of peace than in times of war and revolution, and in times of economic instability and recession rather than in times of prosperity. Durkheim concluded that the suicide rates of a society reflected the extent to which people were or were not integrated into the group life of the society.

Émile Durkheim, like many other social scientists, developed a theory to explain how individual behavior can be understood within a social context. He pointed out the influence of groups and societal forces on what had always been viewed as a highly personal act. Clearly, Durkheim offered a more *scientific* explanation for the causes of suicide than that of inherited tendencies or sunspots. His theory has predictive power, since it suggests that suicide rates will rise or fall in conjunction with certain social and economic changes.

Of course, a theory—even the best of theories—is not a final statement about human behavior. Durkheim's theory of suicide is no exception. Sociologists continue to examine factors that contribute to differences in suicide rates around the world and to a particular society's rate of suicide. They have observed that in Las Vegas, for example, the chances of dying by suicide are strikingly high—twice as high as in the United States as a whole. Noting Durkheim's emphasis on the relationship between suicide and social isolation, researchers have suggested that Las Vegas's rapid growth and constant influx of tourists have undermined the community's sense of permanence, even among longtime residents. Although gambling—or more accurately, losing while gambling—may seem a likely precipitating factor in suicides there, careful study of the data has allowed researchers to dismiss that explanation. What happens in Vegas may stay in Vegas, but the sense of community cohesiveness that the rest of the country enjoys may be lacking (Wray et al. 2008).

thinking CRITICALLY

Can you think of any other explanation for the high suicide rate in Las Vegas? Does that explanation agree with Durkheim's theory?

The Development of Sociology

People have always been curious about sociological matters—how we get along with others, what we do for a living, whom we select as our leaders. Philosophers and religious authorities of ancient and medieval societies made countless observations about human behavior. They did not test or verify those observations scientifically; nevertheless, their observations often became the foundation for moral codes. Several of these early social philosophers correctly predicted that a systematic study of human behavior would emerge one day. Beginning in the 19th century, European theorists made pioneering contributions to the development of a science of human behavior.

Early Thinkers

Auguste Comte The 19th century was an unsettling time in France. The French monarchy had been deposed in the revolution of 1789, and Napoleon had suffered defeat in his effort to conquer Europe. Amid this chaos, philosophers considered how society might be improved. Auguste Comte (1798–1857), credited with being the most influential of the philosophers of the

early 1800s, believed that a theoretical science of society and a systematic investigation of behavior were needed to improve society. He coined the term *sociology* to apply to the science of human behavior.

Writing in the 1800s, Comte feared that the excesses of the French Revolution had permanently impaired France's stability. Yet he hoped that the systematic study of social behavior would eventually lead to more rational human interactions. In Comte's hierarchy of the sciences, sociology was at the top. He called it the "queen," and its practitioners "scientist-priests." This French theorist did not simply give sociology its name; he presented a rather ambitious challenge to the fledgling discipline.

Harriet Martineau Scholars learned of Comte's works largely through translations by the English sociologist Harriet Martineau (1802–1876). But Martineau was a pathbreaker in her own right: she offered insightful observations of the customs and social practices of both her native Britain and the United States. Martineau's book *Society in America* ([1837] 1962) examined religion, politics, child rearing, and immigration in the young nation. It gave special attention to social class distinctions and to such factors as gender and race. Martineau ([1838] 1989) also wrote the first book on sociological methods.

Martineau's writings emphasized the impact that the economy, law, trade, health, and population could have on social problems. She spoke out in favor of the rights of women, the emancipation of slaves, and religious tolerance. Later in life, deafness did not keep her from being an activist. In Martineau's ([1837] 1962) view, intellectuals and scholars should not simply offer observations of social conditions; they should *act* on their convictions in a manner that will benefit society. That is why Martineau conducted research on the nature of female employment and pointed to the need for further investigation of the issue (Deegan 2003; Hill and Hoecker-Drysdale 2001).

Harriet Martineau, an early pioneer of sociology who studied social behavior both in her native England and in the United States, proposed some of the methods still used by sociologists.

Herbert Spencer Another important early contributor to the discipline of sociology was Herbert Spencer (1820–1903). A relatively prosperous Victorian Englishman, Spencer (unlike Martineau) did not feel compelled to correct or improve society; instead, he merely hoped to understand it better. Drawing on Charles Darwin's study *On the Origin of Species,* Spencer applied the concept of evolution of the species to societies in order to explain how they change, or evolve, over time. Similarly, he adapted Darwin's evolutionary view of the "survival of the fittest" by arguing that it is "natural" that some people are rich while others are poor.

Spencer's approach to societal change was extremely popular in his lifetime. Unlike Comte, Spencer suggested that since societies are bound to change eventually, one need not be highly critical of present social arrangements or work actively for social change. This viewpoint appealed to many influential people in England and the United States who had a vested interest in the status quo and were suspicious of social thinkers who endorsed change.

Émile Durkheim

Émile Durkheim made many pioneering contributions to sociology, including his important theoretical work on suicide. The son of a rabbi, Durkheim (1858–1917) was educated in both France and Germany. He established an impressive academic reputation and was appointed one of the first professors of sociology in France. Above all, Durkheim will be remembered for his insistence that behavior must be understood within a larger social context, not just in individualistic terms.

To give one example of this emphasis, Durkheim ([1912] 2001) developed a fundamental thesis to help explain all forms of society. Through intensive study of the Arunta, an Australian tribe, he focused on the functions that religion performed and underscored the role of group life in defining what we consider to be religion. Durkheim concluded that like other forms of group behavior, religion reinforces a group's solidarity.

Another of Durkheim's main interests was the consequences of work in modern societies. In his view, the growing division of labor in industrial societies, as workers became much more specialized in their tasks, led to what he called "anomie." **Anomie** refers to the loss of direction felt in a society when social control of individual behavior has become ineffective. Often, the state of anomie occurs during a time of profound social change, when people have lost their sense of purpose or direction. In a period of anomie, people are so confused and unable to cope with the new social environment that they may resort to suicide.

Durkheim was concerned about the dangers that alienation, loneliness, and isolation might pose for modern industrial societies. He shared Comte's belief that sociology should provide direction for social change. As a result, he advocated the creation of new

social groups—mediators between the individual's family and the state—that would provide a sense of belonging for members of huge, impersonal societies. Unions would be an example of such groups.

Like many other sociologists, Durkheim did not limit his interests to one aspect of social behavior. Later in this book we will consider his thinking on crime and punishment, religion, and the workplace. Few sociologists have had such a dramatic impact on so many different areas within the discipline.

Max Weber

Another important early theorist was Max Weber (pronounced VAY-ber). Born in Germany, Weber (1864–1920) studied legal and economic history, but gradually developed an interest in sociology. Eventually, he became a professor at various German universities. Weber taught his students that they should employ **verstehen** (pronounced fair-SHTAY-en), the German word for "understanding" or "insight," in their intellectual work. He pointed out that we cannot analyze our social behavior by the same type of objective criteria we use to measure weight or temperature. To fully comprehend behavior, we must learn the subjective meanings people attach to their actions—how they themselves view and explain their behavior.

For example, suppose that a sociologist was studying the social ranking of individuals in a fraternity. Weber would expect the researcher to employ *verstehen* to determine the significance of the fraternity's social hierarchy for its members. The researcher might examine the effects of athleticism or grades or social skills or seniority on standing within the fraternity. He or she would seek to learn how the fraternity members relate to other members of higher or lower status. While investigating these questions, the researcher would take into account people's emotions, thoughts, beliefs, and attitudes (L. Coser 1977).

We also owe credit to Weber for a key conceptual tool: the ideal type. An **ideal type** is a construct or model for evaluating specific cases. In his works, Weber identified various characteristics of bureaucracy as an ideal type (discussed in detail in Chapter 6). In presenting this model of bureaucracy, Weber was not describing any particular organization, nor was he using the term *ideal* in a way that suggested a positive evaluation. Instead, his purpose was to provide a useful standard for measuring how bureaucratic an actual organization is (Gerth and Mills 1958). Later in this book, we will use the concept of *ideal type* to study the family, religion, authority, and economic systems, as well as to analyze bureaucracy.

Although their professional careers coincided, Émile Durkheim and Max Weber never met and probably were unaware of each other's existence, let alone ideas. Such was not true of the work of Karl Marx. Durkheim's thinking about the impact of the division of labor in industrial societies was related to Marx's writings, while Weber's concern for a

FIGURE 1-1 CONTRIBUTORS TO SOCIOLOGY

11

Understanding Sociology

	Émile Durkheim 1858–1917	**Max Weber 1864–1920**	**Karl Marx 1818–1883**	**W. E. B. DuBois 1868–1963**
Academic training	Philosophy	Law, economics, history, philosophy	Philosophy, law	Sociology
Key works	1893–*The Division of Labor in Society* 1897–*Suicide: A Study in Sociology* 1912–*Elementary Forms of Religious Life*	1904-1905–*The Protestant Ethic and the Spirit of Capitalism* 1921–*Economy and Society*	1848–*The Communist Manifesto* 1867–*Das Kapital*	1899–*The Philadelphia Negro* 1903–*The Negro Church* 1903–*Souls of Black Folk*

value-free, objective sociology was a direct response to Marx's deeply held convictions. Thus, it is not surprising that Karl Marx is viewed as a major figure in the development of sociology, as well as several other social sciences (Figure 1-1).

Karl Marx

Karl Marx (1818–1883) shared with Durkheim and Weber a dual interest in abstract philosophical issues and the concrete reality of everyday life. Unlike them, however, Marx was so critical of existing institutions that a conventional academic career was impossible. He spent most of his life in exile from his native Germany.

Marx's personal life was a difficult struggle. When a paper he had written was suppressed, he fled to France. In Paris, he met Friedrich Engels (1820–1895), with whom he formed a lifelong friendship. The two lived at a time when European and North American economic life was increasingly dominated by the factory rather than the farm.

While in London in 1847, Marx and Engels attended secret meetings of an illegal coalition of labor unions known as the Communist League. The following year they prepared a platform called *The Communist Manifesto,* in which they argued that the masses of people with no resources other than their labor (whom they referred to as the *proletariat*) should unite to fight for the overthrow of capitalist societies. In the words of Marx and Engels:

> The history of all hitherto existing society is the history of class struggles.... The proletarians have nothing to lose but their chains. They have a world to win. WORKING MEN OF ALL COUNTRIES, UNITE! (Tucker 1978:473, 500).

After completing *The Communist Manifesto,* Marx returned to Germany, only to be expelled. He then moved to England, where he continued to write books and essays. Marx lived there in extreme poverty; he pawned most of his possessions, and several of his children died of malnutrition and disease. Marx

clearly was an outsider in British society, a fact that may well have influenced his view of Western cultures.

In Marx's analysis, society was fundamentally divided between two classes that clashed in pursuit of their own interests. When he examined the industrial societies of his time, such as Germany, England, and the United States, he saw the factory as the center of conflict between the exploiters (the owners of the means of production) and the exploited (the workers). Marx viewed these relationships in systematic terms; that is, he believed that a system of economic, social, and political relationships maintained the power and dominance of the owners over the workers. Consequently, Marx and Engels argued that the working class should overthrow the existing class system. Marx's influence on contemporary thinking has been dramatic. His writings inspired those who would later lead communist revolutions in Russia, China, Cuba, Vietnam, and elsewhere.

Even apart from the political revolutions that his work fostered, Marx's significance is profound. Marx emphasized the *group* identifications and associations that influence an *individual's* place in society. This area of study is the major focus of contemporary sociology. Throughout this textbook, we will consider how membership in a particular gender classification, age group, racial group, or economic class affects a person's attitudes and behavior. In an important sense, we can trace this way of understanding society back to the pioneering work of Karl Marx.

W. E. B. DuBois

Marx's work encouraged sociologists to view society through the eyes of those segments of the population that rarely influence decision making. In the United States, some early Black sociologists, including W. E. B. DuBois (1868–1963), conducted research that they hoped would assist in the struggle for a racially egalitarian society. DuBois (pronounced doo-BOYSS) believed that knowledge was essential in combating prejudice and achieving tolerance and justice. Sociologists, he contended, needed to draw on scientific principles to study social problems such as those experienced by Blacks in the United States. To separate opinion from fact, he advocated basic research on the lives of Blacks. Through his in-depth studies of urban life, both White and Black, in cities such as Philadelphia and Atlanta, DuBois ([1899] 1995) made a major contribution to sociology.

Like Durkheim and Weber, DuBois saw the importance of religion to society. However, he tended to focus on religion at the community level and the role of the church in the lives of its members ([1903] 2003). DuBois had little patience with theorists such as Herbert Spencer, who seemed content with the status quo. He believed that the granting of full political rights to Blacks was essential to their social and economic progress.

Because many of his ideas challenged the status quo, DuBois did not find a receptive audience within either the government or the academic world. As a result, he became increasingly involved with organizations whose members questioned the established social order. In 1909 he helped to found the National Association for the Advancement of Colored People, better known today as the NAACP (Wortham 2008).

DuBois's insights have been lasting. In 1897 he coined the term **double consciousness** to refer to the division of an individual's identity into two or more social realities. He used the term to describe the experience of being Black in White America. Today, an African American holds the most powerful office in the nation, President of the United States. Yet for millions of African Americans, the reality of being Black in the United States typically is not one of power (DuBois [1903] 1961).

Twentieth-Century Developments

Sociology today builds on the firm foundation developed by Émile Durkheim, Max Weber, Karl Marx, and W. E. B. DuBois. However, the field certainly has not remained stagnant over the past hundred years. While Europeans have continued to make contributions to the discipline, sociologists from throughout the world and especially the United States have advanced sociological theory and research. Their new insights have helped us to better understand the workings of society.

Charles Horton Cooley Charles Horton Cooley (1864–1929) was typical of the sociologists who came to prominence in the early 1900s. Born in Ann Arbor, Michigan, Cooley received his graduate training in economics but later became a sociology professor at the University of Michigan. Like other early sociologists, he had become interested in this new discipline while pursuing a related area of study.

Cooley shared the desire of Durkheim, Weber, and Marx to learn more about society. But to do so effectively, he preferred to use the sociological perspective to look first at smaller units—intimate, face-to-face groups such as families, gangs, and friendship networks. He saw these groups as the seedbeds of society, in the sense that they shape people's ideals, beliefs, values, and social nature. Cooley's work increased our understanding of groups of relatively small size.

Jane Addams In the early 1900s, many leading sociologists in the United States saw themselves as social reformers dedicated to systematically studying and then improving a corrupt society. They were genuinely concerned about the lives of immigrants in the nation's growing cities, whether those immigrants came from Europe or from the rural American South. Early female sociologists,

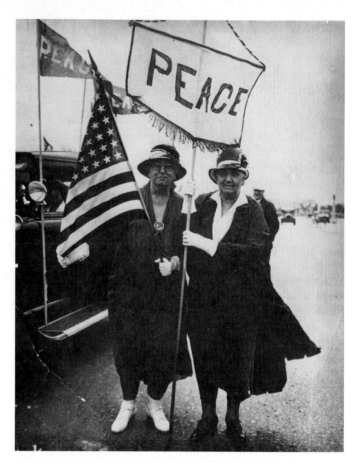

Jane Addams (right) was an early pioneer both in sociology and in the settlement house movement. She was also an activist in the campaign for women's right to vote, as this photograph shows.

in particular, often took active roles in poor urban areas as leaders of community centers known as *settlement houses.* For example, Jane Addams (1860–1935), a member of the American Sociological Society, cofounded the famous Chicago settlement, Hull House.

Addams and other pioneering female sociologists commonly combined intellectual inquiry, social service work, and political activism—all with the goal of assisting the underprivileged and creating a more egalitarian society. For example, working with the Black journalist and educator Ida Wells-Barnett, Addams successfully prevented racial segregation in the Chicago public schools. Addams's efforts to establish a juvenile court system and a women's trade union reveal the practical focus of her work (Addams 1910, 1930; Deegan 1991; Lengermann and Niebrugge-Brantley 1998).

By the middle of the 20th century, however, the focus of the discipline had shifted. Sociologists for the most part restricted themselves to theorizing and gathering information; the aim of transforming society was left to social workers and activists. This shift away from social reform was accompanied by a growing commitment to scientific methods of research and to value-free interpretation of data. Not all sociologists were happy with this emphasis. A new organization, the Society for the Study of Social Problems, was created in 1950 to deal more directly with social inequality and other social problems.

Robert Merton Sociologist Robert Merton (1910–2003) made an important contribution to the discipline by successfully combining theory and research. Born to Slavic immigrant parents in Philadelphia, Merton won a scholarship to Temple University.

He continued his studies at Harvard, where he acquired his lifelong interest in sociology. Merton's teaching career was based at Columbia University.

Merton (1968) produced a theory that is one of the most frequently cited explanations of deviant behavior. He noted different ways in which people attempt to achieve success in life. In his view, some may deviate from the socially approved goal of accumulating material goods or the socially accepted means of achieving that goal. For example, in Merton's classification scheme, *innovators* are people who accept the goal of pursuing material wealth but use illegal means to do so, including robbery, burglary, and extortion. Although Merton based his explanation of crime on individual behavior that has been influenced by society's approved goals and means, it has wider applications. His theory helps to account for the high crime rates among the nation's poor, who may see no hope of advancing themselves through traditional roads to success. Chapter 8 discusses Merton's theory in greater detail.

Merton also emphasized that sociology should strive to bring together the *macro-level* and *micro-level* approaches to the study of society. **Macrosociology** concentrates on large-scale phenomena or entire civilizations. Émile Durkheim's cross-cultural study of suicide is an example of macro-level research. More recently, macrosociologists have examined international crime rates (see Chapter 8) and the stereotype of Asian Americans as a "model minority" (see Chapter 11). In contrast, **microsociology** stresses the study of small groups, often through experimental means. Sociological research on the micro level has included studies of how divorced men and women disengage from significant social roles (see Chapter 5); of how conformity can influence the expression of prejudiced attitudes (see Chapter 8); and of how a teacher's expectations can affect a student's academic performance (see Chapter 16).

Pierre Bourdieu Increasingly, scholars in the United States have been drawing on the insights of sociologists in other countries. The ideas of the French sociologist Pierre Bourdieu (1930–2002) have found a broad following in North America and elsewhere. As a young man, Bourdieu did fieldwork in Algeria during its struggle for independence from France. Today, scholars study Bourdieu's research techniques as well as his conclusions.

Bourdieu wrote about how capital in its many forms sustains individuals and families from one generation to the next. To Bourdieu, *capital* included not just material goods, but cultural and social assets. **Cultural capital** refers to noneconomic goods, such as family background and education, which are reflected in a knowledge of language and the arts. Not necessarily book knowledge, cultural capital refers to the kind of education that is valued by the socially elite. Though a knowledge of Chinese cuisine is culture, for example, it is not the prestigious kind of culture that is valued by the elite. In the United States, immigrants—especially those who arrived in large numbers and settled in ethnic enclaves—have generally taken two or three generations to develop the same level of cultural capital enjoyed by more established groups. In comparison, **social capital** refers to the collective benefit of social networks, which are built on reciprocal trust. Much has been written about the importance of family and friendship networks in providing people with an opportunity to advance. In his emphasis on cultural and social capital, Bourdieu's work extends the insights of early social thinkers such as Marx and Weber (Bourdieu and Passerson 1990; Field 2008).

Today sociology reflects the diverse contributions of earlier theorists. As sociologists approach such topics as divorce, drug addiction, and religious cults, they can draw on the theoretical insights of the discipline's pioneers. A careful reader can hear Comte, Durkheim, Weber, Marx, DuBois, Cooley, Addams, and many others speaking through the pages of current research. Sociology has also broadened beyond the intellectual confines of North America and Europe. Contributions to the discipline now come from sociologists studying and researching human behavior in other parts of the world. In describing the work of these sociologists, it is helpful to examine a number of influential *theoretical perspectives,* also known as *approaches* or *views.*

thinking CRITICALLY

What kinds of social and cultural capital do you possess?

Major Theoretical Perspectives

Sociologists view society in different ways. Some see the world basically as a stable and ongoing entity. They are impressed with the endurance of the family, organized religion, and other social institutions. Other sociologists see society as composed of many groups in conflict, competing for scarce resources. To still other sociologists, the most fascinating aspects of the social world are the everyday, routine interactions among individuals that we sometimes take for granted. These three views, the ones most widely used by sociologists, are the functionalist, conflict, and interactionist perspectives. Together, these approaches will provide an introductory look at the discipline.

Functionalist Perspective

Think of society as a living organism in which each part of the organism contributes to its survival. This view is the **functionalist perspective**, which emphasizes the way in which the parts of a society are structured to maintain its stability.

Talcott Parsons (1902–1979), a Harvard University sociologist, was a key figure in the development of functionalist theory. Parsons was greatly influenced by the work of Émile Durkheim, Max Weber, and other European sociologists. For more than four decades, he dominated sociology in the United States with his advocacy of functionalism. Parsons saw any society as a vast network of connected parts, each of which helps to maintain the system as a whole. His approach, carried forward by German sociologist Niklas Luhmann (1927–1998), holds that if an aspect of social life does not contribute to a society's stability or survival—if it does not serve some identifiably useful function or promote value consensus among members of society—it will not be passed on from one generation to the next (Joas and Knöbl 2009; Knudsen 2010).

Let's examine an example of the functionalist perspective. Many Americans have difficulty understanding the Hindu prohibition against slaughtering cows (specifically, zebu). Cattle browse unhindered through Indian street markets, helping themselves to oranges and mangoes while people bargain for the little food they can afford. What explains this devotion to the cow in the face of human deprivation—a devotion that appears to be dysfunctional?

Chapter 1

The simple explanation is that cow worship is highly functional in Indian society, according to economists, agronomists, and social scientists who have studied the matter. Cows perform two essential tasks: plowing the fields and producing milk. If eating their meat were permitted, hungry families might be tempted to slaughter their cows for immediate consumption, leaving themselves without a means of cultivation. Cows also produce dung, which doubles as a fertilizer and a fuel for cooking. Finally, cow meat sustains the neediest group in society, the *Dalit,* or untouchables, who sometimes resort to eating beef in secrecy. If eating beef were socially acceptable, higher-status Indians would no doubt bid up its price, placing it beyond the reach of the hungriest.

Manifest and Latent Functions A college catalog typically states various functions of the institution. It may inform you, for example, that the university intends to "offer each student a broad education in classical and contemporary thought, in the humanities, in the sciences, and in the arts." However, it would be quite a surprise to find a catalog that declared, "This university was founded in 1895 to assist people in finding a marriage partner." No college catalog will declare this as the purpose of the university. Yet societal institutions serve many functions, some of them quite subtle. The university, in fact, *does* facilitate mate selection.

Robert Merton (1968) made an important distinction between manifest and latent functions. **Manifest functions** of institutions are open, stated, and conscious functions. They involve the intended, recognized consequences of an aspect of society, such as the university's role in certifying academic competence and excellence. In contrast, **latent functions** are unconscious or unintended functions that may reflect hidden purposes of an institution. One latent function of universities is to hold down unemployment. Another is to serve as a meeting ground for people seeking marital partners.

Dysfunctions Functionalists acknowledge that not all parts of a society contribute to its stability all the time. A **dysfunction** refers to an element or process of a society that may actually disrupt the social system or reduce its stability.

Cows (zebu), considered sacred in India, wander freely through this city, respected by all who encounter them. The sanctity of the cow is functional in India, where plowing, milking, and fertilizing are far more important to subsistence farmers than a diet that includes beef.

We view many dysfunctional behavior patterns, such as homicide, as undesirable. Yet we should not automatically interpret them in this way. The evaluation of a dysfunction depends on one's own values, or as the saying goes, on "where you sit." For example, the official view in prisons in the United States is that inmate gangs should be eradicated because they are dysfunctional to smooth operations. Yet some guards have come to view prison gangs as a functional part of their jobs. The danger posed by gangs creates a "threat to security," requiring increased surveillance and more overtime work for guards, as well as requests for special staffing to address gang problems (G. Scott 2001).

Conflict Perspective

Where functionalists see stability and consensus, conflict sociologists see a social world in continual struggle. The **conflict perspective** assumes that social behavior is best understood in terms of tension between groups over power or the allocation of resources, including housing, money, access to services, and political representation. The tension between competing groups need not be violent; it can take the form of labor negotiations, party politics, competition between religious groups for new members, or disputes over the federal budget.

Throughout most of the 1900s, the functionalist perspective had the upper hand in sociology in the United States. However, the conflict approach has become increasingly persuasive since the late 1960s. The widespread social unrest resulting from battles over civil rights, bitter divisions over the war in Vietnam, the rise of the feminist and gay liberation movements, the Watergate political scandal, urban riots, and confrontations at abortion clinics have offered support for the conflict approach—the view that our social world is characterized by continual struggle between competing groups. Currently, the discipline of sociology accepts conflict theory as one valid way to gain insight into a society.

The Marxist View As we saw earlier, Karl Marx viewed struggle between social classes as inevitable, given the exploitation of workers that he perceived under capitalism. Expanding on Marx's work, sociologists and other social scientists have come to see conflict not merely as a class phenomenon but as a part of everyday life in all societies. In studying any culture, organization, or social group, sociologists want to know who benefits, who suffers, and who dominates at the expense of others. They are concerned with the conflicts between women and men, parents and children, cities and suburbs, Whites and Blacks, to name only a few. Conflict theorists are interested in how society's institutions—including the family, government, religion, education, and the media—may help to maintain the privileges of some groups and keep others in a subservient position. Their emphasis on social change and the redistribution of resources makes conflict theorists more radical and activist than functionalists (Dahrendorf 1959).

The Feminist View Sociologists began embracing the feminist perspective only in the 1970s, although it has a long tradition in many other disciplines. The **feminist view** sees inequity in gender as central to all behavior and organization. Because it focuses clearly on one aspect of inequality, it is often allied with the conflict perspective. Proponents of the feminist view tend to focus on the macro level, just as conflict theorists do. Drawing on the work of Marx and Engels, contemporary feminist theorists often view women's subordination as inherent in capitalist societies.

Some radical feminist theorists, however, view the oppression of women as inevitable in *all* male-dominated societies, whether capitalist, socialist, or communist.

An early example of this perspective (long before the label came into use by sociologists) can be seen in the life and writings of Ida Wells-Barnett (1862–1931). Following her groundbreaking publications in the 1890s on the practice of lynching Black Americans, she became an advocate in the women's rights campaign, especially the struggle to win the vote for women. Like feminist theorists who succeeded her, Wells-Barnett used her analysis of society as a means of resisting oppression. In her case, she researched what it meant to be Black, a woman in the United States, and a Black woman in the United States (Giddings 2008; Wells-Barnett 1970).

Feminist scholarship has broadened our understanding of social behavior by extending the analysis beyond the male point of view. Consider sports, for example. Feminist theorists consider how watching or participating in sports reinforces the roles that men and women play in the larger society:

- Although sports generally promote fitness and health, they may also have an adverse effect on participants' health. Men are more likely to resort to illegal steroid use (among body-builders and baseball players, for example); women, to excessive dieting (among gymnasts and figure skaters, for example).

- Gender expectations encourage female athletes to be passive and gentle, qualities that do not support the emphasis on competitiveness in sports. As a result, women find it difficult to enter sports traditionally dominated by men, such as Indy or NASCAR.

- Although professional women athletes' earnings are increasing, they typically trail those of male athletes.

Ida Wells-Barnett explored what it meant to be female and Black in the United States. Her work established her as one of the earliest feminist theorists.

use your sociological *imagination*

You are a sociologist who takes the conflict perspective. How would you interpret the practice of prostitution? How would your view of prostitution differ if you took the functionalist perspective? The feminist perspective?

The Marxist view asks "Who benefits, who suffers, and who dominates?"

Interactionist Perspective

Workers interacting on the job, encounters in public places like bus stops and parks, behavior in small groups—all these aspects of microsociology catch the attention of interactionists. Whereas functionalist and conflict theorists both analyze large-scale, society-wide patterns of behavior, theorists who take the **interactionist perspective** generalize about everyday forms of social interaction in order to explain society as a whole. Today, given rising concern over the cost and availability of gas, interactionists have begun to study a form of commuter behavior called "slugging." To avoid driving to work, commuters gather at certain preappointed places to seek rides from complete strangers. When a driver pulls into the parking area or vacant lot and announces his destination, the first slug in line who is headed for that destination jumps in. Rules of etiquette have emerged to smooth the social interaction between driver and passenger: neither the driver nor the passenger may eat or

FIGURE 1-2 SOCIOLOGY DEGREES CONFERRED IN THE UNITED STATES BY GENDER

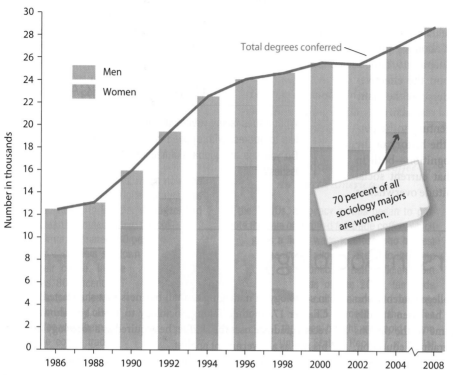

Source: National Center for Education Statistics 2010:Table 275 on p. 413.

engage in four to seven years of intensive work, including the time required to complete the dissertation. Yet even this effort is no guarantee of a job as a sociology professor.

The good news is that over the next 10 years, the demand for instructors is expected to increase because of high rates of retirement among faculty from the baby boom generation, as well as the anticipated slow but steady growth in the college student population in the United States. Nonetheless, anyone who launches an academic career must be prepared for considerable uncertainty and competition in the college job market (American Sociological Association 2009).

Of course, not all people who work as sociologists teach or hold doctoral degrees. Take government, for example. The Census Bureau relies on people with sociological training to interpret data for other government agencies and the general public. Virtually every agency depends on survey research—a field in which sociology students can specialize—in order to assess everything from community needs to the morale of the agency's workers. In addition, people with sociological training can put their academic knowledge to effective use in probation and

in sociology that offer PhD and/or master's degrees. These programs differ greatly in their areas of specialization, course requirements, costs, and the research and teaching opportunities available to graduate students. About 71 percent of the graduates are women (American Sociological Association 2005, 2010).

Higher education is an important source of employment for sociologists with graduate degrees. About 83 percent of recent PhD recipients in sociology seek employment in colleges and universities. These sociologists teach not only majors who are committed to the discipline but also students hoping to become doctors, nurses, lawyers, police officers, and so forth (American Sociological Association 2005).

Sociologists who teach in colleges and universities may use their knowledge and training to influence public policy. For example, sociologist Andrew Cherlin (2003) has commented on the debate over proposed federal funding to promote marriage among welfare recipients. Citing the results of two of his studies, Cherlin questioned the potential effectiveness of such a policy in strengthening low-income families. Because many single mothers choose to marry someone other than the father of their children—sometimes for good reason—their children often grow up in stepfamilies. Cherlin's research shows that children who are raised in stepfamilies are no better off than those in single-parent families. He sees government efforts to promote marriage as a politically motivated attempt to foster traditional social values in a society that has become increasingly diverse.

For sociology graduates who are interested in academic careers, the road to a PhD (or doctorate) can be long and difficult. This degree symbolizes competence in original research; each candidate must prepare a book-length study known as a dissertation. Typically, a doctoral student in sociology will

FIGURE 1-3 OCCUPATIONS OF GRADUATING SOCIOLOGY MAJORS

Note: Based on a national survey conducted in early 2007 of 1,800 sociology majors who graduated in 2005.
Source: Spalter-Roth and Van Vooren 2008a, p. 3.

parole, health sciences, community development, and recreational services. Some people working in government or private industry have a master's degree (MA or MS) in sociology; others have a bachelor's degree (BA or BS).

Currently, about 15 percent of the members of the American Sociological Association use their sociological skills outside the academic world, whether in social service agencies or in marketing positions for business firms. Increasing numbers of sociologists with graduate degrees are employed by businesses, industry, hospitals, and nonprofit organizations. Studies show that many sociology graduates are making career changes from social service areas to business and commerce. For an undergraduate major, sociology is excellent preparation for employment in many parts of the business world (Spalter-Roth and Van Vooren 2008b).

Whether you take a few courses in sociology or complete a degree, you will benefit from the critical thinking skills developed in this discipline. Sociologists emphasize the value of being able to analyze, interpret, and function within a variety of working situations—an asset in virtually any career. Moreover, given rapid technological change and the expanding global economy, all of us will need to adapt to substantial social change, even in our own careers. Sociology provides a rich conceptual framework that can serve as a foundation for flexible career development and assist you in taking advantage of new employment opportunities.

 Connect Learn Succeed™

For more information on career opportunities for individuals with a background in sociology, visit the Online Learning Center at www.mhhe.com/schaefer13e. Go to "Student Edition," and in the section titled "Course-wide Content," click on "Web Resources." Then click on "Career Opportunities," which will provide you with numerous links to sites offering career advice and information.

MASTERING THIS CHAPTER

Summary

Sociology is the scientific study of social behavior and human groups. This chapter examines the nature of sociological theory, the founders of the discipline, theoretical perspectives in contemporary sociology, practical applications for sociological theory and research, and ways to exercise the *sociological imagination.*

1. The **sociological imagination** is an awareness of the relationship between an individual and the wider society. It is based on the ability to view our own society as an outsider might, rather than from the perspective of our limited experiences and cultural biases.

2. In contrast to other **social sciences,** sociology emphasizes the influence that groups can have on people's behavior and attitudes and the ways in which people shape society.

3. Knowledge that relies on common sense is not always reliable. Sociologists must test and analyze each piece of information they use.

4. Sociologists employ **theories** to examine relationships between observations or data that may seem completely unrelated.

5. Nineteenth-century thinkers who contributed sociological insights included Auguste Comte, a French philosopher; Harriet Martineau, an English sociologist; and Herbert Spencer, an English scholar.

6. Other important figures in the development of sociology were Émile Durkheim, who pioneered work on suicide; Max Weber, who taught the need for insight in intellectual work; Karl Marx, who emphasized the importance of the economy and social conflict; and W. E. B. DuBois, who advocated the usefulness of basic research in combating prejudice and fostering racial tolerance and justice.

7. In the 20th century, the discipline of sociology was indebted to the U.S. sociologists Charles Horton Cooley and Robert Merton, as well as to the French sociologist Pierre Bourdieu.

8. **Macrosociology** concentrates on large-scale phenomena or entire civilizations; **microsociology** stresses the study of small groups.

9. The **functionalist perspective** emphasizes the way in which the parts of a society are structured to maintain its stability.

10. The **conflict perspective** assumes that social behavior is best understood in terms of conflict or tension between competing groups.

11. The **feminist view,** which is often allied with the conflict perspective, sees inequity in gender as central to all behavior and organization.

12. The **interactionist perspective** is concerned primarily with fundamental or everyday forms of interaction, including symbols and other types of **nonverbal communication.**

13. Sociologists make use of all four perspectives, since each offers unique insights into the same issue.

14. **Applied** and **clinical sociology** apply the discipline of sociology to the solution of practical problems in human behavior and organizations. In contrast, **basic sociology** is sociological inquiry that seeks only a deeper knowledge of the fundamental aspects of social phenomena.

15. This textbook makes use of the sociological imagination by showing theory in practice and in current research; by thinking globally; by focusing on the significance of social inequality; by speaking across race, gender, and religious boundaries; and by highlighting social policy around the world.

Key Terms

Anomie The loss of direction felt in a society when social control of individual behavior has become ineffective. (page 10)

Applied sociology The use of the discipline of sociology with the specific intent of yielding practical applications for human behavior and organizations. (18)

Basic sociology Sociological inquiry conducted with the objective of gaining a more profound knowledge of the fundamental aspects of social phenomena. Also known as *pure sociology.* (19)

Clinical sociology The use of the discipline of sociology with the specific intent of altering social relationships or restructuring social institutions. (19)

Conflict perspective A sociological approach that assumes that social behavior is best understood in terms of tension between groups over power or the allocation of resources, including housing, money, access to services, and political representation. (14)

Cultural capital Noneconomic goods, such as family background and education, which are reflected in a knowledge of language and the arts. (13)

Double consciousness The division of an individual's identity into two or more social realities. (12)

Dramaturgical approach A view of social interaction in which people are seen as theatrical performers. (16)

Dysfunction An element or process of a society that may disrupt the social system or reduce its stability. (14)

Feminist view A sociological approach that views inequity in gender as central to all behavior and organization. (14)

Functionalist perspective A sociological approach that emphasizes the way in which the parts of a society are structured to maintain its stability. (13)

Globalization The worldwide integration of government policies, cultures, social movements, and financial markets through trade and the exchange of ideas. (19)

Ideal type A construct or model for evaluating specific cases. (10)

Interactionist perspective A sociological approach that generalizes about everyday forms of social interaction in order to explain society as a whole. (15)

Latent function An unconscious or unintended function that may reflect hidden purposes. (14)

Macrosociology Sociological investigation that concentrates on large-scale phenomena or entire civilizations. (13)

Manifest function An open, stated, and conscious function. (14)

Microsociology Sociological investigation that stresses the study of small groups, often through experimental means. (13)

Natural science The study of the physical features of nature and the ways in which they interact and change. (6)

Nonverbal communication The sending of messages through the use of gestures, facial expressions, and postures. (16)

Science The body of knowledge obtained by methods based on systematic observation. (5)

Social capital The collective benefit of social networks, which are built on reciprocal trust. (13)

Social inequality A condition in which members of society have differing amounts of wealth, prestige, or power. (19)

Social science The study of the social features of humans and the ways in which they interact and change. (6)

Sociological imagination An awareness of the relationship between an individual and the wider society, both today and in the past. (5)

Sociology The scientific study of social behavior and human groups. (5)

Theory In sociology, a set of statements that seeks to explain problems, actions, or behavior. (8)

Verstehen The German word for "understanding" or "insight"; used to stress the need for sociologists to take into account the subjective meanings people attach to their actions. (10)

TAKING SOCIOLOGY with you

1. Research! Find out who makes the sports apparel sold at your school's bookstore. What can you learn (perhaps from a company website) about where such products are manufactured and what the working conditions are?

2. In what ways have you been affected by the recent spate of home mortgage foreclosures? Has the widespread loss of home ownership made you and others more aware of the problem of homelessness, or has it pushed the issue out of sight?

3. Consider some group or organization that you participate in. Using Robert Merton's concepts, list its manifest and latent functions.

Self-Quiz

Read each question carefully and then select the best answer.

1. Sociology is
   a. very narrow in scope.
   b. concerned with what one individual does or does not do.
   c. the systematic study of social behavior and human groups.
   d. an awareness of the relationship between an individual and the wider society.

2. Which of the following thinkers introduced the concept of the sociological imagination?
   a. Émile Durkheim
   b. Max Weber
   c. Karl Marx
   d. C. Wright Mills

3. Émile Durkheim's research on suicide suggested that
   a. people with religious affiliations had a higher suicide rate than those who were unaffiliated.
   b. suicide rates seemed to be higher in times of peace than in times of war and revolution.
   c. civilians were more likely to take their lives than soldiers.
   d. suicide is a solitary act, unrelated to group life.

4. Max Weber taught his students that they should employ which of the following in their intellectual work?
   a. anomie
   b. *verstehen*
   c. the sociological imagination
   d. microsociology

5. Robert Merton's contributions to sociology include
   a. successfully combining theory and research.
   b. producing a theory that is one of the most frequently cited explanations of deviant behavior.
   c. an attempt to bring macro-level and micro-level analyses together.
   d. all of the above

6. Which sociologist made a major contribution to society through his in-depth studies of urban life, including both Blacks and Whites?
   a. W. E. B. DuBois
   b. Robert Merton
   c. Auguste Comte
   d. Charles Horton Cooley

7. In the late 19th century, before the term *feminist view* was even coined, the ideas behind this major theoretical approach appeared in the writings of
   a. Karl Marx.
   b. Ida Wells-Barnett.
   c. Charles Horton Cooley.
   d. Pierre Bourdieu.

8. Thinking of society as a living organism in which each part of the organism contributes to its survival is a reflection of which theoretical perspective?
   a. the functionalist perspective
   b. the conflict perspective
   c. the feminist perspective
   d. the interactionist perspective

9. Karl Marx's view of the struggle between social classes inspired the contemporary
   a. functionalist perspective.
   b. conflict perspective.
   c. interactionist perspective.
   d. dramaturgical approach.

10. Erving Goffman's dramaturgical approach, which postulates that people present certain aspects of their personalities while obscuring other aspects, is a derivative of what major theoretical perspective?
   a. the functionalist perspective
   b. the conflict perspective
   c. the feminist perspective
   d. the interactionist perspective

11. While the findings of sociologists may at times seem like common sense, they differ because they rest on _____ analysis of facts.

12. Within sociology, a(n) _____ is a set of statements that seeks to explain problems, actions, or behavior.

13. In _____ _____ 's hierarchy of the sciences, sociology was the "queen," and its practitioners were "scientist-priests."

14. In *Society in America,* originally published in 1837, English scholar _____ _____ examined religion, politics, child rearing, and immigration in the young nation.

15. _____ _____ adapted Charles Darwin's evolutionary view of the "survival of the fittest" by arguing that it is "natural" that some people are rich while others are poor.

16. Sociologist Max Weber coined the term _____ _____ in referring to a construct or model that serves as a measuring rod against which actual cases can be evaluated.

17. In *The Communist Manifesto,* _____ _____ and _____ _____ argued that the masses of people who have no resources other than their labor (the proletariat) should unite to fight for the overthrow of capitalist societies.

18. _____ _____, an early female sociologist, cofounded the famous Chicago settlement house called Hull House and also tried to establish a juvenile court system.

19. The university's role in certifying academic competence and excellence is an example of a(n) _____ function.

20. The _____ _____ draws on the work of Karl Marx and Friedrich Engels in that it often views women's subordination as inherent in capitalist societies.

Answers

1 (c); 2 (d); 3 (b); 4 (b); 5 (d); 6 (a); 7 (b); 8 (a); 9 (b); 10 (d); 11 systematic; 12 theory; 13 Auguste Comte; 14 Harriet Martineau; 15 Herbert Spencer; 16 ideal type; 17 Karl Marx, Friedrich Engels; 18 Jane Addams; 19 manifest; 20 feminist view

THINKING ABOUT MOVIES

Brokeback Mountain

In the rural West, two men struggle to reconcile their social roles with their personal identities.

Frozen River

Two working-class women overcome racial prejudice to form an unlikely friendship.

When the Levees Broke

Spike Lee directs this documentary about the devastating social costs of Hurricane Katrina.

A U.S. census worker introduces herself to the householder she is about to interview. Note the handheld electronic device she carries to record and transmit data. The census is a survey, one of the many methods sociologists, governments, and businesses use to collect data.

Sociological Research

RESEARCH TODAY

2-2 What's in a Name?

Sociologists can learn a great deal using available information. For example, every year the Social Security Administration receives thousands of registrations for newborn babies. Using these data, we can identify some cultural trends in the popularity of children's names.

As the accompanying figure shows, for example, John has been an extremely popular boy's name for over a century. In 2009 about 4,000 babies were named John, making it the 26th most popular boy's name that year. Though less than half as many babies were named Juan in 2009, that name has been gaining in popularity in recent generations, reflecting the growing impact of the Latino population in the United States.

In 2009 about 4,000 babies were named John, making it the 26th most popular name that year.

The public data contained in name registries also reveal a trend toward "American-sounding" names among immigrants to the United States. In Italy, for example, Giuseppe is a very popular boy's name. Among Italian immigrants to the United States, the English form of Giuseppe, Joseph, is the 3rd most popular boy's name, though it ranks only 11th among non-Italian immigrants. The pattern of selecting names that will allow children to fit in is not uniform, however.

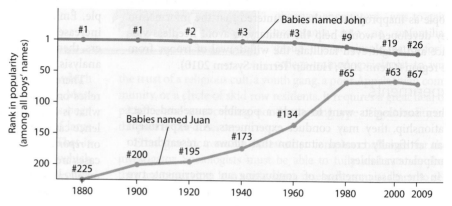

Popularity of John versus Juan

Source: Baby Name Wizard 2010.

In some immigrant groups, parents tend to favor names that symbolize their ethnicity. For example, Kelly is popular among Irish Americans, even though it isn't a traditional girl's name in Ireland. Thus, the available data on newborns' names allow sociologists to detect cultural trends that reflect changing group identities.

Records kept by the Social Security Administration also reveal some regional variations in names. Given the large Hispanic population in Texas, we probably should not be surprised to find that Juan ranks 9th as a name for baby boys in that state. In states like Alabama, Delaware, and Mississippi, however, John is on the top 10 list.

LET'S DISCUSS

1. Visit www.babynamewizard.com on the Internet, and click on "NameVoyager." According to this website, how popular is your first name? Is it becoming more or less fashionable over time?

2. Using the Name Mapper feature at www.babynamewizard.com, find out how popular your name is in the state where you were born. Is your name even more popular in some other states?

Sources: Baby Name Wizard 2010; S. Levitt and Dubner 2006; Lieberson 2000.

---

sources, researchers employ a technique known as **content analysis**, which is the systematic coding and objective recording of data, guided by some rationale.

Content analysis can be revealing. We might think that in the 21st century, blatant favoritism in media representations of men versus women is a thing of the past. However, research suggests otherwise. An analysis of hundreds of characters in children's coloring books shows that males are more likely than females to be shown taking an active role. Gender-stereotyped behavior dominates, with only 3 percent of males engaged in stereotypically female behavior, and only 6 percent of females engaged in stereotypically male behavior (Fitzpatrick and McPherson 2010).

Similarly, despite women's participation in all sports, content analysis of televised sports coverage shows that even when a men's sport is out of season (for example, men's basketball in late summer), it gets more coverage than women's sports in season (for example, women's basketball in July). Furthermore, coverage of female cheerleaders and athletes' wives exceeds coverage of the female athletes who compete in sports (Messner and Cooky 2010).

Table 2-3 summarizes the major research designs, along with their advantages and limitations.

use your sociological *imagination*

Imagine you are a legislator or government policymaker working on a complex social problem. What might happen if you were to base your decision on faulty research?

Ethics of Research

A biochemist cannot inject a drug into a human being unless it has been thoroughly tested and the subject agrees to the shot. To do otherwise would be both unethical and illegal. Sociologists, too, must abide by certain specific standards in conducting research, called a **code of ethics**. The professional society of the discipline, the American Sociological Association (ASA), first published the society's *Code of Ethics* in 1971 and revised it most recently in 1997. It puts forth the following basic principles:

1. Maintain objectivity and integrity in research.
2. Respect the subject's right to privacy and dignity.

TABLE **2-3** MAJOR RESEARCH DESIGNS summing**up** 39

Sociological Research

Method	Examples	Advantages	Limitations
Survey	Questionnaires Interviews	Yields information about specific issues	Can be expensive and time-consuming
Ethnography	Observation	Yields detailed information about specific groups or organizations	Involves months if not years of labor-intensive data
Experiment	Deliberate manipulation of people's social behavior	Yields direct measures of people's behavior	Ethical limitations on the degree to which subjects' behavior can be manipulated
Existing sources/ Secondary analysis	Analysis of census or health data Analysis of films or TV commercials	Cost-efficiency	Limited to data collected for some other purpose

3. Protect subjects from personal harm.

4. Preserve confidentiality.

5. Seek informed consent when data are collected from research participants or when behavior occurs in a private context.

6. Acknowledge research collaboration and assistance.

7. Disclose all sources of financial support (American Sociological Association 1997).

These basic principles probably seem clear-cut. How could they lead to any disagreement or controversy? Yet many delicate ethical questions cannot be resolved simply by reading these seven principles. For example, should a sociologist who is engaged in participant-observation research always protect the confidentiality of subjects? What if the subjects are members of a religious cult allegedly involved in unethical and possibly illegal activities? What if the sociologist is interviewing political activists and is questioned by government authorities about the research?

Because most sociological research uses *people* as sources of information—as respondents to survey questions, subjects of ethnography, or participants in experiments—these sorts of questions are important. In all cases, sociologists need to be certain they are not invading their subjects' privacy. Generally, they do so by assuring subjects of anonymity and by guaranteeing the confidentiality of personal information. In addition, research proposals that involve human subjects must now be overseen by a review board, whose members seek to ensure that subjects are not placed at an unreasonable level of risk. If necessary, the board may ask researchers to revise their research designs to conform to the code of ethics.

We can appreciate the seriousness of the ethical problems researchers confront by considering the experience of sociologist Rik Scarce, described in the next section. Scarce's vow to protect his subjects' confidentiality got him into considerable trouble with the law.

Confidentiality

Like journalists, sociologists occasionally find themselves subject to questions from law enforcement authorities because of knowledge they have gained in the course of their work. This uncomfortable situation raises profound ethical questions.

In May 1993, Rik Scarce, a doctoral candidate in sociology at Washington State University, was jailed for contempt of court. Scarce had declined to tell a federal grand jury what he knew—or even whether he knew anything—about a 1991 raid on a university research laboratory by animal rights activists. At the time, Scarce was conducting research for a book about environmental protesters and knew at least one suspect in the break-in. Curiously, although he was chastised by a federal judge, Scarce won respect from fellow prison inmates, who regarded him as a man who "wouldn't snitch" (Monaghan 1993:A8).

The American Sociological Association supported Scarce's position when he appealed his sentence. Scarce maintained his silence. Ultimately the judge ruled that nothing would be gained by further incarceration, and Scarce was released after serving 159 days in jail. In January 1994, the U.S. Supreme Court declined to hear Scarce's case on appeal. The Court's failure to consider his case led Scarce (2005) to argue that federal legislation is needed to clarify the right of scholars and members of the press to preserve the confidentiality of those they interview.

Conflict of Interest

Sometimes disclosing all the sources of funding for a study, as required in principle 7 of the ASA's *Code of Ethics,* is not a sufficient guarantee of ethical conduct. Especially in the case of both corporate and government funding, money given ostensibly for the support of basic research may come with strings attached. Accepting funds from a private organization or even a government agency that stands to benefit from a study's results can call into question a researcher's objectivity and integrity (principle 1). The controversy surrounding the involvement of social scientists in the U.S. Army's Human Terrain System is one example of this conflict of interest.

Another example is the Exxon Corporation's support for research on jury verdicts. In 1989, the Exxon oil tanker *Valdez* hit a reef off the coast of Alaska, spilling more than 11 million gallons of oil into Prince William Sound. Five years later a federal court ordered Exxon to pay $5.3 billion in damages for the accident. Exxon appealed the verdict and began approaching legal scholars, sociologists, and psychologists who might be willing to study jury deliberations. The corporation's objective was to develop academic support for its lawyers' contention that the punitive judgments in such cases result from faulty deliberations and do not have a deterrent effect.

Some scholars have questioned the propriety of accepting funds under these circumstances, even if the source is disclosed. In at least one case, an Exxon employee explicitly told a

TAKING SOCIOLOGY TO WORK

Dave Eberbach, **Research Coordinator, United Way of Central Iowa**

As a research specialist, Dave Eberbach uses his training in sociology to work for social change. Eberbach looks for small pockets of poverty that are generally hidden in state and county statistics. By zeroing in on conditions in specific neighborhoods, he empowers state and local agencies that work on behalf of the disadvantaged.

Eberbach, who is based in Des Moines, Iowa, was hired to establish a "data warehouse" of social statistics for the local United Way. Part of his job has been to demonstrate to agencies how the information in the database can be of use to them. "We have moved most of our data presentations away from charts and graphs, and on to maps of the county, the city, and the neighborhood," he explains. "This allows people to truly 'see' the big picture."

When Eberbach entered Grinnell College in 1985, he had already taken a sociology course and knew that the subject interested him. Still, he could not have foreseen all the practical uses he might have had for what he learned. "Never assume that you'll never need to know something (including statistics)," he advises. "Life has a funny way of bringing things around again."

At Grinnell, Eberbach benefited from the presence of several visiting professors who exposed him to a variety of cultural and racial perspectives. His personal acquaintance with them complemented the concepts he was learning in his sociology classes. Today, Eberbach draws on his college experiences at the United Way, where his work brings him into contact with a diverse group of people.

Sociology has also helped Eberbach in his chosen specialty, research. "I believe that I am a better 'data person' because of my sociology background," he claims. "The human context for data is as important and can get lost or misdirected by pure statistics," he explains. "My sociology background has helped me ask the appropriate questions to make effective change in our community."

LET'S DISCUSS

1. Do you know what you want to be doing 10 years from now? If so, how might a knowledge of statistics help you in your future occupation?
2. What kinds of statistics, specifically, might you find in the United Way's data warehouse? Where would they come from?

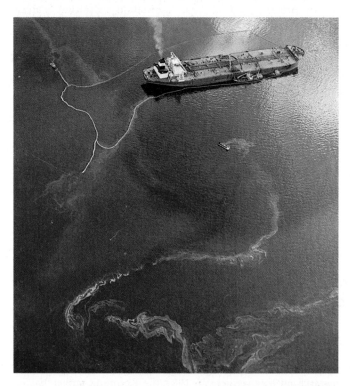

A floating containment barrier (or boom) encircles the Exxon oil tanker *Valdez* after its grounding on a reef off the coast of Alaska. Exxon was found negligent in the environmental disaster and was ordered to pay $5.3 billion for the cleanup. But the corporation's executives spent $1 million to fund academic research that lawyers used to reduce the penalty to $500 million. We will have to see how research results are used or abused to resolve damage claims arising from BP's 2010 oil spill in the Gulf of Mexico.

sociologist that the corporation offers financial support to scholars who have shown the tendency to express views similar to its own. An argument can also be made that Exxon was attempting to set scholars' research agendas with its huge war chest. Rather than funding studies on the improvement of cleanup technologies or the assignment of long-term environmental costs, Exxon chose to shift scientists' attention to the validity of the legal awards in environmental cases.

The scholars who accepted Exxon's support deny that it influenced their work or changed their conclusions. Some received support from other sources as well, such as the National Science Foundation and Harvard University's Olin Center for Law, Economics, and Business. Many of their findings were published in respected academic journals after review by a jury of peers. Still, at least one researcher who participated in the studies refused monetary support from Exxon to avoid even the suggestion of a conflict of interest.

Exxon has spent roughly $1 million on the research, and at least one compilation of studies congenial to the corporation's point of view has been published. As ethical considerations require, the academics who conducted the studies disclosed Exxon's role in funding them. Nevertheless, the investment appears to have paid off. In 2006, drawing on these studies, Exxon's lawyers succeeded in persuading an appeals court to reduce the corporation's legal damages from $5.3 to $2.5 billion. In 2008 Exxon appealed that judgment to the Supreme Court, which further reduced the damages to $500 million. The final award, which is to be shared by about 32,000 plaintiffs, will result in payments of about $15,000 to each person (Freudenburg 2005; Liptak 2008).

Value Neutrality

The ethical considerations of sociologists lie not only in the methods they use and the funding they accept, but also in the way they interpret their results. Max Weber ([1904] 1949) recognized that personal values would influence the questions that sociologists select for research. In his view, that was perfectly acceptable, but under no conditions could a researcher allow his or her personal feelings to influence the *interpretation* of data. In Weber's phrase, sociologists must practice **value neutrality** in their research.

As part of this neutrality, investigators have an ethical obligation to accept research findings even when the data run counter to their personal views, to theoretically based explanations, or to widely accepted beliefs. For example, Émile Durkheim challenged popular conceptions when he reported that social (rather than supernatural) forces were an important factor in suicide.

Although some sociologists believe that neutrality is impossible, ignoring the issue would be irresponsible. Let's consider what might happen if researchers brought their own biases to the investigation. A person investigating the impact of intercollegiate sports on alumni contributions, for example, might focus only on the highly visible revenue-generating sports of football and basketball and neglect the so-called minor sports, such as tennis or soccer, which are more likely to involve women athletes. Despite the early work of W. E. B. DuBois and Jane Addams, sociologists still need to be reminded that the discipline often fails to adequately consider all people's social behavior.

In her book *The Death of White Sociology* (1973), Joyce Ladner called attention to the tendency of mainstream sociology to treat the lives of African Americans as a social problem. More recently, feminist sociologist Shulamit Reinharz (1992) has argued that sociological research should be not only inclusive but also open to bringing about social change and to drawing on relevant research by nonsociologists. Both Ladner and Reinharz maintain that researchers should always analyze whether women's unequal social status has affected their studies in any way. For example, one might broaden the study of the impact of education on income to consider the implications of the unequal pay status of men and women. The issue of value neutrality does not mean that sociologists can't have opinions, but it does mean that they must work to overcome any biases, however unintentional, that they may bring to their analysis of research.

Sociologist Peter Rossi (1987) admits to having liberal inclinations that direct him to certain fields of study. Yet in line with Weber's view of value neutrality, Rossi's commitment to rigorous research methods and objective interpretation of data has sometimes led him to controversial findings that are not necessarily supportive of his liberal values. For example, his measure of the extent of homelessness in Chicago in the mid-1980s fell far below the estimates of the Chicago Coalition for the Homeless. Coalition members bitterly attacked Rossi for hampering their social reform efforts by minimizing the extent of homelessness. Rossi (1987:79) concluded that "in the short term, good social research will often be greeted as a betrayal of one or another side to a particular controversy."

Feminist theorists see the global trafficking of sex workers as one sign of a close relationship between the two supposedly separate worlds of industrial nations and the developing nations that depend on them.

on the current generation of social researchers. How might this perspective influence research? Although researchers must be objective, their theoretical orientation may influence the questions they ask—or, just as important, the questions they fail to ask. Until recently, for example, researchers frequently studied work and the family separately. Yet feminist theorists see the two spheres of activity as being closely integrated. Similarly, work and leisure, paid and unpaid domestic work may be seen not as two separate spheres, but as two sides of the same coin.

Feminist theorists have also drawn researchers' attention to their tendency to overlook women in their studies. For most of the history of sociology, researchers conducted studies of male subjects or male-led groups and organizations and then generalized their findings to all people. For many decades, for example, ethnographic studies of urban life focused on street corners, neighborhood taverns, and bowling alleys—places where men typically congregated. Although researchers gained some valuable insights in this way, they did not form a true impression of city life, because they overlooked the areas where women were likely to gather, such as playgrounds, grocery stores, and front stoops. These are the arenas that the feminist perspective focuses on.

The feminist perspective has also had an impact on global research. To feminist theorists, the traditional distinction between industrial nations and developing nations overlooks the close relationship between these two supposedly separate worlds. Feminist theorists have called for more research on the special role that immigrant women play in maintaining their households; on the use of domestic workers from less developed nations by households in industrial nations; and on the global trafficking of sex workers (Cheng 2003; Cooper et al. 2007; Sprague 2005).

Feminist researchers tend to involve and consult their subjects more than other researchers, and they are more oriented toward seeking change, raising the public consciousness, and influencing policy. They are particularly open to a multidisciplinary approach, such as making use of historical evidence or legal studies (T. Baker 1999; Lofland 1975; Reinharz 1992).

thinking CRITICALLY

If you were planning to do research on human sexuality, which of the seven principles in the ASA's *Code of Ethics* would particularly concern you? What ethical problems might arise in such a study, and how would you attempt to prevent them?

Feminist Methodology

Of the four theoretical approaches to sociology introduced in Chapter 1, the feminist perspective has had the greatest impact

The Data-Rich Future

Advances in technology have affected all aspects of our lives, and sociological research is no exception. Massive increases in available data have allowed sociologists to undertake research that was virtually impossible just a decade ago. In the recent past, only people with grants or major institutional support could work easily with large amounts of data. Now anyone with a computer can access huge amounts of data and learn more about social behavior. Moreover, data from foreign countries are sometimes as available as information from the United States.

In the latter part of 2009, the world experienced an intense burst of influenza initially referred to as "swine flu," but later identified as the H1N1 flu strain. How did medical researchers track the virus's spread across a nation, much less the world? Epidemiologists typically rely on reports that originate in doctors' offices and are funneled through government agencies. Data collection is a time-consuming process, with many days passing between the detection of symptoms and the publication of official statistics. However, public health researchers found a way to track contagious diseases using Google. By monitoring the topics people search for and compensating for the relative access to computers in different countries (high in Sweden and low in Nigeria, for example), they can monitor the spread of disease almost in real time (Dukić et al. 2011).

Similarly, in the past sociologists had to rely on victims' complaints or police reports to understand crime patterns. Now they are beginning to access real-time, geocoded (that is, location-specific) incident reports. These new data will offer sociologists much more information, which they can interpret and relate to other aspects of the social environment (G. King 2011).

One ethical concern raised by all these data involves individual privacy. Sociologists now have access to information about people's real estate transactions, campaign contributions, online product purchases, and even travel along toll ways. What steps should they take to protect the privacy of the individuals whose data they

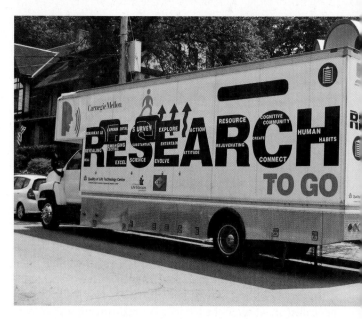

Carnegie Mellon University's Data Truck lets researchers go where their subjects are—from nightclubs to marathon races. Equipped with the latest technology, the truck allows social scientists to enter the responses to their community surveys into their databases on site. It also gives them access to online social networks in the area, and even lets them videotape street activity.

are using? This is not an academic question. Today, 87 percent of the people in the United States can be personally identified given only their gender, date of birth, and ZIP code (G. King 2011).

We have seen that researchers rely on a number of tools, from time-tested observational research and use of existing sources to the latest in computer technologies. The Social Policy section that follows will describe researchers' efforts to survey the general population about a controversial aspect of social behavior: human sexuality. This investigation was complicated by its potential social policy implications. Because in the real world, sociological research can have far-reaching consequences for public policy and public welfare, each of the following chapters in this book will close with a Social Policy section.

socialpolicy and Sociological Research

Studying Human Sexuality

Looking at the Issue

Is sex only as far away as your cable box? The latest content analysis of sexual content on television shows that more than two-thirds of all TV shows include some sexual content—up from about half of all shows seven years earlier (Figure 2-5). Yet a national survey showed that only 17 percent of parents use electronic means, such as the V-chip, to block TV content that may be inappropriate for children. Media

representations of sexual behavior are important, because surveys of teens and young adults tell us that television is one of their top sources of information and ideas about sex. TV has more influence on young people's conceptions of sex than schools, parents, or peers (Kaiser Family Foundation 2007).

In this age of devastating sexually transmitted diseases, there is no time more important to increase our scientific understanding of

THINKING ABOUT MOVIES

And the Band Played On

In the early years of the AIDS crisis, researchers employ the scientific method to understand how the disease is transmitted.

An Inconvenient Truth

In this documentary about global warming, Al Gore argues that certain social groups are already paying the price for climate change.

Kinsey

A researcher struggles with the ethical challenges of studying human sexual behavior.

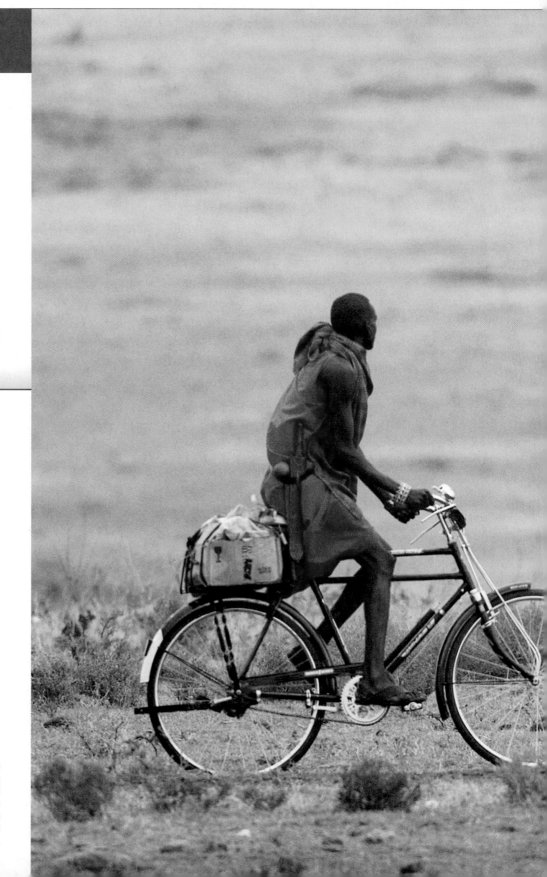

In Africa, Maasai tribesmen ride bicycles through Masai Mara National Park in Kenya. Shared learned behavior—what we call culture—can move across international borders to become part of other societies.

❝ Nacirema culture is characterized by a highly developed market economy which has evolved in a rich natural habitat. While much of the people's time is devoted to economic pursuits, a large part of the fruits of these labors and a considerable portion of the day are spent in ritual activity. The focus of this activity is the human body, the appearance and health of which loom as a dominant concern in the ethos of the people. While such a concern is certainly not unusual, its ceremonial aspects and associated philosophy are unique.

The fundamental belief underlying the whole system appears to be that the human body is ugly and that its natural tendency is to debility and disease. Incarcerated in such a body, man's only hope is to avert these characteristics through the use of the powerful influences of ritual and ceremony. Every household has one or more shrines devoted to this purpose. The more powerful individuals in the society have several shrines in their houses and, in fact, the opulence of a house is often referred to in terms of the number of such ritual centers it possesses. Most houses are of wattle and daub construction, but the shrine rooms of the more wealthy are walled with stone. Poorer families imitate the rich by applying pottery plaques to their shrine walls.

The focal point of the shrine is a box or chest which is built into the wall. In this chest are kept the many charms and magical potions without which no native believes he could live.

While each family has at least one such shrine, the rituals associated with it are not family ceremonies but are private and secret. The rites are normally only discussed with children, and then only during the period when they are being initiated into these mysteries. I was able, however, to establish sufficient rapport with the natives to examine these shrines and to have the rituals described to me.

The focal point of the shrine is a box or chest which is built into the wall. In this chest are kept the many charms and magical potions without which no native believes he could live. These preparations are secured from a variety of specialized practitioners. The most powerful of these are the medicine men, whose assistance must be rewarded with substantial gifts. However, the medicine men do not provide the curative potions for their clients, but decide what the ingredients should be and then write them down in an ancient and secret language. This writing is understood only by the medicine men and by the herbalists who, for another gift, provide the required charm.

The charm is not disposed of after it has served its purpose, but is placed in the charm-box of the household shrine. As these magical materials are specific for certain ills, and the real or imagined maladies of the people are many, the charm-box is usually full to overflowing. The magical packets are so numerous that people forget what their purposes were and fear to use them again. While the natives are very vague on this point, we can only assume that the idea in retaining all the old magical materials is that their presence in the charm-box, before which the body rituals are conducted, will in some way protect the worshipper. ❞

(Miner 1956:503–504) Additional information about this excerpt can be found on the Online Learning Center at www.mhhe.com/schaefer13e.

In this excerpt from his journal article "Body Ritual among the Nacirema," anthropologist Horace Miner casts his observant eye on the intriguing rituals of an exotic culture. If some aspects of this culture seem familiar to you, however, you are right, for what Miner is describing is actually the culture of the United States ("Nacirema" is "American" spelled backward). The "shrine" Miner writes of is the bathroom; he correctly informs us that in this culture, one measure of wealth is how many bathrooms one's home has. In their bathroom rituals, he goes on, the Nacirema use charms and magical potions (beauty products and prescription drugs) obtained from specialized practitioners (such as hair stylists), herbalists (pharmacists), and medicine men (physicians). Using our sociological imaginations, we could update Miner's description of the Nacirema's charms, written in 1956, by adding tooth whiteners, anti-aging creams, Waterpiks, and hair gel.

When we step back and examine a culture thoughtfully and objectively, whether it is our own culture in disguise or another less familiar to us, we learn something new about society. Take Fiji, an island in the Pacific where a robust, nicely rounded body has always been the ideal for both men and women. This is a society in which "You've gained weight" traditionally has been considered a compliment, and "Your legs are skinny," an insult. Yet a recent study shows that for the first time, eating disorders have been showing up among young people in Fiji. What has happened to change their body image? Since the introduction of cable television in 1995, many Fiji islanders, especially young women, have begun to emulate not their mothers and aunts, but the small-waisted stars of television programs currently airing there, like *Grey's Anatomy* and *Desperate Housewives*. Studying culture in places like Fiji, then, sheds light on our society as well (A. Becker 2007; Fiji TV 2010).

In this chapter we will study the development of culture around the world, including the cultural effects of the worldwide trend toward globalization. We will see just how basic the study of culture is to sociology. Our discussion will focus both on general cultural practices found in all societies and on the wide variations that can distinguish one society from another. We will define and explore the major aspects of culture, including language, norms, sanctions, and values. We will see how cultures develop a dominant ideology, and how functionalist and conflict theorists view culture. We'll also see what can happen when a major corporation ignores cultural variations. Then, in the Social Policy section, we will look at the conflicts in cultural values that underlie current debates over bilingualism.

What Is Culture?

Culture is the totality of learned, socially transmitted customs, knowledge, material objects, and behavior. It includes the ideas, values, and artifacts (for example, DVDs, comic books, and birth control devices) of groups of people. Patriotic attachment to the flag of the United States is an aspect of culture, as is a national passion for the tango in Argentina.

Sometimes people refer to a particular person as "very cultured" or to a city as having "lots of culture." That use of the term *culture* is different from our use in this textbook. In sociological terms, culture does not refer solely to the fine arts and refined intellectual taste. It consists of *all* objects and ideas within a society, including slang words, ice-cream cones, and rock music. Sociologists consider both a portrait by Rembrandt and the work of graffiti spray painters to be aspects of culture. A tribe that cultivates soil by hand has just as much culture as a people that relies on computer-operated machinery. Each people has a distinctive culture with its own characteristic ways of gathering and preparing food, constructing homes, structuring the family, and promoting standards of right and wrong.

The fact that you share a similar culture with others helps to define the group or society to which you belong. A fairly large number of people are said to constitute a **society** when they live in the same territory, are relatively independent of people outside their area, and participate in a common culture. Metropolitan Los Angeles is more populous than at least 150 nations, yet sociologists do not consider it a society in its own right. Rather, they see it as part of—and dependent on—the larger society of the United States.

A society is the largest form of human group. It consists of people who share a common heritage and culture. Members of the society learn this culture and transmit it from one generation to the next. They even preserve their distinctive culture through literature, art, video recordings, and other means of expression.

Sociologists have long recognized the many ways in which culture influences human behavior. Through what has been termed a tool kit of habits, skills, and styles, people of a common culture construct their acquisition of knowledge, their interactions with kinfolk, their entrance into the job market—in short, the way in which they live. If it were not for the social transmission of culture, each generation would have to reinvent television, not to mention the wheel (Swidler 1986).

Having a common culture also simplifies many day-to-day interactions. For example, when you buy an airline ticket, you know you don't have to bring along hundreds of dollars in cash. You can pay with a credit card. When you are part of a society, you take for granted many small (as well as more important) cultural patterns. You assume that theaters will provide seats for the

Navigating cultural differences can be a challenge. During a visit to Tokyo, President Obama was criticized for his deep bow to Emperor Akihito. And at the 2010 Winter Olympics, Russian ice dancers Domnina and Shabalin were criticized for their interpretation of Aboriginal dress. Favored to win, they took only third place.

audience, that physicians will not disclose confidential information, and that parents will be careful when crossing the street with young children. All these assumptions reflect basic values, beliefs, and customs of the culture of the United States.

Today, when text, sound, and video can be transmitted around the world instantaneously, some aspects of culture transcend national borders. The German philosopher Theodor Adorno and others have spoken of the worldwide **culture industry** that standardizes the goods and services demanded by consumers. Adorno contends that globally, the primary effect of popular culture is to limit people's choices. Yet others have shown that the culture industry's influence does not always permeate international borders. Sometimes the culture industry is embraced; at other times, soundly rejected (Adorno [1971] 1991:98–106; Horkheimer and Adorno [1944] 2002).

Cultural Universals

All societies have developed certain common practices and beliefs, known as **cultural universals.** Many cultural universals are, in fact, adaptations to meet essential human needs, such as the need for food, shelter, and clothing. Anthropologist George Murdock (1945:124) compiled a list of cultural universals, including athletic sports, cooking, dancing, visiting, personal names, marriage, medicine, religious ritual, funeral ceremonies, sexual restrictions, and trade.

The cultural practices Murdock listed may be universal, but the manner in which they are expressed varies from culture to culture. For example, one society may let its members choose their marriage partners; another may encourage marriages arranged by the parents.

Not only does the expression of cultural universals vary from one society to another; within a society, it may also change dramatically over time. Each generation, and each year for that matter, most human cultures change and expand.

Ethnocentrism

Many everyday statements reflect our attitude that our culture is best. We use terms such as *underdeveloped, backward,* and *primitive* to refer to other societies. What "we" believe is a religion; what "they" believe is superstition and mythology.

It is tempting to evaluate the practices of other cultures on the basis of our perspectives. Sociologist William Graham Sumner (1906) coined the term **ethnocentrism** to refer to the tendency to assume that one's culture and way of life represent the norm or are superior to all others. The ethnocentric person sees his or her group as the center or defining point of culture and view all other cultures as deviations from what is "normal." Westerners who think cattle are to be used for food might look down on India's Hindu religion and culture, which view the cow as sacred. Or people in one culture may dismiss as unthinkable the mate selection or child-rearing practices of another culture. In sum, our view of the world is dramatically influenced by the society in which we were raised.

Conflict theorists point out that ethnocentric value judgments serve to devalue groups and to deny equal opportunities. Functionalists, on the other hand, point out that ethnocentrism serves to maintain a sense of solidarity by promoting group pride. Denigrating other nations and cultures can enhance our patriotic feelings and belief that our way of life is superior. Yet this type of social stability is established at the expense of other peoples. In extreme cases, ethnocentrism can lead to the destruction of an entire culture. Box 3-1 describes several instances of what social scientists have termed *cultural genocide.*

Ethnocentrism is hardly limited to citizens of the United States. Visitors from many African cultures are surprised at the disrespect that children in the United States show their parents. People from India may be repelled by our practice of living in the same household with dogs and cats. Many Islamic fundamentalists in the Arab world and Asia view the United States as corrupt, decadent, and doomed to destruction. All these people may feel comforted by membership in cultures that in their view are superior to ours.

Cultural Relativism

While ethnocentrism means evaluating foreign cultures using the familiar culture of the observer as a standard of correct behavior, **cultural relativism** means viewing people's behavior from the perspective of their own culture. It places a priority on understanding other cultures, rather than dismissing them as "strange" or "exotic." Unlike ethnocentrists, cultural relativists employ the kind of value neutrality in scientific study that Max Weber saw as so important.

Cultural relativism stresses that different social contexts give rise to different norms and values. Thus, we must examine practices such as polygamy, bullfighting, and monarchy within the particular contexts of the cultures in which they are found. Although cultural relativism does not suggest that we must unquestionably accept every cultural variation, it does require a serious and unbiased effort to evaluate norms, values, and customs in light of their distinctive culture.

Consider the practice of children marrying adults. Most people in North America cannot fathom the idea of a 12-year-old girl marrying. The custom, which is illegal in the United States, is common in West Africa and South Asia. Should the United States respect such marriages? The apparent answer is no. In 2006 the U.S. government spent $623 million to discourage the practice in many of the countries with the highest child-marriage rates (Figure 3-1, page 56).

From the perspective of cultural relativism, we might ask whether one society should spend its resources to dictate the norms of another. However, federal officials have defended the government's actions. They contend that child marriage deprives girls of education, threatens their health, and weakens public health efforts to combat HIV/AIDS (Jain and Kurz 2007; B. Slavin 2007).

Sociobiology and Culture

While sociology emphasizes diversity and change in the expression of culture, another school of thought, sociobiology, stresses the universal aspects of culture. **Sociobiology** is the systematic study of how biology affects human social behavior. Sociobiologists assert that many of the cultural traits humans display, such as the almost universal expectation that women will be nurturers and men will be providers, are not learned but are rooted in our genetic makeup.

Sociobiology is founded on the naturalist Charles Darwin's (1859) theory of evolution. In traveling the world, Darwin had noted small variations in species—in the shape of a bird's beak, for example—from one location to another. He theorized that over hundreds of generations, random variations in genetic makeup had helped certain members of a species to survive in a particular environment. A bird with a differently shaped beak might have been better at gathering seeds than other birds, for

SOCIOLOGY IN THE GLOBAL COMMUNITY

3-1 Cultural Genocide

Usually, the term **genocide** refers to the deliberate, systematic killing of an entire people or nation. However, social scientists have long recognized another form of genocide, called *cultural genocide,* in which a nation's culture is eliminated even though the people live on.

Cultural genocide refers to the systematic destruction of a group's culture. Social scientists have used the term to describe one nation's efforts to suppress another nation's language. Japan's attempt to eliminate the Korean people's language, history, and even names during its occupation of Korea in the early 20th century is one example. However, the term also applies to government efforts to eliminate indigenous peoples' traditions. Australia, Canada, New Zealand, and the United States illustrate this second form of cultural genocide.

Agents of the U.S. government took American Indian children from their parents' homes and sent them to be raised in families far from their native culture.

In the United States, government officials encouraged White families to "adopt" indigenous children and raise them in the dominant culture. Agents of the U.S. government took American Indian children from their parents' homes and sent them to be raised in families far from their native culture. Sometimes the children were removed with their parents' permission, but often they were taken against their parents' will. Government officials assumed that the supposed benefit of familiarizing the children with the dominant culture would outweigh and ultimately excuse the personal and cultural losses the children experienced.

Inevitably, the forced removal of generations of American Indian children from their families led to the near extinction of their culture. Only in 1968, following political pressure by Native Americans, did Congress call a halt to the program. Under the Indian Child Welfare Act (ICWA), even if a family agrees to a child's removal from the home, the tribe must also agree. In placing children for adoption and foster care, social workers must give priority first to the child's extended family, then to members of the child's tribe, and finally to all American Indian families.

LET'S DISCUSS

1. Can you imagine being taken from your parents' home by a government agent and moved to a different family with a different culture? How would you react?
2. What might be the long-term consequences of American Indian children's removal from their families, besides the destruction of their culture?

Sources: Cantzler 2008; National Indian Child Welfare Association 2010.

---

instance. In reproducing, these lucky individuals had passed on their advantageous genes to succeeding generations. Eventually, given their advantage in survival, individuals with the variation began to outnumber other members of the species. The species was slowly adapting to its environment. Darwin called this process of adaptation to the environment through random genetic variation *natural selection.*

Sociobiologists apply Darwin's principle of natural selection to the study of social behavior. They assume that particular forms of behavior become genetically linked to a species if they contribute to its fitness to survive (van den Berghe 1978). In its extreme form, sociobiology suggests that *all* behavior is the result of genetic or biological factors, and that social interactions play no role in shaping people's conduct.

Sociobiologists do not seek to describe individual behavior on the level of "Why is Fred more aggressive than Jim?" Rather, they focus on how human nature is affected by the genetic composition of a *group* of people who share certain characteristics (such as men or women, or members of isolated tribal bands). In general, sociobiologists have stressed the basic genetic heritage that *all* humans share and have shown little interest in speculating about alleged differences between racial groups or nationalities. A few researchers have tried to trace specific behaviors, like

criminal activity, to certain genetic markers, but those markers are not deterministic. Family cohesiveness, peer group behavior, and other social factors can override genetic influences on behavior (Guo et al. 2008; E. Wilson 1975, 1978).

Some researchers insist that intellectual interest in sociobiology will only deflect serious study of the more significant influence on human behavior, the social environment. Yet Lois Wladis Hoffman (1985), in her presidential address to the Society for the Psychological Study of Social Issues, argued that sociobiology poses a valuable challenge to social scientists to better document their research. Interactionists, for example, could show how social behavior is not programmed by human biology, but instead adjusts continually to the attitudes and responses of others.

Certainly most social scientists would agree that there is a biological basis for social behavior. But there is less support for the extreme positions taken by certain advocates of sociobiology. Like interactionists, conflict theorists and functionalists believe that people's behavior rather than their genetic structure defines social reality. Conflict theorists fear that the sociobiological approach could be used as an argument against efforts to assist disadvantaged people, such as schoolchildren who are not competing successfully (Freese 2008; Machalek and Martin 2010; E. Wilson 2000).

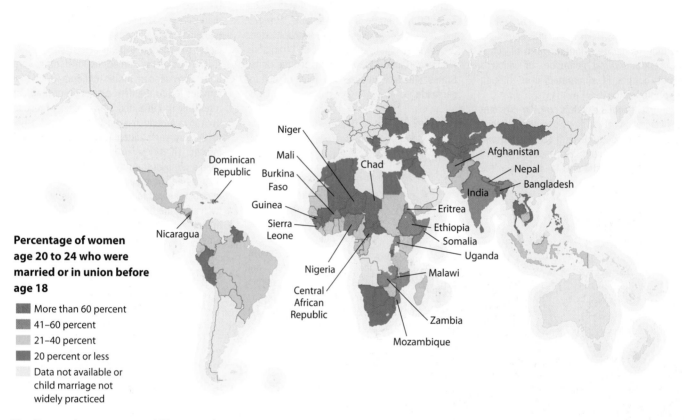

Percentage of women age 20 to 24 who were married or in union before age 18

- More than 60 percent
- 41–60 percent
- 21–40 percent
- 20 percent or less
- Data not available or child marriage not widely practiced

Note: Data are the most recent available, ranging from 1987 to 2006.
Source: UNICEF 2010.
In 21 countries, 40 percent or more of the women under 18 are married.

thinking CRITICALLY

Select three cultural universals from George Murdock's list (page 54) and analyze them from a functionalist perspective. Why are these practices found in every culture? What functions do they serve?

Development of Culture around the World

We've come a long way from our prehistoric heritage. The human species has produced such achievements as the novels of Leo Tolstoy, the art of Pablo Picasso, and the films of Ang Lee. A decade into the new millennium, we can transmit an entire book around the world via the Internet, clone cells, and prolong lives through organ transplants. We can peer into the outermost reaches of the universe or analyze our innermost feelings. In this section we will examine two of the social processes that make these remarkable achievements possible: innovation and the diffusion of culture through globalization and technology.

Innovation

The process of introducing a new idea or object to a culture is known as **innovation.** Innovation interests sociologists because of the social consequences of introducing something new. There are two forms of innovation: discovery and invention. **Discovery** involves making known or sharing the existence of an aspect of reality. The finding of the structure of the DNA molecule and the identification of a new moon of Saturn are both acts of discovery. A significant factor in the process of discovery is the sharing of newfound knowledge with others. In contrast, an **invention** results when existing cultural items are combined into a form that did not exist before. The bow and arrow, the automobile, and the television are all examples of inventions, as are Protestantism and democracy.

use your sociological *imagination*

If you grew up in your parents' generation—without computers, e-mail, MP3 players, and cell phones—how would your daily life differ from the one you lead today?

3-2 Life in the Global Village

Imagine a "borderless world" in which culture, trade, commerce, money, and even people move freely from one place to another. Popular culture is widely shared, whether it be Japanese sushi or U.S. running shoes, and the English speaker who answers questions over the telephone about your credit card account is as likely to be in India or Ireland as in the United States. In this world, even the sovereignty of nations is at risk, challenged by political movements and ideologies that span nations.

What caused this great wave of cultural diffusion? First, sociologists take note of advances in communications technology. Satellite TV, cell phones, the Internet, and the like allow information to flow freely across the world, linking global markets. In 2008, this process reached the point where consumers could view videos on handheld devices and surf the Internet on their wireless cell phones, shopping online at Amazon.com, eBay, and other commercial websites from cars, airports, and cafeterias. Second, corporations in the industrial nations have become multinational, with both factories and markets in developing countries. Business leaders welcome the opportunity to sell consumer goods in populous countries such as China. Third, these multinational firms have cooperated with global financial institutions, organizations, and governments to promote free trade—unrestricted or lightly restricted commerce across national borders.

Globalization is not universally welcomed. Many critics see the dominance of "businesses without borders" as benefiting the rich, particularly the very wealthy in industrial countries, at the expense of the poor in less developed nations. They consider globalization to be a

Even James Bond movies and Taylor Swift may be seen as threats to native cultures.

successor to the imperialism and colonialism that oppressed Third World nations for centuries.

Another criticism of globalization comes from people who feel overwhelmed by global culture. Embedded in the concept of globalization is the notion of the cultural domination of developing nations by more affluent nations. Simply put, people lose their traditional values and begin to identify with the culture of dominant nations. They may discard or neglect their native languages and dress as they attempt to copy the icons of mass-market entertainment and fashion. Even James Bond movies and Taylor Swift may be seen as threats to native cultures, if they dominate the media at the expense of local art forms. As Sembene Ousmane, one of Africa's most prominent writers and filmmakers, noted, "[Today] we are more familiar with European fairy tales than with our own traditional stories" (World Development Forum 1990:4).

Globalization has its positive side, too. Many developing nations are taking their place in the world of commerce and bringing in much needed income. The communications revolution helps people to stay connected and gives them access to knowledge that can improve living standards and even save lives.

LET'S DISCUSS

1. How are you affected by globalization? Which aspects of globalization do you find advantageous and which objectionable?
2. How would you feel if the customs and traditions you grew up with were replaced by the culture or values of another country? How might you try to protect your culture?

Sources: Dodds 2000; Giddens 1991; Hirst and Thompson 1996; D. Martin et al. 2006; Ritzer 2004; Sernau 2001; Tedeschi 2006.

Globalization, Diffusion, and Technology

The recent emergence of Starbucks, the worldwide chain of coffeehouses, is just one illustration of the rapidly escalating trend toward globalization (see Chapter 1). While people in Asia are beginning to enjoy coffee, people in North America are discovering sushi. Some have become familiar with the *bento box,* a small lunchbox that is often used to serve sushi. A trademark Japanese cuisine, sushi has evolved from a once-exotic dish in the United States to a mainstream food commonly found in supermarket refrigerators. Yet its move across the Pacific has changed the delicacy. Americans tend to treat sushi as a take-out or menu item. The authentic way to eat sushi is to sit at a bar and engage the chef in conversation about the day's catch before choosing which fish or shellfish to eat.

More and more cultural expressions and practices are crossing national borders and having an effect on the traditions and customs of the societies exposed to them. Sociologists use the term **diffusion** to refer to the process by which a cultural item spreads from group to group or society to society. Diffusion can occur through a variety of means, among them exploration, military conquest, missionary work, and the influence of the mass media, tourism, and the Internet (Box 3-2). It has also been hastened by the spread of the fast-food restaurant.

Sociologist George Ritzer coined the term *McDonaldization of society* to describe how the principles of fast-food restaurants, developed in the United States, have come to dominate more and more sectors of societies throughout the world (see Chapter 5). For example, hair salons and medical clinics now take walk-ins. In Hong Kong, sex selection clinics offer a menu of items, from fertility enhancement to methods of increasing the likelihood of having a child of the desired sex. And religious groups—from evangelical preachers on local stations or websites to priests at the Vatican Television Center—use marketing techniques similar to those that are used to sell Happy Meals.

The fictional Spider-Man first appeared in comic books in the United States in 1962. Since then, the superhero's image and the legends surrounding him have circled the globe through the process of cultural diffusion. In this photograph, taken at a fairground in Iran, a girl enjoys a Spider-Man ride.

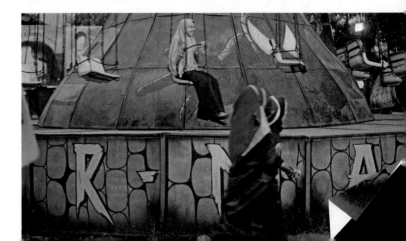

SOCIOLOGY IN THE GLOBAL COMMUNITY

3-3 Cultural Survival in Brazil

When the first Portuguese ships landed on the coast of what we now know as Brazil, more than 2 million people inhabited the vast, mineral-rich land. The natives lived in small, isolated settlements, spoke a variety of languages, and embraced many different cultural traditions.

Today, over five centuries later, Brazil's population has grown to more than 180 million, only about 500,000 of whom are indigenous peoples descended from the original inhabitants. Over 200 different indigenous groups have survived, living a life tied closely to the land and the rivers, just as their ancestors did. But over the past two generations, their numbers have dwindled as booms in mining, logging, oil drilling, and agriculture have encroached on their land and their settlements.

Many indigenous groups were once nomads, moving around from one hunting or fishing ground to another. Now they are hemmed in on the reservations the government confined them to, surrounded by huge farms or ranches whose owners deny their right to live off the land. State officials may insist that laws restrict the development of indigenous lands, but indigenous peoples tell a different story. In Mato Grosso, a heavily forested state near the Amazon River, loggers have been clear-cutting the land at a rate that alarms the Bororo, an indigenous group that has lived in the area for centuries. According to one elder, the Bororo are now confined to six small reservations of about 500 square miles—much less than the area officially granted them in the 19th century.

In Mato Grosso, a heavily forested state near the Amazon River, loggers have been clear-cutting the land at a rate that alarms the Bororo.

In the face of dwindling resources, indigenous groups like the Bororo struggle to maintain their culture. Though the tribe still observes the traditional initiation rites for adolescent boys, members are finding it difficult to continue their hunting and fishing rituals, given the scarcity of game and fish in the area. Pesticides in the runoff from nearby farms have poisoned the water they fish and bathe in, threatening both their health and their culture's survival.

LET'S DISCUSS

1. Compare the frontier in Brazil today to the American West in the 1800s. What similarities do you see?
2. What does society lose when indigenous cultures die?

Sources: Brazier and Hamed 2007; Chu 2005.

McDonaldization is associated with the melding of cultures, through which we see more and more similarities in cultural expression. In Japan, for example, African entrepreneurs have found a thriving market for hip-hop fashions popularized by teens in the United States. Similarly, the familiar Golden Arches of McDonald's can be seen around the world. Yet corporations like McDonald's have had to make some adjustments of their own. Until 2001, McDonald's ran its overseas operations from corporate headquarters in suburban Chicago. After a few false starts, executives recognized the need to develop the restaurant's menus and marketing strategies overseas, relying on advice from local people. Now, at over 3,700 restaurants in Japan, customers can enjoy the Mega Tamago Burger—beef, bacon, and fried egg with special sauces. In India, patrons who don't eat beef can order a double chicken-patty sandwich known as the Maharaja Mac. And in Austria, the locals' love of coffee, cake, and conversation has inspired the McCafé (Hughlett 2008; Ritzer 2002, 2011).

Technology in its many forms has increased the speed of cultural diffusion and broadened the distribution of cultural elements. Sociologist Gerhard Lenski has defined **technology** as "cultural information about the ways in which the material resources of the environment may be used to satisfy human needs and desires" (Nolan and Lenski 2009:357). Today's technological developments no longer await publication in journals with limited circulation. Press conferences, often carried simultaneously on the Internet, trumpet the new developments.

Technology not only accelerates the diffusion of scientific innovations but also transmits culture. The English language and North American culture dominate the Internet and World Wide Web. Such control, or at least dominance, of technology influences the direction of cultural diffusion. For example, websites cover even the most superficial aspects of U.S. culture but offer little information about the pressing issues faced by citizens of other nations. People all over the world find it easier to visit electronic chat rooms about the latest reality TV shows than to learn about their own governments' policies on day care or infant nutrition.

Sociologist William F. Ogburn (1922) made a useful distinction between the elements of *material* and *nonmaterial culture*. **Material culture** refers to the physical or technological aspects of our daily lives, including food, houses, factories, and raw materials. **Nonmaterial culture** refers to ways of using material objects, as well as to customs, beliefs, philosophies, governments, and patterns of communication. Generally, the nonmaterial culture is more resistant to change than the material culture. Consequently, Ogburn introduced the term **culture lag** to refer to the period of maladjustment when the nonmaterial culture is still struggling to adapt to new material conditions. For example, in 2010, manufacturers introduced electronic cigarettes, battery-powered tubes that turn nicotine-laced liquid into a vapor mist. The innovation soon had officials at airlines (which ban smoking) and the Food and Drug Administration scrambling to respond to the latest technology (Kesmodel and Yadron 2010).

Resistance to technological change can lead not only to culture lag, but to some real questions of cultural survival (Box 3-3).

thinking CRITICALLY

Name one culturally significant discovery and one culturally significant invention that occurred in your lifetime. Explain how these innovations have affected the culture to which you belong.

When a society's nonmaterial culture (its values and laws) does not keep pace with rapid changes in its material culture, people experience an awkward period of maladjustment called culture lag. The transition to nuclear power generation that began in the second half of the 20th century brought widespread protests against the new technology, as well as serious accidents that government officials were poorly prepared to deal with. Tensions over the controversial technology have not run as high in some countries as in others, however. France, where this nuclear power plant is situated, generates 78 percent of all its electricity through nuclear power. The technology is not as controversial there as in the United States and Canada, which generate less than 20 percent of their electricity through nuclear reaction.

Cultural Variation

Each culture has a unique character. Inuit tribes in northern Canada, wrapped in furs and dieting on whale blubber, have little in common with farmers in Southeast Asia, who dress for the heat and subsist mainly on the rice they grow in their paddies. Cultures adapt to meet specific sets of circumstances, such as climate, level of technology, population, and geography. Thus, despite the presence of cultural universals such as courtship and religion, great diversity exists among the world's many cultures. Moreover, even *within* a single nation, certain segments of the populace develop cultural patterns that differ from the patterns of the dominant society.

Subcultures

Rodeo riders, residents of a retirement community, workers on an offshore oil rig—all are examples of what sociologists refer to as *subcultures*. A **subculture** is a segment of society that shares a distinctive pattern of customs, rules, and traditions that differs from the pattern of the larger society. In a sense, a subculture can be thought of as a culture existing within a larger, dominant culture. The existence of many subcultures is characteristic of complex societies such as the United States.

Members of a subculture participate in the dominant culture while engaging in unique and distinctive forms of behavior. Frequently, a subculture will develop an **argot,** or specialized language, that distinguishes it from the wider society. Athletes who play *parkour,* an extreme sport that combines forward running with fence leaping and the vaulting of walls, water barriers, and even moving cars, speak an argot they devised especially to describe their feats. Parkour runners talk about doing *King Kong vaults*—diving arms first over a wall or grocery cart and landing in a standing position. They may follow this maneuver with

a *tic tac*—kicking off a wall to overcome some kind of obstacle (Tschorn 2010).

Such argot allows insiders—the members of the subculture—to understand words with special meanings. It also establishes patterns of communication that outsiders can't understand. Sociologists associated with the interactionist perspective emphasize that language and symbols offer a powerful way for a subculture to feel cohesive and maintain its identity.

In India, a new subculture has developed among employees at the international call centers established by multinational corporations. To serve customers in the United States and Europe, the young men and women who work there must be fluent speakers of English. But the corporations that employ them demand more than proficiency in a foreign language; they expect their Indian employees to adopt Western values and work habits, including the grueling pace U.S. workers take for granted. In return they offer perks such as Western-style dinners, dances, and coveted consumer goods. Significantly, they allow employees to take the day off only on U.S. holidays, like Labor Day and Thanksgiving—not on Indian holidays like Diwali, the Hindu festival of lights. While most Indian families are home celebrating, call center employees see only each other; when they have the day off, no one else is free to socialize with them. As a result, these employees have formed a tight-knit subculture based on hard work and a taste for Western luxury goods and leisure-time pursuits.

Another shared characteristic among some employees at Indian call centers is their contempt for the callers they serve. In performing their monotonous, repetitive job day after day, hundreds of thousands of these workers have come to see the faceless Americans they deal with as slow, often rude customers. Such shared understandings underpin this emerging subculture (Bhagat 2007; Gentleman 2006).

Functionalist and conflict theorists agree that variation exists within cultures. Functionalists view subcultures as variations of particular social environments and as evidence that differences can exist within a common culture. However, conflict theorists suggest that variations often reflect the inequality of social arrangements within a society. A conflict theorist would view the challenges to dominant social norms by African

Employees of an international call center in India socialize after their shift has ended. Call center employees, whose odd working hours isolate them from others, tend to form tight-knit subcultures.

American activists, the feminist movement, and the gay rights movement as reflections of inequity based on race, gender, and sexual orientation. Conflict theorists also argue that subcultures sometimes emerge when the dominant society unsuccessfully tries to suppress a practice, such as the use of illegal drugs.

Countercultures

By the end of the 1960s, an extensive subculture had emerged in the United States, composed of young people turned off by a society they believed was too materialistic and technological. This group included primarily political radicals and hippies who had dropped out of mainstream social institutions. These young men and women rejected the pressure to accumulate cars, homes, and an endless array of material goods. Instead, they expressed a desire to live in a culture based on more humanistic values, such as sharing, love, and coexistence with the environment. As a political force, this subculture opposed the United States' involvement in the war in Vietnam and encouraged draft resistance (Flacks 1971; Roszak 1969).

When a subculture conspicuously and deliberately opposes certain aspects of the larger culture, it is known as a **counterculture.** Countercultures typically thrive among the young, who have the least investment in the existing culture. In most cases, a 20-year-old can adjust to new cultural standards more easily than someone who has spent 60 years following the patterns of the dominant culture (Zellner 1995).

In the last decade, counterterrorism experts have become concerned about the growth of ultraconservative militia groups in the United States. Secretive and well armed, members of these countercultural groups tend to be antigovernment, and they often tolerate racism in their midst. Watchdogs estimate that 127 militias are operating in the United States today (Southern Poverty Law Center 2010).

Culture Shock

Anyone who feels disoriented, uncertain, out of place, or even fearful when immersed in an unfamiliar culture may be experiencing **culture shock.** For example, a resident of the United States who visits certain areas in China and wants local meat for dinner may be stunned to learn that the specialty is dog meat. Similarly, someone from a strict Islamic culture may be shocked by the comparatively provocative dress styles and open displays of affection common in the United States and various European cultures.

All of us, to some extent, take for granted the cultural practices of our society. As a result, it can be surprising and even disturbing to realize that other cultures do not follow our way of life. The fact is, customs that seem strange to us may be considered normal and proper in other cultures, which may see our social practices as odd.

---

use your sociological *imagination*

You arrive in a developing African country as a Peace Corps volunteer. What aspects of a very different culture do you think would be the hardest to adjust to? What might the citizens of that country find shocking about your culture?

Role of Language

Language is one of the major elements of culture that underlie cultural variations. It is also an important component of cultural capital. Recall from Chapter 1 that Pierre Bourdieu used the term *cultural capital* to describe noneconomic assets, such as family background and past educational investments, which are reflected in a person's knowledge of language and the arts.

Members of a society generally share a common language, which facilitates day-to-day exchanges with others. When you ask a hardware store clerk for a flashlight, you don't need to draw a picture of the instrument. You share the same cultural term for a small, portable, battery-operated light. However, if you were in England and needed this item, you would have to ask for an electric torch. Of course, even within the same society, a term can have a number of different meanings. In the United States, *pot* signifies both a container that is used for cooking and an intoxicating drug. In this section we will examine the cultural influence of language, which includes both the written and spoken word and nonverbal communication.

Language: Written and Spoken

Seven thousand languages are spoken in the world today—many more than the number of countries. For the speakers of each one, whether they number 2,000 or 200 million, language is fundamental to their shared culture.

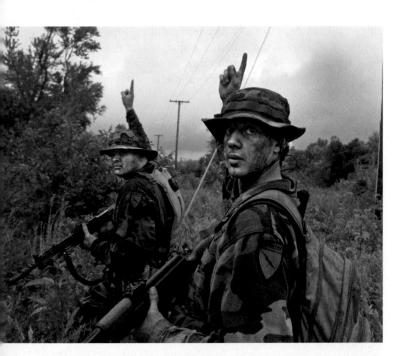

Counterculture in uniform. Members of the militia group Ohio Defense Force engage in paramilitary exercises imagining they are destroying a threatening Muslim stronghold in the United States.

The English language, for example, makes extensive use of words dealing with war. We speak of "conquering" space, "fighting" the "battle" of the budget, "waging war" on drugs, making a "killing" on the stock market, and "bombing" an examination; something monumental or great is "the bomb." An observer from an entirely different and warless culture could gauge the importance that war and the military have had in our lives simply by recognizing the prominence that militaristic terms have in our language. Similarly, the Sami people of northern Norway and Sweden have a rich diversity of terms for snow, ice, and reindeer (Haviland et al. 2008; Magga 2006).

Language is, in fact, the foundation of every culture. **Language** is an abstract system of word meanings and symbols for all aspects of culture. It includes speech, written characters, numerals, symbols, and nonverbal gestures and expressions. Because language is the foundation of every culture, the ability to speak other languages is crucial to intercultural relations. Throughout the Cold War era, beginning in the 1950s and continuing well into the 1970s, the U.S. government encouraged the study of Russian by developing special language schools for diplomats and military advisers who dealt with the Soviet Union. And following September 11, 2001, the nation recognized how few skilled translators it had for Arabic and other languages spoken in Muslim countries. Language quickly became a key not only to tracking potential terrorists, but also to building diplomatic bridges with Muslim countries willing to help in the war against terrorism.

Language does more than simply describe reality; it also serves to *shape* the reality of a culture. For example, most people in the United States cannot easily make the verbal distinctions concerning snow and ice that are possible in the Sami culture. As a result, they are less likely to notice such differences.

The **Sapir-Whorf hypothesis,** named for two linguists, describes the role of language in shaping our interpretation of reality. According to Sapir and Whorf, because people can conceptualize the world only through language, language *precedes* thought. Thus, the word symbols and grammar of a language organize the world for us. The Sapir-Whorf hypothesis also holds that language is not a given. Rather, it is culturally determined, and it encourages a distinctive interpretation of reality by focusing our attention on certain phenomena (Sapir 1929).

For decades, the Navajo have referred to cancer as *lood doo na'dziihii.* Now, through a project funded by the National Cancer Institute, the tribal college is seeking to change the phrase. Why? Literally, the phrase means "the sore that does not heal," and health educators are concerned that tribal members who have been diagnosed with cancer view it as a death sentence. Their effort to change the Navajo language, not easy in itself, is complicated by the Navajo belief that to talk about the disease is to bring it on one's people (Fonseca 2008).

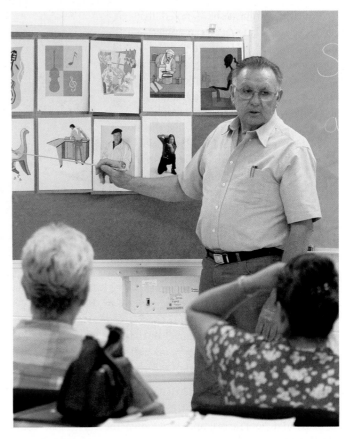

A native speaker trains instructors from the Oneida Nation of New York in the Berlitz method of language teaching. Many Native American tribes are taking steps to recover their seldom-used languages, realizing that language is the essential foundation of any culture. Their efforts are helping to reverse the cultural genocide they endured in the past.

TREND SPOTTING

Linguistic Isolation

In 2006, a severe winter storm hit the northwest United States, knocking out electrical power in many communities. Residents turned on their generators, some without heeding warnings about the risk of carbon monoxide poisoning. Although local media ran public service announcements about the need for adequate ventilation of the generators, six people died and several others fell ill from exposure to carbon monoxide. Investigators later determined that the victims had been unable to understand the English-only warnings. In response to the discovery, the *Seattle Times* took the unprecedented step of publishing the front-page story in six languages: English, Vietnamese, Chinese, Spanish, Russian, and Somali.

Although most immigrants can communicate effectively in English, language does isolate a small percentage of them. Social scientists use the term *linguistic isolation* to refer to households in which all members age 14 and older speak a non-English language and at the same time do not speak English very well. They have found that the proportion of the U.S. population that is linguistically isolated has been increasing steadily, from 3.2 percent in 2000 to 8.6 percent in 2008.

Studies show that those who are linguistically isolated are cut off from many public services. For example, public health professionals find that even after controlling for education and income, members of linguistically isolated households are less likely than others to receive adequate health care, or even to participate in basic health screening. And as the 2006 power outage in the Northwest showed, in some cases linguistic isolation can be deadly.

Similarly, feminists have noted that gender-related language can reflect—although in itself it does not determine—the traditional acceptance of men and women in certain occupations. Each time we use a term such as *mailman, policeman,* or *fireman,* we are implying (especially to young children) that these occupations can be filled only by males. Yet many women work as *mail carriers, police officers,* and *firefighters*—a fact that is being increasingly recognized and legitimized through the use of such non-sexist language.

Language can shape how we see, taste, smell, feel, and hear. It also influences the way we think about the people, ideas, and objects around us. Language communicates a culture's most important norms, values, and sanctions. That's why the decline of an old language or the introduction of a new one is such a sensitive issue in many parts of the world (see the Social Policy section at the end of this chapter).

Using American Sign Language, a form of nonverbal communication, a football coach discusses a play with his team. The Silent Warriors, four-time national champions and the pride of the Alabama School for the Deaf, have defeated both hearing and nonhearing teams.

Nonverbal Communication

If you don't like the way a meeting is going, you might suddenly sit back, fold your arms, and turn down the corners of your mouth. When you see a friend in tears, you may give a quick hug. After winning a big game, you probably high-five your teammates. These are all examples of *nonverbal communication,* the use of gestures, facial expressions, and other visual images to communicate.

We are not born with these expressions. We learn them, just as we learn other forms of language, from people who share our same culture. This statement is as true for the basic expressions of happiness and sadness as it is for more complex emotions, such as shame or distress (Fridlund et al. 1987).

Like other forms of language, nonverbal communication is not the same in all cultures. For example, sociological research done at the micro level documents that people from various cultures differ in the degree to which they touch others during the course of normal social interactions. Even experienced travelers are sometimes caught off guard by these differences. In Saudi Arabia, a middle-aged man may want to hold hands with a partner after closing a business deal. In Egypt, men walk hand in hand in the street; in cafés, they fall asleep while lounging in each other's arms. These gestures, which would shock an American businessman, are considered compliments in those cultures. The meaning of hand signals is another form of nonverbal communication that can differ from one culture to the next. In Australia, the thumbs-up sign is considered rude (Passero 2002; Vaughan 2007).

A related form of communication is the use of symbols to convey meaning to others. **Symbols** are the gestures, objects, and words that form the basis of human communication. The thumbs-up gesture, a gold star sticker, and the smiley face in an e-mail are all symbols. Often deceptively simple, many symbols are rich in meaning and may not convey the same meaning in all social contexts. Around someone's neck, for example, a cross can symbolize religious reverence; over a grave site, a belief in everlasting life; or set in flames, racial hatred.

thinking CRITICALLY

Do you agree with Sapir and Whorf's hypothesis that language precedes thought? What kind of evidence might you cite to refute their hypothesis? Could language shape our interpretation of reality without preceding thought?

Norms and Values

"Wash your hands before dinner." "Thou shalt not kill." "Respect your elders." All societies have ways of encouraging and enforcing what they view as appropriate behavior while discouraging and punishing what they consider to be inappropriate behavior. They also have a collective idea of what is good and desirable in life—or not. In this section we will learn to distinguish between the closely related concepts of norms and values.

Norms

Norms are the established standards of behavior maintained by a society. For a norm to become significant, it must be widely shared and understood. For example, in movie theaters in the United States, we typically expect that people will be quiet while the film is shown. Of course, the application of this norm can vary, depending on the particular film and type of audience. People who are viewing a serious artistic film will be more likely to insist on the norm of silence than those who are watching a slapstick comedy or horror movie.

One persistent social norm in contemporary society is that of heterosexuality. Children are socialized to accept this norm from a very young age. Overwhelmingly, parents describe adult romantic relationships to their children exclusively as heterosexual relationships. That is not necessarily because they consider same-sex relationships unacceptable, but more likely because they see heterosexuality as the norm in marital partnerships. According to a national survey of mothers of three- to six-year-olds, one in five mothers teaches her young children that homosexuality is wrong. The same survey showed that parenting reflects the dominant ideology, in which homosexuality is treated as a rare exception. Most parents assume that their children are heterosexual; only one in four had even considered whether his or her child might grow up to be gay or lesbian (K. Martin 2009).

Types of Norms Sociologists distinguish between norms in two ways. First, norms are classified as either formal or informal. **Formal norms** generally have been written down and specify strict punishments for violators. In the United States, we often formalize norms into laws, which are very precise in defining proper and improper behavior. Sociologist Donald Black (1995) has termed **law** "governmental social control," meaning that laws are formal norms enforced by the state. Laws are just one example of formal norms. The requirements for a college major and the rules of a card game are also considered formal norms.

In contrast, **informal norms** are generally understood but not precisely recorded. Standards of proper dress are a common example of informal norms. Our society has no specific punishment, or *sanction*, for a person who comes to school, say, wearing a monkey suit. Making fun of the nonconforming student is usually the most likely response.

Norms are also classified by their relative importance to society. When classified in this way, they are known as *mores* and *folkways*. **Mores** (pronounced "*MOR*-ays") are norms deemed highly necessary to the welfare of a society, often because they embody the most cherished principles of a people. Each society demands obedience to its mores; violation can lead to severe penalties. Thus, the United States has strong mores against murder, treason, and child abuse, which have been institutionalized into formal norms.

Folkways are norms governing everyday behavior. Folkways play an important role in shaping the daily behavior of members of a culture. Society is less likely to formalize folkways than mores, and their violation raises comparatively little concern. For example, walking up a down escalator in a department store challenges our standards of appropriate behavior, but it will not result in a fine or a jail sentence.

Acceptance of Norms People do not follow norms, whether mores or folkways, in all situations. In some cases, they can evade a norm because they know it is weakly enforced. It is illegal for U.S. teenagers to drink alcoholic beverages, yet drinking by minors is common throughout the nation. (In fact, teenage alcoholism is a serious social problem.)

In some instances, behavior that appears to violate society's norms may actually represent adherence to the norms of a particular group. Teenage drinkers are conforming to the standards of their peer group when they violate norms that condemn underage drinking. Similarly, business executives who use shady accounting techniques may be responding to a corporate culture that demands the maximization of profits at any cost, including the deception of investors and government regulatory agencies.

Norms are violated in some instances because one norm conflicts with another. For example, suppose that you live in an apartment building and one night hear the screams of the woman next door, who is being beaten by her husband. If you decide to intervene by ringing their doorbell or calling the police, you are violating the norm of minding your own business, while following the norm of assisting a victim of violence.

Acceptance of norms is subject to change as the political, economic, and social conditions of a culture are transformed. Until the 1960s, for example, formal norms throughout much of the United States prohibited the marriage of people from different racial groups. Over the past half century, however, such legal prohibitions were cast aside. The process of change can be seen today in the increasing acceptance of single parents and growing support for the legalization of marriage between same-sex couples (see Chapter 14).

When circumstances require the sudden violation of long-standing cultural norms, the change can upset an entire population. In Iraq, where Muslim custom strictly forbids touching by strangers for men and especially for women, the war that began in 2003 has brought numerous daily violations of the norm. Outside important mosques, government offices, and other facilities likely to be targeted by terrorists, visitors must now be patted down and have their bags searched by Iraqi security guards. To reduce the discomfort caused by the procedure, women are searched by female guards and men by male guards. Despite that

use your sociological *imagination*

You are a high school principal. What norms would you want to govern the students' behavior? How might those norms differ from norms appropriate for college students?

thinking CRITICALLY

In the United States, is the norm of heterosexuality a formal norm or an informal norm? Would you categorize it with mores or folkways? Explain your reasoning.

concession, and the fact that many Iraqis admit or even insist on the need for such measures, people still wince at the invasion of their personal privacy. In reaction to the searches, Iraqi women have begun to limit the contents of the bags they carry or simply to leave them at home (Rubin 2003).

Sanctions

Suppose a football coach sends a 12th player onto the field. Imagine a college graduate showing up in shorts for a job interview at a large bank. Or consider a driver who neglects to put any money into a parking meter. These people have violated widely shared and understood norms. So what happens? In each of these situations, the person will receive sanctions if his or her behavior is detected.

Sanctions are penalties and rewards for conduct concerning a social norm. Note that the concept of *reward* is included in this definition. Conformity to a norm can lead to positive sanctions such as a pay raise, a medal, a word of gratitude, or a pat on the back. Negative sanctions include fines, threats, imprisonment, and stares of contempt.

Table 3-1 summarizes the relationship between norms and sanctions. As you can see, the sanctions that are associated with formal norms (which are written down and codified) tend to be formal as well. If a college coach sends too many players onto the field, the team will be penalized 15 yards. The driver who fails to put money in the parking meter will receive a ticket and have to pay a fine. But sanctions for violations of informal norms can vary. The college graduate who goes to the bank interview in shorts will probably lose any chance of getting the job; on the other hand, he or she might be so brilliant that bank officials will overlook the unconventional attire.

The entire fabric of norms and sanctions in a culture reflects that culture's values and priorities. The most cherished values

TABLE **3-1** NORMS AND SANCTIONS

Norms	Sanctions	
	Positive	Negative
Formal	Salary bonus	Demotion
	Testimonial dinner	Firing from a job
	Medal	Jail sentence
	Diploma	Expulsion
Informal	Smile	Frown
	Compliment	Humiliation
	Cheers	Bullying

will be most heavily sanctioned; matters regarded as less critical will carry light and informal sanctions.

Values

Though we each have a personal set of values—which may include caring or fitness or success in business—we also share a general set of values as members of a society. Cultural **values** are these collective conceptions of what is considered good, desirable, and proper—or bad, undesirable, and improper—in a culture. They indicate what people in a given culture prefer as well as what they find important and morally right (or wrong). Values may be specific, such as honoring one's parents and owning a home, or they may be more general, such as health, love, and democracy. Of course, the members of a society do not uniformly share its values. Angry political debates and billboards promoting conflicting causes tell us that much.

In Iraq, a female member of the U.S. Army searches a covered Muslim woman. The searches, which are necessary to prevent terrorist attacks, violate a Muslim norm that forbids touching by strangers.

FIGURE 3-2 LIFE GOALS OF FIRST-YEAR COLLEGE STUDENTS IN THE UNITED STATES, 1966–2010

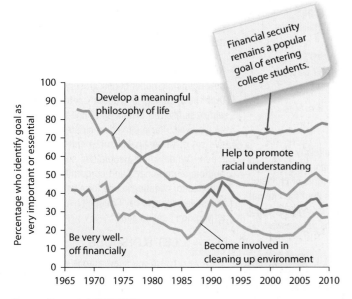

Sources: Pryor et al. 2007, 2010.

Think about It

Why do you think values have shifted among college students in the past few decades? Which of these values is important to you?

Values influence people's behavior and serve as criteria for evaluating the actions of others. The values, norms, and sanctions of a culture are often directly related. For example, if a culture places a high value on the institution of marriage, it may have norms (and strict sanctions) that prohibit the act of adultery or make divorce difficult. If a culture views private property as a basic value, it will probably have stiff laws against theft and vandalism.

The values of a culture may change, but most remain relatively stable during any one person's lifetime. Socially shared, intensely felt values are a fundamental part of our lives in the United States. Sociologist Robin Williams (1970) has offered a list of basic values. It includes achievement, efficiency, material comfort, nationalism, equality, and the supremacy of science and reason over faith. Obviously, not all 309 million people in this country agree on all these values, but such a list serves as a starting point in defining the national character.

Each year more than 200,000 entering college students at nearly 300 of the nation's four-year colleges fill out a questionnaire about their values. Because this survey focuses on an array of issues, beliefs, and life goals, it is commonly cited as a barometer of the nation's values. The respondents are asked what values are personally important to them. Over the past half century, the value of "being very well-off financially" has shown the strongest gain in popularity; the proportion of first-year college students who endorse this value as "essential" or "very important" rose from 42 percent in 1966 to 77.4 percent in 2010 (Figure 3-2).

In contrast, the value that has shown the most striking decline in endorsement by students is "developing a meaningful philosophy of life." While this value was the most popular in the 1967 survey, endorsed by 85 percent of the respondents, it had fallen to seventh place on the list by 2010, when it was endorsed by less than 47 percent of students entering college.

During the 1980s and 1990s, support for values having to do with money, power, and status grew. At the same time, support for certain values having to do with social awareness and altruism, such as "helping others," declined. According to the 2010 nationwide survey, only 41.6 percent of first-year college students stated that "influencing social values" was an "essential" or "very important" goal. The proportion of students for whom "helping to promote racial understanding" was an essential or very important goal reached a record high of 46 percent in 1992, then fell to 33.8 percent in 2010. Like other aspects of culture, such as language and norms, a nation's values are not necessarily fixed.

Whether the slogan is "Think Green" or "Reduce Your Carbon Footprint," students have been exposed to values associated with environmentalism. How many of them accept those values? Poll results over the past 40 years show fluctuations, with a high of nearly 46 percent of students indicating a desire to become involved in cleaning up the environment. By the 1980s, however, student support for embracing this objective had dropped to around 20 percent or even lower (see Figure 3-2). Even with recent attention to global warming, the proportion remains level at only 27.3 percent of first-year students in 2010.

Recently, cheating has become a hot issue on college campuses. Professors who take advantage of computerized services that can identify plagiarism, such as the search engine Google, have been shocked to learn that many of the papers their students hand in are plagiarized in whole or in part. Box 3-4 examines the shift in values that underlies this decline in academic integrity.

Another value that has begun to change recently, not just among students but among the public in general, is the right to privacy. Americans have always valued their privacy and resented government intrusions into their personal lives. In the aftermath of the terrorist attacks of September 11, 2001, however, many citizens called for greater protection against the threat of terrorism. In response, the U.S. government broadened its surveillance powers and increased its ability to monitor people's behavior without court approval. In 2001, shortly after the attacks, Congress passed the Patriot Act, which empowers the FBI to access individuals' medical, library, student, and phone records without informing them or obtaining a search warrant.

Antiterrorism campaigns, especially efforts to acquire information from suspected terrorists, have fueled debate about yet another value, freedom from torture. In the past few years, the use of torture to obtain information has become controversial around the world. As Figure 3-3 on page 67 shows, public opinion regarding the use of torture varies dramatically from one country to another.

Global Culture War

For almost a generation, public attention in the United States has focused on **culture war,** or the polarization of society over controversial cultural elements. Originally, in the 1990s, the term referred to political debates over heated issues such as abortion, religious expression, gun control, and sexual

SOCIOLOGY ON CAMPUS

3-4 A Culture of Cheating?

On November 21, 2002, after issuing several warnings, officials at the U.S. Naval Academy seized the computers of almost 100 midshipmen suspected of downloading movies and music illegally from the Internet. Officers at the school may have taken the unusually strong action to avoid liability on the part of the U.S. government, which owns the computers students were using. But across the nation, college administrators have been trying to restrain students from downloading pirated entertainment for free. The practice is so widespread, it has been slowing down the high-powered computer networks colleges and universities depend on for research and admissions.

Illegal downloading is just one aspect of the growing problem of copyright violation, both on campus and off. Now that college students can use personal computers to surf the Internet, most do their research online. Apparently, the temptation to cut and paste passages from website postings and pass them off as one's own is irresistible to many.

Surveys done by the Center for Academic Integrity show that from 1999 to 2005, the percentage of students who approved of this type of plagiarism rose from 10 percent to 41 percent. At the same time, the percentage who considered cutting and pasting from the Internet to be a serious form of cheating fell from 68 percent to 23 percent. Perhaps the worst form of Internet plagiarism is the purchase of entire papers from other writers. Increasingly, the websites that sell essays to students are based in other countries, including India, Ukraine, Nigeria, and the Philippines.

The Center for Academic Integrity estimates that at most schools, more than 75 percent of the students engage in some form of cheating.

The Center for Academic Integrity estimates that at most schools, more than 75 percent of the students engage in some form of cheating. Students not only cut passages from the Internet and paste them into their papers without citing the source; they share questions and answers on

exams, collaborate on assignments they are supposed to do independently, and even falsify the results of their laboratory experiments.

To address what they consider an alarming trend, many schools are rewriting or adopting new academic honor codes. Observers contend that the increase in student cheating reflects widely publicized instances of cheating in public life, which have served to create an alternative set of values in which the end justifies the means. When young people see sports heroes, authors, entertainers, and corporate executives exposed for cheating in one form or another, the message seems to be "Cheating is okay, as long as you don't get caught."

LET'S DISCUSS

1. Do you know anyone who has engaged in Internet plagiarism? What about cheating on tests or falsifying laboratory results? If so, how did the person justify these forms of dishonesty?
2. Even if cheaters aren't caught, what negative effects does their academic dishonesty have on them? What effects does it have on students who are honest? Could an entire college or university suffer from students' dishonesty?

Sources: Argetsinger and Krim 2002; Bartlett 2009; Center for Academic Integrity 2006; R. Thomas 2003; Toppo 2011; Zernike 2002.

---

orientation. Soon, however, it took on a global meaning—especially after 9/11, as Americans wondered, "Why do they hate us?" Through 2000, global studies of public opinion had reported favorable views of the United States in countries as diverse as Morocco and Germany. But by 2003, in the wake of the U.S. invasion of Iraq, foreign opinion of the United States had become quite negative (J. Hunter 1991; Kohut et al. 2005, 2007).

In the past 20 years, extensive efforts have been made to compare values in different nations, recognizing the challenges in interpreting value concepts in a similar manner across cultures. Psychologist Shalom Schwartz has measured values in more than 60 countries. Around the world, certain values are widely shared, including benevolence, which is defined as "forgiveness and loyalty." In contrast, power, defined as "control or dominance over people and resources," is a value that is endorsed much less often (Hitlin and Piliavin 2004; S. Schwartz and Bardi 2001).

Despite this evidence of shared values, some scholars have interpreted the terrorism, genocide, wars, and military occupations of the early 21st century as a "clash of civilizations." According to this thesis, cultural and religious identities, rather than national or political loyalties, are becoming the prime source of international conflict. Critics of this thesis point out that conflict over values is nothing new; only our ability to create havoc and violence has grown. Furthermore, speaking of a clash of "civilizations" disguises the sharp divisions that exist within large groups. Christianity, for example, runs the gamut from Quaker-style pacifism to certain elements of the Ku Klux Klan's ideology (Berman 2003; Huntington 1993; Said 2001).

thinking CRITICALLY

Do you believe that the world is experiencing a clash of civilizations rather than of nations, as some scholars assert? Why or why not?

FIGURE **3-3** TORTURE VALUES BY COUNTRY

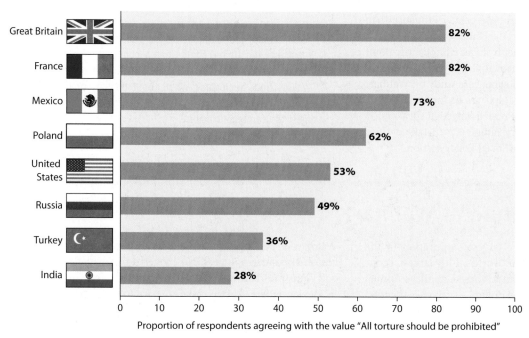

Proportion of respondents agreeing with the value "All torture should be prohibited"

Country	Percentage
Great Britain	82%
France	82%
Mexico	73%
Poland	62%
United States	53%
Russia	49%
Turkey	36%
India	28%

Source: World Public Opinion 2008.

Conflict theorists agree that a common culture may exist, but they argue that it serves to maintain the privileges of certain groups. Moreover, while protecting their self-interest, powerful groups may keep others in a subservient position. The term **dominant ideology** describes the set of cultural beliefs and practices that helps to maintain powerful social, economic, and political interests. This concept was first used by Hungarian Marxist Georg Lukacs (1923) and Italian Marxist Antonio Gramsci (1929), but it did not gain an audience in the United States until the early 1970s. In Karl Marx's view, a capitalist society has a dominant ideology that serves the interests of the ruling class.

Culture and the Dominant Ideology

Functionalist and conflict theorists agree that culture and society are mutually supportive, but for different reasons. Functionalists maintain that social stability requires a consensus and the support of society's members; strong central values and common norms provide that support. This view of culture became popular in sociology beginning in the 1950s. It was borrowed from British anthropologists who saw cultural traits as a stabilizing element in a culture. From a functionalist perspective, a cultural trait or practice will persist if it performs functions that society seems to need or contributes to overall social stability and consensus.

From a conflict perspective, the dominant ideology has major social significance. Not only do a society's most powerful groups and institutions control wealth and property; even more important, they control the means of producing beliefs about reality through religion, education, and the media. Feminists would also argue that if all a society's most important institutions tell women they should be subservient to men, that dominant ideology will help to control women and keep them in a subordinate position. Table 3-2 summarizes the major sociological perspectives on culture.

A growing number of social scientists believe that it is not easy to identify a core culture in the United States. For support, they point to the lack of consensus on national values, the diffusion of cultural

TABLE **3-2** SOCIOLOGICAL PERSPECTIVES ON CULTURE   summing**up**

	Functionalist Perspective	Conflict Perspective	Feminist Perspective	Interactionist Perspective
Cultural Variation	Subcultures serve the interests of subgroups; ethnocentrism reinforces group solidarity	Countercultures question the dominant social order; ethnocentrism devalues groups	Cultural relativism respects variations in the way men and women are viewed in different societies	Customs and traditions are transmitted through intergroup contact and through the media
Norms	Reinforce societal standards	Reinforce patterns of dominance	Reinforce roles of men and women	Are maintained through face-to-face interaction
Values	Are collective conceptions of what is good	May perpetuate social inequality	May perpetuate men's dominance	Are defined and redefined through social interaction
Culture and Society	Culture reflects a society's strong central values	Culture reflects a society's dominant ideology	Culture reflects society's view of men and women	A society's core culture is perpetuated through daily social interactions
Walmart	Provides goods and services to customers	Opposes labor unions; slow to provide employee health benefits, promote women	Limits role of women in leadership	History of insensitivity to cultural variations in store-customer relationships

traits, the diversity within our culture, and the changing views of young people (look again at Figure 3-2). Yet there is no way of denying that certain expressions of values have greater influence than others, even in as complex a society as the United States.

How one views a culture—whether from an ethnocentric point of view or through the lens of cultural relativism—can have serious consequences in business, as the following case study on Walmart demonstrates. It also has important implications for social policy. Should a nation accommodate non-native-language speakers by sponsoring bilingual programs, for example? We'll take a close look at this controversial issue in the Social Policy section.

thinking CRITICALLY

Look around your campus. Do the people you see suggest that the United States has a core culture with a dominant ideology, or a diverse culture with differing values and ideologies? What about the city or town where your college or university is located—does it suggest the same conclusion?

casestudy Culture at Walmart

By some measures, Walmart is the largest corporation in the world. By other measures, it is the world's 14th largest economy. Indeed, the Bentonville, Arkansas–based retailer's annual revenue—over one-third of a trillion dollars—surpasses the total value of goods and services produced in many countries, such as Sweden.

Walmart's rise to the status of an economic superpower has not been without criticism. To keep prices low, the corporation pays store clerks as little as possible and has determinedly shut out labor organizers who seek to better their wages. Recently, the debate has expanded to include health care benefits. Given Walmart's wage levels, a large proportion of employees simply cannot afford health insurance, even if the corporation offers it. Also, Walmart has been noted for its lack of commitment to equal opportunity: very few women occupy managerial positions at the company (Barbaro 2008).

Although U.S. consumers have embraced Walmart's "everyday low prices," the reaction has not been as positive in countries where consumers hold different cultural values. The company, now located in 15 countries, has not been an unqualified success abroad. Consider the following missteps in three very different countries. In 2006, the company sold all its facilities in South Korea, where its warehouse-style stores were not appreciated by shoppers accustomed to more elegant surroundings. Today,

Walmart is learning not to impose its corporate culture on foreign customers and employees. No longer do managers plan to sell golf clubs in Brazil, where the game is rarely played, or ice skates in Mexico, where skating rinks are hard to find. More important, the corporate giant has begun to study the culture and social patterns of potential customers (Landler and Barbaro 2006; Saporito 2007; Walmart 2010; A. Zimmerman and Nelson 2006).

Walmart also pulled out of Germany, due in part to its failure to adjust to the national culture. German shoppers, accustomed to no-nonsense, impersonal service, found Walmart employees' smiling, outgoing style off-putting. The company's "ten-foot attitude"—a salesperson who comes within 10 feet of a customer must look the person in the eye, greet the person, and ask if he or she needs help—simply did not play well there. Food shoppers, used to bagging their own groceries, were turned off by Walmart's practice of allowing clerks to handle their purchases. Furthermore, German employees, who had grown up in a culture that accepts workplace romances, found the company's prohibition against on-the-job relationships bizarre.

Today, rather than risk another mistake abroad, Walmart is considering buying Massmart, a retailer with 288 existing stores in Africa. Time will tell whether the proposed takeover is welcomed, or Walmart is again rejected as the "Beast of Bentonville," as critics in Germany and South Africa called it (Stewart 2010).

socialpolicy and Culture

Bilingualism

Looking at the Issue

All over the world, nations face the challenge of how to deal with minorities who speak a different language from that of mainstream culture. Because languages know no political boundaries, minority languages are common. In India, for example, Hindi is the most widely spoken language, while English is used widely for official purposes. Yet 18 other languages are officially recognized in this nation of about 1 billion people.

Throughout the world, then, schools must deal with incoming students who speak many languages. **Bilingualism** refers

to the use of two languages in a particular setting, such as the workplace or schoolroom, treating each language as equally legitimate. Thus, a teacher of bilingual education may instruct children in their native language while gradually introducing them to the language of the host society. If the curriculum is also bicultural, children will learn about the mores and folkways of both the dominant culture and the subculture.

To what degree should schools in the United States present the curriculum in a language other than English? This issue has prompted a great deal of debate among educators and

FIGURE **3-4**   PERCENTAGE OF PEOPLE WHO SPEAK A LANGUAGE OTHER THAN ENGLISH AT HOME, BY STATE

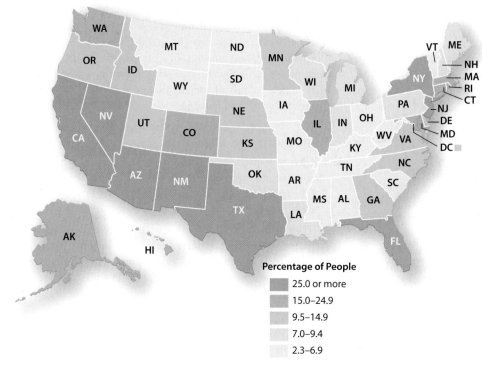

Percentage of People

- 25.0 or more
- 15.0–24.9
- 9.5–14.9
- 7.0–9.4
- 2.3–6.9

Note: Data drawn from the 2009 American Community Survey of people five years and over. National average was 20.0 percent.
Source: American Community Survey 2010: Table R1601.

Recent decades have seen challenges to this pattern of forced obedience to the dominant ideology. Beginning in the 1960s, active movements for Black pride and ethnic pride insisted that people regard the traditions of all racial and ethnic subcultures as legitimate and important. Conflict theorists explain this development as a case of subordinated language minorities seeking opportunities for self-expression. Partly as a result of these challenges, people began to view bilingualism as an asset. It seemed to provide a sensitive way of assisting millions of non-English-speaking people in the United States to *learn* English in order to function more effectively within the society.

The perspective of conflict theory also helps us to understand some of the attacks on bilingual programs. Many of them stem from an ethnocentric point of view, which holds that any deviation from the majority is bad. This attitude tends to be expressed by those who wish to stamp out foreign influence wherever it occurs, especially in our schools. It does not take into account that success in bilingual education may actually have beneficial results, such as decreasing the number of high school dropouts and increasing the number of Hispanics in colleges and universities.

policymakers. According to the Bureau of the Census, 59 million U.S. residents over age five—that's about 20 percent of the population—spoke a language other than English as their primary language at home in 2009 (Figure 3-4). Indeed, 32 other languages are each spoken by at least 200,000 U.S. residents (Shin and Bruno 2003).

Do bilingual programs help the children of these families to learn English? It is difficult to reach firm conclusions because bilingual programs in general vary so widely in their quality and approach. They differ in the length of the transition to English and in how long they allow students to remain in bilingual classrooms. Moreover, results have been mixed. In the years since California effectively dismantled its bilingual education program, reading and math scores of students with limited English proficiency rose dramatically, especially in the lower grades. Yet a major overview of 17 studies, done at Johns Hopkins University, found that students who are offered lessons in both English and their home languages make better progress than similar students who are taught only in English (R. Slavin and Cheung 2003).

Applying Sociology

For a long time, people in the United States demanded conformity to a single language. This demand coincided with the functionalist view that language serves to unify members of a society. Little respect was granted to immigrants' cultural traditions; a young person would often be teased about his or her "funny" name, accent, or style of dress.

Initiating Policy

Bilingualism has policy implications largely in two areas: efforts to maintain language purity and programs to enhance bilingual education. Nations vary dramatically in their tolerance for a variety of languages. China continues to tighten its cultural control over Tibet by extending instruction of Mandarin, a Chinese dialect, from high school into the elementary schools, which will now be bilingual along with Tibetan. In contrast, nearby Singapore establishes English as the medium of instruction but allows students to take their mother tongue as a second language, be it Chinese, Malay, or Tamil.

One bilingual hot spot is Québec, the French-speaking province of Canada. The Québécois, as they are known, represent 83 percent of the province's population, but only 25 percent of Canada's total population. A law implemented in 1978 mandated education in French for all Québec's children except those whose parents or siblings had learned English elsewhere in Canada. While special laws like this one have advanced French in the province, dissatisfied Québécois have tried to form their own separate country. In 1995, the people of Québec indicated their preference of remaining united with Canada by only the narrowest of margins (50.5 percent). Language and language-related cultural areas both unify and divide this nation of 33 million people (*The Economist* 2005b; R. Schaefer 2011).

Policymakers in the United States have been somewhat ambivalent in dealing with the issue of bilingualism. In 1965, the Elementary and Secondary Education Act (ESEA) provided for bilingual, bicultural education. In the 1970s, the federal government took an active role in establishing the proper form for bilingual programs. However, more recently, federal policy has been less supportive of bilingualism, and local school districts have been forced to provide an increased share of funding for their bilingual programs. Yet bilingual programs are an expense that many communities and states are unwilling to pay for and are quick to cut back. In 1998, voters in California approved a proposition that all but eliminated bilingual education: it requires instruction in English for 1.4 million children who are not fluent in the language.

In the United States, repeated efforts have been made to introduce a constitutional amendment declaring English as the nation's official language. As of 2011, 30 states had declared English their official language—an action that is now more symbolic than legislative in its significance.

Public concern over a potential decline in the use of English appears to be overblown. In reality, most immigrants and their offspring quickly become fluent in English and abandon their mother tongue. Nevertheless, many people are impatient with those immigrants who continue to use their mother tongue. The release in 2006 of *"Nuestro Himno,"* the Spanish-language version of the "Star-Spangled Banner," produced a strong public reaction: 69 percent of those who were surveyed on the topic said the anthem should be sung only in English. In reaction against the Spanish version, at least one congressman defiantly sang the national anthem in English—with incorrect lyrics. And the proprietor of a restaurant in Philadelphia posted signs advising patrons that he would accept orders for his famous steak sandwiches only in English. Throughout the year, passions ran high as policymakers debated how much support to afford people who speak other languages (J. Carroll 2006; U.S. English 2010).

In the end, the immigrant's experience is not only about learning a new language. It is about learning a whole new culture—a new totality of socially transmitted customs, knowledge, material objects, and behavior (Viramontes 2007).

Take the Issue with You

1. Have you attended a school with students for whom English is a second language? If so, did the school set up a special bilingual program? Was it effective? What is your opinion of such programs?

2. The ultimate goal of both English-only and bilingual programs is for foreign-born students to become proficient in English. Why should the type of program students attend matter so much to so many people? List all the reasons you can think of for supporting or opposing such programs. What do you see as the primary reason?

3. Besides bilingualism, can you think of another issue that has become controversial recently because of a clash of cultures? If so, analyze the issue from a sociological point of view.

MASTERING THIS CHAPTER

Summary

Culture is the totality of learned, socially transmitted customs, knowledge, material objects, and behavior. This chapter examines social practices common to all cultures, variations that distinguish one culture from another, and the basic elements that make up a culture.

1. A shared culture helps to define the group or **society** to which we belong.

2. Anthropologist George Murdock compiled a list of **cultural universals,** or common practices found in every culture, including marriage, sports, cooking, medicine, and sexual restrictions.

3. People who assume that their culture is superior to others engage in **ethnocentrism.** In contrast, **cultural relativism** is the practice of viewing other people's behavior from the perspective of their own culture.

4. Culture is constantly expanding through the process of **innovation,** which includes both **discovery** and **invention.**

5. **Diffusion**—the spread of cultural items from one place to another—has fostered globalization. Still, people resist ideas that seem too foreign, as well as those they perceive as threatening to their values and beliefs.

6. In a sense, a **subculture** can be thought of as a small culture that exists within a larger, dominant culture. **Countercultures** are subcultures that deliberately oppose aspects of the larger culture.

7. **Language,** an important element of culture, includes speech, written characters, numerals, and **symbols,** as well as gestures and other forms of nonverbal communication. Language both describes culture and shapes it.

8. Sociologists distinguish between **norms** in two ways, classifying them as **formal** or **informal** and as **mores** or **folkways**.

9. The formal norms of a culture will carry the heaviest **sanctions;** informal norms will carry light sanctions.

10. The **dominant ideology** of a culture is the set of cultural beliefs and practices that help to maintain powerful social, economic, and political interests.

11. The social policy of **bilingualism** calls for the use of two languages, treating each as equally legitimate. It is supported by those who want to ease the transition of non-native-language speakers into a host society, but opposed by those who adhere to a single cultural tradition and language.

Key Terms

Argot Specialized language used by members of a group or subculture. (page 59)

Bilingualism The use of two languages in a particular setting, such as the workplace or schoolroom, treating each language as equally legitimate. (68)

Counterculture A subculture that deliberately opposes certain aspects of the larger culture. (60)

Cultural genocide The systematic destruction of a group's culture. (55)

Cultural relativism The viewing of people's behavior from the perspective of their culture. (54)

Cultural universal A common practice or belief found in every culture. (54)

Culture The totality of learned, socially transmitted customs, knowledge, material objects, and behavior. (53)

Culture industry The worldwide media industry that standardizes the goods and services demanded by consumers. (54)

Culture lag A period of maladjustment when the nonmaterial culture is still struggling to adapt to new material conditions. (58)

Culture shock The feeling of surprise and disorientation that people experience when they encounter cultural practices that are different from their own. (60)

Culture war The polarization of society over controversial cultural elements. (65)

Diffusion The process by which a cultural item spreads from group to group or society to society. (57)

Discovery The process of making known or sharing the existence of an aspect of reality. (56)

Dominant ideology A set of cultural beliefs and practices that helps to maintain powerful social, economic, and political interests. (67)

Ethnocentrism The tendency to assume that one's culture and way of life represent the norm or are superior to all others. (54)

Folkway A norm governing everyday behavior whose violation raises comparatively little concern. (63)

Formal norm A norm that has been written down and that specifies strict punishments for violators. (63)

Genocide The deliberate, systematic killing of an entire people or nation. (55)

Informal norm A norm that is generally understood but not precisely recorded. (63)

Innovation The process of introducing a new idea or object to a culture through discovery or invention. (56)

Invention The combination of existing cultural items into a form that did not exist before. (56)

Language An abstract system of word meanings and symbols for all aspects of culture; includes gestures and other nonverbal communication. (61)

Law Governmental social control. (63)

Material culture The physical or technological aspects of our daily lives. (58)

Mores Norms deemed highly necessary to the welfare of a society. (63)

Nonmaterial culture Ways of using material objects, as well as customs, beliefs, philosophies, governments, and patterns of communication. (58)

Norm An established standard of behavior maintained by a society. (62)

Sanction A penalty or reward for conduct concerning a social norm. (64)

Sapir-Whorf hypothesis A hypothesis concerning the role of language in shaping our interpretation of reality. It holds that language is culturally determined. (61)

Society A fairly large number of people who live in the same territory, are relatively independent of people outside their area, and participate in a common culture. (53)

Sociobiology The systematic study of how biology affects human social behavior. (54)

Subculture A segment of society that shares a distinctive pattern of customs, rules, and traditions that differs from the pattern of the larger society. (59)

Symbol A gesture, object, or word that forms the basis of human communication. (62)

Technology Cultural information about the ways in which the material resources of the environment may be used to satisfy human needs and desires. (58)

Value A collective conception of what is considered good, desirable, and proper—or bad, undesirable, and improper—in a culture. (64)

TAKING SOCIOLOGY with you

1. Locate ethnocentrism. For two days, bearing in mind what sociologists mean by *ethnocentrism,* systematically record the places where you see or hear evidence of it.

2. Document a subculture. For two days, record the norms, values, sanctions, and argot evident in a subculture you are familiar with.

3. Analyze popular culture. For two days, record whatever evidence of the dominant culture you see on the Internet or in literature, music, movies, theater, television programs, and sporting events.

Self-Quiz

Read each question carefully and then select the best answer.

1. Which of the following is an aspect of culture?
   a. a comic book
   b. the patriotic attachment to the flag of the United States
   c. slang words
   d. all of the above

2. People's adaptations to meet the needs for food, shelter, and clothing are examples of what George Murdock referred to as
   a. norms.
   b. folkways.
   c. cultural universals.
   d. cultural practices.

3. What term do sociologists use to refer to the process by which a cultural item spreads from group to group or society to society?
   a. diffusion
   b. globalization
   c. innovation
   d. cultural relativism

4. The appearance of Starbucks coffeehouses in China is a sign of what aspect of culture?
   a. innovation
   b. globalization
   c. diffusion
   d. cultural relativism

5. Which of the following statements is true according to the Sapir-Whorf hypothesis?
   a. Language simply describes reality.
   b. Language does not transmit stereotypes related to race.
   c. Language precedes thought.
   d. Language is not an example of a cultural universal.

6. Which of the following statements about norms is correct?
   a. People do not follow norms in all situations. In some cases, they evade a norm because they know it is weakly enforced.
   b. In some instances, behavior that appears to violate society's norms may actually represent adherence to the norms of a particular group.
   c. Norms are violated in some instances because one norm conflicts with another.
   d. all of the above

7. Which of the following statements about values is correct?
   a. Values never change.
   b. The values of a culture may change, but most remain relatively stable during any one person's lifetime.
   c. Values are constantly changing; sociologists view them as being very unstable.
   d. all of the above

8. Which of the following terms describes the set of cultural beliefs and practices that help to maintain powerful social, economic, and political interests?
   a. mores
   b. dominant ideology
   c. consensus
   d. values

9. Terrorist groups are examples of
   a. cultural universals.
   b. subcultures.
   c. countercultures.
   d. dominant ideologies.

10. What is the term used when one places a priority on understanding other cultures, rather than dismissing them as "strange" or "exotic"?
   a. ethnocentrism
   b. culture shock
   c. cultural relativism
   d. cultural value

11. _____ are gestures, objects, and/or words that form the basis of human communication.

12. _____ is the process of introducing a new idea or object to a culture.

13. The bow and arrow, the automobile, and the television are all examples of _____ .

14. Sociologists associated with the _____ perspective emphasize that language and symbols offer a powerful way for a subculture to maintain its identity.

15. "Put on some clean clothes for dinner" and "Thou shalt not kill" are both examples of _____ found in U.S. culture.

16. The United States has strong _____ against murder, treason, and other forms of abuse that have been institutionalized into formal norms.

17. From a(n) _____ perspective, the dominant ideology has major social significance. Not only do a society's most powerful groups and institutions control wealth and property; more important, they control the means of production.

18. Countercultures (e.g., hippies) are typically popular among the _____, who have the least investment in the existing culture.

19. A person experiences _____ when he or she feels disoriented, uncertain, out of place, even fearful when immersed in an unfamiliar culture.

20. From the _____ perspective, enthocentrism serves to maintain a sense of solidarity by promoting group pride.

THINKING ABOUT MOVIES

Smoke Signals

Members of the Coeur d'Alene Indian tribe hold to their own norms and values.

Sugar

A baseball player from the Dominican Republic copes with culture shock after being drafted into the U.S. Major Leagues.

The Wrestler

Through his sport's subculture, a professional wrestler who has passed his prime travels away from the mainstream.

A *father teaches* his daughter to ride a bike. Around the world, the family is the most important agent of socialization.

▶ INSIDE

A rowing team practices for a race in Samoa. Around the world, much of people's social activity takes place in groups.

66 As each of the blind-folded prisoners is escorted down the flight of steps in front of Jordan Hall into our little jail, our guards order them to strip and remain standing naked with their arms outstretched against the wall and legs spread apart. They hold that uncomfortable position for a long time as the guards ignore them because they are busy with last-minute chores, like packing away the prisoners' belongings for safekeeping, fixing up their guards quarters, and arranging beds in the three cells. Before being given his uniform, each prisoner is sprayed with powder, alleged to be a delouser, to rid him of lice that might be brought in to contaminate our jail. . . . The humiliation of being a prisoner has begun, much as it does in many institutions from military boot camps to prisons, hospitals, and low-level jobs. . . .

The morning shift comes on in the middle of the night, 2 a.m. . . .

The prisoners are sound asleep. Some are snoring in their dark, cramped cells. Suddenly the silence is shattered. Loud whistles shriek, voices yell, "Up and at 'em." "Wake up and get out here for the count!" "Okay, you sleeping beauties, it's time to see if you learned how to count." Dazed prisoners line up against the wall and count off mindlessly as the three guards alternate in coming up with new variations on count themes. The count and its attendant push-ups and jumping jacks for failures continue on and on for nearly a weary hour. Finally, the prisoners are ordered back to sleep—until reveille a few hours later. . . .

[By Tuesday] our prisoners are looking raggedy and bleary-eyed, and our little prison is beginning to smell like a men's toilet in a New York subway station. Seems that some guards have made toilet visits a privilege to be awarded infrequently and never after lights out. During the night, prisoners have to urinate and defecate in buckets in their cells, and some guards refuse to allow them to be emptied till morning. Complaints are coming fast and furiously from many of the prisoners. . . .

After less than three days into this bizarre situation, some of the students role-playing prison guards have moved far beyond mere play-acting. They have internalized the hostility, negative affect, and mind-set characteristic of some real prison guards, as is evident from their shift reports, retrospective diaries, and personal reflections. . . .

The depersonalization of the prisoners and the spreading extent of dehumanization are beginning to affect [one of the guards], too: "As I got angrier and angrier, I didn't question this behavior as much. I couldn't let it affect me, so I started hiding myself deeper behind my role. It was the only way of not hurting yourself. I was really lost on what was happening but didn't even think about quitting."

Blaming the victims for their sorry condition—created by our failure to provide adequate shower and sanitation facilities—became common among the staff. We see this victim blame in operation as [the guard] complains, "I got tired of seeing the prisoners in rags, smelling bad, and the prison stink. 99

After less than three days into this bizarre situation, some of the students role-playing prison guards have moved far beyond mere playacting. They have internalized the hostility, negative affect, and mind-set characteristic of some real prison guards.

(Zimbardo 2007b:40, 41, 52, 53, 80, 86) Additional information about this excerpt can be found on the Online Learning Center at www.mhhe.com/schaefer13e.

In this study, directed and described by social psychologist Philip Zimbardo, college students adopted the patterns of social interaction expected of guards and prisoners when they were placed in a mock prison. Sociologists use the term **social interaction** to refer to the ways in which people respond to one another, whether face-to-face or over the telephone or on the computer. In the mock prison, social interactions between guards and prisoners were highly impersonal. The guards addressed the prisoners by number rather than name, and they wore reflective sunglasses that made eye contact impossible.

As in many real-life prisons, the simulated prison at Stanford University had a social structure in which guards held virtually total control over prisoners. The term **social structure** refers to the way in which a society is organized into predictable relationships. The social structure of Zimbardo's mock prison influenced how the guards and prisoners interacted. Zimbardo and his colleagues (2009:516) note that it was a real prison "in the minds of the jailers and their captives." His simulated prison experiment, first conducted more than 30 years ago, has subsequently been repeated (with similar findings) both in the United States and in other countries.

Zimbardo's experiment took on new relevance in 2004, in the wake of shocking revelations of prisoner abuse at the U.S.-run Abu Ghraib military facility in Iraq. Graphic "trophy photos" showed U.S. soldiers humiliating naked Iraqi prisoners and threatening to attack them with police dogs. The structure of the wartime prison, coupled with intense pressure on military intelligence officers to secure information regarding terrorist plots, contributed to the breakdown in the guards' behavior. But Zimbardo himself noted that the guards' depraved conduct could have been predicted simply on the basis of his research. So strong was public reaction to the Abu Ghraib scandal that in 2009, during his first week in office, President Barack Obama declared that henceforth interrogators will use only noncoercive methods for questioning suspected terrorists (Zimbardo 2007a).

The two concepts of social interaction and social structure are central to sociological study. They are closely related to socialization (see Chapter 4), the process through which people learn the attitudes, values, and behaviors appropriate to their culture. When the students in Zimbardo's experiment entered the mock prison, they began a process of resocialization. In that process, they adjusted to a new social structure and learned new rules for social interaction.

In this chapter we will study social structure and its effect on our social interactions. What determines a person's status in society? How do our social roles affect our social interactions? What is the place of social institutions such as the family, religion, and government in our social structure? How can we better understand and manage large

In Zimbardo's mock prison experiment, a guard orders prisoners to line up against the wall. The social interactions fostered by the prison's social structure quickly led to a breakdown in the guards' and prisoners' behavior.

organizations such as multinational corporations? We'll begin by considering how social interactions shape the way we view the world around us. Next, we'll focus on the five basic elements of social structure: statuses, social roles, groups, social networks, and social institutions such as the family, religion, government and the mass media. We'll see that functionalists, conflict theorists, and interactionists approach social institutions quite differently. We'll also touch on a new element of social structure, *virtual worlds*. In a special case study, we'll examine the Second Life virtual world. Finally, we'll compare our modern social structure with simpler forms, using typologies developed by Émile Durkheim, Ferdinand Tönnies, and Gerhard Lenski. The Social Policy section at the end of the chapter focuses on the recent concentration of the mass media in the hands of a few large corporations.

Social Interaction and Reality

When someone in a crowd shoves you, do you automatically push back? Or do you consider the circumstances of the incident and the attitude of the instigator before you react? Chances are you do the latter. According to sociologist Herbert Blumer (1969:79), the distinctive characteristic of social interaction among people is that "human beings interpret or 'define' each other's actions instead of merely reacting to each other's actions." In other words, our response to someone's behavior is based on the *meaning* we attach to his or her actions. Reality is shaped by our perceptions, evaluations, and definitions.

These meanings typically reflect the norms and values of the dominant culture and our socialization experiences within that culture. As interactionists emphasize, the meanings that we attach to people's behavior are shaped by our interactions with them and with the larger society. Social reality is literally constructed from our social interactions (Berger and Luckmann 1966).

How do we define our social reality? Consider something as simple as how we regard tattoos. At one time, most of us in the United States considered tattoos weird or kooky. We associated them with fringe countercultural groups, such as punk rockers, biker gangs, and skinheads. Among many people, a tattoo elicited an automatic negative response. Now, however, so many people have tattoos—including society's trendsetters and major sports figures—and the ritual of getting a tattoo has become so legitimized, that mainstream culture regards tattoos differently.

At this point, as a result of increased social interaction with tattooed people, tattoos look perfectly at home to us in a number of settings.

The nature of social interaction and what constitutes reality varies across cultures. In Western societies, with their emphasis on romantic love, couples see marriage as a relationship as well as a social status. From Valentine's Day flowers to more informal, everyday gestures, professions of love are an expected part of marriage. In Japan, however, marriage is considered more a social status than a relationship. Although many or most Japanese couples undoubtedly do love each other, saying "I love you" does not come easily to them, especially not to husbands. Nor do most husbands call their wives by name (they prefer "Mother") or look them in the eyes. In 2006, in an effort to change these restrictive customs, some Japanese men formed the Devoted Husband Organization, which has been sponsoring a new holiday, Beloved Wives Day. In 2008, this group organized an event called Shout Your Love from the Middle of a Cabbage Patch Day. Dozens of men stood in a cabbage patch north of Tokyo and shouted, "I love you!" to their wives, some of whom had never heard their husbands say those words (Kambayashi 2008).

The ability to define social reality reflects a group's power within a society. In fact, one of the most crucial aspects of the relationship between dominant and subordinate groups is the ability of the dominant or majority group to define a society's values. Sociologist William I. Thomas (1923), an early critic of theories of racial and gender differences, recognized that the "definition of the situation" could mold the thinking and personality of the individual. Writing from an interactionist perspective, Thomas observed that people respond not only to the objective features of a person or situation but also to the *meaning* that person or situation has for them. For example, in Philip Zimbardo's mock prison experiment, student "guards" and "prisoners" accepted the definition of the situation (including the traditional roles and behavior associated with being a guard or prisoner) and acted accordingly.

As we have seen throughout the past 60 years—first in the civil rights movement of the 1950s and 1960s and since then among such groups as women, the elderly, gays and lesbians, and people with disabilities—an important aspect of the process of social change involves redefining or reconstructing social reality. Members of subordinate groups challenge traditional definitions and begin to perceive and experience reality in a new way.

thinking CRITICALLY

Think back over the events of the past few days. Identify two occasions on which different people defined the same social reality differently.

Elements of Social Structure

All social interaction takes place within a social structure, including those interactions that redefine social reality. For purposes of study, we can break down any social structure into five elements: statuses, social roles, groups, social networks, and social institutions. These elements make up social structure just as a foundation, walls, and ceilings make up a building's structure. The elements of social structure are developed through the lifelong process of socialization described in Chapter 4.

Statuses

We normally think of a person's *status* as having to do with influence, wealth, and fame. However, sociologists use the term **status** to refer to any of the full range of socially defined positions within a large group or society, from the lowest to the highest. Within our society, a person can occupy the status of president of the United States, fruit picker, son or daughter, violinist, teenager, resident of Minneapolis, dental technician, or neighbor. A person can hold a number of statuses at the same time.

Ascribed and Achieved Status Sociologists view some statuses as *ascribed* and others as *achieved* (Figure 5-1). An **ascribed status** is assigned to a person by society without regard for the person's unique talents or characteristics. Generally, the assignment takes place at birth; thus, a person's racial background, gender, and age are all considered ascribed statuses. Though these characteristics are biological in origin, they are significant mainly because of the *social* meanings they have in our culture. Conflict theorists are especially interested in ascribed statuses, since they often confer privileges or reflect a person's membership in a subordinate group. The social meanings of race, ethnicity, and gender will be analyzed more fully in Chapters 11 and 12.

In most cases, we can do little to change an ascribed status, but we can attempt to change the traditional constraints associated with it. For example, the Gray Panthers—an activist political

FIGURE **5-1** SOCIAL STATUSES

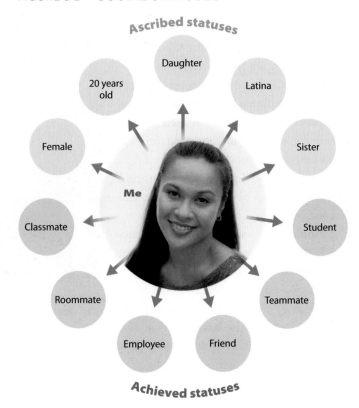

Think about It

The young woman in this figure—"me"—occupies many positions in society, each of which involves distinct statuses. How would you define your statuses? Which have the most influence in your life?

group founded in 1971 to work for the rights of older people—have tried to modify society's negative and confining stereotypes of the elderly. As a result of their work and that of other groups supporting older citizens, the ascribed status of "senior citizen" is no longer as difficult for millions of older people.

An ascribed status does not necessarily have the same social meaning in every society. In a cross-cultural study, sociologist Gary Huang (1988) confirmed the long-held view that respect for the elderly is an important cultural norm in China. In many cases, the prefix "old" is used respectfully: calling someone "old teacher" or "old person" is like calling a judge in the United States "your honor." Huang points out that positive age-seniority language distinctions are uncommon in the United States; consequently, we view the term *old man* as more of an insult than a celebration of seniority and wisdom.

Unlike ascribed statuses, an **achieved status** comes to us largely through our own efforts. Both "computer programmer" and "prison guard" are achieved statuses, as are "lawyer," "pianist," "sorority member," "convict," and "social worker." We must do something to acquire an achieved status—go to school, learn a skill, establish a friendship, invent a new product. But as we will see in the next section, our ascribed status heavily influences our achieved status. Being male, for example, would decrease the likelihood that we would consider child care as a career.

Master Status Each person holds many different and sometimes conflicting statuses; some may connote higher social position and some, lower position. How, then, do others view one's overall social position? According to sociologist Everett Hughes (1945), societies deal with inconsistencies by agreeing that certain statuses are more important than others. A **master status** is a status that dominates others and thereby determines a person's general position in society. For example, Arthur Ashe, who died of AIDS in 1993, had a remarkable career as a tennis star, but at the end of his life, his status as a well-known personality with AIDS may have outweighed his statuses as a retired athlete, author, and political activist. Throughout the world, many people with disabilities find that their status as disabled receives undue weight, overshadowing their actual ability to perform successfully in meaningful employment (Box 5-1).

Our society gives such importance to race and gender that they often dominate our lives. These ascribed statuses frequently influence our achieved status. The Black activist Malcolm X (1925–1965), an eloquent and controversial advocate of Black power and Black pride during the early 1960s, recalled that his feelings and perspectives changed dramatically while in eighth grade. When his English teacher, a White man, advised him that his goal of becoming a lawyer was "no realistic goal for a nigger" and encouraged him instead to become a carpenter, Malcolm X ([1964] 1999:37) found that his being a Black man (ascribed status) was an obstacle to his dream of becoming a lawyer (achieved status). In the United States, the ascribed statuses of race and gender can function as master statuses that have an important impact on one's potential to achieve a desired professional and social status.

Ascribed status may intersect with a person's achieved status. As this doorman greets a resident, the worker's achieved status as a low-wage worker combines with his ethnic status as an African American, an identity that many in this society consider to be lower than that of Whites.

thinking CRITICALLY

Describe a specific master status and explain how it was established. Is it a negative status? If so, how would a person overcome it?

Social Roles

What Are Social Roles? Throughout our lives, we acquire what sociologists call social roles. A **social role** is a set of expectations for people who occupy a given social position or status. Thus, in the United States, we expect that cab drivers will know how to get around a city, that receptionists will be reliable in handling phone messages, and that police officers will take action if they see a citizen being threatened. With each distinctive social status—whether ascribed or achieved—come particular role expectations. However, actual performance varies from individual to individual. One secretary may assume extensive administrative responsibilities, while another may focus on clerical duties. Similarly, in Philip Zimbardo's mock prison experiment, some students were brutal and sadistic guards; others were not.

Roles are a significant component of social structure. Viewed from a functionalist perspective, roles contribute to a society's stability by enabling members to anticipate the behavior of others and to pattern their actions accordingly. Yet social roles can also be dysfunctional if they restrict people's interactions and relationships. If we view a person *only* as a "police officer" or "supervisor," it will be difficult to relate to him or her as a friend or neighbor.

Role Conflict Imagine the delicate situation of a woman who has worked for a decade on an assembly line in an electrical plant, and has recently been named supervisor of her unit. How is this woman expected to relate to her longtime friends and co-workers? Should she still go out to lunch with them, as she has done almost daily for years? Is it her responsibility to recommend the firing of an old friend who cannot keep up with the demands of the assembly line?

Role conflict occurs when incompatible expectations arise from two or more social positions held by the same person. Fulfillment of the roles associated with one status may directly violate the roles linked to a second status. In the example just given, the newly promoted supervisor will most likely experience a sharp conflict between her social and occupational roles. Such role conflicts call for important ethical choices. The new supervisor will have to make a difficult decision about how much allegiance she owes her friend and how much she owes her employers, who have given her supervisory responsibilities.

Another type of role conflict occurs when individuals move into occupations that are not common among people with their ascribed status. Male preschool teachers and female police officers experience this type of role conflict. In the latter case, female officers must strive to reconcile their workplace role in law enforcement with the societal view of a woman's role, which does not embrace many skills needed in police work. And while female police officers encounter sexual harassment, as women do throughout the labor force, they must also deal with the "code of silence," an informal norm that precludes their implicating fellow officers in wrongdoing (Fletcher 1995; S. Martin 1994).

101

RESEARCH TODAY

5-1 Disability as a Master Status

Throughout history and around the world, people with disabilities have been subjected to cruel and inhuman treatment. For example, in the 20th century, the disabled were frequently viewed as subhuman creatures who were a menace to society. In Japan more than 16,000 women with disabilities were involuntarily sterilized with government approval from 1945 to 1995. Sweden apologized for the same action taken against 62,000 of its citizens in the 1970s.

Such blatantly hostile treatment of people with disabilities has given way to a *medical model,* in which the disabled are viewed as chronic patients. Increasingly, however, people concerned with the rights of the disabled have criticized this model as well. In their view, it is the unnecessary and discriminatory barriers present in the environment—both physical and attitudinal—that stand in the way of people with disabilities, more than any biological limitations. Applying a *civil rights model,* activists emphasize that those with disabilities face widespread prejudice, discrimination, and segregation. For example, most voting places are inaccessible to wheelchair users and fail to provide ballots that can be used by those unable to read print.

Drawing on the earlier work of Erving Goffman, contemporary sociologists have suggested that society attaches a stigma to many forms of disability, a stigma that leads to prejudicial treatment. People with disabilities frequently observe that the nondisabled see them only as blind, wheelchair users, and so forth, rather than as complex human beings with individual

In Japan more than 16,000 women with disabilities were involuntarily sterilized with government approval from 1945 to 1995.

strengths and weaknesses, whose blindness or use of a wheelchair is merely one aspect of their lives.

Although discrimination against the disabled occurs around the world, attitudes are changing. The African nation of Botswana has plans to assist its disabled, most of whom live in rural areas and need special services for mobility and economic development. In many countries, disability rights activists are targeting issues essential to overcoming this master status and becoming a full citizen, including

employment, housing, education, and access to public buildings.

LET'S DISCUSS

1. Does your campus present barriers to disabled students? If so, what kinds of barriers—physical, attitudinal, or both? Describe some of them.
2. Why do you think nondisabled people see disability as the most important characteristic of a disabled person? What can be done to help people see beyond the wheelchair and the Seeing Eye dog?

Sources: Albrecht 2004; Goffman 1963; D. Murphy 1997; *Newsday* 1997; Schaefer 2012; Joseph Shapiro 1993.

---

use your sociological *imagination*

If you were a male nurse, what aspects of role conflict might you experience? Now imagine you are a professional boxer and a woman. What conflicting role expectations might that involve? In both cases, how well do you think you would handle role conflict?

Role Strain Role conflict describes the situation of a person dealing with the challenge of occupying two social positions simultaneously. However, even a single position can cause problems. Sociologists use the term **role strain** to describe the difficulty that arises when the same social position imposes conflicting demands and expectations.

People who belong to minority cultures may experience role strain while working in the mainstream culture. Criminologist Larry Gould (2002) interviewed officers of the Navajo Nation Police Department about their relations with conventional law enforcement officials, such as sheriffs and FBI agents. Besides enforcing the law, Navajo Nation officers practice an alternative form of justice known as Peacemaking, in which they seek reconciliation between the parties to a crime. The officers expressed great confidence in Peacemaking, but worried that if they did not make arrests, other law enforcement officials would think they were too soft, or "just taking care of their own." Regardless of the strength of their ties to traditional Navajo ways, all felt the strain of being considered "too Navajo" or "not Navajo enough."

Role Exit Often, when we think of assuming a social role, we focus on the preparation and anticipatory socialization a person undergoes for that role. Such is true if a person is about to become an attorney, a chef, a spouse, or a parent. Yet until recently, social scientists have given little attention to the adjustments involved in *leaving* social roles.

Sociologist Helen Rose Fuchs Ebaugh (1988) developed the term **role exit** to describe the process of disengagement from a role that is central to one's self-identity in order to establish a new role and identity. Drawing on interviews with 185 people—among them ex-convicts, divorced men and women, recovering alcoholics, ex-nuns, former doctors, retirees, and transexuals—Ebaugh (herself an ex-nun) studied the process of voluntarily exiting from significant social roles.

Ebaugh has offered a four-stage model of role exit. The first stage begins with *doubt.* The person experiences frustration, burnout, or simply unhappiness with an accustomed status and the roles associated with the social position. The second stage involves a *search for alternatives.* A person who is unhappy with his or her career may take a leave of absence; an unhappily married couple may begin what they see as a temporary separation.

TAKING SOCIOLOGY TO WORK

Danielle Taylor, Account Manager, Cash Cycle Solutions

When Danielle Taylor entered Clemson University, she was planning to study medicine, but then she discovered that sociology was "ten times more interesting." Today she is an account manager with a company in Charlotte, North Carolina, that provides transaction processing services.

Taylor began her business career as a restaurant manager, a job that involved a good deal of interaction with the public. Sociology prepared her for a diverse work environment, she says, and helped her to handle customer complaints, allowing her to "defuse these often delicate situations more easily and with much less struggle" than managers without her background.

Taylor was managing a corporate restaurant when she made the connection that led to her present position as an account manager. "I was privy to meeting many people with lots of connections in other fields," she explains. "Networking is never as formal as it sounds and just simply conversing with my customers led to me finding a much better suited career."

Taylor thinks she is a more open and understanding person thanks to her sociological training. "I tend to judge less and analyze more," she says. She also sees the big picture that other people might miss. "Managing a restaurant with a degree in sociology was an eye-opening experience," she concludes.

LET'S DISCUSS

1. Before you read this box, would you have thought that a sociology major could be successful as a business manager? Why or why not?

2. Take the skills that Danielle Taylor gained from studying sociology and apply them to the job you hope to get when you graduate. Do they apply just as well to your chosen field?

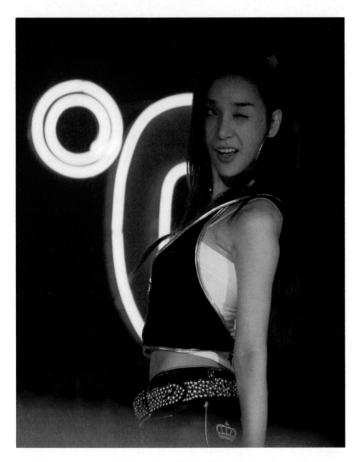

According to sociologist Helen Rose Fuchs Ebaugh, role exit is a four-stage process. Is this transexual in the first or the fourth stage of changing genders?

The third stage of role exit is the *action stage* or *departure*. Ebaugh found that the vast majority of her respondents could identify a clear turning point that made them feel it was essential to take final action and leave their jobs, end their marriages, or engage in another type of role exit. Twenty percent of respondents saw their role exit as a gradual, evolutionary process that had no single turning point.

The fourth stage of role exit involves the *creation of a new identity*. Many of you participated in a role exit when you made the transition from high school to college. You left behind the role of offspring living at home and took on the role of a somewhat independent college student living with peers in a dorm. Sociologist Ira Silver (1996) has studied the central role that material objects play in this transition. The objects students choose to leave at home (like stuffed animals and dolls) are associated with their prior identities. They may remain deeply attached to those objects, but do not want them to be seen as part of their new identities at college. The objects they bring with them symbolize how they now see themselves and how they wish to be perceived. iPods and wall posters, for example, are calculated to say, "This is me."

Groups

In sociological terms, a **group** is any number of people with similar norms, values, and expectations who interact with one another on a regular basis. The members of a women's basketball team, a hospital's business office, a synagogue, or a symphony orchestra constitute a group. However, the residents of a suburb would not be considered a group, since they rarely interact with one another at one time.

Groups play a vital part in a society's social structure. Much of our social interaction takes place within groups and is influenced by their norms and sanctions. Being a teenager or a retired person takes on special meanings when we interact within groups designed for people with that particular status. The expectations associated with many social roles, including those accompanying the statuses of brother, sister, and student, become more clearly defined in the context of a group. We will examine groups more closely in Chapter 6.

Social Institutions

The mass media, the government, the economy, the family, and the health care system are all examples of social institutions found in our society. **Social institutions** are organized patterns of beliefs and behavior centered on basic social needs, such as replacing personnel (the family) and preserving order (the government).

A close look at social institutions gives sociologists insight into the structure of a society. Consider religion, for example. The institution of religion adapts to the segment of society that it serves. Church work has very different meanings for ministers who serve a skid row area and those who serve a suburban middle-class community. Religious leaders assigned to a skid row mission will focus on tending to the ill and providing food and shelter. In contrast, clergy in affluent suburbs will be occupied with counseling those considering marriage and divorce, arranging youth activities, and overseeing cultural events (R. Schaefer 2008b).

Functionalist View One way to understand social institutions is to see how they fulfill essential functions. Anthropologists and sociologists have identified five major tasks, or functional prerequisites, that a society or relatively permanent group must accomplish if it is to survive:

1. *Replacing personnel.* Any group or society must replace personnel when they die, leave, or become incapacitated. This task is accomplished through such means as immigration, annexation of neighboring groups, acquisition of slaves, or sexual reproduction. The Shakers, a religious sect that came to the United States in 1774, are a conspicuous example of a group that has *failed* to replace personnel. Their religious beliefs commit the Shakers to celibacy; to survive, the group must recruit new members. At first, the Shakers proved quite successful in attracting members, reaching a peak of about 6,000 members in the United States during the 1840s. As of 2011, however, the only Shaker community left in this country was a farm in Maine with three members—one man and two women (R. Schaefer and Zellner 2011).

2. *Teaching new recruits.* No group or society can survive if many of its members reject the group's established behavior and responsibilities. Thus, finding or producing new members is not sufficient; the group or society must also encourage recruits to learn and accept its values and customs. Such learning can take place formally, within schools (where learning is a manifest function), or informally, through interaction in peer groups (where learning is a latent function).

3. *Producing and distributing goods and services.* Any relatively permanent group or society must provide and distribute desired goods and services to its members. Each society establishes a set of rules for the allocation of financial and other resources. The group must satisfy the needs of most members to some extent, or it will risk the possibility of discontent and ultimately disorder.

4. *Preserving order.* Throughout the world, indigenous and aboriginal peoples have struggled to protect themselves from outside invaders, with varying degrees of success. Failure to preserve order and defend against conquest leads to the death not only of a people, but of a culture as well.

5. *Providing and maintaining a sense of purpose.* People must feel motivated to continue as members of a group or society in order to fulfill the first four requirements. On January 20, 2009, in the midst of what would prove the worst economic crisis since the Great Depression, some 2 million Americans crowded the National Mall to witness the inauguration of President Barack Obama, the first African American to be elected to the nation's highest office. The celebration, an expression of

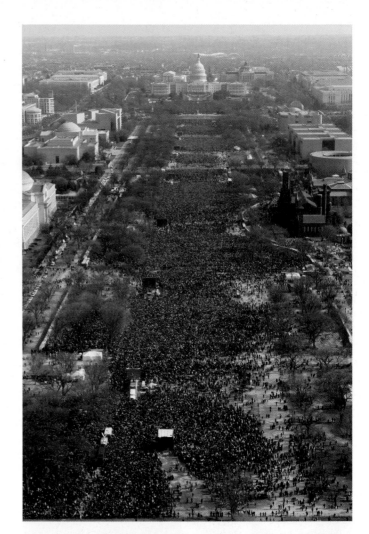

Waving flags and dressed in red, white, and blue, nearly 2 million Americans came together to celebrate the inauguration of President Barack Obama, the nation's first African American president, in January 2009. In the midst of a deepening economic and financial crisis, at that time Obama's election brought hope to Americans of all races, helping them to maintain a sense of purpose in the face of adversity.

both patriotism and Black pride, convinced people of all races that change was possible and better times lay ahead. Faced with huge layoffs and massive home foreclosures, Americans heard the new president's call to serve their nation. Patriotism and racial pride, then, can help people to develop and maintain a sense of purpose. For others, tribal identities, religious values, or personal moral codes are especially meaningful. Whatever the motivator, in any society there remains one common and critical reality: if an individual does not have a sense of purpose, he or she has little reason to contribute to a society's survival.

This list of functional prerequisites does not specify *how* a society and its corresponding social institutions will perform each task. For example, one society may protect itself from external attack by amassing a frightening arsenal of weaponry, while another may make determined efforts to remain neutral in world politics and to promote cooperative relationships with its neighbors. No matter what its particular strategy, any society or relatively permanent group must attempt to satisfy all these functional prerequisites for survival. If it fails on even one condition, the society runs the risk of extinction (Aberle et al. 1950; R. Mack and Bradford 1979).

Perspective	Role of Social Institutions	Focus
Functionalist	Meeting basic social needs	Essential functions
Conflict	Meeting basic social needs	Maintenance of privileges and inequality
Interactionist	Fostering everyday behavior	Influence of the roles and statuses we accept

Conflict View Conflict theorists do not agree with the functionalist approach to social institutions. Although proponents of both perspectives agree that social institutions are organized to meet basic social needs, conflict theorists object to the idea that the outcome is necessarily efficient and desirable.

From a conflict perspective, the present organization of social institutions is no accident. Major institutions, such as education, help to maintain the privileges of the most powerful individuals and groups within a society, while contributing to the powerlessness of others. To give one example, public schools in the United States are financed largely through property taxes. This arrangement allows more affluent areas to provide their children with better-equipped schools and better-paid teachers than low-income areas can afford. As a result, children from prosperous communities are better prepared to compete academically than children from impoverished communities. The structure of the nation's educational system permits and even promotes such unequal treatment of schoolchildren.

Conflict theorists argue that social institutions such as education have an inherently conservative nature. Without question, it has been difficult to implement educational reforms that promote equal opportunity—whether bilingual education, school desegregation, or mainstreaming of students with disabilities. From a functionalist perspective, social change can be dysfunctional, since it often leads to instability. However, from a conflict view, why should we preserve the existing social structure if it is unfair and discriminatory?

Social institutions also operate in gendered and racist environments, as conflict theorists, as well as feminists and interactionists, have pointed out. In schools, offices, and government institutions, assumptions about what people can do reflect the sexism and racism of the larger society. For instance, many people assume that women cannot make tough decisions—even those in the top echelons of corporate management. Others assume that all Black students at elite colleges represent affirmative action admissions. Inequality based on gender, economic status, race, and ethnicity thrives in such an environment—to which we might add discrimination based on age, physical disability, and sexual orientation. The truth of this assertion can be seen in routine decisions by employers on how to advertise jobs, as well as whether to provide fringe benefits such as child care and parental leave.

Interactionist View Social institutions affect our everyday behavior, whether we are driving down the street or waiting in a long shopping line. Sociologist Mitchell Duneier (1994a, 1994b) studied the social behavior of the word processors, all women, who work in the service center of a large Chicago law firm. Duneier was interested in the informal social norms that emerged in this work environment and the rich social network these female employees created.

The Network Center, as it is called, is a single, windowless room in a large office building where the law firm occupies seven floors. The center is staffed by two shifts of word processors, who work either from 4:00 p.m. to midnight or from midnight to 8:00 a.m. Each word processor works in a cubicle with just enough room for her keyboard, terminal, printer, and telephone. Work assignments for the word processors are placed in a central basket and then completed according to precise procedures.

At first glance, we might think that these women labor with little social contact, apart from limited breaks and occasional conversations with their supervisor. However, drawing on the interactionist perspective, Duneier learned that despite working in a large office, these women find private moments to talk (often in the halls or outside the washroom) and share a critical view of the law firm's attorneys and day-shift secretaries. Indeed, the word processors routinely suggest that their assignments represent work that the "lazy" secretaries should have completed during the normal workday. Duneier (1994b) tells of one word processor who resented the lawyers' superior attitude and pointedly refused to recognize or speak with any attorney who would not address her by name.

Interactionist theorists emphasize that our social behavior is conditioned by the roles and statuses we accept, the groups to which we belong, and the institutions within which we function. For example, the social roles associated with being a judge occur within the larger context of the criminal justice system. The status of judge stands in relation to other statuses, such as attorney, plaintiff, defendant, and witness, as well as to the social institution of government. Although courts and jails have great symbolic importance, the judicial system derives its continued significance from the roles people carry out in social interactions (Berger and Luckmann 1966).

Table 5-1 summarizes the three major sociological perspectives on social institutions.

Social Networks

Groups do not merely serve to define other elements of the social structure, such as roles and statuses; they also link the individual with the larger society. We all belong to a number of different groups, and through our acquaintances make connections with people in different social circles. These connections are known as a **social network**—a series of social relationships that links a person directly to others, and through them indirectly to still more people. Social networks are one of the five basic elements of social structure.

Social networks can center on virtually any activity, from sharing job information to exchanging news and gossip, or even sharing sex. In the mid-1990s, sociologists studied romantic relationships at a high school with about 1,000 students. They found that about 61 percent of the girls had been sexually active over

5-2 Social Networks and Obesity

Over the past two generations, obesity has become a public health problem in the United States. To explain the trend toward excess weight, researchers have focused on Americans' nutritional practices, as well as on their genetic tendencies. Another variable that contributes to obesity, less obvious than diet and heredity, is social networking.

Researchers identified this last variable in the course of a long-term heart health survey, during which they tracked the weight of 12,067 respondents. At the same time, they mapped the social networks that respondents belonged to (see the accompanying figure). Over the three decades since the survey began, they have

> *Weight gain in one person is often associated with weight gain in his or her friends, siblings, spouse, and neighbors.*

noted that weight gain in one person is often associated with weight gain in his or her friends, siblings, spouse, and neighbors. In fact, a person's chances of becoming obese increased by 57 percent if a friend became overweight during the same period. This association, they found, was attributable solely to selectivity in the choice of friends—that is, to people of a certain weight seeking out others of roughly the same weight.

This study shows that social networks do influence the way people behave. More important, the results suggest that networking could be exploited to spread positive health behaviors—for example, by recruiting friends to participate in a person's weight-loss plan. Through a similar approach, health practitioners

A NETWORK OF THE OBESE

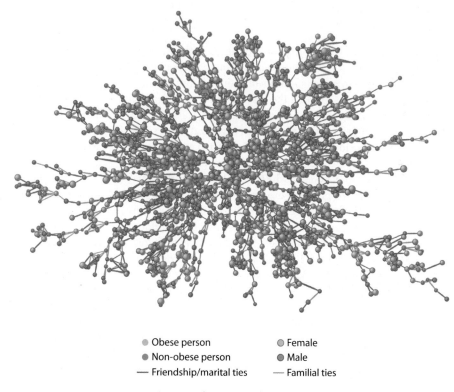

- Obese person
- Non-obese person
- — Friendship/marital ties
- Female
- Male
- — Familial ties

Larger circles represent heavier people.

could include social networking in efforts to control smoking, drinking, and drug abuse.

LET'S DISCUSS

1. Have you ever tried to lose weight, and if so, did your cluster of friends and family help or hinder you? In your experience, do people who are overweight tend to cluster in separate groups from those of normal weight?

2. Besides public health campaigns, what applications can you think of for research on social networking?

Sources: Christakis and Fowler 2007, 2009; Haas et al. 2010.

Sources: Christakis and Fowler 2007, 2009; Haas et al. 2010.

TREND SPOTTING

The Growth of Online Societies

Sociologists and other scholars who study social structure are turning their attention to online societies. Why? These virtual societies have been growing exponentially. India and China, whose roots go back for thousands of years, both have well over a billion people—an enormous population compared to most other countries. By 2011, however, over 600 million people per month were active in Facebook, an online society that has existed for less than a decade. Facebook's competitor, MySpace, had over 300 million members worldwide that year—a number comparable to the population of the United States. Twitter had 190 million users, more than the population of Pakistan.

the past 18 months. Among the sexually active respondents, the researchers counted only 63 steady couples, or pairs with no other partners. A much larger group of 288 students—almost a third of the sample—was involved in a free-flowing network of relationships (Bearman et al. 2004).

This research on high schoolers' sexual activity, an example of applied sociology, has clear implications for public health. Box 5-2 describes a similar but longer-term study in which public health officials used network analysis to curb obesity.

Involvement in social networks—commonly known as *networking*—is especially valuable in finding employment.

Albert Einstein was successful in finding a job only when a classmate's father put him in touch with his future employer. These kinds of contacts—even those that are weak and distant—can be crucial in establishing social networks and facilitating the transmission of information.

During the recent economic downturn, electronic social networks have served a new purpose, encouraging the jobless. Websites and chat rooms that cannot locate jobs for those who have been thrown out of work concentrate instead on helping them to stick together, support one another, and maintain a positive attitude. For the unemployed, online conversations with friends or even strangers in the same predicament can be an invaluable morale booster (Scherer 2010b).

Virtual Worlds

Today, with recent advances in technology, people can maintain their social networks electronically; they don't need face-to-face contacts. Whether through text-messaging, handheld devices, or social networking sites like Facebook, a significant amount of networking occurs online. Adolescents can now interact freely with distant friends, even under close scrutiny by parents or teachers. Without leaving their cubicles, employees with a taste for adventure can escape their work environments. In Box 4-3 (page 88), we considered the impact of online social networks on the process of socialization.

Virtual networks also can help to preserve real-world networks interrupted by war and other dislocations. The recent deployment of U.S. troops in the Middle East and Afghanistan increased many people's reliance on e-mail. Today, digital photos

and sound files accompany e-mail messages between soldiers and their families and friends. GIs can even view siblings' graduations or children's birthday parties live, via webcams. And U.S. soldiers and Iraqi citizens have been posting their opinions of the war in Iraq in online journals called web logs, or blogs. Though critics are skeptical of the identity of some of the authors, these postings have become yet another source of news about the war (Faith 2005; O'Connor 2004; Sisson 2007).

Case Study The Second Life Virtual World

E-mail, webcams, and blogs are only the first stage in the creation of alternative forms of social reality. Recently a whole new society, the Second Life® world, has sprung up in virtual space. web-based and three-dimensional, the Second Life virtual world included about 18 million networked "players" as of November 2010. In this game, players assume avatars that may represent looking-glass selves very different from their actual identities. Once equipped with an avatar, they go about their lives in the

virtual world, establishing businesses, even buying and decorating homes.

Just like real worlds, virtual worlds have become politicized and commercialized. In 2007, Sweden became the first real-world country to place an "embassy" in the Second Life world. Elsewhere in this virtual world, virtual protesters have paraded on behalf of a far-right French group in a confrontation with anti-Nazi protesters. The Second Life virtual world is now open

Virtual worlds have just begun to test our imaginations. On the left, a group of avatars interacts in the Second Life® world. On the right, in the blockbuster film *Avatar*, the Na'vi people interact in the screen-based virtual world of Pandora.

Media Concentration

One of the most pervasive social institutions in our society, the mass media encompass information outlets ranging from printed leaflets to online virtual worlds. Perhaps more than any other institution, they exemplify our postmodern society. According to Lenski's theory of sociocultural evolution, all societies undergo continual change, whether rapid or slow. In today's postmodern world, one of the more noticeable changes—and a potentially undesirable one—is the trend toward control of the media by fewer and fewer corporations.

Looking at the Issue

Who owns the media production and distribution process? Increasingly, the answer is a small number of very large corporations. The social consequences of this trend toward the concentration of media ownership are a reduction in the number of information outlets.

True, the United States still has thousands of independent media outlets—small-town newspapers, radio stations, and television broadcasters—but the clear trend in the media industry is toward the consolidation of ownership. The fact is, a few multinational corporations dominate the publishing, broadcasting, and film industries, although their influence may be hard to identify, since global conglomerates manage many different product names. Consider Time Warner (HBO, CNN, AOL, *Time* and *People* magazines); Rupert Murdoch's News Corporation, founded in Australia (Fox Network Television, several book publishers, numerous newspapers and magazines, MySpace.com, Second Life virtual world, and 20th Century Fox); Sony of Japan (Columbia Pictures, IMAX, CBS Records, and Columbia Records); and Viacom/CBS (Paramount, DreamWorks SKG, MTV, and Black Entertainment Television), and the extent of their power becomes clear.

Similar concerns have been raised about the situation in countries such as China, Cuba, Iraq, and North Korea, where the ruling party owns and controls the media. The difference, which is considerable, is that in the United States the gatekeeping process lies in the hands of private individuals, whose main desire is to maximize profits. In totalitarian countries, the gatekeeping process belongs to political leaders, whose desire is to maintain control of the government.

We should note one significant exception to the centralization and concentration of the media: the Internet. Today, more and more people receive their media content through the Internet. The World Wide Web is now accessible to millions of producers of media content, through independent outlets. Obviously, the producer must be technologically proficient and must have access to a computer, but compared to other media outlets, the Internet is much more readily available. Media conglomerates, well aware of the Internet's potential, are already delivering their material via the web. But for now, the Internet is the only medium that allows the average individual to become a media entrepreneur with a potential audience of millions. Some media scholars warn, however, that it is only a matter of time before corporate giants like AT&T and Comcast begin to dominate the Internet (Noam 2009; Wu 2010).

Applying Sociology

Concentration of ownership is not unique to the media (think about aircraft and automobile manufacturers). However, the media deserve special attention given the way they filter our view of reality. New media technologies also form the basis for group membership and networking, making them a powerful influence on today's society.

Functionalists see media concentration—or the consolidation of any business—as a step toward greater economic efficiency. In their view, consolidation reduces the cost of operations, freeing capital for the development of new creative outlets. Furthermore, they believe that global trade in the media facilitates the free exchange of intellectual property, which is often hampered by arbitrary local restrictions (Croteau and Hoynes 2006).

Conflict theorists believe that media concentration stifles opportunities for minority ownership. According to the most recent FCC data, less than 4 percent of television stations in the United States are owned by racial and ethnic minorities; less than 5 percent are owned by women. Minority owners are underrepresented even in markets where minorities make up the majority of the audience (S. Turner and Cooper 2006).

Interactionists see a change in the way people get their news, although not in their interest in it. In the past people may have met or called one another to discuss the latest episode of *Survivor*; now they share the latest Internet news via e-mail or buddy list. Why wait for the evening news when online sources are at your fingertips? Because savvy media users can seek out the media they consume, interactionists suggest that warnings about media concentration may be overdone (Bielby and Harrington 2008).

Initiating Policy

Any discussion of media regulation must begin with the Telecommunications Act of 1996, which marked the first overhaul of media policy since the early 1930s. The act, which covers everything from cable service to social issues such as obscenity and violence, made a significant distinction between information services, such as the Internet, and promoters of telecommunications service—that is, traditional telephone and wireless phone companies, as well as cable companies that offer phone service. Nevertheless, rapid technological development has rendered the act obsolete in many people's minds. With the convergence of telephone service, videocasting, and the Internet, not to mention the delivery of motion pictures online, such distinctions became archaic only a decade after the act was passed.

Significantly, the act eliminated most restrictions on media ownership; those that remain appear to be on their way out, as well. In 2007 the Federal Communications Commission went even further by allowing the consolidation of newspaper and television ownership in cities with only one local newspaper and one local television station. Critics worried that once the transition to digital television was completed in 2009, a single local media outlet could transmit a dozen signals *and* deliver the daily newspaper (Rice 2008).

The lack of governmental restraint of media concentration—indeed, the move toward deregulation of the media under several recent administrations—has been ascribed to the unique relationship politicians have with the media industry, compared to other industries. Elected leaders fear the impact that the media may have on their careers, given the control the media exercise over the flow of information to voters. Although they often complain about bias in the media, they shrink from attacking the corporate and commercial interests that lie behind the media (McChesney 2008).

Take the Issue with You

1. Are you aware of who owns or manages the media you watch or listen to? If not, find out.

2. Do concerns about media concentration differ from concerns over the monopoly of certain products or services? Explain.

3. Does the trend toward media concentration affect traditional media outlets (print, radio, and broadcast television) differently from the Internet? Why or why not?

MASTERING THIS CHAPTER

Summary

Social interaction refers to the ways in which people respond to one another. **Social structure** refers to the way in which a society is organized into predictable relationships. This chapter examines the five basic elements of social structure: **statuses, social roles, groups, social networks,** and **social institutions.**

1. People shape their social reality based on what they learn through their **social interactions**. Social change comes from redefining or reconstructing social reality.

2. An **ascribed status** is generally assigned to a person at birth, whereas an **achieved status** is largely attained through one's own effort. Some ascribed statuses, such as race and gender, can function as **master statuses** that affect one's potential to achieve a certain professional or social status.

3. With each distinctive status—whether ascribed or achieved—comes a particular **social role**, the set of expectations for people who occupy that status.

4. Much of our social behavior takes place in **groups**, which are often linked to **social networks** and their vast resources.

5. **Social institutions** fulfill essential functions, such as replacing personnel, training new recruits, and preserving order. The mass media, the government, the economy, the family, and the health care system are all examples of social institutions.

6. Conflict theorists charge that social institutions help to maintain the privileges of the powerful while contributing to the powerlessness of others.

7. Interactionist theorists stress that our social behavior is conditioned by the roles and statuses we accept, the groups to which we belong, and the institutions within which we function.

8. Recent advances in technology have created virtual worlds in which people can socialize electronically, without face-to-face contacts. Sociologist Manual Castells sees these emerging social networks as fundamental to new organizations and the growth of existing businesses and associations.

9. Émile Durkheim thought that social structure depends on the division of labor in a society. According to Durkheim, societies with minimal division of labor have a collective consciousness called **mechanical solidarity**; those with greater division of labor show an interdependence called **organic solidarity**.

10. Ferdinand Tönnies distinguished the close-knit community of *Gemeinschaft* from the impersonal mass society known as *Gesellschaft*.

11. Gerhard Lenski thinks that a society's social structure changes as its culture and technology become more sophisticated, a process he calls **sociocultural evolution**.

12. The Internet is the one significant exception to the trend toward media concentration, allowing millions of people to produce their own media content.

Key Terms

Achieved status A social position that a person attains largely through his or her own efforts. (page 100)

Agrarian society The most technologically advanced form of preindustrial society. Members engage primarily in the production of food, but increase their crop yields through technological innovations such as the plow. (110)

Ascribed status A social position assigned to a person by society without regard for the person's unique talents or characteristics. (100)

Gemeinschaft A close-knit community, often found in rural areas, in which strong personal bonds unite members. (108)

Gesellschaft A community, often urban, that is large and impersonal, with little commitment to the group or consensus on values. (109)

Group Any number of people with similar norms, values, and expectations who interact with one another on a regular basis. (103)

Horticultural society A preindustrial society in which people plant seeds and crops rather than merely subsist on available foods. (110)

Hunting-and-gathering society A preindustrial society in which people rely on whatever foods and fibers are readily available in order to survive. (109)

Industrial society A society that depends on mechanization to produce its goods and services. (110)

Master status A status that dominates others and thereby determines a person's general position in society. (101)

Mechanical solidarity A collective consciousness that emphasizes group solidarity, characteristic of societies with minimal division of labor. (108)

Organic solidarity A collective consciousness that rests on mutual interdependence, characteristic of societies with a complex division of labor. (108)

Postindustrial society A society whose economic system is engaged primarily in the processing and control of information. (110)

Postmodern society A technologically sophisticated society that is preoccupied with consumer goods and media images. (111)

Role conflict The situation that occurs when incompatible expectations arise from two or more social positions held by the same person. (101)

Role exit The process of disengagement from a role that is central to one's self-identity in order to establish a new role and identity. (102)

Role strain The difficulty that arises when the same social position imposes conflicting demands and expectations. (102)

Social institution An organized pattern of beliefs and behavior centered on basic social needs. (103)

Social interaction The ways in which people respond to one another. (98)

Social network A series of social relationships that links a person directly to others, and through them indirectly to still more people. (105)

Social role A set of expectations for people who occupy a given social position or status. (101)

Social structure The way in which a society is organized into predictable relationships. (98)

Sociocultural evolution Long-term trends in societies resulting from the interplay of continuity, innovation, and selection. (109)

Status A term used by sociologists to refer to any of the full range of socially defined positions within a large group or society. (100)

Technology Cultural information about the ways in which the material resources of the environment may be used to satisfy human needs and desires. (109)

TAKING SOCIOLOGY with you

1. For one day, categorize every media message you receive in terms of its function: Does it socialize, enforce a social norm, confer status, or promote consumption? Keep a record and tally the results. Which function was the most common? What can you conclude from the results?

2. People in certain professions seem particularly susceptible to role conflict. For example, journalists commonly experience role conflict during disasters, crimes, and other distressing situations. Should they offer assistance to the needy or cover breaking news? Select two occupations you may wish to enter and discuss the role conflicts people in them might experience.

3. The functionalist, conflict, and interactionist perspectives can all be used in analyzing social institutions. What are the strengths and weaknesses in each perspective's analysis of those institutions?

Self-Quiz

Read each question carefully and then select the best answer.

1. In the United States, we expect that cab drivers will know how to get around a city. This expectation is an example of which of the following?
   a. role conflict
   b. role strain
   c. social role
   d. master status

2. What occurs when incompatible expectations arise from two or more social positions held by the same person?
   a. role conflict
   b. role strain
   c. role exit
   d. both a and b

3. In sociological terms, what do we call any number of people with similar norms, values, and expectations who interact with one another on a regular basis?
   a. a category
   b. a group
   c. an aggregate
   d. a society

4. Which sociological perspective argues that the present organization of social institutions is no accident?
   a. the functionalist perspective
   b. the conflict perspective
   c. the interactionist perspective
   d. the global perspective

5. The Shakers, a religious sect that came to the United States in 1774, has seen its group membership diminish significantly due to its inability to
   a. teach new recruits.
   b. preserve order.
   c. replace personnel.
   d. provide and maintain a sense of purpose.

6. Which sociologist saw that the "definition of the situation" could mold the thinking and personality of the individual?
   a. Philip Zimbardo
   b. Herbert Blumer
   c. William I. Thomas
   d. Erving Goffman

7. In Zimbardo's mock prison experiment at Stanford University,
   a. the social interactions between the prisoners and the guards influenced the social structure of the prison.
   b. the social structure of the prison influenced the social interactions between the prisoners and the guards.
   c. there was no relationship between social interaction and social structure.
   d. Zimbardo believed that social structure and social interaction influence each other.

8. Social control in what Ferdinand Tönnies termed a *Gemeinschaft* community is maintained through all but which of the following means?
   a. moral persuasion
   b. gossip
   c. legally defined punishment
   d. gestures

9. Sociologist Daniel Bell uses which of the following terms to refer to a society whose economic system is engaged primarily in the processing and control of information?
   a. postmodern
   b. horticultural
   c. industrial
   d. postindustrial

10. A key challenge for sociologists who study virtual social networks is that
   a. people using online social networking often lie about themselves.
   b. technology changes too rapidly.
   c. due to their rapid growth and lack of historical record, reconstructing these virtual worlds as they existed when they were first populated will be impossible.
   d. it's expensive to join a virtual social network.

11. The term _____ _____ refers to the way in which a society is organized into predictable relationships.

12. The Black activist Malcolm X wrote in his autobiography that his position as a Black man, a(n) _____ status, was an obstacle to his dream of becoming a lawyer, a(n) _____ status.

13. Sociologist Helen Rose Fuchs Ebaugh developed the term _____ _____ to describe the process of disengagement from a role that is central to one's self-identity in order to establish a new role and identity.

14. The mass media, the government, the economy, the family, and the health care system are all examples of _____ _____ found in the United States.

15. According to Herbert Blumer, our response to someone's behavior is based on the _____ we attach to his or her actions.

16. In studying the social behavior of word processors in a Chicago law firm, sociologist Mitchell Duneier drew on the _____ perspective.

17. Public health researchers have studied the relationship between social networks and _____.

18. According to Émile Durkheim, societies with a minimal division of labor are characterized by _____ solidarity, while societies with a complex division of labor are characterized by _____ solidarity.

19. In Gerhard Lenski's theory of sociocultural evolution, a society's level of _____ is critical to the way it is organized.

20. A(n) _____ society is a technologically sophisticated society that is preoccupied with consumer goods and media images.

Answers
1 (c); 2 (a); 3 (b); 4 (b); 5 (c); 6 (c); 7 (b); 8 (c); 9 (d); 10 (c); 11 social structure; 12 ascribed; achieved; 13 role exit; 14 social institutions; 15 meaning; 16 interactionist; 17 obesity; 18 mechanical; organic; 19 technology; 20 postmodern

THINKING ABOUT MOVIES

Invictus

In post-apartheid South Africa, a rugby team helps Nelson Mandela to build national unity.

The Social Network

This dramatization of the rise of Facebook illustrates the way people connect to one another in the 21st century.

Wendy and Lucy

A young woman wanders through life disconnected from social institutions.

The women's rugby team of Brown University struggles for victory. Groups help individuals to navigate through the larger social world, including complex social organizations like educational institutions.

Groups and Organizations 6

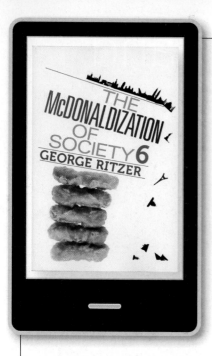

Ray Kroc (1902–1984), the genius behind the franchising of McDonald's restaurants, was a man with big ideas and grand ambitions. But even Kroc could not have anticipated the astounding impact of his creation. McDonald's is the basis of one of the most influential developments in contemporary society. Its reverberations extend far beyond its point of origin in the United States and in the fast-food business. It has influenced a wide range of undertakings, indeed the way of life, of a significant portion of the world. And having rebounded from some well-publicized economic difficulties, that impact is likely to expand at an accelerating rate in the early 21st century.

... I devote all this attention to McDonald's ... because it serves here as the major example of, and the paradigm for, a wide-ranging process I call McDonaldization. ... McDonaldization has shown every sign of being an inexorable process, sweeping through seemingly impervious institutions (e.g., religion) and regions (European nations such as France) of the world.

Other types of business are increasingly adapting the principles of the fast-food industry to their needs. Said the vice chairman of Toys "R" Us, "We want to be thought of as a sort of McDonald's of toys." ... Other chains with similar ambitions include Gap, Jiffy Lube, AAMCO Transmissions, Midas Muffler & Brake Shops, Great Clips, H&R Block, Pearle Vision, Bally's. ...

Other nations have developed their own variants on the McDonald's chain. ... Paris, a city whose love for fine cuisine might lead you to think it would prove immune to fast food, has a large number of fast-food croissanteries; the revered French bread has also been McDonaldized. India has a chain of fast-food restaurants, Nirula's, that sells mutton burgers (about 80% of Indians are Hindus, who eat no beef) as well as local Indian cuisine. Mos Burger is a Japanese chain with 1,373 restaurants that, in addition to the usual fare, sell Teriyaki chicken burgers, rice burgers, and "Oshiruko with brown rice cake." ...

McDonald's is such a powerful model that many businesses have acquired nicknames beginning with Mc. Examples include "McDentists" and "McDoctors," meaning drive-in clinics designed to deal quickly and efficiently with minor dental and medical problems; "McChild" care centers, meaning child care centers such as KinderCare; "McStables," designating the nationwide race horse–training operation of D. Wayne Lucas; and "McPaper," describing the newspaper *USA TODAY*. 99

Ray Kroc (1902–1984), the genius behind the franchising of McDonald's restaurants, was a man with big ideas and grand ambitions.

(Ritzer 2011:1, 3, 5, 12) Additional information about this excerpt can be found on the Online Learning Center at www.mhhe.com/schaefer13e.

In this excerpt from *The McDonaldization of Society,* sociologist George Ritzer contemplates the enormous influence of a well-known fast-food organization on modern-day culture and social life. Ritzer defines **McDonaldization** as "the process by which the principles of the fast-food restaurant are coming to dominate more and more sectors of American society as well as of the rest of the world" (Ritzer 2011:1). In his book, he shows how the business principles on which the fast-food industry is founded—efficiency, calculability, predictability, and control—have changed not only the way Americans do business and run their organizations, but the way they live their lives. Today, busy families rely on the takeout meals served up by fast-food establishments, and McDonald's has become a regular meeting place for social groups from adolescents to senior citizens.

Despite the runaway success of McDonald's and its imitators, and the advantages these enterprises bring to millions of people around the world (see Box 6-2, page 127), Ritzer is critical of their effect on society. The waste and environmental degradation created by billions of disposable containers and the dehumanized work routines of fast-food crews are two of the disadvantages he cites in his critique. Would the modern world be a better one, Ritzer asks, if it were less McDonaldized?

This chapter considers the impact of groups and organizations on social interaction. Do we behave differently in large groups than in small ones? How do we make large organizations manageable? What effect are current social changes having on the structure of groups? We'll begin by noting the distinctions between various types of groups, with particular attention to the dynamics of small groups. We'll examine how and why formal organizations came into existence and describe Max Weber's model of the modern bureaucracy. Finally, we'll look at recent changes in the workplace, some of which are designed to counteract the failures of bureaucracies. The Social Policy section at the end of the chapter focuses on the status of organized labor today.

Understanding Groups

Most of us use the term *group* loosely to describe any collection of individuals, whether three strangers sharing an elevator or hundreds attending a rock concert. However, in sociological terms a **group** is any number of people with similar norms, values, and expectations who interact with one another on a regular basis. College sororities and fraternities, dance companies, tenants' associations, and chess clubs are all considered groups. The important point is that members of a group share some sense of belonging. This characteristic distinguishes groups from mere *aggregates* of people, such as passengers who happen to be together on an airplane flight, or from *categories* of people, such as those who share a common feature (such as being retired) but otherwise do not act together.

Consider the case of a college singing group. It has agreed-on values and social norms. All members want to improve their singing skills and schedule lots of performances. In addition, like many groups, the singing ensemble has both a formal and an informal structure. The members meet regularly to rehearse; they choose leaders to run the rehearsals and manage their affairs. At the same time, some group members may take on unofficial leadership roles by coaching new members in singing techniques and performing skills.

The study of groups has become an important part of sociological investigation because they play such a key role in the transmission of culture. As we interact with others, we pass on our ways of thinking and acting—from language and values to ways of dressing and leisure activities.

Types of Groups

Sociologists have made a number of useful distinctions between types of groups—primary and secondary groups, in-groups and out-groups, and reference groups.

Primary and Secondary Groups Charles Horton Cooley (1902) coined the term **primary group** to refer to a small group characterized by intimate, face-to-face association and cooperation. The members of a street gang constitute a primary group; so do members of a family living in the same household, as do a group of "sisters" in a college sorority.

Primary groups play a pivotal role both in the socialization process (see Chapter 4) and in the development of roles and statuses. Indeed, primary groups can be instrumental in a person's day-to-day existence. When we find ourselves identifying closely with a group, it is probably a primary group.

We also participate in many groups that are not characterized by close bonds of friendship, such as large college classes and business associations. The term **secondary group** refers to a formal, impersonal group in which there is little social intimacy or mutual understanding (Table 6-1). Secondary groups often emerge in the workplace among those who share special understandings about their occupation. The distinction between primary and secondary groups is not always clear-cut, however. Some social clubs may become so large and impersonal that they no longer function as primary groups.

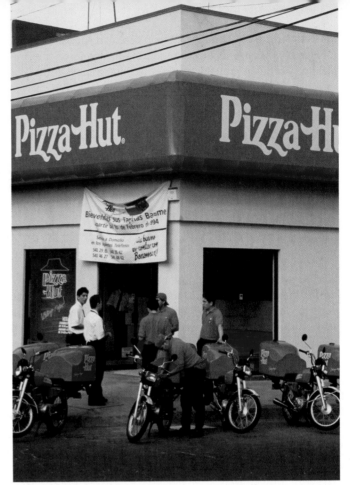

A pizza delivery crew is an example of a *secondary group*—a formal, impersonal group in which there is little social intimacy or mutual understanding. While waiting for the next delivery, members of this crew will become well enough acquainted to distinguish those who see the job as temporary from those who view it as permanent. They will learn who looks forward to deliveries in perceived high-risk areas and who does not. They may even spend time together after work, joking or boasting about their exploits on the job, but their friendships typically will not develop beyond that point.

A significant amount of sociological research has been done on people's behavior in groups. Box 6-1 on page 122 describes the findings on one well-known but short-lived group, the jury.

TABLE **6-1** COMPARISON OF PRIMARY AND SECONDARY GROUPS

Primary Group	Secondary Group
Generally small	Usually large
Relatively long period of interaction	Relatively short duration, often temporary
Intimate, face-to-face association	Little social intimacy or mutual understanding
Some emotional depth to relationships	Relationships generally superficial
Cooperative, friendly	More formal and impersonal

summingup

In-Groups and Out-Groups A group can hold special meaning for members because of its relationship to other groups. For example, people in one group sometimes feel antagonistic toward or threatened by another group, especially if that group is perceived as being different, either culturally or racially. To identify these "we" and "they" feelings, sociologists use two terms first employed by William Graham Sumner (1906): *in-group* and *out-group*.

An **in-group** can be defined as any group or category to which people feel they belong. Simply put, it comprises everyone who is regarded as "we" or "us." The in-group may be as narrow as a teenage clique or as broad as an entire society. The very existence of an in-group implies that there is an out-group that is viewed as "they" or "them." An **out-group** is a group or category to which people feel they do *not* belong.

In-group members typically feel distinct and superior, seeing themselves as better than people in the out-group. Proper behavior for the in-group is simultaneously viewed as unacceptable behavior for the out-group. This double standard enhances the sense of superiority. Sociologist Robert Merton (1968) described this process as the conversion of "in-group virtues" into "out-group vices." We can see this differential standard operating in worldwide discussions of terrorism. When a group or a nation takes aggressive actions, it usually justifies them as necessary, even if civilians are hurt or killed. Opponents are quick to label such actions with the emotion-laden term of *terrorist* and appeal to the world community for condemnation. Yet these same people may themselves retaliate with actions that hurt civilians, which the first group will then condemn.

"So long, Bill. This is my club. You can't come in."

An exclusive social club is an in-group whose members consider themselves superior to others.

use your sociological *imagination*

Try putting yourself in the shoes of an out-group member. What does your in-group look like from that perspective?

Conflict between in-groups and out-groups can turn violent on a personal as well as a political level. In 1999 two disaffected students at Columbine High School in Littleton, Colorado, launched an attack on the school that left 15 students and teachers dead, including themselves. The gunmen, members of an out-group that other students referred to as the Trenchcoat Mafia, apparently resented taunting by an in-group referred to as the Jocks. Similar episodes have occurred in schools across the nation, where rejected adolescents, overwhelmed by personal and family problems, peer group pressure, academic responsibilities, or media images of violence, have struck out against more popular classmates.

Reference Groups Both primary groups and in-groups can dramatically influence the way an individual thinks and behaves. Sociologists call any group that individuals use as a standard for evaluating themselves and their own behavior a **reference group**. For example, a high school student who aspires to join a social circle of hip-hop music devotees will pattern his or her behavior after that of the group. The student will begin dressing like these peers, listening to the same downloads and DVDs, and hanging out at the same stores and clubs.

Reference groups have two basic purposes. They serve a normative function by setting and enforcing standards of conduct

At a powwow, a drum circle breathes spirit into an ancient tribal tradition. These accomplished ceremonial musicians may serve as a reference group for onlookers who want to know more about drumming.

and belief. The high school student who wants the approval of the hip-hop crowd will have to follow the group's dictates, at least to some extent. Reference groups also perform a comparison function by serving as a standard against which people can measure themselves and others. An actor will evaluate himself or herself against a reference group composed of others in the acting profession (Merton and Kitt 1950).

Reference groups may help the process of anticipatory socialization. For example, a college student majoring in finance may read the *Wall Street Journal,* study the annual reports of corporations, and listen to midday stock market news on the radio. Such a student is using financial experts as a reference group to which he or she aspires.

Often, two or more reference groups influence us at the same time. Our family members, neighbors, and co-workers all shape different aspects of our self-evaluation. In addition, reference group attachments change during the life cycle. A corporate executive who quits the rat race at age 45 to become a social worker will find new reference groups to use as standards for evaluation. We shift reference groups as we take on different statuses during our lives.

Coalitions As groups grow larger, coalitions begin to develop. A **coalition** is a temporary or permanent alliance geared toward a common goal. Coalitions can be broad-based or narrow and can take on many different objectives. Sociologist William Julius Wilson (1999) has described community-based organizations in Texas that include Whites and Latinos, working class and affluent, who have banded together to work for improved sidewalks, better drainage systems, and comprehensive street paving. Out of this type of coalition building, Wilson hopes, will emerge better interracial understanding.

Some coalitions are intentionally short-lived. For example, short-term coalition building is a key to success in popular TV programs like *Survivor.* In the program's first season, *Survivor: Borneo,* broadcast in 2000, the four members of the "Tagi alliance" banded together to vote fellow castaways off the island. The political world is also the scene of many temporary coalitions. For example, in 1997 big tobacco companies joined with anti-smoking groups to draw up a settlement for reimbursing states for tobacco-related medical costs. Soon after the settlement was announced the coalition members returned to their decades-long fight against each other (Pear 1997).

use your sociological *imagination*

Describe an experience you have had with coalition building, or one that you have read about—perhaps in politics. Was the coalition effective? What problems did the members need to overcome?

Studying Small Groups

Sociological research done on the micro level and research done from the interactionist perspective usually focus on the study of small groups. Box 6-1, for example, describes microsociological research on juries. The term **small group** refers to a group small enough for all members to interact simultaneously—that is, to talk with one another or at least be well acquainted.

In 2010, when 33 Chilean miners were trapped together far beneath the earth's surface, their plight created a highly unusual opportunity for scholars to study their small group. Researchers were especially interested in how the 33 men would form coalitions or subgroups. The miners first divided into work groups, to move rocks and debris and prepare for their eventual rescue. There were some rifts in their social structure. Five men who worked for a different subcontractor chose to live apart from the others and to collaborate on their own escape strategy. And friction developed when the overstressed miners sent their first videos up to the surface, and some men felt that others were showing off. As the details of the escape plan being developed aboveground became clear, however, the group united around their shared goal of survival and escape (R. Carroll and Franklin 2010).

Throughout the 70-day ordeal, the miners remained aware of the attention their story was drawing in the international news media. To prepare themselves to speak to the press when they surfaced, they studied a manual called *Tactics for Public Speaking.* As their rescue drew closer, the anticipatory socialization intensified. Via closed-circuit TV, the men received training on how to remain poised during interviews and on how to indicate politely that they preferred not to answer a question (Jonathan Franklin 2010, 2011; Kluger 2010).

Size of a Group At what point does a collection of people become too large to be called a small group? That is not clear. In a group with more than 20 members, it is difficult for individuals to interact regularly in a direct and intimate manner. But even within a range of 2 to 20 people, group size can substantially alter the quality of social relationships. For example, as the number of group participants increases, the most active communicators become even more active relative to others. Therefore, a person who dominates a group of 3 or 4 members will be relatively more dominant in a 15-person group.

Can you outwit, outplay, outlast your competition? Maybe a coalition can help. In *Survivor: Redemption Island,* coalition building continued to be one of the keys to success in the long-running television series, now in its 22nd season.

RESEARCH TODAY

6-1   The Drinking Rape Victim: Jury Decision Making

She was heavily intoxicated. He had drunk a few beers. They had sex. She said she was raped. He said it was consensual. The jury deliberated, and the verdict was. . . .

This is not an actual case, but an experiment in group decision making. Few small groups have received as much attention from sociologists over the past decade and a half as juries. Scholars have used several research methods to investigate juries' decision making: interviews with jury members after they have reached a verdict; observation of jurors as they sit through and react to courtroom events; observation of actual jury deliberations, which presiding judges have permitted in a few instances; and experiments involving mock juries. The findings indicate that jurors do not always make decisions the way they are supposed to.

How do jurors form impressions in rape cases, especially those that involve intoxication?

To find out, legal scholars Emily Finch and Vanessa Munro simulated a rape trial in which intoxication was an issue. The two researchers varied the story to see what the effect might be on the verdict. In one version the alleged victim was drunk; in another

Finch and Munro found that male or female, the mock jurors in their study followed a double standard.

she was drugged by a third person; in another she was drugged by the defendant.

Finch and Munro found that male or female, the mock jurors in their study followed a double standard. The more intoxicated the *defendant* was said to have been, the less likely jurors were to regard him as culpable. They were far more likely to regard a *victim* who had drunk too much as having contributed to her rape. This finding applied even in cases in which the victim's drink had been

spiked. In short, before jurors could summon up much sympathy for the victim, the defendant had to engage in a great deal of bad behavior.

Today, research on juries is expanding to deal with generational changes in the experience of being a juror. Some jurors arrive at court expecting to see the kind of sophisticated DNA analysis or investigative methods featured on televised crime shows, such as *CSI*. Improved methods of documenting crime scenes, including the use of computer-generated re-creations, mean that today's jurors are more likely than past jurors to be exposed to images of graphic violence and gore.

LET'S DISCUSS

1. Have you ever served on a jury? If so, were you aware of jurors who made up their minds early in the trial, despite the judge's instructions? Did you experience stress from being exposed to graphic images of violence and bloodshed?
2. Is a jury a typical group? Why or why not?

Sources: S. Diamond and Rose 2005; Finch and Munro 2005, 2007, 2008; McGlynn and Munro 2010.

Group size also has noticeable social implications for members who do not assume leadership roles. In a larger group, each member has less time to speak, more points of view to absorb, and a more elaborate structure to function in. At the same time, an individual has greater freedom to ignore certain members or viewpoints than he or she would in a smaller group. It is harder to disregard someone in a 4-person workforce than someone in an office with 30 employees, harder to disregard someone in a string quartet than someone in a college band with 50 members.

The German sociologist Georg Simmel (1858–1918) is credited as the first sociologist to emphasize the importance of interactive processes within groups and to note how they change as the group's size changes. The simplest of all social groups or relationships is the **dyad**, or two-member group. A wife and husband constitute a dyad, as does a business partnership or a singing duo. The dyad offers a special level of intimacy that cannot be duplicated in larger groups. However, as Simmel ([1917] 1950) noted, a dyad, unlike any other group, can be destroyed by the loss of a single member. Therefore, the threat of termination hangs over a dyadic relationship perhaps more than over any other.

Obviously, the introduction of one additional person to a dyad dramatically transforms the character of the small group. The dyad becomes a three-member group, or **triad.** The third member has many ways of interacting with and influencing the dynamics of the group. The new person may play a *unifying* role in the triad. When a married couple has their first child, the baby may serve to bind the group closer together. A newcomer also may play a *mediating* role

Miners trapped underground in Chile raise a flag, putting a brave face on their plight in a video made for their friends and families. Their extended stay together gave scholars a rare opportunity to study a small group under stress.

in a three-person group. If two roommates are perpetually sniping at each other, the third roommate may attempt to remain on good terms with both and to arrange compromise solutions to problems. Finally, a member of a triad can choose to employ a *divide-and-rule* strategy. Such is the case, for example, with a coach who tries to gain greater control over two assistants by making them rivals (Lawler et al. 2008; H. Nixon 1979).

Groupthink Can mere membership in a group cause those who belong to reach faulty decisions? William H. Whyte Jr. (1952) thought so. To describe the uncritical acceptance of or conformity to the prevailing viewpoint—a phenomenon that too often characterizes group decision making—Whyte coined the term **groupthink.** Simply put, group members experience a collective pressure to conform to the predominant line of thought. This social pressure effectively discourages the open expression of dissent.

In Whyte's opinion, high-level government leaders and their advisers are particularly prone to groupthink. These people confer regularly with one another, often in closed meetings in which they hear no one else's viewpoint. When decision makers are isolated from others in this way, they are liable to adopt unpopular or even disastrous policies. Of course, groupthink is not limited to the upper echelons of government. It occurs in jury rooms, corporate boardrooms, and even among high school students selecting a theme for their senior prom.

There are ways to avoid the illusion of unanimity created by groupthink. Small-group studies have shown the value of having outside facilitators lead groups. Dividing an established group into smaller units also encourages the expression of new perspectives (Janis 1967; Street 1997).

The effects of group size and groupthink on group dynamics are but two of the many aspects of the small group that sociologists have studied. Another aspect, conformity and deviance, is examined in Chapter 8. Although it is clear that small-group encounters have considerable influence on our lives, we are also deeply affected by much larger groups of people, as we'll see in the next section.

Focus Groups Sociological study of small groups led to the development of the *focus group,* a research tool commonly used in marketing and politics. A **focus group** is a carefully selected discussion group led by a trained moderator. Typically composed of 8 to 10 participants, focus groups are used to collect qualitative data on people's opinions, feelings, and ideas. Often, they are used to gauge the attractiveness of a new consumer product, such as a car, or to evaluate a 30-second TV ad for a political candidate.

Focus groups were developed by the sociologist Robert Merton during World War II. Merton was doing government-funded research to determine how military and civilian morale could be improved during wartime. The groups allowed researchers to gather data quickly, by interviewing several people at once rather than individually. They also allowed researchers to observe how people make decisions in groups rather than as individuals. Today, the techniques for selecting groups, moderating discussions, and interpreting participants' comments have evolved to the point that many researchers specialize in

Researchers watch members of a focus group through a one-way mirror. The idea of observing or monitoring a group's discussion of an idea or product was conceived by the sociologist Robert Merton.

the creation of focus groups. In fact, focus groups are one of the most widespread, if often unheralded practical applications not only of the study of groups, but of the entire discipline of sociology (R. Lee 2010; Merton and Kendall 1946).

Focus groups reflect Merton's belief in the integration of macrosociology and microsociology (see Chapter 1). Although the observation of focus groups is an application of microsociology, it has implications for society as a whole. For example, in the jury study described in this chapter (see Box 6-1), focus groups served as mock juries, allowing researchers to observe how jurors make decisions. The researchers then used this microsociological data to generalize about how the judicial system as a whole handles rape cases involving drinking or illegal drugs.

Understanding Organizations

Formal Organizations and Bureaucracies

As contemporary societies have shifted to more advanced forms of technology and their social structures have become more complex, our lives have become increasingly dominated by large secondary groups referred to as *formal organizations.* A **formal organization** is a group designed for a special purpose and structured for maximum efficiency. The U.S. Postal Service, McDonald's, and the Boston Pops orchestra are examples of formal organizations. Though organizations vary in their size, specificity of goals, and degree of efficiency, they are all structured to facilitate the management of large-scale operations. They also have a bureaucratic form of organization, described in the next section.

In our society, formal organizations fulfill an enormous variety of personal and societal needs, shaping the lives of every one of us. In fact, formal organizations have become such a dominant force that we must create organizations to supervise other organizations, such as the Securities and Exchange Commission (SEC) to regulate brokerage companies. Although it sounds more exciting to say that we live in the "computer age" than to say that we live in the "age of formal organization," the latter is probably a more accurate description (Azumi and Hage 1972; Etzioni 1964).

Ascribed statuses such as gender, race, and ethnicity can influence how we see ourselves within formal organizations. For example, a study of female lawyers in the nation's largest law firms found significant differences in the women's self-images, depending on the relative presence or absence of women in positions of power. In firms in which less than 15 percent of partners were women, the female lawyers were likely to believe that "feminine" traits were strongly devalued and that "masculine" traits were equated with success. As one female attorney put it, "Let's face it: this is a man's environment, and it's sort of Jock City, especially at my firm." Women in firms where female lawyers were better represented in positions of power had a stronger desire for and higher expectations of promotion (Ely 1995:619).

Characteristics of a Bureaucracy

A **bureaucracy** is a component of formal organization that uses rules and hierarchical ranking to achieve efficiency. Rows of desks staffed by seemingly faceless people, endless lines and forms, impossibly complex language, and frustrating encounters with red tape—all these unpleasant images have combined to make *bureaucracy* a dirty word and an easy target in political campaigns. As a result, few people want to identify their occupation as "bureaucrat," despite the fact that all of us perform various bureaucratic tasks. In an industrial society, elements of bureaucracy enter into almost every occupation.

Max Weber ([1913–1922] 1947) first directed researchers to the significance of bureaucratic structure. In an important sociological advance, Weber emphasized the basic similarity of structure and process found in the otherwise dissimilar enterprises of religion, government, education, and business. Weber saw bureaucracy as a form of organization quite different from the family-run business. For analytical purposes, he developed an ideal type of bureaucracy that would reflect the most characteristic aspects of all human organizations. By **ideal type** Weber meant a construct or model for evaluating specific cases. In actuality, perfect bureaucracies do not exist; no real-world organization corresponds exactly to Weber's ideal type.

Weber proposed that whether the purpose is to run a church, a corporation, or an army, the ideal bureaucracy displays five basic characteristics. A discussion of those characteristics, as well as the dysfunctions of a bureaucracy, follows.

1. **Division of labor.** Specialized experts perform specific tasks. In your college bureaucracy, the admissions officer does not do the job of registrar; the guidance counselor does not see to the maintenance of buildings. By working at a specific task, people are more likely to become highly skilled and carry out a job with maximum efficiency. This emphasis on specialization is so basic a part of our lives that we may not realize it is a fairly recent development in Western culture.

The downside of division of labor is that the fragmentation of work into smaller and smaller tasks can divide workers and remove any connection they might feel to the overall objective of the bureaucracy. In *The Communist Manifesto* (written in 1848), Karl Marx and Friedrich Engels charged that the capitalist system reduces workers to a mere

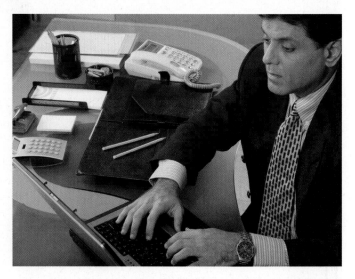

Being an accountant in a large corporation may be a relatively high-paying occupation. In Marxist terms, however, accountants are vulnerable to alienation, since they are far removed from the product or service that the corporation creates.

"appendage of the machine" (Tucker 1978). Such a work arrangement, they wrote, produces extreme **alienation**—a condition of estrangement or dissociation from the surrounding society. According to both Marx and conflict theorists, restricting workers to very small tasks also weakens their job security, since new employees can easily be trained to replace them.

Although division of labor has certainly enhanced the performance of many complex bureaucracies, in some cases it can lead to **trained incapacity;** that is, workers become so specialized that they develop blind spots and fail to notice obvious problems. Even worse, they may not care about what is happening in the next department. Some observers believe that such developments have caused workers in the United States to become less productive on the job.

In some cases, the bureaucratic division of labor can have tragic results. In the wake of the coordinated attacks on the World Trade Center and the Pentagon on September 11, 2001, Americans wondered aloud how the FBI and CIA could have failed to detect the terrorists' elaborately planned operation. The problem, in part, turned out to be the division of labor between the FBI, which focuses on domestic matters, and the CIA, which operates overseas. Officials at these intelligence-gathering organizations, both of which are huge bureaucracies, are well known for jealously guarding information from one another. Subsequent investigations revealed that they knew about Osama bin Laden and his Al-Qaeda terrorist network in the early 1990s. Unfortunately, five federal agencies—the CIA, FBI, National Security Agency, Defense Intelligence Agency, and National Reconnaissance Office—failed to share their leads on the network. Although the hijacking of the four commercial airliners used in the massive attacks may not have been preventable, the bureaucratic division of labor definitely hindered efforts to defend against terrorism, undermining U.S. national security.

2. Hierarchy of authority. Bureaucracies follow the principle of hierarchy; that is, each position is under the supervision of a higher authority. A president heads a college bureaucracy; he or she selects members of the administration, who in turn hire their own staff. In the Roman Catholic Church, the pope is the supreme authority; under him are cardinals, bishops, and so forth.

3. Written rules and regulations. What if your sociology professor gave your classmate an A for having such a friendly smile? You might think that wasn't fair, that it was against the rules. Through written rules and regulations, bureaucracies generally offer employees clear standards for an adequate (or exceptional) performance. In addition, procedures provide a valuable sense of continuity in a bureaucracy. Individual workers will come and go, but the structure and past records of the organization give it a life of its own that outlives the services of any one bureaucrat.

Of course, rules and regulations can overshadow the larger goals of an organization to the point that they become dysfunctional. What if a hospital emergency room physician failed to treat a seriously injured person because he or she had no valid proof of U.S. citizenship? If blindly applied, rules no longer serve as a means to achieving an objective, but instead become important (and perhaps too important) in their own right. Robert Merton (1968) used the term **goal displacement** to refer to overzealous conformity to official regulations.

4. Impersonality. Max Weber wrote that in a bureaucracy, work is carried out *sine ira et studio*, "without hatred or passion." Bureaucratic norms dictate that officials perform their duties without giving personal consideration to people as individuals. Although this norm is intended to guarantee equal treatment for each person, it also contributes to the often cold and uncaring feeling associated with modern organizations. We typically think of big government and big business when we think of impersonal bureaucracies. In some cases, the impersonality that is associated with a bureaucracy can have tragic results. More frequently, bureaucratic impersonality produces frustration and disaffection. Today, even small firms filter callers with electronic menus.

5. Employment based on technical qualifications. Within the ideal bureaucracy, hiring is based on technical qualifications rather than on favoritism, and performance is measured against specific standards. Written personnel policies dictate who gets promoted, and people often have a right to appeal if they believe that particular rules have been violated. Such procedures protect bureaucrats against arbitrary dismissal, provide a measure of security, and encourage loyalty to the organization.

Although ideally, any bureaucracy will value technical and professional competence, personnel decisions do not always follow that ideal pattern. Dysfunctions within bureaucracy have become well publicized, particularly because of the work of Laurence J. Peter. According to the **Peter principle,** every employee within a hierarchy tends to rise to his or her level of incompetence (Peter and Hull 1969). This hypothesis, which has not been directly or systematically tested, reflects a possible dysfunctional outcome of advancement on the basis of merit. Talented people receive promotion after promotion, until sadly, some of them finally achieve positions that they cannot handle with their usual competence.

Table 6-2 summarizes the five characteristics of bureaucracy. These characteristics, developed by Max Weber more than 80 years ago, describe an ideal type rather than an actual bureaucracy. Not every formal organization will possess all five of Weber's characteristics. In fact, wide variation exists among actual bureaucratic organizations.

Bureaucracy pervades modern life; through McDonaldization, it has reached new heights. As Box 6-2 on page 127 shows, the McDonald's organization provides an excellent illustration of Weber's concept of bureaucracy (Ritzer 2011).

---

use your sociological *imagination*

Your school or workplace suddenly ceases to exhibit one of the five characteristics of bureaucracy. Which characteristic is it, and what are the consequences?

Bureaucratization as a Process Have you ever had to speak to 10 or 12 individuals in a corporation or government agency just to find out which official has jurisdiction over a particular problem? Ever been transferred from one department to another until you finally hung up in disgust? Sociologists have used the term **bureaucratization** to refer to the process by which a group, organization, or social movement becomes increasingly bureaucratic.

Normally, we think of bureaucratization in terms of large organizations. But bureaucratization also takes place within small-group settings. Sociologist Jennifer Bickman Mendez (1998)

TREND SPOTTING

Joining Up: Voluntary Associations in the United States

One alternative to the formal, bureaucratic organization is the *voluntary association*, a collection of people with a common interest whose members volunteer or even pay to join. Voluntary associations have always been popular in the United States. By 2011, more than 25,000 such nonprofit associations existed, from the Girl Scouts of America to the American Association of Aardvark Aficionados.

What accounts for the popularity of the voluntary association? Some scholars see Americans as individualists who prefer to pursue their own interests on their own terms. Others see the United States as a nation of joiners. Data tend to support the second explanation. Since 1974, fully 70 percent of adults in the United States have belonged to at least one voluntary association; more than 25 percent belong to three or more. This proportion has not changed over time. In other countries, the willingness to join is not as great as in the United States, largely because of lower participation in religious groups.

Characteristic	Positive Consequence	Negative Consequence	
		For the Individual	For the Organization
Division of labor	Produces efficiency in a large-scale corporation	Produces trained incapacity	Produces a narrow perspective
Hierarchy of authority	Clarifies who is in command	Deprives employees of a voice in decision making	Permits concealment of mistakes
Written rules and regulations	Let workers know what is expected of them	Stifle initiative and imagination	Lead to goal displacement
Impersonality	Reduces bias	Contributes to feelings of alienation	Discourages loyalty to company
Employment based on technical qualifications	Discourages favoritism and reduces petty rivalries	Discourages ambition to improve oneself elsewhere	Fosters Peter principle

studied domestic houseworkers employed in central California by a nationwide franchise. She found that housekeeping tasks were minutely defined, to the point that employees had to follow 22 written steps for cleaning a bathroom. Complaints and special requests went not to the workers, but to an office-based manager.

Oligarchy: Rule by a Few Conflict theorists have examined the bureaucratization of social movements. The German sociologist Robert Michels (1915) studied socialist parties and labor unions in Europe before World War I and found that such organizations were becoming increasingly bureaucratic. The emerging leaders of the organizations—even some of the most radical—had a vested interest in clinging to power. If they lost their leadership posts, they would have to return to full-time work as manual laborers. (For a discussion of the status of labor unions today, see the Social Policy section at the end of this chapter.)

Through his research, Michels originated the idea of the **iron law of oligarchy,** which describes how even a democratic organization will eventually develop into a bureaucracy ruled by a few, called an oligarchy. Why do oligarchies emerge? People who achieve leadership roles usually have the skills, knowledge, or charismatic appeal (as Weber noted) to direct, if not control, others. Michels argued that the rank and file of a movement or organization look to leaders for direction and thereby reinforce the process of rule by a few. In addition, members of an oligarchy are strongly motivated to maintain their leadership roles, privileges, and power.

Bureaucracy and Organizational Culture

How does bureaucratization affect the average individual who works in an organization? The early theorists of formal organizations tended to neglect this question. Max Weber, for example, focused on the management personnel in bureaucracies, but had little to say about workers in industry or clerks in government agencies.

According to the **classical theory,** or **scientific management approach,** of formal organizations, workers are motivated almost entirely by economic rewards. This theory stresses that only the physical constraints on workers limit their productivity. Therefore, workers may be treated as a resource, much like the machines that began to replace them in the 20th century. Under the scientific management approach, management attempts to achieve maximum work efficiency through scientific planning, established performance standards, and careful supervision of workers and production. Planning involves efficiency studies but not studies of workers' attitudes or job satisfaction.

SOCIOLOGY IN THE GLOBAL COMMUNITY

6-2 McDonald's and the Worldwide Bureaucratization of Society

In his book *The McDonaldization of Society*, sociologist George Ritzer notes the enormous influence of a well-known fast-food organization on modern-day culture and social life.

Not surprisingly, Max Weber's five characteristics of bureaucracy are apparent in McDonald's restaurants, as well as in the global corporation behind them. Food preparation and order-taking reflect a painstaking *division of labor*, implemented by a *hierarchy of authority* that stretches from the food workers up to the store operator, and ultimately to the corporate board of directors. Store operators learn McDonald's *written rules and regulations*, which govern even the amount of ketchup or mustard placed on a hamburger, at McDonald's Hamburger University. Little bonding occurs between servers and customers, creating a pervasive sense of *impersonality*. Finally, employees are expected to have specific *technical qualifications*, although most of the skills they need to perform routine tasks can be learned in a brief training period.

The real significance of McDonaldization is that it is not confined to the food-service industry or to coffee shops like Starbucks. Worldwide, McDonald's brand of predictability, efficiency, and dependence on nonhuman technology have become customary in a number of services, ranging from medical care to wedding planning to education. Even sporting events reflect the influence of bureaucratization. Around the world, stadiums are becoming increasingly similar, both physically and in the way they present the sport to spectators. All seats offer spectators an unrestricted view, and a big screen guarantees them access to instant replays. Scores, player statistics, and attendance figures are updated automatically by computer and displayed on an automated scoreboard or fed to people's smartphones. Spectator enthusiasm is manufactured through digital displays urging

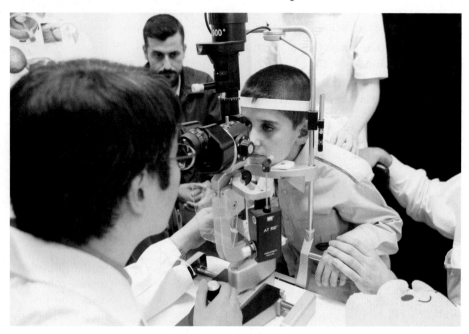

The worldwide success of highly efficient fast-food operations has led to the bureaucratization of many other services, including eye care and other forms of medical treatment.

applause or rhythmic chanting. And of course, the merchandising of teams' and even players' names and images is highly controlled.

> *Worldwide, McDonald's brand of predictability, efficiency, and dependence on nonhuman technology have become customary in a number of services, ranging from medical care to wedding planning to education.*

McDonald's reliance on the five characteristics of bureaucracy is not revolutionary.

What is new is the bureaucratization of services and life events that once were highly individualized, at times even spontaneous. More and more, society itself is undergoing McDonaldization.

LET'S DISCUSS

1. What features of fast-food restaurants do you appreciate? Do you have any complaints about them?
2. Analyze life at your college using Weber's model of bureaucracy. What elements of McDonaldization do you see? Do you wish life were less McDonaldized?

Sources: Ormond 2005; Ritzer 2008, 2011.

Not until workers organized unions—and forced management to recognize that they were not objects—did theorists of formal organizations begin to revise the classical approach. Social scientists became aware that along with management and administrators, informal groups of workers have an important impact on organizations. An alternative way of considering bureaucratic dynamics, the **human relations approach,** emphasizes the role of people, communication, and participation in a bureaucracy. This type of analysis reflects the interest of interactionist theorists in small-group behavior. Unlike planning under the scientific management approach, planning based on the human relations approach focuses on

workers' feelings, frustrations, and emotional need for job satisfaction.

The gradual move away from a sole focus on the physical aspects of getting the job done—and toward the concerns and needs of workers—led advocates of the human relations approach to stress the less formal aspects of bureaucratic structure. Informal groups and social networks within organizations develop partly as a result of people's ability to create more direct forms of communication than under the formal structure. Charles Page (1946) used the term *bureaucracy's other face* to refer to the unofficial activities and interactions that are such a basic part of daily organizational life.

Today, research on formal organizations is following new avenues. Among them are

- the recent arrival of a small number of women and minority group members in high-level management;
- in large corporations, the decision-making role of groups that lie outside the top ranks of leadership;
- the loss of fixed boundaries in organizations that have outsourced key functions; and
- the role of the Internet and virtual worlds in influencing business and consumer preferences.

Though research on organizations still embraces Max Weber's insights, then, it has gone well beyond them (Hamm 2007; Kleiner 2003; W. Scott and Davis 2007).

thinking CRITICALLY

Select an organization that is familiar to you—for example, your college, workplace, religious institution, or civic association—and apply Weber's five characteristics of bureaucracy to it. To what degree does it correspond to Weber's ideal type of bureaucracy?

The Changing Workplace

Weber's work on bureaucracy and Michels's thinking on oligarchy are still applicable to the organizational structure and culture of the workplace. However, today's factories and offices are undergoing rapid, profound changes unanticipated a century or more ago. Besides the far-reaching impact of technological advances such as computerization, workers must cope with organizational restructuring. This section will detail the dramatic changes evident in today's workplace.

Organizational Restructuring

To some extent, individual businesses, community organizations, and government agencies are always changing, if only because of personnel turnover. Since the late 20th century, however, formal organizations have been experimenting with new ways of getting the job done, some of which have significantly altered the workplace.

Collective decision making, or the active involvement of employee problem-solving groups in corporate management, first became popular in the United States in the 1980s. Management gurus had noted the dazzling success of Japanese automobile and consumer products manufacturers. In studying these companies, they found that problem-solving groups and an emphasis on continuous improvement were two keys to success. However, even the most successful Japanese corporations must constantly retool. Over the last few years, a series of embarrassing recalls at Toyota has forced the world's largest automobile company to restructure. Now, even a single consumer complaint receives quick attention, and problems with a product in one country are communicated worldwide (Maynard 2010).

Another innovation in the workplace, called *minimal hierarchy*, replaces the traditional bureaucratic hierarchy of authority with a flatter organizational structure. Minimal hierarchy offers workers

Work teams are a part of formal organizations.

greater access to those in authority, giving them an opportunity to voice concerns that might not be heard in a traditional bureaucracy. This new organizational structure is thought to minimize the potential for costly and dangerous bureaucratic oversights.

Finally, organizational *work teams* have become increasingly common, even in smaller organizations. There are two types of work team. *Project teams* address ongoing issues, such as safety or compliance with the Americans with Disabilities Act. *Task forces* pursue nonrecurring issues, such as a major building renovation. In both cases, team members are released to some degree from their regular duties in order to contribute to the organizationwide effort (W. Scott and Davis 2007; Huff 2007).

The common purpose of work teams, minimal hierarchy, and collective decision making is to empower workers. For that reason, these new organizational structures can be exciting for the employees who participate in them. But these innovations rarely touch the vast numbers of workers who perform routine jobs in factories and office buildings. The 1.7 million who are paid by the hour and who earn the minimum wage or lower know little about organizational restructuring (Bureau of Labor Statistics 2009).

Together with organizational restructuring, societal changes well in place at the beginning of the 21st century have weakened the impact of bureaucratization on the workplace. As a result of globalization, today's formal organizations are less likely than those of the past to be self-contained. New information technologies have both increased employers' reliance on outside providers and facilitated direct communication between those at the very top and the very bottom of corporate hierarchies.

The Postmodern Job

As we saw in Chapter 5, today many societies have moved into a postmodern stage of sociocultural development, one that is dominated by high technology. For workers, this transition has manifested itself in a greater reliance on electronic communication—even if the co-workers involved are separated only by a cubicle wall. The transition to postmodern society has also fostered telecommuting, or *homeshoring*, as it has come to be called in a play on the term *offshoring* (see Chapter 18). **Telecommuters** are employees who work

TAKING SOCIOLOGY TO WORK

Sarah Levy, Owner, Sarah's Pastries & Candies

Sarah Levy didn't know anything about sociology when she entered Northwestern University, but she knew that someday she wanted to start a bakery. After graduating from Northwestern with a major in sociology, she enrolled in Chicago's French Pastry School and spent some time interning at local bakeries and restaurants. A year later she started her own bakery in her mother's kitchen. Today Sarah owns and manages two locations in downtown Chicago, one on Oak Street and a second in Macy's, on State Street. Sarah's Pastries & Candies makes fine pastries and chocolates from scratch, along with custom-made wedding cakes and gift baskets.

Like many small business owners, Sarah does anything and everything in a typical workweek, from consulting with brides to helping in the kitchen. She manages 20 employees and provides her own marketing and public relations services. A gifted publicist, Sarah has welcomed Martha Stewart to her store and participated in a Food Network challenge that involved baking a three-foot animated dinosaur cake. Sarah's Pastries & Candies gives back to the community by contributing to several charities, including Meals on Wheels, Common Threads, and For the Love of Chocolate Foundation.

Sarah saw the connection between business and sociology in her introductory sociology course, in which she used this textbook. Learning about how people interact, she says, has broadened her horizons and taught her how to step back and analyze a situation from a sociological perspective. "In my job, I am constantly interacting with people—employees, customers, vendors," she explains. "I think one of my greatest strengths is my ability to get along with people from all sorts of backgrounds, and make everyone get along with each other and work together towards the same goal."

LET'S DISCUSS

1. Have you ever thought of starting your own business? If so, what do you think the key to your success would be?
2. Would business have been a more practical major for Sarah? Why or why not?

---

full-time or part-time at home rather than in an outside office, and who are linked to their supervisors and colleagues through phone lines, Wi-Fi, the Internet, and smartphones. Not surprisingly, the number of telecommuters increased from 8.5 million in 1995 to 40 million in 2008 and an estimated 63 million by 2011 (Schadler 2009).

What are the social implications of this shift toward the virtual office? Table 6-3 summarizes the pros and cons. From an interactionist perspective, the workplace is a major source of friendships; restricting face-to-face social opportunities could destroy the trust that is created by "handshake agreements." Thus, telecommuting may move society further along the continuum from *Gemeinschaft* to *Gesellschaft*. And like it or not, when employees work at home, they tend to become available 24/7. On a more positive note, telecommuting may be the first social change that pulls fathers and mothers back into the home rather than pushing them out. The trend, if it continues, should also increase autonomy and job satisfaction for many employees (Castells 2001; DiMaggio et al. 2001).

Electronic communication in the workplace has generated some heat lately. On the one hand, e-mailing is a convenient way to push messages around, especially with the copy button. It's democratic, too: lower-status employees are more likely to participate in e-mail discussions than in face-to-face communications, giving organizations the benefit of their experience and views. But e-mail doesn't convey body language, which in face-to-face communication can soften insensitive phrasing and make unpleasant messages (such as a reprimand) easier to take. It also leaves a permanent record, which can be a problem if messages are written thoughtlessly (DiMaggio et al. 2001).

Electronic communication has contributed significantly to the fragmentation of work. Today, work is frequently interrupted by e-mail, pagers, and pop-up windows, as well as face-to-face interruptions. In one observation study of office workers, researchers found that employees spent an average of only 11 minutes on any given project before being interrupted.

Typically, 25 minutes passed before they returned to their original tasks. While multitasking may increase a person's efficiency in some situations, it has become an integral and not necessarily helpful feature of work for many employees (Mark et al. 2005; C. Thompson 2005).

use your sociological *imagination*

If your first full-time job after college involved telecommuting, what do you think would be the advantages and disadvantages of working out of a home office? Do you think you would be satisfied as a telecommuter? Why or why not?

TABLE 6-3 TELECOMMUTING: PROS AND CONS

Pros	Cons
Flexible schedule	Disconnectedness from fellow employees
Freedom to work anywhere	"At home" means still at work
Reduced expense and stress from commuting	For promotions, out of sight may mean out of mind
Environmental benefits of reduced commuting	Requires excellent Internet connectivity
Facilitates caregiving for children and aged parents	Loss of managerial control
Reduces terrorist targets	Downgraded security of electronic information
	Scams that masquerade as telecommuting opportunities

summingup

129

How many people do you know who belong to a labor union? Chances are you can name a lot fewer people than someone could 50 years ago. In 1954 unions represented 39 percent of workers in the private sector of the U.S. economy; in 2010 they represented only 11.9 percent—the lowest share in more than 70 years. As Figure 6-1 shows, the decline in unionization is common to virtually all industrial nations. What has happened to diminish the importance of organized labor? Have unions outlived their usefulness in a rapidly changing global economy that is dominated by the service sector?

Looking at the Issue

Labor unions consist of organized workers who share either the same skill (as in electronics) or the same employer (as in the case of postal employees). Unions began to emerge during the Industrial Revolution in England, in the 1700s. Groups of workers banded together to extract concessions from employers (for example, safer working conditions, a shorter workweek), as well as to protect their positions.

Historically, labor unions have engaged in restrictive practices that are regarded today as discriminatory. They frequently tried to protect their jobs by limiting entry to their occupation based on

gender, race, ethnicity, citizenship, age, and sometimes rather arbitrary measures of skill levels. Today we see less of this protection of special interests, but individual labor unions are still the target of charges of discrimination, as are employers (J. Rosenfeld 2010).

The power of labor unions varies widely from country to country. In some countries, such as Britain and Mexico, unions play a key role in the foundation of governments. In others, such as Japan and Korea, their role in politics is very limited, and even their ability to influence the private sector is relatively weak. In the United States, unions can sometimes have a significant influence on employers and elected officials, but their effect varies dramatically by type of industry and even region of the country (S. Zimmerman 2008c).

Few people today would dispute the fact that union membership is declining. Among the reasons for the decline are the following:

1. **Changes in the type of industry.** Manufacturing jobs, the traditional heart of the labor union, have declined, giving way to postindustrial service jobs.

2. **Growth in part-time jobs.** Between 1982 and 1998 the number of temporary jobs in the United States rose 577 percent, while total employment increased only 41 percent. Only in 2000 did laws governing collective bargaining allow temporary workers to join a union.

3. **The legal system.** The United States has not made it particularly easy for unions to organize and bargain, and some government measures have made it more difficult. A dramatic example was President Ronald Reagan's firing of 11,000 air traffic controllers in 1981, when their union threatened they would walk off the job while seeking a new contract.

4. **Globalization.** The threat of jobs leaving the country has undercut the ability of union leaders to organize workers at home. Some say that labor union demands for wage increases and additional benefits have themselves spurred the exodus of jobs to developing nations, where wages are significantly lower and unions are virtually nonexistent.

5. **Employer offensives.** Increasingly hostile employers have taken court action to block unions' efforts to represent their members.

6. **Union rigidity and bureaucratization.** In the past, labor has been slow to embrace women, minorities, and immigrants. Furthermore, in some unions the election of leaders seems to dominate the organization's activity.

Around the world, the economic downturn that began in 2008 has had special consequences for labor unions. Like nonunion workers, many union members lost their jobs in the recession; others saw their contracts renegotiated. As part of the $17.4 billion auto bailout legislation passed by the U.S. Congress, the United Auto Workers (UAW) accepted a nearly 20 percent pay cut. This and other rollbacks of benefits were largely accepted by U.S. unions, but in Europe, thousands of workers turned out in protest. In a few highly publicized cases, unions took the company bosses hostage.

FIGURE **6-1**   LABOR UNION MEMBERSHIP WORLDWIDE

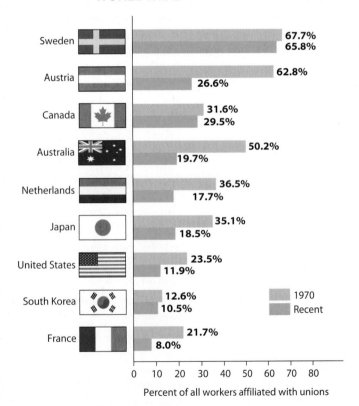

Percent of all workers affiliated with unions

Note: Recent data from 2008–2010, except for Sweden and the Netherlands (2007).
Sources: Bureau of Labor Statistics 2011; New Unionism Network 2011; Visser 2006:45.

Although some union leaders in the United States expect the hardship caused by the economic slowdown to raise union membership, how well unions will be able to represent their members through tough times remains to be seen (Greenhouse 2008a, 2009).

Applying Sociology

Both Marxists and functionalists would view unions as a logical response to the emergence of impersonal, large-scale, formal, and often alienating organizations. This view certainly characterized the growth of unions in major manufacturing industries with a sharp division of labor. However, as manufacturing has declined, unions have had to look elsewhere for growth.

Worldwide, today's labor unions bear little resemblance to those early unions organized spontaneously by exploited workers. In line with Robert Michels's iron law of oligarchy (see page 126), unions have become increasingly bureaucratized under a self-serving leadership. Conflict theorists would point out that the longer union leaders are in office, the less responsive they are to the needs and demands of the rank and file, and the more concerned with maintaining their own positions and power. Yet research shows that under certain circumstances, union leadership can change significantly. Smaller unions are vulnerable to changes in leadership, as are unions whose membership shifts in composition from predominantly White to African American or Latino.

Initiating Policy

U.S. law grants workers the right to self-organize via unions. However, the United States is unique among industrial democracies in allowing employers to actively oppose their employees' decision to organize. The recent economic recession has compounded employers' opposition to unions and is even threatening workers' rights in established unions. Today, state and local governments across the United States are facing significant budget deficits. In an effort to cut costs, many elected officials are moving to shrink the pensions that government workers gained through collective bargaining. In some states, officials want not only to reduce retirees' benefits, but also to curtail union workers' collective bargaining rights.

In Europe, labor unions tend to play a major role in political elections. The ruling party in Great Britain, in fact, is called the Labour Party. Unions play a lesser role in U.S. politics, although they have recently been attacked for their large financial contributions to political campaigns. In addition to the role of unions in national politics, international trade unions sometimes speak out on common issues. In 2009 one of them condemned "corporate grand theft"—a reference to corporate executives who spend lavishly on themselves while laying off workers. Despite efforts dating back to Karl Marx and Friedrich Engels's call for the workers of all countries to unite (1847), no global union has emerged (International Trade Union Confederation 2009).

Though unions are a global force, their form and substance varies from country to country. In China, where there is only one political party, the government ordered Walmart's 31,000 workers to unionize, over the corporation's objections. Chinese unions are controlled by the Communist Party, whose membership has declined as the party's pervasive control has weakened. Nevertheless, these unions are more likely to listen to the government than independent unions, which listen to the workers who are their members (Zhang 2009).

Take the Issue with You

1. What unions are represented on your college campus? Have you been aware of union activity? Has there been any opposition to the unions on the part of the administration?

2. Do you think nurses should be allowed to strike? Why or why not? What about teachers or police officers?

3. Should state and local officials be allowed to reduce government workers' retirement benefits and take away their right to collective bargaining?

MASTERING THIS CHAPTER

Summary

Social interaction among human beings is necessary to the transmission of culture and the survival of every society. This chapter examines the social behavior of **groups and formal organizations.**

1. When we find ourselves identifying closely with a group, it is probably a **primary group.** A **secondary group** is more formal and impersonal.

2. People tend to see the world in terms of **in-groups** and **out-groups,** a perception often fostered by the very groups to which they belong.

3. **Reference groups** set and enforce standards of conduct and serve as a source of comparison for people's evaluations of themselves and others.

4. Interactionist researchers have noted distinct and predictable processes in the functioning of **small groups.** The simplest group is a **dyad,** composed of two members. **Triads** and larger groups increase the ways of interacting and allow for **coalitions** to form.

5. The **focus group,** developed by sociologist Robert Merton to collect qualitative data on people's opinions, feelings, and ideas, also allows researchers to observe how people make decisions in small groups.

6. As societies have become more complex, large **formal organizations** have become more powerful and pervasive.

7. Max Weber argued that in its ideal form, every **bureaucracy** has five basic characteristics: division of labor, hierarchical authority, written rules and regulations, impersonality, and employment based on technical qualifications.

8. Bureaucracy can be understood both as a process and as a matter of degree. Thus, an organization may be more or less bureaucratic than other organizations.

9. When leaders of an organization build up their power, the result can be *oligarchy* (rule by a few).

10. The informal structure of an organization can undermine and redefine official bureaucratic policies.

11. Organizational restructuring and new technologies have transformed the workplace through innovations such as *collective decision making* and *telecommuting*.

12. **Labor unions** are on the decline because of major shifts in the economy.

Key Terms

Alienation A condition of estrangement or dissociation from the surrounding society. (page 124)

Bureaucracy A component of formal organization that uses rules and hierarchical ranking to achieve efficiency. (124)

Bureaucratization The process by which a group, organization, or social movement becomes increasingly bureaucratic. (125)

Classical theory An approach to the study of formal organizations that views workers as being motivated almost entirely by economic rewards. (126)

Coalition A temporary or permanent alliance geared toward a common goal. (121)

Dyad A two-member group. (122)

Focus group A carefully selected discussion group led by a trained moderator. (123)

Formal organization A group designed for a special purpose and structured for maximum efficiency. (123)

Goal displacement Overzealous conformity to official regulations of a bureaucracy. (125)

Group Any number of people with similar norms, values, and expectations who interact with one another on a regular basis. (119)

Groupthink Uncritical acceptance of or conformity to the prevailing viewpoint. (123)

Human relations approach An approach to the study of formal organizations that emphasizes the role of people, communication, and participation in a bureaucracy and tends to focus on the informal structure of the organization. (127)

Ideal type A construct or model for evaluating specific cases. (124)

In-group Any group or category to which people feel they belong. (120)

Iron law of oligarchy A principle of organizational life under which even a democratic organization will eventually develop into a bureaucracy ruled by a few individuals. (126)

Labor union Organized workers who share either the same skill or the same employer. (130)

McDonaldization The process by which the principles of the fast-food restaurant are coming to dominate more and more sectors of American society as well as of the rest of the world. (118)

Out-group A group or category to which people feel they do not belong. (120)

Peter principle A principle of organizational life according to which every employee within a hierarchy tends to rise to his or her level of incompetence. (125)

Primary group A small group characterized by intimate, face-to-face association and cooperation. (119)

Reference group Any group that individuals use as a standard for evaluating themselves and their own behavior. (120)

Scientific management approach Another name for the classical theory of formal organizations. (126)

Secondary group A formal, impersonal group in which there is little social intimacy or mutual understanding. (119)

Small group A group small enough for all members to interact simultaneously—that is, to talk with one another or at least be well acquainted. (121)

Telecommuter An employee who works full-time or part-time at home rather than in an outside office, and who is linked to supervisor and colleagues through phone lines, Wi-Fi, the Internet, and smartphones. (128)

Trained incapacity The tendency of workers in a bureaucracy to become so specialized that they develop blind spots and fail to notice obvious problems. (124)

Triad A three-member group. (122)

TAKING SOCIOLOGY with you

1. Are primary groups, secondary groups, in-groups, out-groups, and reference groups likely to be found within a formal organization? What functions do these groups serve for a formal organization? What dysfunctions might occur as a result of their presence?

2. Max Weber identified five basic characteristics of bureaucracy. Select an actual organization familiar to you (for example, your college, a workplace, or a religious institution or civic association you belong to) and apply Weber's five characteristics to that organization. To what degree does it correspond to Weber's ideal type of bureaucracy?

3. Talk with two or three business students or businesspeople about the bureaucratization of business. On balance, do they see bureaucratization as a positive or negative trend? What bureaucratic dysfunctions are common in business, and how do managers attempt to counteract them?

Self-Quiz

Read each question carefully and then select the best answer.

1. George Ritzer's belief that business principles of the fast-food industry have greatly influenced how we live and do business has been coined
   a. Fast Food Nation.
   b. Drive-Through Life.
   c. McDonaldization.
   d. Burger USA.

2. _____ groups often emerge in the workplace among those who share special understandings about their occupation.
   a. Primary
   b. Secondary
   c. Out-
   d. Formal

3. The purpose of a reference group is to serve a(n)
   a. normative function by enforcing standards of conduct and belief.
   b. comparison function by setting a standard against which people can measure themselves and others.
   c. elimination function by dissolving groups that no longer have a social purpose.
   d. both a and b

4. The president of the United States need not be a good typist, and a surgeon need not be able to fill a cavity, because of the bureaucratic characteristic of
   a. division of labor.
   b. impersonality.
   c. employment based on technical qualifications.
   d. written rules and regulations.

5. Which pioneer of sociology first directed researchers to the significance of bureaucratic structure?
   a. Émile Durkheim
   b. Max Weber
   c. Karl Marx
   d. Ferdinand Tönnies

6. Minimal hierarchy involves a(n)
   a. traditional bureaucracy.
   b. lack of rules in the workplace.
   c. flatter organizational structure.
   d. absence of traditional job titles.

7. The U.S. Postal Service, the Boston Pops orchestra, and the college or university in which you are currently enrolled as a student are all examples of
   a. primary groups.
   b. reference groups.
   c. formal organizations.
   d. triads.

8. One positive consequence of bureaucracy is that it reduces bias. Reduction of bias results from which characteristic of a bureaucracy?
   a. impersonality
   b. hierarchy of authority
   c. written rules and regulations
   d. employment based on technical qualifications

9. According to the Peter principle,
   a. all bureaucracies are notoriously inefficient.
   b. if something *can* go wrong, it *will*.
   c. every employee within a hierarchy tends to rise to his or her level of incompetence.
   d. all line workers get burned in the end.

10. What are the social implications of a shift toward the virtual office as a result of the increasing number of telecommuters?
   a. Supervisors will find that performance goals must be defined more clearly, which may lead to further bureaucratization.
   b. It should increase autonomy and job satisfaction for many employees.
   c. It will lead to greater worker privacy and job security.
   d. both a and b

11. William Graham Sumner distinguished between _____ and _____.

12. Formal organizations have a(n) _____ form of organization.

13. Sociologist Robert Merton devised the often-used methodology of monitoring a discussion that is called a _____ _____.

14. _____ groups often emerge in the workplace among those who share special understandings about their occupation.

15. In many cases, people model their behavior after groups to which they may not belong. These groups are called _____ groups.

16. Trained incapacity, goal displacement, and the Peter principle are all examples of bureaucratic _____.

17. The iron law of oligarchy was developed by German sociologist _____ _____.

18. People who happen to be in the same place at the same time, such as members of a Broadway theater audience, are a(n) _____.

19. When we find ourselves identifying closely with a group, it is probably a(n) _____ group.

20. Max Weber developed a(n) _____ _____ of bureaucracy, which reflects the most characteristic aspects of all human organizations.

The answers appear upside down.

Answers

1 (c); 2 (b); 3 (d); 4 (a); 5 (b); 6 (c); 7 (c); 8 (a); 9 (c); 10 (b); 11 in-groups; out-groups; 12 bureaucratic; 13 focus group; 14 Secondary; 15 reference; 16 dysfunctions; 17 Robert Michels; 18 aggregate; 19 primary; 20 ideal type

THINKING ABOUT **MOVIES**

Bread and Roses

Poorly paid janitors in Los Angeles struggle to unionize.

Restrepo

This documentary shows a U.S. military platoon serving in a dangerous part of Afghanistan.

Toy Story 3

Rejected toys band together to improve their social circumstances.

The mass media are an
integral part of modern
culture. In Alaska, an Inuit
man checks his laptop.

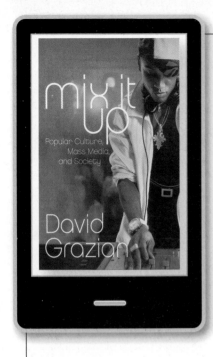

mix it up
Popular Culture,
Mass Media
and Society

David Grazian

Over forty years ago communications theorist Marshall McLuhan (1967) developed a pathbreaking idea—media not only pass along messages from sender to receiver but actively reshape how we process information, knowledge, and text. . . .

. . . For instance, about $60 billion is illegally gambled in Internet poker games each year, a pursuit that draws in an estimated 1.6 million U.S. college students. . . . In 2005 Lehigh University sophomore class president Greg Hogan, Jr., lost $7,500 playing online poker, and out of desperation, in December of that year he held up a Wachovia bank for $2,871 in cash. With no casino dealers, card shuffling, or friendly table partners to distract him, Hogan found the seamless, fast-paced action of digital poker "paralyzing" and "narcotic," a familiar sensation among addicts, men and women alike. According to M. Schwartz (2006), "Many, like Lauren Patrizi, a 21-year-old senior at Loyola University in Chicago, have had weeks when they're playing poker during most of their waking hours. Rarely leaving their rooms, they take their laptops with them to bed, fall asleep each night in the middle of a hand and think, talk and dream nothing but poker."

According to cultural anthropologist Natasha Dow Schull (2005, p. 73), digital technologies succeed in creating what consumers call the *zone,* a dissociated subjective state marked by a suspension of normative parameters—monetary, bodily, temporal, and spatial. Gambling sites rely on cashless transactions (performed with credit and debit card numbers) in which financial stakes are transformed into pixilated "chips" that no longer seem like real money. Unlike dorm-lounge poker games in which classmates eventually get tired, punch-drunk, or else lose their shirts, online casinos never close, but consistently and relentlessly maintain a steady rhythm of play that keeps addicts glued to their screens alone for hours, nights, and weeks on end. With only computer keys to depress, players never drop their cards;

With no casino dealers, card shuffling, or friendly table partners to distract him, Hogan found the seamless, fast-paced action of digital poker "paralyzing" and "narcotic," a familiar sensation among addicts, men and women alike.

moreover, gambling software allows gamers to bet multiple hands simultaneously, further increasing the hypnotic speed and tempo with which one gains and (more often) loses.

How else do goings-on within the virtual world impact our everyday lives offline? Certainly, the ease with which information flows online among otherwise discrete interpersonal networks has obvious consequences for how we maintain control over our reputations and identities. . . . Since anyone with an Internet connection can post intimate photographs, juicy gossip, or vicious rumors on the Web for a potential worldwide audience of billions, personal reputations can easily be maligned within hours. In 2003 Kelley D. Parker, a partner at the elite New York law firm of Paul, Weiss, Rifkind, Wharton and Garrison, allegedly ordered a paralegal to conduct research on nearby sushi restaurants after eating some bad takeout. The underling wrote up a three-page memo replete with interview quotes, footnotes, and exhibitions, and the scanned document later appeared on the Web site Gawker for her colleagues to mock. . . . While it was never determined whether the infamous "sushi memo" was a hoax or a prank, it presumably hardly matters to Ms. Parker, whose reputation has been forever marred by the online posting.

Of course, rumors of bad behavior among celebrities likely travel faster online than any other kind of hearsay. Web sites like Gawker, The Smoking Gun, TMZ, and YouTube are veritable clearinghouses for such gossip, as actor Christian Bale learned after he cursed out the director of photography on the movie set of *Terminator: Salvation* in 2008 for nearly four minutes, and a full-length audio recording of his tantrum resurfaced on YouTube the following year. (Bale has since apologized for the outburst, but notably did so only after its public airing.) The Web site Bitter Waitress provides an ongoing list of celebrity (as well as civilian) diners who have stingily tipped less than 15 percent of their check: famous cheapskates shamed by the site include actresses Lindsay Lohan and Helena Bonham Carter, former Miami Dolphins quarterback Dan Marino, rock singer David Lee Roth, and reality TV figure Dog the Bounty Hunter. In March 2009, People for the Ethical Treatment of Animals (or PETA) published an online list of celebrities who unabashedly wear fur, including Madonna, Maggie Gyllenhaal, Kanye West, Elizabeth Hurley, Kate Moss, Demi Moore, Ashton Kutcher, Mary J. Blige, and Mary-Kate and Ashley Olsen. ❞❞

(Grazian 2010:197, 200, 203; see also Glater 2003; Schull 2005; M. Schwartz 2006) Additional information about this excerpt can be found on the Online Learning Center at www.mhhe.com/schaeferbrief13e.

In this excerpt from *Mix It Up: Popular Culture, Mass Media, and Society,* sociologist David Grazian describes how today's mass media are actively reshaping the way we process information, as Marshall McLuhan predicted they would in 1967. Playing poker and video games online, Grazian writes, is a qualitatively different experience from playing them in person. He also discusses the social consequences of the instant dissemination of information through the mass media, from the embarrassment of an attorney who assigned a paralegal to research a lunch locale to the humiliation of an actor whose four-minute tantrum went viral on YouTube. In this age, thanks to digital recording, anyone can become a global personality for any reason, at any time.

We have come a long way from the 1950s, when rabbit-ear antennas sat atop black-and-white television sets. Both television and the Net are forms of **mass media,** a term that refers to the print and electronic means of communication that carry messages to widespread audiences. Print media include newspapers, magazines, and books; electronic media include radio, satellite radio, television, motion pictures, and the Internet. Advertising, which falls into both categories, is also a form of mass media.

The social impact of the mass media is obvious. Consider a few examples. TV dinners were invented to accommodate the millions of couch potatoes who can't bear to miss their favorite television programs. Today, *screen time* encompasses not just television viewing but playing video games and surfing the Internet as well. Candidates for political office rely on their media consultants to project a winning image both in print and in the electronic media. World leaders use all forms of media for political advantage, whether to gain territory or to bid on hosting the Olympics. In parts of Africa and Asia, AIDS education projects owe much of their success to media campaigns. And during the 2003 war in Iraq, both the British and U.S. governments allowed journalists to be embedded with frontline troops as a means of "telling their story."

Few aspects of society are as central as the mass media. Through the media we expand our understanding of people and events beyond what we experience in person. The media inform us about different cultures and lifestyles and about the latest forms of technology. For sociologists, the key questions are how the mass media affect our social institutions and how they influence our social behavior.

The social impact of the mass media has become so huge, in fact, that scholars have begun to speak of *cultural convergence.* The term **cultural convergence** refers to the flow of content across multiple media, and the accompanying migration of media audiences. As you watch a television program, for example, you wonder what the star of the show is doing at the moment, and turn to the Internet. Later, while texting your best friend, you tell her what you learned, accompanied by a Google Earth map showing the celebrity's location. Using Photoshop, you may even include the star's image next to your own, post the photo on your Facebook page, and then tweet your friends (send them a mini-blog) to create a caption. Media convergence is not orchestrated by the media, sophisticated though they may be. You initiate it, using techniques you likely learned by interacting with others, either face-to-face or through the media (H. Jenkins 2006).

Why are the media so influential? Who benefits from media influence and why? How do we maintain cultural and ethical standards in the face of negative media images? In this chapter we will consider the ways sociology helps us to answer these questions. First we will look at how proponents of the various sociological perspectives view the media. Then we will examine just who makes up the media's audience, not just at home but around the world. The chapter closes with a Social Policy section on the right to privacy in a digital age.

Sociological Perspectives on the Media

Over the past decade, new technologies have made new forms of mass media available to U.S. households. These new technologies have changed people's viewing and listening habits. People spend a lot of time with the media, more and more of it on the Internet. Media consumers have moved away from television and toward digital images downloaded to their computers and portable devices. Increasingly, they learn not just about the famous but about ordinary people by viewing their Facebook or MySpace pages or by keeping in touch with their friends via Twitter.

In studying the impact of the mass media on socialization, sociologists must consider the wide variety of contact people have with communication outlets, from immersion in all types of media to relative isolation, especially from recent innovations. In 2007 the Pew Research Center released a report that sorted U.S. residents into 10 categories based on their use of information and communications technologies (ICTs; Table 7-1). According to the report, about 32 percent of the adult population falls into the top four categories, from the "Omnivores," who use these devices as a means of self-expression, to the "Productivity Enhancers," who use them to get the job done. Middle-of-the-road users, who represent about 19 percent of the population, take advantage of new technologies but aren't as excited about them. They range from the "Mobile Centrics," who are strongly attached to their cell phones, to the "Connected but Hassled."

Close to half the people in the nation have few if any technology devices, or if they do, they are not wedded to them. Typically, younger people embrace technological change more than older people, who tend either to be indifferent toward new technologies or to find them annoying.

How do people's viewing and listening habits affect their social behavior? In the following sections we'll use the four major sociological perspectives to examine the impact of the mass media and changes in their usage patterns (Nelson 2004).

Functionalist View

One obvious function of the mass media is to entertain. Except for clearly identified news or educational programming, we often think the explicit purpose of the mass media is to occupy our leisure time—from newspaper comics and crossword puzzles to the latest music releases on the Internet. While that is true, the media have other important functions. They also socialize us, enforce social norms, confer status, and promote consumption. An important dysfunction of the mass media is that they may act as a narcotic, desensitizing us to distressing events (Lazarsfeld and Merton 1948; C. Wright 1986).

Agent of Socialization The media increase social cohesion by presenting a common, more or less standardized view of culture through mass communication. Sociologist Robert Park (1922) studied how newspapers helped immigrants to the United States adjust to their environment by changing their customary habits

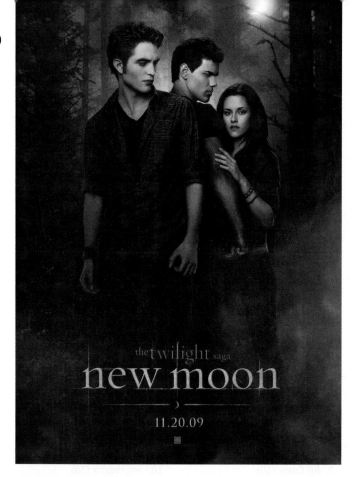

the twilight saga
new moon
11.20.09

Product placement ("brand casting") is an increasingly important source of revenue for motion picture studios. The movie *New Moon* (2009), which was geared toward teens, featured many brands, including Coca-Cola and Apple. But the real winner was Burger King, which integrated its entire marketing strategy with the film's release (Brandchannel.com 2010).

home country, shows that 51 of them originated in the United States; 49 others come from 12 different countries (Figure 7-1).

Media advertising has several clear functions: it supports the economy, provides information about products, and underwrites the cost of media. In some cases, advertising becomes part of the entertainment. A national survey showed that one-half of viewers watch the Super Bowl primarily for the commercials, and one-third of online conversations about the Super Bowl the day of and the day after the event are driven by Super Bowl advertising. Yet advertising's functions are related to dysfunctions. Media advertising contributes to a consumer culture that creates needs and raises unrealistic expectations of what is required to be happy or satisfied. Moreover, because the media depend heavily on advertising revenue, advertisers can influence media content (Carey and Gelles 2010; Nielsen Company 2009).

use your sociological *imagination*

You are a news junkie. Where do you gather your facts or information—from newspapers, tabloids, magazines, TV newscasts, blogs, or the Internet? Why did you choose that medium?

Dysfunction: The Narcotizing Effect In addition to the functions just noted, the media perform a *dysfunction*. Sociologists Paul Lazarsfeld and Robert Merton (1948) created the term **narcotizing dysfunction** to refer to the phenomenon in which the media provide such massive amounts of coverage that the audience becomes numb and fails to act on the information, regardless of how compelling the issue. Interested citizens may take in the information but make no decision or take no action.

Consider how often the media initiate a great outpouring of philanthropic support in response to natural disasters or family crises. But then what happens? Research shows that as time passes, viewer fatigue sets in. The mass media audience becomes numb, desensitized to the suffering, and may even conclude that a solution to the crisis has been found (Moeller 1999).

The media's narcotizing dysfunction was identified 70 years ago, when just a few homes had television—well before the advent of electronic media. At that time, the dysfunction went largely unnoticed, but today commentators often point out the ill effects of addiction to television or the Internet, especially among young people. Street crime, explicit sex, war, and HIV/AIDS apparently are such overwhelming topics that some in the audience may feel they have acted—or at the very least learned all they need to know—simply by watching the news.

Conflict View

Conflict theorists emphasize that the media reflect and even exacerbate many of the divisions in our society and world, including those based on gender, race, ethnicity, and social class. They point in particular to the media's ability to decide what is transmitted, through a process called *gatekeeping*. Conflict theorists also stress the way interest groups monitor media content; the way powerful groups transmit society's dominant ideology through the mass media; and the technological gap between the haves and have-nots, which limits people's access to the Internet.

Gatekeeping What story appears on page 1 of the morning newspaper? What motion picture plays on three screens rather than one at the local cineplex? What picture isn't released at all? Behind these decisions are powerful figures—publishers, editors, and other media moguls.

The mass media constitute a form of big business in which profits are generally more important than the quality of the programming. Within the mass media, a relatively small number of people control what eventually reaches the audience through **gatekeeping.** This term describes how material must travel through a series of gates (or checkpoints) before reaching the public. Thus, a select few decide what images to bring to a broad audience. In many countries the government plays a gatekeeping role. A study done for the World Bank found that in 97 countries, 60 percent of the top five TV stations and 72 percent of the largest radio stations are government-owned (World Bank 2001:183).

Gatekeeping, which prevails in all kinds of media, is not a new concept. The term was coined by a journalism scholar in the 1940s to refer to the way that small-town newspaper editors control which events receive public attention. As sociologist C. Wright Mills ([1956] 2000b) observed, the real power of the media is that they can control what is being presented. In the recording industry, gatekeepers may reject a popular local band because it competes with a group already on their label. Even if

MAPPING LIFE WORLDWIDE
FIGURE **7-1** BRANDING THE GLOBE

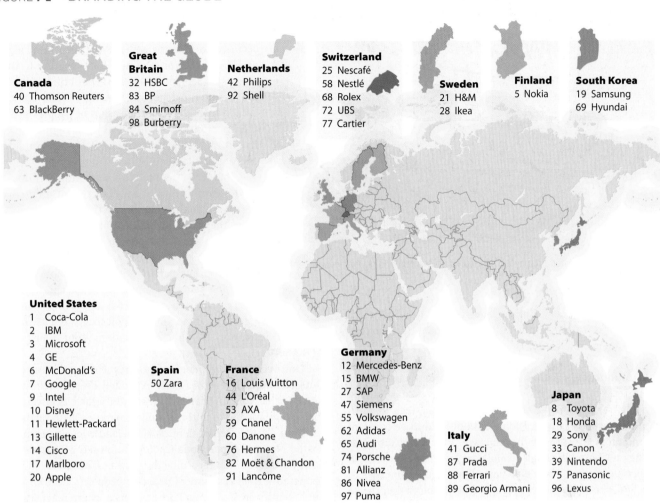

Canada
40 Thomson Reuters
63 BlackBerry

Great Britain
32 HSBC
83 BP
84 Smirnoff
98 Burberry

Netherlands
42 Philips
92 Shell

Switzerland
25 Nescafé
58 Nestlé
68 Rolex
72 UBS
77 Cartier

Sweden
21 H&M
28 Ikea

Finland
5 Nokia

South Korea
19 Samsung
69 Hyundai

United States
1 Coca-Cola
2 IBM
3 Microsoft
4 GE
6 McDonald's
7 Google
9 Intel
10 Disney
11 Hewlett-Packard
13 Gillette
14 Cisco
17 Marlboro
20 Apple

Spain
50 Zara

France
16 Louis Vuitton
44 L'Oréal
53 AXA
59 Chanel
60 Danone
76 Hermes
82 Moët & Chandon
91 Lancôme

Germany
12 Mercedes-Benz
15 BMW
27 SAP
47 Siemens
55 Volkswagen
62 Adidas
65 Audi
74 Porsche
81 Allianz
86 Nivea
97 Puma

Italy
41 Gucci
87 Prada
88 Ferrari
89 Georgio Armani

Japan
8 Toyota
18 Honda
29 Sony
33 Canon
39 Nintendo
75 Panasonic
96 Lexus

Note: Map shows the top 100 brands in the world by country of ownership, except for the United States, for which only brands in the top 20 are shown.
Source: Based on Interbrand 2010.
Based on revenue and name recognition, these are the brands that dominate the global marketplace. Just 13 nations account for all the top 100 brands.

Think about It
How many of these brands do you recognize?

the band is recorded, radio programmers may reject the music because it does not fit the station's sound. Television programmers may keep a pilot for a new TV series off the air because they believe it does not appeal to the target audience (which is sometimes determined by advertising sponsors). Similar decisions are made by gatekeepers in the publishing industry (Hanson 2005; White 1950).

Gatekeeping is not as dominant in at least one form of mass media, the Internet. You can send virtually any message to an electronic bulletin board, and create a web page or web log (blog) to advance any argument, including one that insists the earth is flat. The Internet is a means of quickly disseminating information (or misinformation) without going through any significant gatekeeping process.

Nevertheless, the Internet is not totally without restrictions. In many nations, laws regulate content on issues such as gambling, pornography, and even politics. And popular Internet service providers will terminate accounts for offensive behavior. After the terrorist attacks in 2001, eBay did not allow people to sell parts of the World Trade Center via its online auction. Despite such interference, growing numbers of people are actively involved in online communities. These **netizens** are committed to the free flow of information, with few outside controls.

Today, many countries try to control political dissent by restricting citizens' access to online comments unfavorable to the government. In 2011, online criticism fueled dissent in Arab countries like Egypt, Tunisia, Libya, and Bahrain. Using social media, activists in these countries encouraged their followers to demonstrate against the government at predetermined locales. To further encourage the opposition, they posted cell phone videos of the protests on the Internet. Even in China, where the government limits or even bans access to Google, Facebook,

Social media have facilitated both public criticism of government and government attempts to monitor dissent.

and Twitter, media-savvy Chinese have created local networks to share their dissatisfaction with the government (C. MacLeod 2010; Preston and Stelter 2011).

Media Monitoring The term *media monitoring* is used most often to refer to interest groups' monitoring of media content. The public reaction to the shootings at Virginia Tech in April 2007 provides one example. People did not need to be constant news monitors to learn of the rampage. Ever since the mass shootings at Columbine High School near Littleton, Colorado, in 1999, news outlets of every type have descended on the sites of such school shootings, offering insight into the perpetrators and their families, covering the mass expressions of grief, and following the communities' efforts to recover. Once again, though media outlets provided valuable information and quickly reassured viewers, listeners, and readers that the shooters posed no further danger, many people criticized the reality that they constructed through their coverage.

Reactions ran the gamut. Some observers, including groups representing Asian Americans, questioned the recurring racial identifier used to describe the shooter at Virginia Tech. Indeed, when the news began to leak out that the shooter was "foreign" or "Asian," many people of color commented that they hoped he would not turn out to be one of their own, since people of color appear so rarely, if at all, in news coverage. Other observers objected to another form of stigmatization, the detailed disclosure of the shooter's history of mental illness, which seemed to some to vilify anyone who has ever had a mental health problem. Others objected to what they saw as the media's heavily antigun posture, which damned those who work to preserve the right to own firearms. In such emotional circumstances, the media's construction of reality certainly is not to everyone's liking and rarely satisfies anyone completely (Asian American Journalists Association 2007; Groening 2007; Stanley 2007).

The term *media monitoring* can also be applied to government monitoring of individuals' phone calls without their

knowledge. For example, the federal government has been criticized for authorizing wiretaps of U.S. citizens' telephone conversations without judicial approval. Government officials argue that the wiretaps were undertaken in the interest of national security, to monitor contacts between U.S. citizens and known terrorist groups following the terrorist attacks of September 11, 2001. But critics who take the conflict perspective, among others, are concerned by the apparent invasion of people's privacy (Gertner 2005). We will examine the right to privacy in greater detail in the Social Policy section at the end of this chapter.

What are the practical and ethical limits of media monitoring? In daily life, parents often oversee their children's online activities and scan the blogs they read—which are, of course, available for anyone to see. Most parents see such monitoring of children's media use and communications as an appropriate part of adult supervision. Yet their snooping sets an example for their children, who may use the technique for their own ends. Some media analysts have noted a growing trend among adolescents: the use of new media to learn not-so-public information about their parents (Delaney 2005).

One unanticipated benefit of government monitoring of private communications has been expedited disaster relief. As in the aftermath of Hurricane Katrina in 2005, the U.S. government turned to media monitoring following the 2010 earthquake in Haiti. At the Department of Homeland Security, employees at the National Operations Center monitored 31 social media sites for information regarding the disaster. The intelligence they gathered helped responders to locate people in need of rescue and identify areas outside Port-au-Prince where relief was necessary (Department of Homeland Security 2010).

Government media monitoring isn't always sinister. In the days following the 2010 earthquake in Haiti, the Department of Homeland Security monitored social media sites to identify potential locations for rescue missions and supply deliveries.

Dominant Ideology: Constructing Reality Conflict theorists argue that the mass media maintain the privileges of certain groups. Moreover, powerful groups may limit the media's representation of others to protect their own interests. The term **dominant ideology** describes a set of cultural beliefs and practices that helps to maintain powerful social, economic, and political interests. The media transmit messages that essentially define what we regard as the real world, even though those images frequently vary from the ones that the larger society experiences.

Mass media decision makers are overwhelmingly White, male, and wealthy. It may come as no surprise, then, that the media tend to ignore the lives and ambitions of subordinate groups, among them working-class people, African Americans, Hispanics, gays and lesbians, people with disabilities, overweight people, and older people. Worse yet, media content may create false images or stereotypes of these groups that then become accepted as accurate portrayals of reality. **Stereotypes** are unreliable generalizations about all members of a group that do not recognize individual differences within the group. Some broadcasters use stereotypes deliberately in a desperate bid for attention, with the winking approval of media executives. Shock radio host Don Imus may have been banned from the airwaves for his stereotyped description of Black female athletes, but within 10 months he was back on the air, earning a seven-figure income.

Television content is another example of this tendency to ignore reality. How many overweight TV characters can you name? Even though in real life 1 out of every 4 women is obese (30 or more pounds over a healthy body weight), only 3 out of 100 TV characters are portrayed as obese. Heavyset television characters have fewer romances, talk less about sex, eat more often, and are more often the object of ridicule than their thin counterparts (Hellmich 2001).

On the other hand, television news and other media outlets do alert people to the health implications of obesity. As with constructions of reality, whether some of this coverage is truly educational is debatable. Increasingly, the media have framed the problem not merely as an individual or personal one, but as a broad structural problem involving, for example, the manner in which food is processed and sold (Saguy and Almeling 2008).

As of 2011, 45 percent of all youths in the United States were children of color, yet few of the faces they saw on television reflected their race or cultural heritage. Using content analysis, sociologists have found that only 2 of the nearly 60 prime-time series aired in recent years—*Ugly Betty* and *George Lopez*—focused on minority performers. What is more, programs that are shown earlier in the evening, when young people are most likely to watch television, are the least diverse. Researchers have noted one positive trend, however. Today, television is dominated by reality shows, which are particularly popular among younger viewers. Box 7-1 shows how the diverse audience for these shows is reflected in the programs themselves.

Another concern about the media, from the conflict perspective, is that television distorts the political process. Until the U.S. campaign finance system is truly reformed, the candidates with the most money (often backed by powerful lobbying groups) will be able to buy exposure to voters and saturate the air with commercials attacking their opponents.

Dominant Ideology: Whose Culture? In the United States, on the popular television contest *The Apprentice,* the dreaded dismissal line is "You're fired." In Finland, on *Dilli (The Deal),* it's "*Olet vapautettu*" ("You're free to leave"); in Germany, on *Big Boss,* it's "*Sie haben frei*" ("You're off"). Although people throughout the world decry U.S. exports, from films to language to Bart Simpson, the U.S. media are still widely imitated. Sociologist Todd Gitlin describes American popular culture as something that "people love, and love to hate" (2002:177; Wentz and Atkinson 2005).

We risk being ethnocentric if we overstress U.S. dominance, however. For example, *Survivor, Who Wants to Be a Millionaire, Big Brother,* and *Iron Chef*—immensely popular TV programs in the United States—came from Sweden, Britain, the Netherlands, and Japan, respectively. Even *American Idol* originated in Britain as *Pop Idol,* featuring Simon Cowell. And the steamy telenovelas of Mexico and other Spanish-speaking countries owe very little of their origin to the soap operas on U.S. television. Unlike motion pictures, television is gradually moving away from U.S. domination and is now more likely to be locally produced. By 2003, all the top 50 British TV shows were locally produced. *Medium* may appear on television in London, but it is shown late at night. Even U.S.-owned TV ventures such as Disney, MTV, and CNN had dramatically increased their locally produced programming overseas. Still, *CSI: NY* was on top in

Despite the popularity of Hollywood entertainment, media that are produced abroad for local consumption also do well. The animated series *Freej* features Muslim grandmothers who stumble on a cursed book while tackling their culture's wedding traditions. Produced in Dubai, the United Arab Emirates, for adult viewers, the series was launched in 2006.

RESEARCH TODAY

7-1 Diversity in Reality Television

The underrepresentation of racial and ethnic minorities in the television industry is well documented. Not only are minorities less likely than Whites to play recurring roles; they are also underrepresented among key decision makers, such as directors, producers, and casting agents.

The new media phenomenon of reality TV may be an exception to this rule. Reality, or unscripted, television dominated prime-time television during the first decade of the 21st century. Popular with consumers and relatively inexpensive to produce, it soon became a staple on both broadcast and cable networks. Shows featured ordinary people or C-list celebrities confronting various challenges.

Although these series have been criticized on artistic grounds, they do present a diverse cast of characters. Content analysis shows that as a group, reality programs accurately represent the diversity of the general population. As such, they offer a new and significant exception to television programming that is otherwise dominated by White actors and actresses. One show, *America's Got Talent*, even has a minority host, African American Nick Cannon.

Reality shows do not necessarily promote racial and ethnic enlightenment. Instead, the broad collection of players often seems to fuel friction and build racial, social class, or sexual tension, based on either explicit or implicit issues. Far from being a multicultural paradise, reality TV is a low-wage segment of the industry in which the stars, unlike the actors in scripted dramas, receive little to no compensation. Perhaps not much has changed after all.

The color line remains in place in one segment of the reality genre, shows that promote

A rare sight on prime-time television: people of color playing leading roles. Reality shows such as *America's Next Top Model* are one of the few categories in network TV that Whites do not dominate.

romantic partnerships. For the first 17 seasons (through 2009), *The Bachelor* and *The Bachelorette* featured an all-White dating gallery. Like

> *Far from being a multicultural paradise, reality TV is a low-wage segment of the industry in which the stars, unlike the actors in scripted dramas, receive little to no compensation.*

scripted TV, these shows are likely to remain White-only. Of the nearly 70 scripted pilot projects under development by the four major networks in 2009, just 4 featured a minority person in a starring role.

LET'S DISCUSS

1. Do you watch reality TV? If so, what do you like about the shows? Have you noted any tension or conflict based on race, social class, or sex? What about friendship and support that cross those lines—have you seen it?
2. What does the popularity of reality TV shows tell us about our culture and society?

Sources: Belton 2009; Braxton 2009; Grazian 2010:129; NAACP 2008; Wyatt 2009.

France, where only sports programs had a higher rating (Bielby and Harrington 2008; Colucci 2008; *The Economist* 2003).

Nations that feel a loss of identity may try to defend against the cultural invasion from foreign countries, especially the economically dominant United States. Yet as sociologists know, audiences are not necessarily passive recipients of foreign cultural messages, either in developing nations or in industrial nations. Thus, research on consumers of cultural products like television, music, and film must be placed in social context. Although people may watch and even enjoy media content, that does not mean that they will accept values that are alien to their own (Bielby and Harrington 2008).

Many developing nations have long argued for a greatly improved two-way flow of news and information between industrial nations and developing nations. They complain that news from the Third World is scant, and what news there is reflects unfavorably on the developing nations. For example, what do you know about South America? Most people in the United States will mention the two topics that dominate the news from countries south of the border: revolution and drugs. Most know little else about the continent.

To remedy this imbalance, a resolution to monitor the news and content that cross the borders of developing nations was passed by the United Nations Educational, Scientific, and Cultural Organization (UNESCO) in the 1980s. The United States disagreed with the proposal, which became one factor in the U.S. decision to withdraw from UNESCO in the mid-1980s. In 2005, the United States opposed another UNESCO plan, meant

SOCIOLOGY IN THE GLOBAL COMMUNITY

7-2 The Global Disconnect

Bogdan Ghirda, a Romanian, is paid 50 cents an hour to participate in multiplayer Internet games like City of Heroes and Star Wars. He is sitting in for someone in an industrialized country who does not want to spend days ascending to the highest levels of competition in order to compete with players who are already "well armed." This arrangement is not unusual. U.S.-based services can earn hundreds of dollars for recruiting someone in a less developed country, like Ghirda, to represent a single player in an affluent industrial country.

Meanwhile, villagers in Arumugam, India, are beginning to benefit from their new Knowledge Centre. The facility, funded by a nonprofit organization, contains five computers that offer Internet access—an amenity unknown until now to thousands of villagers.

These two situations illustrate the technological disconnect between the developing and industrial nations. Around the world, developing nations lag far behind industrial nations in their access to and use of new technologies. The World Economic Forum's Networked Readiness Index (NRI), a ranking of 139 nations, shows the relative preparedness of individuals, businesses, and governments to benefit from information technologies. As the accompanying table shows, the haves of the world—countries like Singapore, the United States, and Denmark—are network ready; the have-nots—countries like Zimbabwe, Chad, and Nepal—are not.

For developing nations, the consequences of the global disconnect are far more serious than an inability to surf the Net. Thanks to the Internet, multinational organizations can now function as a single global unit, responding instantly in real time, 24 hours a day. This new capability has fostered the emergence of what sociologist Manuel Castells calls a "global economy." But if large numbers of people—indeed, entire

> *For developing nations, the consequences of the global disconnect are far more serious than an inability to surf the Net.*

nations—are disconnected from the new global economy, their economic growth will remain slow and the well-being of their people will remain retarded. Those citizens who are educated and skilled will immigrate to other labor markets, deepening the impoverishment of nations on the periphery.

LET'S DISCUSS

1. For nations on the periphery, what are some of the social and economic consequences of the global disconnect?

NETWORKED READINESS INDEX

Top 10 Countries	Bottom 10 Countries
1. Switzerland	130. Nepal
2. Sweden	131. Mozambique
3. Singapore	132. Mali
4. United States	133. Timor-Leste
5. Germany	134. Burkina Faso
6. Japan	135. Mauritania
7. Finland	136. Zimbabwe
8. Netherlands	137. Burundi
9. Denmark	138. Angola
10. Canada	139. Chad

2. What factors might complicate efforts to remedy the global disconnect in developing nations?

Sources: Castells 2010a; Dutta and Mia 2010; *The Economist* 2005c; Lim 2007; Tony Thompson 2005; World Economic Forum 2010.

---

to reduce the diminishment of cultural differences. Hailed as an important step toward protecting threatened cultures, particularly the media markets in developing nations, the measure passed the UN's General Assembly by a vote of 148–2. The United States, one of the two dissenters, objected officially to the measure's vague wording, but the real concern was clearly the measure's potential impact on a major U.S. export (Dominick 2009; Riding 2005).

The Digital Divide Finally, as numerous studies have shown, advances in communications technology are not evenly distributed. Worldwide, low-income groups, racial and ethnic minorities, rural residents, and the citizens of developing countries have far less access than others to the latest technologies—a gap that is called the **digital divide.** People in low-income households and developing countries, for example, are less likely than others to have Internet access. When marginalized people do gain Internet access, they are still likely to trail the privileged. They may have dial-up service instead of broadband, or broadband instead of wireless Internet.

The implications of the digital divide go well beyond an inability to check sports results or celebrity comings and goings. The Internet and other new media are becoming essential to economic progress, whether it is finding a job or accessing information needed to improve one's skills.

The digital divide is most evident in developing countries. In Africa, 4 percent of the population has Internet access. These fortunate few typically pay the highest rates in the world—$250 to $300 a month—for the slowest connection speeds. Box 7-2 examines the global disconnect between the haves and have-nots of the information age (Robinson and Crenshaw 2010; P. Schaefer 2008).

use your sociological *imagination*

How do your favorite media reflect U.S. culture? How do they reflect the cultures of the rest of the world?

Feminist View

Feminists share the view of conflict theorists that the mass media stereotype and misrepresent social reality. According to

145

FIGURE 7-2 NETWORK COVERAGE OF WOMEN'S VERSUS MEN'S SPORTS

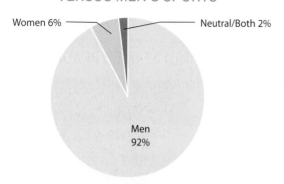

Women 6% — — Neutral/Both 2%

Men 92%

Note: Based on a content analysis of 2004 televised sports news and highlights shows.
Source: Messner et al. 2006:35.

this view, the media powerfully influence how we look at men and women, communicating unrealistic, stereotypical, and limiting images of the sexes.

Educators and social scientists have long noted the stereotypical portrayal of women and men in the mass media. Women are often shown as being shallow and obsessed with beauty. They are more likely than men to be presented unclothed, in danger, or even physically victimized. When women achieve newsworthy feats in fields traditionally dominated by men, such as professional sports, the media are often slow to recognize their accomplishments. As Figure 7-2 shows, only about 6 percent of network sports coverage is devoted to women. The situation is even worse on ESPN's *SportsCenter*, where content analysis shows that only 2 percent of airtime is devoted to women's sports.

Even when they are covered by the press, female athletes are not treated equally by television commentators. Communications researchers conducted a content analysis of over 200 hours of nationally televised coverage of professional golf events. The study showed that when female golfers are successful, they are more likely than male golfers to be called strong and intelligent. When they are not successful, they are more likely than men to be described as lacking in athletic ability. In contrast, male golfers receive more comments on their concentration and commitment. These findings suggest a subtle sexism, with women being portrayed as innately talented and men being portrayed as superior in mental or emotional makeup (T. Jacobs 2009).

Another aim of feminist research is to determine whether the media have a different impact on women than on men. Recently, researchers found that adolescent boys are almost three times as likely as adolescent girls to participate in online gaming. Young females who do participate are more likely than boy gamers to get into serious fights and report obesity. Clearly, this topic deserves further study (R. Desai et al. 2010).

A continuing, troubling issue for feminists and society as a whole is pornography. Feminists tend to be very supportive of freedom of expression and self-determination, rights that are denied to women more often than to men. Yet pornography presents women as sex objects and seems to make viewing women that way acceptable. Nor are concerns about

pornography limited to this type of objectification and imagery, as well as their implicit endorsement of violence against women. The industry that creates risqué adult images for videos, DVDs, and the Internet is largely unregulated, even putting its performers at risk.

Feminist scholars are cautiously optimistic about new media. Although women are represented among bloggers, by some measures they are responsible for only about 10 percent of the most popular blogs. Still, in conservative cultures like Saudi Arabia, online media offer women the opportunity to explore lifestyles that traditional media outlets largely ignore (Jesella 2008; Worth 2008).

As in other areas of sociology, feminist researchers caution against assuming that what holds true for men's media use is true for everyone. Researchers, for example, have studied the different ways that women and men approach the Internet. Though men are only slightly more likely than women ever to have used the Internet, they are much more likely to use it daily. Yet according to a 2009 study, more women than men use the Internet. Not surprisingly, men account for 91 percent of the players in online sports fantasy leagues. Perhaps more socially significant, however, is the finding that women are more likely than men to maintain friendship networks through e-mail (Boase et al. 2006; Fallows 2006; Pew Internet Project 2009; Rainie 2005).

Interactionist View

Interactionists are especially interested in shared understandings of everyday behavior. These scholars examine the media on the micro level to see how they shape day-to-day social behavior. Increasingly, researchers point to the mass media as the source of major daily activity; some argue that television serves essentially as a primary group for many individuals who share TV viewing. Other mass-media participation is not necessarily face-to-face. For example, we usually listen to the radio or read the newspaper as a solitary activity, although it is possible to share either with others (Cerulo et al. 1992; Waite 2000).

Online social networks, in fact, have become a new way of promoting consumption. As Figure 7-3 shows, advertisers have traditionally marketed products and services through spot ads, mass mailings, or billboards, whether they are promoting flat-screen televisions or public service messages like "Don't drink and drive." Now, using social networks (see Box 4-3, page 88), they can find consumers online and attempt to develop a relationship with them there. Through Facebook, for example, Burger King awarded a free Whopper to anyone who would delete 10 friends. Facebook's staff was not happy with Burger King's promotion, which notified 239,906 Facebook users that they had been dropped for a burger—an action that violated the network's policy. Nevertheless, Burger King created a vast network of consumers who enjoy Whoppers. Similarly, Kraft Foods encouraged people to post images of the Wiener-mobile on the photo site Flickr (Bacon Lovers' Talk 2009; Burger King 2009; Gaudin 2009).

Interactionists note, too, that friendship networks can emerge from shared viewing habits or from recollection of a cherished television series from the past. Family members and friends often gather for parties centered on the broadcasting of popular events such as the Super Bowl or the Academy Awards. And as

FIGURE 7-3 MARKETING ONLINE THROUGH SOCIAL NETWORKS

Traditional Marketing

Advertiser

Online Marketing

Advertiser

Traditional forms of advertising (left) allow only one-way communication, from the advertiser to the consumer. Online social networks (right) offer two-way communication, allowing advertisers to develop a relationship with consumers.

be a less tolerant society. If we read, see, and hear only what we know and agree with, we may be much less prepared to meet people from different backgrounds or converse with those who express new viewpoints.

Furthermore, while many people in the United States embrace the Internet, we should note that information is not evenly distributed throughout the population. The same people, by and large, who experience poor health and have few job opportunities have been left off the information highway. Figure 7-4 breaks down Internet usage by gender, age, race, income, education, and community type. Note the large disparities in usage between those with high and low incomes, and between those with more and less education. The data also show a significant racial disparity. Though educators and politicians have touted the potential benefits to the disadvantaged, Internet usage may be reinforcing existing social-class and racial barriers.

The interactionist perspective helps us to understand one important aspect of the entire mass media system—the audience. How do we actively participate in media events? How do we construct with others the meaning of media messages? We will explore these questions in the section that follows. (Table 7-3 on page 149 summarizes the various sociological perspectives on the media.)

we've seen, television often serves as a babysitter or playmate for children and even infants.

The rise of the Internet has also facilitated new forms of communication and social interaction. Grandparents can now keep up with their grandchildren via e-mail, or even watch them on their laptops via Skype. Gay and lesbian teens have online resources for support and information. People can even find their lifetime partners through computer dating services.

Some troubling issues have been raised about day-to-day life on the Internet, however. What, if anything, should be done about terrorists and other extremist groups who use the Internet to exchange messages of hatred and even bomb-making recipes? What, if anything, should be done about the issue of sexual expression on the Internet? How can children be protected from it? Should "hot chat" and X-rated film clips be censored? Or should expression be completely free?

Though the Internet has created a new platform for extremists, hate groups, and pornographers, it has also given people greater control over what they see and hear. That is, the Internet allows people to manage their media exposure so as to avoid sounds, images, and ideas they do not enjoy or approve of. The legal scholar Cass Sunstein (2002) has referred to this personalized approach to news information gathering as *egocasting*. One social consequence of this trend may

thinking CRITICALLY

What do you think is the most important function of the mass media in our society? Why? Which of the problems associated with the media troubles you most, and why?

TREND SPOTTING

Internet Dropouts

Although more and more people are surfing the Internet, the number of people who are going offline has also been rising. In 2009, one out of five nonusers had once surfed the Net and even used e-mail. For some of these people, the cost or lack of reliable access to the Internet was the reason for dropping offline. A significant number, however, simply lost interest. The overwhelming majority of these dropouts—89 percent—had no desire ever to go online again.

Surprisingly, almost one out of three people under age 30 take this attitude toward the Net. Some have a spouse or other relative who goes online for them, but others have deliberately distanced themselves from the online world. Their reasons vary from embarrassment over their lack of skill with computers to fear of being victimized by online crime and bad experiences online in the past. The Internet may be popular, but it is not for everyone.

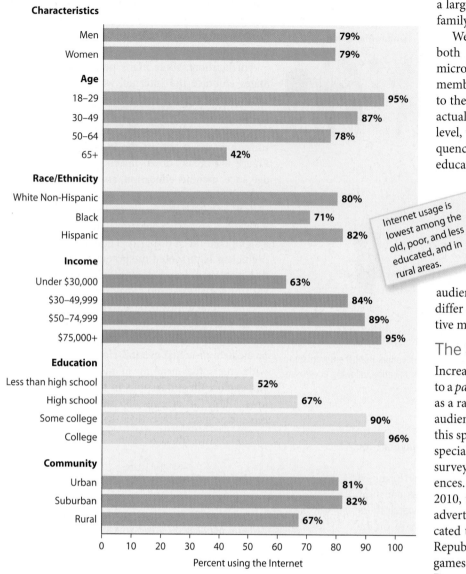

Characteristics

Note: Based on a national survey taken April–May 2010. Hispanic data limited to English-speaking respondents.
Source: Pew Internet Project 2010.

Internet usage is lowest among the old, poor, and less educated, and in rural areas.

audience may be a secondary group gathered in a large auditorium or a primary group, such as a family watching the latest Disney video at home.

We can look at the audience from the level of both *microsociology* and *macrosociology*. At the micro level, we might consider how audience members, interacting among themselves, respond to the media, or in the case of live performances, actually influence the performers. At the macro level, we might examine broader societal consequences of the media, such as the early childhood education delivered through programming like *Sesame Street.*

Even if an audience is spread out over a wide geographic area and members don't know one another, it is still distinctive in terms of age, gender, income, political party, formal schooling, race, and ethnicity. The audience for a ballet, for example, would likely differ substantially from the audience for alternative music.

The Segmented Audience

Increasingly, the media are marketing themselves to a *particular* audience. Once a media outlet, such as a radio station or a magazine, has identified its audience, it targets that group. To some degree, this specialization is driven by advertising. Media specialists have sharpened their ability, through survey research, to identify particular target audiences. Thus, during the midterm elections in 2010, the two major political parties placed TV advertisements in markets where surveys indicated they would find support. For example, the Republican Party placed ads on college football games and *America's Funniest Home Videos.* The Democratic Party bought time on *Brothers & Sisters* and *Dr. Phil* (Ashley Parker 2010).

The Audience

Ever feel like text-messaging everyone you know, to encourage them to vote for your favorite performer on a certain reality program? Ever looked over someone's shoulder as he watched last week's episode of *American Idol* on his iPhone—and been tempted to reveal the ending to him? Ever come across an old CD and tried to remember the last time you or a friend listened to one, or heard the songs in the order in which they were recorded? In this and many other ways, we are reminded that we are all part of a larger audience.

Who Is in the Audience?

The mass media are distinguished from other social institutions by the necessary presence of an audience. It can be an identifiable, finite group, such as an audience at a jazz club or a Broadway musical, or a much larger and undefined group, such as VH-1 viewers or readers of the same issue of *USA Today.* The

The specialized targeting of audiences has led some scholars to question the "mass" in mass media. For example, the British social psychologist Sonia Livingstone (2004) has written that the media have become so segmented, they have taken on the appearance almost of individualization. Are viewing audiences so segmented that large collective audiences are a thing of the past? That is not yet clear. Even though we seem to be living

TABLE **7-3** SOCIOLOGICAL PERSPECTIVES ON THE MASS MEDIA

Theoretical Perspective	Emphasis
Functionalist	Socialization
	Enforcement of social norms
	Conferral of status
	Promotion of consumption
	Narcotizing effect (dysfunction)
Conflict	Gatekeeping
	Media monitoring
	Construction of reality
	Digital divide
Feminist	Misrepresentation of women
	Differential impact on women
Interactionist	Impact on social behavior
	Source of friendship networks

Where's the President? The media target audience interests, so in 2009 *Us Weekly* featured the new family in the White House on its cover, but blocked out President Barack Obama with photos of the supposedly overweight Jessica Simpson and a single Jennifer Anniston. If you look closely, you can see the President's white-shirted arm behind First Lady Michelle Obama.

in an age of *personal* computers and *personal* digital assistants (PDAs), large formal organizations still do transmit public messages that reach a sizable, heterogeneous, and scattered audience.

use your sociological *imagination*

How might you use the concept of audience segmentation in your future occupation?

Audience Behavior

Sociologists have long researched how audiences interact with one another and how they share information after a media event. The role of audience members as opinion leaders particularly intrigues social researchers. An **opinion leader** is someone who influences the opinions and decisions of others through day-to-day personal contact and communication. For example, a movie or theater critic functions as an opinion leader. Sociologist Paul Lazarsfeld and his colleagues (1948) pioneered the study of opinion leaders in their research on voting behavior in the 1940s. They found that opinion leaders encourage their relatives, friends, and co-workers to think positively about a particular candidate, perhaps pushing them to listen to the politician's speeches or read the campaign literature.

Despite the role of opinion leaders, members of an audience do not all interpret media in the same way. Often their response is influenced by their social characteristics, such as occupation,

race, education, and income. Take the example of the televised news coverage of the riots in Los Angeles in 1992. The riots were an angry response to the acquittal of two White police officers accused of severely beating a Black motorist. Sociologist Darnell Hunt (1997) wondered how the social composition of audience members would affect the way they interpreted the news coverage. Hunt gathered 15 groups from the Los Angeles area, whose members were equally divided among Whites, Blacks, and Latinos. He showed each group a 17-minute clip from the televised coverage of the riots and asked members to discuss how they would describe what they had just seen to a 12-year-old. In analyzing the discussions, Hunt found that although gender and class did not cause respondents to vary their answers much, race did.

Hunt went beyond noting simple racial differences in perceptions; he analyzed how the differences were manifested. For example, Black viewers were much more likely than Latinos or Whites to refer to the events in terms of "us" versus "them." Another difference was that Black and Latino viewers were more animated and critical than White viewers as they watched the film clip. White viewers tended to sit quietly, still and unquestioning, suggesting that they were more comfortable with the news coverage than the Blacks or Latinos.

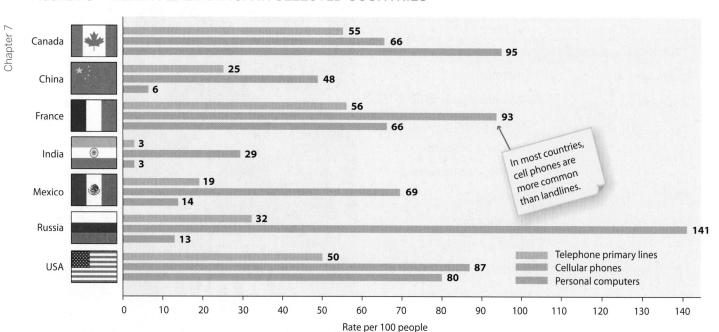

FIGURE 7-5 MEDIA PENETRATION IN SELECTED COUNTRIES

Canada: 55, 66, 95

China: 25, 48, 6

France: 56, 93, 66

India: 3, 29, 3

Mexico: 19, 69, 14

Russia: 32, 141, 13

USA: 50, 87, 80

In most countries, cell phones are more common than landlines.

Legend:
- Telephone primary lines
- Cellular phones
- Personal computers

Rate per 100 people (x-axis: 0 to 140)

Note: Personal computer data for 2006, released in 2009; for 2008, released in 2011.
Sources: Bureau of the Census 2009a:Table 1345; 2010a:Table 1392.

Think about It
What is the economic and political significance of media penetration?

thinking CRITICALLY

What kind of audience is targeted by the producers of televised professional wrestling? By the creators of an animated film? By a rap group? What factors determine who makes up a particular audience?

The Media's Global Reach

Has the rise of the electronic media created a *global village*? Canadian media theorist Marshall McLuhan predicted it would nearly 50 years ago. Today, physical distance is no longer a barrier, and instant messaging is possible across the world. The mass media have indeed created a global village. Not all countries are equally connected, as Figure 7-5 shows, but the progress has

In 2010, hip-hop artist UnK's "2 Step" was one of the most frequently downloaded cell phone ringtones. Because today's media provide multiple services, music fans can use the Internet to access recorded music and listen to it on their cell phones.

SOCIOLOGY IN THE GLOBAL COMMUNITY

7-3 Al Jazeera Is on the Air

A 24-hour-a-day televised news network with short bulletins every hour, followed by a fast-paced montage of news clips—all broadcast globally by satellite-linked cable stations. This could be CNN, but it's Al Jazeera, the Arabic-language television news network founded in 1996 and based in the small Persian Gulf state of Qatar. The name Al Jazeera means "island" or "peninsula," in reference to the network's home country.

Most people in the United States had never heard of Al Jazeera until October 7, 2001. That was when the channel aired the first of several videotaped messages from Osama bin Laden, the mastermind of the Al-Qaeda terrorist network. U.S. news outlets also televised the messages, but stopped after the government objected to the airing of bin Laden's calls for violence against U.S. citizens.

Though many media observers see Al Jazeera as biased, many viewers around the world might see CNN, ABC, and Fox News as biased. According to Kenton Keith, a former

> "You have to be a supporter of Al Jazeera, even if you have to hold your nose sometimes."

U.S. ambassador to Qatar, Al Jazeera has a slant, but no more than other news organizations. It just happens to be a slant that most Americans aren't comfortable with.

Al Jazeera does offer diverse views. On its popular talk show *The Opposing View*, two

In 2006, Al Jazeera expanded its programming to include an all-English channel; since then its following has grown. Israel's top cable company, for example, dropped CNN and added AJE to its lineup.

women hotly debated polygamy among Muslim men. On another popular program, *Shari'a [Islamic Law] and Life,* the speaker dared to reassure Muslim women that the Koran does not force them to marry suitors designated by their parents. Ambassador Keith believes that "for the long-range importance of press freedom in the Middle East and the advantages that will ultimately have for the West, you have to be a supporter of Al Jazeera, even if you have to hold your nose sometimes" (Barr 2002:7).

LET'S DISCUSS

1. Do you find news outlets in the United States biased? How would you judge?
2. What do you think of the Al Jazeera network? Could the news coverage it provides and the editorial perspectives it takes be useful to the U.S. government? Explain.

Sources: Al Jazeera 2010; Barr 2002; Daniszewski 2003; S. MacLeod and Walt 2005; H. Rosenberg 2003; Urbina 2002.

---

been staggering, considering that voice transmission was just beginning 100 years ago (McLuhan 1964, 1967).

Sociologist Todd Gitlin considers *global torrent* a more apt metaphor for the media's reach than *global village*. The media permeate all aspects of everyday life. Take advertising, for example. Consumer goods are marketed vigorously worldwide, from advertisements on airport baggage carriers to imprints on sandy beaches. Little wonder that people around the world develop loyalty to a brand and are as likely to sport a Nike, Coca-Cola, or Harley-Davidson logo as they are their favorite soccer or baseball insignia (Gitlin 2002; Klein 1999).

A highly visible part of the media, whether it be print or electronic, is news. In the past, most people in the United States had little familiarity with news outlets outside their own country, with the possible exception of the British-based Reuters and BBC News.

Like so many other things, however, that changed after September 11, 2001, when an Arab news network took center stage (Box 7-3).

The Internet has facilitated all forms of communication. Reference materials and data banks can now be made accessible across national boundaries. Information related to international finance, marketing, trade, and manufacturing is literally just a keystroke away. We have seen the emergence of true world news outlets and the promotion of a world music that is not clearly identifiable with any single culture. Even the most future-oriented thinker would find the growth in the reach of the mass media in postindustrial and postmodern societies remarkable (Castells 2001, 2010b; Croteau and Hoynes 2003, 2006).

Although in the United States we may take television for granted, even thinking of it as an old-fashioned medium, worldwide that is not necessarily the case. In India, half of all households

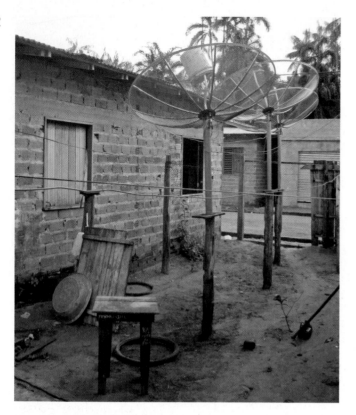

New technologies can create new social norms. In Gurupá, Brazil, television watching became a community social activity when three new TV owners agreed to share their sets with the community of 3,000.

do not have television; in Nigeria and Bangladesh, more than 70 percent of households go without. Two technological advances are likely to change this pattern, however. First, advances in battery power now allow viewers to watch television even in areas where there is no electricity. Second, digital signal transmission permits television reception via cable or satellite.

In some developing countries, people manage to watch television even though they don't own one. Consider the town of Gurupá, in the remote Amazon area of Brazil. In 1982, the wealthiest three households in this community bought televisions. To please the rest of the town, they agreed to place their TVs near the window so that their neighbors could watch them as well. As the TV owners proudly displayed their new status symbol, TV watching became a community social activity. The introduction of a new technology had created a new social norm (Kenny 2009; Pace 1993, 1998).

Around the world, people rely increasingly on digital media, from cell phones to the Internet. This trend toward online communication has raised new concerns about the right to privacy. The Social Policy section that follows examines the social implications of digital media, from censorship to criminal activity.

thinking CRITICALLY

Use the functionalist, conflict, and interactionist perspectives to assess the effects of global TV programming on developing countries.

social**policy** and the Mass Media

The Right to Privacy

In 2010, humans added 1.2 zettabytes of digital information to the world's already huge data library. A zettabyte equals 1 trillion gigabytes—a quantity which, if placed on DVDs, would require a stack of disks stretching to the moon and back. By 2020, the size of this imaginary DVD tower will triple, quadruple, or even quintuple (Acohido 2010).

Within this mound of data lies personal information about people's finances, health, and individual tastes. In the postmodern digital age, do people have a right to keep that kind of information private? If so, can they expect others to respect that right?

Looking at the Issue

Although much of the sweeping change that accompanied the transition to digital media has benefited society, scholars have noted some negative effects. In particular, recent advances in computer technology have made it increasingly easy for business firms, government agencies, and even criminals to retrieve and store information about private individuals. In public places, at work, and on the Internet, surveillance devices track our every move, whether it is a keystroke or an ATM withdrawal. The

information they accumulate includes everything from our buying habits to our web-surfing patterns.

As these technologies increase the power to monitor our behavior, they raise fears of their misuse for criminal or even undemocratic purposes. In short, they threaten not just our privacy, but our freedom from crime and censorship as well. Some obvious violations of privacy, such as identity theft—the misuse of credit card and Social Security numbers to masquerade as another person—have been well documented. Other violations involve online surveillance of dissident political groups by authoritarian regimes and the unauthorized release of classified government documents. In 2010, WikiLeaks released thousands of classified U.S. foreign policy documents on its website, causing some people to condemn the action as treasonous and others to praise it as a blow against government censorship (O'Harrow Jr. 2005).

Other privacy violations are subtler, and not strictly illegal. For example, many commercial websites use "cookies" and tracking technology to monitor visitors' websurfing. Using that information, marketers can estimate a visitor's age, gender, and zip code, and from that data, the person's income. They can then

It's for an electronic poll, sir. How do you feel about anyone anywhere having access to your private data?

Our society's growing dependence on electronic transactions has greatly increased concerns about our privacy.

select advertisements that will appeal specifically to that person. So depending on who we are, or at least appear to be, one of us might see ads about weight-loss products and another, ads about travel to exotic locations.

Is this approach to online marketing just effective advertising, or is it an invasion of privacy? Because the information that marketers gather in this way can be tied to other devices a person uses, such as a cell phone or computer, some critics see online tracking as a form of fingerprinting (Angwin 2010; Angwin and Valentino-DeVries 2010a).

Applying Sociology

From a sociological point of view, the complex issues of privacy and censorship can be considered illustrations of culture lag. As usual, the material culture (technology) is changing faster than the nonmaterial culture (norms for controlling the use of technology). Too often, the result is an anything-goes approach to the use of new technologies.

Sociologists' views on the use and abuse of new technologies differ depending on their theoretical perspective. Functionalists take a generally positive view of the Internet, pointing to its manifest function of facilitating communication. From their perspective, the Internet performs the latent function of empowering people with few resources—from hate groups to special-interest organizations—to communicate with the masses.

In contrast, conflict theorists stress the danger that the most powerful groups in a society will use technology to violate the privacy of the less powerful.

Initiating Policy

Legislation regarding the surveillance of electronic communications has not always upheld citizens' right to privacy. In 1986, the federal government passed the Electronic Communications Privacy Act, which outlawed the surveillance of telephone calls except with the permission of both the U.S. attorney general and a federal judge. Telegrams, faxes, and e-mails did not receive the same degree of protection, however. In 2001, one month after the terrorist attacks of September 11, Congress passed the Patriot Act, which relaxed existing legal checks on surveillance by law enforcement officers. Federal agencies are now freer to gather data electronically, including people's credit card receipts and banking records (Gertner 2005).

Today, most other types of online monitoring have yet to be tested in court, including the use of tracking technologies and the compilation and sale of personal profiles. Consistent with the concept of culture lag, privacy advocates complain that the law hasn't kept pace with advancing technology. In 2010, Congress began to draft federal legislation to inform cell phone and computer owners that their devices are being "fingerprinted," and to allow them to opt out of being monitored. The next year, seeking to head off the measure, some tracking organizations began voluntarily to allow people to edit the information collected in their online profiles. At the same time, the Federal Trade Commission issued a report that faulted the industry for not doing enough to protect consumers' privacy online (Angwin and Valentino-DeVries 2010b; Federal Trade Commission 2010; Steel 2010; *The Week* 2010b).

If anything, however, people seem to be less vigilant about maintaining their privacy today than they were before the information age. Young people who have grown up browsing the Internet seem to accept the existence of the "cookies" and "spyware" they may pick up while surfing. They have become accustomed to adult surveillance of their conversation in electronic chat rooms. And many see no risk in providing personal information about themselves to strangers they meet online. Little wonder that college professors find their students do not appreciate the political significance of their right to privacy (Turkle 2004, 2011).

Compared to online tracking, most people seem more worried about government surveillance and crimes like identity theft. Although online piracy is a real threat, in the long run, online tracking and other questionable forms of surveillance may pose a greater threat to society. As Nicholas Carr (2010:W2), former editor of the *Harvard Business Review,* has noted, "The continuing erosion of personal privacy . . . may lead us as a society to devalue the concept of privacy, to see it as outdated and unimportant . . . merely as a barrier to efficient shopping and socializing." From the point of view of many technology companies, however, abandoning the right to privacy is only realistic. As Sun Microsystems CEO Scott McNealy remarked in 1999, "You have no privacy. Get over it" (Carr 2010:W2).

Take the Issue with You

1. How would you react if you discovered that the government was monitoring your use of the mass media?

2. If your safety were in jeopardy, would you be willing to sacrifice your privacy?

3. Which do you consider the greatest threat to society: government censorship, cybercrime, or Internet surveillance? Explain.

Summary

The **mass media** are print and electronic instruments of communication that carry messages to often widespread audiences. They pervade all social institutions, from entertainment to education to politics. This chapter examines how the mass media affect those institutions and influence our social behavior.

1. From the functionalist perspective, the media entertain, socialize, enforce social norms, confer status, and promote consumption. They can be dysfunctional to the extent that they desensitize us to serious events and issues, a phenomenon called the **narcotizing dysfunction.**

2. Conflict theorists think the media reflect and even deepen the divisions in society through **gatekeeping,** or control over which material reaches the public; media monitoring, the covert observation of people's media usage and choices; and support of the **dominant ideology,** which defines reality, overwhelming local cultures.

3. Feminist theorists point out that media images of the sexes communicate unrealistic, stereotypical, limiting, and sometimes violent perceptions of women.

4. Interactionists examine the media on the micro level to see how they shape day-to-day social behavior. Interactionists have studied shared TV viewing and intergenerational e-mail.

5. The mass media require the presence of an audience, whether it is small and well defined or large and amorphous. With increasing numbers of media outlets has come more and more targeting of segmented (or specialized) audiences.

6. Social researchers have studied the role of **opinion leaders** in influencing audiences.

7. The media have a global reach thanks to new communications technologies, especially the Internet. Some people are concerned that this global reach will spread unhealthy influences to other cultures.

8. In the postmodern digital age, new technologies that facilitate the collection and sharing of personal information are threatening people's right to privacy.

Key Terms

Cultural convergence The flow of content across multiple media, and the accompanying migration of media audiences. (page 137)

Digital divide The relative lack of access to the latest technologies among low-income groups, racial and ethnic minorities, rural residents, and the citizens of developing countries. (145)

Dominant ideology A set of cultural beliefs and practices that helps to maintain powerful social, economic, and political interests. (143)

Gatekeeping The process by which a relatively small number of people in the media industry control what material eventually reaches the audience. (140)

Mass media Print and electronic means of communication that carry messages to widespread audiences. (136)

Narcotizing dysfunction The phenomenon in which the media provide such massive amounts of coverage that the audience becomes numb and fails to act on the information, regardless of how compelling the issue. (140)

Netizen A person who is actively involved in online communities and is committed to the free flow of information, with few outside controls. (141)

Opinion leader Someone who influences the opinions and decisions of others through day-to-day personal contact and communication. (149)

Stereotype An unreliable generalization about all members of a group that does not recognize individual differences within the group. (143)

TAKING SOCIOLOGY with you

1. For one day, categorize every media message you receive in terms of its function: Does it socialize, enforce a social norm, confer status, or promote consumption? Keep a record and tally the results. Which function was the most common? What can you conclude from the results?

2. Pick a specific audience—residents of your dorm, for example—and track their media preferences over the next day or two. Which mass media are they watching, reading, or listening to? Which media are the most popular and which the least popular? How segmented is this particular mass media audience?

3. Pick a foreign film, television program, or Internet site and study it from the point of view of a sociologist. What does it tell you about the culture that produced it?

Self-Quiz

Read each question carefully and then select the best answer.

1. From the functionalist perspective, the media can be dysfunctional in what way?
   a. They enforce social norms.
   b. They confer status.
   c. They desensitize us to events.
   d. They are agents of socialization.

2. Sociologist Robert Park studied how newspapers helped immigrants to the United States adjust to their environment by changing their customary habits and by teaching them the opinions held by people in their new home country. His study was conducted from which sociological perspective?
   a. the functionalist perspective
   b. the conflict perspective
   c. the interactionist perspective
   d. the dramaturgical perspective

3. There are problems inherent in the socialization function of the mass media. For example, many people worry about
    a. the effect of using the television as a babysitter.
    b. the impact of violent programming on viewer behavior.
    c. the unequal ability of all individuals to purchase televisions.
    d. both a and b.

4. Media advertising has several clear functions, but it also has dysfunctions. Sociologists are concerned that
    a. it creates unrealistic expectations of what is required to be happy.
    b. it creates new consumer needs.
    c. advertisers are able to influence media content.
    d. all of the above

5. Gatekeeping, the process by which a relatively small number of people control what material reaches an audience, is largely dominant in all but which of the following media?
    a. television
    b. the Internet
    c. publishing
    d. music

6. Which sociological perspective is especially concerned with the media's ability to decide what gets transmitted through gatekeeping?
    a. the functionalist perspective
    b. the conflict perspective
    c. the interactionist perspective
    d. the dramaturgical perspective

7. Which of the following is *not* a problem feminist theorists see with media coverage?
    a. Women are underrepresented, suggesting that men are the cultural standard and that women are insignificant.
    b. Men and women are portrayed in ways that reflect and perpetuate stereotypical views of gender.
    c. Female athletes are treated differently from male athletes in television commentary.
    d. The increasing frequency of single moms in the media is providing a negative role model for women.

8. Which of the following is *not* true concerning how men and women use the Internet?
    a. Men are more likely to use the Internet daily.
    b. Women are more likely to use e-mail to maintain friendships.
    c. Men account for 100 percent of players in online sports fantasy leagues.
    d. Men are slightly more likely to have ever used the Internet than women are.

9. Sociologist Paul Lazarsfeld and his colleagues pioneered the study of
    a. the audience.
    b. opinion leaders.
    c. the media's global reach.
    d. media violence.

10. In his study of how the social composition of audience members affected how they interpreted the news coverage of riots in Los Angeles in 1992, sociologist Darnell Hunt found what kind of differences in perception?
    a. racial
    b. gender
    c. class
    d. religious

11. The mass media increase social cohesion by presenting a more or less standardized, common view of culture through mass communication. This statement reflects the _____ perspective.

12. Paul Lazarsfeld and Robert Merton created the term _____ _____ to refer to the phenomenon in which the media provide such massive amounts of information that the audience becomes numb and generally fails to act on the information, regardless of how compelling the issue.

13. _____ is the term used to describe the set of cultural beliefs and practices that helps to maintain powerful social, economic, and political interests.

14. Sociologists blame the mass media for the creation and perpetuation of _____, or generalizations about all members of a group that do not recognize individual differences within the group.

15. The _____ perspective contends that television distorts the political process.

16. We risk being _____ if we overstress U.S. dominance and assume that other nations do not play a role in media cultural exports.

17. Both _____ and _____ theorists are troubled that the victims depicted in violent imagery are often those who are given less respect in real life: women, children, the poor, racial minorities, citizens of foreign countries, and even the physically disabled.

18. The _____ perspective examines the media on the micro level to see how they shape day-to-day social behavior.

19. From a sociological point of view, the current controversy over privacy and media censorship illustrates the concept of _____ _____.

20. Nearly 50 years ago, Canadian media theorist _____ _____ predicted that the rise of the electronic media would create a "global village."

THINKING ABOUT MOVIES

Pirate Radio

In the 1960s, an independent English radio station broadcasts from international waters, threatening the British Broadcasting Corporation's monopoly.

Talk to Me

In Washington, D.C., an R&B station struggles to keep its radio audience during the massive social change that followed the civil rights movement.

We Live in Public

This documentary traces the rise and fall of an Internet entrepreneur.

A potential shopper examines
a marijuana plant at the
Cannabis Crown competition
for medical marijuana growers
in Aspen, Colorado. Although
deviant behavior violates the
standards of conduct of a group
or society, it is not necessarily
criminal behavior.

(1963, 1975) suggests that most of us *would* obey such orders. In his words (1975:xi), "Behavior that is unthinkable in an individual . . . acting on his own may be executed without hesitation when carried out under orders."

Milgram placed advertisements in New Haven, Connecticut, newspapers to recruit subjects for a learning experiment at Yale University. Participants included postal clerks, engineers, high school teachers, and laborers. They were told that the purpose of the research was to investigate the effects of punishment on learning. The experimenter, dressed in a gray technician's coat, explained that in each test, one subject would be randomly selected as the "learner," while another would function as the "teacher." However, the experiment was rigged so that the real subject would always be the teacher, while an associate of Milgram's served as the learner.

At this point, the learner's hand was strapped to an electric apparatus. The teacher was taken to an electronic "shock generator" with 30 levered switches labeled from 15 to 450 volts. Before beginning the experiment, all subjects received sample shocks of 45 volts, to convince them of the authenticity of the experiment. The experimenter then instructed the teacher to apply shocks of increasing voltage each time the learner gave an incorrect answer on a memory test. Teachers were told that "although the shocks can be extremely painful, they cause no permanent tissue damage." In reality, the learner did not receive any shocks.

In a prearranged script, the learner deliberately gave incorrect answers and expressed pain when "shocked." For example, at 150 volts, the learner would cry out, "Get me out of here!" At 270 volts, the learner would scream in agony. When the shock reached 350 volts, the learner would fall silent. If the teacher wanted to stop the experiment, the experimenter would insist that the teacher continue, using such statements as "The experiment requires that you continue" and "You have no other choice; you *must* go on" (Milgram 1975:19–23).

Reflecting on the Milgram Experiment The results of this unusual experiment stunned and dismayed Milgram and other social scientists. A sample of psychiatrists had predicted that virtually all subjects would refuse to shock innocent victims. In their view, only a "pathological fringe" of less than 2 percent would continue administering shocks up to the maximum level. Yet almost *two-thirds* of participants fell into the category of "obedient subjects."

Why did these subjects obey? Why were they willing to inflict seemingly painful shocks on innocent victims who had never done them any harm? There is no evidence that these subjects were unusually sadistic; few seemed to enjoy administering the shocks. Instead, in Milgram's view, the key to obedience was the experimenter's social role as a "scientist" and "seeker of knowledge."

Milgram pointed out that in the modern industrial world, we are accustomed to submitting to impersonal authority figures whose status is indicated by a title (professor, lieutenant, doctor) or by a uniform (the technician's coat). Because we view the authority as larger and more important than the individual, we shift responsibility for our behavior to the authority figure. Milgram's subjects frequently stated, "If it were up to me, I would not have administered shocks." They saw themselves as merely doing their duty (Milgram 1975).

From a conflict perspective, our obedience may be affected by the value we place on those whom our behavior affects. While Milgram's experiment shows that in general, people are willing

In one of Stanley Milgram's experiments, the learner supposedly received an electric shock from a shock plate when he answered a question incorrectly. At the 150-volt level, the learner would demand to be released and would refuse to place his hand on the shock plate. The experimenter would then order the actual subject, the teacher, to force the hand onto the plate, as shown in the photo. Though 40 percent of the true subjects stopped complying with Milgram at this point, 30 percent did force the learner's hand onto the shock plate, despite his pretended agony.

to obey authority figures, other studies show that they are even more willing to obey if they feel the "victim" is deserving of punishment. Sociologist Gary Schulman (1974) re-created Milgram's experiment and found that White students were significantly more likely to shock Black learners than White learners. By a margin of 70 percent to 48 percent, they imposed more shocks on the Black learners than on the White learners.

From an interactionist perspective, one important aspect of Milgram's findings is the fact that subjects in follow-up studies were less likely to inflict the supposed shocks as they were moved physically closer to their victims. Moreover, interactionists emphasize the effect of *incrementally* administering additional dosages of 15 volts. In effect, the experimenter negotiated with the teacher and convinced the teacher to continue inflicting higher levels of punishment. It is doubtful that anywhere near the two-thirds rate of obedience would have been reached had the experimenter told the teachers to administer 450 volts immediately (B. Allen 1978; Katovich 1987).

Milgram launched his experimental study of obedience to better understand the involvement of Germans in the annihilation of 6 million Jews and millions of other people during World War II. In an interview conducted long after the publication of his study, he suggested that "if a system of death camps were set up in the United States of the sort we had seen in Nazi Germany, one would be able to find sufficient personnel for those camps in any medium-sized American town." Though many people questioned his remark, the revealing photos taken at Iraq's Abu Ghraib prison in 2004, showing U.S. military guards humiliating if not torturing Iraqi prisoners, recalled the experiment Milgram had done two generations earlier. Under conducive circumstances, otherwise normal people can and often do treat one another inhumanely (CBS News 1979:7–8; Hayden 2004; Zimbardo 2007a).

How willing would participants in this experiment be to shock learners today? Although many people may be skeptical of the high levels of conformity Milgram found, recent replications of his experiment confirm his findings. In 2006, using additional safeguards to protect participants' welfare, psychologist Jerry Burger (2009) repeated part of Milgram's experiment with college undergraduates. To avoid biasing the participants, Burger was careful to screen out students who had heard of Milgram's study. The results of the replication were startlingly similar to Milgram's: participants showed a high level of willingness to shock the learner, just as the participants in Milgram's experiment had almost half a century earlier. At the most comparable point in the two studies, Burger measured a rate of 70 percent full obedience—lower, but not significantly so, than the rate of 82.5 percent measured two generations earlier.

---

use your sociological *imagination*

If you were a participant in Milgram's research on conformity, how far do you think you would go in carrying out orders? Do you see any ethical problem with the experimenter's manipulation of the subjects?

Informal and Formal Social Control

The sanctions that are used to encourage conformity and obedience—and to discourage violation of social norms—are carried out through both informal and formal social control. As the term implies, people use **informal social control** casually to enforce norms. Examples include smiles, laughter, a raised eyebrow, and ridicule.

In the United States and many other cultures, adults often view spanking, slapping, or kicking children as a proper and necessary means of informal social control. Child development specialists counter that such corporal punishment is inappropriate because it teaches children to solve problems through violence. They warn that slapping and spanking can escalate into more serious forms of abuse. Yet, despite a 1998 policy statement by the American Academy of Pediatrics that corporal punishment is not effective and can indeed be harmful, 59 percent of pediatricians support the use of corporal punishment, at least in certain situations. Our culture widely accepts this form of informal social control (Chung et al. 2009).

Formal social control is carried out by authorized agents, such as police officers, judges, school administrators, employers, military officers, and managers of movie theaters. It can serve as a last resort when socialization and informal sanctions do not bring about desired behavior. Sometimes, informal social control can actually undermine formal social control, encouraging people to violate social norms. Box 8-1 examines binge drinking among college students, who receive conflicting messages about the acceptability of the behavior from sources of social control.

An increasingly significant means of formal social control in the United States is to imprison people. During the course of a year, over 7 million adults undergo some form of

correctional supervision—jail, prison, probation, or parole. Put another way, almost 1 out of every 30 adult Americans is subject to this very formal type of social control every year (Sabol et al. 2009).

In 2007, in the wake of the mass shootings at Virginia Tech, many college officials reviewed security measures on their campuses. Administrators were reluctant to end or even limit the relative freedom of movement students on their campuses enjoyed. Instead, they concentrated on improving emergency communications between campus police and students, faculty, and staff. Reflecting a reliance on technology to maintain social control, college leaders called for replacement of the "old" technology of e-mail with instant alerts that could be sent to people's cell phones via instant messaging.

Six years earlier, in the aftermath of September 11, 2001, new measures of social control became the norm in the United States. Some of them, such as stepped-up security at airports and high-rise buildings, were highly visible to the public. The federal government has also publicly urged citizens to engage in informal social control by watching for and reporting people whose actions seem suspicious.

Many people think this kind of social control goes too far. Civil rights advocates worry that the government's request for information on suspicious activities may encourage negative stereotyping of

Though formal social control usually involves fines, probation, or incarceration, some judges have used public humiliation as a sanction.

SOCIOLOGY ON CAMPUS

8-1   Binge Drinking

About 1,700 college students die each year of unintentional alcohol-related injuries. According to a study published by the Harvard School of Public Health, 44 percent of college students indulge in binge drinking (defined as at least five drinks in a row for men and four in a row for women). These numbers represent an increase from 1990s data, despite efforts on many campuses across the nation to educate students about the risks of binge drinking.

The problem is not confined to the United States—Britain, Russia, and South Africa all report regular "drink till you drop" alcoholic consumption among young people. According to a study that compared data from 22 countries, however, college students in the United States have the highest rate of drinking and driving. Nor does binge drinking begin in college. A national study found that over a 30-day period, 29 percent of high school students engaged in binge drinking.

Binge drinking on campus presents a difficult social problem. On the one hand, it can be regarded as *deviant,* violating the standards of conduct expected of those in an academic setting. In fact, Harvard researchers consider binge drinking the most serious public health hazard facing colleges. On the other hand, binge drinking represents *conformity* to the peer culture, especially in fraternities and sororities, which serve as social centers on many campuses. Most students seem to take an "everybody does it—no big deal" attitude toward the behavior.

Some colleges and universities are taking steps to make binge drinking a bit less "normal" by means of *social control*—banning

kegs, closing fraternities and sororities, encouraging liquor retailers not to sell in high volume to students, and expelling students

44 percent of college students indulge in binge drinking.

after three alcohol-related infractions. Despite privacy laws, many schools are notifying parents whenever their underage children are caught drinking. Even with these measures, however, curbing underage drinking is a challenge.

LET'S DISCUSS

1. Why do you think most college students regard binge drinking as a normal rather than a deviant behavior?
2. Which do you think would be more effective in stopping binge drinking on your campus, informal or formal social control?

Sources: E. Bernstein 2007; Centers for Disease Control and Prevention 2010; J. Miller et al. 2007; National Center on Addiction and Substance Abuse at Columbia University 2007; Outside the Classroom 2009; Wechsler et al. 2002, 2004.

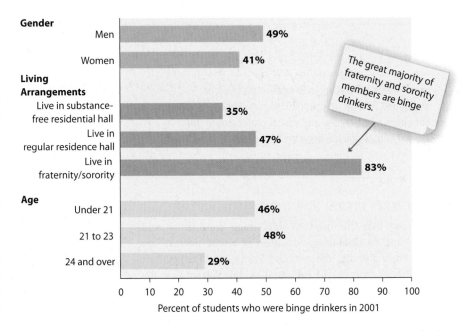

The great majority of fraternity and sorority members are binge drinkers.

Note: Based on a 2001 national survey of more than 10,000 college students. Binge drinking was defined as one drinking session of at least five drinks for men or four drinks for women during the two weeks prior to the self-administered questionnaire.
Source: Wechsler et al. 2002:208.

Muslims and Arab Americans. Clearly, there is a trade-off between the benefits of surveillance and the right to privacy.

thinking CRITICALLY

Think about a job you once held. How did your employer exercise social control over the employees? How did you, as an employee, use social control in relating to those around you?

Law and Society

Some norms are so important to a society that they are formalized into laws regarding people's behavior. **Law** may be

defined as governmental social control (Black 1995). Some laws, such as the prohibition against murder, are directed at all members of society. Others, such as fishing and hunting regulations, affect particular categories of people. Still others govern the behavior of social institutions (for instance, corporate law and laws regarding the taxing of nonprofit enterprises).

Sociologists see the creation of laws as a social process. Because laws are passed in response to a perceived need for formal social control, sociologists have sought to explain how and why such a perception arises. In their view, law is not merely a static body of rules handed down from generation to generation. Rather, it reflects continually changing standards of what is right and wrong, of how violations are to be determined, and of what sanctions are to be applied (Schur 1968).

Sociologists representing varying theoretical perspectives agree that the legal order reflects the values of those in a position to exercise authority. Therefore, the creation of civil and criminal law can be a most controversial matter. Should it be against the law to employ illegal immigrants, to have an abortion (see Chapter 12), to allow prayer in public schools, or to smoke on an airplane? Such issues have been bitterly debated, because they require a choice among competing values. Not surprisingly, laws that are unpopular—such as the one-time prohibition of alcohol under the Eighteenth Amendment and the widespread establishment of a 55-mile-per-hour speed limit on highways—become difficult to enforce when there is no consensus supporting the norms.

One current and controversial debate over laws governing behavior is whether people should be allowed to use marijuana legally, for medical purposes. Although the majority of adults polled in national surveys support such a use, the federal government continues to regard all uses of marijuana as illegal. In 2005 the Supreme Court upheld the federal government's position. Nevertheless, 15 states and the District of Columbia have granted citizens the right to use marijuana for medical purposes—even if that privilege rests on dubious legal grounds (Figure 8-1).

In Singapore, a custodian removes a bit of litter from an otherwise spotless floor. Strict social controls prevail in the city-state, where the careless disposal of a cigarette butt or candy wrapper carries a $200 fine.

thinking CRITICALLY

Should some illegal drugs be decriminalized? Why or why not?

Socialization is the primary source of conforming and obedient behavior, including obedience to law. Generally, it is not external pressure from a peer group or authority figure that makes us go along with social norms. Rather, we have internalized such norms as valid and desirable and are committed to observing them. In a profound sense, we want to see ourselves (and to be seen) as loyal, cooperative, responsible, and respectful of others. In the United States and other societies around the world, people are socialized both to want to belong and to fear being viewed as different or deviant.

Control theory suggests that our connection to members of society leads us to systematically conform to society's norms. According to sociologist Travis Hirschi and other control theorists, our bonds to family members, friends, and peers induce us to follow the mores and folkways of our society. We give little conscious thought to whether we will be sanctioned if we fail to conform. Socialization develops our self-control so well that we don't need further pressure to obey social norms. Although control theory does not effectively explain the rationale for every conforming act, it nevertheless reminds us that while the media may focus on crime and disorder, most members of most societies conform to and obey basic norms (Brewis et al. 2011; Gottfredson and Hirschi 1990; Hirschi 1969).

TREND SPOTTING

Incarceration Nation

Since 1980, through prosperity and recession, war and peace, the United States has been sending more and more people to prison. Today, about 1.6 million people reside in federal or state institutions. That number is higher than the population of the fifth largest U.S. city, Phoenix.

Both the number of prisoners and the rate of incarceration have grown steadily. From 1980 through the end of 2008, the prison population increased from just over 1 in 1,000 to 1 in 198. If only adults are counted, the current proportion is 1 in every 100. The trend becomes even more disturbing when we consider the growing reliance on early-release programs. If cash-strapped states were not using electronic monitoring devices, like ankle bracelets, to lower their prison populations, the statistics would be even more dismal.

Internationally, the United States' incarceration rate stands out as one of the highest in the world—more than three times as high as that of Mexico or Canada. Even China with its huge population does not have as many people behind bars as the United States.

death row inmates, and reimbursed far fewer lawyers for their defense of condemned criminals.

Internationally, attention has focused on those nations where executions are relatively common, such as China and Iran. Foes of the death penalty see these nations as violators of human rights. In the United States, which usually regards itself as a champion of human rights, pressure to abolish capital punishment has grown both at home and abroad.

Take the Issue with You

1. Does the death penalty deter crime? If so, why are crime rates in the United States high compared to those in other nations?

2. What is your position on the death penalty—should it be legal or should it be abolished? Explain your reasoning.

3. Should youths who have been convicted of violent crimes be subject to the death penalty? Why or why not?

MASTERING THIS CHAPTER

Summary

Conformity and **deviance** are two ways in which people respond to real or imagined pressure from others. In this chapter we examined the relationships among deviance and conformity, **crime** and **social control.** We studied the mechanisms societies use, both formal and informal, to encourage conformity and discourage deviance, paying particular attention to the law and how it reflects our social values.

1. Deviant behavior violates social norms. Some forms of **deviance** carry a negative social **stigma,** while other forms are more or less accepted.

2. A society uses **social control** to encourage the acceptance of basic norms.

3. Stanley Milgram defined **conformity** as going along with one's peers; **obedience** is defined as compliance with higher authorities in a hierarchical structure.

4. Some norms are so important to a society, they are formalized into **laws.** Socialization is a primary source of conforming and obedient behavior, including obedience to law.

5. From a functionalist point of view, deviance and its consequences help to define the limits of proper behavior.

6. Some interactionists maintain that people learn criminal behavior by interacting with others (**cultural transmission**). To them, deviance results from exposure to attitudes that are favorable to criminal acts (**differential association**).

7. Other interactionists attribute increases in crime and deviance to the absence or breakdown of communal relationships and social institutions, such as the family, school, church, and local government (**social disorganization theory**).

8. An important aspect of **labeling theory** is the recognition that some people are viewed as deviant, while others who engage in the same behavior are not.

9. From the conflict perspective, laws and punishments are a reflection of the interests of the powerful.

10. The feminist perspective emphasizes that cultural attitudes and differential economic relationships help to explain gender differences in deviance and crime.

11. **Crime** represents a deviation from formal social norms administered by the state.

12. Sociologists differentiate among **victimless crimes** (such as drug use and prostitution), *professional crime,* **organized crime, white-collar crime, hate crime,** and **transnational crime.**

13. Crime statistics are among the least reliable social data, partly because so many crimes are not reported to law enforcement agencies. Rates of violent crime are higher in the United States than in other Western societies, although they have been dropping.

14. The death penalty is the ultimate sanction, one that functionalists believe deters serious crime. However, it is applied disproportionately to the economically disadvantaged and to racial minorities. Worldwide, many countries have renounced the death penalty.

Key Terms

Anomie Durkheim's term for the loss of direction felt in a society when social control of individual behavior has become ineffective. (page 166)

Anomie theory of deviance Robert Merton's theory of deviance as an adaptation of socially prescribed goals or of the means governing their attainment, or both. (167)

Conformity Going along with peers—individuals of our own status who have no special right to direct our behavior. (161)

Control theory A view of conformity and deviance that suggests that our connection to members of society leads us to systematically conform to society's norms. (165)

Crime A violation of criminal law for which some governmental authority applies formal penalties. (171)

Cultural transmission A school of criminology that argues that criminal behavior is learned through social interactions. (168)

Deviance Behavior that violates the standards of conduct or expectations of a group or society. (159)

Differential association A theory of deviance that holds that violation of rules results from exposure to attitudes favorable to criminal acts. (168)

Differential justice Differences in the way social control is exercised over different groups. (171)

Formal social control Social control that is carried out by authorized agents, such as police officers, judges, school administrators, and employers. (163)

Hate crime A criminal offense committed because of the offender's bias against a race, religion, ethnic group, national origin, or sexual orientation. Also referred to as *bias crime.* (174)

Index crimes The eight types of crime reported annually by the FBI in the *Uniform Crime Reports:* murder, rape, robbery, assault, burglary, theft, motor vehicle theft, and arson. (172)

Informal social control Social control that is carried out casually by ordinary people through such means as laughter, smiles, and ridicule. (163)

Labeling theory An approach to deviance that attempts to explain why certain people are viewed as deviants while others engaged in the same behavior are not. (169)

Law Governmental social control. (164)

Obedience Compliance with higher authorities in a hierarchical structure. (161)

Organized crime The work of a group that regulates relations among criminal enterprises involved in illegal activities, including prostitution, gambling, and the smuggling and sale of illegal drugs. (173)

Professional criminal A person who pursues crime as a day-to-day occupation, developing skilled techniques and enjoying a certain degree of status among other criminals. (172)

Sanction A penalty or reward for conduct concerning a social norm. (161)

Social constructionist perspective An approach to deviance that emphasizes the role of culture in the creation of the deviant identity. (170)

Social control The techniques and strategies for preventing deviant human behavior in any society. (161)

Social disorganization theory The theory that crime and deviance are caused by the absence or breakdown of communal relationships and social institutions. (169)

Societal-reaction approach Another name for *labeling theory*. (169)

Stigma A label used to devalue members of certain social groups. (160)

Transnational crime Crime that occurs across multiple national borders. (175)

Victimization survey A questionnaire or interview given to a sample of the population to determine whether people have been victims of crime. (176)

Victimless crime A term used by sociologists to describe the willing exchange among adults of widely desired but illegal goods and services. (172)

White-collar crime Illegal acts committed by affluent, "respectable" individuals in the course of business activities. (173)

TAKING SOCIOLOGY with you

1. Describe the mechanisms of social control, both formal and informal, on your campus. Which is more effective, formal or informal control?

2. Explain the presence of both criminals and law-abiding citizens in an inner-city neighborhood in terms of the interactionist perspective.

3. Pay a visit to your local courthouse and observe a trial by jury from the point of view of a sociologist. Then describe what you saw and heard using sociological concepts.

Self-Quiz

Read each question carefully and then select the best answer.

1. Society brings about acceptance of basic norms through techniques and strategies for preventing deviant human behavior. This process is termed
   a. stigmatization.
   b. labeling.
   c. law.
   d. social control.

2. Which sociological perspective argues that people must respect social norms if any group or society is to survive?
   a. the conflict perspective
   b. the interactionist perspective
   c. the functionalist perspective
   d. the feminist perspective

3. Stanley Milgram used the word *conformity* to mean
   a. going along with peers.
   b. compliance with higher authorities in a hierarchical structure.
   c. techniques and strategies for preventing deviant human behavior in any society.
   d. penalties and rewards for conduct concerning a social norm.

4. Which sociological theory suggests that our connection to members of society leads us to conform systematically to society's norms?
   a. feminist theory
   b. control theory

   c. interactionist theory
   d. functionalist theory

5. Which of the following statements is true of deviance?
   a. Deviance is always criminal behavior.
   b. Deviance is behavior that violates the standards of conduct or expectations of a group or society.
   c. Deviance is perverse behavior.
   d. Deviance is inappropriate behavior that cuts across all cultures and social orders.

6. Which sociologist illustrated the boundary-maintenance function of deviance in his study of Puritans in 17th-century New England?
   a. Kai Erikson
   b. Émile Durkheim
   c. Robert Merton
   d. Edwin Sutherland

7. Which of the following is *not* one of the basic forms of adaptation specified in Robert Merton's anomie theory of deviance?
   a. conformity
   b. innovation
   c. ritualism
   d. hostility

8. Which sociologist first advanced the idea that an individual undergoes the same basic socialization process whether learning conforming or deviant acts?
   a. Robert Merton
   b. Edwin Sutherland
   c. Travis Hirschi
   d. William Chambliss

9. Which of the following theories contends that criminal victimization increases when communal relationships and social institutions break down?
   a. labeling theory
   b. conflict theory
   c. social disorganization theory
   d. differential association theory

10. Which of the following conducted observation research on two groups of high school males (the Saints and the Roughnecks) and concluded that social class played an important role in the varying fortunes of the two groups?
   a. Richard Quinney
   b. Edwin Sutherland
   c. Émile Durkheim
   d. William Chambliss

11. If we fail to respect and obey social norms, we may face punishment through informal or formal _____.

12. Police officers, judges, administrators, employers, military officers, and managers of movie theaters are all instruments of _____ social control.

13. Some norms are considered so important by a society that they are formalized into _____ controlling people's behavior.

14. It is important to underscore the fact that _____ is the primary source of conformity and obedience, including obedience to law.

15. _____ is a state of normlessness that typically occurs during a period of profound social change and disorder, such as a time of economic collapse.

16. Labeling theory is also called the _____ _____ approach.

17. _____ theorists view standards of deviant behavior as merely reflecting cultural norms, whereas _____ and _____ theorists point out that the most powerful groups in a society can shape laws and standards and determine who is (or is not) prosecuted as a criminal.

18. Feminists contend that prostitution and some forms of pornography are not _____ crimes.

19. Daniel Bell used the term _____ _____ to describe the process during which leadership of organized crime was transferred from Irish Americans to Jewish Americans and later to Italian Americans and others.

20. Consumer fraud, bribery, and income tax evasion are considered _____ _____ crimes.

THINKING ABOUT MOVIES

American Gypsy

This documentary sheds light on the Romani, a minority group whose members are often stereotyped as criminals.

Hurt Locker

During the Iraq War, a U.S. Army sergeant who uses unorthodox methods assumes command of a bomb squad.

Temple Grandin

An autistic woman fights for animal rights.

Pedestrians pass by a man panhandling for change in Las Vegas. The United States is a society of contrasts among great wealth, modest means, and deep poverty.

5. British sociologist Ralf Dahrendorf views social classes as groups of people who share common interests resulting from their authority relationships. Dahrendorf's ideology aligns best with which theoretical perspective?
   a. the functionalist perspective
   b. the conflict perspective
   c. the interactionist perspective
   d. sociocultural evolution

6. The respect or admiration that an occupation holds in a society is referred to as
   a. status.
   b. esteem.
   c. prestige.
   d. ranking.

7. Approximately how many out of every nine people in the United States live(s) below the poverty line established by the federal government?
   a. one
   b. two
   c. three
   d. four

8. Which sociologist has applied functionalist analysis to the existence of poverty and argues that various segments of society actually benefit from the existence of the poor?
   a. Émile Durkheim
   b. Max Weber
   c. Karl Marx
   d. Herbert Gans

9. A measure of social class that is based on income, education, and occupation is known as
   a. the objective method.
   b. stratification.
   c. socioeconomic status.
   d. the open system.

10. A plumber whose father was a physician is an example of
   a. downward intergenerational mobility.
   b. upward intergenerational mobility.
   c. downward intragenerational mobility.
   d. upward intragenerational mobility.

11. _____ is the most extreme form of legalized social inequality for individuals or groups.

12. In the _____ system of stratification, or feudalism, peasants were required to work land leased to them by nobles in exchange for military protection and other services.

13. Karl Marx viewed _____ differentiation as the crucial determinant of social, economic, and political inequality.

14. _____ _____ is the term Thorstein Veblen used to describe the extravagant spending patterns of those at the top of the class hierarchy.

15. _____ poverty is the minimum level of subsistence that no family should be expected to live below.

16. _____ poverty is a floating standard of deprivation by which people at the bottom of a society, whatever their lifestyles, are judged to be disadvantaged in comparison with the nation as a whole.

17. Sociologist William Julius Wilson and other social scientists have used the term _____ to describe the long-term poor who lack training and skills.

18. Max Weber used the term _____ _____ to refer to people's opportunities to provide themselves with material goods, positive living conditions, and favorable life experiences.

19. An open class system implies that the position of each individual is influenced by the person's _____ status.

20. _____ mobility involves changes in social position within a person's adult life.

Answers
1 (d); 2 (c); 3 (b); 4 (a); 5 (b); 6 (c); 7 (a); 8 (d); 9 (c); 10 (a); 11 Slavery; 12 estate; 13 class; 14 Conspicuous consumption; 15 Absolute; 16 Relative; 17 underclass; 18 life chances; 19 achieved; 20 Intragenerational

THINKING ABOUT MOVIES

The Fighter

Two working-class brothers strive for upward mobility in the world of professional boxing.

Pursuit of Happyness

A homeless man struggles to climb out of the underclass and make a life for his son.

Titanic

Social class pervades this story of two lovers on the ill-fated luxury liner.

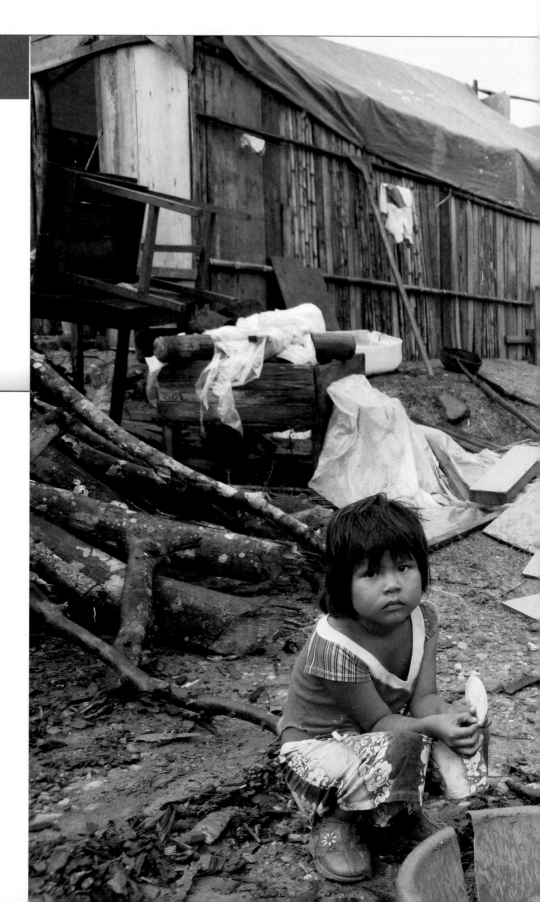

In Trinidad, Bolivia, open drains
threaten children's health.
Bolivia is a highly stratified
society in which a significant
portion of the population lives
in poverty.

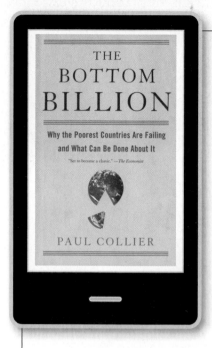

THE
BOTTOM
BILLION

Why the Poorest Countries Are Failing
and What Can Be Done About It

"Set to become a classic." —*The Economist*

PAUL COLLIER

> The third world has shrunk. For forty years the development challenge has been a rich world of one billion people facing a poor world of five billion people.... By 2015, however, it will be apparent that this way of conceptualizing development has become outdated. Most of the five billion, about 80 percent, live in countries that are indeed developing, often at amazing speed. The real challenge of development is that there is a group of countries at the bottom that are falling behind, and often falling apart.
>
> The countries at the bottom coexist with the twenty-first century, but their reality is the fourteenth century: civil war, plague, ignorance. They are concentrated in Africa and Central Asia, with a scattering elsewhere. Even during the 1990s, in retrospect the golden decade between the end of the Cold War and 9/11, incomes in this group declined by 5 percent. We must learn to turn the familiar numbers upside down: a total of five billion people who are already prosperous, or at least are on track to be so, and one billion who are stuck at the bottom.
>
> This problem matters, and not just to the billion people who are living and dying in fourteenth-century conditions. It matters to us.
>
> The twenty-first-century world of material comfort, global travel, and economic interdependence will become increasingly vulnerable to these large islands of chaos. And it matters now. As the bottom billion diverges from an increasingly sophisticated world economy, integration will become harder, not easier.
>
> And yet it is a problem denied, both by development *biz* and by development *buzz*. Development biz is run by the aid agencies and the companies that get the contracts for their projects. They will fight this thesis with the tenacity of bureaucracies endangered, because they like things the way they are. A definition of development that encompasses five billion people gives them license to be everywhere, or more honestly, everywhere but the bottom billion. At the bottom, conditions are rather rough. Every development agency has difficulty getting its staff to serve in Chad and Laos; the glamour postings are for countries such as Brazil and China. The World Bank has large offices in every major middle-income country but not a single person resident in the Central African Republic....
>
> What of the governments of the countries at the bottom? The prevailing conditions bring out extremes. Leaders are sometimes psychopaths who have shot their way to power, sometimes crooks who have bought it, and sometimes brave people who, against the odds, are trying to build a better future. Even the appearance of modern government in these states is sometimes a façade, ... the government of Somalia continued to be officially "represented" in the international arena for years after Somalia ceased to have a functioning government in the country itself. So don't expect the governments of the bottom billion to unite in formulating a practical agenda.

The real challenge of development is that there is a group of countries at the bottom that are falling behind, and often falling apart.

(Collier 2007:3–5) Additional information about this excerpt can be found on the Online Learning Center at www.mhhe.com/schaefer13e.

How should we help the poor—not just a poor household or a poor neighborhood, but hundreds of millions of the world's poorest people? For most of his adult life, Paul Collier, an economist at Oxford University, has pondered this question. In this excerpt from his book *The Bottom Billion: Why the Poorest Countries Are Failing and What Can Be Done About It,* Collier outlines the magnitude of the challenge. He thinks that the answer lies in avoiding the traps that developing countries often fall into: wasteful depletion of their natural resources, ineffective government, prolonged internal conflict, protracted wars, and insufficient economic development.

In this chapter we will consider social inequality both *between* developing and developed nations and *within* them. Inequality exists within all countries, not just in the United States. Even in the poorest countries, Collier writes, the very wealthy rub shoulders with the very poor.

What economic and political conditions explain the divide between rich nations and poor? Within developing nations, how are wealth and income distributed, and how much opportunity does the average worker have to move up the social ladder? How do race and gender affect social mobility in these countries? In this chapter we will focus on global inequality, beginning with the global divide. We will consider the impact of colonialism and neocolonialism, globalization, the rise of multinational corporations, and the trend toward modernization. Then we will focus on stratification within nations, in terms of the distribution of wealth and income as well as social mobility. In a special case study, we will look closely at social stratification in Mexico, including the social impact of race and gender and the economic effects of industrialization. The chapter closes with a Social Policy section on welfare reform in Europe and North America.

The Global Divide

FIGURE **10-1** FUNDAMENTAL GLOBAL INEQUALITY   215

Global Inequality

In some parts of the world, the people who have dedicated their lives to fighting starvation refer to what they call "coping mechanisms"—ways in which the desperately poor attempt to control their hunger. Eritrean women will strap flat stones to their stomachs to lessen their hunger pangs. In Mozambique, people eat the grasshoppers that have destroyed their crops, calling them "flying shrimp." Though dirt eating is considered a pathological condition (called *pica*) among the well-fed, the world's poor eat dirt to add minerals to their diet. And in many countries, mothers have been known to boil stones in water, to convince their hungry children that supper is almost ready. As they hover over the pot, these women hope that their malnourished children will fall asleep (McNeil 2004).

Around the world, inequality is a significant determinant of human behavior, opening doors of opportunity to some and closing them to others. Indeed, disparities in life chances are so extreme that in some places, the poorest of the poor may not be aware of them. Western media images may have circled the globe, but in extremely depressed rural areas, those at the bottom of society are not likely to see them.

A few centuries ago, such vast divides in global wealth did not exist. Except for a very few rulers and landowners, everyone in the world was poor. In much of Europe, life was as difficult as it was in Asia or South America. This was true until the Industrial Revolution and rising agricultural productivity produced explosive economic growth. The resulting rise in living standards was not evenly distributed across the world.

Figure 10-1 compares the industrialized nations of the world to the developing nations. Using total population as a yardstick, we see that the developing countries have more than their fair

Note: In this comparison, industrialized nations include the United States and Canada, Japan, western Europe, and Australasia. Developing nations include Africa, Asia (except for Japan), Latin America, eastern Europe, the Caribbean, and the Pacific.
Source: Adapted from Sutcliffe 2002:18.

Think about It
What is the relationship between health spending, disease, and deaths of children? Between CO_2 emissions, income, and exports?

share of rural population, as well as of total births, disease, and childhood deaths. At the same time, the industrialized nations of the world, with a much smaller share of total population, have much more income and exports than the developing nations. Industrialized nations also spend more on health and the military than other nations, and they emit more carbon dioxide (CO_2; Sachs 2005; Sutcliffe 2002).

What do we stand in line for? People's needs and desires differ dramatically depending on where they live. On the left, eager customers line up outside a store in New York City to purchase the newly released version of X-Box 360. On the right, residents of Ethiopia line up to receive water.

Self-Quiz

Read each question carefully and then select the best answer.

1. The maintenance of political, social, economic, and cultural domination over a people by a foreign power for an extended period is referred to as
   a. neocolonialism.
   b. government-imposed stratification.
   c. colonialism.
   d. dependency.

2. In viewing the global economic system as divided between nations that control wealth and those that are controlled and exploited, sociologist Immanuel Wallerstein draws on the
   a. functionalist perspective.
   b. conflict perspective.
   c. interactionist perspective.
   d. dramaturgical approach.

3. Which of the following nations would Immanuel Wallerstein classify as a *core* country within the world economic system?
   a. Germany
   b. South Korea
   c. Ireland
   d. Mexico

4. Which sociological perspective argues that multinational corporations can actually help the developing nations of the world?
   a. the interactionist perspective
   b. the feminist perspective
   c. the functionalist perspective
   d. the conflict perspective

5. Which of the following terms is used by contemporary social scientists to describe the far-reaching process by which peripheral nations move from traditional or less developed institutions to those characteristic of more developed societies?
   a. dependency
   b. globalization
   c. industrialization
   d. modernization

6. In at least 24 nations around the world, the most affluent 10 percent receives at least what percentage of all income?
   a. 20 percent
   b. 30 percent
   c. 40 percent
   d. 50 percent

7. Karuna Chanana Ahmed, an anthropologist from India who has studied developing nations, calls which group the most exploited of oppressed people?
   a. children
   b. women
   c. the elderly
   d. the poor

8. Which of the following terms is used to refer to Mexico's large, impoverished majority, most of whom have brown skin and a mixed racial lineage due to intermarriage?
   a. *criollo*
   b. *indio*
   c. *mestizo*
   d. *zapatista*

9. In Mexico, women now constitute what percentage of the labor force?
   a. 15 percent
   b. 23 percent
   c. 34 percent
   d. 46 percent

10. Which of the following terms refers to the foreign-owned factories established just across the border in Mexico, where the companies that own them don't have to pay taxes or provide insurance or benefits for their workers?
    a. *maquiladoras*
    b. *hombres*
    c. *mujeres*
    d. *toreadors*

11. Colonial domination established patterns of economic exploitation leading to former colonies remaining dependent on more industrialized nations. Such continuing dependence and foreign domination are referred to as _____.

12. According to Immanuel Wallerstein's analysis, the United States is at the _____ while neighboring Mexico is on the _____ of the world economic system.

13. Wallerstein's world systems analysis is the most widely used version of _____ theory.

14. _____ factories are factories found throughout the developing world that are run by multinational corporations.

15. As _____ industries become a more important part of the international marketplace, many companies have concluded that the low costs of overseas operations more than offset the expense of transmitting information around the world.

16. Viewed from a(n) _____ perspective, the combination of skilled technology and management provided by multinationals and the relatively cheap labor available in developing nations is ideal for a global enterprise.

17. In 2000 the United Nations launched the _____ _____; its objective is to eliminate extreme poverty worldwide by the year 2015.

18. Modernization theory reflects the _____ perspective.

19. At the top of the color hierarchy in Mexico are the _____, the 10 percent of the population who are typically White, well-educated members of the business and intellectual elites, and who have familial roots in Spain.

20. The term _____ refers to the area of a common culture along the border between Mexico and the United States.

THINKING ABOUT MOVIES

The End of Poverty?

This documentary asks whether we can close the gap between rich and poor nations by redistributing the world's wealth.

Hotel Rwanda

A hotel becomes a safe haven from the Rwandan genocide.

Slumdog Millionaire

Authorities question a young man's victory on India's version of Who Wants to Be a Millionaire? because of his low socioeconomic status.

In Boise, Idaho, proud new citizens take the oath of allegiance during their naturalization ceremony. U.S. society is becoming increasingly diverse as immigrants from around the world bring their skills, languages, and cultures with them to their new home.

Racial and Ethnic Inequality 11

35 years after the end of the Vietnam War, sharp differences of opinion remain among Vietnamese Americans, especially the older ones, concerning the war and the present government of Vietnam (Pfeifer 2008).

Korean Americans At over 1.3 million, the population of Korean Americans now exceeds that of Japanese Americans. Yet Korean Americans are often overshadowed by other groups from Asia.

Today's Korean American community is the result of three waves of immigration. The initial wave arrived between 1903 and 1910, when Korean laborers migrated to Hawai'i. The second wave followed the end of the Korean War in 1953; most of those immigrants were wives of U.S. servicemen and war orphans. The third wave, continuing to the present, has reflected the admissions priorities set up in the 1965 Immigration Act. These well-educated immigrants arrive in the United States with professional skills. Yet because of language difficulties and discrimination, many must settle at least initially for positions of lower responsibility than those they held in Korea and must suffer through a period of disenchantment. Stress, loneliness, and family strife may accompany the pain of adjustment.

In the early 1990s, the apparent friction between Korean Americans and another subordinate racial group, African Americans, attracted nationwide attention. Conflict between the two groups was dramatized in Spike Lee's 1989 movie *Do the Right Thing*. The situation stemmed from Korean Americans' position as the latest immigrant group to cater to the needs of inner-city populations abandoned by those who have moved up the economic ladder. This type of friction is not new; generations of Jewish, Italian, and Arab merchants have encountered similar hostility from what to outsiders seems an unlikely source—another oppressed minority (Kim 1999).

Japanese Americans Approximately 100,000 Japanese Americans live in the United States. As a people, they are relatively recent arrivals. In 1880, only 148 Japanese lived in the United States, but by 1920 there were more than 110,000. Japanese immigrants—called the *Issei* (pronounced EE-say), or first generation—were usually males seeking employment opportunities. Many Whites saw them (along with Chinese immigrants) as a "yellow peril" and subjected them to prejudice and discrimination.

In 1941, the attack on Hawai'i's Pearl Harbor by Japan had severe repercussions for Japanese Americans. The federal government decreed that all Japanese Americans on the West Coast must leave their homes and report to "evacuation camps." In effect, Japanese Americans became scapegoats for the anger that other people in the United States felt concerning Japan's role in World War II. By August 1943, in an unprecedented application of guilt by virtue of ancestry, 113,000 Japanese Americans had been forced into hastily built camps. In striking contrast, only a few German Americans and Italian Americans were sent to evacuation camps (Hosokawa 1969).

In 1983, a federal commission recommended government payments to all surviving Japanese Americans who had been held in detention camps. The commission reported that the detention was motivated by "race prejudice, war hysteria, and a failure of political leadership." It added that "no documented acts of espionage, sabotage, or fifth-column activity were shown to have been committed" by Japanese Americans. In 1988, President Ronald Reagan signed the Civil Liberties Act, which required the federal government to issue individual apologies for all violations of Japanese Americans' constitutional rights, and established a $1.25 billion trust fund to pay reparations to the approximately 77,500 surviving Japanese Americans who had been interned (Department of Justice 2000).

Arab Americans

Arab Americans are immigrants, and their descendants, from the 22 nations of the Arab world. As defined by the League of Arab States, these are the nations of North Africa and what is popularly known as the Middle East, including Lebanon, Syria, Palestine, Morocco, Iraq, Saudi Arabia, and Somalia. Not all residents of those countries are Arab; for example, the Kurds, who live in northern Iraq, are not Arab. And some Arab Americans may have immigrated to the United States from non-Arab countries such as Great Britain or France, where their families have lived for generations.

The Arabic language is the single most unifying force among Arabs, although not all Arabs, and certainly not all Arab Americans, can read and speak Arabic. Moreover, the language has evolved over the centuries so that people in different parts of the Arab world speak different dialects. Still, the fact that the Koran (or Qur'an) was originally written in Arabic gives the language special importance to Muslims, just as the Torah's composition in Hebrew gives that language special significance to Jews.

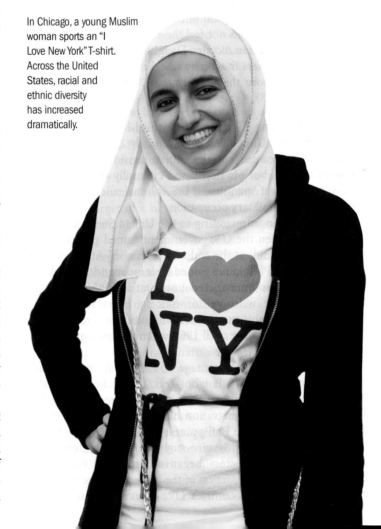

In Chicago, a young Muslim woman sports an "I Love New York" T-shirt. Across the United States, racial and ethnic diversity has increased dramatically.

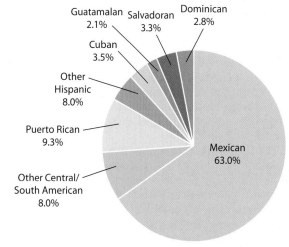

Notes: Roman/Eastern Catholic includes Roman Catholic, Maronite, and Mel
kite (Greek Catholic); Eastern Orthodox includes Antiochian, Syrian, Greek,
and Coptic; Muslim includes Sunni, Shi'a, and Druze.
Source: Arab American Institute 2010, based on 2002 Zogby International Survey.

Unlike Arabs in other parts of the world, most Arab Americans are Christian.

Note: "Other Hispanic" includes Spanish Americans and Latinos identified as
mixed ancestry as well as other Central and South Americans not otherwise
indicated by specific country.
Source: 2010 census data in Ennis et al. 2011:33.

> **Think about It**
> Do Hispanic Americans really have a common identity?

Estimates of the size of the Arab American community differ widely. By some estimates, up to 3 million people of Arab ancestry reside in the United States. Among those who identify themselves as Arab Americans, the most common country of origin is Lebanon, followed by Syria, Egypt, and Palestine. In 2000, these four countries of origin accounted for two-thirds of all Arab Americans. Their rising numbers have led to the development of Arab retail centers in several cities, including Dearborn and Detroit, Michigan; Los Angeles; Chicago; New York City; and Washington, D.C.

As a group, Arab Americans are extremely diverse. Many families have lived in the United States for several generations; others are foreign born. Their points of origin range from the metropolis of Cairo, Egypt, to the rural villages of Morocco. Despite the stereotype, most Arab Americans are *not* Muslim (Figure 11-6). Nor can Arab Americans be characterized as having a specific family type, gender role, or occupational pattern (David 2004, 2008).

Despite this great diversity, profiling of potential terrorists at airports has put Arab and Muslim Americans under special surveillance. For years, a number of airlines and law enforcement authorities have used appearance and ethnic-sounding names to identify and take aside Arab Americans and search their belongings. After the terrorist attacks of September 2001, criticism of this practice declined as concern for the public's safety mounted.

Latinos

Together, the various groups included under the general category *Latinos* represent the largest minority in the United States. There are more than 50 million Hispanics in this country, including 30 million Mexican Americans, more than 4 million Puerto

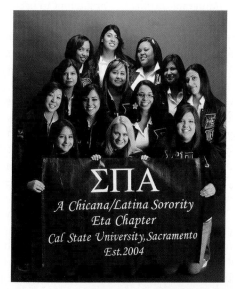

Ricans, and smaller numbers of Cuban Americans and people of Central and South American origin (Figure 11-7). The latter group represents the fastest-growing and most diverse segment of the Hispanic community.

According to Census Bureau data, the Latino population now outnumbers the African American population in 6 of the 10 largest cities of the United States: Los Angeles, Houston, Phoenix, San Diego, Dallas, and San Antonio. Hispanics are now the majority of residents in cities such as Miami, Florida; El Paso, Texas; and Santa Ana, California. The rise in the Hispanic population of the United States—fueled by comparatively high birthrates and levels of immigration—has intensified debates over public policy issues such as bilingualism and immigration. Coincidentally, these discussions are taking place just as Latinos are beginning to flex their muscles as voters (Box 11-2).

The various Latino groups share a heritage of Spanish language and culture, which can cause serious problems in their assimilation. An intelligent student whose first language is Spanish may be presumed slow or even unruly by English-speaking schoolchildren, and frequently by English-speaking teachers as well. The labeling of Latino children as underachievers, as learning disabled, or as emotionally disturbed can act as a self-fulfilling prophecy for some children. Bilingual education aims at easing the educational difficulties experienced by Hispanic children and others whose first language is not English.

The educational difficulties of Latino students certainly contribute to Hispanics' generally low economic status. In 2008, about 17 percent of all Hispanic households earned

11-2 Latinos in the Voting Booth

Over the past 40 years, the two major political parties have slowly acknowledged Latinos as a force at the ballot box. The rapid growth of the Hispanic population, together with policies that facilitate voting by non-English speakers, underlie this shift.

In 1975, Congress moved to recognize the multilingual background of the U.S. population. Federal law now requires bilingual or even multilingual ballots in voting districts where at least 10,000 people or 5 percent of the voting-age population do not speak English.

These voting reforms have not had the impact many advocates hoped, however, and turnout remains poor. Hispanics are interested in voting, but many are ineligible because they are not citizens. Thus, in the 2008 presidential election, Hispanics accounted for 15.4 percent of the total U.S. population but only 9.5 percent of the eligible electorate.

Apathy is another hurdle to voter participation. Like African Americans, many Latinos resent the fact that political movers and shakers seem to recognize their existence only once every four years. Between major elections, they hear little except from Latino elected officials.

Like African Americans, many Latinos resent the fact that political movers and shakers seem to recognize their existence only once every four years.

Although national surveys show that Latino policy concerns mirror those of the general electorate—the economy, education, health care, national security, the environment, and energy—there is one exception. Immigration policy usually ranks among Latinos' top five or six concerns. Latinos want less restrictive immigration laws that will speed up the immigration and naturalization process. Non-Hispanics tend to see immigration as either an economic threat or a national security concern.

The potential for a stronger Latino political presence is great. In anticipation of a larger turnout, both political parties are now nominating more Hispanic candidates. As a rule, Democrats have been more successful than Republicans in attracting the Hispanic vote. In the 2010 congressional elections, 60 percent of Latino voters backed Democratic candidates, compared to 37 percent of Whites.

LET'S DISCUSS

1. Do you vote in a community where polling places offer multilingual ballots? If so, do the names on the ballot mirror the community's multiethnic background?
2. If you were a campaign worker, how would you go about appealing to the Latino vote?

Sources: Connelly 2008; Lopez 2010.

---

less than $15,000, compared to 11 percent of White non-Hispanic households; and the poverty rate was 25.3 percent for Hispanics, compared to 9.4 percent for White non-Hispanics. Overall, Latinos are not as affluent as White non-Hispanics, but a middle class is beginning to emerge (DeNavas-Walt et al. 2010:15, 35, 38).

Mexican Americans The largest Latino population is Mexican Americans, who can be further subdivided into those descended from residents of the territories annexed after the Mexican American War of 1848 and those who have immigrated from Mexico to the United States. The opportunity for a Mexican to earn in one hour what it would take an entire day to earn in Mexico has pushed millions of legal and illegal immigrants north.

Aside from the family, the most important social organization in the Mexican American (or Chicano) community is the church, specifically the Roman Catholic Church. This strong identification with the Catholic faith has reinforced the already formidable barriers between Mexican Americans and their predominantly White and Protestant neighbors in the Southwest. At the same time, the Catholic Church helps many immigrants to develop a sense of identity and assists their assimilation into the norms and values of the dominant culture of the United States. The complexity of the Mexican American community is underscored by the fact that Protestant churches—especially those that endorse expressive, open worship—have attracted increasing numbers of Mexican Americans.

Puerto Ricans The second-largest segment of Latinos in the United States is Puerto Ricans. Since 1917, residents of Puerto Rico have held the status of American citizens; many have migrated to New York and other eastern cities. Unfortunately, Puerto Ricans have experienced serious poverty both in the United States and on the island. Those who live in the continental United States earn barely half the family income of Whites. As a result, a reverse migration began in the 1970s, when more Puerto Ricans were leaving for the island than were coming to the mainland (Torres 2008).

Politically, Puerto Ricans in the United States have not been as successful as Mexican Americans in organizing for their rights. For many mainland Puerto Ricans—as for many residents of the island—the paramount political issue is the destiny of Puerto Rico itself: should it continue in its present commonwealth status, petition for admission to the United States as the 51st state, or attempt to become an independent nation? This question has divided Puerto Rico for decades and remains a central issue in Puerto Rican elections. In a 1998 referendum, voters supported a "none of the above" option, effectively favoring continuation of the commonwealth status over statehood or independence.

Cuban Americans Cuban immigration to the United States dates back as far as 1831, but it began in earnest following Fidel Castro's assumption of power in the Cuban revolution (1959). The first wave of 200,000 Cubans included many professionals with relatively high levels of schooling; these men and women were largely welcomed as refugees from communist tyranny. However, more recent waves of immigrants have aroused growing concern, partly because they were less likely to be skilled professionals. Throughout these waves of immigration, Cuban Americans have been encouraged to locate around the United States. Nevertheless, many continue to settle in (or return to) metropolitan Miami, Florida, with its warm climate and proximity to Cuba.

The Cuban experience in the United States has been mixed. Some detractors worry about the vehement anticommunism of Cuban Americans and the apparent growth of an organized crime syndicate that engages in the drug trade and ganglike violence. Recently, Cuban Americans in Miami have expressed concern over what they view as the indifference of the city's Roman Catholic hierarchy. Like other Hispanics, Cuban Americans are underrepresented in leadership positions within the church. Also—despite many individual success stories—as a group, Cuban Americans in Miami remain behind Whites in income, rate of employment, and proportion of professionals (Masud-Piloto 2008).

Central and South Americans Immigrants from Central and South America are a diverse population that has not been closely studied. Indeed, most government statistics treat members of this group collectively as "other," rarely differentiating among them by nationality. Yet people from Chile and Costa Rica have little in common other than their hemisphere of origin and the Spanish language—if that. The fact is, not all Central and South Americans speak Spanish. Immigrants from Brazil, for example, speak Portuguese; immigrants from French Guyana speak French; and immigrants from Suriname speak Dutch.

Racially, many of the nations of Central and South America follow a complex classification system that recognizes a multitude of color gradients. Experience with this multiracial system does not prepare immigrants to the United States for the stark Black–White racial divide that characterizes U.S. society. Beyond their diversity in color and language, immigrants from Central and South America are differentiated by social class distinctions, religious differences, urban or rural upbringings, and dialects. Some of them may come from indigenous populations, especially in Guatemala and Belize. If so, their social identity would be separate from any national allegiance.

In short, social relations among Central and South Americans, who collectively number nearly 7 million people, defy generalization. The same can be said about their relations with other Latinos and with non-Latinos. Central and South Americans do not form, nor should they be expected to form, a cohesive group. Nor do they easily form coalitions with Cuban Americans, Mexican Americans, or Puerto Ricans.

Jewish Americans

Jews constitute about 2 percent of the population of the United States. They play a prominent role in the worldwide Jewish community, because the United States has the world's largest concentration of Jews. Like the Japanese, many Jewish immigrants came to this country and became white-collar professionals in spite of prejudice and discrimination.

Anti-Semitism—that is, anti-Jewish prejudice—has often been vicious in the United States, although rarely so widespread and never so formalized as in Europe. In many cases, Jews have been used as scapegoats for other people's failures. Not surprisingly, Jews have not achieved equality in the United States. Despite high levels of education and professional training, they

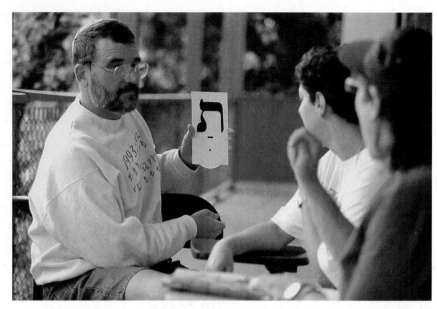

For practicing Jews, the Hebrew language is an important part of religious instruction. This teacher is showing flashcards of Hebrew alphabetic characters to deaf students.

are still conspicuously absent from the top management of large corporations (except for the few firms founded by Jews). Nonetheless, a national survey in 2009 showed that one out of four people in the United States blames "the Jews" for the financial crisis. In addition, private social clubs and fraternal groups frequently continue to limit membership to Gentiles (non-Jews), a practice upheld by the Supreme Court in the 1964 case *Bell v. Maryland* (Malhotra and Margalit 2009).

The Anti-Defamation League (ADL) of B'nai B'rith coordinates an annual tally of reported anti-Semitic incidents. Although the number has fluctuated, in 2009 the tabulation of the total reported incidents of harassment, threats, vandalism, and assaults came to 1,211. Some incidents were inspired and carried out by neo-Nazi skinheads—groups of young people who champion racist and anti-Semitic ideologies. Such threatening behavior only intensifies the fears of many Jewish Americans, who remember the Holocaust—the extermination of 6 million Jews by the Nazi Third Reich during World War II (Anti-Defamation League 2010).

As is true for other minorities discussed in this chapter, Jewish Americans face the choice of maintaining ties to their long religious and cultural heritage or becoming as indistinguishable as possible from Gentiles. Many Jews have tended to assimilate, as is evident from the rise in marriages between Jews and Christians. In marriages that occurred in the 1970s, more than 70 percent of Jews married Jews or people who converted to Judaism. In marriages since 1996, that proportion has dropped to 53 percent. This trend means that today, American Jews are almost as likely to marry a Gentile as a Jew. For many, religion is a nonissue—neither parent practices religious rituals. Two-thirds of the children of these Jewish–Gentile marriages are not raised as Jews. Finally, in 2005, two-thirds of Jews felt that the biggest threat to Jewish life was anti-Semitism; only one-third named intermarriage as the biggest threat (American Jewish Committee 2005; Sanua 2007).

White Ethnics

A significant segment of the population of the United States is made up of White ethnics whose ancestors arrived from Europe within the past century. The nation's White ethnic population includes about 50 million people who claim at least partial German ancestry, 36 million Irish Americans, 18 million Italian Americans, and 10 million Polish Americans, as well as immigrants from other European nations. Some of these people continue to live in close-knit ethnic neighborhoods, whereas others have largely assimilated and left the "old ways" behind.

Many White ethnics today identify only sporadically with their heritage. **Symbolic ethnicity** refers to an emphasis on concerns such as ethnic food or political issues rather than on deeper ties to one's ethnic heritage. It is reflected in the occasional family trip to an ethnic bakery, the celebration of a ceremonial event such as St. Joseph's Day among Italian Americans, or concern about the future of Northern Ireland among Irish Americans. Such practices are another example of the social construction of race and ethnicity. Except in cases in which new immigration reinforces old traditions, symbolic ethnicity tends to decline with each passing generation (Alba 1990; Winter 2008).

Although the White ethnic identity may be a point of pride to those who share it, they do not necessarily celebrate it at the expense of disadvantaged minorities. It is all too easy to assume that race relations are a zero-sum game in which one group gains at the expense of the other. Rather, the histories of several White ethnic groups, such as the Irish and the Italians, show that once marginalized people can rise to positions of prestige and influence (Alba 2009).

That is not to say that White ethnics and racial minorities have not been antagonistic toward one another because of economic competition—an interpretation that agrees with the conflict approach to sociology. As Blacks, Latinos, and Native Americans emerge from the lower class, they must compete with working-class Whites for jobs, housing, and educational opportunities. In times of high unemployment or inflation, any such competition can easily generate intense intergroup conflict.

In many respects, the plight of White ethnics raises the same basic issues as that of other subordinate people in the United States. How ethnic can people be—how much can they deviate from an essentially White, Anglo-Saxon, Protestant norm—before society punishes them for their willingness to be

White Americans often express their ethnicity with special celebrations, such as this Scandinavian Festival parade in Junction City, Oregon. Participants proudly display the flag of Denmark.

different? Our society does seem to reward people for assimilating, yet as we have seen, assimilation is no easy process. In the years to come, more and more people will face the challenge of fitting in, not only in the United States but around the world, as the flow of immigrants from one country to another continues to increase. In the Social Policy section that follows, we focus on global immigration and its implications for the future.

thinking CRITICALLY

Summarize the major differences (a) among Asian Indian, Vietnamese, Chinese, Japanese, and Korean Americans, or (b) among Mexican Americans, Puerto Ricans, Cuban Americans, and Central and South Americans.

social policy and Racial and Ethnic Inequality

Global Immigration

Worldwide, immigration is at an all-time high. Each year, about 191 million people move from one country to another—a number that is roughly the equivalent of the total populations of Russia and Italy. A million of these immigrants enter the United States legally, to join the 13 percent of the U.S. population who are foreign born. Perhaps more significantly, one-fourth of the U.S. labor force is foreign born—the largest proportion in at least 120 years (Passel and Cohn 2011).

Globally, these mass migrations have had a tremendous social impact. The constantly increasing numbers of immigrants and the pressure they put on job opportunities and welfare capabilities in the countries they enter raise troubling questions for many of the world's economic powers. Who should be allowed

in? At what point should immigration be curtailed (United Nations 2009)?

Looking at the Issue

The migration of people is not uniform across time or space. At certain times, war or famine may precipitate large movements of people, either temporarily or permanently. Temporary dislocations occur when people wait until it is safe to return to their home areas. However, more and more migrants who cannot make an adequate living in their home nations are making permanent moves to developed nations. The major migration streams flow into North America, the oil-rich areas of the Middle East, and the industrial economies of western Europe and Asia. Currently, seven of the world's wealthiest nations (including Germany, France, the United Kingdom, and the United States) shelter about one-third of the world's migrant population, but less than one-fifth of the world's total population. As long as disparities in job opportunities exist among countries, there is little reason to expect this international trend to reverse.

One consequence of global immigration is the emergence of **transnationals**—immigrants who sustain multiple social relationships that link their societies of origin with the society of settlement. The industrial tycoons of the early 20th century, whose power outmatched that of many nation-states, were among the world's first transnationals. Today, millions of people, many of very modest means, move back and forth between countries much as commuters do between city and suburbs. More and more of these people have dual citizenship. Rather than being shaped by allegiance to one country, their identity is rooted in their struggle to survive—and in some instances prosper—by transcending international borders (Croucher 2004; Sassen 2005). We will take a closer look at these citizens of the world in the Social Policy section of Chapter 22.

Countries that have long been a destination for immigrants, such as the United States, usually have policies regarding who has preference to enter. Often, clear racial and ethnic biases are built into these policies. In the 1920s, U.S. policy gave preference to people from western Europe, while making it difficult for residents of southern and eastern Europe, Asia, and Africa to enter the country. During the late 1930s and early 1940s, the federal government refused to lift or loosen restrictive immigration quotas in order to allow Jewish refugees to escape the terror of the Nazi regime. In line with this policy, the SS *St. Louis*, with more than 900 Jewish refugees on board, was denied permission to land in the United States in 1939. The ship was forced to sail back to Europe, where it is estimated that at least a few hundred of its passengers later died at the hands of the Nazis (Morse 1967; G. Thomas and Witts 1974).

Since the 1960s, U.S. policy has encouraged the immigration of relatives of U.S. residents as well as of people who have desirable skills. This change has significantly altered the pattern of sending nations. Previously, Europeans dominated, but for the past 40 years, immigrants have come primarily from Latin America and Asia. Thus, an ever-growing proportion of the U.S. population will be Asian or Hispanic (Figure 11-8). To a large degree, fear and resentment of growing racial and ethnic diversity is a key factor in opposition to immigration. In many nations, people are concerned that the new arrivals do not reflect their own cultural and racial heritage.

Applying Sociology

Research suggests that immigrants adapt well to life in the United States, becoming an asset to the nation's economy. In some areas, heavy immigration may drain a local community's resources, but in other areas it revitalizes the local economy.

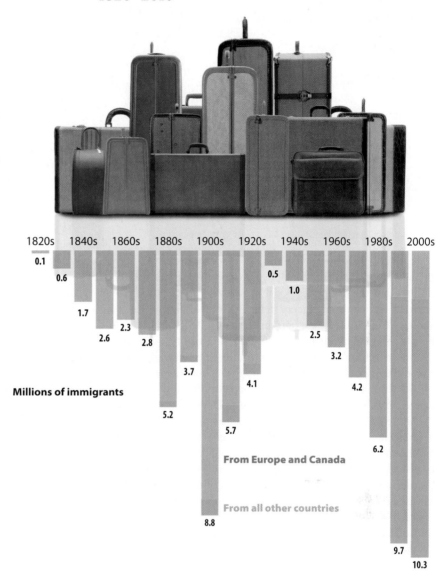

FIGURE **11-8** LEGAL MIGRATION TO THE UNITED STATES, 1820–2010

1820s 1840s 1860s 1880s 1900s 1920s 1940s 1960s 1980s 2000s
0.1
0.6
1.7
2.6 2.3
2.8
3.7
5.2
5.7
8.8
0.5
1.0
4.1
2.5
3.2
4.2
6.2
9.7
10.3

Millions of immigrants

From Europe and Canada

From all other countries

Sources: Office of Immigration Statistics 2011.

Despite people's fears, immigration performs many valuable functions. For the receiving society, it alleviates labor shortages, as it does in health care and technology in the United States. For the sending nation, migration can relieve an economy unable to support large numbers of people. Often overlooked is the large amount of money *(remittances),* that immigrants send *back* to their home nations.

Immigration can be dysfunctional as well. Although studies generally show that it has a positive impact on the receiving nation's economy, areas that accept high concentrations of immigrants may find it difficult to meet short-term social service needs. And when migrants with skills or educational potential leave developing countries, their departure can be dysfunctional for those nations. No amount of payments sent back home can make up for the loss of valuable human resources from poor nations (Borjas et al. 2006; Kochhar 2006; Sum et al. 2006).

Conflict theorists note how much of the debate over immigration is phrased in economic terms. But the debate intensifies when the arrivals are of a different racial and ethnic background from

U.S. employers' demand for low-paid labor fuels illegal immigration.

the host population. For example, Europeans often refer to "foreigners," but the term does not necessarily mean one of foreign birth. In Germany, "foreigners" refers to people of non-German ancestry, even if they were *born* in Germany; it does not refer to people of German ancestry born in another country, who may choose to return to their mother country. Fear and dislike of "new" ethnic groups divides countries throughout the world.

The feminist perspective pays special attention to the role that women play in global immigration. Immigrant women face all the challenges that immigrant men do, and some additional ones. Typically, they bear the responsibility for obtaining services for their families, particularly their children. Because the men are likely to be consumed with work, the women are left to navigate through the bureaucratic tangle of schools, city services, and medical facilities, as well as the unfamiliar stores and markets they must visit to feed their families. Women who need special medical services or are victims of domestic violence are often reluctant to seek outside help. Yet they are more likely than the men to serve as the liaison between their households and community and religious associations. Also, because many new immigrants view the United States as a dangerous place to raise a family, women must be especially watchful over their children's lives (Hondagneu-Sotelo 2003).

Initiating Policy

The long border with Mexico provides ample opportunity for illegal immigration into the United States. Throughout the 1980s, the public perception that the United States had lost control of its borders grew. Feeling pressure for immigration control, Congress ended a decade of debate by approving the Immigration Reform and Control Act of 1986. The act marked a historic change in the nation's immigration policy. For the first time, the hiring of illegal aliens was outlawed, and employers caught violating the law became subject to fines and even prison sentences. Just as significant a change was the extension of amnesty and legal status to many illegal immigrants already living in the United States. More than 20 years later, however, the act appears to have had mixed results. Substantial numbers of illegal immigrants continue to enter the country each year, with an estimated 11 million or more present at any given time—a marked increase since 2000, when their number was estimated at close to 8 million (Passel and Cohn 2011).

In 2010, frustrated by the continuing flow of illegal immigrants across the Mexican border, Arizona enacted a law empowering police to detain without authorization people whom they reasonably suspect of being illegal immigrants and to verify their immigration status. Immediately, opponents charged that the new law would lead to racial profiling. Legal experts questioned whether state enforcement of immigration law was constitutional. Although implementation of the law has been problematic, it has highlighted the resolve of those seeking to tighten control of the nation's borders. It has also galvanized those seeking to reform the nation's immigration law.

Recently, immigrants have staged massive marches to pressure Congress to speed the naturalization process and develop ways for illegal immigrants to gain legal residency. Counterdemonstrations by those who oppose illegal immigration have called for more resources with which to detect and deport illegal immigrants and to strengthen the U.S.–Mexican border. Despite this widespread public dissatisfaction with the nation's immigration policy, little progress has been made. Congress has had difficulty reaching a bipartisan compromise that pleases both sides: both supporters of strict social control and those who would allow illegal immigrants to remain in the country legally, under some circumstances.

The entire world feels the overwhelming impact of globalization on immigration patterns. The European Union agreement of 1997 gave the governing commission authority to propose a Europe-wide policy on immigration. An EU policy that allows residents of one EU country to live and work in another EU country is expected to complicate efforts by sending nations, such as Turkey, to become members of the EU. Immigrants from Turkey's predominantly Muslim population are not welcome in many EU countries (Denny 2004).

In the wake of the attacks of September 11, 2001, on the World Trade Center and the Pentagon, immigration procedures were complicated by the need to detect potential terrorists. Illegal immigrants especially, but even legal immigrants, have felt increased scrutiny by government officials around the world. For would-be immigrants to many nations, the wait to receive the right to enter a country—even to join relatives—has increased substantially, as immigration officials scrutinize more closely what were once routine applications.

The intense debate over immigration reflects deep value conflicts in the cultures of many nations. One strand of our culture, for example, has traditionally emphasized egalitarian principles and a desire to help people in time of need. At the same time, hostility to potential immigrants and refugees—whether the Chinese in the 1880s, European Jews in the 1930s and 1940s, or Mexicans, Haitians, and Arabs today—reflects not only racial, ethnic, and religious prejudice, but a desire to maintain the dominant culture of the in-group by keeping out those viewed as outsiders.

Take the Issue with You

1. Did you or your parents or grandparents immigrate to the United States from another nation? If so, when and where did your family come from, and why?

2. On balance, do the functions of immigration to the United States outweigh the dysfunctions?

3. Do you live, work, or study with recent immigrants to the United States? If so, are they well accepted in your community, or do they face prejudice and discrimination?

Summary

The social dimensions of race and ethnicity are important factors in shaping people's lives, both in the United States and in other countries. In this chapter, we examine the meaning of race and ethnicity and study the major **racial** and **ethnic groups** of the United States.

1. A **racial group** is set apart from others by physical differences; an **ethnic group** is set apart primarily by national origin or cultural patterns.

2. When sociologists define a **minority group,** they are concerned primarily with the economic and political power, or powerlessness, of the group.

3. The meaning people attach to the physical differences between races gives social significance to race, producing **stereotypes.**

4. **Prejudice** often but not always leads to **discrimination.** Sometimes, through **color-blind racism,** prejudiced people try to use the principle of racial neutrality to defend a racially unequal status quo.

5. **Institutional discrimination** results from the normal operations of a society.

6. Functionalists point out that discrimination is both functional and dysfunctional for a society. Conflict theorists explain racial subordination through **exploitation theory.** Interactionists pose the **contact hypothesis** as a means of reducing prejudice and discrimination.

7. **Racial profiling** is any arbitrary action initiated by an authority based on race, ethnicity, or national origin rather than on a person's behavior. Based on false stereotypes of certain racial and ethnic groups, the practice is not an effective way to fight crime.

8. Four patterns describe typical intergroup relations in North America and elsewhere: **segregation, amalgamation, assimilation,** and **pluralism.** Pluralism remains more of an ideal than a reality.

9. Contemporary prejudice and discrimination against African Americans are rooted in the history of slavery in the United States.

10. Asian Americans are commonly viewed as a **model** or **ideal minority,** a false stereotype that is not necessarily beneficial to members of that group.

11. The various groups included under the general term *Latinos* represent the largest ethnic minority in the United States.

12. Worldwide, immigration is at an all-time high, fueling controversy not only in the United States but in the European Union as well. A new kind of immigrant, the **transnational,** moves back and forth across international borders in search of a better job or an education.

Key Terms

Affirmative action Positive efforts to recruit minority group members or women for jobs, promotions, and educational opportunities.   (page 244)

Amalgamation The process through which a majority group and a minority group combine to form a new group. (248)

Anti-Semitism Anti-Jewish prejudice. (257)

Apartheid A former policy of the South African government, designed to maintain the separation of Blacks and other non-Whites from the dominant Whites. (248)

Assimilation The process through which a person forsakes his or her cultural tradition to become part of a different culture. (248)

Black power A political philosophy, promoted by many younger Blacks in the 1960s, that supported the creation of Black-controlled political and economic institutions. (249)

Color-blind racism The use of the principle of race neutrality to defend a racially unequal status quo. (241)

Contact hypothesis An interactionist perspective which states that in cooperative circumstances, interracial contact between people of equal status will reduce prejudice. (246)

Discrimination The denial of opportunities and equal rights to individuals and groups because of prejudice or other arbitrary reasons. (241)

Ethnic group A group that is set apart from others primarily because of its national origin or distinctive cultural patterns. (237)

Ethnocentrism The tendency to assume that one's own culture and way of life represent the norm or are superior to all others. (240)

Exploitation theory A Marxist theory that views racial subordination in the United States as a manifestation of the class system inherent in capitalism. (245)

Genocide The deliberate, systematic killing of an entire people or nation. (247)

Glass ceiling An invisible barrier that blocks the promotion of a qualified individual in a work environment because of the individual's gender, race, or ethnicity. (242)

Institutional discrimination The denial of opportunities and equal rights to individuals and groups that results from the normal operations of a society. (244)

Minority group A subordinate group whose members have significantly less control or power over their lives than the members of a dominant or majority group have over theirs. (237)

Model, or ideal, minority A subordinate group whose members supposedly have succeeded economically, socially, and educationally despite past prejudice and discrimination, and without resorting to confrontations with Whites. (252)

Pluralism Mutual respect for one another's cultures among the various groups in a society, which allows minorities to express their cultures without experiencing prejudice. (248)

Prejudice A negative attitude toward an entire category of people, often an ethnic or racial minority. (240)

Racial formation A sociohistorical process in which racial categories are created, inhabited, transformed, and destroyed. (238)

Racial group A group that is set apart from others because of physical differences that have taken on social significance. (237)

Racial profiling Any arbitrary action initiated by an authority based on race, ethnicity, or national origin rather than on a person's behavior. (246)

Racism The belief that one race is supreme and all others are innately inferior. (240)

Segregation The physical separation of two groups of people in terms of residence, workplace, and social events; often imposed on a minority group by a dominant group. (248)

Stereotype An unreliable generalization about all members of a group that does not recognize individual differences within the group. (239)

Symbolic ethnicity An ethnic identity that emphasizes concerns such as ethnic food or political issues rather than deeper ties to one's ethnic heritage. (258)

Transnational An immigrant who sustains multiple social relationships that link his or her society of origin with the society of settlement. (259)

White privilege Rights or immunities granted to people as a particular benefit or favor simply because they are White. (243)

TAKING SOCIOLOGY with you

1. Consider one or more jobs you have had, or an occupation you aspire to. How diverse is the staff you worked or would work with? What about your clients or customers? Do you expect racial and ethnic diversity to play an important role in your future career?

2. Talk with an older relative about your family's past. Did your ancestors experience prejudice or discrimination because of their race or ethnicity, and if so, in what way? Did they ever use racial or ethnic slurs to refer to people of other races or ethnicities? Have your family's attitudes toward members of other groups changed over the years, and if so, why?

3. Look up the census statistics on the racial and ethnic composition of your community. What are the predominant racial and ethnic groups? How many other groups are represented? How many members of your community are immigrants, and where do they come from?

Self-Quiz

Read each question carefully and then select the best answer.

1. Sociologists have identified five basic properties of a minority group. Which of the following is *not* one of those properties?
   a. unequal treatment
   b. physical traits
   c. ascribed status
   d. cultural bias

2. The largest racial minority group in the United States is
   a. Asian Americans.
   b. African Americans.
   c. Native Americans.
   d. Jewish Americans.

3. Racism is a form of which of the following?
   a. ethnocentrism
   b. discrimination
   c. prejudice
   d. both b and c

4. Suppose that a White employer refuses to hire a qualified Vietnamese American but hires an inferior White applicant. This decision is an act of
   a. prejudice.
   b. ethnocentrism.
   c. discrimination.
   d. stigmatization.

5. Suppose that a workplace requires that only English be spoken, even when it is not a business necessity to restrict the use of other languages. This requirement would be an example of
   a. prejudice.
   b. scapegoating.
   c. a self-fulfilling prophecy.
   d. institutional discrimination.

6. Working together as computer programmers for an electronics firm, a Hispanic woman and a Jewish man overcome their initial prejudices and come to appreciate each other's strengths and talents. This scenario is an example of
   a. the contact hypothesis.
   b. a self-fulfilling prophecy.
   c. amalgamation.
   d. reverse discrimination.

7. Intermarriage over several generations, resulting in various groups combining to form a new group, would be an example of
   a. amalgamation.
   b. assimilation.
   c. segregation.
   d. pluralism.

8. Alphonso D'Abruzzo changed his name to Alan Alda. His action is an example of
   a. amalgamation.
   b. assimilation.
   c. segregation.
   d. pluralism.

9. In which of the following racial or ethnic groups has one teenager in every six attempted suicide?
   a. African Americans
   b. Asian Americans
   c. Native Americans
   d. Latinos

10. Advocates of *Marxist class theory* argue that the basis for racial subordination in the United States lies within the capitalist economic system. Another representation of this point of view is reflected in which of the following theories?
    a. exploitation
    b. functionalist
    c. interactionist
    d. contact

11. Sociologists consider race and ethnicity to be _____ statuses, since people are born into racial and ethnic groups.

12. The one-drop rule was a vivid example of the social _____ of race—the process by which people come to define a group as a race based in part on physical characteristics, but also on historical, cultural, and economic factors.

13. _____ are unreliable generalizations about all members of a group that do not recognize individual differences within the group.

14. Sociologists use the term _____ to refer to a negative attitude toward an entire category of people, often an ethnic or racial minority.

15. When White Americans can use credit cards without suspicion and browse through stores without being shadowed by security guards, they are enjoying _____ _____.

16. _____ _____ refers to positive efforts to recruit minority group members or women for jobs, promotions, and educational opportunities.

17. After the Civil War, the Southern states passed "_____ _____" laws to enforce official segregation, and the Supreme Court upheld them as constitutional in 1896.

18. In the 1960s, proponents of _____ _____ rejected the goal of assimilation into White, middle-class society. They defended the beauty and dignity of Black and African cultures and supported the creation of Black-controlled political and economic institutions.

19. Asian Americans are held up as a(n) _____ or _____ minority group, supposedly because despite past suffering from prejudice and discrimination, they have succeeded economically, socially, and educationally without resorting to confrontations with Whites.

20. Together, the various groups included under the general category _____ represent the largest minority group in the United States.

_____

Answers

1 (d); 2 (b); 3 (c); 4 (c); 5 (d); 6 (d); 7 (a); 8 (b); 9 (c); 10 (a); 11 ascribed; 12 construction; 13 Stereotypes; 14 prejudice; 15 White privilege; 16 Affirmative action; 17 Jim Crow; 18 Black power; 19 model; ideal; 20 Latinos OR Hispanics

THINKING ABOUT MOVIES

Amreeka

A Palestinian family that has immigrated to the United States struggles with judgments against their ethnicity.

Pride

In the 1970s, an African American swim team battles racial prejudice in the United States.

Crash

The lives of multiple characters collide, revealing layers of prejudice directed at a wide range of races and ethnicities.

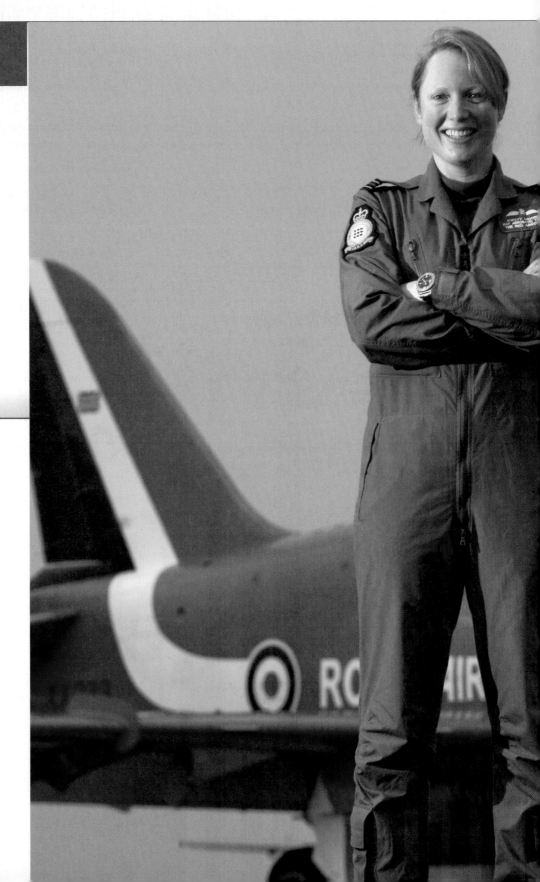

▶ INSIDE

Around the world, most occupations are dominated by either men or women. Men still predominate in military organizations, although women occupy many roles. Pictured here is Kirsty Moore, a female pilot with the RAF acrobatic display team the Red Arrows of Great Britain.

❝Her hair is in child-like pigtails, her tattoos glare through strategically placed holes in fishnet stockings, and a short skirt reveals the pink panties that match the tight T-shirt altered to provide the most potent view of breast cleavage. The image portrays the outlandish, extravagant conventions of sexuality associated with the tawdriness of "pin-up girls." And yet the salience of knee pads, shin pads, elbow pads, and helmets resist simple assessments of sexualized femininity, as do facial scowls and the brutish postures through which she powers her way around the skating rink. This roller derby girl is ready to "kick ass," and she's going to do it in a sports environment that is described as "women's space" despite large numbers of burly roaring male fans.

The recent emergence of women's roller derby onto the popular scene provides an opportunity to explore the dynamics through which alternative femininities are constructed and reinforced within a social context. . . . At a derby bout, skaters . . . make conscious efforts to disassociate their sport from ones that are "feminized softer" sports where one does not play too rough. As one skater describes it, "We are tough girls fighting their way through it. Not like other sports." Another boasts, "This is not synchronized swimming. It feels good to hit a girl and you're still standing; that's the evil part." Taunting danger and injury is normative in derby. When designated emergency rescue teams, who are present at all the bouts due to the large number of injuries, carry off skaters, skaters complain that "I just want to get back in there and skate." Derby Web sites often contain pictures of bruises presented as works of art in an Internet gallery. Skaters wear injuries like badges of honor. A young skater who is usually serene off the rink explains, "We're mean. You have a flame inside you. I think the fans know it. I think they're scared of us." Ferocious intimidation is part of the performance; skulls and crossbones adorn clothing and are embedded in logos.

Yet their skulls and crossbones have pink bows. Skaters are not striving for the image of the "gender neutral" tough athlete; this image is intentionally feminized. The bruises have fishnet patterns made from sliding across a rink floor with hosiery on one's legs. "Rink rash is sexy," says the poster. Uniforms are complemented by gold panties, Catholic schoolgirl skirts, and heavy makeup; there are pink shoelaces in their black skates. The quintessential posturing of the derby girl juxtaposes caricatured expressions of physical strength with teasing exposure of cleavage and clothes that mock conventional feminine modesty but that also serve as markers of femininity. As one skater sees it, "It wouldn't be the same to me if I were wearing pants".
. . .

One salient humorous pattern in derby is also one of the most bountiful areas for the juxtaposition of gender resistance and accommodation—the selection of a skater name. Everyone must select a skater name, such as "Harm School Teacher," "Maria Von Slap," "Calamity Jam," "Lola Fellonya," "Naturally Blood," and "Bomb Bastic," that mocks violence, sexuality, and convention while simultaneously claiming them. Names often blur the boundaries between masculine and feminine or reclaim pariah labels used to control women who are contaminating the gender order—"Wicked Wonder" or "Bitch Barbie." For some the name and character they use to skate becomes an alternate identity they can take off and put on with their skater garb. One skater said, "It definitely feels like being someone else; outfits and all." Several skaters said that they felt like a celebrity when they were in persona; several called it feeling like a "superhero" or "rock star." More than one mentioned that their persona made them feel "sexier than I ever have before." It is in sharp contrast to their daily lives, but as one confided, "I'm more like my derby self than people knew.❞

"This is not synchronized swimming. It feels good to hit a girl and you're still standing; that's the evil part."

(Finley 2010:359–360, 371–372, 377) Additional information about this excerpt can be found on the Online Learning Center at www.mhhe.com/schaefer13e.

For two years sociologist Nancy Finley attended women's flat-track roller-derby games, practices, fund-raisers, and public appearances. A fan of the sport, Finley was fascinated by the roller skaters' seemingly contradictory gender images. Through her fieldwork, which included in-depth interviews with skaters, referees, and volunteers, she learned how the women manage to observe conventional definitions of femininity while mocking them. In this excerpt from her journal article "Skating Femininity," Finley explains how "derby girls" manipulate gender meanings, embracing heightened feminism even as they exhibit the masculine values traditionally associated with violent team sports (Finley 2010; Women's Flat Track Derby Association 2011).

Obviously, women with skater names like Wicked Wonder or Bomb Bastic don't fit the conventional gender roles played by female athletes, much less by women in general. What are the accepted gender roles in today's society? Have men's and women's positions in society changed? How do gender roles differ from one culture or subculture to another? In this chapter we will study these and other questions by looking first at how various cultures, including our own, assign women and men to particular social roles. Then we will consider sociological explanations for gender stratification. We will see that around the world, women constitute an oppressed majority of the population. We'll learn that only recently have women begun to develop a collective consciousness of their oppression and the way in which their gender combines with other factors to create social inequality. Finally, we will close the chapter with a Social Policy section on the controversy over a woman's right to abortion.

Social Construction of Gender

How many airline passengers do you think are startled on hearing a female captain's voice from the cockpit? What do we make of a father who announces that he will be late for work because his son has a routine medical checkup? Consciously or unconsciously, we are likely to assume that flying a commercial plane is a *man's* job and that most parental duties are, in fact, a *woman's*. Gender is such a routine part of our everyday activities that we typically take notice only when someone deviates from conventional behavior and expectations.

Although a few people begin life with an unclear sexual identity, the overwhelming majority begin with a definite sex and quickly receive societal messages about how to behave. In fact, virtually all societies have established social distinctions between females and males that do not inevitably result from biological differences between the sexes (such as women's reproductive capabilities).

In studying gender, sociologists are interested in the gender-role socialization that leads females and males to behave differently. In Chapter 4, **gender roles** were defined as expectations regarding the proper behavior, attitudes, and activities of males and females. The application of dominant gender roles leads to many forms of differentiation between women and men. Both sexes are capable of learning to cook and sew, yet most Western societies determine that women should perform those tasks. Both men and women are capable of learning to weld and to fly airplanes, but those functions are generally assigned to men.

As we will see throughout this chapter, however, social behavior does not mirror the mutual exclusivity suggested by these gender roles. Nor are gender roles independent: in real life, the way men behave influences women's behavior, and the way women behave affects men's behavior. Thus, most people do not display strictly "masculine" or "feminine" qualities all the time. Indeed, such standards can be ambiguous. For instance, though men are supposed to be unemotional, they are allowed to become emotional when their favorite athletic team wins or loses a critical game. Yet our society still focuses on "masculine" and "feminine" qualities as if men and women must be evaluated in those terms. Despite recent inroads by women into male-dominated occupations, our construction of gender continues to define significantly different expectations for females and males (J. Howard and Hollander 1997; West and Zimmerman 1987).

Gender roles are evident not only in our work and behavior but also in how we react to others. We are constantly "doing gender" without realizing it. If the father mentioned earlier sits in the doctor's office with his son in the middle of a workday, he will probably receive approving glances from the receptionist and from other patients. "Isn't he a wonderful father?" runs through their minds. But if the boy's mother leaves *her* job and sits with the son in the doctor's office, she will not receive such silent applause.

We socially construct our behavior so as to create or exaggerate male/female differences. For example, men and women come in a variety of heights, sizes, and ages. Yet traditional norms regarding marriage and even casual dating tell us that in heterosexual couples, the man should be older, taller, and wiser than the woman. As we will see throughout this chapter, such social norms help to reinforce and legitimize patterns of male dominance.

Gender Roles in the United States

Gender-Role Socialization Male babies get blue blankets; females get pink ones. Boys are expected to play with trucks, blocks, and toy soldiers; girls receive dolls and kitchen goods. Boys must be masculine—active, aggressive, tough, daring, and dominant—but girls must be feminine—soft, emotional, sweet, and submissive. These traditional gender-role patterns have been influential in the socialization of children in the United States.

An important element in traditional views of proper "masculine" and "feminine" behavior is **homophobia,** fear of and prejudice against homosexuality. Homophobia contributes significantly to rigid gender-role socialization, since many people stereotypically associate male homosexuality with femininity and lesbianism with masculinity. Consequently, men and women who deviate from traditional expectations about gender roles are often presumed to be gay. Despite the advances made by the gay liberation movement, the continuing stigma attached to homosexuality in our culture places pressure on all males (whether gay or not) to exhibit only narrow masculine behavior and on all females (whether lesbian or not) to exhibit only narrow feminine behavior (Seidman 1994; see also Lehne 1995).

It is *adults,* of course, who play a critical role in guiding children into those gender roles deemed appropriate in a society. Parents are normally the first and most crucial agents of socialization. But other adults, older siblings, the mass media, and religious and educational institutions also exert an important influence on gender-role socialization, in the United States and elsewhere.

It is not hard to test how rigid gender-role socialization can be. Just try transgressing some gender norm—say, by smoking a cigar in public if you are female, or by carrying a purse if you are male. That was exactly the assignment given to sociology students at the University of Colorado and Luther College in Iowa. Professors asked students to behave in ways that they thought violated the norms of how a man or woman should act. The students had no trouble coming up with gender-norm transgressions (Table 12-1), and they kept careful notes on others' reactions to their behavior, ranging from amusement to disgust (Nielsen et al. 2000).

Women's Gender Roles How does a girl come to develop a feminine self-image, while a boy develops one that is masculine? In part, they do so by identifying with females and males in their families and neighborhoods and in the media. If a young girl regularly sees female television characters of all ages and body types, she is likely to grow up with a normal body image. And it will not hurt if the women she knows—her mother, sister, parents' friends, and neighbors—are comfortable with their body types, rather than constantly obsessed with their weight. In contrast, if this young girl sees only wafer-thin actresses and models on television, her self-image will be quite different. Even if she grows up to become a well-educated professional, she may secretly regret falling short of the media stereotype—a thin, sexy young woman in a bathing suit.

Television is far from alone in stereotyping women. Studies of children's books published in the United States in the 1940s, 1950s, and 1960s found that females were significantly underrepresented in central roles and illustrations. Virtually all female characters were portrayed as helpless, passive, incompetent, and

Chapter 12

of Jane Addams and Ida Wells-Barnett, but they generally worked outside the discipline, focusing on what we would now call applied sociology and social work. At the time, their efforts, while valued as humanitarian, were seen as unrelated to the research and conclusions being reached in academic circles, which of course were male academic circles (Andersen 2007; J. Howard 1999).

Intersections with Race, Class, and Other Social Factors

Contemporary feminists recognize the differential treatment of some women not only because of their gender, but also because of the intersection of their race, ethnicity, and socioeconomic status. Simply put, Whites dominate these poor, non-White women because they are non-White; men dominate them because they are women; and the affluent dominate them because they are poor. The African American feminist theorist Patricia Hill Collins (2000) has termed the convergence of social forces that contributes to the subordinate status of these low-status women the **matrix of domination** (Figure 12-1).

Gender, race, and social class are not the only sources of oppression in the United States, though they profoundly affect women and people of color. Other forms of categorization and stigmatization that might be included in the matrix are sexual orientation, religion, disability, and age. If we apply the matrix to the world as a whole, we might add citizenship status or perceived colonial or neocolonial status to the list (Winant 2006).

Though feminists have addressed themselves to the needs of minority women, these women are oppressed much more by their race and ethnicity than by their gender. The question for Latinas (Hispanic women), African American women, Asian American women, and Native American women appears to be whether they should unite with their brothers against racism or challenge them for their sexism. The answer is that our society must eradicate both sexism and racism (Beisel and Kay 2004; Breines 2007; Epstein 1999).

The discussion of gender roles among African Americans has always provoked controversy. Advocates of Black nationalism contend that feminism only distracts women from participating fully in the African American struggle. The existence of feminist groups among Blacks, in their view, simply divides the Black community, thereby serving the dominant White majority. In contrast, Black feminists such as bell hooks (1994) argue that little is to be gained by accepting the gender-role divisions of the dominant society, which place women in a separate, subservient position. Though the media commonly portray Black women in a negative light—as illiterates, welfare queens, or prostitutes—Black feminists emphasize that it is not solely Whites and the White-dominated media who focus on such negative images. Black men (most recently, Black male rap artists) have also portrayed Black women in a negative way (Raybon 1989; Threadcraft 2008).

Historically, Native Americans stand out as an exception to the patriarchal tradition in North America. At the time of the European settlers' arrival, Native American gender roles varied greatly from tribe to tribe. Southern tribes, for reasons unclear to today's scholars, were usually matriarchal and traced their descent through the mother. European missionaries, who sought to make

FIGURE **12-1**   MATRIX OF DOMINATION

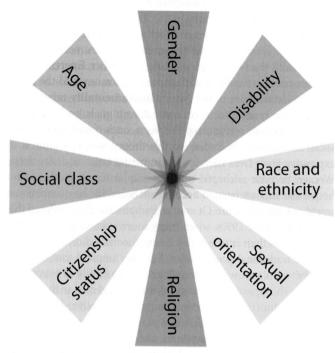

Source: Developed by author.

The matrix of domination illustrates how several social factors, including gender, social class, and race and ethnicity, can converge to create a cumulative impact on a person's social standing.

the native peoples more like Europeans, set out to transform this arrangement, which was not entirely universal. Like members of other groups, some Native American women have resisted gender stereotypes (Marubbio 2006).

Latinas are usually considered as part of either the Hispanic or feminist movements, and their distinctive experience ignored. In the past, they have been excluded from decision making in the two social institutions that most affect their daily lives: the family and the church. Particularly in the lower class, the Hispanic family suffers from the pervasive tradition of male domination. And the Catholic Church relegates women to supportive roles, while reserving the leadership positions for men (Browne 2001; De Anda 2004).

Prior to this chapter, much of our discussion has focused on the social effects of race and ethnicity, coupled with poverty, low incomes, and meager wealth. The matrix of domination highlights the confluence of these factors with gender discrimination, which we must include to fully understand the plight of women of color.

use your sociological *imagination*

Which elements of the matrix of domination privilege you? Which place you at a disadvantage?

FIGURE **12-2** GE

50   40   30

Poorest

Note: Housework includ

Source: Adapted from H

Around the world, rich c

in developing nati
is performed by w
hours for low pay, I
incomes (Chubb e

In industrialize
seen in the divisio
hold and the pay th
gender inequality
and the poor (the k
Typically, poor mei
Figure 12-2 shows,
than women.

thinkin

What are th
women acro

Women in th
of the Unite

More than 30 year
(1976:1) concluded
dence proclaiming
too literally for too I
tunities for employ
bias has limited woi
home, at the same ti
ate burden inside th

	TABLE **12-2**	SOCIOLOGICAL PERSPECTIVES ON GENDER
	Theoretical Perspective	Emphasis
summing**up**	Functionalist	Gender differentiation contributes to social stability
	Conflict	Gender inequality is rooted in the female–male power relationship
	Feminist	Women's subjugation is integral to society and social structure
	Interactionist	Gender distinctions and "doing gender" are reflected in people's everyday behavior

Interactionist Approach

While functionalists and conflict theorists who study gender stratification typically focus on macro-level social forces and institutions, interactionist researchers tend to examine gender stratification on the micro level of everyday behavior. The key to this approach is the way gender is socially constructed in everyday interactions. We "do gender" by reinforcing traditionally masculine and feminine actions. For example, a man "does masculinity" by opening a door for his girlfriend; she "does femininity" by consenting to his assistance. Obviously, the social construction of gender goes beyond these relatively trivial rituals. Interactionists recognize, too, that people can challenge traditional gender roles. A female golfer who uses the men's tees and a man who actively arranges a birthday luncheon at work are redoing gender (Deutsch 2007; West and Zimmerman 1987).

One continuing subject of investigation is the role of gender in cross-sex conversations (sometimes referred to as "cross-talk"), specifically the idea that men interrupt women more than women interrupt men. Interestingly, empirical research does not clearly support this assertion. True, people in positions of authority or status—who are much more likely to be male than female—dominate interpersonal conversations. That does not necessarily mean that women per se cannot be heard, however. Future research results may deemphasize the clichéd advice that women must speak up and focus instead on the situational structures that cast men in dominant positions (Cameron 2007; Hyde 2005; Tannen 1990).

Table 12-2 summarizes the major sociological perspectives on gender.

Women: The Oppressed Majority

Many people, both male and female, find it difficult to conceive of women as a subordinate and oppressed group. Yet take a look at the political structure of the United States: women remain noticeably underrepresented. As of mid-2011, for example, only 6 of the nation's 50 states had a female governor (Arizona, New Mexico, North Carolina, Oklahoma, South Carolina, and Washington).

Women have made slow but steady progress in certain political arenas. In 1981, out of 535 members of Congress, there were only 21 women: 19 in the House of Representatives and 2 in the Senate. In contrast, the Congress that held office in mid-2011 had 88 women: 71 in the House and 17 in the Senate. Yet the membership and leadership of Congress remain overwhelmingly male.

In October 1981, Sandra Day O'Connor was sworn in as the nation's first female Supreme Court justice. Still, no woman has ever served as president of the United States, vice president, or chief justice of the Supreme Court.

Sexism and Sex Discrimination

Just as African Americans are victimized by racism, women in our society are victimized by sexism. **Sexism** is the ideology that one sex is superior to the other. The term is generally used to refer to male prejudice and discrimination against women. In Chapter 11, we noted that Blacks can suffer from both individual acts of racism and institutional discrimination. **Institutional discrimination** was defined as the denial of opportunities and equal rights to individuals and groups that results from the normal operations of a society. In the same sense, women suffer from both individual acts of sexism (such as sexist remarks and acts of violence) and institutional sexism.

It is not simply that particular men in the United States are biased in their treatment of women. All the major institutions of our society—including the government, armed forces, large corporations, the media, universities, and the medical establishment—are controlled by men. These institutions, in their normal, day-to-day operations, often discriminate against women and perpetuate sexism. For example, if the central office of a nationwide bank sets a policy that single women are a bad risk for loans—regardless of their incomes and investments—that bank will discriminate against women in state after state. It will do so even at branches where loan officers hold no personal biases toward women, but are merely "following orders."

Our society is run by male-dominated institutions, yet with the power that flows to men come responsibility and stress. Men have higher reported rates of certain types of mental illness than women, and a greater likelihood of death due to heart attack or stroke. The pressure on men to succeed, and then to remain on top in the competitive world of work, can be especially intense. That is not to suggest that gender stratification is as damaging to men as it is to women. But it is clear that the power and privilege men enjoy are no guarantee of personal well-being.

The Status of Women Worldwide

A detailed overview of the status of the world's women, issued by the United Nations, noted that women and men live in two

SOCIO

12-1 The

The wearing of
is common to n
societies. All M
are expected to
revealing clothe
body's contour
beauty. The Kora
revealing garmer
or with members

The Prophet
women cover al
face, hands, an
woman's headco
and upper chest
ments comply w
attire; collective
hijab. Face veils
tion, however—n

In effect, the
the beauty myth
prevalent in W
themselves almo
assure themselv
physical appear
their contacts o
women will be k
intellect, and the

The veil was
movements that
against tradition
instance, in the
officials attempt
ethnic and religi
alistic goals. Tho
to wear the veil,
themselves in pu
Muslims resented

different world
pay, sexually h
because they a
where such tre
their rights are
tests. To achiev
must hold the
Development F

This critique
tries. Although
ple, Muslim cou
that perception
are exceedingly
types created by
the status of Mu

Regardless
from second-cl
world's food, bu

FIGURE 12-3 TRENDS IN U.S. WOMEN'S PARTICIPATION IN THE PAID LABOR FORCE, 1890–2009

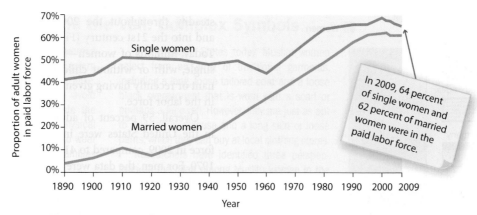

In 2009, 64 percent of single women and 62 percent of married women were in the paid labor force.

Sources: Bureau of the Census 1975, 2010a:Table 598.

employees to prove what they can do." The goal was not complete equity for women, but 40 percent representation by 2008. By 2010 the percentage stood at 10 percent (Crumley 2010).

Compensation

He works. She works. Both are physicians—a high-status occupation with considerable financial rewards. He makes $140,000. She makes $88,000.

These median annual earnings for physicians in the United States were released by the Census Bureau. They are typical of the results of the bureau's detailed study of occupations and income. Take air traffic controllers. He makes $67,000; she makes $56,000. Or housekeepers: he makes $19,000; she makes $15,000. What about teachers' assistants? He makes $20,000; she makes $15,000. Statisticians at the

bureau looked at the median annual earnings for no fewer than 821 occupations ranging from dishwasher to chief executive. After adjusting for workers' ages, education, and work experience, they came to an unmistakable conclusion: across the board, there is a substantial gender gap in the median earnings of full-time workers.

Men do not always earn more than women for doing the same work. Researchers at the Census Bureau found 2 occupations out of 821 in which women typically earn about 1 percent more income than men: hazardous materials recovery and telecommunications line installation. These two occupations employed less than 1 out of every 1,000 workers the bureau studied. Forecasting analyses show no convincing evidence that the wage gap is narrowing.

What accounts for these yawning wage gaps between men and women in the same occupation? Scholars at the Census Bureau studied the following characteristics of men and women in the same occupation:

- Age and degree of formal education
- Marital status and the presence of children at home
- Specialization within the occupation (for example, family practice versus surgical practice)
- Years of work experience
- Hours worked per year

TABLE 12-3 U.S. WOMEN IN SELECTED OCCUPATIONS: WOMEN AS A PERCENTAGE OF ALL WORKERS IN THE OCCUPATION

Underrepresented		Overrepresented	
Aircraft pilots	1%	High school teachers	55%
Firefighters	3	Cashiers	74
Civil engineers	9	Social workers	81
Police officers	16	Elementary teachers	82
Clergy	17	File clerks	82
Chefs and head cooks	21	Librarians	82
Computer systems analysts	27	Tellers	87
Dentists	30	Registered nurses	92
Coaches and umpires	32	Receptionists	92
Lawyers	32	Word processors and typists	92
Physicians	32	Child care workers	95
Mail carriers	35	Dental assistants	98

Note: Women constitute 47 percent of the entire labor force.
Source: Data for 2009 reported in Bureau of the Census 2010a:Table 615.

Taking all these factors into consideration reduced the pay gap between men and women by only 3 cents. Women still earned 80 cents for every dollar earned by men. In sum, the disparity in pay between men and women cannot be explained by pointing to women's career choices (Government Accountability Office 2003; Weinberg 2004, 2007).

Legally, sex discrimination in wage payments is difficult to prove. Witness the case of former Goodyear worker Lilly Ledbetter, who learned 19 years after she was hired that she was being paid less than men doing the same job. Ledbetter sued and was awarded damages, only to have the Supreme Court overturn the decision on the grounds that she made her claim more than six months after the first discriminatory paycheck was issued. Congress relaxed this restriction in 2009 (Pear 2009).

Not all the obstacles women face in the workplace originate with management. Unfortunately, many workers, both male and female, would prefer not to work for a woman (Box 12-2).

While women are at a disadvantage in male-dominated occupations, the same is not true for men in female-dominated occupations. Sociologist Michelle Budig (2002) examined a national

RESEARCH TODAY

12-2 Give Me a Male Boss, Please

As women increased their presence in the managerial ranks from 19.7 percent in 1972 to 51.4 percent in 2009, the desirability of having a male supervisor became a topic of casual conversation. Numerous studies suggest that compared to all the other social factors present in the workplace, the boss's gender has little effect on the nature and quality of the manager–employee relationship. However, that fact does not prevent potential workers—male or female—from preferring a male boss. National opinion polls consistently show that in general—that is, without reference to particular people—workers prefer to take orders from a man by a two-to-one margin. If anything, women are more likely than men to prefer a male supervisor.

National opinion polls consistently show that in general, workers prefer to take orders from a man by a two-to-one margin.

This preference is so strong that many people are willing to accept less pay to get a male boss. Researchers at the University of Chicago's business school asked college students who were about to graduate to consider hypothetical job opportunities at consulting firms. The positions varied in terms of their starting salary, location, paid holidays, and the boss's sex. The results showed that students' choices matched their stated preferences for salary, location, and

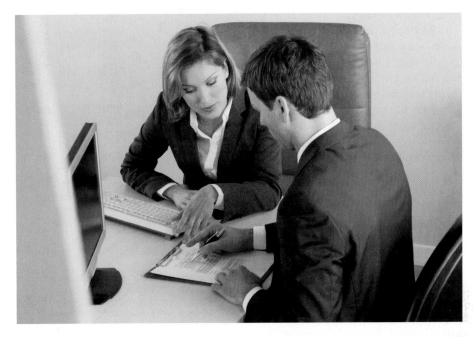

holidays. Surprisingly, the boss's sex turned out to be a far more important variable than the other three, whether students were male or female. In a variety of scenarios describing both salary and the boss's characteristics, students chose to take a 22 percent reduction in starting salary to get a male boss.

LET'S DISCUSS

1. Have you ever worked for a female boss? If so, were you comfortable taking orders from her? Did you notice any differences in the way your boss was treated, compared to men on her level?

2. What might explain the strong preference for a male boss? Do you expect this preference to remain stable or disappear over time? Explain.

Sources: Bureau of the Census 2010a:Table 615; Bureau of Labor Statistics 2003; Caruso et al. 2009; N. Gibbs 2009:31; Powell 2010; Whittaker 2006.

---

database containing career information on more than 12,000 men, collected over the course of 15 years. She found that men were uniformly advantaged in female occupations. Though male nurses, grade school teachers, and librarians may experience some scorn in the larger society, they are much more likely than women to be encouraged to become administrators. Observers of the labor force have termed this advantage for men in female-dominated occupations the *glass escalator*—quite a contrast to the glass ceiling (J. Jacobs 2003; C. L. Williams 1992, 1995).

Social Consequences of Women's Employment

Today, many women face the challenge of trying to juggle work and family. Their situation has many social consequences. For one thing, it puts pressure on child care facilities, public financing of day care, and even the fast-food industry, which provides many of the meals women used to prepare themselves. For another, it raises questions about what responsibility male wage earners have in the household.

Who does the housework when women become productive wage earners? Studies indicate that there is a clear gender gap in the performance of housework, although it has been narrowing (see Figure 12-2, page 275). Women do more housework and spend more time on child care than men do, whether on a workday or a nonworkday. Taken together, then, a woman's workday on and off the job is much longer than a man's (Sayer et al. 2004).

Sociologist Arlie Hochschild (1989, 1990, 2005) has used the phrase **second shift** to describe the double burden—work outside the home followed by child care and housework—that many women face and few men share equitably. Unfortunately, today's workplace is becoming a 24/7 virtual office thanks to the advent of mobile information technologies. As these devices take over what little personal time employees have left, the physical toll on women becomes even more burdensome.

What is life like for these women? On the basis of interviews with and observations of 52 couples over an eight-year period, Hochschild reports that the wives (and not their husbands) drive home from the office while planning domestic schedules and play dates for children—and then begin their second shift. Drawing on national studies, she concludes that women spend 15 fewer hours each week in leisure activities than their husbands. In a year, these women work an extra month of 24-hour days because of the second shift; over a dozen years, they work an extra year of 24-hour days. Hochschild found that the married couples she studied were fraying at the edges, and so were their careers and their marriages. With such reports in mind, many feminists have advocated greater governmental and corporate support for child care, more flexible family leave policies, and other reforms designed to ease the burden on the nation's families (Eby et al. 2010).

The greater amounts of time women put into caring for their children, and to a lesser degree into housework, take a special toll on women who are pursuing careers. In a survey published in the *Harvard Business Review,* about 40 percent of women indicated that they had voluntarily left work for months or years, compared to only 24 percent of men. As Figure 12-4 shows, women were much more likely than men to take time off for family reasons.

FIGURE **12-4** WHY LEAVE WORK?

	Women	Five Top Reasons for Leaving	Men
	44%	Family time	12%
	16%	Change in career	29%
	23%	Earn a degree, other training	25%
	17%	Work not enjoyable, satisfying	24%
	*	Not interested in field	18%
	17%	Moved away	*

＊ Not one of top 5 reasons

Note: Based on a representative Harris Interactive survey of "highly qualified" workers, defined as those with a graduate degree, a professional degree, or a high honors undergraduate degree.
Source: Figure adapted from Sylvia Ann Hewlett and Carolyn Burk Luce, 2005. "Off-Ramps and On-Ramps: Keeping Talented Women on the Road to Success," *Harvard Business Review,* March 2005. Copyright © 2005 by the Harvard Business School Publishing Corporation, all rights reserved. Reprinted by permission of *Harvard Business Review.*

thinking CRITICALLY

How would you argue that women have come either very far or not far enough in their labor force participation?

TREND SPOTTING

Working Mothers

Women in the labor force, either working or seeking employment, is an established fact in the United States. So too is the participation of women with young children. Such was not always the case, however. Forty years ago only 30 percent of married mothers with children under age 6 were working outside the home. By 1995—just 25 years later—that proportion had more than doubled. For married mothers, work outside the home has been the norm ever since.

This rising trend has also affected single mothers, whose labor force participation has always been high. In 1970 the proportion of single mothers of preschoolers who worked outside the home was 52 percent—22 percent higher than for married mothers of young children. Today the proportion has climbed to 72 percent.

Another way to look at these statistics is to note the narrowing gap between the two groups' labor force participation rates. Today, a married woman with at least one child under age 6 is *more likely to be working* than a single mother was in 1970.

Emergence of a Collective Consciousness

Feminism is the belief in social, economic, and political equality for women. The feminist movement of the United States was born in upstate New York, in a town called Seneca Falls, in the summer of 1848. On July 19, the first women's rights convention began, attended by Elizabeth Cady Stanton, Lucretia Mott, and other pioneers in the struggle for women's rights. This first wave of *feminists,* as they are currently known, battled ridicule and scorn as they fought for legal and political equality for women. They were not afraid to risk controversy on behalf of their cause; in 1872, Susan B. Anthony was arrested for attempting to vote in that year's presidential election.

Ultimately, the early feminists won many victories, among them the passage and ratification of the Nineteenth Amendment to the Constitution, which granted women the right to vote in national elections beginning in 1920. But suffrage did not lead to other reforms in women's social and economic position, and in the early and middle 20th century the women's movement became a much less powerful force for social change.

TAKING SOCIOLOGY TO WORK

Abigail E. Drevs, **Former Program and Volunteer Coordinator, Y-ME Illinois**

For two and a half years, Abigail Drevs served as the program and volunteer coordinator for the Illinois affiliate of Y-ME National Breast Cancer Organization. Y-ME's mission is to provide support and educational outreach through workshops and peer-led support groups, to ensure that no one faces breast cancer alone.

As the coordinator, Drevs was responsible for recruiting, training, and retaining the volunteers who staff the organization's support groups. She also presented workshops about breast cancer and how to detect it early. To make sure that services were available to all and that funding was being managed effectively, she met with community leaders and organizations, corporate partners, and medical institutions. "A typical workweek, in one word, was juggling," she says. "In a small nonprofit, few people do the work of many."

Occasionally, Drevs traveled to conferences to network with other organizations dedicated to working with certain populations of breast cancer survivors, including young women. These organizations have banded together to develop a pilot program that will address young women's concerns with intimacy and infertility after breast cancer.

In Chicago, Drevs strove to raise the awareness of breast cancer among African American women from all walks of life. "As a middle-class white woman, the issue of race had been a very academic one in my experience," she says. "I read Studs Terkel and took racial disparities curricula, but never truly understood the issues until I became immersed in the community." Drevs's experience with Y-ME helped her to understand the position of thousands of underinsured African American women in that city: "limited access to health care, distrust of the system, and the importance of their community and social networks."

Asked what insights she has drawn from her training in sociology, Drevs replies, "It reaffirmed my belief that no one perspective is the only perspective. From fundamental social theory to social conflict to developing nations, there are many ways to explain something, and oftentimes, there is something that can be gained from each perspective."

Drevs is now working for her alma mater, Dartmouth College, as the program manager for young alumni, students, and diversity at the Office of Alumni Relations. Her advice to current students of sociology: "Even if you don't major in this, make sure to take it with you wherever you go. Many of the world's problems can be traced to not communicating properly and not understanding another group's perspective. A good basis in sociology can serve you well, no matter what you do."

LET'S DISCUSS

1. Do some research on breast cancer. Does the survival rate differ among different racial and ethnic groups? What about different social classes? Why are education and early detection important?
2. Relate what you have learned about breast cancer to what you have learned about gender. What social patterns does your research illustrate?

The second wave of feminism in the United States emerged in the 1960s and came into full force in the 1970s. In part, the movement was inspired by three pioneering books arguing for women's rights: Simone de Beauvoir's *The Second Sex,* Betty Friedan's *The Feminine Mystique,* and Kate Millett's *Sexual Politics.* In addition, the general political activism of the 1960s led women—many of whom were working for Black civil rights or against the war in Vietnam—to reexamine their own powerlessness. The sexism often found within even allegedly progressive and radical political circles convinced many women that they needed to establish a movement for women's liberation (Breines 2007; Freeman 1973, 1975).

As more and more women became aware of sexist attitudes and practices, including attitudes they themselves had accepted through socialization into traditional gender roles, they began to challenge male dominance. A sense of sisterhood, much like the class consciousness that Marx hoped would emerge in the proletariat, became evident. Individual women identified their interests with those of the collectivity *women.* No longer were women happy in submissive, subordinate roles ("false consciousness" in Marxist terms).

National surveys done today, however, show that while women generally endorse feminist positions, they do not necessarily accept the label *feminist.* Some 57 percent of women considered themselves feminists in 1987; the proportion had dropped to about 25 percent in 2001. Feminism as a unified political cause, requiring one to accept a similar stance on everything from abortion to sexual harassment to pornography to welfare, has fallen out of favor. Both women and men prefer to express their views on these complex issues individually, rather than under a convenient umbrella like feminism. Still, feminism is very much alive in the growing acceptance of women in nontraditional roles, and even the basic acknowledgment that a married mother not only can work outside the home but perhaps *belongs* in the labor force. A majority of women say that given the choice, they would prefer to work outside the home rather than stay home and take care of a house and family, and about one-quarter of women prefer *Ms.* to *Miss* or *Mrs.* (Feminist Majority Foundation 2007; Robison 2002).

The women's movement has undertaken public protests on a wide range of issues. Feminists have endorsed passage of the equal rights amendment, government subsidies for child care (see Chapter 4), affirmative action for women and minorities (see Chapter 18), federal legislation outlawing sex discrimination in education (see Chapter 16), greater representation of women in government (see Chapter 17), and the right to a legal abortion (discussed in the Social Policy section of this chapter).

thinking CRITICALLY

Today, is feminism more likely to produce social change or to respond to social change? Explain.

Few issues seem to stir as much intense conflict as abortion. A critical victory in the struggle for legalized abortion in the United States came in 1973, when the Supreme Court granted women the right to terminate pregnancies. This ruling, known as *Roe v. Wade,* was based on a woman's right to privacy. The Court's decision was generally applauded by pro-choice groups, which believe women should have the right to make their own decisions about their bodies and should have access to safe and legal abortions. It was bitterly condemned by those opposed to abortion. For these pro-life groups, abortion is a moral and often a religious issue. In their view, human life begins at the moment of conception, so that its termination through abortion is essentially an act of murder.

Looking at the Issue

The debate that has followed *Roe v. Wade* revolves around prohibiting abortion altogether, or at the very least, limiting it. In 1979, for example, Missouri required parental consent for minors wishing to obtain an abortion, and the Supreme Court upheld the law. Parental notification and consent have become especially sensitive issues in the debate. Pro-life activists argue that the parents of teenagers should have the right to be notified about—and to permit or prohibit—abortions. In their view, parental authority deserves full support at a time when the traditional nuclear family is embattled. However, pro-choice activists counter that many pregnant teenagers come from troubled families where they have been abused. These young women may have good reason to avoid discussing such explosive issues with their parents.

In the United States, people support a woman's right to a legal abortion, but with reservations. According to a 2009 national survey, 46 percent say that abortion should be legal in most or all cases; 44 percent say it should be illegal in most or all cases. There is no gender difference in opinion on this issue: women are just as likely as men to embrace a right-to-life orientation (Pew Research Center 2009).

The United States is not alone in debating abortion. Latin American countries typically have the strictest measures against the practice, but occasionally changes occur. In 2007, Mexico loosened decade-old restrictions to permit legal abortions during the first three months of a pregnancy, for any reason (M. Davis 2010).

MAPPING LIFE NATIONWIDE

FIGURE **12-5**   RESTRICTIONS ON PUBLIC FUNDING FOR ABORTION

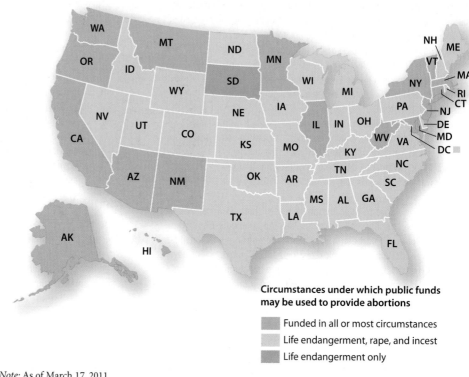

Circumstances under which public funds may be used to provide abortions

- Funded in all or most circumstances
- Life endangerment, rape, and incest
- Life endangerment only

Note: As of March 17, 2011.
Source: NARAL Pro-Choice America 2011.

Applying Sociology

Sociologists see gender and social class as the defining issues surrounding abortion. That is, the intense conflict over abortion reflects broader differences over women's position in society. Feminists involved in defending abortion rights typically believe that men and women are essentially similar. They support women's full participation in work outside the home and oppose all forms of sex discrimination. Feminists also claim that pregnancy and childbirth have been socially constructed by male-centered health care systems and patriarchal religious traditions. In contrast, most antiabortion activists believe that men and women are fundamentally different. In their view, men are best suited to the public world of work, while women are best suited to the demanding and crucial task of rearing children. These activists are troubled by women's growing participation in work outside the home, which they view as destructive to the family, and ultimately to society (Lorber 2005).

In regard to social class, the first major restriction on the legal right to terminate a pregnancy affected poor people. In 1976, Congress passed the Hyde Amendment, which banned the use of Medicaid and other federal funds for abortions. The Supreme Court upheld this legislation in 1980. State laws also restrict the use of public funds for abortions (Figure 12-5).

FIGURE **12-6**   THE GLOBAL DIVIDE ON ABORTION

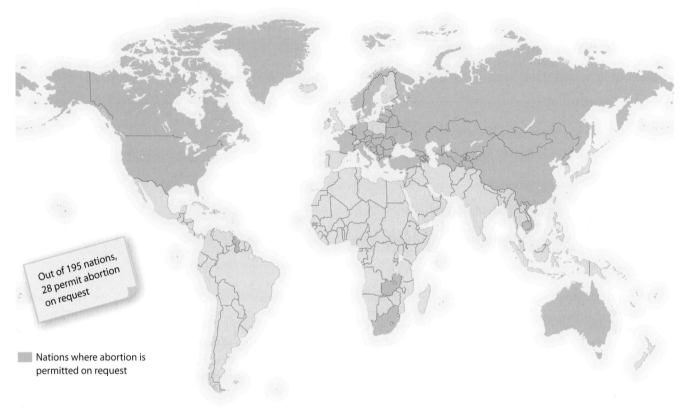

Out of 195 nations, 28 permit abortion on request

■ Nations where abortion is permitted on request

Note: Data current as of November 2007.
Source: Developed by the author based on United Nations Population Division 2007.

Another obstacle facing the poor is access to abortion providers. In the face of vocal pro-life sentiment, fewer and fewer hospitals throughout the world are allowing physicians to perform abortions, except in extreme cases. Moreover, some doctors who work in clinics, intimidated by death threats and murders, have stopped performing abortions. For poor people in rural areas, this reduction in service makes it more difficult to locate and travel to a facility that will accommodate their wishes. Viewed from a conflict perspective, this is one more financial burden that falls especially heavily on low-income women.

Finally, some antiabortion activists have charged that family-planning agencies and health care professionals are targeting young African American women for abortions. These pro-life proponents use the emotion-laden phrase "womb lynchings" to call attention to the issue. Abortion rights advocates counter that the campaign falsely portrays young Black women as naive and not in control of their own decisions (Dewan 2010).

Initiating Policy

In 1973 the Supreme Court supported the general right to terminate a pregnancy by a narrow 5–4 majority. Although pro-life activists continue to hope for an overruling of *Roe v. Wade,* they have focused in the interim on weakening the decision through tactics such as limiting the use of fetal tissue in medical experiments and prohibiting certain late-term abortions, which they term "partial-birth" abortions. The Supreme Court continues to hear cases involving such restrictions.

What is the policy in other countries? As in the United States, many European nations responded to public opinion and liberalized abortion laws beginning in the 1970s. However, many of those nations limit the procedure to the first 12 weeks of a pregnancy. (The United States, in contrast, allows abortions up to about the 24th week and beyond.) Inspired by the strong antiabortion movement in the United States, antiabortion activists in Europe have become more outspoken, especially in Great Britain, France, Portugal, Spain, Italy, and Germany.

The policies of the United States are intertwined with those of developing nations. From the 1980s through January 2009, members of Congress who opposed abortion successfully blocked foreign aid to countries that might use the funds to encourage abortion. Yet developing nations generally have the most restrictive abortion laws. As Figure 12-6 shows, it is primarily in Africa, Latin America, and parts of Asia that women are not allowed to terminate a pregnancy on request. As might be expected, illegal abortions are most common in those nations. An estimated quarter of the world's women live in countries where abortion is illegal or is permitted only if a woman's life is in jeopardy. Indeed, the rate of abortions in countries with legal restrictions on the procedure matches the rate in countries that permit it. Hence, 40 percent of abortions worldwide—about 16 million procedures each year—are performed illegally (P. Baker 2009; Guttmacher Institute 2008).

Take the Issue with You

1. How easy do you think it is for a young adult woman to obtain an abortion? What do you think should be the first step she takes in considering one?

2. Do you think teenage girls should be required to get their parents' consent before having an abortion? Why or why not?

3. Under what circumstances should abortions be allowed? Explain your reasoning.

MASTERING THIS CHAPTER

Summary

Gender is an ascribed status that provides a basis for social differentiation. This chapter examines the social construction of gender, theories of stratification by gender, women as an oppressed majority group, women in the workforce of the United States, and the emergence of a collective consciousness.

1. In the United States, the social construction of gender continues to define significantly different expectations for females and males.

2. **Gender roles** show up in our work and behavior and in how we react to others. Throughout history, these roles have restricted women much more than they have men.

3. Though men may exhibit a variety of different gender roles, called **multiple masculinities,** society reinforces their traditional role of dominating women.

4. Anthropological research points to the importance of cultural conditioning in defining the social roles of males and females.

5. Functionalists maintain that sex differentiation contributes to overall social stability, but conflict theorists charge that the relationship between females and males is one of unequal power, with men dominating women. This dominance shows up in people's everyday interactions.

6. Many women experience differential treatment, not only because of their gender but because of their race, ethnicity, and social class as well. Patricia Hill Collins has termed this convergence of social forces the **matrix of domination.**

7. As one example of their micro-level approach to the study of gender stratification, interactionists have analyzed men's verbal dominance over women through conversational interruptions.

8. Women around the world live and work with pervasive **sexism** and **institutional discrimination.**

9. In the United States today, almost as many women as men participate in the paid labor force, but women are underrepresented in managerial positions and underpaid compared to men in the same jobs.

10. As women have taken on more and more hours of paid employment outside the home, they have been only partially successful in getting their husbands to take on more homemaking duties, including child care.

11. Many women agree with the positions of the feminist movement but reject the label *feminist.*

12. The issue of abortion has bitterly divided the United States (as well as other nations), pitting pro-choice activists against pro-life activists.

Key Terms

Expressiveness Concern for the maintenance of harmony and the internal emotional affairs of the family.   (page 271)

Feminism The belief in social, economic, and political equality for women.   (278)

Gender role Expectations regarding the proper behavior, attitudes, and activities of males and females.   (267)

Glass ceiling An invisible barrier that blocks the promotion of a qualified individual in a work environment because of the individual's gender, race, or ethnicity.   (275)

Homophobia Fear of and prejudice against homosexuality.   (267)

Institutional discrimination The denial of opportunities and equal rights to individuals and groups that results from the normal operations of a society.   (273)

Instrumentality An emphasis on tasks, a focus on more distant goals, and a concern for the external relationship between one's family and other social institutions.   (271)

Matrix of domination The cumulative impact of oppression because of race and ethnicity, gender, and social class, as well as religion, sexual orientation, disability, age, and citizenship status.   (272)

Multiple masculinities A variety of male gender roles, including nurturing-caring and effeminate-gay roles, that men may play along with their more pervasive traditional role of dominating women.   (269)

Second shift The double burden—work outside the home followed by child care and housework—that many women face and few men share equitably.   (277)

Sexism The ideology that one sex is superior to the other.   (273)

1. For a day or two, watch for examples of people "doing gender" on your campus. Record your sightings in a journal and compare them with those of your classmates.

2. Find out what percentage of the faculty members at your college are women. What percentage of the women has tenure, compared to the men? What percentage holds full professorships? Do the percentages vary much from one department to another, and if so, why?

3. Use your school's alumni network to get in touch with graduates who have entered the workforce. Are mothers of young children having difficulty balancing work and parenting? Do both men and women feel they have a chance to get ahead? Are both men and women well compensated?

Self-Quiz

Read each question carefully and then select the best answer.

1. Both males and females are physically capable of learning to cook and sew, yet most Western societies determine that women should perform these tasks. This illustrates the operation of
   a. gender roles.
   b. sociobiology.
   c. homophobia.
   d. comparable worth.

2. An important element in traditional views of proper "masculine" and "feminine" behavior is fear of homosexuality. This fear, along with accompanying prejudice, is referred to as
   a. lesbianism.
   b. femme fatalism.
   c. homophobia.
   d. claustrophobia.

3. The most crucial agents of socialization in teaching gender roles in the United States are
   a. peers.
   b. teachers.
   c. media personalities.
   d. parents.

4. Research by anthropologists Margaret Mead and Peggy Reeves Sanday has shown that
   a. biology is the most important factor in determining the social roles of males and females.
   b. cultural conditioning is the most important factor in determining the social roles of males and females.
   c. biology and cultural conditioning have an equal impact in determining the social roles of males and females.
   d. biology and cultural conditioning have a negligible impact in determining the social roles of males and females.

5. Which sociological perspective acknowledges that it is not possible to change gender roles drastically without dramatic revisions in a culture's social structure?
   a. functionalist perspective
   b. conflict perspective
   c. interactionist perspective
   d. both a and b

6. The term *sexism* is generally used to refer to
   a. female prejudice and discrimination against men.
   b. male prejudice and discrimination against women.
   c. female discrimination against men and male discrimination against women equally.
   d. discrimination between members of the same sex.

7. Which of these statements is true?
   a. More boys than girls take AP exams.
   b. Women in the United States are more likely than men to attend college.
   c. Women in the United States are less likely than men to obtain doctoral degrees.
   d. all of the above

8. Which sociological perspective distinguishes between instrumental and expressive roles?
   a. functionalist perspective
   b. conflict perspective
   c. interactionist perspective
   d. labeling theory

9. Contemporary feminists recognize the differential treatment of some women not only because of their gender, but also because of their
   a. race.
   b. ethnicity.
   c. socioeconomic status.
   d. all of the above

10. The sense of sisterhood that became evident during the rise of the contemporary feminist movement resembled the Marxist concept of
    a. alienation.
    b. dialectics.
    c. class consciousness.
    d. false consciousness.

11. Talcott Parsons and Robert Bales contend that women take the _____, emotionally supportive role in the family and that men take the _____, practical role, with the two complementing each other.

12. A significant component of the _____ approach to gender stratification draws on feminist theory.

13. It is not simply that particular men in the United States are biased in their treatment of women. All the major institutions of our society—including the government, the armed forces, large corporations, the media, the universities, and the medical establishment—are controlled by men. This situation is symptomatic of institutional _____.

14. Women from all groups and men from minority groups sometimes encounter attitudinal or organizational bias that prevents them from reaching their full potential. This is known as the _____ _____.

15. Sociologist Arlie Hochschild has used the phrase _____ _____ to describe the double burden that many women face and few men share equitably: work outside the home followed by child care and housework.

16. Within the general framework of their theory, _____ sociologists maintain that gender differentiation has contributed to overall social stability.

17. Through the rise of contemporary _____, women are developing a greater sense of group solidarity.

18. _____ contributes significantly to rigid gender-role socialization, since many people stereotypically associate male homosexuality with femininity and lesbianism with masculinity.

19. The term _____ _____ _____ was coined by feminist theorist Patricia Hill Collins to describe the convergence of social forces that contributes to the subordinate status of poor, non-White women.

20. The author of the pioneering argument for women's rights, *The Feminine Mystique,* was _____ _____.

_____

THINKING ABOUT **MOVIES**

Easy A

A high school student is accused of being sexually promiscuous.

La Mission

A man redefines his masculinity after he learns that his son is gay.

North Country

A woman who works in an iron mine fights against sexual harassment.

Several generations enjoy rafting on the Penobscot River in Maine. Age serves as a basis for social stratification, sometimes separating the old from the young more than is necessary or desirable. To a great extent, older people's quality of life, including their livelihoods, their social relationships, and their leisure pursuits, depends on society's view of aging.

286

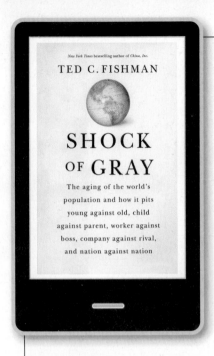

❝ Now in her eighties, my mother still dances at her grandsons' Led Zeppelin tribute concerts, swims Lake Michigan when the water is brisk, hikes among penguins in Patagonia, and dons cross-country skis as soon as the snow is deep enough. My late father, in contrast, was at the peak of his professional and creative success in his early sixties, but a barrage of ailments hit him hard at sixty-three. He began a cruel fifteen-year decline that left him blind, immobile, slow of speech, and utterly dependent. That he never lost his wit or kindness or his ability to hold on to the joys of life was, to me, heroic.

My parents' different experiences neatly represent what is happening to millions of Americans and to vast portions of the globe's population. The world is going gray. Getting not just older but *old*. Sometime after sixty, it seems to happen to everyone: life-altering events cascade one after another. In some combination, family nests are emptied; jobs end or change; spouses, friends, and kin grow gravely ill or die; bodies and minds decline; one's status and power in the family and in social circles inverts; money draws down; and, as remaining years grow fewer, relationships with time and eternity shift.

And yet new worlds can open up, too. Time can expand, social circles grow bigger, new passions take root. Freed from the relentless demands of family and work, older people may experience a sweet rejuvenation. People whom one might expect to be decrepit and infirm are, well, dancing at Led Zeppelin tribute concerts; Or even performing in them.

The aging of the globe is having profound economic, political, cultural, and familial effects that are only going to intensify.

Meanwhile, although the world well understands how young people shape social life and business, it is just now beginning to see how the arrival of a historically enormous older population will affect all of us. Many old people, like my mother, will be healthy and vibrant, but many others, like my father, will need extraordinary resources to make it from one day to the next. The aging of the globe is having profound economic, political, cultural, and familial effects that are only going to intensify. Some of these changes will be welcome and others will not. Certain people will benefit and others will be harmed. Money and power are at stake, of course, as well as the well-being of millions of older people who have worked and loved and given themselves to all that life offers. But the well-being of the globe's young is also at stake, because it is they who need resources also required by the old, and because in the end, it is largely the young who, as family members, friends, and citizens traveling the continuum of an aging world, will eventually care for the old. And in time their older selves.

The signs of the shift, large and small, are everywhere, if we only will see them. Consider:

In a room full of telephones and flat-panel displays, where staff is on hand twenty-four hours a day, calls begin to pick up around 9:00 a.m. That's when the more than 6 million elderly customers of Philips Lifeline tend to begin their daily routines. The service allows its clients to alert the company if anything threatens them. The morning is rife with dangers. The average age of a customer is eighty-two, but thousands of centenarians use the service, too. The large majority are women, a predictable reality in an older group. The mornings see millions of Lifeline clients head to the showers, step out on slippery tiles, and then make their way to the kitchen, where fire, knives, tall cabinets, area rugs, and wood flooring are mortal threats. If customers slip and fall, or a sleeve catches fire, or if they are overcome with anxiety and fear as the day begins, devices around their necks or on their wrists let them send signals, sometimes automatically, to the Lifeline call center. By midmorning on a beautiful fall day, Lifeline has handled nearly seven hundred thousand *calls*. ❞

(Fishman 2010a:1–2) *Additional information about this excerpt can be found on the Online Learning Center at www.mhhe.com/schaefer13e.*

Journalist Ted C. Fishman, author of this opening excerpt, is known for his reporting on global trade and finance. During the course of his work, he became aware of a powerful demographic trend, the aging of the world's population. In his book *Shock of Gray,* Fishman confronts the consequences of the rise in the proportion of elderly, not only for elders themselves and their families, but for entire societies and economies. He predicts a growing conflict between young and old, developed and developing nations, over limited resources.

As Fishman notes, not all older people are frail and dependent, in need of support; many, like his mother, are healthy, energetic, and engaged. Unfortunately, younger people tend to stereotype the aged. Like race or gender, age is socially constructed, an ascribed status that dominates people's perceptions of others, obscuring individual differences. Rather than suggesting that a particular elderly person is no longer competent to drive, for instance, we may condemn the entire age group: "Those old codgers shouldn't be allowed on the road." Unless people can begin to look at the life course as a continuum, rather than as a series of finite stages with predictable consequences, such stereotypical attitudes toward age and aging are not likely to change.

How do people's roles change as they age? What are the social implications of the growing number of elderly in the United States? How does ageism affect an older person's employment opportunities? In this chapter we will look at the process of aging throughout the life course. We will examine aging around the world, focusing primarily on the United States. After exploring various theories of the impact of aging, both on the individual and on society, we will discuss the role transitions typical of the major stages in the life course. In the process we will consider the challenges facing the "sandwich generation," middle-aged people who care for both their children and their aging parents. We will pay particular attention to the effects of prejudice and discrimination on older people, and to the rise of a political consciousness among the elderly. Finally, in the Social Policy section we will discuss the controversial issue of the right to die.

Aging and Society

The Sherpas—a Tibetan-speaking Buddhist people in Nepal—live in a culture that idealizes old age. Almost all elderly members of the Sherpa culture own their homes, and most are in relatively good physical condition. Typically, older Sherpas value their independence and prefer not to live with their children. Among the Fulani of Africa, however, older men and women move to the edge of the family homestead. Since that is where people are buried, the elderly sleep over their own graves, for they are viewed socially as already dead. Like gender stratification, age stratification varies from culture to culture. One society may treat older people with great reverence, while another sees them as unproductive and "difficult" (M. Goldstein and Beall 1981; Stenning 1958; Tonkinson 1978).

It is understandable that all societies have some system of age stratification that associates certain social roles with distinct periods in life. Some of this age differentiation seems inevitable; it would make little sense to send young children off to war, or to expect most older citizens to handle physically demanding tasks, such as loading freight at shipyards. However, as is the case with stratification by gender, in the United States age stratification goes far beyond the physical constraints on human beings at different ages.

"Being old" is a master status that commonly overshadows all others in the United States. Thus, the insights of labeling theory can help us in analyzing the consequences of aging. Once people have been labeled "old," the designation has a major impact on how others perceive them, and even on how they view themselves. Negative stereotypes of the elderly contribute to their position as a minority group subject to discrimination, as we will see later in the chapter.

The model of five basic properties of a minority or subordinate group (introduced in Chapter 11) can be applied to older people in the United States to clarify their subordinate status:

1. Older people experience unequal treatment in employment and may face prejudice and discrimination.

2. Older people share physical characteristics that distinguish them from younger people. In addition, their cultural preferences and leisure-time activities often differ from those of the rest of society.

3. Membership in this disadvantaged group is involuntary.

4. Older people have a strong sense of group solidarity, as is reflected in the growth of senior citizens' centers, retirement communities, and advocacy organizations.

5. Older people generally are married to others of comparable age.

There is one crucial difference between older people and other subordinate groups, such as racial and ethnic minorities or women: *all* of us who live long enough will eventually assume the ascribed status of an older person (Barron 1953; Levin and Levin 1980; Wagley and Harris 1958).

Sociological Perspectives on Aging

Aging is one important aspect of socialization—the lifelong process through which an individual learns the cultural norms and values of a particular society. There are no clear-cut definitions for different periods of the aging cycle in the United States. *Old age* has typically been regarded as beginning at 65, which corresponds to the retirement age for many workers, but not everyone in the United States accepts that definition. With the increase in life expectancy, writers are beginning to refer to people in their 60s as the "young old," to distinguish them from those in their 80s and beyond (the "old old").

The particular problems of the elderly have become the focus of a specialized field of research and inquiry known as gerontology. **Gerontology** is the scientific study of the sociological and psychological aspects of aging and the problems of the aged. It

Extended family arrangements are important to Americans, especially Latinos. Thirty-one percent of Hispanic women age 65 and older live with their relatives, compared to 13 percent of White non-Hispanic women. Among men of the same age, the rate is 15 percent for Hispanics, compared to 6 percent for White non-Hispanics (Jacobsen et al. 2011).

TAKING SOCIOLOGY TO WORK

A. David Roberts, **Social Worker**

Dave Roberts admits to being a "people person," a trait that sociology courses fostered by showing how "everybody has differences; there are little bits of different cultures in all of us." He also had the benefit of "a lot of great teachers" at Florida State University, including Dr. Jill Quadagno in a course on aging. It was this class that sparked his interest in aging issues, which led to a certificate in gerontology in addition to a sociology degree in 1998. He realized that there was a good job market in working with the aging baby boom generation.

Volunteer work with the Meals on Wheels program steered him toward working with the elderly. Today Roberts is a social worker in a nursing home, where he is responsible for patients' care plans. In the course of his work, he meets regularly with patients, family members, and medical residents. Roberts finds that the concept of teamwork he learned in group projects in college has helped him in his job. Also, the projects he had to do in school taught him to work on a schedule. Perhaps most important, sociology has helped him "to grow as a person, to explore different angles, different theories. . . . I'm a better person."

His advice to sociology students: "Just give it a chance; they throw everything into an intro course. Don't get overwhelmed; take it as it comes."

LET'S DISCUSS

1. What other types of employment might be open to a college graduate with a certificate in gerontology?
2. What might be the special rewards of working with elderly people?

---

originated in the 1930s, as an increasing number of social scientists became aware of the plight of the elderly.

Gerontologists rely heavily on sociological principles and theories to explain the impact of aging on the individual and society. They also draw on psychology, anthropology, physical education, counseling, and medicine in their study of the aging process. Two influential views of aging—disengagement theory and activity theory—can best be understood in terms of the sociological perspectives of functionalism and interactionism, respectively. The conflict perspective also contributes to our sociological understanding of aging.

use your sociological *imagination*

Time has passed, and you are now in your 70s or 80s. How does old age in your generation compare with your parents' or grandparents' experience of old age?

Functionalist Approach: Disengagement Theory

After studying elderly people in good health and relatively comfortable economic circumstances, Elaine Cumming and William Henry (1961) introduced their **disengagement theory,** which implicitly suggests that society and the aging individual mutually sever many of their relationships. In keeping with the functionalist perspective, disengagement theory emphasizes that passing social roles on from one generation to another ensures social stability.

According to this theory, the approach of death forces people to drop most of their social roles—including those of worker, volunteer, spouse, hobby enthusiast, and even reader. Younger members of society then take on these functions. The aging person, it is held, withdraws into an increasing state of inactivity while preparing for death.

Since it was first outlined five decades ago, disengagement theory has generated considerable controversy. Today, gerontologists and sociologists are more likely to see the elderly in terms of social connectedness, postretirement employment, and volunteerism. For their part, producers and retailers of electronic products are likely to see the older set as e-savvy consumers. Since 2008, they note, growth in computer and digital camera sales has been greatest in that market segment. And retirement homes have had to make room for residents who want to bowl or play tennis on Nintendo's Wii system (Cornwell et al. 2008; NPD Group 2008).

Interactionist Approach: Activity Theory

How important is it for older people to stay actively involved, whether at a job or in other pursuits? A tragic disaster in Chicago in 1995 showed that it can be a matter of life and death. An intense heat wave lasting more than a week—with a heat index exceeding 115 degrees on two consecutive days—resulted in 733 heat-related deaths. About three-fourths of the deceased were 65 and older. Subsequent analysis showed that older people who lived alone had the highest risk of dying, suggesting that support networks for the elderly literally help to save lives. Older Hispanics and Asian Americans had lower death rates from the heat wave than other racial and ethnic groups. Their stronger social networks probably resulted in more regular contact with family members and friends (Klinenberg 2002; R. Schaefer 1998).

Often seen as an opposing approach to disengagement theory, **activity theory** suggests that those elderly people who remain active and socially involved will be best adjusted. Proponents of this perspective acknowledge that a person age 70 may not have the ability or desire to perform various social roles that he or she had at age 40. Yet they contend that old people have essentially the same need for social interaction as any other group.

The improved health of older people—sometimes overlooked by social scientists—has strengthened the arguments of activity theorists. Illness and chronic disease are no longer quite the scourge of the elderly that they once were. The recent emphasis on fitness, the availability of better medical care, greater control of infectious diseases, and the reduction of fatal strokes and heart attacks have combined to mitigate the traumas of growing old.

These "silver surfers" in California still enjoy life to the fullest, just as they did when they were young. According to activity theory, staying active and involved is healthy for the older population.

Accumulating medical research also points to the importance of remaining socially involved. Among those who decline in their mental capacities later in life, deterioration is most rapid in those who withdraw from social relationships and activities. Fortunately, older people are finding new ways to remain socially engaged, as evidenced by their increasing use of the Internet, especially to keep in touch with family and friends (Clifford 2009b).

Admittedly, many activities open to older adults involve unpaid labor, for which younger adults may receive salaries. Unpaid elderly workers include hospital volunteers (versus aides and orderlies), drivers for charities such as the Red Cross (versus chauffeurs), tutors (as opposed to teachers), and craftspeople for charity bazaars (as opposed to carpenters and dressmakers). However, some companies have recently begun programs to hire retirees for full-time or part-time work.

Though disengagement theory suggested that older people find satisfaction in withdrawal from society, conveniently receding into the background and allowing the next generation to take over, proponents of activity theory view such withdrawal as harmful to both the elderly and society. Activity theorists focus on the potential contributions of older people to the maintenance of society. In their opinion, aging citizens will feel satisfied only when they can be useful and productive in society's terms—primarily by working for wages (Charles and Carstensen 2009; Quadagno 2011).

Labeling Theory

Just who are "the elderly"? Labeling theorists, who study the way reality is constructed through our culture and social interactions, have noted that recently, our society has begun to reconsider what makes a person old.

As early as 1975, social scientists were suggesting that old age should be defined not in terms of how old one is, but in terms of how long one can be expected to live. As life expectancy lengthens, then, the age at which one is labeled old rises. Some have suggested that the threshold of old age should begin in the last 10 or 15 years of a person's expected life. Using that definition, old age would begin at about age 70 or 75, at least for those of us who live in the United States.

Is this new definition of old age likely to be accepted? From the labeling perspective, it all depends on who you are.

Understandably, many people would prefer to be considered old later rather than sooner. Those who advocate for the elderly would prefer a broader definition. For example, the AARP (see pages 298–299) offers membership to anyone age 50 or older. It argues that people should begin planning for old age in their 50s, but clearly, encouraging the "young old" to join gives them strength in numbers.

The labeling of old age also differs from one culture to the next, due in part to differences in physical health and life opportunities. In relatively prosperous cultures like the United States, 70 is the new 60. But in countries whose health and social support systems have been significantly weakened over the past 20 years—Russia, for example—50 is the new 60 (Sanderson and Scherbov 2008).

thinking CRITICALLY

Is labeling the same as stereotyping? Why or why not?

Conflict Approach

Conflict theorists have criticized both disengagement theorists and activity theorists for failing to consider the impact of social structure on aging patterns. Neither approach, they say, questions why social interaction must change or decrease in old age. In addition, they often ignore the impact of social class on the lives of elderly people.

The privileged upper class generally enjoys better health and vigor and less likelihood of dependency in old age. Affluence cannot forestall aging indefinitely, but it can soften the economic hardships people face in later years. Although pension plans, retirement packages, and insurance benefits may be developed to assist older people, those whose wealth allows them access to investment funds can generate the greatest income for their later years.

In contrast, the working class often faces greater health hazards and a greater risk of disability; aging is particularly difficult for those who suffer job-related injuries or illnesses. Working-class people also depend more heavily on Social Security benefits and private pension programs. During inflationary times, their relatively fixed incomes from these sources barely keep pace with the escalating costs of food, housing, utilities, and other necessities (Atchley and Barusch 2004).

According to the conflict approach, the treatment of older people in the United States reflects the many divisions in our society. The low status of older people is seen in prejudice and discrimination against them, in age segregation, and in unfair job practices—none of which are directly addressed by either disengagement or activity theory.

Conflict theorists have noted, too, that in the developing world, the transition from agricultural economies to industrialization and capitalism has not always been beneficial to the

292 elderly. As a society's production methods change, the traditionally valued role of older people tends to erode. Their wisdom is no longer relevant in the new economy.

In sum, the four perspectives considered here take different views of the elderly. Functionalists portray older people as socially isolated, with reduced social roles; interactionists see them as involved in new networks and changing social roles. Labeling theorists see old age as a life stage that is defined by society. Conflict theorists see it as a time when people are victimized and their social roles devalued. Table 13-1 summarizes these perspectives.

use your sociological *imagination*

Have you noticed signs of second-class treatment of older people? If so, in what ways?

Aging Worldwide

Today the world's population is evenly divided between those people who are under age 28 and those who are over age 28. By the middle of the 21st century, the median age will have risen to 40. Even though the United Nations held the first world assembly on aging in 1982, few people gave much thought to this prospect of whole populations—that is, nations—growing older until the 1990s. By 2010, the world had more than 551 million people age 65 and over. Together they constituted about 8 percent of the world's population. By 2045, nearly twice that proportion, or 15.2 percent of the world's people, will be over 65.

In an important sense, this trend toward the aging of the world's population represents a major success story, one that unfolded during the latter years of the 20th century. Through the efforts of national governments and international agencies, many societies have drastically reduced their incidence of disease, and with it their rate of death. As a result, these nations—particularly the industrialized countries of Europe and North America—have a high and steadily rising proportion of older members (Figure 13-1); (Fishman 2010b; Haub 2010).

Overall, Europe's population is older than that of any other continent. Though many European countries have long prided themselves on their generous pension programs, as the proportion of older people continues to rise, government officials have reluctantly begun to reduce pension benefits and raise the age at which workers can receive them. Japan, too, has a relatively old population; the Japanese enjoy a life expectancy of 83 years, compared to 78 in the United States.

In most developing countries, people over 60 are likely to be in poorer health than their counterparts in industrialized nations. Yet few of those countries are in a position to offer extensive financial

TABLE **13-1** SOCIOLOGICAL PERSPECTIVES ON AGING

summing up

Sociological Perspective	View of Aging	Social Roles	Portrayal of Elderly
Functionalist	Disengagement	Reduced	Socially isolated
Interactionist	Activity	Changed	Involved in new networks
Labeling	Socially constructed	Changing	Varies by audience
Conflict	Competition	Relatively unchanged	Victimized, organized to confront their victimization

support to the elderly. Ironically, though the modernization of the developing world has brought many social and economic advances, it has undercut the traditionally high status of the elderly. In many cultures, the earning power of younger adults now exceeds that of their older relatives (Beck 2009).

Role Transitions throughout the Life Course

Socialization is a lifelong process. We simply do not experience things the same way at different points in the life course. For example, one study found that even falling in love differs according to where we are in the life course. Young unmarried adults tend to treat love as a noncommittal game or an obsession characterized by possessiveness and dependency. People over age 50 are much more likely to see love as involving commitment, and they tend to take a practical approach to finding a partner who meets a set of rational criteria. That does not mean that romance is dead among the older

FIGURE **13-1** WORLD'S "OLDEST" COUNTRIES VERSUS THE UNITED STATES

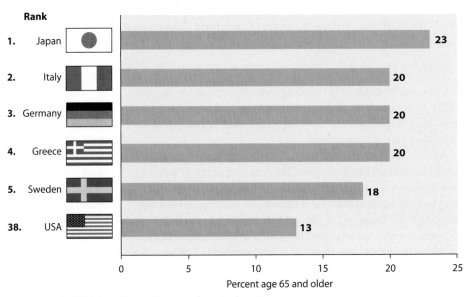

Rank		Percent age 65 and older
1.	Japan	23
2.	Italy	20
3.	Germany	20
4.	Greece	20
5.	Sweden	18
38.	USA	13

Source: Data for 2009 or earliest available year from Haub 2010.

This sandwich-generation mom cares for both her aging parent and her children. Increasingly, members of the baby boom generation find themselves caring for two generations at once.

generation, however. Among those age 65 and over, 39 percent are "head over heels in love," compared to only 25 percent of those ages 18 to 34. The life course, then, affects the manner in which we relate to one another (G. Anderson 2009; Montgomery and Sorell 1997).

How we move through the life course varies dramatically, depending on our personal preferences and circumstances. Some of us marry early, others late; some have children and some don't. These individual patterns are influenced by social factors such as class, race, and gender. Only in the most general terms, then, can we speak of stages or periods in the life course.

One transitional stage, identified by psychologist Daniel Levinson, begins at the time at which an individual gradually enters the adult world, perhaps by moving out of the parental home, beginning a career, or entering a marriage. The next transitional period, the midlife transition, typically begins at about age 40. Men and women often experience a stressful period of self-evaluation, commonly known as the **midlife crisis,** in which they realize that they have not achieved basic goals and ambitions and have little time left to do so. Thus, Levinson (1978, 1996) found that most adults surveyed experienced tumultuous midlife conflicts within the self and with the external world.

Not all the challenges at this time of life come from career or one's partner. In the next section we will examine a special challenge faced by a growing number of middle-aged adults: caring for two generations at once.

The Sandwich Generation

During the late 1990s social scientists focused on the **sandwich generation**—adults who simultaneously try to meet the competing needs of their parents and their children. That is, caregiving goes in two directions: (1) to children, who even as young adults may still require significant direction, and (2) to aging parents, whose health and economic problems may demand intervention by their adult children. By 2010, 13 million Americans were caring for both their children *and* their parents.

Like the role of caring for children, the role of caring for aging parents falls disproportionately on women. Overall, women provide 66 percent of the care their parents receive, and even more as the demands of the role grow more intense and time-consuming. Increasingly, middle-aged women and younger are finding themselves on the "daughter track," as their time and attention are diverted by the needs of their aging mothers and fathers. So significant have the challenges of caring for two generations become that in his 2010 State of the Union message, President Obama called for tax credits for families who care for both children and parents (National Alliance for Caregiving 2009).

The last major transition identified by Levinson occurs after age 60—sometimes well after that age, given advances in health care, greater longevity, and gradual acceptance within society of older people. Nonetheless, there is a point at which people transition to a different lifestyle. As we will see, this is a time of dramatic changes in people's everyday lives.

Adjusting to Retirement

Retirement is a rite of passage that marks a critical transition from one phase of a person's life to another. Typically, symbolic events are associated with this rite of passage, such as retirement gifts, a retirement party, and special moments on the last day on the job. The preretirement period itself can be emotionally charged, especially if the retiree is expected to train his or her successor (Atchley 1976).

From 1950 to the mid-1990s, the average age at retirement in the United States declined, but over the past few years it has reversed direction. By 2011, 5 percent of women and 10 percent of men over 75 were still working. A variety of factors explains this reversal: changes in Social Security benefits, the recent economic recession, and workers' concern with maintaining their health insurance and pension benefits. At the same time, longevity has increased, and the quality of people's health has improved (Department of Labor 2011).

Phases of Retirement Gerontologist Robert Atchley (1976) has identified several phases of the retirement experience:

- *Preretirement,* a period of anticipatory socialization as the person prepares for retirement
- *The near phase,* when the person establishes a specific departure date from his or her job
- *The honeymoon phase,* an often euphoric period in which the person pursues activities that he or she never had time for before
- *The disenchantment phase,* in which retirees feel a sense of letdown or even depression as they cope with their new lives, which may include illness or poverty
- *The reorientation phase,* which involves the development of a more realistic view of retirement alternatives
- *The stability phase,* a period in which the person has learned to deal with life after retirement in a reasonable and comfortable fashion

- *The termination phase,* which begins when the person can no longer engage in basic, day-to-day activities such as self-care and housework

Retirement is not a single transition, then, but rather a series of adjustments that varies from one person to another. The length and timing of each phase will differ for each individual, depending on such factors as financial status and health. A particular person will not necessarily go through all the phases identified by Atchley (Reitzes and Mutran 2006).

Some factors, such as being forced into retirement or being burdened with financial difficulties, can further complicate the retirement process. People who enter retirement involuntarily or without the necessary means may never experience the honeymoon phase. In the United States, many retirees continue in the paid labor force, often taking part-time jobs to supplement their pensions. Although most younger workers expect to retire—in a 2009 national survey, only 6 percent of respondents ages 18 to 29 said they would never retire—16 percent of those ages 50 to 64 do not expect to retire (Morin 2009; Figure 13-2).

Like other aspects of life in the United States, the experience of retirement varies according to gender, race, and ethnicity. White males are most likely to benefit from retirement wages, as well as to have participated in a formal retirement preparation program. As a result, anticipatory socialization for retirement is most complete for White men. In contrast, members of racial and ethnic minority groups—especially African Americans—are more likely to exit the paid labor force through disability than through retirement. Because of their comparatively lower incomes and smaller savings, men and women from racial and ethnic minority groups work intermittently after retirement more often than older Whites (National Institute on Aging 1999; Quadagno 2011).

Naturally Occurring Retirement Communities (NORCs)

With recent improvements in health care, older Americans have gained new choices in where to live. Today, rather than residing in nursing homes or planned retirement communities, many of them congregate in areas that have gradually become informal centers for senior citizens. Social scientists have dubbed such areas **naturally occurring retirement communities (NORCs).**

"Have you given much thought to what kind of job you want after you retire?"

thinking CRITICALLY

Today, many young adults continue to live with their parents after finishing their schooling. Contrast their situation with that of the elderly who live with their children. Does society treat dependent adult children in the same way as dependent parents? Why or why not?

use your sociological *imagination*

How have people close to you, such as relatives, personally handled their retirement from the labor force?

FIGURE **13-2** EXPECTED RETIREMENT AGE

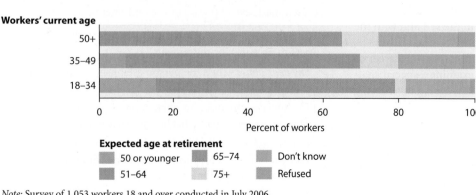

Workers' current age

	0	20	40	60	80	100
50+						
35–49						
18–34						

Percent of workers

Expected age at retirement

50 or younger	65–74	Don't know
51–64	75+	Refused

Note: Survey of 1,053 workers 18 and over conducted in July 2006.
Source: S. K. Brown 2006.

Think about It
At what age do you expect to retire completely, without working for pay at all?

Using observation research, census data, and interviews, sociologists have developed some interesting conclusions about NORCs in the United States, which numbered approximately 300 in 2009. These communities can be as small as a single apartment building or as large as a neighborhood in a big city. Often, they emerge as singles and young couples move out and older people move in. Sometimes couples simply remain where they are; as they grow older, the community becomes noticeably grayer. In time, business establishments that cater to the elderly—pharmacies, medical supply outlets, small restaurants—relocate to NORCs, making them even more attractive to older citizens.

Unfortunately, residents of some of these communities are threatened by gentrification, or the takeover of low-income neighborhoods by higher-income residents. In Chicago, a high-rise building known as Ontario Place is converting to a condominium, at prices that current residents cannot afford. About half the building's occupants are Russian immigrants; most of the others are elderly or disabled people living on fixed incomes. These people are distressed not just because they will need to move, but because their community is being destroyed (Lansprey 1995; P. Moeller 2009; P. Morrison and Bryan 2010; Sheehan 2005).

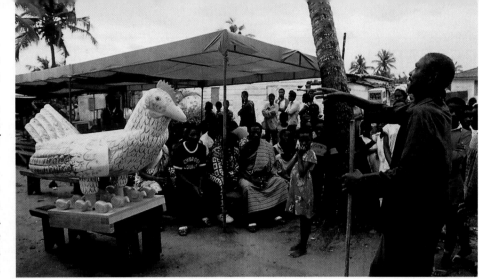

Coffins in Ghana sometimes reflect the way the dead lived their lives. This Methodist burial service honors a woman who died at age 85, leaving behind 11 children, 82 grandchildren, and 60 great-grandchildren. Her coffin, designed to resemble a mother hen, features 11 chicks nestling beneath the wings (Secretan 1995).

Death and Dying

Among the role transitions that typically (but not always) come later in life is death. Until recently, death was viewed as a taboo topic in the United States. However, psychologist Elisabeth Kübler-Ross (1969), through her pioneering book *On Death and Dying,* greatly encouraged open discussion of the process of dying. Drawing on her work with 200 cancer patients, Kübler-Ross identified five stages of the experience: denial, anger, bargaining, depression, and finally acceptance.

Despite its popular appeal, the five-stage theory of dying has been challenged. Observers often cannot substantiate these stages. Moreover, research suggests that each person declines in his or her own way. Thus, one should not expect—much less counsel—a person to approach death in any particular way. Cross-culturally, the variation in approaches is even more marked. Box 13-1 describes some of the ways in which different Native American tribes acknowledge death (R. Epstein 2005; Fitchett 1980).

Functionalist analysis brings to mind the cherished yet controversial concept of a "good death." One researcher described a good death among the Kaliai, a people of the South Pacific. In that culture, the dying person calls together all his relatives, settles his debts, disposes of his possessions, and then announces that it is time for him to die (Counts 1977).

The Kaliai concept of a good death has a parallel in Western societies, where people may speak of a "natural death," an "appropriate death," or "death with dignity." The practice of **hospice care,** introduced in London, England, in 1967, is founded on this concept. Hospice workers seek to improve the quality of a dying person's last days by offering comfort and by helping the person to remain at home, or in a homelike setting at a hospital or other special facility, until the end. Currently, more than 3,200

hospice programs serve over 960,000 people a year in the United States through federal programs such as Medicare and Medicaid (Hospice Association of America 2008).

Although the Western ideal of the good death makes the experience of dying as positive as possible, some critics fear that acceptance of the concept of a good death may direct both individual efforts and social resources away from attempts to extend life. Still others argue that fatally ill older people should not just passively accept death, but should forgo further treatment in order to reduce public health care expenditures. Such issues are at the heart of current debates over the right to die and physician-assisted suicide.

Today, in many varied ways, people have broken through the historic taboos about death and are attempting to arrange certain aspects of the idealized good death. For example, bereavement practices—once highly structured—are becoming increasingly varied and therapeutic. More and more people are actively addressing the inevitability of death by making wills, leaving "living wills" (health care proxies that explain their feelings about the use of life-support equipment), donating organs, and providing instructions for family members about funerals, cremations, and burials. Given medical and technological advances and a breakthrough in open discussion and negotiation regarding death and dying, it is possible that good deaths may become a social norm in the United States.

Age Stratification in the United States

The "Graying of America"

When Lenore Schaefer, a ballroom dancer, tried to get on the *Tonight Show,* she was told she was "too young": she was in her early 90s. When she turned 101, she made it. But even at that age, Lenore is no longer

RESEARCH TODAY

13.1 Native Americans and Death

The native peoples of North America include hundreds of distinctive cultures, as different from one another as English culture is from Turkish culture. Their practices with respect to death and dying reflect this cultural diversity. Sociologist Gerry Cox conducted ethnographic fieldwork and interviews with tribal peoples on 42 reservations throughout the United States and Canada. He found that among the Creek and some other tribes, those closest to the deceased accompany the body in the days before the burial. In other tribes, such as the Navajo, Apache, and Hopi, relatives spend little time with the body.

In many cases, these practices evolved after contact with European Americans. Religious proselytizing, intermarriage, and the enforcement of colonial regulations all had an impact on cultural traditions. Among the first to experience Hispanic contact in the 16th century were the Zuni and other Pueblo peoples of present-day Arizona and New Mexico. In those cultures, burials that had once been done quickly, with little ceremony, moved onto church grounds or to graveyards consecrated by Christian ritual. At the same time, Native Americans continued their traditional burial practices, in secret when necessary.

Family members smudge the body with ashes immediately after death, then go with it to a funeral home for embalming.

Among the Flathead of Montana, who converted to Roman Catholicism a century ago, traditional practices persist. Family members smudge the body with ashes immediately after death, then go with it to a funeral home for embalming. Before the body is placed in a coffin, they wash it in rose water. The Catholic funeral mass that precedes the burial includes native songs and ceremonial drums.

Today, Native Americans have won some concessions from hospitals that care for the dying. Lakota patients are allowed to have more relatives in the room than other patients. They may ask to use smoke for ceremonial purposes, even though smoking is strictly forbidden. Apaches, in contrast, prefer to die alone. Navajos may want to hold a "sing."

Native American rituals demonstrate reverence and respect for life as well as death. Despite the great diversity in their values, beliefs, and normative behavior regarding death, one broad belief unites Native Americans: death is a natural and accepted part of the life cycle. Native Americans also share the belief that their dear ones continue to love, care for, and protect families and friends after death.

LET'S DISCUSS

1. Does your own family observe traditional cultural practices regarding death and dying, independent of formal religious ritual? If so, explain their meaning and importance to your family.
2. Apply the concepts you learned in Chapter 3 to Native American burial practices. Which of them do you find most useful in understanding these practices?

Sources: G. Cox 2010; Sharon Kaufman and Morgan 2005; A. Walker and Balk 2007.

---

unusual in our society. Today, people over 100 constitute, proportionately, the country's fastest-growing age group. They are part of the increasing proportion of the population of the United States that is composed of older people (Himes 2001; Rimer 1998).

As Figure 13-3 shows, in the future, an increasing proportion of the U.S. population will be composed of older people. This trend is expected to continue well into the 21st century, as the mortality rate declines and members of the postwar baby boom age. At the same time, the "oldest old"—that is, the segment of the population representing those who are age 85 or older—will grow at an even faster rate.

Compared with the rest of the population, the elderly are more likely to be female than male. Men tend to have higher death rates than women at every age. By old age, women outnumber men by a ratio of 3 to 2. The gap widens with advancing age, so that among the oldest old, the ratio is 5 to 2.

The elderly are also more likely than others to be White: about 80 percent of the elderly are White and non-Hispanic. Although this segment of the population is becoming more racially and ethnically diverse, the higher death rates of racial and ethnic minorities, together with the continuing immigration of younger Latinos and Asians, is likely to keep it more White than the nation as a whole. Yet the overall pattern of an increasingly diversified population will show up among older Americans. As the projections in Figure 13-4 show, as the 21st century advances, non-Whites and Latinos will make up an increasing proportion of those who are 65 and over.

Finally, the elderly are more likely than the rest of the population to live in certain states. The highest proportions of

FIGURE 13-3 PERCENTAGE OF U.S. POPULATION IN SELECTED AGE GROUPS, 1970–2050

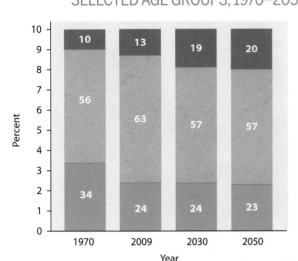

Source: Population Reference Bureau analysis of Bureau of the Census data, in Jacobsen et al. 2011:3.

FIGURE 13-4 MINORITY POPULATION AGE 65 AND OLDER, 2010–2050

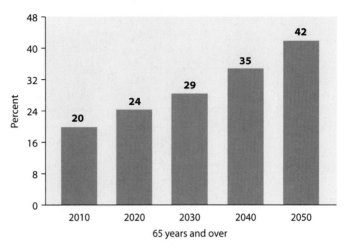

Source: Bureau of the Census in Vincent and Velkoff 2010.

older people are found in Florida, Pennsylvania, Rhode Island, Iowa, West Virginia, and Arkansas. However, that will soon change. In 2000, Florida was the state most populated by the elderly, with 17.6 percent of the population over age 65. Yet as Figure 13-5 shows, in less than 20 years, more than half the states will have an even greater proportion of elderly people than Florida does now.

The graying of the United States is a phenomenon that can no longer be ignored, either by social scientists or by government policymakers. Advocates for the elderly have spoken out on a wide range of issues. Politicians court the votes of older people, since they are the age group most likely to register and vote. In fact, in the 2008 presidential election, despite the upsurge in the youth vote, people over 60 made up 23 percent of those who voted, compared to 18 percent for those under 30 (Connelly 2008).

Wealth and Income

There is significant variation in wealth and poverty among the nation's older people. Some individuals and couples find themselves poor in part because of fixed pensions and sky-rocketing health care costs (see Chapter 19). Nevertheless, as a group, older people in the United States are neither homogeneous nor poor. The typical elderly person enjoys a standard of living that is much higher now than at any point in the nation's past. Class differences among the elderly remain evident, but tend to narrow somewhat: those older people who enjoyed middle-class incomes while younger tend to remain better off after retirement, but less so than before (Denise Smith and Tillipman 2000).

To some extent, older people owe their overall improved standard of living to a greater accumulation of wealth—in the form of home ownership, private pensions, and other financial assets. But much of the improvement is due to more generous Social Security benefits. While modest when compared with

other countries' pension programs, Social Security nevertheless provides 39 percent of all income received by older people in the United States. Still, about 9 percent of the nation's elderly population lives below the federal government's poverty line. At the extremes of poverty are those groups who were more likely to be poor at earlier points in the life cycle: female-headed households and racial and ethnic minorities (He et al. 2005).

Viewed from a conflict perspective, it is not surprising that older women experience a double burden; the same is true of elderly members of racial and ethnic minorities. For example, in 2009 the proportion of older Latinos with incomes below the poverty level (18.3 percent) was almost three times as large as the proportion of older White non-Hispanics (6.6 percent). Moreover, 18.9 percent of older African Americans fell below the federal government's poverty line (Issa and Zedlewski 2011).

Ageism

Physician Robert Butler (1990) became concerned 49 years ago when he learned that a housing development near his home in metropolitan Washington, D.C., barred the elderly. Butler coined the term **ageism** to refer to prejudice and discrimination based on a person's age. Research shows that in the United States, a large majority of people over age 60—84 percent—have experienced ageism, from insulting jokes to outright disrespect (Roscigno 2010:7).

Ageism is especially difficult for the old, because at least youthful recipients of prejudice know that in time they will be "old enough." For many, old age symbolizes disease. With ageism all too common in the United States, it is hardly surprising that older people are barely visible on television. In 2002, the Senate Special Committee on Aging convened a panel on the media's portrayal of older people and sharply criticized media and marketing executives for bombarding audiences with negative images of the aged. The social consequences of such images

MAPPING LIFE NATIONWIDE

FIGURE **13-5**   TWENTY-EIGHT FLORIDAS BY 2030

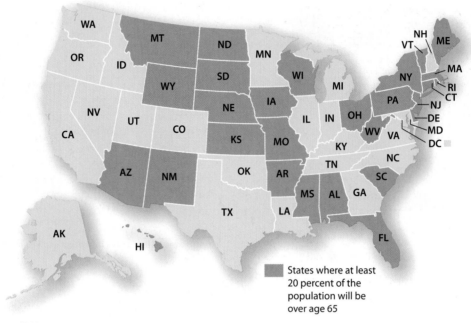

States where at least 20 percent of the population will be over age 65

Source: Bureau of the Census 2005a.

are significant. Research shows that older people who have positive perceptions of aging live an average of 7.5 years longer than those who have negative perceptions (M. Gardner 2003; Levy et al. 2002; Ramirez 2002).

Competition in the Labor Force

Although paid employment is not typical after age 65, since the 1980s it has become increasingly common. Concerned over their pension benefits, more and more people who are healthy enough to continue working have decided to postpone their retirement. Their decision has further eroded job opportunities for younger workers, already handicapped by the highest unemployment rates in a generation. Unfortunately, some people view older workers as "job stealers"—a biased judgment similar to that directed against illegal immigrants—instead of as experienced contributors to the labor force. Moreover, unemployed workers in their 50s find that potential employers rarely give them serious consideration. These difficulties not only intensify age conflict but lead to age discrimination as well (Jacobsen et al. 2011).

The federal Age Discrimination in Employment Act (ADEA), which went into effect in 1968, was passed to protect workers who are age 40 and older from being fired because of their age and replaced with younger workers, who would presumably receive lower salaries. The Supreme Court strengthened federal protection against age discrimination in 1996, ruling unanimously that such lawsuits can be successful even if an older worker is replaced by someone who is older than 40. Consequently, firing a 65-year-old employee to make way for a 45-year-old can be construed as age discrimination.

While firing people simply because they are old violates federal law, courts have upheld the right to lay off older workers

for economic reasons. Critics contend that later, the same firms hire young, cheaper workers to replace experienced older workers. When economic growth began to slow in 2008 and companies cut back on their workforces, complaints of age bias grew sharply as older workers began to suspect they were bearing a disproportionate share of the layoffs (Roscigno 2010).

Given recent legislative and legal advances, has the climate changed significantly for older workers? Box 13-2 on page 300 presents several studies that have attempted to assess the extent of ageism, both in everyday life and in hiring.

use your sociological *imagination*

It is September and you are channel-surfing through the new fall TV series. How likely are you to watch a television show that is based on older characters who spend a lot of time together?

The Elderly: Emergence of a Collective Consciousness

During the 1960s, students at colleges and universities across the country, advocating "student power," collectively demanded a role in the governance of educational institutions. In the following decade, many older people became aware that *they* were being treated as second-class citizens and turned to collective action.

The AARP is a major voice for the elderly. By featuring Bruce Springsteen (born in 1949) on the cover of its widely distributed magazine, the organization is signaling a desire to represent the younger members of the older generation, as well as to portray the active lives many older people lead.

voters in the United States. The AARP has endorsed voter registration campaigns, nursing home reforms, and pension reforms. In acknowledgment of its difficulties recruiting members of racial and ethnic minority groups, the AARP recently began a Minority Affairs Initiative. The spokeswoman for the initiative, Margaret Dixon, became the AARP's first African American president in 1996 (Birnbaum 2005).

People grow old in many different ways. Not all elderly people face the same challenges or enjoy the same resources. While the AARP lobbies to protect the elderly in general, other groups work in more specific ways. For example, the National Committee to Preserve Social Security and Medicare, founded in 1982, has successfully lobbied Congress to keep Medicare benefits for the ailing poor elderly. Other large special interest groups represent retired federal employees, retired teachers, and retired union workers (Quadagno 2011).

Still another manifestation of the new awareness of older people is the formation of organizations for elderly homosexuals. One such group, Senior Action in a Gay Environment (SAGE), was established in New York City in 1977 and now oversees a nationwide network of community groups, as well as affiliates in Canada and Germany. Like traditional senior citizens' groups, SAGE sponsors workshops, classes, dances, and food deliveries to the homebound. At the same time, the group must deal with special concerns, such as informing gay people of their rights, supporting gay people with Alzheimer's, and advocating for gays who face eviction (Senior Action in a Gay Environment 2010).

The elderly in the United States are better off today both financially and physically than ever before. Many of them have strong financial assets and medical care packages that will meet almost any health need. But as we have seen, a significant segment is impoverished, faced with the prospect of declining health and mounting medical bills. And some older people must now add being aged to a lifetime of disadvantage. Like people in all other stages of the life course, the aged constitute a diverse group in the United States and around the world.

The largest organization representing the nation's elderly is the AARP, founded in 1958 by a retired school principal who was having difficulty getting insurance because of age prejudice. Many of the AARP's services involve discounts and insurance for its 40 million members (43 percent of Americans age 50 and older), but the organization is also a powerful lobbying group. Recognizing that many elderly people are still gainfully employed, it has dropped its full name, American Association of *Retired* Persons (Donnelly 2007; Eggen 2009).

The potential power of the AARP is enormous. It is the third-largest voluntary association in the United States (behind only the Roman Catholic Church and the American Automobile Association), representing one out of every four registered

TREND SPOTTING

Job Wanted—Over 65

From the 1940s through the early 1990s, the proportion of people over age 65 who were working declined steadily, and the rate dropped faster for men than for women. Since the 1990s this pattern has reversed for both men and women. In little more than a decade, the percentage of older people who are working doubled.

Even more remarkable is the shift of older workers to full-time employment. In 2002, for the first time, more older people were working full-time than part-time. This trend has continued through the recession that began in 2008. Older workers face high unemployment rates, but more and more have continued to seek work, perhaps to offset losses to their retirement savings.

As the baby boom generation ages, the share of workers in the 55-years-and-older age group is expected to increase dramatically, at least through 2018. Despite this trend, the participation rates of older workers are not expected to reach the working levels of those in their 40s.

RESEARCH TODAY

13-2 Elderspeak and Other Signs of Ageism

"Who did you used to be?" This comment reveals an unflattering assumption about what happens to people when they grow old. Unfortunately, such remarks are far too frequent. In fact, condescending language is so often directed at elderly people that gerontologists have come to call it *elderspeak*.

According to scholars who have done observation research in nursing homes and retirement facilities, staff in these institutions tend to relate to the elderly residents in a manner befitting infants, calling them "dear," "good girl," and "sweetie." Medical professionals may patronize elderly patients, asking "Did you understand what I said?" or cajole them with "You don't want to upset your family, do you?" Although the people who make these remarks do not regard them as derogatory, older people find the unintended insults demoralizing.

Many older people experience ageism long before they retire. They may find that past a certain age, they will not be hired or even interviewed for a job. Yet research has shown that older workers can be an asset to employers. In response to such findings, some U.S. corporations, including Home Depot, are actively recruiting retired people.

Still, many older people have difficulty finding work, often as the result of ageism. Economist Johanna Lahey sent similar résumés for fictitious women of different ages to employers in Boston and St. Petersburg, Florida. The results were striking. In Boston, a younger worker was 42 percent more likely than an older worker to be offered an interview for an entry-level job, such as a clerical position. In St. Petersburg, the difference was 46 percent.

To determine why the older applicants had more difficulty getting an interview, Lahey tried making them look more desirable.

To prevent a 62-year-old applicant from being seen as inflexible, undependable, or out of touch, she added a certificate of completion of a recent computer course to the person's application, along with an indication of health insurance coverage. However, these "extras" had no effect on the call-back rate.

About 30 percent of older workers choose to remain on the job past the usual retirement age. Research shows they can be retrained in new technologies and are more dependable than younger workers.

Many older people experience ageism long before they retire. They may find that past a certain age, they will not be hired or even interviewed for a job.

This study mirrored the results of one done two decades earlier, which showed that younger applicants are significantly more welcome in the job market than older applicants. Although further research might be done, the pattern seems clear: ageism is entrenched in our society.

LET'S DISCUSS

1. Have you ever worked alongside an older person? If so, did that person's age affect the way he or she did the job? In what ways?
2. Are older people the only ones who experience ageism? What signs of ageism might those who are not old experience?

Sources: Bendick et al. 1993; Charness and Villeval 2009; Freudenheim 2005; Lahey 2006; Leland 2008; Lohr 2008; Roscigno 2010; K. Williams et al. 2009.

---

social**policy** and Age Stratification

The Right to Die Worldwide

On August 4, 1993, Dr. Jack Kevorkian, a retired pathologist, helped a 30-year-old Michigan man with Lou Gehrig's disease to commit suicide in a van. The patient died after inhaling carbon monoxide through a mask designed by Dr. Kevorkian; in doing so, he became the 17th person to commit suicide with Kevorkian's assistance. Kevorkian was openly challenging a Michigan law (aimed at him) that makes it a felony—punishable by up to four years in jail—to assist in a suicide. Since then Kevorkian has assisted in numerous other suicides, but not until he did it on television in 1998 did the charges brought against him result in his imprisonment for second-degree murder. Kevorkian completed his sentence in 2007 and died of circulatory problems in 2011.

Looking at the Issue

The issue of physician-assisted suicide is but one aspect of the larger debate in the United States and other countries over the ethics of suicide and euthanasia. The term **euthanasia** has been defined as the "act of bringing about the death of a hopelessly ill and suffering person in a relatively quick and painless way for reasons of mercy" (Council on Ethical and Judicial Affairs, American Medical Association 1992:229). This type of mercy killing reminds us of the ideal of the "good death" discussed earlier in the chapter. The debate over euthanasia and assisted suicide often focuses on cases involving older people, although it can involve younger adults with terminal and degenerative diseases, or even children.

National surveys show that public opinion on this controversial practice is divided. In 2007, 71 percent of respondents said that a physician should be legally permitted to end a patient's life if both the patient and the patient's family make such a request. However, an earlier survey found that only half of respondents could even imagine a situation in which they themselves would request physician-assisted suicide (J. Carroll 2007; Jost 2005).

Currently, public policy in the United States does not permit *active euthanasia* (such as a deliberate injection of lethal drugs into a terminally ill patient) or physician-assisted suicide. Although suicide itself is no longer a crime, assisting suicide is illegal in at least 29 states. There is greater legal tolerance for *passive euthanasia* (such as disconnecting life-support equipment from a comatose patient).

Applying Sociology

Many societies are known to have practiced *senilicide*—"killing of the aged"—because of extreme difficulties in providing basic necessities such as food and shelter. In a study of the treatment of elderly people in 41 nonindustrialized societies, Anthony Glascock (1990) found some form of "death-hastening" behavior in 21 of them. Killing of elderly people was evident in 14 of the societies; abandoning them was evident in 8. Typically, death hastening occurs when older people become decrepit and are viewed as already dead. In these nonindustrialized cultures it is open and socially approved. Family members generally make the decisions, often after open consultation with those who are about to die.

Although formal norms against euthanasia are still strict, informal norms seem to permit mercy killings. According to an estimate by the American Hospital Association, as many as 70 percent of all deaths in the United States are quietly negotiated, with patients, family members, and physicians agreeing not to use life-support technology. In an informal poll of internists, one in five reported that he or she had assisted or helped cause the death of a patient. In a period in which AIDS-related deaths are common, an AIDS underground is known to share information and assistance regarding suicide (N. Gibbs 1993; Martinez 1993).

Conflict theorists ask questions about the values raised by such decisions. By endorsing physician-assisted suicide, are we devaluing the disabled through an acceptance of their premature death? Critics note that we are all only temporarily able-bodied; disease or a speeding automobile can place any one of us among the disabled. By establishing a precedent for ending the lives of selected disabled people, we may unwittingly contribute to negative social views and labeling of all disabled people. Further reflecting the conflict perspective, gerontologist Elizabeth Markson (1992:6) argues that the "powerless, poor or undesirable are at special risk of being 'encouraged' to choose assisted death."

Despite these concerns, research to date shows little bias. In studies of physician-assisted suicide in Oregon and the Netherlands, researchers looked at how implementation of the controversial policy might affect people who were vulnerable because of their disability, age, mental health, or race and ethnicity. People with AIDS proved to be the only vulnerable group with a heightened use of physician-assisted suicide. Overall, those people who died with a doctor's help were more likely to be socially, economically, and educationally privileged than to be particularly vulnerable (Battin et al. 2007).

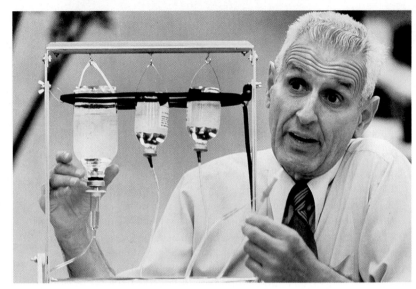

Dr. Jack Kevorkian with the apparatus that administered a lethal injection to those who wanted assistance in committing suicide.

Initiating Policy

In the industrialized world, euthanasia is legal and widely accepted in only three countries: the Netherlands, where about 3,800 such procedures are carried out legally each year; Belgium, which records about 350 procedures a year; and Switzerland, which records 200 a year. Unlike the Netherlands and Belgium, Switzerland allows foreigners to be euthanized; about 55 foreign nationals are euthanized there every year. While physician-assisted suicide is accepted by the public in all three countries, the "suicide tourism" that occurs in Switzerland is controversial (*The Economist* 2005a).

In the United States, the first state to allow assisted suicide was Oregon, where the Death with Dignity Act became law in 1997. By mid-2009, more than 400 terminally ill Oregonians had taken their lives with the assistance of a physician. President George W. Bush's administration had made an unsuccessful attempt to stop the prescription of lethal drugs to terminally ill patients in Oregon. In 2006, the Supreme Court ruled 6–3 that the federal government had overstepped its authority in punishing doctors in Oregon who had helped terminally ill patients to end their lives. Two years later, voters in Washington State passed a law similar to Oregon's, which took effect in 2009. Some local courts and state legislatures are also moving to legalize the practice, despite strong opposition (Fausset 2009; *The Week* 2009; W. Yardley 2009).

Advances in technology now allow us to prolong life in ways that were unimaginable decades ago. But should people be forced or expected to prolong lives that are unbearably painful, or that are in effect "lifeless"? Unfortunately, medical and technological advances cannot provide answers to these complex ethical, legal, and political questions.

Take the Issue with You

1. Why do you think "death-hastening" behavior is common in nonindustrialized countries?

2. In what ways are conflict theory and disengagement theory relevant to the debate over the "right to die"?

3. Do you think someone should be allowed to choose to die? Why or why not?

MASTERING THIS CHAPTER

Summary

Age, like gender and race, is an ascribed status that serves as a basis for social differentiation. This chapter examines sociological perspectives on aging, role transitions in the life course, age stratification in the United States, the growing political activism of the nation's elderly population, and the controversy surrounding the right to die.

1. Like other forms of stratification, age stratification varies from culture to culture.

2. In the United States, being old is a master status that seems to overshadow all others.

3. The particular problems of the aged have become the focus for a specialized area of research and inquiry known as **gerontology.**

4. **Disengagement theory** implicitly suggests that society should help older people to withdraw from their accustomed social roles. In contrast, **activity theory** suggests that the elderly person who remains active and socially involved will be better adjusted.

5. Labeling theorists note that people of the same age are labeled differently in different societies, based largely on differences in physical health, life opportunities, and life expectancy in those societies.

6. From a conflict perspective, the low status of older people is reflected in prejudice and discrimination against them and in unfair job practices.

7. About 40 percent of those who look after their elderly relatives still have children to care for; these people have been dubbed the **sandwich generation.**

8. As we age, we go through role transitions, including adjustment to retirement and preparation for death.

9. An increasing proportion of the population of the United States is composed of older people.

10. **Ageism** reflects a deep uneasiness about growing old on the part of younger people.

11. The AARP is a powerful lobbying group that backs legislation to benefit senior citizens.

12. The "right to die" often entails physician-assisted suicide, a controversial issue worldwide.

Key Terms

Activity theory An interactionist theory of aging that suggests that those elderly people who remain active and socially involved will be best adjusted. (page 290)

Ageism Prejudice and discrimination based on a person's age. (297)

Disengagement theory A functionalist theory of aging that suggests that society and the aging individual mutually sever many of their relationships. (290)

Euthanasia The act of bringing about the death of a hopelessly ill and suffering person in a relatively quick and painless way for reasons of mercy. (300)

Gerontology The scientific study of the sociological and psychological aspects of aging and the problems of the aged. (289)

Hospice care Treatment of the terminally ill in their own homes, or in special hospital units or other facilities, with the goal of helping them to die easily, without pain. (295)

Midlife crisis A stressful period of self-evaluation that begins at about age 40. (293)

Naturally occurring retirement community (NORC) An area that has gradually become an informal center for senior citizens. (294)

Sandwich generation The generation of adults who simultaneously try to meet the competing needs of their parents and their children. (293)

TAKING SOCIOLOGY with you

1. Think about your grandparents: Would you describe them as active or disengaged? Do you think their social class has had an impact on the way they have aged? Explain. How well have they adjusted to retirement?

2. What public agency or organization—the senior center, council on aging—is responsible for serving seniors in your community? Visit the site and learn about the programs offered there. Then relate your findings to what you learned in this chapter.

3. Find out the percentage of people age 65 and over who live in your community. How does that percentage compare to your state or to the United States as a whole? If you can, determine whether residents in this age bracket are clustered in particular areas. Are you aware of any naturally occurring retirement communities (NORCs) where you live?

Self-Quiz

Read each question carefully and then select the best answer.

1. Activity theory is associated with the
   a. functionalist perspective.
   b. conflict perspective.
   c. interactionist perspective.
   d. labeling perspective.

2. What is the one crucial difference between older people and other subordinate groups, such as racial and ethnic minorities or women?
   a. Older people do not experience unequal treatment in employment.
   b. Older people have a strong sense of group solidarity and other groups do not.
   c. All of us who live long enough will eventually assume the ascribed status of being an older person.
   d. Older people are generally married to others of comparable age and other minorities do not marry within their group.

3. Which field of study was originally developed in the 1930s as an increasing number of social scientists became aware of the plight of the elderly?
   a. sociology
   b. gerontology
   c. gerontocracy
   d. senilicide

4. Which sociological perspective is most likely to emphasize the important role of social networks in providing life satisfaction for elderly people?
   a. functionalist perspective
   b. conflict perspective
   c. interactionist perspective
   d. labeling theory

5. Elaine Cumming and William Henry introduced an explanation of the impact of aging known as
   a. disengagement theory.
   b. activity theory.
   c. labeling theory.
   d. the contact hypothesis.

6. According to psychologist Elisabeth Kübler-Ross, the first stage of the experience of dying that a person may undergo is
   a. denial.
   b. anger.
   c. depression.
   d. bargaining.

7. Which of the following statements about the elderly is correct?
   a. Being old is a master status.
   b. Once people are labeled as "old," the designation has a major impact on how others perceive them, and even on how they view themselves.
   c. Negative stereotypes of the elderly contribute to their position as a minority group subject to discrimination.
   d. all of the above

8. The text points out that the model of five basic properties of a minority or subordinate group can be applied to older people in the United States. Which of the following is *not* one of those basic properties?
   a. Older people experience unequal treatment in employment and may face prejudice and discrimination.
   b. Statistically, the elderly represent a majority.
   c. Membership in this group is involuntary.
   d. Older people have a strong sense of group solidarity.

9. Which of the following theories argues that elderly people have essentially the same need for social interaction as any other group and that those who remain active and socially involved will be best adjusted?
   a. conflict theory
   b. functionalist theory
   c. activity theory
   d. disengagement theory

10. According to your text, which of the following statements is true?
   a. Functionalists portray the elderly as being socially isolated, with reduced social roles.
   b. Interactionists see older people as being involved in new networks of people and in changing social roles.
   c. Conflict theorists regard older people as being victimized by social structure, with their social roles relatively unchanged but devalued.
   d. all of the above

11. The elderly are _____ regarded in the traditional Sherpa (Tibet) culture.

12. In keeping with the _____ perspective of sociology, disengagement theory emphasizes that a society's stability is ensured when social roles are passed on from one generation to another.

13. The final phase of retirement, according to Robert Atchley, is the _____ phase, which begins when the person can no longer engage in basic, day-to-day activities such as self-care and housework.

14. _____ theorists argue that both the disengagement and the activity perspectives often ignore the impact of social class in the lives of elderly people.

15. The fastest-growing age group in the United States is people over age _____.

16. _____ is the scientific study of the sociological and psychological aspects of aging and the problems of the aged. It originated in the 1930s as an increasing number of social scientists became aware of the plight of elderly people.

17. Based on a study of elderly people in good health and relatively comfortable economic circumstances, _____ theory suggests that society and the aging individual mutually sever many of their relationships.

18. During the late 1990s, social scientists focused on the _____ _____—adults who simultaneously try to meet the competing needs of their parents and their children.

19. In 2000, _____ was the state most populated by the elderly, with 17.6 percent of the population over age 65.

20. Physician Robert Butler coined the term _____ to refer to prejudice and discrimination based on a person's age.

_____

THINKING ABOUT MOVIES

Gran Torino

A retired automotive worker overcomes his racism and learns to accept his immigrant neighbors.

Joan Rivers: A Piece of Work

This documentary shows a popular comedian trying to maintain her success as she ages.

Please Give

Characters from different stages in the life course grow together.

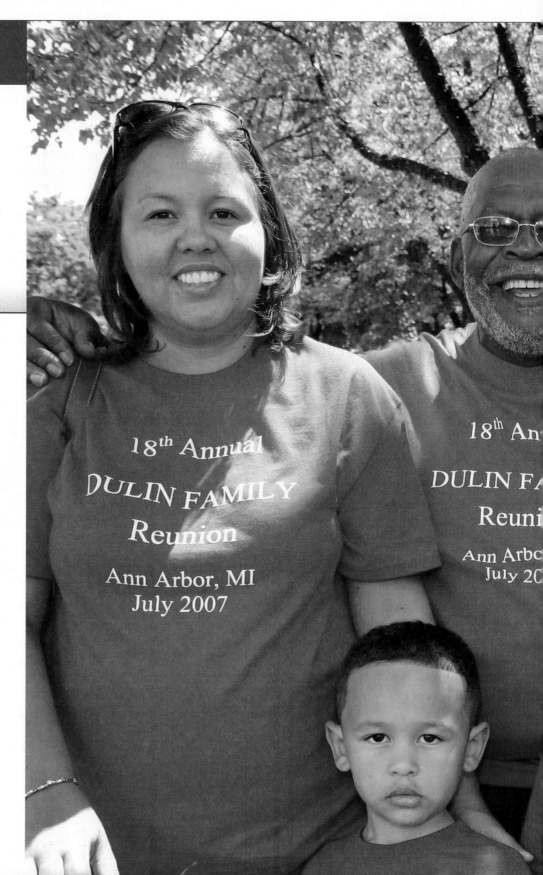

In Ann Arbor, Michigan, several generations of Dulins celebrate their 18th family reunion. Despite marital strains and geographical separation, countless families come together every year to reaffirm the importance of this social institution.

FIGURE 14-1 U.S. HOUSEHOLDS BY FAMILY TYPE, 1940–2010

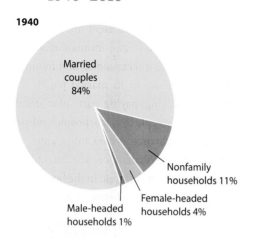

1940

Married couples 84%

Nonfamily households 11%

Female-headed households 4%

Male-headed households 1%

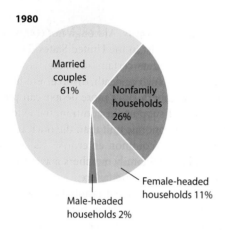

1980

Married couples 61%

Nonfamily households 26%

Female-headed households 11%

Male-headed households 2%

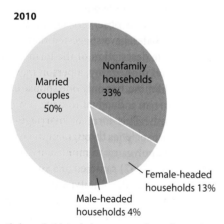

2010

Married couples 50%

Nonfamily households 33%

Female-headed households 13%

Male-headed households 4%

Note: Nonfamily households include women and men living alone or exclusively with people to whom they are not related, as in a college dormitory, homeless shelter, or military base.
Source: Bureau of the Census 2010b:Table HH1.

Box 14-1. Polyandry, however, is exceedingly rare today, though it is accepted in some extremely poor societies. Like many other societies, polyandrous cultures devalue the social worth of women (Zeitzen 2008).

Kinship Patterns: To Whom Are We Related?

Many of us can trace our roots by looking at a family tree or by listening to elderly family members talk about their lives—and about the lives of ancestors who died long before we were born. Yet a person's lineage is more than simply a personal history; it

also reflects societal patterns that govern descent. In every culture, children encounter relatives to whom they are expected to show an emotional attachment. The state of being related to others is called **kinship.** Kinship is culturally learned, however, and is not totally determined by biological or marital ties. For example, adoption creates a kinship tie that is legally acknowledged and socially accepted.

The family and the kin group are not necessarily one and the same. Whereas the family is a household unit, kin do not always live together or function as a collective body on a daily basis. Kin groups include aunts, uncles, cousins, in-laws, and so forth. In a society such as the United States, the kinship group may come together only rarely, for a wedding or funeral. However, kinship ties frequently create obligations and responsibilities. We may feel compelled to assist our kin, and we may feel free to call on them for many types of aid, including loans and babysitting.

How do we identify kinship groups? The principle of descent assigns people to kinship groups according to their relationship to a mother or father. There are three primary ways of determining descent. The United States follows the system of **bilateral descent,** which means that both sides of a person's family are regarded as equally important. For example, no higher value is given to the brothers of one's father than to the brothers of one's mother.

Most societies—according to George Murdock, 64 percent—give preference to one side of the family or the other in tracing descent. In **patrilineal** (from the Latin *pater,* "father") **descent,** only the father's relatives are significant in terms of property, inheritance, and emotional ties. Conversely, in societies that favor **matrilineal** (from the Latin *mater,* "mother") **descent,** only the mother's relatives are significant.

New forms of reproductive technology will necessitate a new way of looking at kinship. Today, a combination of biological and social processes can "create" a family member, requiring that more distinctions be made about who is related to whom.

use your sociological *imagination*

In your family, which relatives do you have a significant relationship with? Which do you hardly ever see?

Authority Patterns: Who Rules?

Imagine that you have recently married and must begin to make decisions about the future of your new family. You and your spouse face many questions. Where will you live? How will you furnish your home? Who will do the cooking, the shopping, the cleaning? Whose friends will be invited to dinner? Each time a decision must be made, an issue is raised: Who has the power to make the decision? In simple terms, who rules the family? Conflict theorists examine these questions in the context of traditional gender stratification, under which men have held a dominant position over women.

Societies vary in the way power is distributed within the family. A society that expects males to dominate in all family decision

14-1 One Wife, Many Husbands: The Nyinba

The Nyinba culture of Nepal and Tibet is an agrarian society located in the remote valleys of the Himalaya Mountains, more than 9,000 feet above sea level. Despite the Nyinba's isolation, they have been closely studied. Scholars from around the world have traveled to the Himalayas to observe this people, one of the few remaining cultures on earth to practice polyandry.

In the physically challenging environment of the Himalayas, polyandry seems to work well. Because the land and climate make it difficult

> *Favoritism toward a particular husband is frowned on by the Nyinba. Thus, it is the wife's responsibility to see that each husband shares time with her in a rotational fashion.*

to sustain crops, farming is labor-intensive: many Nyinba laborers must work the fields to support a single family. Thus, a typical marriage involving three brothers and one wife provides the necessary adult male laborers, yet minimizes the number of offspring—a necessity in a place where the food supply is limited.

While an outsider might suppose that Nyinba women dominate their families, in fact authority and inheritance rest on the husband or son. The birth of a son is celebrated; the birth of a daughter, regardless of who might be the father, brings disappointment. Paternity appears to be a nonissue in this culture, since households are shared by brothers from the same family. The literal head of the household is the oldest brother, who typically chooses a wife from outside his extended family.

Favoritism toward a particular husband is frowned on by the Nyinba. Thus, it is the wife's

A Nyinba family threshing buckwheat in the field. At left is the wife; in the center, one of her five husbands (with raised mallet); at right, her mother-in-law.

responsibility to see that each husband shares time with her in a rotational fashion. Often, over the morning meal, she will indicate which husband will sleep with her that night. To avoid any confusion, the chosen husband will place his shoes outside her bedroom door.

As in any society (for example, the United States), not all Nyinba households conform to the social norm. If a family has only one son, he must of necessity marry monogamously—an unfortunate outcome in this society. If a wife is unable to have children, a second wife, typically her sister or cousin, may be welcomed into the marriage.

LET'S DISCUSS

1. Why would a monogamous marriage be considered an unfortunate one in the Nyinba culture?
2. What might be some other ways for a society to handle the physical constraints of life in a mountainous terrain?

Sources: N. Levine 1988; Stockard 2002; Zeitzen 2008.

---

making is termed a **patriarchy.** In patriarchal societies, such as Iran, the eldest male often wields the greatest power, although wives are expected to be treated with respect and kindness. An Iranian woman's status is typically defined by her relationship to a male relative, usually as a wife or daughter. In many patriarchal societies, women find it more difficult to obtain a divorce than a man does. In contrast, in a **matriarchy,** women have greater authority than men. Matriarchies, which are very uncommon, emerged among Native American tribal societies and in nations in which men were absent for long periods because of warfare or food-gathering expeditions (Farr 1999).

In a third type of authority pattern, the **egalitarian family,** spouses are regarded as equals. That does not mean, however, that all decisions are shared in such families. Wives may hold authority in some spheres, husbands in others. Many sociologists believe the egalitarian family has begun to replace the patriarchal family as the social norm in the United States.

thinking CRITICALLY

From a woman's point of view, what are the economic advantages and disadvantages of monogamous, polygamous, and polyandrous families? What are the advantages and disadvantages of each of these family situations for men?

Although spouses in an egalitarian family may not share all their decisions, they regard themselves as equals. This pattern of authority is becoming more common in the United States.

2. **Protection.** In all cultures, the family assumes the ultimate responsibility for the protection and upbringing of children.

3. **Socialization.** Parents and other kin monitor a child's behavior and transmit the norms, values, and language of their culture to the child.

4. **Regulation of sexual behavior.** Sexual norms are subject to change both over time (for instance, in the customs for dating) and across cultures (compare strict Saudi Arabia to the more permissive Denmark). However, whatever the time period or cultural values of a society, standards of sexual behavior are most clearly defined within the family circle.

5. **Affection and companionship.** Ideally, the family provides members with warm and intimate relationships, helping them to feel satisfied and secure. Of course, a family member may find such rewards outside the family—from peers, in school, at work—and may even perceive the home as an unpleasant or abusive setting. Nevertheless, we expect our relatives to understand us, to care for us, and to be there for us when we need them.

6. **Provision of social status.** We inherit a social position because of the family background and reputation of our parents and siblings. The family presents the newborn child with an ascribed status based on race and ethnicity that helps to determine his or her place within society's stratification system. Moreover, family resources affect children's ability to pursue certain opportunities, such as higher education.

Sociological Perspectives on the Family

Do we really need the family? Over a century ago, Friedrich Engels ([1884] 1959), a colleague of Karl Marx, described the family as the ultimate source of social inequality because of its role in the transfer of power, property, and privilege. More recently, conflict theorists have argued that the family contributes to societal injustice, denies women opportunities that are extended to men, and limits freedom in sexual expression and mate selection. In contrast, the functionalist view focuses on the ways in which the family gratifies the needs of its members and contributes to social stability. The interactionist view considers the intimate, face-to-face relationships that occur in the family. And the feminist approach examines the role of the wife and mother, especially in the absence of an adult male.

Functionalist View

The family performs six paramount functions, first outlined nearly 80 years ago by sociologist William F. Ogburn (Ogburn and Tibbits 1934):

1. **Reproduction.** For a society to maintain itself, it must replace dying members. In this sense, the family contributes to human survival through its function of reproduction.

Traditionally, the family has fulfilled a number of other functions, such as providing religious training, education, and recreational outlets. But Ogburn argued that other social institutions have gradually assumed many of those functions. Education once took place at the family fireside; now it is the responsibility of professionals working in schools and colleges. Even the family's traditional recreational function has been transferred to outside groups such as Little Leagues, athletic clubs, and Twitter.

Conflict View

Conflict theorists view the family not as a contributor to social stability, but as a reflection of the inequality in wealth and power that is found within the larger society. Feminist and conflict theorists note that the family has traditionally legitimized and perpetuated male dominance. Throughout most of human history—and in a wide range of societies—husbands have exercised overwhelming power and authority within the family. Not until the first wave of contemporary feminism in the United States, in the mid-1800s, was there a substantial challenge to the historic status of wives and children as the legal property of husbands.

While the egalitarian family has become a more common pattern in the United States in recent decades—owing in good part to the activism of feminists beginning in the late 1960s and early 1970s—male dominance over the family has hardly disappeared.

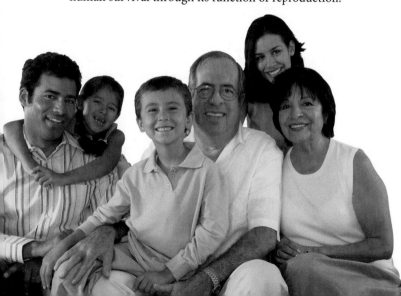

Sociologists have found that while married men are increasing their involvement in child care, their wives still perform a disproportionate amount of it. Furthermore, for every stay-at-home dad there are 38 stay-at-home moms. And unfortunately, many husbands reinforce their power and control over wives and children through acts of domestic violence (Jason Fields 2004: 11–12; Garcia-Moreno et al. 2005; Sayer et al. 2004).

Conflict theorists also view the family as an economic unit that contributes to societal injustice. The family is the basis for transferring power, property, and privilege from one generation to the next. Although the United States is widely viewed as a land of opportunity, social mobility is restricted in important ways. Children inherit the privileged or less-than-privileged social and economic status of their parents (and in some cases, of earlier generations as well). The social class of parents significantly influences children's socialization experiences and the degree of protection they receive. Thus, the socioeconomic status of a child's family will have a marked influence on his or her nutrition, health care, housing, educational opportunities, and in many respects, life chances as an adult. For this reason, conflict theorists argue that the family helps to maintain inequality.

Interactionist View

Interactionists focus on the micro level of family and other intimate relationships. They are interested in how individuals interact with one another, whether they are cohabiting partners or longtime married couples. For example, in a study of both Black and White two-parent households, researchers found that when fathers are more involved with their children (reading to them, helping them with homework, or restricting their television viewing), the children have fewer behavior problems, get along better with others, and are more responsible (Mosley and Thomson 1995).

Another interactionist study might examine the role of the stepparent. The increased number of single parents who remarry has sparked an interest in those who are helping to raise other people's children. Studies have found that stepmothers are more likely than stepfathers to accept the blame for bad relations with their stepchildren. Interactionists theorize that stepfathers (like most fathers) may simply be unaccustomed to interacting directly with children when the mother isn't there (Bray and Kelly 1999; F. Furstenberg and Cherlin 1991).

Feminist View

Because "women's work" has traditionally focused on family life, feminist sociologists have taken a strong interest in the family as a social institution. As we saw in Chapter 12, research on gender roles in child care and household chores has been extensive. Sociologists have looked particularly closely at how women's work outside the home impacts their child care and housework—duties Arlie Hochschild (1989, 1990, 2005) has referred to as the "second shift." Today, researchers recognize that for many women, the second shift includes the care of aging parents as well.

Feminist theorists have urged social scientists and social agencies to rethink the notion that families in which no adult male is present are automatically a cause for concern, or even dysfunctional. They have also contributed to research on single women, single-parent households, and lesbian couples. In the case of single mothers, researchers have focused on the resiliency of many such households, despite economic stress. According to Velma McBride Murray and her colleagues (2001) at the University of Georgia, such studies show that among African Americans, single mothers draw heavily on kinfolk for material resources, parenting advice, and social support. Considering feminist research on the family as a whole, one researcher concluded that the family is the "source of women's strength" (V. Taylor et al. 2009).

Finally, feminists who take the interactionist perspective stress the need to investigate neglected topics in family studies. For instance, in a growing number of dual-income households, the wife earns a higher income than the husband. In 2005, a study of 58 married couples revealed that 26 percent of the wives earned more than their husbands. In 1981, the proportion was just 16 percent. Yet beyond individual case studies, little research has been done on how these families may differ from those in which the husband is the major breadwinner (Wills and Risman 2006).

Table 14-1 summarizes the four major theoretical perspectives on the family.

Interactionists are particularly interested in the ways in which parents relate to each other and to their children. The close and loving relationship illustrated here is one of the foundations of a strong family.

TABLE **14-1** SOCIOLOGICAL PERSPECTIVES ON THE FAMILY

Theoretical Perspective	Emphasis
Functionalist	The family as a contributor to social stability Roles of family members
Conflict	The family as a perpetuator of inequality Transmission of poverty or wealth across generations
Interactionist	Relationships among family members
Feminist	The family as a perpetuator of gender roles Female-headed households

summingup

Marriage and Family

Currently, over 95 percent of all men and women in the United States marry at least once during their lifetimes. Historically, the most consistent aspect of family life in this country has been the high rate of marriage. In fact, despite the high rate of divorce, there are some indications of a miniboom in marriages of late.

In this part of the chapter, we will examine various aspects of love, marriage, and parenthood in the United States and contrast them with cross-cultural examples. Though we're used to thinking of romance and mate selection as strictly a matter of individual preference, sociological analysis tells us that social institutions and distinctive cultural norms and values also play an important role.

Courtship and Mate Selection

In the past, most couples met their partners through family, friends, or their neighborhood or workplace. Today, however, many couples meet on the Internet. According to a national survey done in 2010, the Internet is second only to friends as a source of romantic partners—ahead of family, workplace, and neighborhood. Significantly, online networking is just as important to mate-seekers in their 40s and 50s as to those under age 30. It is especially important to gays and lesbians, given the limited number of meeting places available to them: 61 percent of same-sex couples meet online, compared to 23 percent of heterosexual couples (Rosenfeld 2010).

Internet romance is only the latest courtship practice. In the central Asian nation of Uzbekistan and many other traditional cultures, courtship is defined largely through the interaction of two sets of parents, who arrange marriages for their children. Typically, a young Uzbekistani woman will be socialized to eagerly anticipate her marriage to a man whom she has met only once, when he is presented to her family at the time of the final inspection of her dowry. In the United States, in contrast, courtship is conducted primarily by individuals who have a romantic interest in each other. In our culture, courtship often requires these individuals to rely heavily on intricate games, gestures, and signals. Despite such differences, courtship—whether in the United States, Uzbekistan, or elsewhere—is influenced by the norms and values of the larger society (Carol J. Williams 1995).

One unmistakable trend in mate selection is that the process appears to be taking longer today than in the past. A variety of factors, including concerns about financial security and personal independence, has contributed to this delay in marriage. Most people are now well into their 20s before they marry, both in the United States and in other countries (Figure 14-2).

Aspects of Mate Selection Many societies have explicit or unstated rules that define potential mates as acceptable or unacceptable. These norms can be distinguished in terms of endogamy and exogamy. **Endogamy** (from the Greek *endon*, "within") specifies the groups within which a spouse must be found and prohibits marriage with others. For example, in the United States, many people are expected to marry within their racial, ethnic, or religious group, and are strongly discouraged or even prohibited from marrying outside the group. Endogamy is intended to reinforce the cohesiveness of the group by suggesting to the young that they should marry someone "of their own kind." Although interracial and interethnic marriages are still the exception, about one in every seven new marriages in the United States is either interracial or an interethnic union between Hispanics and non-Hispanics. About one-fourth of Latinos and one-third of Asian Americans now marry outside their group (Pew Research Center 2010).

In contrast, **exogamy** (from the Greek *exo*, "outside") requires mate selection outside certain groups, usually one's family or certain kinfolk. The **incest taboo,** a social norm common to virtually all societies, prohibits sexual relationships between certain culturally specified relatives. For those of us in the United States, this taboo means

FIGURE 14-2 MEDIAN AGE AT FIRST MARRIAGE IN EIGHT COUNTRIES

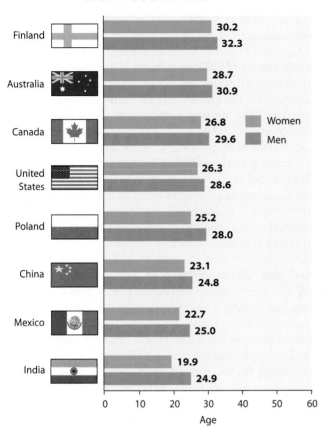

Country	Women	Men
Finland	30.2	32.3
Australia	28.7	30.9
Canada	26.8	29.6
United States	26.3	28.6
Poland	25.2	28.0
China	23.1	24.8
Mexico	22.7	25.0
India	19.9	24.9

Source: United Nations Statistics Division 2008.

Think about It
Why do people marry earlier in India than in Finland?

Although most interracial couples are not as visible as Seal and Heidi Klum, such unions are becoming increasingly common and accepted. They are also blurring the definitions of race. Will the children of these couples be considered Black or White? Why do you think so?

that we must marry outside the nuclear family. We cannot marry our siblings, and in most states we cannot marry our first cousins.

Another factor that influences the selection of a marriage partner is **homogamy,** the conscious or unconscious tendency to select a mate with personal characteristics similar to one's own. The "like marries like" rule can be seen in couples with similar personalities and cultural interests. However, mate selection is unpredictable. Though some people may follow the homogamous pattern, others observe the "opposites attract" rule: one person is dependent and submissive—almost childishly so—while the other is dominant and controlling.

Recently, the concept of homogamy has been incorporated into the process of seeking a date or marital partner online. The Internet dating site eHarmony, which claims to be the first to use a "scientific approach" to matching people based on a variety of abilities and interests, says that it "facilitates" 46 marriages a day. Sociologist Pepper Schwartz, a consultant for the competing site PerfectMatch.com, has developed a 48-question survey that covers everything from prospective mates' decision-making style to their degree of impulsivity (Gottlieb 2006; Kalmijn 1998).

The Love Relationship Today's generation of college students seems more likely to hook up or cruise in large packs than to

engage in the romantic dating relationships of their parents and grandparents. Still, at some point in their adult lives, the great majority of today's students will meet someone they love and enter into a long-term relationship that focuses on creating a family.

Parents in the United States tend to value love highly as a rationale for marriage, so they encourage their children to develop intimate relationships based on love and affection. Songs, films, books, magazines, television shows, and even cartoons and comic books reinforce the theme of love. At the same time, our society expects parents and peers to help a person confine his or her search for a mate to "socially acceptable" members of the opposite sex.

Though most people in the United States take the importance of falling in love for granted, the coupling of love and marriage is by no means a cultural universal. Many of the world's cultures give priority in mate selection to factors other than romantic feelings. In societies with *arranged marriages* engineered by parents or religious authorities, economic considerations play a significant role. The newly married couple is expected to develop a feeling of love *after* the legal union is formalized, if at all.

Throughout the world, even where marital arrangements differ from our own, new media technologies are changing the mating game. In a rural Turkish village, where a small minority of the population still practices polygyny, the search for a second wife has moved from neighboring Syria to an Internet café where local men can contact prospective brides in faraway Morocco. Moroccan women watch Turkish soap operas on television and tend to see Turkish men as more romantic than others. They have become familiar with Turkey's culture and religion, politics and economy through the international news media. With a weak economy at home, many of these women must look elsewhere for marriage, so they turn to the Arabic website Habibti.com ("Mydear.com") to find a traditional marriage in an untraditional way (Schleifer 2009).

---

use your sociological *imagination*

Your parents and/or a matchmaker are going to arrange a marriage for you. What kind of mate will they select? Will your chances of having a successful marriage be better or worse than if you selected your own mate?

Variations in Family Life and Intimate Relationships

Within the United States, social class, race, and ethnicity create variations in family life. Studying these variations will give us a more sophisticated understanding of contemporary family styles in our country.

Social Class Differences Various studies have documented the differences in family organization among social classes in the United States. In the upper class, the emphasis is on lineage and maintenance of family position. If you are in the upper class, you are not simply a member of a nuclear family, but rather a member of a larger family tradition (think of the Rockefellers or the Kennedys). As a result, upper-class families are quite concerned about what they see as proper training for children.

Lower-class families do not often have the luxury of worrying about the "family name"; they must first struggle to pay their bills and survive the crises often associated with a life of poverty. Such families are more likely to have only one parent at home, which creates special challenges in child care and financial management. Children from lower-class families typically assume adult responsibilities—including marriage and parenthood—at an earlier age than children from affluent homes. In part, that is because they may lack the money needed to remain in school.

Social class differences in family life are less striking today than they once were. In the past, family specialists agreed that the contrasts in child-rearing practices were pronounced. Lower-class families were found to be more authoritarian in rearing children and more inclined to use physical punishment. Middle-class families were more permissive and more restrained in punishing their children. And compared to lower-class families, middle-class families tended to schedule more of their children's time, or even to overstructure it. However, these differences may have narrowed as more and more families from all social classes turned to the same books, magazines, and even television talk shows for advice on rearing children (Kronstadt and Favreault 2008; Luster et al. 1989).

Among the poor, women often play a significant role in the economic support of the family. Men may earn low wages, may be unemployed, or may be entirely absent from the family. In 2009, 30 percent of all families headed by women with no husband present fell below the federal government's poverty line. In comparison, the poverty rate for married couples was only 5.5 percent. The disproportionate representation of female-headed households among the poor is a persistent and growing trend, referred to by sociologists as the *feminization of poverty* (see Chapter 9; DeNavas-Walt et al. 2010:15).

Many racial and ethnic groups appear to have distinctive family characteristics. However, racial and class factors are often closely related. In examining family life among racial and ethnic minorities, keep in mind that certain patterns may result from class as well as cultural factors.

Racial and Ethnic Differences The subordinate status of racial and ethnic minorities in the United States profoundly affects their family lives. For example, the lower incomes of African Americans, Native Americans, most Hispanic groups, and selected Asian American groups make creating and maintaining successful marital unions a difficult task. The economic restructuring of the past 60 years, described by sociologist William Julius Wilson (1996, 2009) and others, has especially affected people living in inner cities and desolate rural areas, such as reservations. Furthermore, the immigration policy of the United States has complicated the successful relocation of intact families from Asia and Latin America.

The African American family suffers from many negative and inaccurate stereotypes. It is true that in a significantly higher proportion of Black than White families, no husband is present in the home (Figure 14-3). Yet Black single mothers often belong to stable, functioning kin networks, which mitigate the pressures of sexism and racism. Members of these networks—predominantly female kin such as mothers, grandmothers, and aunts—ease financial strains by sharing goods and services. In addition to these strong kinship bonds, Black family life has emphasized deep religious commitment and high aspirations for achievement (DuBois [1909] 1970; F. Furstenberg 2007).

Like African Americans, Native Americans draw on family ties to cushion many of the hardships they face. On the Navajo reservation, for example, teenage parenthood is not regarded as the crisis that it is elsewhere in the United States. The Navajo trace their descent matrilineally. Traditionally, couples reside with the wife's family after marriage, allowing the grandparents to help with the child rearing. While the Navajo do not approve of teenage parenthood, the deep emotional commitment of their extended families provides a warm home environment for children, even when no father is present or involved (Dalla and Gamble 2001).

Sociologists also have taken note of differences in family patterns among other racial and ethnic groups. For example, Mexican American men have been described as exhibiting a sense of virility, personal worth, and pride in their maleness that is called **machismo.** Mexican Americans are also described as

FIGURE **14-3** RISE OF SINGLE-PARENT FAMILIES IN THE UNITED STATES, 1970–2010

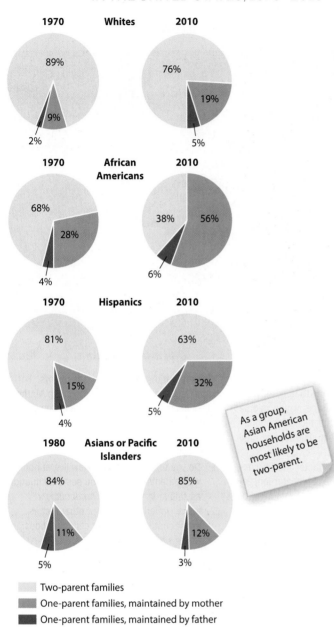

Two-parent families
One-parent families, maintained by mother
One-parent families, maintained by father

As a group, Asian American households are most likely to be two-parent.

Note: Families are groups with children under 18. Early data for Asian Americans are for 1980. Hispanics can be of any race. Not included are unrelated people living together with no children present. All data exclude the 11 percent of children in nonparental households.
Sources: Bureau of the Census 2008a:56, 2010c:Table FG10.

being more familistic than many other subcultures. **Familism** refers to pride in the extended family, expressed through the maintenance of close ties and strong obligations to kinfolk outside the immediate family. Traditionally, Mexican Americans have placed proximity to their extended families above other needs and desires.

Although familism is often seen as a positive cultural attribute, it may also have negative consequences. Sociologists who have studied the relatively low college application rates of Hispanic students have found they have a strong desire to stay at home. Even the children of college-educated parents express this preference, which diminishes the likelihood of their

getting a four-year degree and dramatically reduces the possibility that they will apply to a selective college (Desmond and Turley 2009).

These family patterns are changing, however, in response to changes in Latinos' social class standing, educational achievements, and occupations. Like other Americans, career-oriented Latinos in search of a mate but short on spare time are turning to Internet sites. As Latinos and other groups assimilate into the dominant culture of the United States, their family lives take on both the positive and negative characteristics associated with White households (Landale and Oropesa 2007).

Child-Rearing Patterns

The Nayars of southern India acknowledge the biological role of fathers, but the mother's eldest brother is responsible for her children. In contrast, uncles play only a peripheral role in child care in the United States. Caring for children is a universal function of the family, yet the ways in which different societies assign this function to family members can vary significantly. Even within the United States, child-rearing patterns are varied. We'll take a look here at parenthood and grandparenthood, adoption, dual-income families, single-parent families, and stepfamilies.

Parenthood and Grandparenthood The socialization of children is essential to the maintenance of any culture. Consequently, parenthood is one of the most important (and most demanding) social roles in the United States. Sociologist Alice Rossi (1968, 1984) has identified four factors that complicate the transition to parenthood and the role of socialization. First, there is little anticipatory socialization for the social role of caregiver. The normal school curriculum gives scant attention to the subjects most relevant to successful family life, such as child care and home maintenance. Second, only limited learning occurs during the period of pregnancy itself. Third, the transition to parenthood is quite abrupt. Unlike adolescence, it is not prolonged; unlike the transition to work, the duties of caregiving cannot be taken on gradually. Finally, in Rossi's view, our society lacks clear and helpful guidelines for successful parenthood. There is little consensus on how parents can produce happy and well-adjusted offspring—or even on what it means to be well adjusted. For these reasons, socialization for parenthood involves difficult challenges for most men and women in the United States.

One recent development in family life in the United States has been the extension of parenthood, as single adult children continue to live at home or return home after college. In 2009, 33 percent of men and 22 percent of women in their 20s lived with their parents. Some of these adult children were still pursuing an education, but in many instances, financial difficulties lay at the heart of these living arrangements. For younger job seekers, employment is often short-term or low paying. (This problem, along with the trend toward adult children living with their parents, is not unique to the United States; see Box 14-2.) Moreover, with many marriages now ending in divorce—most commonly in the first seven years of marriage—divorced sons and daughters often return to live with their parents, sometimes with their own children (Bureau of the Census 2010b:Table A2).

14-2 Family Life, Italian Style: Thirty-Something and Living with Mom

Bamboccioni—adult children who live with their parents—are no longer socially unacceptable in Italy. In fact, they're not even unusual. In December 2009, the Italian government released new data showing that 40 percent of Italian men between ages 30 and 34 live with their parents. So do 20 percent of Italian women in this age bracket. Among those a little older, ages 35 to 39, 17.5 percent of men and 9.3 percent of women live with their parents.

> *About 40 percent of* bamboccioni *live with their parents not because of financial need, but because they enjoy the company.*

This state of affairs is not a recent phenomenon. What is new is that 80 percent of these adult children say they cannot afford to leave their parents' homes. Salaries in Italy are low but rents are high, so these not-so-young adults linger on with mama and papa. As one of them, a 30-year-old biologist, put it, "We are the €1,000-per-month generation—who can afford spending more than €800 for an apartment?"

About 40 percent of *bamboccioni* live with their parents not because of financial need, but because they enjoy the company. Others feel responsible for their aging parents. Among the women ages 35 to 40, more than half feel it is a duty. Sociologist Giampiero dalla Zuanna says their commitment to the family means the elderly in Italy are much more likely to remain in their own homes than those in northern Europe, many of whom must move to retirement communities.

The pattern of adult children staying home with their parents is not unique to Italy. In North America and throughout Europe, young people are feeling the impact of the recent economic downturn. Many are delaying childbearing until their job prospects improve.

One relatively unnoticed factor that is contributing to the trend is parents' greater longevity. Today, more parents survive long enough for their children to become adults, and remain healthy enough to maintain a home for them.

What happens when adult children finally do leave the nest? So close are the ties between parent and child in Italy that services have emerged to support their relationship through the separation in living arrangements. For a small fee, special couriers will pick up Mother's fresh homemade pasta and even homegrown greens and deliver them to her adult children.

LET'S DISCUSS

1. Do you or someone you know live at home with parents? If so, do you see the situation as similar to that of the *bamboccioni*?
2. In the United States, what other factors might contribute to adult children choosing to live with their parents?

Sources: Meichtry 2011; Momigliana 2010; S. Roberts 2010.

Is this living arrangement a positive development for family members? Social scientists have just begun to examine the phenomenon, sometimes called the "boomerang generation" or the "full-nest syndrome" in the popular press. One survey in Virginia seemed to show that neither the parents nor their adult children were happy about continuing to live together. The children often felt resentful and isolated, but the parents suffered too: learning to live without children in the home is an essential stage of adult life and may even be a significant turning point for a marriage (*Berkeley Wellness Letter* 1990; Mogelonsky 1996).

In some homes, the full nest holds grandchildren. In 2009, 7 million children, or 9 percent of all children in the United States, lived in a household with a grandparent. In about a third of these homes, no parent was present to assume responsibility for the youngsters. Special difficulties are inherent in such relationships, including legal custodial concerns, financial issues, and emotional problems for adults and youths alike. It is not surprising that support groups such as Grandparents as Parents have emerged to provide assistance (Bureau of the Census 2010b:Table C4).

thinking CRITICALLY

How do both cultural and socioeconomic factors contribute to the "boomerang generation"?

Adoption In a legal sense, **adoption** is a "process that allows for the transfer of the legal rights, responsibilities, and privileges of parenthood" to a new legal parent or parents (E. Cole 1985:638).

When nine-year-old Blake Brunson shows up for a basketball game, so do his *eight* grandparents—the result of his parents' remarriages. Blended families can be very supportive to children, but what message do they send to them on the permanency of marriage?

In many cases, these rights are transferred from a biological parent or parents (often called birth parents) to an adoptive parent or parents. At any given time, about 2 million adults in the United States are raising adopted children (Jo Jones 2009).

Viewed from a functionalist perspective, government has a strong interest in encouraging adoption. Policymakers, in fact, have both a humanitarian and a financial stake in the process. In theory, adoption offers a stable family environment for children who otherwise might not receive satisfactory care. Moreover, government data show that unwed mothers who keep their babies tend to be of lower socioeconomic status and often require public assistance to support their children. The government can lower its social welfare expenses, then, if children are transferred to economically self-sufficient families. From an interactionist perspective, however, adoption may require a child to adjust to a very different family environment and parental approach to child rearing.

About 4 percent of all people in the United States are adopted, about half of whom were adopted by persons not related to them at birth. There are two legal methods of adopting an unrelated person: the adoption may be arranged through a licensed agency, or in some states it may be arranged through a private agreement sanctioned by the courts. Adopted children may come from the United States or from abroad. In 2009, over 12,700 children entered the United States as the adopted children of U.S. citizens. International adoptions began to decline in 2004 after a long and steady increase. Recently China, the source for about one-fourth of overseas adoptions, tightened the rules for foreign adoptions, effectively reducing their number. Applicants for adoption who are single, obese, or older than 50 are now automatically disqualified (Department of State 2010a).

The 2010 earthquake in Haiti drew attention to the foreign perspective on international adoptions, which is not always positive. When well-meaning people from the United States arrived in Haiti to rescue alleged orphans and arrange for their adoption in other countries, government officials objected. Some of the children, it turned out, were not orphans; their parents were simply too poor to care for them. For the governments of overstressed developing nations, adoption can be both a solution and a problem.

Adoption is controversial not only abroad but at home as well. In some cases, those who adopt children are not married. In 1995, an important court decision in New York held that a couple does not need to be married to adopt a child. Under this ruling, unmarried heterosexual couples, lesbian couples, and gay couples can all adopt children in New York. Today, most states permit gay and lesbian couples to adopt. Florida is the only state that explicitly forbids it; five others (Arkansas, Michigan, Mississippi, Nebraska, and Utah) prohibit couples who are not legally married from adopting (National Gay and Lesbian Task Force 2008).

For every child who is adopted, many more remain the wards of state-sponsored child protective services. At any given time, around half a million children in the United States are living in foster care. Every year, about 57,000 of them are adopted; another 103,000 are eligible and waiting to be adopted (Department of Health and Human Services 2011b).

Dual-Income Families The idea of a family consisting of a wage-earning husband and a wife who stays at home has largely given way to the dual-income household. Among married people between ages 25 and 34, 96 percent of the men and 69 percent of the women were in the labor force in 2007 (Bureau of the Census 2008a:375).

Why has there been such a rise in the number of dual-income couples? A major factor is economic need, coupled with a desire by both men *and* women to pursue their careers. Evidence of this trend can be found in the rise in the number of married couples living apart for reasons other than marital discord. The 3.6 million couples who now live apart represent 1 out of every 33 marriages. More than half of them live farther than 100 miles apart, and half of those live 1,000 or more miles apart. Of course, couples living apart are nothing new; men have worked at transient jobs for generations as soldiers, truck drivers, or traveling salesmen. Now, however, the woman's job is often the one that creates the separation. The existence of such household arrangements reflects an acceptance of the egalitarian family type (Higgins et al. 2010; Holmes 2009; Silverman 2009).

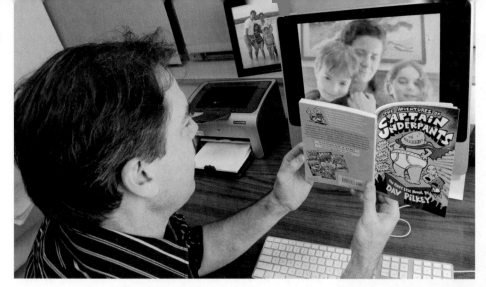

Miles Harvey reads to his children via Skype. Harvey, who is happily married, lives 900 miles from his family in Chicago. He accepted a job in New Orleans for economic reasons.

worth in our society is limited at best. Given the barriers that many young women face because of their gender, race, ethnicity, and class, many teenagers may believe they have little to lose and much to gain by having a child.

According to a widely held stereotype, "unwed mothers" and "babies having babies" in the United States are predominantly African American. However, this view is not entirely accurate. African Americans account for a disproportionate share of births to unmarried women and teenagers, but the majority of all babies born to unmarried teenage mothers are born to White adolescents. Moreover, since 1980, birthrates among Black teenagers have generally declined (J. Martin et al. 2009).

Although 84 percent of single parents in the United States are mothers, the number of households headed by single fathers more than quadrupled from 1987 to 2010. Though single mothers often develop social networks, single fathers are typically more isolated. In addition, they must deal with schools and social service agencies that are more accustomed to women as custodial parents (Bureau of the Census 1994, 2010b).

Stepfamilies Approximately 45 percent of all people in the United States will marry, divorce, and then remarry. The rising rates of divorce and remarriage have led to a noticeable increase in stepfamily relationships.

The exact nature of blended families has social significance for adults and children alike. Certainly resocialization is required when an adult becomes a stepparent or a child becomes a stepchild and stepsibling. Moreover, an important distinction must be made between first-time stepfamilies and households where there have been repeated divorces, breakups, or changes in custodial arrangements.

In evaluating the rise of stepfamilies, some observers have assumed that children would benefit from remarriage because they would be gaining a second custodial parent, and would potentially enjoy greater economic security. However, after reviewing many studies of stepfamilies, sociologist Andrew J. Cherlin (2009:5) concluded that "children whose parents have remarried do not have higher levels of well-being than children in lone-parent families."

Stepparents can play valuable and unique roles in their stepchildren's lives, but their involvement does not guarantee an improvement in family life. In fact, standards may decline. Studies suggest that children raised in families with stepmothers are likely to have less health care, education, and money spent on their food than children raised by biological mothers. The measures are also negative for children raised by stepfathers, but only half as negative as in the case of stepmothers. These results don't mean that stepmothers are "evil"—it may be that the stepmother holds back out of concern for seeming too intrusive, or relies mistakenly on the biological father to carry out parental duties (Schmeeckle 2007; Schmeeckle et al. 2006).

---

use your sociological *imagination*

What personal experience do you have with child rearing by grandparents, adoptive parents, or dual-income families? Describe what you observed using sociological concepts.

Single-Parent Families The 2004 *American Idol* winner Fantasia Barrino's song "Baby Mama" offers a tribute to young single mothers—a subject she knows about. Barrino was 17 when she became pregnant with her daughter. Though critics charged that the song sends the wrong message to teenage girls, Barrino says it is not about encouraging teens to have sex. Rather, she sees the song as an anthem for young mothers courageously trying to raise their children alone (Cherlin 2006).

In recent decades, the stigma attached to unwed mothers and other single parents has significantly diminished. **Single-parent families,** in which only one parent is present to care for the children, can hardly be viewed as a rarity in the United States. In 2010, a single parent headed about 24 percent of White families with children under 18, 37 percent of Hispanic families with children, and 62 percent of African American families with children (see Figure 14-3 on page 315).

The lives of single parents and their children are not inevitably more difficult than life in a traditional nuclear family. It is as inaccurate to assume that a single-parent family is necessarily deprived as it is to assume that a two-parent family is always secure and happy. Nevertheless, life in a single-parent family can be extremely stressful, in both economic and emotional terms. A family headed by a single mother faces especially difficult problems when the mother is a teenager.

Why might low-income teenage women wish to have children and face the obvious financial difficulties of motherhood? Viewed from an interactionist perspective, these women tend to have low self-esteem and limited options; a child may provide a sense of motivation and purpose for a teenager whose economic

Divorce

In the United States, the pattern of family life includes commitments both to marriage and to self-expression and personal growth. Needless to say, the tension between those competing commitments can undermine a marriage, working against the establishment of a lasting relationship. This approach to family life is distinctive to the United States. In some nations, such as Italy, the culture strongly supports marriage and discourages divorce. In others, such as Sweden, people treat marriage the same way as cohabitation, and both arrangements are just as lasting (Cherlin 2009).

Statistical Trends in Divorce

Just how common is divorce? Surprisingly, this is not a simple question; divorce statistics are difficult to interpret. The media frequently report that one out of every two marriages ends in divorce, but that figure is misleading. It is based on a comparison of all divorces that occur in a single year (regardless of when the couples were married) with the number of new marriages in the same year.

In many countries, divorce began to increase in the late 1960s but then leveled off; since the late 1980s, it has declined by 30 percent. (Figure 14-4 shows the pattern in the United States.) This trend is due partly to the aging of the baby boomer population and the corresponding decline in the proportion of people of marriageable age. But it also indicates an increase in marital stability in recent years (Coontz 2006).

Getting divorced obviously does not sour people on marriage. About 63 percent of all divorced people in the United States have remarried. Women are less likely than men to remarry because many retain custody of their children after a divorce, which complicates a new adult relationship (Bianchi and Spain 1996; Saad 2004).

Most households in the United States do not consist of two parents living with their unmarried children.

Some people regard the nation's high rate of remarriage as an endorsement of the institution of marriage, but it does lead to the new challenges of a kin network composed of both current and prior marital relationships. Such networks can be particularly complex if children are involved or if an ex-spouse remarries.

Factors Associated with Divorce

Perhaps the most important factor in the increase in divorce over the past hundred years has been the greater social *acceptance* of divorce. It is no longer considered necessary to endure an unhappy marriage. More important, various religious denominations have relaxed their negative attitudes toward divorce, so that most religious leaders no longer treat it as a sin.

The growing acceptance of divorce is a worldwide phenomenon. A decade ago, Sunoo, South Korea's foremost matchmaking service, had no divorced clients. Few Koreans divorced; those who did felt social pressure to resign themselves to the single life. But in one recent seven-year period, South Korea's divorce rate doubled. Today, 15 percent of Sunoo's membership are divorced (Onishi 2003; United Nations Statistics Division 2009:Table 23).

In the United States, several factors have contributed to the growing social acceptance of divorce:

- Most states have adopted more liberal divorce laws in the past three decades. No-fault divorce laws, which allow a couple to end their marriage without fault on either side (by specifying adultery, for instance), accounted for an initial surge in the divorce rate after they were introduced in the 1970s, but appear to have had little effect beyond that.

- Divorce has become a more practical option in newly formed families, since families tend to have fewer children now than in the past.

- A general increase in family incomes, coupled with the availability of free legal aid to some poor people, has meant that more couples can afford costly divorce proceedings.

FIGURE **14-4**   TRENDS IN MARRIAGE AND DIVORCE IN THE UNITED STATES, 1920–2009

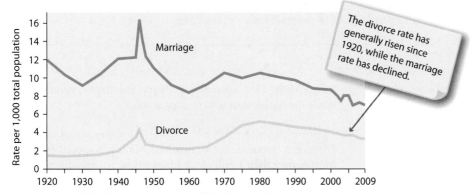

The divorce rate has generally risen since 1920, while the marriage rate has declined.

Sources: Bureau of the Census 1975:64; *National Vital Statistics Reports* 2010.

14-3   Divorce and Military Deployment

Whenever soldiers talk about the hardships of foreign deployment, separation from their families and the toll on their marital relationships are the main topic. Too often, military couples marry just before a deployment, following a brief romance. Then, when they are suddenly separated, the relationship begins to fall apart. To keep wives from worrying or to reduce their own homesickness, many soldiers avoid calling home. Those couples who do communicate by phone, letter, or e-mail often argue; some talk about divorce. Impulsively, a soldier may throw his wedding ring away. A wife struggling to manage on her own may empty the family's bank account.

Yet many couples make heroic efforts to hold together despite the hardship. Those who are left home continue to care for their families, coping with life as a single parent and

23 percent of soldiers stationed in Iraq in 2009 say they plan to divorce or separate after returning home.

Welcome home! Military families reunite after a long, anxious separation.

comforting children who miss their father or mother. They will themselves to overcome loneliness and anxiety. For these couples, every new deployment is a challenge; being apart doesn't get easier as they get older.

On balance, does overseas deployment affect the divorce rate among military couples? Current research delivers a mixed message. One long-term study published recently indicates that the longer the deployment, the lower the risk of divorce. Studies of soldiers who served in the Vietnam War and the 1991 Persian Gulf War came to the same conclusion. Yet 2009 data show that the current divorce rate among those in the military is 3.6 percent a year—slightly higher than the national rate of 3.4 percent. Furthermore, 23 percent of soldiers stationed in Iraq in 2009 say they plan to divorce or separate after returning home, compared to 12 percent in 2003.

There were other negative findings of the study. Female service members were found to be twice as likely as male service members to end their marriages. Moreover, enlisted service members were more likely than officers to end their marriages. This second disparity may be due to the fact that officers tend to be older than enlisted personnel, and older couples are less likely than younger couples to divorce.

Studies of the impact of overseas deployment on couples' children have not been reassuring. In 2007, an Army-funded study found that the rate of child neglect among military families was almost four times higher when husbands were deployed than when they were home. Physical abuse of children in those cases was nearly twice as high when husbands were away. Given these findings, one can only hope that support programs for families separated by war will be strengthened.

There is a need for further research on this topic. The information that researchers have covers only the short term and pertains only to those soldiers who remained in the military. Could the long-term impact on military couples be more telling? Could the outcome be different for those who leave the military soon after a war? And might soldiers consider marriage more carefully than the average person, knowing that their futures are uncertain? As with even the most detailed research, this study's conclusions raise new questions for scientific investigation.

LET'S DISCUSS

1. Do you know any married couples who have been separated by military deployment overseas? If so, how did they cope? What was the effect on their children?
2. Can you think of some other reasons why military marriages might survive the strain of war as well as they do?

Sources: Block 2009; Bowman 2009; D. Gibbs et al. 2007; Karney and Crown 2007; Krauss 1993; Perry 2007; Priest 2008; RAND 2007; Stone and Bello 2009; Wheller 2009; Zoroya 2009.

- As society provides greater opportunities for women, more and more wives are becoming less dependent on their husbands, both economically and emotionally. They may feel more able to leave a marriage if it seems hopeless.

What about the stress of separation caused by military duty? Forced transfer overseas, the tension of war, new duties at home, and anxiety over a spouse's return might seem a recipe for marital failure. Box 14-3 considers military marriages' vulnerability while the husband or wife is away at war.

Impact of Divorce on Children

Divorce is traumatic for all involved, but it has special meaning for the more than 1 million children whose parents divorce each year. Of course, for some of these children, divorce signals the welcome end to a very dysfunctional relationship. Perhaps that

FIGURE **14-5** UNMARRIED-COUPLE HOUSEHOLDS BY STATE

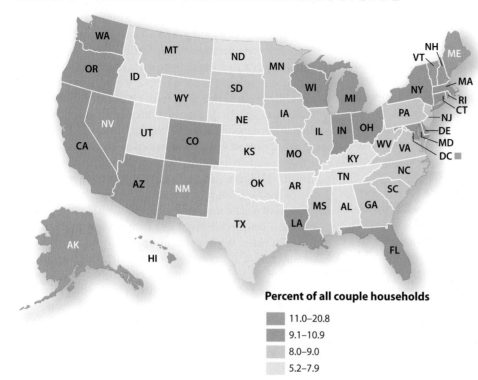

Percent of all couple households

- 11.0–20.8
- 9.1–10.9
- 8.0–9.0
- 5.2–7.9

Note: Data are for 2000 and include both opposite-sex and same-sex partners. U.S. average is 9.1 percent.
Source: Simmons and O'Connell 2003:4.

Cohabitation

In the United States, testing the marital waters by living together before making a commitment is a common practice among marriage-wary 20- and 30-somethings. The tremendous increase in the number of male–female couples who choose to live together without marrying, a practice called **cohabitation,** is one of the most dramatic trends of recent years.

About half of all *currently* married couples in the United States say that they lived together before marriage. This percentage is likely to increase. The number of households in the United States that are headed by unmarried opposite-sex couples has been rising steadily; in 2010 it was 6.7 million. Figure 14-5 shows regional variations in the rate of cohabitation (Kreider 2010).

In much of Europe, cohabitation is so common that the general sentiment seems to be "Love, yes; marriage, maybe." In Iceland, 62 percent of all children are born to single mothers; in France, Great Britain, and Norway, about 40 percent. Government policies in these countries make few legal distinctions between married and unmarried couples or households. Perhaps as a result, partnerships between cohabiting adults are not necessarily brief or lacking in commitment. Children born to a cohabiting couple in Sweden, for example, are less likely than children born to a cohabiting couple in the United States to see their parents break up (Cherlin 2009; Lyall 2002; M. Moore 2006).

People commonly associate cohabitation with younger couples. But according to a study done in Los Angeles, working couples are almost twice as likely to cohabit as college students. And census data show that in 2003, 45 percent of unmarried couples had one or more children present in the household. These cohabitants are more like spouses than dating partners. Moreover, in contrast to the common perception that people who cohabit have never been married, researchers report that about half of all people involved in cohabitation in the United States have been previously married. Cohabitation serves as a temporary or permanent alternative to matrimony for many men and women who have experienced their own or their parents' divorces (Jason Fields 2004; Popenoe and Whitehead 1999).

Periodically, legislators attempt to bolster the desirability of a lifelong commitment to marriage. In 2002, President George W. Bush backed funding for an initiative to promote marriage among those who receive public assistance. Under the Healthy Marriage Initiative, the federal government created a resource center that promoted marriage-related programs. Critics charged

is why a national study that tracked 6,332 children both before and after their parents' divorce found that their behavior did not suffer from the marital breakups. Other studies have shown greater unhappiness among children who live amid parental conflict than among children whose parents are divorced. Still, it would be simplistic to assume that children are automatically better off following the breakup of their parents' marriage. The interests of the parents do not necessarily serve children well (Zi 2007).

thinking CRITICALLY

In a society that maximizes the welfare of all family members, how easy should it be for couples to divorce? How easy should it be to get married?

Diverse Lifestyles

Marriage is no longer the presumed route from adolescence to adulthood. Instead, it is treated as just one of several paths to maturity. As a result, the marriage ceremony has lost much of its social significance as a rite of passage. The nation's marriage rate has declined since 1960 because people are postponing marriage until later in life, and because more couples, including same-sex couples, are deciding to form partnerships without marriage (Haq 2011).

that the effort was underfunded or an inappropriate mission for the federal government. Still, the Obama administration has indicated a desire to continue the initiative, although the fragile economy may jeopardize its funding (Jayson 2009).

Remaining Single

Looking at TV programs today, you would be justified in thinking that most households are composed of singles. Although that is not the case, it is true that more and more people in the United States are postponing entry into a first marriage. Over one out of three households with children in the United States is a single-parent household. Even so, less than 4 percent of women and men in the United States are likely to remain single throughout their lives (Bureau of the Census 2008a).

The trend toward maintaining a single lifestyle for a longer period is related to the growing economic independence of young people. This trend is especially significant for women. Freed from financial needs, women don't necessarily need to marry to enjoy a satisfying life. Divorce, late marriage, and longevity also figure into this trend.

There are many reasons why a person may choose not to marry. Some singles do not want to limit their sexual intimacy to one lifetime partner. Some men and women do not want to become highly dependent on any one person—and do not want anyone depending heavily on them. In a society that values individuality and self-fulfillment, the single lifestyle can offer certain freedoms that married couples may not enjoy. Even divorced parents may not feel the need to remarry. Andrew J. Cherlin (2009) contends that a single parent who connects with other adults, such as grandparents, to form a solid, supportive relationship for child rearing should not feel compelled to re-partner.

Nevertheless, remaining single represents a clear departure from societal expectations; indeed, it has been likened to "being single on Noah's Ark." A single adult must confront the inaccurate view that he or she is always lonely, is a workaholic, or is immature. These stereotypes help to support the traditional assumption in the United States and most other societies that to be truly happy and fulfilled, a person must get married and raise a family. To counter these societal expectations, singles have formed numerous support groups (Hertz 2006; Lundquist 2006).

Marriage without Children

There has been a modest increase in childlessness in the United States. According to census data, about 16 to 17 percent of women will now complete their childbearing years without having borne any children, compared to 10 percent in 1980. As many as 20 percent of women in their 30s expect to remain childless (Biddlecom and Martin 2006).

Childlessness within marriage has generally been viewed as a problem that can be solved through such means as adoption and artificial insemination. More and more couples today, however, choose not to have children and regard themselves as child-free rather than childless. They do not believe that having children automatically follows from marriage, nor do they feel that reproduction is the duty of all married couples. Childless couples have formed support groups (with names like No Kidding) and set up websites.

Economic considerations have contributed to this shift in attitudes; having children has become quite expensive. According to a government estimate made for 2012, the average middle-class family will spend $229,320 to feed, clothe, and shelter a child from birth to age 18. If the child attends college, that amount could double, depending on the college chosen. In 1960, parents spent only 2 percent of their income on child care and education; now they spend 16 percent, reflecting the rising dependence on nonfamily child care (see the Social Policy section in Chapter 4). Aware of the financial pressures, some couples are weighing the advantages of a child-free marriage (Lino 2010).

Childless couples are beginning to question current practices in the workplace. While applauding employers' efforts to provide child care and flexible work schedules, some nevertheless express concern about tolerance of employees who leave early to take children to doctors, ball games, or after-school classes. As more dual-career couples enter the paid labor force and struggle to balance career and familial responsibilities, conflicts with employees who have no children may increase (Biddlecom and Martin 2006).

use your sociological *imagination*

What would happen to our society if many more married couples suddenly decided not to have children? How would society change if cohabitation and/or singlehood became the norm?

Lesbian and Gay Relationships

Twenty-one-year-old Parke, a junior in college, grew up in a stable, loving family. A self-described fiscal conservative, he credits his parents with instilling in him a strong work ethic. Sound like an average child of an average family? The only break with traditional expectations in this case is that Parke is the son of a lesbian couple (P. Brown 2004).

The lifestyles of lesbians and gay men are varied. Some live in long-term, monogamous relationships; others live alone or with roommates. Some remain in "empty-shell" heterosexual marriages and do not publicly acknowledge their homosexuality. Others live with children from a former marriage or with adopted children. Based on election exit polls, researchers for the National Health and Social Life Survey and the Voter News Service estimate that 2 to 5 percent of the adult population identify themselves as either gay or lesbian. An analysis of the 2000 Census shows a minimum of at least 600,000 gay households, and a gay and lesbian adult population approaching 10 million (Laumann et al. 1994b:293; David M. Smith and Gates 2001).

Gay and lesbian couples face discrimination on both a personal and a legal level. Their inability to marry denies them many rights that married couples take for granted, from the ability to make decisions for an incapacitated partner to the right to receive government benefits to dependents, such as Social Security payments. Though gay couples consider themselves families just like the straight couples who live down the street, they are often treated as if they are not.

Precisely because of such inequities, many gay and lesbian couples are now demanding the right to marry. In the Social Policy section that follows, we will examine the highly controversial issue of gay marriage.

thinking CRITICALLY

How is romantic cohabitation similar to marriage? How is it different? Could gay and lesbian couples achieve all the benefits of marriage without actually marrying?

social policy and the Family

Gay Marriage

In the United States, attitudes toward marriage are complex. As always, society and popular culture suggest that a young man or woman should find the perfect mate, settle down and marry, have children, and live happily ever after. But young people are also bombarded by messages implying the frequency of adultery and the acceptability of divorce. In this atmosphere, the idea of same-sex marriage strikes some people as only the latest of many attacks on traditional marriage. To others, it seems an overdue acknowledgment of the formal relationships that faithful, monogamous gay couples have long maintained.

Looking at the Issue

What has made gay marriage the focus of national attention? Events in two states brought the issue to the forefront. In 1999, Vermont gave gay couples the legal benefits of marriage through civil union, but stopped short of calling the arrangement a marriage. Then, in 2003, the Massachusetts Supreme Court ruled 4–3 that under the state's constitution, gay couples have the right to marry—a ruling the U.S. Supreme Court has refused to review. Now, with gay married couples in this state passing their 5th anniversaries and approaching their 10th, scholars are beginning to study their experiences compared to those of opposite-sex couples.

Recently, national surveys of attitudes toward gay marriage in the United States have shown an almost even split among the public. A 2009 survey showed that 53 percent oppose allowing gay men and lesbians to marry. However, 57 percent favor allowing them to enter legal unions—arrangements that give gay couples many of the same rights as marriage (Kelley and Bazar 2010).

Applying Sociology

Functionalists have traditionally seen marriage as a social institution that is closely tied to human reproduction. Same-sex marriage would at first appear not to fit that arrangement. But many same-sex couples are entrusted with the socialization of young children, whether or not their relationship is recognized by the state. Functionalists also wonder whether religious views toward marriage can be ignored. The courts have focused on civil marriage, but religious views are hardly irrelevant, even in a country like the United States, which observes a separation between religion and the state. Indeed, religious teachings have led even some staunch supporters of gay rights to oppose same-sex marriage on spiritual grounds.

Conflict theorists have charged that denial of the right to marry reinforces the second-class status of gays and lesbians. Some have compared the ban

FIGURE **14-6**   GAY MARRIAGE BY STATE

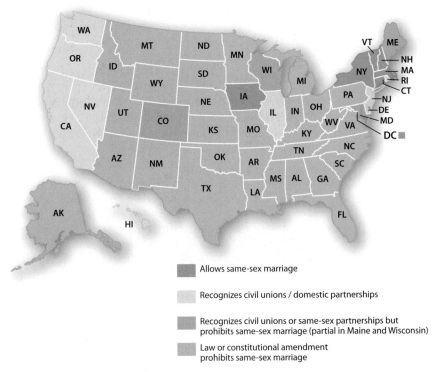

Allows same-sex marriage

Recognizes civil unions / domestic partnerships

Recognizes civil unions or same-sex partnerships but prohibits same-sex marriage (partial in Maine and Wisconsin)

Law or constitutional amendment prohibits same-sex marriage

Sources: As of May 2011, author based on news reports; Clabaugh 2010; Human Rights Campaign 2011; National Conference of State Legislatures 2011.

and have extended employee benefits to those relationships. Under such policies, a **domestic partnership** may be defined as two unrelated adults who share a mutually caring relationship, reside together, and agree to be jointly responsible for their dependents, basic living expenses, and other common necessities. Domestic partnership benefits can apply to couples' inheritance, parenting, pensions, taxation, housing, immigration, workplace fringe benefits such as life insurance, and health care. Even though the most passionate support for domestic partnership legislation has come from lesbian and gay activists, the majority of those eligible for such benefits would be cohabiting heterosexual couples.

In the United States, marriage has traditionally been under the jurisdiction of state lawmakers. But recently, pressure has been mounting for national legislation. The Defense of Marriage Act, passed in 1996, provided that no state is obliged to recognize same-sex marriages performed in another state. However, some legal scholars doubt that the law could withstand a constitutional challenge, since it violates a provision in the Constitution that requires states to recognize one another's laws.

Within the United States, state courts in California, Iowa, and Massachusetts have ruled that there is no state law that precludes same-sex marriage. In California, 18,000 same-sex couples were married before voters amended the state constitution to prohibit such marriages in the future. In August 2010, a federal court weighed in for the first time on gay marriage, ruling that California's ban on same-sex marriage was unconstitutional. Ultimately, the Supreme Court will consider the issue. As of mid-2011, the District of Columbia and six states (Connecticut, Iowa, Massachusetts, New Hampshire, New York, and Vermont) were issuing marriage licenses to same-sex couples. Gay rights activists claim their movement is gathering momentum, but opponents argue that their high-profile actions have galvanized conservatives who wish to define marriage as the union of one man and one woman.

against gay marriage to past policies that until 1967 banned interracial marriage in 32 states. Figure 14-6 illustrates the different ways same-sex partnerships are treated today in different states.

Interactionists generally avoid the policy question and focus instead on the nature of same-sex households. They ask many of the same questions about gay partner relations and child rearing that they ask about conventional couples. Of course, much less research has been done on same-sex households than on other families, but the studies published to date raise the same issues as those that apply to conventional married couples, plus a few more. For gay couples, the support or opposition of family, coworkers, and friends looms large (Dundas and Kaufman 2000; Dunne 2000; B. Powell et al. 2010).

Initiating Policy

The United States is not the first nation to consider this issue. Recognition of same-sex partnerships is common in Europe, and same-sex marriage is recognized in Argentina, Belgium, the Netherlands, Norway, Portugal, Spain, and Sweden. Today, as many as 8 percent of all marriages in the Netherlands are same-sex. The trend is toward recognition in North America as well, since gay couples can marry legally in Canada.

In the United States, many local jurisdictions have passed legislation allowing for the registration of domestic partnerships,

Take the Issue with You

1. If marriage is good for heterosexual couples and their families, why isn't it good for homosexual couples and their families?

2. How can interactionist studies of gay couples and their families inform policymakers who are dealing with the issue of gay marriage? Give a specific example.

3. Who are the stakeholders in the debate over gay marriage, and what do they stand to gain or lose? Whose interest do you think is most important?

Summary

The **family,** in its many varying forms, is present in all human cultures. This chapter examines the state of marriage, the family, and other intimate relationships in the United States and considers alternatives to the traditional **nuclear family.**

1. **Families** vary from culture to culture and even within the same culture.

2. The structure of the **extended family** can offer certain advantages over that of the **nuclear family.**

3. Societies determine **kinship** by descent from both parents (**bilateral descent**), from the father only (**patrilineal descent**), or from the mother only (**matrilineal descent**).

4. Sociologists do not agree on whether the **egalitarian family** has replaced the patriarchal family as the social norm in the United States.

5. William F. Ogburn outlined six basic functions of the family: reproduction, protection, socialization, regulation of sexual behavior, companionship, and the provision of social status.

6. Conflict theorists argue that male dominance of the family contributes to societal injustice and denies women opportunities that are extended to men.

7. Interactionists focus on how individuals interact in the family and in other intimate relationships.

8. Feminists stress the need to broaden research on the family. Like conflict theorists, they see the family's role in socializing children as the primary source of sexism.

9. People select mates in a variety of ways. Some marriages are arranged; in other societies, people choose their own mates. Some societies require mates to be chosen within a certain group (**endogamy**) or outside certain groups (**exogamy**). And consciously or unconsciously, many people look for a mate with similar personal characteristics (**homogamy**).

10. In the United States, family life varies with social class, race, and ethnicity.

11. Currently, in the majority of all married couples in the United States, both husband and wife work outside the home.

12. **Single-parent families** account for an increasing proportion of U.S. families.

13. Among the factors that contribute to the rising divorce rate in the United States are greater social acceptance of divorce and the liberalization of divorce laws in many states.

14. More and more people are living together without marrying, a practice known as **cohabitation.** People are also staying single longer, and some married couples are deciding not to have children.

15. The gay marriage movement, which would confer equal rights on gay and lesbian couples and their dependents, is strongly opposed by conservative religious and political groups.

Key Terms

Adoption In a legal sense, a process that allows for the transfer of the legal rights, responsibilities, and privileges of parenthood to a new legal parent or parents. (page 316)

Bilateral descent A kinship system in which both sides of a person's family are regarded as equally important. (308)

Cohabitation The practice of living together as a male–female couple without marrying. (321)

Domestic partnership Two unrelated adults who share a mutually caring relationship, reside together, and agree to be jointly responsible for their dependents, basic living expenses, and other common necessities. (324)

Egalitarian family An authority pattern in which spouses are regarded as equals. (309)

Endogamy The restriction of mate selection to people within the same group. (312)

Exogamy The requirement that people select a mate outside certain groups. (312)

Extended family A family in which relatives—such as grandparents, aunts, or uncles—live in the same home as parents and their children. (307)

Familism Pride in the extended family, expressed through the maintenance of close ties and strong obligations to kinfolk outside the immediate family. (315)

Family A set of people related by blood, marriage or some other agreed-on relationship, or adoption, who share the primary responsibility for reproduction and caring for members of society. (307)

Homogamy The conscious or unconscious tendency to select a mate with personal characteristics similar to one's own. (313)

Incest taboo The prohibition of sexual relationships between certain culturally specified relatives. (312)

Kinship The state of being related to others. (308)

Machismo A sense of virility, personal worth, and pride in one's maleness. (314)

Matriarchy A society in which women dominate in family decision making. (309)

Matrilineal descent A kinship system in which only the mother's relatives are significant. (308)

Monogamy A form of marriage in which one woman and one man are married only to each other. (307)

Nuclear family A married couple and their unmarried children living together. (307)

Patriarchy A society in which men dominate in family decision making. (309)

Patrilineal descent A kinship system in which only the father's relatives are significant. (308)

Polyandry A form of polygamy in which a woman may have more than one husband at the same time. (307)

Polygamy A form of marriage in which an individual may have several husbands or wives simultaneously. (307)

Polygyny A form of polygamy in which a man may have more than one wife at the same time. (307)

Serial monogamy A form of marriage in which a person may have several spouses in his or her lifetime, but only one spouse at a time. (307)

Single-parent family A family in which only one parent is present to care for the children. (318)

1. Go online and try tracing your family roots using one of the genea-logical search sites. How far back can you go? Why might certain ancestral paths be more difficult to trace than others?

2. Do some research on the divorce law in your state. Has the law changed much over the past few decades, and if so, how? From a sociological perspective, why would the law change? Explain.

3. Talk to a marriage and family counselor or a professor of family law about the benefits of marriage versus cohabitation, or read what practical advice you can find on the Internet or in the library. What advantages does marriage offer that cohabitation does not? How important do those advantages seem to you?

Self-Quiz

Read each question carefully and then select the best answer.

1. Alice, age seven, lives in a private home with her parents, her grandmother, and her aunt. Alice's family is an example of a(n)
   a. nuclear family.
   b. dysfunctional family.
   c. extended family.
   d. polygynous family.

2. In which form of marriage may a person have several spouses in his or her lifetime, but only one spouse at a time?
   a. serial monogamy
   b. monogamy
   c. polygamy
   d. polyandry

3. The marriage of a woman to more than one man at the same time is referred to as
   a. polygyny.
   b. monogamy.
   c. serial monogamy.
   d. polyandry.

4. Which system of descent is followed in the United States?
   a. matrilineal
   b. patrilineal
   c. bilateral
   d. unilateral

5. According to the functionalist perspective, which of the following is *not* one of the paramount functions performed by the family?
   a. mediation
   b. reproduction
   c. regulation of sexual behavior
   d. affection and companionship

6. Which norm requires mate selection outside certain groups, usually one's own family or certain kinfolk?
   a. exogamy
   b. endogamy

   c. matriarchy
   d. patriarchy

7. According to the discussion of social class differences in family life and intimate relationships, which of the following statements is true?
   a. Social class differences in family life are more striking than they once were.
   b. The upper class emphasizes lineage and maintenance of family position.
   c. Among the poor, women usually play an insignificant role in the economic support of the family.
   d. In examining family life among racial and ethnic minorities, most patterns result from cultural, but *not* class, factors.

8. One recent development in family life in the United States has been the extension of parenthood as adult children continue to live at home or return home after college. The reason for this is
   a. the rising divorce rate.
   b. skyrocketing rent and real estate prices.
   c. financial difficulties.
   d. all of the above

9. In the United States, the *majority* of all babies born to unmarried teenage mothers are born to whom?
   a. African American adolescents
   b. White adolescents
   c. Latina adolescents
   d. Asian American adolescents

10. Which of the following factors is associated with the high divorce rate in the United States?
    a. the liberalization of divorce laws
    b. the fact that contemporary families have fewer children than earlier families did
    c. the general increase in family incomes
    d. all of the above

11. The principle of _____ assigns people to kinship groups according to their relationship to an individual's mother or father.

12. _____ emerged among Native American tribal societies, and in nations in which men were absent for long periods because of warfare or food-gathering expeditions.

13. In the view of many sociologists, the _____ family has begun to replace the patriarchal family as the social norm in the United States.

14. As _____ theorists point out, the social class of couples and their children significantly influences the socialization experiences to which the children are exposed and the protection they receive.

15. _____ focus on the micro level of family and other intimate relationships; for example, they are interested in whether people are cohabiting partners or are longtime married couples.

16. The rule of _____ specifies the groups within which a spouse must be found and prohibits marriage with others.

17. Social class differences in family life are less striking today than they once were; however, in the past, _____-class families were found to be more authoritarian in rearing children and more inclined to use physical punishment.

18. Caring for children is a(n) _____ function of the family, yet the ways in which different societies assign this function to family members can vary significantly.

19. Viewed from the _____ perspective, the government has a strong interest in encouraging adoption.

20. The rising rates of divorce and remarriage have led to a noticeable increase in _____ relationships.

_____

Answers

1 (c); 2 (a); 3 (d); 4 (c); 5 (a); 6 (a); 7 (b); 8 (d); 9 (b); 10 (d); 11 descent; 12 Matriarchies; 13 egalitarian; 14 conflict; 15 Interactionists; 16 endogamy; 17 lower; 18 universal; 19 functionalist; 20 stepfamily

THINKING ABOUT MOVIES

Blue Valentine

A marriage unravels under personal and social pressure.

Goodbye Solo

In this moving drama about the role of family in people's lives, two quite different men form an unlikely pair.

The Kids Are Alright

A family copes when the children's birth father, a sperm donor, tries to become part of their lives.

▶ INSIDE

Religion is expressed in a variety of social settings. At this Christian rock festival in New Hampshire, fans pray in response to the music.

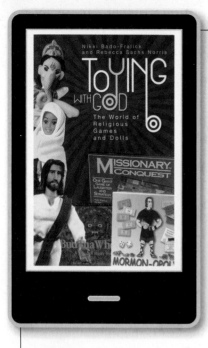

66 There are many types of religious toys: stuffed torahs; Moses, David, and Jesus and the Tomb action figures; Noah's ark collections; and Resurrection Eggs, which supplement a young child's Easter book. "Lead your kids on a fun, faith-filled Easter egg hunt this year—one that teaches them about Jesus' death and resurrection! Each egg carton is filled with a dozen colorful plastic eggs. Pop them open and find miniature symbols of the Easter story inside." One of the dozen plastic eggs contains a crown of thorns, another is empty, representing the disappearance of the body of Jesus from the tomb, and pointing to his resurrection. Muslim toys include a mosque building set, mosque jewelry cases, and a prayer practice chart. Jewish toys include dreidels, wooden Shabbat sets, toy *sukkahs*, and a Plush Plagues Bag that includes "all 10 Plagues!"

Religious dolls are part of this wonderland of sacred fun. There are plush and plastic talking Bible dolls, pumped-up Christian action figures, dolls designed to support a Jewish girl's religious identity and conform to religious requirements, Goddess dolls designed for affluent young feminists, talking Muslim dolls that teach Arabic phrases, and "anti-Barbies"—Muslim dolls deliberately designed to compete with Barbie for the hearts and minds of young girls. There are plush Buddha and Siva dolls, and cuddly Jesus and Esther dolls as well.

Numerous card games and puzzles teach a variety of languages, including Hebrew, Arabic, and Punjabi. The Christian Book Distributors Web site not only offers religiously themed educational materials, they also offer nonreligious toys that appeal to parents with religious consciences who may be looking for nonviolent toys, such as a food groups toy with hand-painted pieces in four wooden crates, a pizza party game with different toppings, and a car towing game.

Not all religious toys are meant for the edification of the young. Many religious games and toys are satirical or simply products meant to be amusing enough to sell in an era where we are oversatiated with things, and any cultural phenomenon is fair game for marketing purposes. These items amuse or appall us, depending on how clever or offensive the item is, and for whom it is intended. . . .

Games and toys not only transmit cultural values but reflect them as well. . . . Games and religion have a long and complex history—they were used for divination and gambling, for this-worldly satire, and in the afterlife. Games were objects and methods used to interpret divine powers and influence supernatural forces. These religious and magical functions reflect the presence and movement of the sacred in the material world, indicators of a complex whole rather than a dualism where sacred and ordinary occupy separate realms.

Contemporary religious games have their roots in ancient practices, but their flavor—their style and substance—as well as their commercial focus reveal a specifically twenty-first century American form of religiosity. 99

Contemporary religious games have their roots in ancient practices, but their flavor—their style and substance—as well as their commercial focus reveal a specifically twenty-first century American form of religiosity.

(Bado-Fralick and Norris 2010:7–8, 29–30) Additional information about this excerpt can be found on the Online Learning Center at www.mhhe.com/schaefer13e.

In this excerpt from *Toying with God: The World of Religious Games and Dolls*, religious studies scholars Nikki Bado-Fralick and Rebecca Sachs Norris consider how religiously themed toys and games reflect both popular and religious culture. Depending on their purpose and design, the authors note, as well as on the social context in which they are used, these dolls and board games can either reinforce or undermine organized religion. Their impact on the children who play with them parallels the broader influence of religion on society. Despite the much-publicized decline of organized religion over the past century, even a casual observer can see that religion still permeates our social environment. As a result, nonbelievers are influenced by believers, whether they want to be or not. Similarly, believers are influenced by nonbelievers and by those of different faiths, despite any attempts they may make to screen out other points of view.

Indeed, religion plays a major role in people's lives, and religious practices of some sort are evident in every society. That makes religion a cultural universal, along with other common practices or beliefs found in every culture, such as dancing, food preparation, the family, and personal names. At present, an estimated 4 billion people belong to the world's many religious faiths.

When religion's influence on other social institutions in a society diminishes, the process of **secularization** is said to be under way. During this process, religion will survive in the private sphere of individual and family life (as in the case of many Native American families); it may even thrive on a personal level. But at the same time, other social institutions—such as the economy, politics, and education—maintain their own sets of norms, independent of religious guidance. Even so, religion is enormously resilient. Although specific faiths or organizations may change, their transformation does not signal the demise of religious faith. Rather, it contributes to the diversity of religious expression and organization (Christian Smith 2008; Stark 2004).

Like religion, education is a cultural universal. As such it is an important aspect of socialization—the lifelong process of learning the attitudes, values, and behavior considered appropriate to members of a particular culture. As we saw in Chapter 4, socialization can occur in the classroom or at home, through interactions with parents, teachers, friends, and even strangers. Exposure to books, toys and games, and other forms of communication also promotes socialization.

What social purposes does religion serve? Does it help to hold society together or foster social change? What happens when religion mixes with politics? Does religion belong in the public schools? In this chapter we will study the formal systems of religion that characterize modern industrial societies. We will begin with a brief description of the sociological perspectives on religion, followed by an overview of the world's major religions. Next, we will explore religion's role in societal integration, social support, social change, and social control. We'll examine three important components of religious behavior—belief, ritual, and experience—as well as the basic forms of religious organization, including new religious movements. In a case study, we'll take a fascinating look at religion in India. The chapter will close with a Social Policy section on religion in the schools.

Durkheim and the Sociological Approach to Religion

If a group believes that it is being directed by a "vision from God," sociologists do not attempt to prove or disprove the revelation. Instead, they assess the effects of the religious experience on the group. What sociologists are interested in is the social impact of religion on individuals and institutions.

Émile Durkheim was perhaps the first sociologist to recognize the critical importance of religion in human societies. He saw its appeal for the individual, but more important, he stressed the *social* impact of religion. In Durkheim's view, religion is a collective act that includes many forms of behavior in which people interact with others. As in his work on suicide, Durkheim was not so interested in the personalities of religious believers as he was in understanding religious behavior within a social context.

Durkheim defined **religion** as a "unified system of beliefs and practices relative to sacred things." In his view, religion involves a set of beliefs and practices that are uniquely the property of religion, as opposed to other social institutions and ways of thinking. Durkheim ([1893] 1933; [1912] 2001) argued that religious faiths distinguish between certain transcending

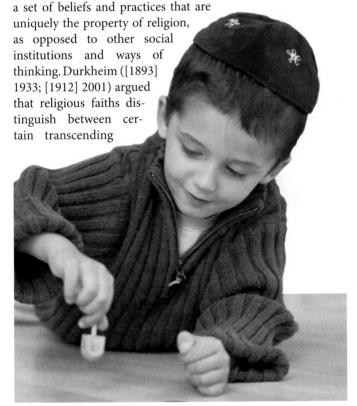

events and the everyday world. He referred to those realms as the *sacred* and the *profane.*

The **sacred** encompasses elements beyond everyday life that inspire awe, respect, and even fear. People become part of the sacred realm only by completing some ritual, such as prayer or sacrifice. Because believers have faith in the sacred, they accept what they cannot understand. In contrast, the **profane** includes the ordinary and commonplace. This concept can be confusing, however, because the same object can be either sacred or profane, depending on how it is viewed. A normal dining room table is profane, but it becomes sacred to some Christians if it bears the elements of a communion. A candelabra becomes sacred to Jews if it is a menorah. For Confucians and Taoists, incense sticks are not mere decorative items, but highly valued offerings to the gods in religious ceremonies that mark the new and full moons.

Following the direction established by Durkheim a century ago, contemporary sociologists view religion in two different ways. First, they study the norms and values of religious faiths by examining their substantive beliefs. For example, it is possible to compare the degree to which Christian faiths interpret the Bible literally, or Muslim groups follow the Qur'an (or Koran), the sacred book of Islam. At the same time, sociologists examine religion in terms of the social functions it fulfills, such as providing social support or reinforcing social norms. By exploring both the beliefs and the functions of religion, we can better understand its impact on the individual, on groups, and on society as a whole.

thinking CRITICALLY

What objects that you regard as profane might others consider to be sacred?

World Religions

Worldwide, tremendous diversity exists in religious beliefs and practices. Overall, about 89 percent of the world's population adheres to some religion; thus, only about 10 percent is nonreligious. This level of adherence changes over time and also varies by country and age group. In the United States today, those who are nonreligious account for about 16 percent of the population; in 1900, they accounted for a mere 1.3 percent of all Americans.

Self-Quiz

Read each question carefully and then select the best answer.

1. Which of the following sociologists stressed the social impact of religion and was perhaps the first to recognize the critical importance of religion in human societies?
   a. Max Weber
   b. Karl Marx
   c. Émile Durkheim
   d. Talcott Parsons

2. A Roman Catholic parish church offers services in the native language of an immigrant community. This is an example of
   a. the integrative function of religion.
   b. the social support function of religion.
   c. the social control function of religion.
   d. none of the above.

3. Sociologist Max Weber pointed out that the followers of John Calvin emphasized a disciplined work ethic, this-worldly concerns, and a rational orientation to life. Collectively, this point of view has been referred to as
   a. capitalism.
   b. the Protestant ethic.
   c. the sacred.
   d. the profane.

4. The use of a church, primarily Roman Catholic, in a political effort to eliminate poverty, discrimination, and other forms of injustice evident in a secular society is referred to as
   a. creationism.
   b. ritualism.
   c. religious experience.
   d. liberation theology.

5. Many people in the United States strongly adhere to the biblical explanation of the beginning of the universe. Adherents of this point of view are known as
   a. liberationists.
   b. creationists.

   c. ritualists.
   d. experimentalists.

6. The Adam and Eve account of creation found in Genesis, the first book of the Old Testament, is an example of a religious
   a. ritual.
   b. experience.
   c. custom.
   d. belief.

7. Which of the following is *not* an example of an ecclesia?
   a. the Lutheran church in Sweden
   b. Islam in Saudi Arabia
   c. Buddhism in Thailand
   d. the Episcopal church in the United States

8. Religion defines the spiritual world and gives meaning to the divine. These are _____ functions of religion.
   a. manifest
   b. latent
   c. positive
   d. negative

9. Which sociological perspective emphasizes the integrative power of religion in human society?
   a. functionalist perspective
   b. conflict perspective
   c. interactionist perspective
   d. all of the above

10. John Calvin, a leader of the Protestant Reformation, emphasized
   a. disciplined work ethic.
   b. this-worldly concerns.
   c. a rational orientation to life.
   d. all of the above.

11. The _____ encompasses elements beyond everyday life that inspire awe, respect, and even fear, as compared to the _____, which includes the ordinary and the commonplace.

12. Wicca is an example of a(n) _____.

13. _____ is the largest single faith in the world; the second largest is _____.

14. _____ _____ are statements to which members of a particular religion adhere.

15. A(n) _____ is a religious organization that claims to include most or all members of a society and is recognized as the national or official religion.

16. Because they are _____, most religions tend to reinforce men's dominance in secular as well as spiritual matters.

17. The single largest denomination in the United States is _____ _____.

18. The big bang theory is challenged by _____, who hold to the biblical account of creation of humans and the universe.

19. Unlike ecclesiae and denominations, _____ require intensive commitments and demonstrations of belief by members.

20. A possible dysfunction of _____ _____ would be the belief that when Roman Catholics focus on political and governmental injustice, the clergy are no longer addressing people's personal and spiritual needs.

THINKING ABOUT MOVIES

Monsieur Ibrahim

In this film, which draws comparisons between Islam and Judaism, a Muslim grocer befriends a Jewish boy.

Saved!

A young woman tries to find her own voice in a Christian high school.

Trembling Before G-D

This documentary explores the tension between religious belief and sexual orientation.

Prospective students and their
parents tour the campus of
the University of Washington,
Seattle. From informal learning
in the family to formal study
at an institution of higher
learning, education is a cultural
universal.

1. Attend a meeting of a local Parent Teacher Association (PTA). What issues are parents talking about? Describe their concerns using one or more sociological perspectives.

2. Make a list of the student subcultures on your campus, then describe them using the concepts you learned in Chapter 3. Do any of these subcultures serve as out-groups for other subcultures?

3. Does your school have a gay–straight alliance? If so, speak with one of the officers. What are members doing to reduce prejudice and foster better relations among gay and straight students? Explain their approach using sociological theory.

Self-Quiz

Read each question carefully and then select the best answer.

1. Which sociological perspective emphasizes that the common identity and social integration fostered by education contribute to overall societal stability and consensus?
   a. the functionalist perspective
   b. the conflict perspective
   c. the interactionist perspective
   d. labeling theory

2. Which one of the following was introduced into school systems to promote social change?
   a. sex education classes
   b. affirmative action programs
   c. Project Head Start
   d. all of the above

3. The correspondence principle was developed by
   a. Max Weber.
   b. Karl Marx and Friedrich Engels.
   c. Samuel Bowles and Herbert Gintis.
   d. James Thurber.

4. The student subculture that is hostile to the college environment and seeks out ideas that may or may not relate to studies is called the
   a. collegiate subculture.
   b. academic subculture.
   c. vocational subculture.
   d. nonconformist subculture.

5. Most recent research on ability grouping raises questions about its
   a. effectiveness, especially for lower-achieving students.
   b. failure to improve the prospects of higher-achieving students.
   c. ability to improve the prospects of lower- and higher-achieving students.
   d. both a and b

6. The most basic *manifest* function of education is
   a. transmitting knowledge.
   b. transmitting culture.
   c. maintaining social control.
   d. serving as an agent of change.

7. Sixty years ago, a high school diploma was the minimum requirement for entry into the paid labor force of the United States. Today, a college diploma is virtually the bare minimum. This change reflects the process of
   a. tracking.
   b. credentialism.
   c. the hidden curriculum.
   d. the correspondence principle.

8. Samuel Bowles and Herbert Gintis have argued that capitalism requires a skilled, disciplined labor force and that the educational system of the United States is structured with that objective in mind. Citing numerous studies, they offer support for what they call
   a. tracking.
   b. credentialism.
   c. the correspondence principle.
   d. the teacher-expectancy effect.

9. The teacher-expectancy effect is most closely associated with
   a. the functionalist perspective.
   b. the conflict perspective.
   c. the interactionist perspective.
   d. anomie theory.

10. Sociologist Max Weber noted five basic characteristics of bureaucracy, all of which are evident in the vast majority of schools, whether at the elementary, secondary, or even college level. Which of the following is *not* one of them?
    a. division of labor
    b. written rules and regulations
    c. impersonality
    d. shared decision making

11. The _____ perspective stresses the importance of education in transmitting culture, maintaining social control, and promoting social change.

12. In the past, the integrative function of education was most obvious through its emphasis on promoting a common _____.

13. The _____ subculture identifies with the intellectual concerns of the faculty and values knowledge for its own sake.

14. A _____ _____ is an experimental school that is developed and managed outside the public school system.

15. Women's education tends to suffer in those cultures with traditional _____ _____.

16. Schools perform a variety of _____ functions, such as transmitting culture, promoting social and political integration, and maintaining social control.

17. Sociologist _____ _____ points out that better-educated people tend to have greater access to information, to hold more diverse opinions, and to possess the ability to make subtle distinctions in analysis.

18. The term _____ _____ refers to standards of behavior that are deemed proper by society and are taught subtly in schools. For example, children must not speak until the teacher calls on them and must regulate their activities according to the clock or the bell.

19. _____ is the practice of placing students in specific curriculum groups on the basis of their test scores and other criteria.

20. Of the four distinctive subcultures among college students discussed in the text, the _____ subculture is interested primarily in career prospects, and views college as a means of obtaining degrees that are essential for advancement.

_____

Answers

1 (a); 2 (d); 3 (c); 4 (d); 5 (a); 6 (a); 7 (b); 8 (b); 9 (c); 10 (d); 11 functionalist; 12 language; 13 academic; 14 charter school; 15 gender roles; 16 latent; 17 Robin Williams; 18 hidden curriculum; 19 Tracking; 20 vocational

THINKING ABOUT MOVIES

Freedom Writers

A teacher attempts to defuse conflict among her students.

Nursery University

This documentary, set in New York City, shows how early childhood education is becoming formalized.

Waiting for Superman

This film documents failures in the American educational system and their personal consequences.

Government affects society at all levels. In 2010, Microsoft founder Bill Gates and former President Bill Clinton testified before the U.S. Senate's Foreign Relations Committee on approaches to global health problems.

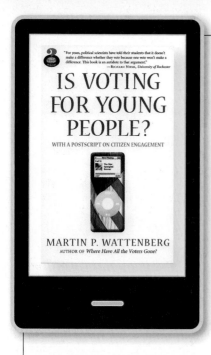

IS VOTING FOR YOUNG PEOPLE?

WITH A POSTSCRIPT ON CITIZEN ENGAGEMENT

MARTIN P. WATTENBERG
AUTHOR OF *Where Have All the Voters Gone?*

❝ Voting is for Old People," proclaimed a T-shirt printed and distributed in 2004 by Urban Outfitters, a popular American clothing company. At Harvard's Kennedy School of Government, the perceived message of the shirt hit a raw nerve. Its director issued a public statement criticizing the slogan, saying that it could not be further from the truth—that voting is for everyone. In response, Urban Outfitters said they never intended to discourage anyone from voting. Rather, they asserted that their goal was to draw attention to the relative lack of participation of young adults in politics, a problem that many analysts and politicians acknowledge but few seem to be genuinely concerned about. . . .

Over the last three decades, politics and voting have indeed become more and more the province of the elderly, which will be shown to be the case not only in the United States but also *throughout the world's advanced industrialized democracies.* There is in fact a rift between politicians and young adults, although not one of mutual contempt but rather of mutual neglect. Many young people don't vote simply because they don't follow politics. Moreover, because so many young people don't follow politics and don't vote, parties and politicians frequently don't bother with young people, thereby further widening the age bias in electoral participation.

All too often, low turnout rates among the young are considered to be a natural part of political life, and hence not worth fretting about. Scholars often write of a life cycle pattern in which people become more aware of the political world as they age, and hence are more likely to vote. As such, it is often thought that today's young nonvoters will eventually show up at the polls and have their voices heard. If such a life cycle truly exists, it ought to be consistently found in: (1) different eras; and (2) across a wide range of democracies. The data . . . from a number of countries in the 1970s contradict the life cycle hypothesis. . . .

Communications technology is one . . . aspect of political life that has undergone transformation throughout the world's advanced industrialized societies . . . in recent years. . . . Changes in media habits from generation to generation have led to a new situation in which young people are far less likely to be exposed to news about public affairs than their elders. Young adults have not consciously decided to avoid political news in recent years; rather, having been socialized in a markedly different communications environment, they just have not picked up the same media habits that their parents and grandparents did. These media habits, which older people developed long ago in a different world, continue to serve them well in today's political environment—making them substantially more likely to follow politics and become familiar with the issues of the day. And the more one learns about public affairs and follows current events, the more one is likely to realize the stakes involved at the polls. ❞

> *All too often, low turnout rates among the young are considered to be a natural part of political life, and hence not worth fretting about.*

(Wattenberg 2008:1–2, 3) Additional information about this excerpt can be found on the Online Learning Center at www.mhhe.com/schaefer13e.

In this excerpt from *Is Voting for Young People?* Martin P. Wattenberg, a professor of political science at the University of California at Irvine, confronts the generation gap in politics, not only in the United States but in industrialized countries around the world. Wattenberg thinks that the absence of young people from the voting booth reflects a generational difference in the way that citizens use the mass media. Few young people nowadays read the newspapers, so few know much about politics or think that it has any relevance to them. Most spend their time surfing the Internet, downloading music to their iPods and MP3s, text-messaging and snapping photos using their cell phones. Only in countries where these technological marvels are not available to the average youth is apathy among young people not a noteworthy phenomenon.

Those who vote (or who choose not to) operate within the framework of the existing political system, be it local, state, national, or international. By **political system,** sociologists mean the social institution that is founded on a recognized set of procedures for implementing and achieving society's goals, such as the allocation of valued resources. Like religion and the family, the political system is a cultural universal: it is found in every society. In the United States, the political system holds the ultimate responsibility for addressing the social policy issues examined in this textbook: child care, immigration, welfare reform, and so forth.

Are young people more interested in what's playing on their portable media players than in the political issues confronting their nation? How does government maintain its power, and how do political parties and public interest groups attempt to exert theirs? Does our campaign finance system put some groups at a disadvantage? In this chapter we will analyze the impact of government on people's lives from a sociological point of view. We will begin with a macro-level analysis of the sources of political power and authority, and the four major types of government in which that power and authority is exerted. We will see how politics works, with particular attention to citizens' participation and the changing role of women and minority groups. We'll look at two models of power in the United States, the elite and the pluralist models. Then we'll touch briefly on war, peace, and terrorism, and see how political activists have begun using the Internet to promote their causes. Finally, the Social Policy section will explore the controversy over campaign financing, an issue that vividly illustrates the close relationship between government and the moneyed elite who seek to influence the political process.

Power and Authority

In any society, someone or some group—whether it be a tribal chief, a dictator, or a parliament—makes important decisions about how to use resources and how to allocate goods. One cultural universal, then, is the exercise of power and authority. Inevitably, the struggle for power and authority involves **politics,** which political scientist Harold Lasswell (1936) tersely defined as "who gets what, when, and how." In their study of politics and government, sociologists are concerned with social interactions among individuals and groups and their impact on the larger political and economic order.

Power

Power lies at the heart of a political system. According to Max Weber, **power** is the ability to exercise one's will over others. To put it another way, whoever can overcome the resistance of others and control their behavior is exercising power. Power relations can involve large organizations, small groups, or even people in an intimate association.

Because Weber developed his conceptualization of power in the early 1900s, he focused primarily on the nation-state and its sphere of influence. Today scholars recognize that the trend toward globalization has brought new opportunities, and with them new concentrations of power. Power is now exercised on a global as well as a national stage, as countries and multinational corporations vie to control access to resources and manage the distribution of capital (R. Schaefer 2008b; Sernau 2001).

There are three basic sources of power within any political system: force, influence, and authority. **Force** is the actual or threatened use of coercion to impose one's will on others. When leaders imprison or even execute political dissidents, they are applying force; so, too, are terrorists when they seize or bomb an embassy or assassinate a political leader.

In the 21st century, force has taken on new meaning as nations clamp down on use of the Internet to oppose the central government or assert freedom of expression, human rights, and minority or religious views. When a military coup overthrew the democratically elected government of Thailand in September 2006, for example, citizens lost access to websites that criticized the takeover. As of 2008, 16 nations maintained selective to pervasive political controls on Internet content (Figure 17-1). Censorship of online content is just as much a use of force as closing down a newspaper or arresting dissidents (Deibert et al. 2008; OpenNet Initiative 2011; Zittrain and Palfrey 2008).

Influence, on the other hand, refers to the exercise of power through a process of persuasion. A citizen may change his or her view of a Supreme Court nominee because of a newspaper editorial, the expert testimony of a law school dean before the Senate Judiciary Committee, or a stirring speech by a political activist at a rally. In each case, sociologists would view such efforts to persuade people as examples of influence. Now let's take a look at the third source of power, *authority.*

Types of Authority

The term **authority** refers to institutionalized power that is recognized by the people over whom it is exercised. Sociologists commonly use the term in connection with those who hold legitimate power through elected or publicly acknowledged positions. A person's authority is often limited. Thus, a referee has the authority to decide whether a penalty should be called during a football game, but has no authority over the price of tickets to the game.

Max Weber ([1913] 1947) developed a classification system for authority that has become one of the most useful and frequently cited contributions of early sociology. He identified three ideal types of authority: traditional, rational-legal, and charismatic. Weber did not insist that only one type applies to a given society or organization. All can be present, but their relative importance will vary. Sociologists have found Weber's typology valuable in understanding different manifestations of legitimate power within a society.

Traditional Authority Until the middle of the past century, Japan was ruled by a revered emperor whose absolute power was passed down from generation to generation. In a political system based on **traditional authority,** legitimate power is conferred by custom and accepted practice. A king or queen is accepted as ruler of a nation simply by virtue of inheriting the crown; a tribal chief rules because that is the accepted practice. The ruler may be loved or hated, competent or destructive; in terms of legitimacy, that does not matter. For the traditional leader, authority rests in custom, not in personal characteristics, technical competence, or even written law. People accept the ruler's authority because that is how things have always been done. Traditional authority is absolute when the ruler has the ability to determine laws and policies.

Rational-Legal Authority The U.S. Constitution gives Congress and our president the authority to make and enforce laws and policies. Power made legitimate by law is known as **rational-legal authority.** Leaders derive their rational-legal authority from the written rules and regulations of political systems, such as a constitution. Generally, in societies based on rational-legal authority, leaders are thought to have specific areas

MAPPING LIFE WORLDWIDE
FIGURE **17-1** FILTERING INFORMATION: POLITICAL CONTENT

Pervasive
Substantial
Selective
Suspected
No evidence
No data (not tested for filtering)

Note: "No data" (see the gray portions of the map) does not necessarily indicate an absence of filtering.
Sources: OpenNet Initiative 2011; see also Deibert et al. 2008; Faris and Villeneuve 2008.

This map highlights nations that filter or restrict content that opposes the current government's views, or that is related to human rights, freedom of expression, minority rights, and religious movements.

of competence and authority but are not thought to be endowed with divine inspiration, as in certain societies with traditional forms of authority.

Charismatic Authority Joan of Arc was a simple peasant girl in medieval France, yet she was able to rally the French people and lead them into major battles against English invaders. How was this possible? As Weber observed, power can be legitimized by the *charisma* of an individual. The term **charismatic authority** refers to power made legitimate by a leader's exceptional personal or emotional appeal to his or her followers.

Charisma lets a person lead or inspire without relying on set rules or traditions. In fact, charismatic authority is derived more from the beliefs of followers than from the actual qualities of leaders. So long as people perceive a charismatic leader such as Jesus, Joan of Arc, Gandhi, Malcolm X, or Martin Luther King Jr. as having qualities that set him or her apart from ordinary citizens, that leader's authority will remain secure and often unquestioned.

Observing charismatic authority from an interactionist perspective, sociologist Carl Couch (1996) points out that the growth of the electronic media has facilitated the development of charismatic authority. During the 1930s and 1940s, the heads of state of the United States, Great Britain, and Germany all used radio to issue direct appeals to citizens. Now, television and the Internet allow leaders to "visit" people's homes and communicate

with them. In both Taiwan and South Korea in 1996, troubled political leaders facing reelection campaigns spoke frequently to national audiences and exaggerated military threats from neighboring China and North Korea, respectively.

As we noted earlier, Weber used traditional, rational-legal, and charismatic authority as ideal types. In reality, particular leaders and political systems combine elements of two or more of these forms. Presidents Franklin D. Roosevelt, John F. Kennedy, and Ronald Reagan wielded power largely through the rational-legal basis of their authority. At the same time, they were unusually charismatic leaders who commanded the personal loyalty of large numbers of citizens.

thinking CRITICALLY

On your campus, what are some examples of the three types of authority?

Types of Government

Each society establishes a political system through which it is governed. In modern industrialized nations, these formal systems of government make a significant number of critical political decisions. We will survey five basic types of government here: monarchy, oligarchy, dictatorship, totalitarianism, and democracy.

Monarchy

A **monarchy** is a form of government headed by a single member of a royal family, usually a king, queen, or some other hereditary ruler. In earlier times, many monarchs claimed that God had granted them a divine right to rule. Typically, they governed on the basis of traditional forms of authority, sometimes accompanied by the use of force. By the beginning of the 21st century, however, monarchs held genuine governmental power in only a few nations, such as Monaco. Most monarchs now have little practical power; they serve primarily ceremonial purposes.

Oligarchy

An **oligarchy** is a form of government in which a few individuals rule. A rather old method of governing that flourished in ancient Greece and Egypt, oligarchy now often takes the form of military rule. In developing nations in Africa, Asia, and Latin America, small factions of military officers will forcibly seize power, either from legally elected regimes or from other military cliques.

Strictly speaking, the term *oligarchy* is reserved for governments that are run by a few selected individuals. However, the People's Republic of China can be classified as an oligarchy if we stretch the meaning of the term. In China, power rests in the hands of a large but exclusive ruling *group,* the Communist Party. In a similar vein, drawing on conflict theory, one might argue that many industrialized nations of the West should be considered oligarchies (rather than democracies), since only a powerful few—leaders of big business, government, and the military—actually rule. Later in this chapter, we will examine the *elite model* of the U.S. political system in greater detail.

North Korea has a totalitarian government whose leadership attempts to control all aspects of people's lives. This billboard, a blatant example of government propaganda, portrays the country's ruthless leader as a benevolent father figure.

Dictatorship and Totalitarianism

A **dictatorship** is a government in which one person has nearly total power to make and enforce laws. Dictators rule primarily through the use of coercion, which often includes torture and executions. Typically, they *seize* power rather than being freely elected (as in a democracy) or inheriting power (as in a monarchy). Some dictators are quite charismatic and manage to achieve a certain popularity, though their supporters' enthusiasm is almost certainly tinged with fear. Other dictators are bitterly hated by the people over whom they rule.

Frequently, dictators develop such overwhelming control over people's lives that their governments are called *totalitarian.* (Monarchies and oligarchies may also achieve this type of dominance.) **Totalitarianism** involves virtually complete government control and surveillance over all aspects of a society's social and political life. Germany during Hitler's reign, the Soviet Union in the 1930s, and North Korea today are classified as totalitarian states.

Democracy

In a literal sense, **democracy** means government by the people. The word *democracy* originated in two Greek roots—*demos,* meaning "the populace" or "the common people," and *kratia,* meaning "rule." Of course, in large, populous nations such as the United States, government by the people is impractical at the national level. Americans cannot vote on every important issue that comes before Congress. Consequently, popular rule is generally maintained through **representative democracy,** a form of government in which certain individuals are selected to speak for the people.

The United States is commonly classified as a representative democracy, since the elected members of Congress and state legislatures make our laws. However, critics have questioned whether our democracy really is representative. Even today, not everyone in the United States feels included. Conspicuous among those who view themselves as excluded are Native Hawaiians (Box 17-1).

Do Congress and the state legislatures genuinely represent the masses, including minorities? Are the people of the United States legitimately self-governing, or has our government become a forum for powerful elites? We will explore these issues in the remainder of the chapter.

thinking CRITICALLY

Contrast the use of power as defined by Max Weber in a dictatorship in a democracy.

Political Behavior in the United States

Citizens of the United States take for granted many aspects of their political system. They are accustomed to living in a nation with a Bill of Rights, two major political parties, voting by secret ballot, an elected president, state and local governments distinct from the national government, and so forth. Yet each society has its own ways of governing itself and making decisions. U.S. residents expect Democratic and Republican candidates to compete for public office; residents of Cuba and the People's Republic of China are accustomed to one-party rule by the Communist Party. In this section, we will examine several aspects of political behavior within the United States.

Participation and Apathy

In theory, a representative democracy will function most effectively and fairly if an informed and active electorate communicates its views to government leaders. Unfortunately, that is hardly the case in the United States. Virtually all citizens are familiar with the basics of the political process, and most tend to identify to some extent with a political party. In 2011, about 29 percent of registered voters in the United States saw themselves as Democrats and 29 percent as Republicans; an impressive 39 percent were independent. However, only a small minority of citizens, often members of the higher social classes, actually participate in political organizations on a local or national level. Studies reveal that only 8 percent of Americans belong to a political club or organization. Not more than 20 percent have ever contacted an official of national, state, or local government about a political issue or problem (Gallup 2011b; Orum and Dale 2009).

By the 1980s, it had become clear that many people in the United States were beginning to be turned off by political parties, politicians, and big government. The most dramatic indication of this growing alienation came from voting statistics. Today, voters of all ages and races appear to be less enthusiastic than ever about elections, even presidential contests. For example, in the presidential election of 1896, almost 80 percent of eligible voters in the United States went to the polls. Yet by the 2008 election, despite its drama and historic nature, turnout was only 62 percent of all eligible voters—well below the levels of the 1960s. Obviously, even modestly higher voter turnout could dramatically change an election outcome, as the razor-thin margin in the 2000 presidential election demonstrated (McDonald 2008, 2009a).

Although a few nations still command high voter turnout, increasingly, national leaders of other countries also complain of voter apathy. Even so, among the 140 countries that held parliamentary elections between 1945 and 1998, the United States ranked 114th in voter turnout. No other industrialized nation has recorded a lower average turnout (Figure 17-2, page 376).

Despite poor voter turnout, participation in politics may be increasing, especially on the Internet. In terms of both antigovernment activities and financial contributions to political parties, online participation rivals the political rallies and doorbell-ringing efforts of yesteryear. Fifty-five percent of the entire adult population of the United States went online in 2008 to get news and information about the presidential election. One in every five of those online participants went so far as to post comments for others to read (A. Smith 2009).

In the end, political participation makes government accountable to the voters. If participation declines, government operates with less of a sense of accountability to society. This issue

TREND SPOTTING

Democracy on the Rise?

The breakup of the Soviet Union in 1991 launched several new countries in Eastern Europe, whose citizens were eager to escape foreign domination. In parts of Europe and Asia, democracy seemed to bloom where it never had grown before. What has happened since then?

Applying our own standards of democracy to nations in other parts of the world can be difficult. If a country holds free elections that are open to all citizens, is that enough to qualify it as a democracy? What if the government bans certain political parties? What if the media cannot criticize the government or report on opposition parties?

Freedom House, founded in 1941, is an international organization that advocates for democracy. Although it receives significant funding from the U.S. government, its annual review of democratic trends is generally regarded as a reasonable barometer of the spread (or lack thereof) of democracy. According to Freedom House, in 1989, only 41 percent of the world's countries could be considered democracies. The percentage rose dramatically after the collapse of the Soviet Union, reaching 60 percent in 1995. Since then, however, little has changed; the percentage of democracies has fluctuated between 59 and 64 percent.

Although recently, citizen-led revolts in countries like Egypt have offered some optimism, the overall trend is not encouraging. The industrialized democracies of North America and Europe often shrink from pressuring developing countries to reform their governments. Furthermore, in some areas of the world, violence and organized crime make democratic reform difficult. On the other hand, although the recent worldwide recession might easily have unsettled some fragile democracies, that fortunately has not happened.

SOCIOLOGY IN THE GLOBAL COMMUNITY

17-1 Sovereignty in the Aloha State

The people of Hawai'i are definitely multiracial. Twenty-three percent of the population is White; 38 percent, Asian American; 9 percent, Hawaiian or other Pacific Islander; 9 percent, Hispanic; and 2 percent, African American. Another 19 percent of the population, including Hawai'i-born Barack Obama, declare themselves to be of two or more races. Yet Hawai'i is not a racial paradise: certain occupations and even social classes tend to be dominated by Whites, Chinese, or Japanese Americans. Nor is Hawai'i immune to intolerance, although compared to the mainland and much of the rest of the world, race relations there are more harmonious than discordant.

For one group in particular, Native Hawaiians, access to any kind of power has been severely limited for generations. Now, through the **sovereignty movement,** the indigenous people of Hawai'i are hoping to win self-government, as well as restoration of—or compensation for—1.2 million acres of ancestral lands they have lost over the last century. Their movement is comparable to efforts made by American Indian tribes in the continental United States, both in its roots and in its significance.

The sovereignty movement began in 1996, when Native Hawaiians held a referendum on the question "Shall the Hawaiian people elect delegates to propose a Native Hawaiian government?" The results indicated that 73 percent of those who voted favored such an effort. Since then, the state Office of Hawaiian Affairs has sought to create a registry of the estimated 200,000 people of significant Hawaiian descent on the islands. Officials are about halfway to reaching their goal of

convincing all Native Hawaiians to come forward and register.

In Washington, D.C., Hawai'i's congressional delegation is seeking passage of the Native Hawaiian Government Reorganization Act, also referred to as the Akaka Bill, after U.S. Senator Daniel Akaka. The act would give people of Hawaiian ancestry more say over the use of local resources, including land and fresh water; provide them with affordable housing; take steps to preserve their culture; and create ways for them to better express their grievances. If the act passes, Native Hawaiians will become the last remaining indigenous group in the United States to be allowed to establish their own government—a right already extended to Alaskan Natives and 564 Native American tribes. As of mid-2011, the measure had passed the U.S. House of

Representatives, but had not yet been discussed on the floor of the Senate.

Meanwhile, Native Hawaiians do what they can to create political pressure for their cause. On occasion, they form alliances with environmental groups that want to halt commercial development on the islands. And in 2008, a Native Hawaiian independence group seized the royal palace in Honolulu to protest the U.S.-backed overthrow of the Hawaiian monarchy in

If the act passes, Native Hawaiians will become the last remaining indigenous group in the United States to be allowed to establish their own government.

1893. Although the occupation lasted barely a day, the political discontent it revealed persists. Little wonder that in 2009, the 50th anniversary of Hawai'i's statehood passed without a single government-sponsored celebration. Instead, Native Hawaiians concentrated their attention on Washington, D.C., and pushed for passage of the Akaka Bill.

LET'S DISCUSS

1. From a mainstream point of view, what might be the advantages and disadvantages of extending sovereignty to an indigenous group? Discuss using sociological concepts.
2. Do some research on the legal basis for tribal sovereignty. How did American Indian tribes gain the status of separate nations?

Sources: Halvalani 2002; Niesse 2008, 2011; Staton 2004; Toensing 2009; Welch 2011.

---

is most serious for the least powerful individuals and groups in the United States. Voter turnout has been particularly low among members of racial and ethnic minorities. In postelection surveys, fewer African Americans and Hispanics than Whites report that they actually voted. Many more potential voters fail to register to vote. The poor—whose focus understandably is on survival—are traditionally underrepresented among voters as well. The low turnout found among these groups is explained at least in part by their common feeling of powerlessness. Yet these low statistics encourage political power brokers to continue to ignore the interests of the less affluent and the nation's minorities. The segment of the voting population that has shown the most voter apathy is the young, as discussed in Box 17-2 on page 377 (File and Crissey 2010).

use your sociological *imagination*

Were you brought up to consider political involvement an important civic duty? If so, do you take that duty seriously by informing yourself about the issues and voting?

Race and Gender in Politics

Because politics is synonymous with power and authority, we should not be surprised that political strength is lacking in marginalized groups, such as women and racial and ethnic minorities. Nationally, women did not get the vote until 1920. Most Chinese Americans

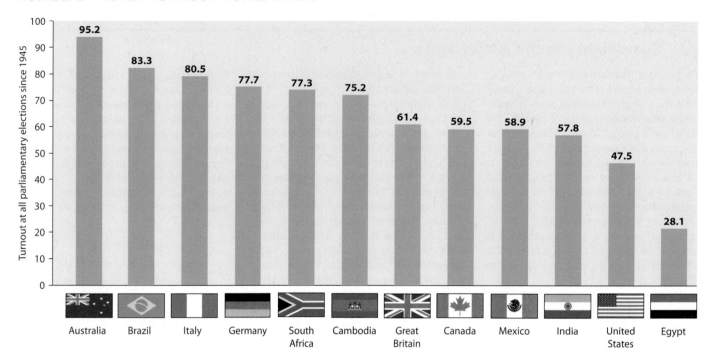

Note: Based on turnout in recent elections for seats in national congress or parliament. Data are for 2008 except for Australia (2007), Brazil, Cambodia, and Mexico (2006), Egypt, Germany, and Great Britain (2005), India (2004), and South Africa (2009).
Source: International Institute for Democracy and Electoral Assistance 2011.

were turned away from the polls until 1926. And African Americans were disenfranchised until 1965, when national voting rights legislation was passed. Predictably, it has taken these groups some time to develop their political power and begin to exercise it effectively.

Progress toward the inclusion of minority groups in government has been slow. As of mid-2011, 17 out of 100 U.S. senators were women; 2 were Latino and 2 were Asian Americans, leaving 79 White non-Hispanic men. Among the 435 members of the U.S. House of Representatives, 310 were White non-Hispanic men; 71 were women, 42 were African Americans (including 13 women), 29 were Latinos (including 7 Latinas), and 7 were Asian Americans (including 4 women). These numbers, although low, represent a high-water mark for most of these groups.

Today, with record-high numbers of Blacks and Latinos holding elective office, many critics still decry what has been termed *fiesta politics.* White power brokers tend to visit racial and ethnic minority communities only when they need electoral support, making a quick appearance on a national or ethnic holiday to get their pictures taken and then vanishing. When the election is over, they too often forget to consult the residents who supported them about community needs and concerns.

Female politicians may be enjoying more electoral success now than in the past, but there is some evidence that the media cover them differently from male politicians. A content analysis of newspaper coverage of recent gubernatorial races showed that reporters wrote more often about a female candidate's personal life, appearance, or personality than a male candidate's, and less often about her political positions and voting record. Furthermore, when political issues were raised in newspaper articles, reporters were more likely to illustrate them with statements made by male candidates than by female candidates (Devitt 1999; Jost 2008).

Minnesota Democrat Keith Ellison created quite a stir in 2007 when he became the first person to take the congressional oath of office on a Qur'an. The newly elected member of the House of Representatives, who is Muslim, thought the Qur'an would make his oath more meaningful than a Bible. Speaker of the House Nancy Pelosi (left) borrowed Thomas Jefferson's two-volume Qur'an for the occasion—a reminder that acknowledging diversity is nothing new in U.S. politics.

RESEARCH TODAY

17-2 Why Don't More Young People Vote?

All through the 1960s, young people in the United States participated actively in a range of political issues, from pushing civil rights to protesting the Vietnam War. They were especially disturbed by the fact that young men were barred from voting but were being drafted to serve in the military and were dying for their country. In response to these concerns, the Twenty-Sixth Amendment to the Constitution was ratified in 1971, lowering the voting age from 21 to 18.

Now, more than 40 years later, we can consider the available research and see what happened. Frankly, what is remarkable is what did *not* happen. First, young voters (those between ages 18 and 21) have not united in any particular political sentiment. We can see in the way the young vote the same divisions of race, ethnicity, and gender that are apparent among older age groups.

Second, while the momentum for lowering the voting age came from college campuses, the majority of young voters are not students. Third, and particularly troubling, is their relatively low turnout. The 2008 presidential election, held against a background of war in Iraq, the historic candidacy of Barack Obama, and a global economic decline, did pique the interest of young voters. In that election, 51.4 percent of eligible voters under age 30 turned out, compared to 49 percent in 2004.

What lies behind voter apathy among the young? The popular explanation is that people—especially young people—are alienated from the political system, turned off by the shallowness and negativity of candidates and campaigns. However, young people do vote as they age.

> *While the momentum for lowering the voting age came from college campuses, the majority of young voters are not students at all.*

Other explanations for the lower turnout among the young seem more plausible. First, the United States is virtually alone in requiring citizens to vote twice, in effect. They must first *register* to vote, often at a time when issues are not on the front burner and candidates haven't even declared. Second, though citizens in the United States tend to be more active in politics at the community level than those in other countries, young people often feel unmoved by local issues such as public school financing.

One way in which youths *are* impacting elections is through their reliance on the Internet for information. Today, every political campaign maintains a presence on the Web, not only through an official website, but on social networking sites. During the 2008 presidential election, two-thirds of young adults with online profiles took part in some form of political activity on those sites. Time will tell whether the Internet will ultimately reduce political apathy among younger citizens.

LET'S DISCUSS

1. How often do you vote? If you do not vote, what accounts for your apathy? Are you too busy to register? Are community issues uninteresting to you?
2. Do you think voter apathy is a serious social problem? What might be done to increase voter participation in your age group and community?

Sources: Alwin 2002; Clymer 2000; Higher Education Research Institute 2004; McDonald 2009b; Niemi and Hanmer 2010; Patterson 2005; A. Smith 2009; Vargas 2007; Wattenberg 2008.

REASONS FOR NOT VOTING, 18- TO 24-YEAR-OLDS

Source: Holder 2006:13.

Figure 17-3 shows the representation of women in selected national legislatures. While the proportion of women in national legislatures has increased in the United States and many other nations, in all but one country women still do not account for half the members of the national legislature. The African Republic of Rwanda, the exception, ranks the highest, with 56.3 percent of its legislative seats held by women. Overall, the United States ranked 89th among 186 nations in the proportion of women serving as national legislators in 2011.

To remedy this situation, many countries have adopted quotas for female representatives. In some, the government sets aside a certain percentage of seats for women, usually from 14 to 30 percent. In others, political parties have decided that 20 to 40 percent of their candidates should be women. Thirty-two countries now have some kind of female quota system (Rubin and Dagher 2009; Vasagar 2005).

thinking CRITICALLY

In the United States, which plays a more significant role in political behavior, gender or race? Explain.

Models of Power Structure in the United States

Who really holds power in the United States? Do "we the people" genuinely run the country through our elected representatives? Or is it true that behind the scenes, a small elite controls both the government and the economic system? It is difficult to determine the location of power in a society as complex as the United States. In exploring this critical question, social scientists have developed two basic views of our nation's power structure: the power elite and the pluralist models.

Power Elite Models

Karl Marx believed that 19th-century representative democracy was essentially a sham. He argued that industrialized societies were dominated by relatively small numbers of people who owned factories and controlled natural resources. In Marx's view, government officials and military leaders were essentially servants of this capitalist class and followed their wishes. Therefore, any key decisions made by politicians inevitably reflected the interests of the dominant bourgeoisie. Like others who share an **elite model** of power relations, Marx believed that society is ruled by a small group of individuals who share a common set of political and economic interests.

Mills's Model Sociologist C. Wright Mills took this model a step further in his pioneering work *The Power Elite* ([1956] 2000b). Mills described a small group of military, industrial, and government leaders who controlled the fate of the United States—the **power elite.** Power rested in the hands of a few, both inside and outside government.

A pyramid illustrates the power structure of the United States in Mills's model (Figure 17-4a). At the top are the corporate rich,

FIGURE **17-3** WOMEN IN NATIONAL LEGISLATURES, SELECTED COUNTRIES

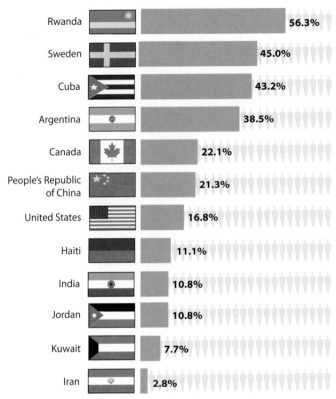

Percent female

Notes: Data are for lower legislative houses only, as of March 31, 2011; data on upper houses, such as the U.S. Senate, are not included. In 2005, the all-male Kuwaiti Parliament granted women the right to vote and serve in elected offices, which allowed women to run for office in 2007.
Source: Inter-Parliamentary Union 2011.

Think about It
Why do you think being elected to Congress is so difficult for women?

leaders of the executive branch of government, and heads of the military (whom Mills called the "warlords"). Directly below are local opinion leaders, members of the legislative branch of government, and leaders of special-interest groups. Mills contended that these individuals and groups would basically follow the wishes of the dominant power elite. At the bottom of the pyramid are the unorganized, exploited masses.

The power elite model is in many respects similar to the work of Karl Marx. The most striking difference is that Mills believed that the economically powerful coordinate their maneuvers with the military and political establishments to serve their common interests. He rejected Marx's belief that by itself, the economic structure of capitalism could create a ruling class. Still, the powerless masses at the bottom of Mills's power elite model certainly bring to mind Marx's portrait of the oppressed workers of the world, who have "nothing to lose but their chains."

A fundamental element in Mills's thesis is that the power elite not only includes relatively few members but also operates as a self-conscious, cohesive unit. Although not necessarily

FIGURE **17-4** POWER ELITE MODELS

379

Government and Politics

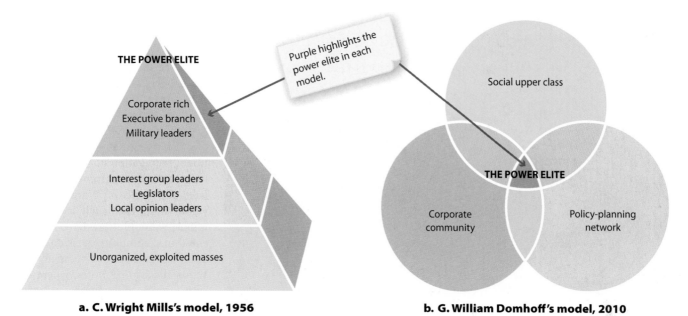

a. C. Wright Mills's model, 1956

b. G. William Domhoff's model, 2010

Source: Left, author based on Mills [1956] 2000b; right, Domhoff 2010:116.

diabolical or ruthless, the elite comprises similar types of people who interact regularly with one another and have essentially the same political and economic interests. Mills's power elite is not a conspiracy, but rather a community of interest and sentiment among a small number of influential people (A. Hacker 1964).

Admittedly, Mills failed to clarify when the elite opposes protests and when it tolerates them; he also failed to provide detailed case studies that would substantiate the interrelationships among members of the power elite. Nevertheless, his challenging theories forced scholars to look more critically at the democratic political system of the United States.

In commenting on the scandals that have rocked major corporations such as Enron and AIG over the past 15 years, observers have noted that members of the business elite *are* closely interrelated. In a study of the members of the boards of directors of *Fortune* 1000 corporations, researchers found that each director can reach *every* other board of directors in just 3.7 steps. That is, by consulting acquaintances of acquaintances, each director can quickly reach someone who sits on each of the other 999 boards. Furthermore, the face-to-face contact directors regularly have in their board meetings makes them a highly cohesive elite. Finally, the corporate elite is not only wealthy, powerful, and cohesive; it is also overwhelmingly White and male (G. Davis 2003, 2004; Kentor and Jang 2004; Mizruchi 1996; R. Schaefer 2008b; Strauss 2002).

One outgrowth of Mills's power elite model is current research on the presence of a *global* power elite—that is, those business, political, and former military leaders who exercise influence across national borders. Because this avenue of scholarship is relatively new, there is some disagreement on the definition of the term. Must the members of the global power elite demonstrate as much consensus as the members of Mills's power elite? Or can the global power elite include such diverse voices as publisher Rupert Murdoch, illegal arms dealer Viktor Bout, and

former President Bill Clinton, in his role as head of the Clinton Global Initiative (L. Miller 2008; Rothkopf 2008)?

Domhoff's Model Over the past three decades, sociologist G. William Domhoff (2010) has agreed with Mills that a powerful elite runs the United States. He finds that it is still largely White, male, and upper class, as he wrote in his book with Richard L. Zweigenhaft (2006). But Domhoff stresses the role played both by elites of the corporate community and by leaders of organizations in the policy-planning network, such as chambers of commerce and labor unions. Many of the people in both groups are also members of the social upper class. And he notes the presence of a small number of women and minority men in key positions—groups that were excluded from Mills's top echelon and are still underrepresented today.

Though the three groups in Domhoff's power elite model overlap, as Figure 17-4b shows, they do not necessarily agree on specific policies. Domhoff notes that in the electoral arena, two coalitions have exercised influence. A *corporate-conservative coalition* has played a large role in both political parties, generating support for particular candidates through direct-mail appeals. A *liberal-labor coalition* is based in unions, local environmental organizations, a segment of the minority group community, liberal churches, and the university and arts communities (Zweigenhaft and Domhoff 2006).

Pluralist Model

Several social scientists insist that power in the United States is shared more widely than the elite models indicate. In their view, a pluralist model more accurately describes the nation's political system. According to the **pluralist model,** many competing groups within the community have access to government, so that no single group is dominant.

The pluralist model suggests that a variety of groups play a significant role in decision making. Typically, pluralists make use of intensive case studies or community studies based on

At the 2011 summit in Paris, world leaders addressed the crisis in Libya.

observation research. One of the most famous—an investigation of decision making in New Haven, Connecticut—was reported by Robert Dahl (1961). Dahl found that although the number of people involved in any important decision was rather small, community power was nonetheless diffuse. Few political actors exercised decision-making power on all issues. One individual or group might be influential in a battle over urban renewal, but have little impact on educational policy.

The pluralist model, however, has not escaped serious questioning. Domhoff (1978, 2010) reexamined Dahl's study of decision making in New Haven and argued that Dahl and other pluralists had failed to trace how local elites who were prominent in decision making belonged to a larger national ruling class. In addition, studies of community power, such as Dahl's work in New Haven, can examine decision making only on issues that

become part of the political agenda. They fail to address the potential power of elites to keep certain matters entirely out of the realm of government debate.

Dianne Pinderhughes (1987) has criticized the pluralist model for failing to account for the exclusion of African Americans from the political process. Drawing on her studies of Chicago politics, Pinderhughes points out that the residential and occupational segregation of Blacks and their long political disenfranchisement violates the logic of pluralism—which would hold that such a substantial minority should always have been influential in community decision making. This critique applies to many cities across the United States, where other large racial and ethnic minorities, among them Asian Americans, Puerto Ricans, and Mexican Americans, are relatively powerless.

Historically, pluralists have stressed ways in which large numbers of people can participate in or influence governmental decision making. New communications technologies like the Internet are increasing the opportunity to be heard, not just in countries such as the United States, but in developing countries the world over. One common point of the elite and pluralist perspectives stands out, however: in the political system of the United States, power is unequally distributed. All citizens may be equal in theory, yet those who are high in the nation's power structure are "more equal." New communications technology may or may not change that distribution of power (A. McFarland 2007).

Perhaps the ultimate test of power, no matter what a nation's power structure, is the decision to go to war. Because the rank and file of any army is generally drawn from the lower classes—the least powerful groups in society—such a decision has life-and-death consequences for people far removed from the center of power. In the long run, if the general population is not convinced that war is necessary, military action is unlikely to succeed. Thus, war is a risky way in which to address conflict between nations. In the following section we will contrast war and peace as ways of addressing societal conflict, and more recently, the threat of terrorism.

thinking CRITICALLY

Which is a better model of the power structure in the United States, the power elite model or the pluralist model? Justify your answer.

Pluralism can be seen in action in the activity of lobbying groups attempting to influence public policy. The highly publicized battle over stem cell research is one example; it has pitted conservative religious groups against health advocacy groups, dividing political leaders in the process. Though legislation to support the controversial research technique had the backing of several prominent Republican lawmakers, including Senator Orrin Hatch (R-Utah), shown here with actor and activist Michael J. Fox, it fell victim to a presidential veto in 2006.

War and Peace

Conflict is a central aspect of social relations. Too often it becomes ongoing and violent, engulfing innocent bystanders as well as intentional participants. Sociologists Theodore

TAKING SOCIOLOGY TO WORK

Joseph W. Drummond, **Management Analyst, U.S. Army Space and Missile Defense Command**

When Joseph Drummond entered Morehouse College, he was planning to major in political science. But after taking an introductory sociology course, he felt that sociology gave him a clearer picture of the complexity and inter-connectedness of society. "The career track that I had in mind was to enter the field of sociology as a researcher/policy maker," he explains. However, he soon ran into "a disconnect between academia and policy making," and an apparent lack of representation of sociologists at the policymaking level.

Drummond credits one of his sociology professors for steering him toward quantitative courses. "If you ever plan on having a job," the professor suggested, "make sure you have a lot of classes with quantitative analysis—for example, statistics and data analysis. These classes tell whatever company you want to work for that you have practical skills." Later, when Drummond asked his current employer why he had gotten the job he now holds, he was told that his data analysis and social statistics courses had made him competitive.

Today, Drummond works at the U.S. Army's Space and Missile Defense Command (SMDC), near Huntsville, Alabama. He began there as an intern, after responding to an email from Morehouse College's career office. Drummond is now a junior analyst with a team that formulates and develops doctrine, organization, and material requirements for Army units assigned to space and missile defense. In a typical workweek, he reviews military force structure—units, battalions, and so on—and helps to implement directives from Department of the Army headquarters. "A lot of what we do is attempting to translate very high-level guidance to something that's practical," he explains.

Drummond values the support and professional development he has received from the Army, including classes on program management, data analysis, national security, and force management. An Army-sponsored Technology and Government in Your Future event emphasized the need for interns to pursue graduate studies in math and science to land the best jobs. Drummond says the real-world experience he got as an intern at SMDC not only brought classroom theory to life; it also made him more attractive to future employers.

Asked how he uses sociology in his work, Drummond replies that his academic training has helped him to look critically at problems and to think about the second- and third-order effects of a decision. Seeing society from a macro-level view is also invaluable to him. "When U.S. leadership began to realize that a 'hearts and mind' campaign means that we need to understand the social-historical context of the people whose country we're occupying, that changed the way that we did business and also impacted the way U.S. military force structure was managed," he explains. "A lot of people had problems making the connection." Finally, sociology has taught Drummond not to take things at face value. "Most problems/issues that we come across very seldom have easy fixes," he notes. "Sociology taught me that thorough analysis means leaving no stone unturned."

LET'S DISCUSS

1. Have you ever considered a career in national defense? Do you know anyone with a college degree who works in the field?
2. Why do you think quantitative analysis is such an important skill to employers? How might you use it in your career?

Caplow and Louis Hicks (2002:3) have defined **war** as conflict between organizations that possess trained combat forces equipped with deadly weapons. This meaning is broader than the legal definition, which typically requires a formal declaration of hostilities.

War

Sociologists approach war in three different ways. Those who take a *global view* study how and why two or more nations become engaged in military conflict. Those who take a *nation-state view* stress the interaction of internal political, socioeconomic, and cultural forces. And those who take a *micro view* focus on the social impact of war on individuals and the groups they belong to (Kiser 1992).

From the nation-state perspective, there is little to be said for the supposed socioeconomic benefits of war. Although armed conflicts increase government expenditures on troops and weapons, which tends to stimulate the economy, they also divert workers from civilian health and medical services. Thus, they have a negative effect on civilians' life chances, causing higher levels of civilian mortality. It is exceedingly difficult for a society to engage in armed conflict while maintaining citizens' well-being at home (Carlton-Ford 2010).

Although the decision to go to war is made by government leaders, public opinion plays a significant role in its execution. By 1971, the number of U.S. soldiers killed in Vietnam had surpassed 50,000, and antiwar sentiment was strong. Surveys done at that time showed the public was split roughly equally on the question of whether war was an appropriate way to settle differences between nations (Figure 17-5). This division in public opinion continued until the United States became involved in the Gulf War following Iraq's invasion of Kuwait in 1990. Since then, U.S. sentiment has been more supportive of war as a means of resolving disputes.

A major change in the composition of the U.S. military is the growing presence of women. Over 197,000 women, or about 14 percent of active U.S. military forces, are now in uniform, serving not just as support personnel but as an integral part of combat units. The first casualty of the war in Iraq, in fact, was Private First Class Lori Piestewa, a member of the Hopi tribe and a descendant of Mexican settlers in the Southwest (Bureau of the Census 2008a:328).

From a micro view, war can bring out the worst as well as the best in people. In 2004, graphic images of the abuse of Iraqi prisoners by U.S. soldiers at Iraq's Abu Ghraib prison shocked the world. For social scientists, the deterioration of the guards' behavior brought to mind Philip Zimbardo's mock prison experiment, done in 1971. Although the results of the experiment, highlighted in Chapter 5, have been applied primarily to civilian correctional facilities, Zimbardo's study was actually funded by the Office of Naval Research. In July 2004, the U.S. military began using a documentary film about the experiment to train military interrogators to avoid mistreatment of prisoners (Zarembo 2004; Zimbardo 2004).

FIGURE **17-5** U.S. PUBLIC OPINION ON THE NECESSITY OF WAR, 1971–2007

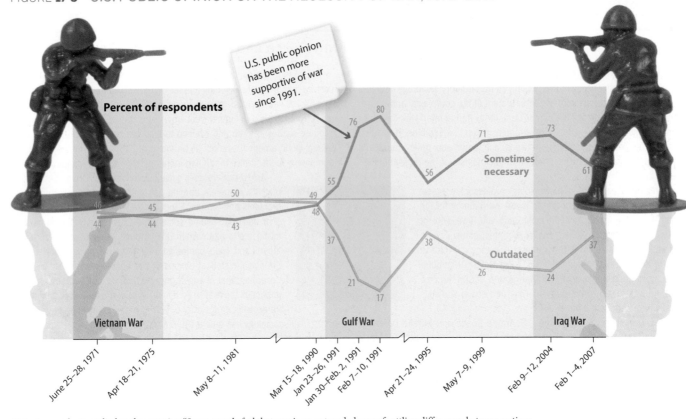

Percent of respondents

U.S. public opinion has been more supportive of war since 1991.

76   80

71   73

Sometimes necessary

55   56   61

50   49
46   45
44   44   48
43

37   38

Outdated

21   26   24   37

17

Vietnam War   Gulf War   Iraq War

June 25–28, 1971
Apr 18–21, 1975
May 8–11, 1981
Mar 15–18, 1990
Jan 23–26, 1991
Jan 30–Feb. 2, 1991
Feb 7–10, 1991
Apr 21–24, 1995
May 7–9, 1999
Feb 9–12, 2004
Feb 1–4, 2007

Note: Respondents replied to the question "Some people feel that war is an outmoded way of settling differences between nations. Others feel that wars are sometimes necessary to settle differences. With which point of view do you agree?"
Source: Gallup 2009b.

Peace

Sociologists have considered **peace** both as the absence of war and as a proactive effort to develop cooperative relations among nations. While we will focus here on international relations, we should note that in the 1990s, 90 percent of the world's armed conflicts occurred *within* rather than between states. Often, outside powers became involved in these internal conflicts, either as supporters of particular factions or in an attempt to broker a peace accord. In at least 28 countries where such conflicts occurred— none of which would be considered core nations in world systems analysis—at least 10,000 people died (Kriesberg 1992; Dan Smith 1999).

Another way of picturing the relative peacefulness of nations around the world is the Global Peace Index (Figure 17-6). This index is based on 24 indicators, including organized internal conflict, violent crime, political instability, the potential for terrorist acts, and a nation's level of military expenditures compared to its neighbors'. Currently, New Zealand is at the top of the index (very peaceful);

Somalia, Afghanistan, and Iraq are at the bottom. The United States ranks 83 on this list of 144 nations, between Ukraine and Kazakhstan.

A representative of the International Red Crescent Society delivers an aid parcel in the southern Iraqi town of Safwan. The Red Crescent provides emergency aid to victims of war and disaster in Muslim communities. Such nongovernmental organizations (NGOs) help to bind countries together, promoting peaceful relations.

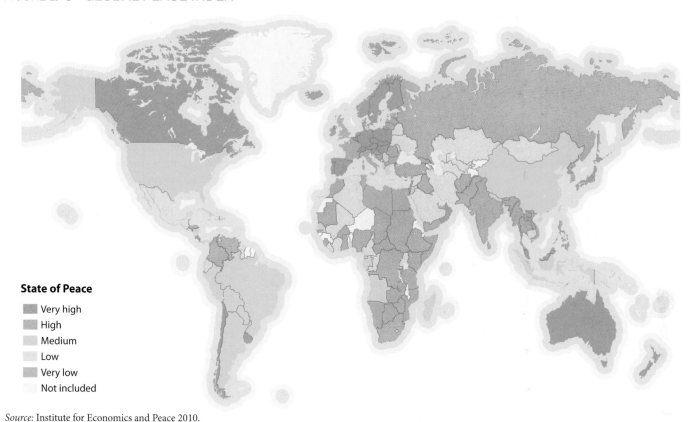

State of Peace

- Very high
- High
- Medium
- Low
- Very low
- Not included

Source: Institute for Economics and Peace 2010.

Sociologists and other social scientists who draw on sociological theory and research have tried to identify conditions that deter war. One of their findings is that international trade may act as a deterrent to armed conflict. As countries exchange goods, people, and then cultures, they become more integrated and less likely to threaten each other's security. Viewed from this perspective, not just trade but immigration and foreign exchange programs have a beneficial effect on international relations.

Another means of fostering peace is the activity of international charities and activist groups called nongovernmental organizations (NGOs). The Red Cross and Red Crescent, Doctors Without Borders, and Amnesty International donate their services wherever they are needed, without regard to nationality. In the past decade or more, these global organizations have been expanding in number, size, and scope. By sharing news of local conditions and clarifying local issues, they often prevent conflicts from escalating into violence and war. Some NGOs have initiated cease-fires, reached settlements, and even ended warfare between former adversaries.

Finally, many analysts stress that nations cannot maintain their security by threatening violence. Peace, they contend, can best be maintained by developing strong mutual security agreements between potential adversaries (Etzioni 1965; Shostak 2002).

In recent years, the United States has begun to recognize that its security can be threatened not just by nation-states, but by political groups that operate outside the bounds of legitimate authority. Indeed, terrorism is now considered the foremost threat to U.S. security—one the U.S. military is unaccustomed to fighting.

use your sociological *imagination*

Do you hear much discussion of how to promote worldwide peace, or do the conversations you hear focus more on ending a particular conflict?

Terrorism

Acts of terror, whether perpetrated by a few or by many people, can be a powerful political force. Formally defined, **terrorism** is the use or threat of violence against random or symbolic targets in pursuit of political aims. For terrorists, the end justifies the means. They believe the status quo is oppressive and that desperate measures are essential to end the suffering of the deprived. Convinced that working through the formal political process will not effect the desired political change, terrorists insist that illegal actions—often directed against innocent people—are needed. Ultimately, they hope to intimidate society and thereby bring about a new political order.

Global terrorism is just that—global in scope and impact. In March 2010, two female suicide bombers from the Caucasus region took 40 lives on the Moscow subway to call attention to their homeland's struggle for political independence from Russia.

about the heightened anxiety created by the vague alerts issued by the federal government from time to time. Worldwide, immigration and the processing of refugees have slowed to a crawl, separating families and preventing employers from filling job openings. As these efforts to combat political violence illustrate, the term *terrorism* is an apt one (R. Howard and Sawyer 2003; Lee 1983; R. Miller 1988).

Increasingly, governments are becoming concerned about another form of political violence, the potential for malicious cyberattacks. In an age in which computer viruses can spread worldwide through the Internet, this kind of attack could render a nation's computer systems useless, or even shut down its power plants. A few years ago, such a scenario would have been considered pulp fiction, but it is now the subject of contingency planning throughout the world. In the next section, we will consider some other ways that the Internet has affected government (Clayton 2011).

An essential aspect of contemporary terrorism involves use of the media. Terrorists may wish to keep secret their individual identities, but they want their political messages and goals to receive as much publicity as possible. Drawing on Erving Goffman's dramaturgical approach, sociologist Alfred McClung Lee has likened terrorism to the theater, where certain scenes are played out in predictable fashion. Whether through calls to the media, anonymous manifestos, or other means, terrorists typically admit responsibility for and defend their violent acts.

Sociologists and others have studied the role of different factors in the development of terrorism. They find that both democratic and repressive regimes can facilitate terrorism, although in different ways. The likelihood of violence is higher in youthful populations and among alienated groups, especially expatriate (overseas) communities (P. Davis and Cragin 2009).

Since September 11, 2001, governments worldwide have renewed their efforts to fight terrorism. Although the public generally regards increased surveillance and social control as a necessary evil, these measures have nonetheless raised governance issues. For example, some citizens in the United States and elsewhere have questioned whether measures such as the USA Patriot Act of 2001 threaten civil liberties. Citizens have also complained

thinking CRITICALLY

What is the greatest threat to world peace, and how would you counter it?

Political Activism on the Internet

By any measure, the Internet has become a force to be reckoned with in politics. Although television and newspapers still serve as sources of political news, 73 percent of adult

Tibetan monks in exile check the news from Tibet at a technological center in Dharamsala, India. Once a military network, the Internet has become a hotbed of political activism.

Internet users in the United States, or 54 percent of all adults, went online to get news about the 2010 election. Surfers are less likely to visit candidates' official websites than to check the chatter on Twitter. By 2010, 22 percent of online adults were using the social media site, which was created in 2006, for political purposes (A. Howard 2011). These developments have turned political campaigning into a 24/7 activity, especially in the United States. President Barack Obama, now a candidate for reelection, has maintained his 13-million-name e-mail list not only to inform and persuade citizens but also to seek campaign donations (M. Scherer/Owings 2010).

On the Internet, political activity is not limited to traditional party politics, and certainly not to domestic politics. In far-flung places including Egypt, Indonesia, Kosovo, and Malaysia, citizens are making themselves heard through *cyberactivism* or Net activism—the use of the Internet for political purposes. In China, 10,000 members of the fast-growing Falun Gong religious sect surprised government officials with a mass rally organized on the web and through YouTube videos. In Kosovo, the staff of Koha Ditore, a dissident newspaper, took to the web after Serbian soldiers closed their office. And in Mexico, the revolutionary Zapatista movement gained support from an online campaign for self-rule in the state of Chiapas.

As these incidents illustrate, organizers find the web especially useful in circumventing the restrictive controls of authoritarian regimes. In fact, groups branded as terrorists in a variety of states have used the web to their advantage. Websites can be established outside a country's borders, beyond the control of government officials yet still accessible to the country's citizens.

The use of online technology by political activists has not been lost on traditional sources of authority, be they charismatic, legal-rational, or traditional. From Queen Elizabeth II to Prime Minister Manmohan Singh of India, legitimate authority figures have mounted a major effort to create an online presence, sometimes called *e-government*. The competition is on, both online and offline (Lucas 2008).

Also growing in importance are borderless organizations that unite people of like mind—from peace activists to terrorists—around the world. These are very tightly knit communities, notes Professor Juan Enriquez of Harvard University. Labor groups and environmental organizations such as Greenpeace have become particularly adept at using e-mail to mobilize activists quickly, wherever they are needed. The result: a completely new kind of power structure, compared to the more familiar face-to-face approach of Washington lobbyists. "The new people with power are those with credibility and an e-mail list," says political consultant Jennifer Laszlo. "You have no idea who they are, where they are, what color they are" (Engardio 1999:145).

use your sociological *imagination*

Imagine a future in which everyone in the United States has access to the Internet, and the Internet is the foremost political medium. How would government in that society differ from government today?

social**policy** and **Politics**

Campaign Financing

How much does it cost to become president of the United States? All told, Barack Obama's 2008 campaign raised $745 million; John McCain's, $768 million. If we include all presidential and congressional candidates in 2008, win or lose, the price tag was over $5.2 billion.

Is the enormous cost of modern political campaigns a big issue with voters? The answer is yes and no. Surveys show that 61 percent of voters favor limits on campaign spending. Yet 38 percent feel that a candidate—maybe their candidate?—should be allowed to spend whatever he or she wants. What is more, over 60 percent of both Republicans and Democrats agree that campaign contributions are free speech, and as such are protected by the First Amendment to the Constitution (Center for Responsive Politics 2010a, 2010b; Saad 2010a).

Looking at the Issue

Regulation of campaign contributions has a long history, beginning with efforts to bar the requirement that government employees contribute to their bosses' campaign funds. More recently, the focus on both the state and national levels has been on remedying the shortcomings of the Federal Campaign Act of 1974, which placed restrictions on so-called *hard money,* or donations made to specific candidates for national office. Hard money is now limited to $10,000 per organization or $2,000 per individual donor per election cycle (the primary and election being separate cycles). These limits were intended to keep national candidates or elected officials from being bought by the wealthy or the powerful.

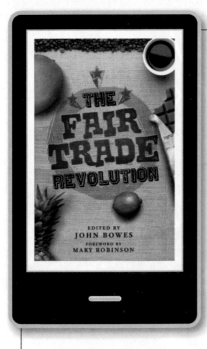

66 It is rare in life to have a moment of personal epiphany. Mine came in the millennium year when, at the Co-op, we had just introduced the UK's first own brand Fairtrade product: a chocolate bar with its key ingredient sourced from Ghana. We had supported the concept of fair trade right from the beginning but, although always empathetic to the ethical agenda, my interest was primarily commercial; the intention was to develop responsible retailing, a holistic approach to this agenda, as a modern day reflection of cooperative values and a vehicle for differentiating the business from its competitors. But in concert with the chocolate initiative a BBC crew visited Kuapa Kokoo in Ghana and their 14-minute film changed my view of the world. At the end of their report they unwrapped a chocolate bar, which was starting to melt in the heat, and gave some to a young woman and her daughter. As they tasted the product their eyes lit up and their faces were transformed into bright smiles and the young woman said 'oh, it's so sweet, so sweet'. This lady had spent her whole life toiling in the fields for a pittance and had never tasted the product of her own labours; she had no concept of what it was about chocolate that made it so important and appealing to the people living thousands of miles away in the northern hemisphere. In one sense the film captured a joyous experience but in another it was extraordinarily sad. I felt a catch in my throat and knew I was hooked for the rest of my life.

. . .

The United States of America is the largest consumer market on Earth. No other country on the planet could do more to address the climate problem and establish a fairer trading system.

It has been estimated that fair trade may, currently, be benefiting more than 7 million people in the developing world. This is an impressive achievement but set in the context of the sheer scale of world poverty it still represents only a relatively small contribution towards addressing an enormous problem.

It is estimated that 1.4 billion people, one fifth of the world's population, are trying to survive at or below the World Bank's official poverty line of just $1.25 a day. And 2.6 billion people, about 40 per cent of humanity, are living on less than $2 a day.

These astonishing numbers are so large that it is difficult to fully comprehend them. They reflect the appalling collective failure of human society. And the scale of the failure becomes even more dramatic when we consider *disparities* in world income. The poorest 40 per cent account for just 5 per cent of global income whilst the richest 20 per cent take three quarters of the pot. The truth is that fair trade is still very much in its infancy. Those who are committed to making a real difference in the developing world will recognise that we are not at the end of a process, or anywhere near the end, but really only at the very beginning. If we strip away all of the commercial spin, and occasional wishful thinking, we might be left with the uncomfortable conclusion that, far from capitalising on a consumer movement, we have perhaps not yet recognised its full potential and have so far failed to put mechanisms into place to ensure that its momentum can be fully realised.

. . .

The United States of America is the largest consumer market on Earth. No other country on the planet could do more to address the climate problem and establish a fairer trading system. While fair trade has experienced strong growth in the States, which in absolute terms is the largest single market for fair trade products, overall market penetration is low. Yet, if we are to have a true revolution in trading practices it is difficult to see how it can be achieved without the US fully on board. This represents the greatest single challenge for fair trade campaigners. . . . 99

(Bowes 2011:ix, 2–3, 231–232) Additional information about this excerpt can be found on the Online Learning Center at www.mhhe.com/schaefer13e.

John Bowes, editor of this excerpt from *The Fair Trade Revolution*, once served as a top executive in a British grocery chain. In the process, he became acutely aware of the low wages paid to those who harvest the food sold in grocery stores. To address their plight, he helped to originate a movement called **fair trade**, in which consumers in industrialized countries voluntarily pay above-market prices for certain foods so that the workers who plant, pick, and pack the crops can receive higher wages. Supporters of fair trade often seek to subsidize export crops grown in developing countries, such as coffee, bananas, and chocolate (A. Stark 2011).

While acknowledging Bowes's point of view, sociologists also try to see foreign agricultural laborers and farm owners from the perspective of their own cultures—an approach called **cultural relativism** (see Chapter 3). That is, besides comparing farm work

in developing countries to similar work in industrial nations, sociologists would compare it to the other jobs available to foreign workers. For example, sweatshops certainly aren't the sort of places where people in industrial countries would want to work, but from the foreign worker's perspective, they may be preferable to a farm in an isolated rural area or a lower-paying job with a local employer. In sum, foreign workers and producers face a different *economic system* from the one in industrial nations, so their attitudes and the choices they make may differ from our own.

The term **economic system** refers to the social institution through which goods and services are produced, distributed, and consumed. As with social institutions such as the family, religion, and government, the economic system shapes other aspects of the social order and is in turn influenced by them.

Throughout this textbook, you have been reminded of the economy's impact on social behavior—for example, on individual and group behavior in factories and offices. You have studied the work of Karl Marx and Friedrich Engels, who emphasized that a society's economic system can promote social inequality. And you have learned that foreign investment in developing countries can intensify inequality among residents.

This chapter will present a sociological analysis of the impact of the economy on people's lives. What makes work satisfying? How has the trend toward deindustrialization changed the work people do? What will the workforce of the 21st century look like? We will begin to answer these questions with a macro-level analysis of two ideal types of economic system—capitalism and socialism—and the real-world institution known as the informal economy. A case study on China, a socialist society that has been moving toward capitalism, follows. Next, we will examine various aspects of work, including worker alienation and worker satisfaction. We will also look at the ways in which the U.S. economy is changing. Finally, in the Social Policy section we will explore the effects of a financial innovation called *microfinancing* on the lives of poor people in developing countries.

Economic Systems

The sociocultural evolution approach developed by Gerhard Lenski categorizes preindustrial society according to the way in which the economy is organized. The principal types of preindustrial society, as you recall, are hunting-and-gathering societies, horticultural societies, and agrarian societies.

As we noted in Chapter 5, the *Industrial Revolution*—which took place largely in England during the period 1760 to 1830—brought about changes in the social organization of the workplace. People left their homesteads and began working in central locations such as factories. As the Industrial Revolution proceeded, a new form of social structure emerged: the **industrial society**, a society that depends on mechanization to produce its goods and services.

Two basic types of economic system distinguish contemporary industrial societies: capitalism and socialism. As described in the following sections, capitalism and socialism serve as ideal types of economic system. No nation precisely fits either model. Instead, the economy of each individual state represents a mixture of capitalism and socialism, although one type or the other is generally more useful in describing a society's economic structure.

Capitalism

In preindustrial societies, land functioned as the source of virtually all wealth. The Industrial Revolution changed all that. It required that certain individuals and institutions be willing to take substantial risks in order to finance new inventions, machinery, and business enterprises. Eventually, bankers, industrialists, and other holders of large sums of money replaced landowners as the most powerful economic force. These people invested their funds in the hope of realizing even greater profits, and thereby became owners of property and business firms.

The transition to private ownership of business was accompanied by the emergence of the capitalist economic system. **Capitalism** is an economic system in which the means of production are held largely in private hands and the main incentive for economic activity is the accumulation of profits. In practice, capitalist systems vary in the degree to which the government regulates private ownership and economic activity (D. Rosenberg 1991).

Immediately following the Industrial Revolution, the prevailing form of capitalism was what is termed **laissez-faire** ("let them do"). Under the principle of laissez-faire, as expounded and endorsed by British economist Adam Smith (1723–1790), people could compete freely, with minimal government intervention in the economy. Business retained the right to regulate itself and operated essentially without fear of government interference (Smelser 1963).

TREND SPOTTING

Occupational Growth and Decline

One of the most closely watched trends in the U.S. economy is the growth or decline of particular occupations. In good economic times and bad, people want to know where the jobs of the future will be. As a result, the Bureau of Labor Statistics regularly projects job growth over the next 10 years.

In the United States today, most new job openings are expected to require little formal education, or at most on-the-job training. Construction laborers, groundskeepers, and food preparers are three occupations that are expected to see a large increase in employment. Skilled occupations such as nurses, accountants, and teachers from preschool through high school are also expected to see strong growth.

The fastest-growing occupations—those that show the highest growth proportionately—are almost all skilled occupations, most of them in health and medicine. They include biomedical engineers—expected to grow 72 percent over the next 10 years—health aides, physician assistants, and physical therapists. Skilled non-health-related occupations, such as financial examiners and computer software engineers, are also expected to grow.

Finally, there is the other side of the ledger—occupations that are declining in number. The steepest decline, down 33 percent, is expected to occur among sewing machine operators. Other occupations that are expected to see big job losses are farmers, postal workers, telemarketers, switchboard operators, and door-to-door sales workers.

For more than a century, the board game of Monopoly has entertained millions of people around the world. In the game, players strive to dominate the fictitious economy, gleefully bankrupting other players. Ironically, Monopoly was actually developed to demonstrate the weaknesses of capitalist economies, such as excessive rents and the tendency for money to accumulate in the hands of a few.

Two centuries later, capitalism has taken on a somewhat different form. Private ownership and maximization of profits still remain the most significant characteristics of capitalist economic systems. However, in contrast to the era of laissez-faire, capitalism today features government regulation of economic relations. Without restrictions, business firms can mislead consumers, endanger workers' safety, and even defraud the companies' investors—all in the pursuit of greater profits. That is why the government of a capitalist nation often monitors prices, sets safety and environmental standards for industries, protects the rights of consumers, and regulates collective bargaining between labor unions and management. Yet under capitalism as an ideal type, government rarely takes over ownership of an entire industry.

Contemporary capitalism also differs from laissez-faire in another important respect: capitalism tolerates monopolistic practices. A **monopoly** exists when a single business firm controls the market. Domination of an industry allows the firm to effectively control a commodity by dictating pricing, quality standards, and availability. Buyers have little choice but to yield to the firm's decisions; there is no other place to purchase the product or service. Monopolistic practices violate the ideal of free competition cherished by Adam Smith and other supporters of laissez-faire capitalism.

Some capitalistic nations, such as the United States, outlaw monopolies through antitrust legislation. Such laws prevent any business from taking over so much of the competition in an industry that it controls the market. The U.S. federal government allows monopolies to exist only in certain exceptional cases, such as the utility and transportation industries. Even then, regulatory agencies scrutinize these officially approved monopolies to protect the

public. The protracted legal battle between the Justice Department and Microsoft, owner of the dominant operating system for personal computers, illustrates the uneasy relationship between government and private monopolies in capitalistic countries.

Conflict theorists point out that although *pure* monopolies are not a basic element of the economy of the United States, competition is still much more restricted than one might expect in what is called a *free enterprise system*. In numerous industries, a few companies largely dominate the field and keep new enterprises from entering the marketplace.

During the severe economic downturn that began in 2008, the United States moved even further away from the laissez-faire ideal. To keep major financial institutions from going under, the federal government invested hundreds of millions of dollars in distressed banking, investment, and insurance companies. Then in 2009, the government bailed out the failing automobile industry, taking a 60 percent interest in General Motors. The Canadian government took another 12 percent.

As we have seen in earlier chapters, globalization and the rise of multinational corporations have spread the capitalistic pursuit of profits around the world. Especially in developing countries, governments are not always prepared to deal with the sudden influx of foreign capital and its effects on their economies. One particularly striking example of how unfettered capitalism can harm developing nations is found in the Democratic Republic of Congo (formerly Zaire). The Congo has significant deposits of the metal columbite-tantalite—coltan, for short—which is used in the production of electronic circuit boards. Until the market for cell phones, pagers, and laptop computers heated up recently, U.S. manufacturers got most of their coltan from Australia. But at the height of consumer demand, they turned to miners in the Congo to increase their supply.

Predictably, the escalating price of the metal—as much as $600 a kilogram at one point, or more than three times the average

A worker mines for coltan with sweat and a stick. The sudden increase in demand for the metal by U.S. computer manufacturers caused incursions into the Congo by neighboring countries hungry for capital to finance a war. Too often, globalization can have unintended consequences for a nation's economy and social welfare.

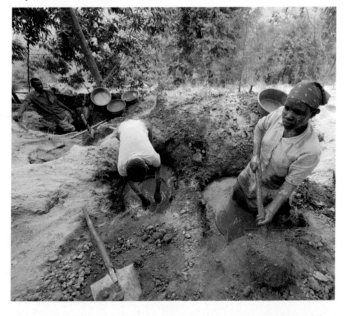

Congolese worker's yearly wages—attracted undesirable attention. Soon the neighboring countries of Rwanda, Uganda, and Burundi, at war with one another and desperate for resources to finance the conflict, were raiding the Congo's national parks, slashing and burning to expose the coltan beneath the forest floor. Indirectly, the sudden increase in the demand for coltan was financing war and the rape of the environment. U.S. manufacturers have since cut off their sources in the Congo in an effort to avoid abetting the destruction. But their action has only penalized legitimate miners in the impoverished country (Austin 2002; Friends of the Congo 2011).

---

use your sociological *imagination*

Which aspects of capitalism do you personally appreciate? Which do you find worrisome?

Socialism

Socialist theory was refined in the writings of Karl Marx and Friedrich Engels. These European radicals were disturbed by the exploitation of the working class that emerged during the Industrial Revolution. In their view, capitalism forced large numbers of people to exchange their labor for low wages. The owners of an industry profit from the labor of workers primarily because they pay workers less than the value of the goods produced.

As an ideal type, a socialist economic system attempts to eliminate such economic exploitation. Under **socialism**, the means of production and distribution in a society are collectively rather than privately owned. The basic objective of the economic system is to meet people's needs rather than to maximize profits. Socialists reject the laissez-faire philosophy that free competition benefits the general public. Instead, they believe that the central government, acting as the representative of the people, should make basic economic decisions. Therefore, government ownership of all major industries—including steel production, automobile manufacturing, and agriculture—is a primary feature of socialism as an ideal type.

In practice, socialist economic systems vary in the extent to which they tolerate private ownership. For example, in Great Britain, a nation with some aspects of both a socialist and a capitalist economy, passenger airline service is concentrated in the government-owned corporation British Airways. Yet private airlines are allowed to compete with it.

Socialist nations differ from capitalist nations in their commitment to social service programs. For example, the U.S. government provides health care and health insurance to the elderly and poor through the Medicare and Medicaid programs. But socialist countries typically offer government-financed medical care to *all* citizens. In theory, the wealth of the people as a collectivity is used to provide health care, housing, education, and other key services to each individual and family.

Marx believed that socialist societies would eventually "wither away" and evolve into *communist* societies. As an ideal type, **communism** refers to an economic system under which all property is communally owned and no social distinctions are made on the basis of people's ability to produce. In recent decades, the Soviet Union, the People's Republic of China, Vietnam, Cuba, and

Economic System	Characteristics	Contemporary Examples
Capitalism	Private ownership of the means of production. Accumulation of profits the main incentive	Canada Mexico United States
Socialism	Collective ownership of the means of production. Meeting people's needs the basic objective	Germany Russia Sweden
Communism	Communal ownership of all property. No social distinctions made on basis of people's ability to produce	Cuba North Korea Vietnam

Note: Countries listed in column 3 are typical of one of the three economic systems, but not perfectly so. In practice, the economies of most countries include a mix of elements from the three major systems.

nations in Eastern Europe were popularly thought of as examples of communist economic systems. However, this usage represents an incorrect application of a term with sensitive political connotations. All nations known as communist in the 20th century actually fell far short of the ideal type (Walder and Nguyen 2008).

By the early 1990s, Communist parties were no longer ruling the nations of Eastern Europe. As of 2010, however, China, Cuba, Laos, North Korea, and Vietnam remained socialist societies ruled by Communist parties. Yet even in those countries, capitalism had begun to make inroads. In Vietnam, for example, the Ho Chi Minh City Stock Exchange, which opened in 1990, now trades 600 stocks representing almost 40 percent of the country's gross domestic product (GDP) (K. Chu 2010).

As we have seen, capitalism and socialism serve as ideal types of economic systems. In reality, the economy of each industrial society—including the United States, the European Union, and Japan—includes certain elements of both capitalism and socialism (Table 18-1). Whatever the differences—whether a society more closely fits the ideal type of capitalism or socialism—all industrial societies rely chiefly on mechanization in the production of goods and services.

The Informal Economy

In many countries, one aspect of the economy defies description as either capitalist or socialist. In the **informal economy**, transfers of money, goods, or services take place but are not reported to the government. Examples of the informal economy include trading services with someone—say, a haircut for a computer lesson; selling goods on the street; and engaging in illegal transactions, such as gambling or drug deals. The informal economy also includes off-the-books work in landscaping, street vending, child care, and housecleaning. Participants in this type of economy avoid taxes and government regulations.

In the United States, the informal economy accounts for about 8 percent of total economic activity. In other industrialized nations it varies, from 11 percent in Great Britain to 20 percent in Spain workers, including professionals, self-employed persons, and even unpaid volunteers. The concept of work-related anxiety now covers alienation even among more affluent workers, who have a greater degree of control over their working conditions. From a conflict perspective, we have masked the fact that alienation falls most heavily on the lower and working classes by making it appear to be endemic, from the boardroom to the shop floor.

Worker Satisfaction

In general, people with greater responsibility for a finished product (such as white-collar professionals and managers) experience more satisfaction than those with less responsibility. For women

Working at the checkout counter may help to pay the bills, but it isn't likely to provide much job satisfaction—especially in a large supermarket where workers enjoy little responsibility or personal recognition.

and men working in blue-collar jobs, the repetitive nature of work can be particularly unsatisfying. Repeatedly assembling parts for a cell phone or laptop computer is monotonous work. Not surprisingly, sociologist Robert Blauner's (1964) classic research study revealed that printers—who often work in small shops and supervise apprentices—were more satisfied with their work than laborers who performed repetitive tasks on automobile assembly lines.

A number of general factors can reduce the level of dissatisfaction of contemporary industrial workers. Higher wages give workers a sense of accomplishment apart from the task before them. A shorter workweek is supposed to increase the amount of time people can devote to recreation and leisure, reducing some of the discontent of the workplace. But the number of hours Americans work actually *increased* in the 1990s, by the equivalent of about one workweek. Short staffing because of low unemployment rates may have accounted for part of the increase in hours worked; however, many Americans took a second job during this period, just to make ends meet (Gerson and Jacobs 2004).

Numerous studies have shown that positive relationships with co-workers can make a boring job tolerable or even enjoyable. In his often cited "banana time" study, sociologist Donald Roy (1959) examined worker satisfaction in a two-month participant observation of a small group of machine operators. Drawing on the interactionist perspective, Roy carefully recorded the social interactions among members of his work group, including many structured "times" and "themes" designed to break up long days of simple, repetitive work. For example, the workers divided their food breaks into coffee time, peach time, banana time, fish time, Coke time, and lunch time—each of which occurred daily and involved distinctive responsibilities, jokes, and insults. Roy (1959:166) concluded that his observations "seem to support the generally accepted notion that one key source of job satisfaction lies in the informal interaction shared by members of a work group." The patterned conversation and horseplay of these workers reduced the monotony of their workdays.

Sociologist George Ritzer (1977, 2000) has suggested that the relatively positive impression many workers present is misleading. In his view, manual workers are so deeply alienated that they come to expect little from their jobs. Their satisfaction comes from nonwork tasks, and any job-related gratification results from receiving wages. Ritzer's interpretation explains why

manual workers—although they say they are satisfied with their occupations—would not choose the same line of work if they could begin their lives over.

The Changing U.S. Economy

As advocates of the power elite model point out, the trend in capitalist societies has been toward concentration of ownership by giant corporations, especially multinational ones. In the following sections, we will examine three outgrowths of this trend in the United States: the changing face of the workforce, deindustrialization, and offshoring. As these trends show, any change in the economy has social and political implications.

The Changing Face of the Workforce

The workforce in the United States is constantly changing. During World War II, when men were mobilized to fight abroad, women entered the workforce in large numbers. And with the rise of the civil rights movement in the 1960s, minorities found numerous job opportunities opening to them. Box 18-2 takes a closer look at the active recruitment of women and minorities into the workplace, known as *affirmative action*.

Although predictions are not always reliable, sociologists and labor specialists foresee a workforce increasingly composed of women and racial and ethnic minorities. In 1960 there were twice as many men in the labor force as women. From 1988 to 2018, however, 52 percent of new workers are expected to be women. The dynamics for minority group workers are even more dramatic, as the number of Black, Latino, and Asian American workers continues to increase at a faster rate than the number of White workers (Toossi 2009).

More and more, then, the workforce reflects the diversity of the population, as ethnic minorities enter the labor force and immigrants and their children move from marginal jobs or employment in the informal economy to positions of greater visibility and responsibility. The impact of this changing labor force is not merely statistical. A more diverse workforce means that relationships between workers are more likely to cross gender, racial, and ethnic lines. Interactionists note that people will soon find themselves supervising and being supervised by people very different from themselves.

RESEARCH TODAY

18-2 Affirmative Action

Jessie Sherrod began picking cotton in the fields of Mississippi when she was eight years old, earning $1.67 for a 12-hour day. Today she is a Harvard-educated pediatrician who specializes in infectious diseases. But the road from the cotton fields to the medical profession was hardly an easy one. "You can't make up for 400 years of slavery and mistreatment and unequal opportunity in 20 years," she says angrily. "We had to ride the school bus for five miles . . . and pass by a white school to get to our black elementary school. Our books were used books. Our instructors were not as good. We didn't have the proper equipment. How do you make up for that?" (Stolberg 1995:A14). Some people think it should be done through affirmative action programs.

The term *affirmative action* first appeared in an executive order issued by President John F. Kennedy in 1961. That order called for contractors to "take affirmative action to ensure that applicants are employed, and that employees are treated during employment, without regard to their race, creed, color, or national origin." In 1967, the order was amended by President Lyndon Johnson to prohibit discrimination on the basis of sex as well, but affirmative action remained a vague concept. Currently, **affirmative action** refers to positive efforts to recruit minority group members or women for jobs, promotions, and educational opportunities.

> *Critics warn against hiring and admissions quotas, complaining that they constitute a kind of "reverse discrimination" against White males.*

Sociologists—especially conflict and feminist theorists—view affirmative action as a legislative attempt to reduce the inequality embedded in the social structure by increasing opportunities for groups who were deprived in the past, such as women and African Americans. Despite the clear disparity in earnings between White males and other groups, however, many people doubt that everything done in the name of affirmative action is desirable. Critics warn against hiring and admissions quotas, complaining that they constitute a kind of "reverse discrimination" against White males.

Affirmative action became a prominent issue in state and national political campaigns in 1996, when California's voters approved by a 54 to 46 percent margin the California Civil Rights Initiative. Better known as Proposition 209, this measure amends the state constitution to *prohibit* any program that gives preference to women and minorities in college admissions, hiring, promotion, or government contracts. In other words, it aims to abolish affirmative action programs. The courts have since upheld the measure. In 1998, voters in Washington State passed a similar anti–affirmative action measure.

In 2003, focusing specifically on college admissions in a pair of decisions involving policies at the University of Michigan, the Supreme Court ruled that colleges may consider race and ethnicity as one factor in their admissions decisions. However, they cannot assign a specific value to being a minority candidate in such a way that race becomes the overriding factor in a decision. The ruling allowed many colleges and universities to continue their existing affirmative action policies.

Increasingly, critics of affirmative action are calling for color-blind policies that would end affirmative action. Presumably, such policies would allow all applicants to be judged fairly. However, opponents warn against the danger of **color-blind racism**—the use of the principle of race neutrality to defend a racially unequal status quo (see Chapter 11). Will "color-blind" policies put an end to institutional practices that now favor Whites, they ask? According to the latest data, for example, Harvard University admits 40 percent of those applicants who are children of alumni—almost all of whom are White—compared to 11 percent of nonalumni children. Ironically, studies show that children of alumni are far more likely than either minority students or athletes to run into trouble academically.

LET'S DISCUSS

1. Is affirmative action part of the admissions policy at the college or university you attend? If so, do you think the policy has helped to level the playing field? Might it have excluded some qualified White applicants?

2. Take a poll of your classmates. What percentage of the class supports affirmative action in hiring and college admissions? How does that group break down in terms of gender, race, and ethnicity?

Sources: Massey and Mooney 2007; Pincus 2003, 2008; Stolberg 1995; University of Michigan 2003.

The Supreme Court's many decisions on the constitutionality of affirmative action programs have made it difficult for organizations to encourage diversity without transgressing the law.

Deindustrialization

What happens when a company decides it is more profitable to move its operations out of a long-established community to another part of the country, or out of the country altogether? People lose jobs; stores lose customers; the local government's tax base declines and it cuts services. This devastating process has occurred again and again in the past decade or so.

The term **deindustrialization** refers to the systematic, widespread withdrawal of investment in basic aspects of productivity, such as factories and plants. Giant corporations that deindustrialize are not necessarily refusing to invest in new economic opportunities. Rather, the targets and locations of investment change, and the need for labor decreases as advances in technology continue to automate production. First, companies may

Especially in India, the extension of microloans to financially questionable projects with little chance for success has left some borrowers in debt. At the other extreme, some lenders have reaped extraordinary profits, both for themselves and for the investment banks they have created.

In some countries, politicians resent microfinancing because it competes with the central government's path to self-sufficiency. In Nicaragua, President Daniel Ortega supports the *movimento no pago,* or no-pay movement, which encourages borrowers not to repay their debts. So successful has the movement been that one of that nation's leading microfinanciers has been driven out of business.

At a workshop in Mumbai, India, Sharda Bhandare cuts the pieces for a pair of gloves from a towel. Microloans make such small businesses possible, and help them to become self-sustaining.

Applying Sociology

Researchers who draw on the interactionist approach have shown that there is more to microfinancing than money. A study done by microfinance expert Daryl Collins and his colleagues (2009) shows how even with modest assistance, poor people can significantly improve their circumstances through mutual support. Collins asked villagers and slum dwellers in Bangladesh, India, and South Africa to keep diaries of how they spent every penny they earned. He and his team found that most of the poor households they studied did not live hand to mouth, spending everything they earned as soon as they got it. Instead, they used financial tools that were linked to their extended families and informal social networks. They saved money, squeezed it out of creditors whenever possible, ran sophisticated savings clubs, and took advantage of microfinancing whenever it was available. Their tactics suggested new methods of fighting poverty and encouraged the development of broader microfinance programs.

Because an estimated 90 percent of the recipients of microcredit are women, feminist theorists are especially interested in the growth of microfinancing. Women's economic status has been found to be critical to the well-being of their children, and the key to a healthy household environment. In developing countries, where women often are not treated as well as men, being entrusted with credit is particularly empowering to them. Research indicates that women recipients are more likely than men to participate in networks and collective action groups, perhaps because they must overcome resistance to women as economic decision makers (Karides 2010; Sanyal 2009).

Drawing on world systems analysis (see Chapter 10), sociologist Marina Karides (2010) contrasts microfinancing with the Western model of economic development, in which multinational corporations based in core countries take advantage of the low wages and natural resources in periphery and semi-periphery countries. The low-wage workers employed by the multinationals rarely escape subsistence living, while the vast majority of people in core nations enjoy a comparatively high standard of living. Microfinanciers hope that in contrast, the cottage industries they help to establish will contribute to the local economies in developing countries, and ultimately to the well-being of those societies, rather than merely serve the economic interests of core nations.

Some critics complain that the creation of small home-based industries reduces the demand for formal employment opportunities. Supporters of microenterprise counter that much time has passed without a significant change in job growth. Microfinancing, they claim, is the best way to create sustainable market opportunities for the poor in developing nations, even if those opportunities are much less attractive than those available in core nations.

Initiating Policy

Even supporters of microfinancing acknowledge the need to reduce overlending and monitor the success of small loans in helping borrowers to escape poverty. Some indicators suggest that many borrowers do not achieve self-sufficiency. If that is true, lenders should increase their oversight and attempt to identify best practices—that is, those types of assistance that are most effective in helping the poor. Less than a decade ago, microfinancing was hailed as the single best solution to world poverty. With modifications, it should continue to reduce hardship and suffering among the poor (Bajaj 2011a, 2011b; Glazer 2011).

Lenders also need to work with political leaders, and vice versa, to ensure that they do not regard one another as competitors for political support from the poor. Some government leaders have gone so far as to charge lenders with profiteering at the expense of the poor, and to take extraordinary measures for the protection of borrowers. In 2010, officials of one state in India required all loans to be approved by the government, and their eventual repayment to be made in person before a public official. To the degree that profiteering is truly a problem, some type of remedy, whether through legislation or self-monitoring, may need to be introduced. Given the cultural, political, and legal differences among nations where microfinanciers operate, the development of this type of government policy will be a major undertaking.

Taking Sociology with You

1. Do you think microfinancing might be useful in the United States? If so, how and under what conditions?

2. Using sociological concepts, explain why some politicians might resent microfinancing programs.

3. What obstacles might prevent poor people, either in the United States or elsewhere, from improving their lives through microfinancing? Might the government have a role to play in removing those obstacles?

Summary

The **economic system** of a society has an important influence on social behavior and on other social institutions. This chapter examines the major economic systems, the rise of **capitalism** in China, work and **alienation** from work, the changing U.S. economy, and **microfinancing,** a strategy for helping the poor to lift themselves out of poverty.

1. With the Industrial Revolution, a new form of social structure emerged: the **industrial society.**

2. Systems of **capitalism** vary in the degree to which the government regulates private ownership and economic activity, but all emphasize the profit motive.

3. The basic objective of **socialism** is to eliminate economic exploitation and meet people's needs.

4. Marx believed that **communism** would evolve naturally out of socialism.

5. In developing nations, the **informal economy** represents a significant part of total economic activity. Yet because this sector depends largely on women's work, it is undervalued.

6. In the 1980s, the Chinese Communist Party began allowing Chinese entrepreneurs to experiment with capitalist ventures. Today, multinational corporations are capitalizing on China's huge workforce to produce goods and services for sale not just to those in industrialized nations, but to the people of China.

7. Industrial jobs can lead to a sense of **alienation** in the workplace. Karl Marx expected that powerless workers would eventually overthrow the capitalist system.

8. **Affirmative action** is intended to remedy the effects of discrimination against minority groups and women in education and the workplace. The concept is controversial, however, because some people see it as reverse discrimination against majority groups.

9. The U.S. economy is changing rapidly. Workers are coping with **deindustrialization** and **downsizing;** employers are training an increasingly diverse workforce. Many companies are turning to **offshoring,** or the outsourcing of work to foreign contractors, to lower their costs so they can compete in a global marketplace.

10. In developing countries, **microfinancing** ("banking the unbanked") is improving the lives of millions of poor people.

Key Terms

Affirmative action Positive efforts to recruit minority group members or women for jobs, promotions, and educational opportunities. (page 401)

Alienation A condition of estrangement or dissociation from the surrounding society. (399)

Capitalism An economic system in which the means of production are held largely in private hands and the main incentive for economic activity is the accumulation of profits. (393)

Color-blind racism The use of the principle of race neutrality to defend a racially unequal status quo. (402)

Communism As an ideal type, an economic system under which all property is communally owned and no social distinctions are made on the basis of people's ability to produce. (395)

Cultural relativism The viewing of people's behavior from the perspective of their own culture. (392)

Deindustrialization The systematic, widespread withdrawal of investment in basic aspects of productivity, such as factories and plants. (401)

Downsizing Reductions taken in a company's workforce as part of deindustrialization. (402)

Economic system The social institution through which goods and services are produced, distributed, and consumed. (392)

Fair trade A movement in which consumers in industrialized countries voluntarily pay above-market prices for certain foods so that the workers who plant, pick, and pack the crops can receive higher wages. (392)

Industrial society A society that depends on mechanization to produce its goods and services. (393)

Informal economy Transfers of money, goods, or services that are not reported to the government. (395)

Laissez-faire A form of capitalism under which people compete freely, with minimal government intervention in the economy. (393)

Microfinancing Lending small sums of money to the poor so they can work their way out of poverty. (403)

Monopoly Control of a market by a single business firm. (394)

Offshoring The transfer of work to foreign contractors. (402)

Socialism An economic system under which the means of production and distribution are collectively owned. (395)

TAKING SOCIOLOGY with you

1. Observe and/or interview some of the service workers in the college or university you attend. Do any of them show signs of alienation from the workplace?

2. Do some original research on the economy of the nearest city using a survey, experiment, or observation research. Then compare the results to what you can learn from existing sources, including this textbook. Did you learn anything new from your research?

3. If your college has a program for study abroad, find someone who has spent time in a developing country and interview him or her. What was the country's economy like? Was there a large informal sector, and if so, what goods or services were exchanged? Was microcredit available to small borrowers? How many people worked for multinational corporations? How many lived in poverty?

Self-Quiz

Read each question carefully and then select the best answer.

1. Which two basic types of economic system distinguish contemporary industrial societies?
   a. capitalism and communism
   b. capitalism and socialism
   c. socialism and communism
   d. capitalism and dictatorship

2. According to the discussion of capitalism in the text, which of the following statements is true?
   a. The means of production are held largely in private hands.
   b. The main incentive for economic activity is the accumulation of profits.
   c. The degree to which the government regulates private ownership and economic activity will vary.
   d. all of the above.

3. Which sociological perspective points out that while *pure* monopolies are not a basic element of the economy of the United States, competition is much more restricted than one might expect in what is called a *free enterprise system*?
   a. the functionalist perspective
   b. the conflict perspective
   c. the interactionist perspective
   d. labeling theory

4. Which of the following is *not* an example of the informal economy?
   a. trading a haircut for a computer lesson
   b. selling illegal drugs on the street
   c. working as a computer programmer for a major corporation
   d. providing child care out of a private home, without reporting the income to the IRS

5. The systematic, widespread withdrawal of investment in basic aspects of productivity such as factories and plants is called
   a. deindustrialization.
   b. downsizing.
   c. postindustrialization.
   d. gentrification.

6. Karl Marx is associated with which of the following concepts?
   a. anomie
   b. assimilation
   c. apartheid
   d. alienation

7. Sociologists and labor specialists foresee a workforce increasingly composed of
   a. women.
   b. racial minorities.
   c. ethnic minorities.
   d. all of the above.

8. Currently, _____ _____ refers to positive efforts to recruit minority group members or women for jobs, promotions, and educational opportunities.
   a. equal rights
   b. affirmative action
   c. work programs
   d. equal action

9. The principle of laissez-faire was expounded and endorsed by the British economist
   a. John Maynard Keynes.
   b. Adam Smith.
   c. Paul Samuelson.
   d. Arthur Scargill.

10. Which sociologist, using the interactionist perspective, noted that "one key source of job satisfaction lies in the informal interaction shared by members of a work group"?
    a. Robert Blauner
    b. Donald Roy
    c. George Ritzer
    d. Karl Marx

11. The term _____ _____ refers to the social institution through which goods and services are produced, distributed, and consumed.

12. The principle of _____ _____, as expounded and endorsed by the British economist Adam Smith, was the prevailing form of capitalism immediately following the Industrial Revolution.

13. Under _____, the means of production and distribution in a society are collectively rather than privately owned, and the basic objective of the economic system is to meet people's needs rather than to maximize profits.

14. _____ is an economic system under which all property is communally owned and no social distinctions are made based on people's ability to produce.

15. The term _____ was introduced in 1987 to refer to reductions taken in a company's workforce as part of deindustrialization.

16. A(n) _____ society depends on mechanization to produce its goods and services.

17. _____ theorists point out that while pure monopolies are not a basic element of the economy of the United States, competition is much more restricted than one might expect in what is called a free enterprise system.

18. Émile Durkheim argued that as labor becomes more and more differentiated, individuals experience _____, or loss of direction.

19. Most studies of _____ have focused on factors that serve to increase or decrease worker satisfaction.

20. Some capitalist nations, such as the United States, outlaw _____ through antitrust legislation.

Answers

1 (b); 2 (d); 3 (b); 4 (c); 5 (a); 6 (d); 7 (d); 8 (b); 9 (b); 10 (b); 11 economic system; 12 laissez-faire; 13 socialism; 14 Communism; 15 downsizing; 16 industrial; 17 Conflict; 18 anomie; 19 alienation; 20 monopolies

406

THINKING ABOUT MOVIES

The Company Men

Corporate downsizing forces a white-collar worker to enter a blue-collar profession.

Inside Job

This documentary explores the near collapse of the global financial industry in 2008.

Up in the Air

The tables are about to turn on a corporate downsizing expert who makes his living by laying people off.

The environment is a major
influence on our health
and well-being. By providing
clean, sustainable energy, this
wind farm in Dhule, India, helps
to preserve our ecosystem. Since
1980, nations around the world
have been turning to wind turbines
as a source of electric power.

409

MAPPING LIFE WORLDWIDE

FIGURE **19-2** PEOPLE LIVING WITH HIV

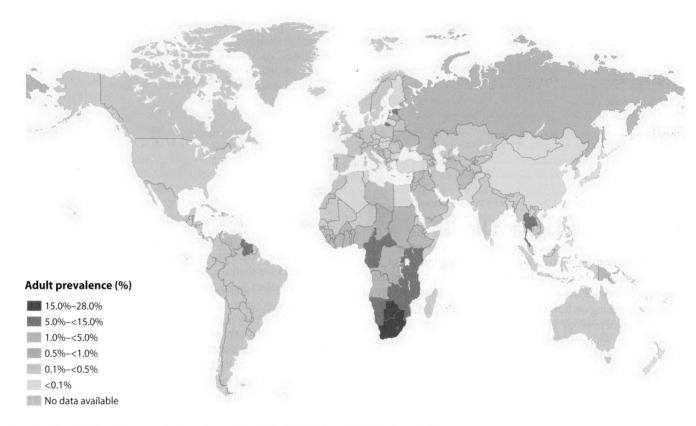

Adult prevalence (%)

- 15.0%–28.0%
- 5.0%–<15.0%
- 1.0%–<5.0%
- 0.5%–<1.0%
- 0.1%–<0.5%
- <0.1%
- No data available

Note: Data for the 33.3 million people (estimated range, 31.4–35.8 million) living with HIV at the end of 2009.
Source: UNAIDS 2010:23.

childhood or young adulthood is likely to mean more illness later in life. The longer that low income presents a barrier to adequate health care, the more chronic and difficult to treat illness becomes (Pampel et al. 2010; Phelan et al. 2010).

Another reason for the link between social class and health is that the poor—many of whom belong to racial and ethnic minorities—are less able than others to afford quality medical care. The affluent are more likely than others to have health insurance, either because they can afford it or because they have jobs that provide it. This situation has been deteriorating over time, as employer-provided coverage (the most common form of health insurance) declined steadily from 2000 through 2009. In 2008, 46.3 million people reported going without health care because they could not pay for it; in 2009, 50.7 million went without. And increasingly, pharmacists reported that people were purchasing only those medications they "needed the most," or were buying in small quantities, such as four pills at a time. Even for children, many of whom are eligible for government-subsidized health insurance, coverage varies widely, ranging from 98.5 percent in Massachusetts to 81.6 percent in Nevada (Figure 19-3).

In 2010, largely in response to the millions of people who do not have health insurance, Congress enacted the Patient Protection and Affordable Care Act. Beginning in 2014, this legislation—the most significant health care reform since passage of Medicare in 1965—will help people who are sick or have

lost a job to afford medical care. In the meantime, certain high-risk people will receive immediate coverage. By 2019, about 95 percent of citizens and legal residents who are not covered by Medicare should have health insurance. In the next few years, researchers will be busy assessing the effect of the legislation on health care inequities (Starr 2010).

Finally, in the view of Karl Marx and contemporary conflict theorists, capitalist societies such as the United States care more about maximizing profits than they do about the health and safety of industrial workers. As a result, government agencies do not take forceful action to regulate conditions in the workplace, and workers suffer many preventable job-related injuries and illnesses. As we will see later in this chapter, research also shows that the lower classes are more vulnerable to environmental pollution than are the affluent, not only where they work but where they live.

use your sociological *imagination*

Does the cost of health care affect the way you receive medical services?

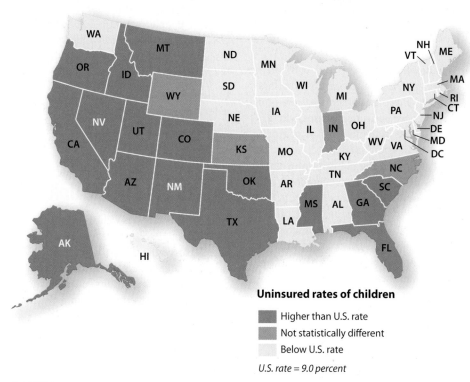

Uninsured rates of children

■ Higher than U.S. rate
■ Not statistically different
□ Below U.S. rate

U.S. rate = 9.0 percent

Source: Mach and Blumenthal 2010:2.

Think about It

Do you know people whose children don't have health insurance? If so, how has the lack of insurance affected their decisions about their children's medical treatment?

Race and Ethnicity

The health profiles of many racial and ethnic minorities reflect the social inequality evident in the United States. The poor economic and environmental conditions of groups such as African Americans, Hispanics, and Native Americans are manifested in high morbidity and mortality rates for those groups. It is true that some diseases, such as sickle-cell anemia among Blacks, have a clear genetic basis. But in most instances, environmental factors contribute to the differential rates of disease and death.

As noted earlier, infant mortality is regarded as a primary indicator of health care. There is a significant gap in the United States between the infant mortality rates of African Americans and Whites. Generally, the rate of infant death is more than twice as high among Blacks (MacDorman and Mathews 2011).

The medical establishment is not exempt from racism. Unfortunately, the media often focus on obvious forms of racism, such as hate crimes, while overlooking more insidious forms in social institutions like the medical establishment. Minorities receive inferior medical care even when they are insured. Despite having access to care, Blacks, Latinos, and Native Americans are treated unequally as a result of racial prejudice and differences in the quality of various health care plans. Furthermore, national clinical studies have shown that even allowing for differences in income and insurance coverage, racial and ethnic minorities are less likely

than other groups to receive both standard health care and life-saving treatment for conditions such as HIV infection (Centers for Disease Control and Prevention 2011b; Long and Masi 2009).

Drawing on the conflict perspective, sociologist Howard Waitzkin (1986) suggests that racial tensions also contribute to the medical problems of Blacks. In his view, the stress that results from racial prejudice and discrimination helps to explain the higher rates of hypertension found among African Americans (and Hispanics) compared to Whites. Hypertension—twice as common in Blacks as in Whites—is believed to be a critical factor in Blacks' high mortality rates from heart disease, kidney disease, and stroke (Centers for Disease Control and Prevention 2011b).

Some Mexican Americans and many other Latinos adhere to cultural beliefs that make them less likely to use the established medical system. They may interpret their illnesses according to **curanderismo**, or traditional Latino folk medicine—a form of holistic health care and healing. *Curanderismo* influences how one approaches health care and even how one defines illness. Most Hispanics probably use *curanderos,* or folk healers, infrequently, but perhaps 20 percent rely on home remedies. Some define such illnesses as *susto* (fright sickness) and *atague* (fighting attack) according to folk beliefs. Because these complaints often have biological bases, sensitive medical practitioners need to deal with them carefully in order to diagnose and treat illnesses accurately. Moreover, it would be a mistake to blame the poor health care that Latinos receive on cultural differences. Latinos are much more likely to seek treatment for pressing medical problems at clinics and emergency rooms than they are to receive regular preventive care through a family physician (Centers for Disease Control and Prevention 2011b; Durden and Hummer 2006; Trotter and Chavira 1997).

Gender

A large body of research indicates that compared with men, women experience a higher prevalence of many illnesses, although they tend to live longer. There are some variations—for example, men are more likely to have parasitic diseases, whereas women are more likely to become diabetic—but as a group, women appear to be in poorer health than men.

The apparent inconsistency between the ill health of women and their greater longevity deserves an explanation, and researchers have advanced a theory. Women's lower rate of cigarette smoking (reducing their risk of heart disease, lung cancer, and emphysema), lower consumption of alcohol (reducing the risk of auto accidents and cirrhosis of the liver), and lower rate of employment in dangerous occupations explain about one-third of their greater longevity than men. Moreover, some clinical studies suggest that the differences in morbidity may actually be less pronounced than the data show. Researchers argue that women are much more likely than men to seek treatment, to be diagnosed as having a disease, and thus to have their illnesses reflected in the data examined by epidemiologists.

From a conflict perspective, women have been particularly vulnerable to the medicalization of society, with everything from birth to beauty being treated in an increasingly medical context. Such medicalization may contribute to women's higher morbidity rates compared to those of men. Ironically, even though women have been especially affected by medicalization, medical researchers have often excluded them from clinical studies. Female physicians and researchers charge that sexism lies at the heart of such research practices, and insist there is a desperate need for studies of female subjects (Centers for Disease Control and Prevention 2011b; Rieker and Bird 2000).

thinking CRITICALLY

Which is a more important factor in the adequate delivery of health care, race or gender?

Age

Health is the overriding concern of the elderly. Most older people in the United States report having at least one chronic illness, but only some of those conditions are potentially life threatening or require medical care. At the same time, health problems can affect the quality of life of older people in important ways. Almost half of older people in the United States are troubled by arthritis, and many have visual or hearing impairments that can interfere with the performance of everyday tasks.

Older people are also especially vulnerable to certain mental health problems. Alzheimer's disease, the leading cause of dementia in the United States, afflicts an estimated 5.1 million people age 65 or over—that is, 13 percent of that segment of the population. While some individuals with Alzheimer's exhibit only mild symptoms, the risk of severe problems resulting

from the disease rises substantially with age (Alzheimer's Association 2010:10).

Not surprisingly, older people in the United States (age 75 and older) are five times more likely to use health services than younger people (ages 15–24). The disproportionate use of the U.S. health care system by older people is a critical factor in all discussions about the cost of health care and possible reforms of the health care system (Bureau of the Census 2010a).

In sum, to achieve greater access and reduce health disparities, federal health officials must overcome inequities that are rooted not just in age, but in social class, race and ethnicity, and gender. If that were not enough, they must also deal with a geographical disparity in health care resources.

Health Care in the United States

As the entire nation is well aware, the costs of health care have skyrocketed. In 1997, total expenditures for health care in the United States crossed the trillion-dollar threshold—more than four times the 1980 total (Figure 19-4). In 2000, the amount spent on health care equaled that spent on education, defense, prisons, farm subsidies, food stamps, and foreign aid combined. By the year 2019,

FIGURE **19-4**   TOTAL HEALTH CARE EXPENDITURES IN THE UNITED STATES, 1970–2019 (PROJECTED)

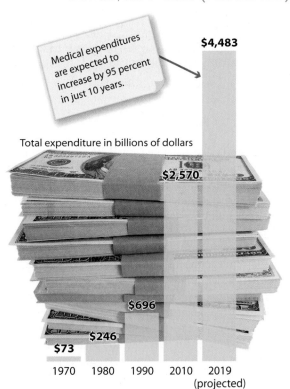

Medical expenditures are expected to increase by 95 percent in just 10 years.

$4,483

Total expenditure in billions of dollars

$2,570

$696

$246

$73

| 1970 | 1980 | 1990 | 2010 | 2019 (projected) |

Sources: Centers for Medicare and Medicaid Services 2010: Table 1 (2004–2019 data); Health Care Financing Administration 2001 (1970–1990 data).

Think about It

What social changes in the United States might account for the rise in health care costs from $73 billion in 1970 to almost 2.6 trillion in 2010?

health care proceeded, the medical profession gained control over both the market for its services and the various organizational hierarchies that govern medical practice, financing, and policy-making. By the 1920s, physicians controlled hospital technology, the division of labor of health personnel, and indirectly, other professional practices such as nursing and pharmacy (R. Coser 1984).

Physicians, Nurses, and Patients

Traditionally, physicians have held a position of dominance in their dealings with both patients and nurses. The functionalist and interactionist perspectives offer a framework for understanding the professional socialization of physicians as it relates to patient care. Functionalists suggest that established physicians and medical school professors serve as mentors or role models who transmit knowledge, skills, and values to the passive learner—the medical student. Interactionists emphasize that students are molded by the medical school environment as they interact with their classmates.

Both approaches argue that the typical training of physicians in the United States leads to rather dehumanizing physician–patient encounters. As Dr. Lori Arviso Alvord, a Navajo physician, writes in *The Scalpel and the Silver Bear,* "I had been trained by a group of physicians who placed much more emphasis on their technical abilities and clinical skills than on their abilities to be caring and sensitive" (Alvord and Van Pelt 1999:13). Despite many efforts to formally introduce a humanistic approach to patient care into the medical school curriculum, patient overload and cost-cutting by hospitals have tended to undercut positive relations. Moreover, widespread publicity about malpractice suits and high medical costs has further strained the physician–patient relationship. Interactionists have closely examined compliance and negotiation between physician and patient. They concur with Talcott Parsons's view that the relationship is generally asymmetrical, with doctors holding a position of dominance and controlling rewards.

Just as physicians have maintained dominance in their interactions with patients, they have controlled interactions with nurses. Despite their training and professional status, nurses commonly take orders from physicians. Traditionally, the

"I'm going to hold up a number of outstanding medical bills. Tell me how many you see."

total expenditures for health care in the United States are expected to exceed $4.4 trillion. The rising costs of medical care are especially burdensome in the event of catastrophic illnesses or confinement to a nursing home. Bills of tens of thousands of dollars are not unusual in the treatment of cancer, Alzheimer's disease, and other chronic illnesses requiring custodial care.

The health care system of the United States has moved far beyond the days when general practitioners living in a neighborhood or community typically made house calls and charged modest fees for their services. How did health care become a big business involving nationwide hospital chains and marketing campaigns? How have these changes reshaped the interactions between doctors, nurses, and patients? We will address these questions in the next section of the chapter.

A Historical View

Today, state licensing and medical degrees confer an authority on medical professionals that is maintained from one generation to the next. However, health care in the United States has not always followed this model. The "popular health movement" of the 1830s and 1840s emphasized preventive care and what is termed "self-help." Strong criticism was voiced of "doctoring" as a paid occupation. New medical philosophies or sects established their own medical schools and challenged the authority and methods of more traditional doctors. By the 1840s, most states had repealed medical licensing laws.

In response, through the leadership of the American Medical Association (AMA), founded in 1848, "regular" doctors attacked lay practitioners, sectarian doctors, and female physicians in general. Once they had institutionalized their authority through standardized programs of education and licensing, they conferred it on all who successfully completed their programs. The authority of the physician no longer depended on lay attitudes or on the person occupying the sick role; increasingly, it was built into the structure of the medical profession and the health care system. As the institutionalization of

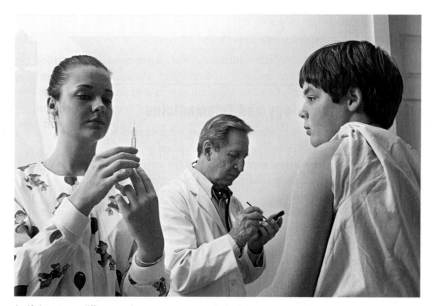

As if the status differences between nurses and physicians were not clear to all, the cheery uniform of nurses and the formal white doctor's coat reinforce the distinction.

One reflection of the interplay between globalization and the environment is the emergence of *environmental refugees.* Europe in particular is beginning to see an influx of such immigrants from developing nations. According to a European Union report, global warming can be viewed as a "threat multiplier" that exacerbates prolonged droughts and a shortage of arable land, and along with them, poverty, poor health, and poor living conditions. Viewed through the lens of world systems analysis, periphery countries may become overburdened by environmental problems, precipitating either migrations to industrial nations or conflicts that cause mass displacements of their populations. "Europe must expect substantially increased migratory pressure" from these environmental refugees, the report concludes (Traynor 2008).

Against these potentially negative effects of globalization we must note the potential for new jobs in what are called green industries. Installing solar panels, weatherizing homes, brewing biofuels, building hybrid cars, growing organic foods, manufacturing organic garments, and erecting giant wind turbines are all classified as *green-collar jobs.* However, skeptics question how many such jobs will be created, and to what degree they will offset job losses in pollution-prone industries like oil, gas, and coal mining (S. Greenhouse 2008b; R. Pinderhughes 2008).

thinking CRITICALLY

Which issue is more significant in your local community, air or water pollution? Why?

social policy and the Environment

Environmentalism

On April 22, 1970, in a dramatic manifestation of growing grassroots concern over preservation of the environment, an estimated 25 million people turned out to observe the nation's first Earth Day. Two thousand communities held planned celebrations, and more than 2,000 colleges and 10,000 schools hosted environmental teach-ins. In many parts of the United States, citizens marched on behalf of specific environmental causes. That same year, the activism of these early environmentalists convinced Congress to establish the Environmental Protection Agency. The Clean Air, Clean Water, and Endangered Species acts soon followed (Brulle and Jenkins 2008).

Looking at the Issue

Sociologist Manual Castells (2010a:72) has declared environmentalism "the most comprehensive, influential movement of our time." Several social trends helped to mobilize the environmental movement. First, the activist subculture of the 1960s and early 1970s encouraged people, especially young people, to engage in direct action regarding social issues. Second, the dissemination of scientific knowledge about serious environmental problems like oil spills and air pollution alarmed many Americans. And third, the growing popularity of outdoor recreation increased the number of people who were concerned about the environment. In this climate of broad-based interest in environmental issues, many organizations that had once focused narrowly on the conservation of natural resources evolved into full-fledged environmental groups (Dunlap and Mertig 1991).

Today, Earth Day has been enshrined on the calendars of city councils, zoos, and museums worldwide. Environmental issues have also moved up the agenda of mainstream political parties. Increasingly, efforts to publicize environmental concerns and create support for action have moved to the Internet. Although times have changed, two beliefs continue to galvanize environmentalists: the environment is in dire need of protection, and the government must take strong action in response. Although environmentalists recognize that they must "think locally" and monitor their own carbon footprints, they also see preservation of the environment as a global challenge. They note that while significant progress has been made toward environmental protection, government regulation of the environment has been curtailed in some ways (Brulle and Jenkins 2008; Rootes 2007; Sieber et al. 2006).

The general public has a mixed reaction to environmental issues. Many people question the scientific arguments behind the theory of global warming. And although the economic cost of environmental protection has always been an issue, the broad economic downturn that began in 2008 tipped the balance of public opinion in favor of economic growth. In 2009, for the first time, a majority of people gave economic growth priority over the environment (Figure 19-7). In times of economic stress, people tend to put off or ignore environmental concerns. Thus, there seems to be little public enthusiasm for the positive, forward-looking approach of ecological modernization. Not surprisingly, the political debate over the environmental movement grew more partisan between 2000 and 2010: Democrats became more sympathetic and Republicans more antagonistic (Dunlap 2010).

Today's college students also show less interest in the environment than students of past decades. In 2010, about 27 percent of first-year college students in the United States wanted to clean up the environment—down from 45.9 percent in 1972 (see Figure 3-2 on page 65). And as Figure 19-8 shows, U.S. high school students' interest in the issue does not compare favorably with that of teens in other major countries. In a 30-nation comparative study, 15-year-olds in the United States tied those in another country for 22nd place in their knowledge of environmental issues.

FIGURE **19-7**   THE ENVIRONMENT VERSUS THE ECONOMY

Source: Gallup Poll 2011, see Jones 2011 in references.

Applying Sociology

Even those who support environmentalists' goals are troubled by the fact that nationwide, the most powerful environmental organizations are predominantly White, male-dominated, and affluent. One study notes that while women are overrepresented in the environmental movement (particularly in grassroots environmental groups), men continue to hold most of the high-profile upper-management positions in mainstream national organizations. The perceived middle-class orientation of the movement is especially relevant given the class, racial, and ethnic factors associated with environmental hazards. As we saw earlier in the context of environmental justice, low-income communities and areas with significant minority populations are more likely than affluent White communities to be located near waste sites. Sociologists Liam Downey and Brian

Hawkins (2008) found that an average Black household with an income of $50,000 to $60,000 a year coped with higher levels of pollution than an average White household with an income of less than $10,000 a year.

Viewed from a conflict perspective, it is significant that some environmental organizations accept funding from oil companies, chemical giants, and other powerful corporations. Perhaps as a result, the environmental movement has often emphasized limited reform rather than profound structural change. Activists may recommend making cars more energy-efficient, for example, instead of drastically reducing the number of vehicles on the road (Navarro 2009; Sale 1996).

Like any social movement, the environmental movement has aroused resistance. Some opponents question the environmentalists' move to replace fossil fuels such as coal and oil with biofuels such as ethanol. They complain that diverting corn and other crops into fuel production will raise food prices, hampering efforts to reduce global hunger (Helvarg 1994; Pontin 2007).

Initiating Policy

The global economic downturn that began in 2008 has been a mixed blessing for environmentalists. As noted earlier, public opinion in the United States currently favors economic growth over environmental protection. Yet at the same time, the recession has sharply reduced the use of fossil fuels such as coal and oil. Moreover, the federal government's efforts to stimulate economic activity have emphasized the creation of green-collar jobs. By one estimate,

FIGURE **19-8**   ARE U.S. TEENS GREEN ENOUGH?

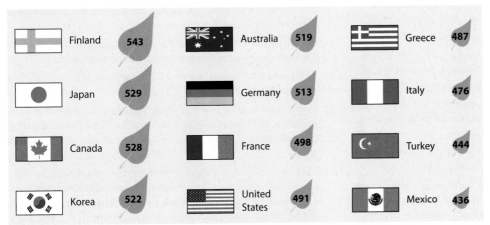

Note: Mean score for 15-year-old students' knowledge of environmental issues = 543.
Source: Organisation for Economic Co-operation and Development 2009b.

every \$1 billion invested in well-conceived green programs generates over 30,000 jobs and \$450 million in cost savings per year. More specific environmental measures, such as raising federal gas mileage standards for automobiles, face a tough battle in Congress (Houser et al. 2009).

Environmentalism has moved onto a much bigger stage than the one it occupied on the first Earth Day. In 2008, for the first time, the leaders of the G8 economic powers (the United States, Japan, Germany, Great Britain, France, Italy, Canada, and Russia) set an explicit long-term target for eliminating greenhouse gases, which scientists have long warned were warming the planet. "Long-term" may be an understatement: their target date for cutting greenhouse gases in half is 2050. Environmentalists sharply criticized the G8's failure to set specific goals for the nearer term. The challenge is significant, given the fact that G8 emissions *increased* 35 percent over the preceding 15 years (Longhofer and Schofer 2010; Stolberg 2008).

Conventional wisdom holds that concern for environmental quality is limited to wealthy industrialized nations. However, the results of a 47-nation survey show that around the world, people are increasingly reluctant to ignore environmental issues. Concern has risen sharply in Latin America and Europe, as well as in Japan and India. The survey also noted a general increase in the percentage of people who cite pollution and environmental problems as a top global threat. Many people in other countries blame the United States, and to a lesser extent China, for environmental problems, and look to Washington, D.C., for a solution. Time will tell whether policymakers in the United States or elsewhere will address their concern for the environment (Pew Global Attitudes Project 2007).

Take the Issue with You

1. In your community, how would you act locally to preserve the environment? Describe your community's environmental problems and explain how you would seek to solve them.

2. How do you see the trade-off between the economy and the environment? Which is more important? Is it possible to improve both at the same time? Explain.

3. Thinking globally about the environment, list what you consider the most pressing priorities. How important are world hunger and economic justice compared to global warming, clean air and water, and economic development? Are some of your priorities related? In what way?

MASTERING THIS CHAPTER

Summary

Both culture and the environment have a significant effect on our **health** and well-being. The concept of health is shaped by social definitions of behavior. This chapter considers sociological perspectives on health and the environment; the distribution of disease in a society; the evolution of the U.S. health care system; mental illness and its treatment; and the environmental issues facing our planet.

1. According to Talcott Parsons's functionalist perspective, physicians function as gatekeepers for the **sick role,** either verifying a person's condition as "illness" or designating the person as "recovered."

2. Conflict theorists use the term *medicalization of society* to refer to medicine's growing role as a major institution of social control.

3. Labeling theorists suggest that the designation of a person as "healthy" or "ill" generally involves social definition by others. These definitions affect how others see us and how we view ourselves.

4. Contemporary **social epidemiology** is concerned not only with epidemics but also with nonepidemic diseases, injuries, drug addiction and alcoholism, suicide, and mental illness.

5. Studies have consistently shown that people in the lower classes have higher rates of mortality and disability than others.

6. Racial and ethnic minorities have higher rates of morbidity and mortality than Whites. Women tend to be in poorer health than men but live longer. Older people are especially vulnerable to mental health problems, such as Alzheimer's disease.

7. The preeminent role of physicians in the U.S. health care system has given them a position of dominance in their dealings with nurses and patients.

8. Many people use alternative health care techniques, such as **holistic medicine** and self-help groups.

9. Mental disorders may be viewed from two different perspectives, the medical model and the sociological model, which is based on labeling theory. In the United States, society has traditionally taken a negative, suspicious attitude toward people with mental disorders.

10. The human ecological perspective stresses the interrelationships between people and their environment.

11. Conflict theorists charge that the most serious threat to the environment comes from Western industrialized nations.

12. **Environmental justice** addresses the disproportionate subjection of minorities to environmental hazards.

13. Four broad areas of environmental concern include air and water pollution, global warming, and globalization. Though globalization can contribute to environmental woes, it can also have beneficial effects.

14. Environmentalism is a social movement that is dominated by affluent White people from industrialized countries. Increasingly, however, people of all races, ethnicities, social classes, and nationalities are becoming concerned about global warming and the threat it poses to our planet's health.

Key Terms

Brain drain The immigration to the United States and other industrialized nations of skilled workers, professionals, and technicians who are desperately needed in their home countries. (page 412)

Curanderismo Latino folk medicine, a form of holistic health care and healing. (417)

Ecological modernization The alignment of environmentally favorable practices with economic self-interest through constant adaptation and restructuring. (425)

Environmental justice A legal strategy based on claims that racial minorities are subjected disproportionately to environmental hazards. (426)

Health As defined by the World Health Organization, a state of complete physical, mental, and social well-being, and not merely the absence of disease and infirmity. (411)

Holistic medicine Therapies in which the health care practitioner considers the person's physical, mental, emotional, and spiritual characteristics. (420)

Human ecology An area of study that is concerned with the interrelationships between people and their environment. (425)

Incidence The number of new cases of a specific disorder that occur within a given population during a stated period. (415)

Infant mortality rate The number of deaths of infants under one year old per 1,000 live births in a given year. (413)

McDonaldization The process by which the principles of the fast-food restaurant are coming to dominate more and more sectors of American society as well as of the rest of the world. (421)

Mental illness A disorder of the brain that disrupts a person's thinking, feeling, and ability to interact with others. (423)

Morbidity rate The incidence of disease in a given population. (415)

Mortality rate The incidence of death in a given population. (415)

Prevalence The total number of cases of a specific disorder that exist at a given time. (415)

Sick role Societal expectations about the attitudes and behavior of a person viewed as being ill. (411)

Social epidemiology The study of the distribution of disease, impairment, and general health status across a population. (415)

1. Do some research on the incidence and prevalence of HIV/AIDS in your city or state. Now look up the corresponding morbidity and mortality rates. How do those rates compare to the rates in other cities or states? What might account for any differences in the rates from one place to another?

2. Visit the emergency room of your local hospital and observe what is going on in the waiting room. How crowded is the waiting room? How many people in the room appear to be severely ill or injured? How many do not seem to have an emergency? What else can you observe about the people who are gathered there, and how might that help to explain their presence?

3. Do an Internet search to locate the hazardous waste sites nearest your school or home. How many of them have been cleaned up, and at what cost? Who paid that cost? How many of these sites are still a problem?

Self-Quiz

Read each question carefully and then select the best answer.

1. Which sociologist developed the concept of the sick role?
   a. Émile Durkheim
   b. Talcott Parsons
   c. Wright Mills
   d. Erving Goffman

2. Regarding health care inequities, the conflict perspective would note that
   a. physicians serve as gatekeepers for the sick role, either verifying a patient's condition as "illness" or designating the patient as "recovered."
   b. patients play an active role in health care by failing to follow a physician's advice.
   c. emigration out of the Third World by physicians is yet another way that the world's core industrialized nations enhance their quality of life at the expense of developing countries.
   d. the designation "healthy" or "ill" generally involves social definition by others.

3. Which one of the following nations has the lowest infant mortality rate?
   a. the United States
   b. Mozambique
   c. Canada
   d. Sweden

4. Compared with Whites, Blacks have higher death rates from
   a. heart disease.
   b. diabetes.
   c. cancer.
   d. all of the above.

5. Which theorist notes that capitalist societies, such as the United States, care more about maximizing profits than they do about the health and safety of industrial workers?
   a. Thomas Szasz
   b. Talcott Parsons
   c. Erving Goffman
   d. Karl Marx

6. Which program is essentially a compulsory health insurance plan for the elderly?
   a. Medicare
   b. Medicaid

    c. Blue Cross

    d. Healthpac

7. Which of the following is a criticism of the sick role?

    a. Patients' judgments regarding their own state of health may be related to their gender, age, social class, and ethnic group.

    b. The sick role may be more applicable to people experiencing short-term illnesses than to those with recurring long-term illnesses.

    c. Even such simple factors as whether a person is employed or not seem to affect the person's willingness to assume the sick role.

    d. all of the above

8. Which of the following terms do conflict theorists use in referring to the growing role of medicine as a major institution of social control?

    a. the sick role

    b. the medicalization of society

    c. medical labeling

    d. epidemiology

9. Which of the following approaches stresses the alignment of environmentally favorable practices with economic self-interest?

    a. conflict theory

    b. human ecology

    c. ecological modernization

    d. environmental justice

10. Conflict theorists would contend that blaming developing countries for the world's environmental deterioration contains an element of

    a. ethnocentrism.

    b. xenocentrism.

    c. separatism.

    d. goal displacement.

11. A _____ _____ studies the effects of social class, race and ethnicity, gender, and age on the distribution of disease, impairment, and general health across a population.

12. From a(n) _____ perspective, "being sick" must be controlled so as to ensure that not too many people are released from their societal responsibilities at any one time.

13. The immigration to the United States and other industrialized nations of skilled workers, professionals, and technicians who are desperately needed by their home countries is known as the _____ _____.

14. Traditionally, the relationship between doctors and nurses has paralleled _____ dominance of the larger society.

15. Sociologists find it useful to consider _____ rates because they reveal that a specific disease occurs more frequently among one segment of a population compared with another.

16. The system of reimbursement used by Medicare has contributed to the controversial practice of "_____," under which patients whose treatment may be unprofitable are transferred by private hospitals to public facilities.

17. As defined by the World Health Organization, _____ is a "state of complete physical, mental, and social well-being, and not merely the absence of disease and infirmity."

18. The biologist _____ _____ blames environmental degradation primarily on technological innovations such as plastics and pesticides.

19. Regarding environmental problems, four broad areas of concern stand out: _____ pollution, _____ pollution, _____ _____, and _____.

20. _____ _____ is a legal strategy based on claims that racial minorities are subjected disproportionately to environmental hazards.

THINKING ABOUT MOVIES

The Cove

This documentary exposes a dark side of the dolphin industry and its health effects on humans.

Food, Inc.

As this film shows, dietary staples such as beef, poultry, and corn are often produced by multinational corporations using methods that maximize profit but dehumanize workers.

Gasland

This documentary shows some of the health consequences of increased drilling for natural gas.

glossary

Numbers following the definitions indicate pages where the terms were identified. Consult the index for further page references.

A

Absolute poverty A minimum level of subsistence that no family should be expected to live below. (199)

Achieved status A social position that a person attains largely through his or her own efforts. (100, 187)

Activity theory An interactionist theory of aging that suggests that those elderly people who remain active and socially involved will be best adjusted. (290)

Adoption In a legal sense, a process that allows for the transfer of the legal rights, responsibilities, and privileges of parenthood to a new legal parent or parents. (316)

Aerotropolis An urban community that is centered around an airport and the hotels, office complexes, entertainment venues, and distribution facilities it supports. (438)

Affirmative action Positive efforts to recruit minority group members or women for jobs, promotions, and educational opportunities. (244, 401)

Ageism Prejudice and discrimination based on a person's age. (297)

Agrarian society The most technologically advanced form of preindustrial society. Members engage primarily in the production of food, but increase their crop yields through technological innovations such as the plow. (110)

Alienation A condition of estrangement or dissociation from the surrounding society. (124, 399)

Amalgamation The process through which a majority group and a minority group combine to form a new group. (248)

Anomie Durkheim's term for the loss of direction felt in a society when social control of individual behavior has become ineffective. (10, 166)

Anomie theory of deviance Robert Merton's theory of deviance as an adaptation of socially prescribed goals or of the means governing their attainment, or both. (167)

Anticipatory socialization Processes of socialization in which a person rehearses for future positions, occupations, and social relationships. (89)

Anti-Semitism Anti-Jewish prejudice. (257)

Apartheid A former policy of the South African government, designed to maintain the separation of Blacks and other non-Whites from the dominant Whites. (248)

Applied sociology The use of the discipline of sociology with the specific intent of yielding practical applications for human behavior and organizations. (18)

Argot Specialized language used by members of a group or subculture. (59)

Ascribed status A social position assigned to a person by society without regard for the person's unique talents or characteristics. (100, 187)

Assembling perspective A theory of collective behavior introduced by McPhail and Miller that seeks to examine how and why people move from different points in space to a common location. (465)

Assimilation The process through which a person forsakes his or her cultural tradition to become part of a different culture. (248)

Authority Institutionalized power that is recognized by the people over whom it is exercised. (371)

B

Basic sociology Sociological inquiry conducted with the objective of gaining a more profound knowledge of the fundamental aspects of social phenomena. Also known as *pure sociology*. (19)

Bilateral descent A kinship system in which both sides of a person's family are regarded as equally important. (308)

Bilingualism The use of two languages in a particular setting, such as the workplace or schoolroom, treating each language as equally legitimate. (68)

Birthrate The number of live births per 1,000 population in a given year. Also known as the *crude birthrate*. (440)

Black power A political philosophy, promoted by many younger Blacks in the 1960s, that supported the creation of Black-controlled political and economic institutions. (249)

Borderlands The area of common culture along the border between Mexico and the United States. (227)

Bourgeoisie Karl Marx's term for the capitalist class, comprising the owners of the means of production. (192)

Brain drain The immigration to the United States and other industrialized nations of skilled workers, professionals, and technicians who are desperately needed in their home countries. (412)

Bureaucracy A component of formal organization that uses rules and hierarchical ranking to achieve efficiency. (124)

Bureaucratization The process by which a group, organization, or social movement becomes increasingly bureaucratic. (125)

C

Capitalism An economic system in which the means of production are held largely in private hands and the main incentive for economic activity is the accumulation of profits. (192, 393)

Caste A hereditary rank, usually religiously dictated, that tends to be fixed and immobile. (185)

Causal logic The relationship between a condition or variable and a particular consequence, with one leading to the other. (30)

Census An enumeration, or counting, of a population. (440)

Charismatic authority Max Weber's term for power made legitimate by a leader's exceptional personal or emotional appeal to his or her followers. (371)

Charter school An experimental school that is developed and managed by individuals, groups of parents, or educational management organizations. (364)

Class A group of people who have a similar level of wealth and income. (193)

Class consciousness In Karl Marx's view, a subjective awareness held by members of a class regarding their common vested interests and the need for collective political action to bring about social change. (192)

Class system A social ranking based primarily on economic position in which achieved characteristics can influence social mobility. (189)

Classical theory An approach to the study of formal organizations that views workers as being motivated almost entirely by economic rewards. (126)

Clinical sociology The use of the discipline of sociology with the specific intent of altering social relationships or restructuring social institutions. (19)

Closed system A social system in which there is little or no possibility of individual social mobility. (203)

Coalition A temporary or permanent alliance geared toward a common goal. (121)

Code of ethics The standards of acceptable behavior developed by and for members of a profession. (38)

Cognitive theory of development Jean Piaget's theory that children's thought progresses through four stages of development. (83)

Cohabitation The practice of living together as a male–female couple without marrying. (321)

Collective behavior In the view of sociologist Neil Smelser, the relatively spontaneous and unstructured behavior of a group of people who are reacting to a common influence in an ambiguous situation. (462)

Colonialism The maintenance of political, social, economic, and cultural domination over a people by a foreign power for an extended period. (216)

Color-blind racism The use of the principle of race neutrality to defend a racially unequal status quo. (241, 402)

Communism As an ideal type, an economic system under which all property is communally owned and no social distinctions are made on the basis of people's ability to produce. (395)

Community A spatial or political unit of social organization that gives people a sense of belonging, based either on shared residence in a particular place or on a common identity. (438)

Concentric-zone theory A theory of urban growth devised by Ernest Burgess that sees growth in terms of a series of rings radiating from the central business district. (448)

Conflict perspective A sociological approach that assumes that social behavior is best understood in terms of tension between groups over power or the allocation of resources, including housing, money, access to services, and political representation. (14)

Conformity Going along with peers—individuals of our own status who have no special right to direct our behavior. (161)

Conspicuous consumption Purchasing and using goods not to survive but to flaunt one's superior wealth and social standing. (193)

Contact hypothesis An interactionist perspective which states that in cooperative circumstances, interracial contact between people of equal status will reduce prejudice. (246)

Content analysis The systematic coding and objective recording of data, guided by some rationale. (38)

Control group The subjects in an experiment who are not introduced to the independent variable by the researcher. (37)

Control theory A view of conformity and deviance that suggests that our connection to members of society leads us to systematically conform to society's norms. (165)

Control variable A factor that is held constant to test the relative impact of an independent variable. (33)

Corporate welfare Tax breaks, bailouts, direct payments, and grants that the government gives to corporations. (230)

Correlation A relationship between two variables in which a change in one coincides with a change in the other. (30)

Correspondence principle A term used by Bowles and Gintis to refer to the tendency of schools to promote the values expected of individuals in each social class and perpetuate social class divisions from one generation to the next. (357)

Counterculture A subculture that deliberately opposes certain aspects of the larger culture. (60)

Craze An exciting mass involvement that lasts for a relatively long period. (468)

Creationism A literal interpretation of the Bible regarding the creation of humanity and the universe, used to argue that evolution should not be presented as established scientific fact. (343)

Credentialism An increase in the lowest level of education needed to enter a field. (356)

Crime A violation of criminal law for which some governmental authority applies formal penalties. (171)

Cross-tabulation A table or matrix that shows the relationship between two or more variables. (44)

Crowd A temporary gathering of people in close proximity who share a common focus or interest. (466)

Cultural capital Noneconomic goods, such as family background and education, which are reflected in a knowledge of language and the arts. (13)

Cultural convergence The flow of content across multiple media, and the accompanying migration of media audiences. (137)

Cultural genocide The systematic destruction of a group's culture. (55)

Cultural relativism The viewing of people's behavior from the perspective of their own culture. (54, 392)

Cultural transmission A school of criminology that argues that criminal behavior is learned through social interactions. (168)

Cultural universal A common practice or belief found in every culture. (54)

Culture The totality of learned, socially transmitted customs, knowledge, material objects, and behavior. (53)

Culture industry The worldwide media industry that standardizes the goods and services demanded by consumers. (54)

Culture lag A period of maladjustment when the nonmaterial culture is still struggling to adapt to new material conditions. (58, 487)

Culture shock The feeling of surprise and disorientation that people experience when they encounter cultural practices that are different from their own. (60)

Culture war The polarization of society over controversial cultural elements. (65)

Curanderismo Latino folk medicine, a form of holistic health care and healing. (417)

D

Death rate The number of deaths per 1,000 population in a given year. Also known as the *crude death rate.* (440)

Degradation ceremony An aspect of the socialization process within some total institutions, in which people are subjected to humiliating rituals. (90)

Deindustrialization The systematic, widespread withdrawal of investment in basic aspects of productivity, such as factories and plants. (401)

Democracy In a literal sense, government by the people. (373)

Demographic transition A term used to describe the change from high birthrates and death rates to low birthrates and death rates. (442)

Demography The scientific study of population. (439)

Denomination A large, organized religion that is not officially linked to the state or government. (339)

Dependency theory An approach that contends that industrialized nations continue to exploit developing countries for their own gain. (216)

Dependent variable The variable in a causal relationship that is subject to the influence of another variable. (30)

Deviance Behavior that violates the standards of conduct or expectations of a group or society. (159)

Dictatorship A government in which one person has nearly total power to make and enforce laws. (373)

Differential association A theory of deviance proposed by Edwin Sutherland that holds that violation of rules results from exposure to attitudes favorable to criminal acts. (168)

Differential justice Differences in the way social control is exercised over different groups. (171)

Diffusion The process by which a cultural item spreads from group to group or society to society. (57)

Digital divide The relative lack of access to the latest technologies among low-income groups, racial and ethnic minorities, rural residents, and the citizens of developing countries. (145)

Disaster A sudden or disruptive event or set of events that overtaxes a community's resources, so that outside aid is necessary. (466)

Discovery The process of making known or sharing the existence of an aspect of reality. (56)

Discrimination The denial of opportunities and equal rights to individuals and groups because of prejudice or other arbitrary reasons. (241)

Disengagement theory A functionalist theory of aging that suggests that society and the aging individual mutually sever many of their relationships. (290)

Domestic partnership Two unrelated adults who share a mutually caring relationship, reside together, and agree to be jointly responsible for their dependents, basic living expenses, and other common necessities. (324)

Dominant ideology A set of cultural beliefs and practices that helps to maintain powerful social, economic, and political interests. (67, 143, 195)

Double consciousness The division of an individual's identity into two or more social realities. (12)

Downsizing Reductions taken in a company's workforce as part of deindustrialization. (402)

Dramaturgical approach A view of social interaction, popularized by Erving Goffman, in which people are seen as theatrical performers. (16, 81)

Dyad A two-member group. (122)

Dysfunction An element or process of a society that may disrupt the social system or reduce its stability. (14)

E

Ecclesia A religious organization that claims to include most or all members of a society and is recognized as the national or official religion. (339)

Ecological modernization The alignment of environmentally favorable practices with economic self-interest through constant adaptation and restructuring. (425)

Economic system The social institution through which goods and services are produced, distributed, and consumed. (392)

Education A formal process of learning in which some people consciously teach while others adopt the social role of learner. (350)

Egalitarian family An authority pattern in which spouses are regarded as equals. (309)

Elite model A view of society as being ruled by a small group of individuals who share a common set of political and economic interests. (378)

Emergent-norm perspective A theory of collective behavior proposed by Turner and Killian that holds that a collective definition of appropriate or inappropriate behavior emerges during episodes of collective behavior. (463)

Endogamy The restriction of mate selection to people within the same group. (312)

Environmental justice A legal strategy based on claims that racial minorities are subjected disproportionately to environmental hazards. (426)

Equilibrium model Talcott Parsons's functionalist view that society tends toward a state of stability or balance. (485)

Established sect J. Milton Yinger's term for a religious group that is the outgrowth of a sect, yet remains isolated from society. (340)

Estate system A system of stratification under which peasants were required to work land leased to them by nobles in exchange for military protection and other services. Also known as *feudalism*. (189)

Esteem The reputation that a specific person has earned within an occupation. (196)

Ethnic group A group that is set apart from others primarily because of its national origin or distinctive cultural patterns. (237)

Ethnocentrism The tendency to assume that one's own culture and way of life represent the norm or are superior to all others. (54, 240)

Ethnography The study of an entire social setting through extended systematic fieldwork. (36)

Euthanasia The act of bringing about the death of a hopelessly ill and suffering person in a relatively quick and painless way for reasons of mercy. (300)

Evolutionary theory A theory of social change that holds that society is moving in a definite direction. (485)

Exogamy The requirement that people select a mate outside certain groups. (312)

Experiment An artificially created situation that allows a researcher to manipulate variables. (37)

Experimental group The subjects in an experiment who are exposed to an independent variable introduced by a researcher. (37)

Exploitation theory A Marxist theory that views racial subordination in the United States as a manifestation of the class system inherent in capitalism. (245)

Expressiveness Concern for the maintenance of harmony and the internal emotional affairs of the family. (271)

Extended family A family in which relatives—such as grandparents, aunts, or uncles—live in the same home as parents and their children. (307)

F

Face-work A term used by Erving Goffman to refer to the efforts people make to maintain the proper image and avoid public embarrassment. (82)

Fad A temporary pattern of behavior that involves large numbers of people and is independent of preceding trends. (468)

Fair trade A movement in which consumers in industrialized countries voluntarily pay above-market prices for certain foods so that

the workers who plant, pick, and pack the crops can receive higher wages. (392)

False consciousness A term used by Karl Marx to describe an attitude held by members of a class that does not accurately reflect their objective position. (192, 472)

Familism Pride in the extended family, expressed through the maintenance of close ties and strong obligations to kinfolk outside the immediate family. (315)

Family A set of people related by blood, marriage or some other agreed-on relationship, or adoption, who share the primary responsibility for reproduction and caring for members of society. (307)

Fashion A pleasurable mass involvement that has a line of historical continuity. (468)

Feminism The belief in social, economic, and political equality for women. (278)

Feminist view A sociological approach that views inequity in gender as central to all behavior and organization. (14)

Feminization of poverty A trend in which women constitute an increasing proportion of the poor people of the United States. (201)

Fertility The level of reproduction in a society. (439)

Focus group A carefully selected discussion group led by a trained moderator. (123)

Folkway A norm governing everyday behavior whose violation raises comparatively little concern. (63)

Force The actual or threatened use of coercion to impose one's will on others. (371)

Formal norm A norm that has been written down and that specifies strict punishments for violators. (63)

Formal organization A group designed for a special purpose and structured for maximum efficiency. (123)

Formal social control Social control that is carried out by authorized agents, such as police officers, judges, school administrators, and employers. (163)

Functionalist perspective A sociological approach that emphasizes the way in which the parts of a society are structured to maintain its stability. (13)

Fundamentalism An emphasis on doctrinal conformity and the literal interpretation of sacred texts. (338)

G

Gatekeeping The process by which a relatively small number of people in the media industry control what material eventually reaches the audience. (140)

Gemeinschaft A term used by Ferdinand Tönnies to describe a close-knit community, often found in rural areas, in which strong personal bonds unite members. (108)

Gender role Expectations regarding the proper behavior, attitudes, and activities of males and females. (184, 267)

Generalized other A term used by George Herbert Mead to refer to the attitudes, viewpoints, and expectations of society as a whole that a child takes into account in his or her behavior. (81)

Genocide The deliberate, systematic killing of an entire people or nation. (55, 247)

Gentrification The resettlement of low-income city neighborhoods by prosperous families and business firms. (456)

Gerontology The scientific study of the sociological and psychological aspects of aging and the problems of the aged. (289)

Gesellschaft A term used by Ferdinand Tönnies to describe a community, often urban, that is large and impersonal, with little commitment to the group or consensus on values. (109)

Glass ceiling An invisible barrier that blocks the promotion of a qualified individual in a work environment because of the individual's gender, race, or ethnicity. (242, 275)

Globalization The worldwide integration of government policies, cultures, social movements, and financial markets through trade and the exchange of ideas. (19, 218)

Goal displacement Overzealous conformity to official regulations of a bureaucracy. (125)

Group Any number of people with similar norms, values, and expectations who interact with one another on a regular basis. (103, 119)

Groupthink Uncritical acceptance of or conformity to the prevailing viewpoint. (123)

Growth rate The difference between births and deaths, plus the difference between immigrants and emigrants, per 1,000 population. (441)

H

Hate crime A criminal offense committed because of the offender's bias against a race, religion, ethnic group, national origin, or sexual orientation. Also referred to as *bias crime*. (174)

Hawthorne effect The unintended influence that observers of experiments can have on their subjects. (37)

Health As defined by the World Health Organization, a state of complete physical, mental, and social well-being, and not merely the absence of disease and infirmity. (411)

Hidden curriculum Standards of behavior that are deemed proper by society and are taught subtly in schools. (354)

Holistic medicine Therapies in which the health care practitioner considers the person's physical, mental, emotional, and spiritual characteristics. (420)

Homogamy The conscious or unconscious tendency to select a mate with personal characteristics similar to one's own. (312)

Homophobia Fear of and prejudice against homosexuality. (267)

Horizontal mobility The movement of an individual from one social position to another of the same rank. (203)

Horticultural society A preindustrial society in which people plant seeds and crops rather than merely subsist on available foods. (110)

Hospice care Treatment of the terminally ill in their own homes, or in special hospital units or other facilities, with the goal of helping them to die easily, without pain. (295)

Human ecology An area of study that is concerned with the interrelationships between people and their environment. (425, 448)

Human relations approach An approach to the study of formal organizations that emphasizes the role of people, communication, and participation in a bureaucracy and tends to focus on the informal structure of the organization. (127)

Hunting-and-gathering society A preindustrial society in which people rely on whatever foods and fibers are readily available in order to survive. (109)

Hypothesis A speculative statement about the relationship between two or more variables. (30)

I

Ideal type A construct or model for evaluating specific cases. (10, 124)

Impression management A term used by Erving Goffman to refer to the altering of the presentation of the self in order to create distinctive appearances and satisfy particular audiences. (81)

Incest taboo The prohibition of sexual relationships between certain culturally specified relatives. (312)

Incidence The number of new cases of a specific disorder that occur within a given population during a stated period. (415)

Income Salaries and wages. (87)

Independent variable The variable in a causal relationship that causes or influences a change in a second variable. (30)

Index crimes The eight types of crime reported annually by the FBI in the *Uniform Crime Reports*: murder, rape, robbery, assault, burglary, theft, motor vehicle theft, and arson. (172)

Industrial city A relatively large city characterized by open competition, an open class system, and elaborate specialization in the manufacturing of goods. (447)

Industrial society A society that depends on mechanization to produce its goods and services. (110, 393)

Infant mortality rate The number of deaths of infants under one year old per 1,000 live births in a given year. (413, 440)

Influence The exercise of power through a process of persuasion. (371)

Informal economy Transfers of money, goods, or services that are not reported to the government. (395)

Informal norm A norm that is generally understood but not precisely recorded. (63)

Informal social control Social control that is carried out casually by ordinary people through such means as laughter, smiles, and ridicule. (163)

In-group Any group or category to which people feel they belong. (120)

Innovation The process of introducing a new idea or object to a culture through discovery or invention. (56)

Institutional discrimination The denial of opportunities and equal rights to individuals and groups that results from the normal operations of a society. (244, 273)

Instrumentality An emphasis on tasks, a focus on more distant goals, and a concern for the external relationship between one's family and other social institutions. (271)

Intelligent design (ID) The idea that life is so complex that it could only have been created by intelligent design. (344)

Interactionist perspective A sociological approach that generalizes about everyday forms of social interaction in order to explain society as a whole. (15)

Intergenerational mobility Changes in the social position of children relative to their parents. (203)

Interview A face-to-face, telephone, or online questioning of a respondent to obtain desired information. (34)

Intragenerational mobility Changes in social position within a person's adult life. (204)

Invention The combination of existing cultural items into a form that did not exist before. (56)

Iron law of oligarchy A principle of organizational life developed by Robert Michels, under which even a democratic organization will eventually develop into a bureaucracy ruled by a few individuals. (126)

K

Kinship The state of being related to others. (308)

L

Labeling theory An approach to deviance that attempts to explain why certain people are viewed as deviants while others engaged in the same behavior are not. (169)

Labor union Organized workers who share either the same skill or the same employer. (130)

Laissez-faire A form of capitalism under which people compete freely, with minimal government intervention in the economy. (393)

Language An abstract system of word meanings and symbols for all aspects of culture; includes gestures and other nonverbal communication. (61)

Latent function An unconscious or unintended function that may reflect hidden purposes. (14)

Law Governmental social control. (63, 164)

Liberation theology Use of a church, primarily Roman Catholicism, in a political effort to eliminate poverty, discrimination, and other forms of injustice from a secular society. (336)

Life chances Max Weber's term for the opportunities people have to provide themselves with material goods, positive living conditions, and favorable life experiences. (202)

Life course approach A research orientation in which sociologists and other social scientists look closely at the social factors that influence people throughout their lives, from birth to death. (89)

Life expectancy The median number of years a person can be expected to live under current mortality conditions. (441)

Looking-glass self A concept used by Charles Horton Cooley that emphasizes the self as the product of our social interactions. (80)

Luddites Rebellious craft workers in 19th-century England who destroyed new factory machinery as part of their resistance to the Industrial Revolution. (488)

M

Machismo A sense of virility, personal worth, and pride in one's maleness. (314)

Macrosociology Sociological investigation that concentrates on large-scale phenomena or entire civilizations. (13)

Manifest function An open, stated, and conscious function. (14)

Mass media Print and electronic means of communication that carry messages to widespread audiences. (136)

Master status A status that dominates others and thereby determines a person's general position in society. (101)

Material culture The physical or technological aspects of our daily lives. (58)

Matriarchy A society in which women dominate in family decision making. (309)

Matrilineal descent A kinship system in which only the mother's relatives are significant. (308)

Matrix of domination The cumulative impact of oppression because of race and ethnicity, gender, and social class, as well as religion, sexual orientation, disability, age, and citizenship status. (272)

McDonaldization The process by which the principles of the fast-food restaurant are coming to dominate more and more sectors of American society as well as the rest of the world. (118, 421)

Mean A number calculated by adding a series of values and then dividing by the number of values. (44)

Mechanical solidarity A collective consciousness that emphasizes group solidarity, characteristic of societies with minimal division of labor. (108)

Median The midpoint or number that divides a series of values into two groups of equal numbers of values. (44)

Mental illness A disorder of the brain that disrupts a person's thinking, feeling, and ability to interact with others. (423)

Microfinancing Lending small sums of money to the poor so they can work their way out of poverty. (403)

Microsociology Sociological investigation that stresses the study of small groups, often through experimental means. (13)

Midlife crisis A stressful period of self-evaluation that begins at about age 40. (293)

Migration The relatively permanent movement of people, with the purpose of changing their place of residence. (445)

Minority group A subordinate group whose members have significantly less control or power over their own lives than the members of a dominant or majority group have over theirs. (237)

Mode The single most common value in a series of scores. (44)

Model, or ideal, minority A subordinate group whose members supposedly have succeeded economically, socially, and educationally despite past prejudice and discrimination, and without resorting to confrontations with Whites. (252)

Modernization The far-reaching process through which periphery nations move from traditional or less developed institutions to those characteristic of more developed societies. (222)

Modernization theory A functionalist approach that proposes that modernization and development will gradually improve the lives of people in developing nations. (222)

Monarchy A form of government headed by a single member of a royal family, usually a king, queen, or some other hereditary ruler. (373)

Monogamy A form of marriage in which one woman and one man are married only to each other. (307)

Monopoly Control of a market by a single business firm. (394)

Morbidity rate The incidence of disease in a given population. (415)

Mores Norms deemed highly necessary to the welfare of a society. (65)

Mortality rate The incidence of death in a given population. (415)

Multinational corporation A commercial organization that is headquartered in one country but does business throughout the world. (218)

Multiple masculinities A variety of male gender roles, including nurturing-caring and effeminate-gay roles, that men may play along with their more pervasive traditional role of dominating women. (269)

Multiple-nuclei theory A theory of urban growth developed by Harris and Ullman that views growth as emerging from many centers of development, each of which reflects a particular urban need or activity. (448)

N

Narcotizing dysfunction The phenomenon in which the media provide such massive amounts of coverage that the audience becomes numb and fails to act on the information, regardless of how compelling the issue. (140)

Natural science The study of the physical features of nature and the ways in which they interact and change. (6)

Naturally occurring retirement community (NORC) An area that has gradually become an informal center for senior citizens. (294)

Neocolonialism Continuing dependence of former colonies on foreign countries. (216)

Netizen A person who is actively involved in online communities and is committed to the free flow of information, with few outside controls. (141)

New religious movement (NRM) or cult A small, secretive religious group that represents either a new religion or a major innovation of an existing faith. (341)

New social movement An organized collective activity that addresses values and social identities, as well as improvements in the quality of life. (473)

New urban sociology An approach to urbanization that considers the interplay of local, national, and worldwide forces and their effect on local space, with special emphasis on the impact of global economic activity. (450)

Nonmaterial culture Ways of using material objects, as well as customs, beliefs, philosophies, governments, and patterns of communication. (58)

Nonperiodic assembly A nonrecurring gathering of people that often results from word-of-mouth information. (465)

Nonverbal communication The sending of messages through the use of gestures, facial expressions, and postures. (16)

Norm An established standard of behavior maintained by a society. (62)

Nuclear family A married couple and their unmarried children living together. (307)

O

Obedience Compliance with higher authorities in a hierarchical structure. (161)

Objective method A technique for measuring social class that assigns individuals to classes on the basis of criteria such as occupation, education, income, and place of residence. (195)

Observation A research technique in which an investigator collects information through direct participation by closely watching a group or community. (36)

Offshoring The transfer of work to foreign contractors. (402)

Oligarchy A form of government in which a few individuals rule. (373)

Open system A social system in which the position of each individual is influenced by his or her achieved status. (203)

Operational definition An explanation of an abstract concept that is specific enough to allow a researcher to assess the concept. (29)

Opinion leader Someone who influences the opinions and decisions of others through day-to-day personal contact and communication. (149)

Organic solidarity A collective consciousness that rests on mutual interdependence, characteristic of societies with a complex division of labor. (108)

Organized crime The work of a group that regulates relations between criminal enterprises involved in illegal activities, including prostitution, gambling, and the smuggling and sale of illegal drugs. (173)

Out-group A group or category to which people feel they do not belong. (120)

P

Panic A fearful arousal or collective flight based on a generalized belief that may or may not be accurate. (468)

Patriarchy A society in which men dominate in family decision making. (309)

Patrilineal descent A kinship system in which only the father's relatives are significant. (308)

Peace The absence of war or, more broadly, a proactive effort to develop cooperative relations among nations. (382)

Percentage A portion of 100. (29)

Periodic assembly A recurring, relatively routine gathering of people, such as a college class. (465)

Personality A person's typical patterns of attitudes, needs, characteristics, and behavior. (77)

Peter principle A principle of organizational life, originated by Laurence J. Peter, according to which every employee within a hierarchy tends to rise to his or her level of incompetence. (125)

Pluralism Mutual respect for one another's cultures among the various groups in a society, which allows minorities to express their cultures without experiencing prejudice. (248)

Pluralist model A view of society in which many competing groups within the community have access to government, so that no single group is dominant. (379)

Political system The social institution that is founded on a recognized set of procedures for implementing and achieving society's goals. (370)

Politics In Harold Lasswell's words, "who gets what, when, and how." (371)

Polyandry A form of polygamy in which a woman may have more than one husband at the same time. (307)

Polygamy A form of marriage in which an individual may have several husbands or wives simultaneously. (307)

Polygyny A form of polygamy in which a man may have more than one wife at the same time. (307)

Population pyramid A special type of bar chart that shows the distribution of a population by gender and age. (442)

Postindustrial city A city in which global finance and the electronic flow of information dominate the economy. (447)

Postindustrial society A society whose economic system is engaged primarily in the processing and control of information. (110)

Postmodern society A technologically sophisticated society that is preoccupied with consumer goods and media images. (111)

Power The ability to exercise one's will over others. (193, 371)

Power elite A term used by C. Wright Mills to refer to a small group of military, industrial, and government leaders who control the fate of the United States. (378)

Precarious work Employment that is poorly paid, and from the worker's perspective, insecure and unprotected. (200)

Preindustrial city A city of only a few thousand people that is characterized by a relatively closed class system and limited mobility. (446)

Prejudice A negative attitude toward an entire category of people, often an ethnic or racial minority. (240)

Prestige The respect and admiration that an occupation holds in a society. (196)

Prevalence The total number of cases of a specific disorder that exist at a given time. (415)

Primary group A small group characterized by intimate, face-to-face association and cooperation. (119)

Profane The ordinary and commonplace elements of life, as distinguished from the sacred. (331)

Professional criminal A person who pursues crime as a day-to-day occupation, developing skilled techniques and enjoying a certain degree of status among other criminals. (172)

Proletariat Karl Marx's term for the working class in a capitalist society. (192)

Protestant ethic Max Weber's term for the disciplined work ethic, this-worldly concerns, and rational orientation to life emphasized by John Calvin and his followers. (335)

Public A dispersed group of people, not necessarily in contact with one another, who share an interest in an issue. (469)

Public opinion Expressions of attitudes on matters of public policy that are communicated to decision makers. (469)

Q

Qualitative research Research that relies on what is seen in field or naturalistic settings more than on statistical data. (36)

Quantitative research Research that collects and reports data primarily in numerical form. (36)

Quasi-religion A scholarly category that includes organizations that may see themselves as religious but are seen by others as "sort of religious." (342)

Questionnaire A printed or written form used to obtain information from a respondent. (34)

R

Racial formation A sociohistorical process in which racial categories are created, inhibited, transformed, and destroyed. (238)

Racial group A group that is set apart from others because of physical differences that have taken on social significance. (237)

Racial profiling Any arbitrary action initiated by an authority based on race, ethnicity, or national origin rather than on a person's behavior. (246)

Racism The belief that one race is supreme and all others are innately inferior. (240)

Random sample A sample for which every member of an entire population has the same chance of being selected. (32)

Rational-legal authority Power made legitimate by law. (371)

Reference group Any group that individuals use as a standard for evaluating themselves and their own behavior. (120)

Relative deprivation The conscious feeling of a negative discrepancy between legitimate expectations and present actualities. (471)

Relative poverty A floating standard of deprivation by which people at the bottom of a society, whatever their lifestyles, are judged to be disadvantaged *in comparison with the nation as a whole.* (199)

Reliability The extent to which a measure produces consistent results. (32)

Religion According to Émile Durkheim, a unified system of beliefs and practices relative to sacred things. (33)

Religious belief A statement to which members of a particular religion adhere. (338)

Religious experience The feeling or perception of being in direct contact with the ultimate reality, such as a divine being, or of being overcome with religious emotion. (338)

Religious ritual A practice required or expected of members of a faith. (338)

Remittances The monies that immigrants return to their families of origin. Also called *migradollars.* (228)

Representative democracy A form of government in which certain individuals are selected to speak for the people. (373)

Research design A detailed plan or method for obtaining data scientifically. (34)

Resocialization The process of discarding former behavior patterns and accepting new ones as part of a transition in one's life. (90)

Resource mobilization The ways in which a social movement utilizes such resources as money, political influence, access to the media, and personnel. (472)

Rite of passage A ritual marking the symbolic transition from one social position to another. (89)

Role conflict The situation that occurs when incompatible expectations arise from two or more social positions held by the same person. (101)

Role exit The process of disengagement from a role that is central to one's self-identity in order to establish a new role and identity. (102)

Role strain The difficulty that arises when the same social position imposes conflicting demands and expectations. (102)

Role taking The process of mentally assuming the perspective of another and responding from that imagined viewpoint. (80)

Rumor A piece of information gathered informally that is used to interpret an ambiguous situation. (469)

S

Sacred Elements beyond everyday life that inspire awe, respect, and even fear. (331)

Sample A selection from a larger population that is statistically representative of that population. (31)

Sanction A penalty or reward for conduct concerning a social norm. (64, 161)

Sandwich generation The generation of adults who simultaneously try to meet the competing needs of their parents and their children. (293)

Sapir-Whorf hypothesis A hypothesis concerning the role of language in shaping our interpretation of reality. It holds that language is culturally determined. (61)

Science The body of knowledge obtained by methods based on systematic observation. (5)

Scientific management approach Another name for the classical theory of formal organizations. (126)

Scientific method A systematic, organized series of steps that ensures maximum objectivity and consistency in researching a problem. (29)

Second shift The double burden—work outside the home followed by child care and housework—that many women face and few men share equitably. (277)

Secondary analysis A variety of research techniques that make use of previously collected and publicly accessible information and data. (37)

Secondary group A formal, impersonal group in which there is little social intimacy or mutual understanding. (119)

Sect A relatively small religious group that has broken away from some other religious organization to renew what it considers the original vision of the faith. (339)

Secularization The process through which religion's influence on other social institutions diminishes. (330)

Segregation The physical separation of two groups of people in terms of residence, workplace, and social events; often imposed on a minority group by a dominant group. (248)

Self According to George Herbert Mead, a distinct identity that sets us apart from others. (80)

Serial monogamy A form of marriage in which a person may have several spouses in his or her lifetime, but only one spouse at a time. (307)

Sexism The ideology that one sex is superior to the other. (273)

Sick role Societal expectations about the attitudes and behavior of a person viewed as being ill. (411)

Significant other A term used by George Herbert Mead to refer to an individual who is most important in the development of the self, such as a parent, friend, or teacher. (81)

Single-parent family A family in which only one parent is present to care for the children. (318)

Slavery A system of enforced servitude in which some people are owned by other people. (187)

Small group A group small enough for all members to interact simultaneously—that is, to talk with one another or at least be well acquainted. (121)

Social capital The collective benefit of social networks, which are built on reciprocal trust. (13)

Social change Significant alteration over time in behavior patterns and culture, including norms and values. (484)

Social constructionist perspective An approach to deviance that emphasizes the role of culture in the creation of the deviant identity. (170)

Social control The techniques and strategies for preventing deviant human behavior in any society. (161)

Social disorganization theory The theory that crime and deviance are caused by the absence or breakdown of communal relationships and social institutions. (169)

Social epidemiology The study of the distribution of disease, impairment, and general health status across a population. (415)

Social inequality A condition in which members of society have differing amounts of wealth, prestige, or power. (19, 186)

Social institution An organized pattern of beliefs and behavior centered on basic social needs. (103)

Social interaction The ways in which people respond to one another. (98)

Social mobility Movement of individuals or groups from one position in a society's stratification system to another. (203)

Social movement An organized collective activity to bring about or resist fundamental change in an existing group or society. (470)

Social network A series of social relationships that links a person directly to others, and through them indirectly to still more people. (105)

Social role A set of expectations for people who occupy a given social position or status. (101)

Social science The study of the social features of humans and the ways in which they interact and change. (6)

Social structure The way in which a society is organized into predictable relationships. (98)

Socialism An economic system under which the means of production and distribution are collectively owned. (395)

Socialization The lifelong process in which people learn the attitudes, values, and behaviors appropriate for members of a particular culture. (76)

Societal-reaction approach Another name for *labeling theory*. (169)

Society A fairly large number of people who live in the same territory, are relatively independent of people outside their area, and participate in a common culture. (53)

Sociobiology The systematic study of how biology affects human social behavior. (54)

Sociocultural evolution Long-term trends in societies resulting from the interplay of continuity, innovation, and selection. (109)

Socioeconomic status (SES) A measure of social class that is based on income, education, and occupation. (197)

Sociological imagination An awareness of the relationship between an individual and the wider society, both today and in the past. (5)

Sociology The scientific study of social behavior and human groups. (5)

Sovereignty movement The effort by the indigenous people of Hawai'i to win self-government, as well as the restoration of—or compensation for—their ancestral lands. (375)

Squatter settlement An area occupied by the very poor on the fringe of a city, in which housing is constructed by the settlers themselves from discarded material. (451)

Status A term used by sociologists to refer to any of the full range of socially defined positions within a large group or society. (100)

Status group A term used by Max Weber to refer to people who have the same prestige or lifestyle, independent of their class positions. (193)

Stereotype An unreliable generalization about all members of a group that does not recognize individual differences within the group. (143, 239)

Stigma A label used to devalue members of certain social groups. (168)

Stratification A structured ranking of entire groups of people that perpetuates unequal economic rewards and power in a society. (186)

Subculture A segment of society that shares a distinctive pattern of customs, rules, and traditions that differs from the pattern of the larger society. (59)

Suburb According to the Census Bureau, any territory within a metropolitan area that is not included in the central city. (453)

Survey A study, generally in the form of an interview or questionnaire, that provides researchers with information about how people think and act. (34)

Symbol A gesture, object, or word that forms the basis of human communication. (62)

Symbolic ethnicity An ethnic identity that emphasizes concerns such as ethnic food or political issues rather than deeper ties to one's ethnic heritage. (258)

T

Teacher-expectancy effect The impact that a teacher's expectations about a student's performance may have on the student's actual achievements. (358)

Technology Cultural information about the ways in which the material resources of the environment may be used to satisfy human needs and desires. (58, 109)

Telecommuter An employee who works full-time or part-time at home rather than in an outside office, and who is linked to supervisor and colleagues through phone lines, Wi-Fi, the Internet, and smartphones. (128)

Terrorism The use or threat of violence against random or symbolic targets in pursuit of political aims. (383)

Theory In sociology, a set of statements that seeks to explain problems, actions, or behavior. (8)

Total fertility rate (TFR) The average number of children born alive to any woman, assuming that she conforms to current fertility rates. (440)

Total institution A term coined by Erving Goffman to refer to an institution that regulates all aspects of a person's life under a single authority, such as a prison, the military, a mental hospital, or a convent. (90)

Totalitarianism Virtually complete government control and surveillance over all aspects of a society's social and political life. (373)

Tracking The practice of placing students in specific curriculum groups on the basis of their test scores and other criteria. (356)

Traditional authority Legitimate power conferred by custom and accepted practice. (371)

Trained incapacity The tendency of workers in a bureaucracy to become so specialized that they develop blind spots and fail to notice obvious problems. (124)

Transnational An immigrant who sustains multiple social relationships that link his or her society of origin with the society of settlement. (259, 495)

Transnational crime Crime that occurs across multiple national borders. (175)

Triad A three-member group. (122)

U

Underclass The long-term poor who lack training and skills. (201)

Urban ecology An area of study that focuses on the interrelationships between people and their environment in urban areas. (448)

Urbanism A term used by Louis Wirth to describe distinctive patterns of social behavior evident among city residents. (447)

V

Validity The degree to which a measure or scale truly reflects the phenomenon under study. (31)

Value A collective conception of what is considered good, desirable, and proper—or bad, undesirable, and improper—in a culture. (64)

Value-added model A theory of collective behavior proposed by sociologist Neil Smelser to explain how broad social conditions are transformed in a definite pattern into some form of collective behavior. (464)

Value neutrality Max Weber's term for objectivity of sociologists in the interpretation of data. (40)

Variable A measurable trait or characteristic that is subject to change under different conditions. (30)

Verstehen The German word for "understanding" or "insight"; used by Max Weber to stress the need for sociologists to take into account the subjective meanings people attach to their actions. (10)

Vertical mobility The movement of an individual from one social position to another of a different rank. (203)

Vested interests Veblen's term for those people or groups who will suffer in the event of social change, and who have a stake in maintaining the status quo. (487)

Victimization survey A questionnaire or interview given to a sample of the population to determine whether people have been victims of crime. (176)

Victimless crime A term used by sociologists to describe the willing exchange among adults of widely desired but illegal goods and services. (172)

Visitability The accessibility of private homes to visitors with disabilities. (477)

Vital statistics Records of births, deaths, marriages, and divorces gathered through a registration system maintained by governmental units. (440)

W

War Conflict between organizations that possess trained combat forces equipped with deadly weapons. (381)

Wealth An inclusive term encompassing all a person's material assets, including land, stocks, and other types of property. (187)

White-collar crime Illegal acts committed by affluent, "respectable" individuals in the course of business activities. (173)

White privilege Rights or immunities granted to people as a particular benefit or favor simply because they are White. (243)

World systems analysis Immanuel Wallerstein's view of the global economic system as one divided between certain industrialized nations that control wealth and developing countries that are controlled and exploited. (216, 450)

Z

Zero population growth (ZPG) The state of a population in which the number of births plus immigrants equals the number of deaths plus emigrants. (444)

references

A

Abercrombie, Nicholas, Bryan S. Turner, and Stephen Hill, eds. 1990. *Dominant Ideologies*. Cambridge, MA: Unwin Hyman.

———, Stephen Hill, and Bryan S. Turner. 1980. *The Dominant Ideology Thesis*. London: Allen and Unwin.

Aberle, David F., A. K. Cohen, A. K. Davis, M. J. Leng, Jr., and F. N. Sutton. 1950. "The Functional Prerequisites of a Society." *Ethics* 60 (January):100–111.

Abramson, David, Irwin Redlener, Tasha Stehling-Ariza, and Elizabeth Fuller. 2007. *The Legacy of Katrina's Children: Estimating the Numbers of At-Risk Children in the Gulf Coast States of Louisiana and Mississippi.* New York: Columbia University Mailman School of Public Health.

Acharya, Meena. 2000. *Labor Market Developments and Poverty: With Focus on Economic Opportunities for Women.* Kathmandu, Nepal: Tanka Prasad Acharya Foundation/FES.

Acohido, Byron. 2010. "Tech-Savvy Put Explosion to Work." *USA Today,* November 17, pp. B1, B2.

Adams, Tyrene L., and Stephen A. Smith. 2008. *Electronic Tribes: The Virtual Worlds of Geeks, Gamas, Shamans, and Scammers.* Austin: University of Texas Press.

Adamy, Janet. 2008. "Starbucks Plans to License 150 Stores in Europe." *New York Times,* June 12, p. B3.

Addams, Jane. 1910. *Twenty Years at Hull-House.* New York: Macmillan.

———. 1930. *The Second Twenty Years at Hull-House.* New York: Macmillan.

Adler, Patricia A., and Peter Adler. 2007. "The Demedicalization of Self-Injury: From Psychopathology to Sociological Deviance." *Journal of Contemporary Ethnography* 36 (October):537–570.

———, and John M. Johnson. 1992. "Street Corner Society Revisited." *Journal of Contemporary Ethnography* 21 (April):3–10.

Adler, Roy D. 2008. "Counting on the Middle-Class." *Miller-McCune* (November–December):20–23.

Adorno, Theodor. [1971] 1991. *The Culture Industry.* London: Routledge.

Aguirre, Benigno E., E. L. Quarantelli, and Jorge L. Mendoza. 1988. "The Collective Behavior of Fads: The Characteristics, Effects, and Career of Streaking." *American Sociological Review* 53 (August):569–584.

Alain, Michel. 1985. "An Empirical Validation of Relative Deprivation." *Human Relations* 38 (8):739–749.

Alba, Richard D. 2009. *Blurring the Color Line: The New Chance for a More Integrated America.* Cambridge, MA: Harvard University Press.

———. 1990. *Ethnic Identity: The Transformation of White America.* New Haven, CT: Yale University Press.

Albas, Cheryl, and Daniel Albas. 1996. "An Invitation to the Ethnographic Study of University Examination Behavior: Concepts, Methodology and Implications." *Canadian Journal of Higher Education* 26 (3):1–26.

Albas, Daniel, and Cheryl Albas. 1988. "Aces and Bombers: The Post-Exam Impression Management Strategies of Students." *Symbolic Interaction* 11 (Fall):289–302.

Albrecht, Gary L. 1995. "Review of Disability Laws, Enabling Acts: Disability Rights in Britain and America." *Contemporary Sociology* 24 (5):627–629.

———. 1997. "Disability Is Area Rich with Sociological Opportunity." *Footnotes* 25 (December):6.

———. 2004. "Disability: Sociological Perspectives." Pp. 3710–3713 in *International Encyclopedia of the Social and Behavioral Sciences,* edited by Neil J. Smelser and Paul B. Baltes. New York: Elsevier.

———, ed. 2005. *Encyclopedia of Disability.* Thousand Oaks, CA: Sage.

Alderman, Liz. 2010. "Dubai Rises from Ashes of Debt Crisis." *International Herald Tribune,* August 30, pp. 1, 20.

Alexander, Karl L. 1997. "Public Schools and the Public Good." *Social Forces* 70 (September):1–30.

Ali, Syed. 2010. "Permanent Impermanence." *Contexts* (Spring):26–31.

Al-Jadda, Souheila. 2006. "A Veil Doesn't Mean 'Oppressed.'" *USA Today,* June 22, p. A13.

Al Jazeera. 2010. Home Page. Accessed February 7 (http://english.aljazeera.net/HomePage).

Allen, Bem P. 1978. *Social Behavior: Fact and Falsehood.* Chicago: Nelson-Hall.

Alliance for Board Diversity. 2008. *Women and Minorities on* Fortune *100 Boards.* Washington, DC: Catalyst, Prout Group, Executive Leadership Council, and Hispanic Association on Corporate Responsibility.

Allport, Gordon W. 1979. *The Nature of Prejudice.* 25th anniversary ed. Reading, MA: Addison-Wesley.

Alon, Sigal. 2009. "The Evolution of Class Inequality in Higher Education: Competition, Exclusion, and Adaptation." *American Sociological Review* 74 (October):731–755.

Alvord, Lori Arviso, and Elizabeth Cohen Van Pelt. 1999. *The Scalpel and the Silver Bear.* New York: Bantam Books.

Alwin, Duane F. 2002. "Generations X, Y, and Z: Are They Changing America?" *Contexts* (Fall–Winter):42–51.

Alzheimer's Association. 2010. *2010 Alzheimer's Disease Facts and Figures.* Chicago: Alzheimer's Association.

American Academy of Cosmetic Surgery. 2010. "New Survey Indicates More than 17 Million Cosmetic Procedures Performed Last Year in U.S." Chicago: AACS.

American Bar Association. 1997. *Section of the Individual Rights and Responsibilities: Section of Litigation (Capital Punishment).* Chicago: Division for Policy Administration, ABA.

American Community Survey. 2010. "2008 American Community Survey." Accessed at http://factfinder.census.gov.

American Jewish Committee. 2005. *2005 Annual Survey of American Jewish Opinion.* New York: AJC.

American Lung Association. 2009. *State of the Air 2009.* Washington, DC: ALA.

American Psychological Association. 2008. "Being Gay Is Just as Healthy as Being Straight." Accessed February 25 (www.apa.org).

American Sociological Association. 1997. *Code of Ethics.* Washington, DC: American Sociological Association. Accessible at www.asanet.org/members/ecoderev.html.

———. 2005. "Need Today's Data Yesterday." Accessed December 17 (www.asanet.org).

———. 2009. *21st Century Careers with an Undergraduate Degree in Sociology.* Washington, DC: ASA.

———. 2010a. *2010 Guide to Graduate Departments of Sociology.* Washington, DC: ASA.

———. 2010b. "What Are Sections?" Accessed January 4 (www.asanet.org/cs/root/leftnav/sections/overview).

American Soybean Association. 2011. "World Soybean Production 2009." Accessed June 1 (www.soystats.com).

Amnesty International. 2009. *Death Sentences and Executions 2009.* London: Amnesty International. Accessible at http://www.amnesty.org/en/library/asset/ACT50/001/2010/en/17348b70-3fc7-40b2-a258-af92778c73e5/act500012010en.pdf.

Andersen, Margaret. 2007. *Thinking about Women: Sociological Perspectives on Sex and Gender.* 7th ed. New York: Allyn and Bacon.

Anderson, Elijah. 1990. *Streetwise: Race, Class, and Change in an Urban Community.* Chicago: University of Chicago Press.

Anderson, Gretchen. 2009. *Love, Actually: A National Survey of Adults 18+ on Love, Relationships, and Romance.* Washington, DC: AARP.

Anderson, John Ward, and Molly Moore. 1993. "The Burden of Womanhood." *Washington Post National Weekly Edition* 10 (March 22–28):6–7.

Anderson, Warwick. 2003. *The Cultivation of Whiteness: Science, Health and Racial Destiny in Australia.* New York: Perseus.

Angier, Natalie. 1998. "Drugs, Sports, Body Image and G.I. Joe." *New York Times,* December 22, pp. D1, D3.

Angwin, Julia. 2010. "The Web's New Gold Mine: Your Secrets." *Wall Street Journal,* July 31, pp. W1, W2.

———, and Jennifer Valentino-DeVries. 2010a. "Race Is On to 'Fingerprint' Phones, PCs." *Wall Street Journal,* December 1, pp. A1, A15.

———, and ———. 2010b. "Web Privacy 'Inadequate.'" *Wall Street Journal,* December 2, pp. B1, B2.

Ansell, Amy E. 2008. "Color Blindness." Pp. 320–321, vol. 1, in *Encyclopedia of Race, Ethnicity, and Society,* edited by Richard T. Schaefer. Thousand Oaks, CA: Sage.

Anti-Defamation League. 2010. "2009 Audit of Anti-Semitic Incidents: Summary of Findings." Accessed March 18, 2011 (www.adl.org/main_anti_semitism_domestic/2009_Audit.htm).

References

Arab American Institute. 2010. "Demographics." Accessed March 7 (www.aaiusa.org/arab-americans/22/demographics).

Archibold, Randal C., and Julia Preston. 2008. "Homeland Security Stands by Its Fence." *New York Times,* May 21.

Argetsinger, Amy, and Jonathan Krim. 2002. "Stopping the Music." *Washington Post National Weekly Edition* 20 (December 2):20.

Arias, Elizabeth. 2010. "United States Life Tables, 2006." *National Vital Statistics Reports* 58 (June 28).

Armer, J. Michael, and John Katsillis. 1992. "Modernization Theory." Pp. 1299–1304, vol. 4, in *Encyclopedia of Sociology,* edited by Edgar F. Borgatta and Marie L. Borgatta. New York: Macmillan.

Ash, Timothy Garton. 2007. "Welcome to a Mixed-Up World." *Globe and Mail* (Toronto), July 14, p. A19.

Asian American Journalists Association. 2007. "Media Advisory: Coverage on Virginia Tech Shooting Incident." Accessed May 16 (www.aaja.org).

Association of American Medical Colleges. 2011. "AAMC Faculty Roster, May 2009" and "AAMC Data Warehouse." Accessible at www.aamc.org.

Association of Theological Schools. 2011. "2010–2011 Annual Data Tables: Table 2-12A." Accessed March 28 (www.ats.edu/Resources/Publications/Documents/AnnualDataTables/2010-11AnnualDataTables.pdf).

Atchley, Robert C. 1976. *The Sociology of Retirement.* New York: Wiley.

———, and Amanda S. Barusch. 2004. *Social Forces and Agency: An Introduction to Social Gerontology.* 10th ed. Belmont, CA: Thomson.

Attwood, Bain. 2003. *Rights for Aborigines.* Crows Nest, Australia: Allen and Unwin.

Aud, Susan, Mary Ann Fox, and Angelina KewalRamani. 2010. *Status and Trends in the Education of Racial and Ethnic Groups.* Washington, DC: National Center for Education Statistics, U.S. Department of Education.

Austin, April. 2002. "Cellphones and Strife in Congo." *Christian Science Monitor,* December 5, p. 11.

Australia. 1997. "Bringing Them Home: Report of the National Inquiry into the Separation of Aboriginal and Torres Strait Islander Children from Their Families." Accessible at www.humanrights.gov.au.

———. 2008. "Apology to Australia's Indigenous Peoples, House of Representatives, Parliament House, Canberra." Accessed February 13 (www.pm.gov.au/media/speech/2008/speech_0073.cfm).

Azumi, Koya, and Jerald Hage. 1972. *Organizational Systems.* Lexington, MA: Heath.

B

Babad, Elisha Y., and P. J. Taylor. 1992. "Transparency of Teacher Expectancies across Language, Cultural Boundaries." *Journal of Educational Research* 86:120–125.

Baby Name Wizard. 2010. "Name Voyager." Accessed January 17 (www.babynamewizard.com).

Bacon Lovers' Talk. 2009. "Bacon Lovers' Talk." Accessed February 4 (www.bacontalk.com/).

Bado-Fralick, Nikki, and Rebecca Sachs Norris. 2010. *Toying with God: The World of Religious Games and Dolls.* Waco, TX: Baylor University Press.

Bajaj, Vikas. 2011a. "15 Years in Microcredit Has Suffered a Black Eye." *New York Times,* January 6, p. B3.

———. 2011b. "Luster Dims for a Public Microlender." *New York Times,* May 11, pp. 1, 4.

Baker, Joseph O., and Buster G. Smith. 2009. "The Names: Social Characteristics of the Religiously Unfaithful." *Social Forces* 87(March):1251–1263.

Baker, Peter. 2009. "Obama Reverses Rules on U.S. Abortion Aid." *New York Times,* January 24.

Baker, Therese L. 1999. *Doing Social Research.* 3rd ed. New York: McGraw-Hill.

Barbaro, Michael. 2008. "Wal-Mart Says Most Workers Have Health Plan." *New York Times,* January 22.

Barboza, David. 2008. "Reform Stalls in Chinese Factories." *New York Times,* January 5, pp. B1, B6.

Barnes, Patricia, Barbara Bloom, and Richard Nahin. 2008. "Complementary and Alternative Medicine Use among Adults and Children: United States, 2007." *National Health Statistics Reports,* December 10.

———, Eve Powell-Griner, Ken McFann, and Richard L. Nation. 2004. "Complementary and Alternative Medicine Use among Adults: United States, 2002." *Advance Data from Vital and Health Statistics,* No. 343. Hyattsville, MD: National Center for Health Statistics.

Barnes, Taylor. 2009. "Rise of the Shadow Economy." *Christian Science Monitor,* November 8, pp. 30–31.

Barr, Cameron W. 2002. "Top Arab TV Network to Hit US Market." *Christian Science Monitor,* December 26, pp. 1, 7.

Barrett, David B., Todd M. Johnson, and Peter F. Crossing. 2008. "The 2007 Annual Megacensus of Religions." Chicago: Encyclopaedia Britannica.

Barron, Milton L. 1953. "Minority Group Characteristics of the Aged in American Society." *Journal of Gerontology* 8:477–482.

Bartlett, Thomas. 2009. "How the International Essay Mill Has Changed Cheating." *Chronicle of Higher Education,* March 20, pp. A1, A22–A25.

Barton, Bernadette. 2006. *Stripped: Inside the Lives of Exotic Dancers.* New York: New York University Press.

Bascara, Victor. 2008. "Model Minority." Pp. 910–912, vol. 2, in *Encyclopedia of Race, Ethnicity, and Society,* edited by Richard T. Schaefer. Thousand Oaks, CA: Sage.

Battin, Margaret P., Agnes van der Heide, and Bregje D. Onwuleaka-Philipsen. 2007. "Legal Physician-Assisted Dying in Oregon and the Netherlands: Evidence Concerning the Impact on Patients in 'Vulnerable' Groups." *Journal of Medical Ethics* 33 (October):591–597.

Bauerlein, Mark. 2008. "Online Literacy Is a Lesser Kind." *Chronicle of Higher Education,* September 19, pp. B10–B11.

Bauerlein, Monika. 1996. "The Luddites Are Back." *Utne Reader* (March–April):24, 26.

Bauman, Kurt J. 1999. "Extended Measures of Well-Being: Meeting Basic Needs." *Current Population Reports,* ser. P-70, no. 67. Washington, DC: U.S. Government Printing Office.

Bazar, Emily. 2009. "Tent Cities Filling up with Casualties of the Economy. *USA Today,* May 5, pp. 1A–2A.

BBC News. 2005. "Indonesian Village Report: January 12, 2005." Accessed January 19 (www.theworld.org).

Beagan, Brenda L. 2001. " 'Even If I Don't Know What I'm Doing I Can Make It Look Like I Know What I'm Doing': Becoming a Doctor in the 1990s." *Canadian Review of Sociology and Anthropology* 38:275–292.

Bearman, Peter S., James Moody, and Katherine Stovel. 2004. "Chains of Affection: The Structure of Adolescent Romantic and Sexual Networks." *American Journal of Sociology* 110 (July):44–91.

Bebchuk, Lucian A., and Jesse M. Fried. 2010. "Tackling the Managerial Power Problem." *Pathways* (Summer):9–12.

Beck, Barbara. 2009. "A Slow-Burning Fuse: A Special Report on Ageing Populations." *The Economist* (June 27).

Becker, Anne E. 2007. "Facets of Acculturation and Their Diverse Relations to Body Shape Concerns in Fiji." *International Journal of Eating Disorders* 40 (1):42–50.

Becker, Howard S. 1952. "Social Class Variations in the Teacher-Pupil Relationship." *Journal of Educational Sociology* 25 (April):451–465.

———. 1963. *The Outsiders: Studies in the Sociology of Deviance.* New York: Free Press.

Beisel, Nicola, and Tamara Kay. 2004. "Abortion, Race, and Gender in Nineteenth-Century America." *American Sociological Review* 69 (4):498–518.

Bell, Daniel. 1953. "Crime as an American Way of Life." *Antioch Review* 13 (Summer):131–154.

———. 1973. *The Coming of Post-Industrial Society.* New York: Basic Books.

———. 1999. *The Coming of Post-Industrial Society: A Venture in Social Forecasting.* With new foreword. New York: Basic Books.

———. 2008. *China's New Confucianism: Politics and Everyday Life in a Changing Society.* Princeton, NJ: Princeton University Press.

Bell, Wendell. 1981. "Modernization." Pp. 186–187 in *Encyclopedia of Sociology.* Guilford, CT: DPG Publishing.

Beller, Emily. 2009. "Bringing Intergenerational Social Mobility Research into the Twenty-first Century: Why Mothers Matter. *America Sociological Review* 74 (August):507–528.

Belton, Danielle C. 2009. "Blacks in Space." *American Prospect* (June):47–49.

Belz, Adam. 2011. "Farm Boom Leaves Main Street Wanting." *USA Today,* June 1, p. 6A.

Bendick, Marc, Jr., Charles W. Jackson, and J. Horacio Romero. 1993. *Employment Discrimination against Older Workers: An Experimental Study of Hiring Practices.* Washington, DC: Fair Employment Council of Greater Washington.

Benford, Robert D. 1992. "Social Movements." Pp. 1880–1887, vol. 4, in *Encyclopedia of Sociology,* edited by Edgar F. Borgatta and Marie Borgatta. New York: Macmillan.

Bennett, Vivienne, S. Dávila-Poblete, and M. N. Rico, eds. 2005. *Opposing Currents: The Politics of Water and Gender in Latin America.* Pittsburgh: University of Pittsburgh Press.

Bergen, Raquel Kennedy. 2006. *Marital Rape: New Research and Directions.* Harrisburg, PA: VAW Net.

Berger, Peter, and Thomas Luckmann. 1966. *The Social Construction of Reality.* New York: Doubleday.

Berk, Richard A., and Howard E. Aldrich. 1972. "Patterns of Vandalism during Civil Disorders as an Indicator of Selection of Targets." *American Sociological Review* 37 (October):533–547.

Berkeley Wellness Letter. 1990. "The Nest Refilled." 6 (February):1–2.

Berman, Paul. 2003. *Terror and Liberalism.* New York: Norton.

Bernat, Frances P., and Tatyana Zhilina. 2011. "Trafficking in Humans: The TIP Report." *Sociology Compass* 5 (June):452–462.

Bernhardt, Annette, et al. (10 additional co-anchors). 2009. *Broken Laws, Unprotected Workers.* New York: Ford, Joyce, Haynes, and Russell Sage Foundations.

Bernstein, Elizabeth. 2007. "Colleges Move Boldly on Student Drinking." *Wall Street Journal,* December 6, pp. D1, D2.

Best, Joel. 2004. *Deviance: Career of a Concept.* Belmont, CA: Wadsworth Thomson.

Bhagat, Chetan. 2007. *One Night at the Call Centre.* London: Black Swan.

Bialik, Carol. 2010. "Seven Careers in a Lifetime? Think Twice, Researchers Say." *Wall Street Journal,* September 4, p. A6.

Bianchi, Suzanne M., and Daphne Spain. 1996. "Women, Work, and Family in America." *Population Bulletin* 51 (December).

Biddlecom, Ann, and Steven Martin. 2006. "Childless in America." *Contexts* 5 (Fall):54.

Bielby, Denise D., and C. Lee Harrington. 2008. *Global TV: Exporting Television and Culture in the World Market.* New York: New York University Press.

Billitteri, Thomas, J. 2009. "Middle-Class Squeeze." *CQ Researcher* 19 (March 6):201–224.

Bilton, Nick. 2011. *I Live in the Future and Here's How It Works.* New York: Crown Business.

Birnbaum, Jeffrey H. 2005. "Listen to the Wallet." *Washington Post National Weekly Edition,* April 4, p. 11.

Bitler, Marianne, and Hilary W. Hoynes. 2010. "The State of the Safety Net in the Post-Welfare Reform Era". Paper prepared for Brooking Papers on Economic Activity, Washington, DC, September 16–20.

Black, Donald. 1995. "The Epistemology of Pure Sociology." *Law and Social Inquiry* 20 (Summer): 829–870.

Blank, Rebecca M. 2010. "Middle Class in America." *Focus* 27 (Summer):1–8.

Blau, Peter M., and Otis Dudley Duncan. 1967. *The American Occupational Structure.* New York: Wiley.

Blauner, Robert. 1964. *Alienation and Freedom.* Chicago: University of Chicago Press.

———. 1972. *Racial Oppression in America.* New York: Harper and Row.

Blumer, Herbert. 1955. "Collective Behavior." Pp. 165–198 in *Principles of Sociology,* 2nd ed., edited by Alfred McClung Lee. New York: Barnes and Noble.

———. 1969. *Symbolic Interactionism: Perspective and Method.* Englewood Cliffs, NJ: Prentice Hall.

———. 1972. *Racial Oppression in America.* New York: Harper and Row.

Block, Melissa. 2009. "Toll of War: Broken Hearts, Marriages for Marines." Accessed August 20 (http://npr.org/templates/transcript/transcript.php?storyly=111988038).

Blumberg, Stephen J., and Julian V. Luke. 2007. "Coverage Bias in Traditional Telephone Surveys of Low-Income and Young Adults." *Public Opinion Quarterly* 71 (5):734–749.

Blumer, Herbert. 1955. "Collective Behavior." Pp. 165–198 in *Principles of Sociology,* 2nd ed., edited by Alfred McClung Lee. New York: Barnes and Noble.

———. 1969. *Symbolic Interactionism: Perspective and Method.* Englewood Cliffs, NJ: Prentice Hall.

Blumstein, Alfred, and Joel Wallman. 2006. "The Crime Drops and Beyond." *Annual Review of Law and Society* 2:125–146.

Boase, Jeffery, John B. Horrigan, Barry Wellman, and Lee Rainie. 2006. *The Strength of Internet Ties.* Washington, DC: Pew Internet and American Life Project.

Boellstorff, Tom. 2008. *Coming of Age in Second Life: An Anthropologist Explores the Virtually Human.* Princeton, NJ: Princeton University Press.

Bonikowski, Bart, and Miller McPherson. 2006. "The Sociology of Voluntary Associations." In 21st Century Sociology (online version accessed February 6, 2010). Thousand Oaks, CA: Sage.

Bonilla-Silva, Eduardo. 2004. "From Bi-Racial to Tri-Racial: Towards a New System of Racial Stratification in the USA." *Ethics and Racial Studies* 27 (November):931–950.

———. 2006. *Racism without Racists.* Lanham, MD: Rowman and Littlefield.

Bonus, Rick. 2000. *Locating Filipino Americans: Ethnicity and the Cultural Politics of Space.* Philadelphia: Temple University Press.

Borjas, George S., Jeffrey Grogger, and Gordon H. Hanson. 2006. "Immigration and African-American Employment Opportunities: The Response of Wages, Employment, and Incarceration to Labor Supply Shocks." Working Paper 12518. Cambridge, MA: National Bureau of Economic Research.

Borrelli, Christopher. 2010. "*Second Life Talk Given Both Locally, Virtually.*" *Chicago Tribune,* November 8, sec. 3, p. 1.

Bottomore, Tom, and Maximilien Rubel, eds. 1956. *Karl Marx: Selected Writings in Sociology and Social Philosophy.* New York: McGraw-Hill.

Boudreaux, Richard. 2002. "Indian Rights Law Is Upheld in Mexico." *Los Angeles Times,* September 7, p. A3.

Bourdieu, Pierre, and Jean-Claude Passeron. 1990. *Reproduction in Education, Society and Culture.* 2nd ed. London. Sage. Originally published as *La reproduction.*

Boushey, Heather. 2005. *Student Debt: Bigger and Bigger.* Washington, DC: Center for Economic and Policy Research.

Bouvier, Leon F. 1980. "America's Baby Boom Generation: The Fateful Bulge." *Population Bulletin* 35 (April).

Bowes, John. 2011. *The Fair Trade Revolution.* London: Pluto Press.

Bowles, Samuel, and Herbert Gintis. 1976. *Schooling in Capitalistic America: Educational Reforms and the Contradictions of Economic Life.* New York: Basic Books.

Bowman, Tom. 2009. "Toll of War: Broken Hearts, Marriages for Marines." Accessed August 20 (http://npr.org/templates/transcript/transcript.php?storyly=111988038).

Brabazon, Tara. 2007. *The University of Google: Education in the (post) Information Age.* Burlingaton, VT: Ashgate.

Brady, Erik. 2010. "Title IX Model Survey Policy to Be Rescinded." *USA Today,* April 20, p. C1.

Brandchannel.com. 2010. "2009 Movie Lust." Accessed February 7 (www.brandchannel.com/brandcameo_films.asp?movie_year_az=2009#movie_list).

Brannigan, Augustine. 1992. "Postmodernism." Pp. 1522–1525 in *Encyclopedia of Sociology,* vol. 3, edited by Edgar F. Borgatta and Marie L. Borgatta. New York: Macmillan.

Brannon, Rush. 1995. "The Use of the Concept of Disability Culture: A Historian's View." *Disability Studies* 15 (Fall):3–15.

Braxton, Gregory. 2009. "'Reality Television' in More Ways than One." *Los Angeles Times,* February 17, pp. A1, A15.

Bray, James H., and John Kelly. 1999. *Stepfamilies: Love, Marriage, and Parenting in the First Decade.* New York: Broadway Books.

Brazier, Chris, and Amir Hamed, eds. 2007. *The World Guide.* 11th ed. Oxford, UK: New Internationalist.

Breines, Winifred. 2007. "Struggling to Connect: White and Black Feminism in the Movement Years." *Contexts* 6 (Winter):18–24.

Brewer, Rose M., and Nancy A. Heitzeg. 2008. "The Racialization of Criminal Punishment." *American Behavioral Scientist* 51 (January):625–644.

Brewis, Alexandra, Amber Wutich, Ashlan Falletta-Cowden, and Isa Rodriguez-Soto. 2011. "Body Norms and Fat Stigma in Global Perspective." *Current Anthropology* 52 (April):269–276.

Brint, Steven. 1998. *Schools and Societies.* Thousand Oaks, CA: Pine Forge Press.

Britannica Online. 2011. "Worldwide Adherents of All Religions by Six Continental Areas. Mid-2010." Accessed March 28.

Brower, Brock. 1988. "The Pernicious Power of the Polls." *Money,* March 17, pp. 144–163.

Brown, David. 2009. "Doing a Number on Surveys." *Washington Post National Weekly Edition* 26 (January 19):37.

Brown, David K. 2001. "The Social Sources of Educational Credentialism: Status Cultures, Labor Markets, and Organizations." *Sociology of Education* 74 (Extra issue):19–34.

Brown, Michael, and Amy Goldin. 1973. *Collective Behavior: A Review and Reinterpretation of the Literature.* Pacific Palisades, CA: Goodyear.

Brown, Patricia Leigh. 2004. "For Children of Gays, Marriage Brings Joy." *New York Times,* March 19, p. A13.

Brown, Robert McAfee. 1980. *Gustavo Gutierrez.* Atlanta: John Knox.

Brown, Roger W. 1954. "Mass Phenomena." Pp. 833–873, vol. 2, in *Handbook of Social Psychology,* edited by Gardner Lindzey. Reading, MA: Addison-Wesley.

Brown, S. Kathi. 2006. *Attitudes toward Work and Job Security.* Washington, DC: AARP.

Browne, Irene, ed. 2001. *Latinas and African American Women at Work: Race, Gender, and Economic Inequality.* New York: Russell Sage Foundation.

Brubaker, Bill. 2008. "Social Insecurity: Many People's Numbers Are Readily Available Online to Identity Thieves." *Washington Post National Weekly Edition,* January 14, p. 34.

Bruinius, Harry. 2010. "March of the Megacities." *Christian Science Monitor,* May 10, pp. 26–30.

Brulle, Robert, and J. Craig Jenkins. 2008. "Fixing the Bungled U.S. Environmental Movement." *Contexts* 7 (Spring):14–18.

510

Buchholz, Barbara Ballinger. 2003. "Expanded Access." *Chicago Tribune*, January 26, sec. 16, pp. 1R, 5R.

Buchmann, Claudia, Thomas A. DiPrete, and Anne McDaniel. 2008. "Gender Inequalities in Education." *Annual Review of Sociology* 34:319–337.

Buckingham, David. 2007. "Selling Childhood? Children and Consumer Culture." *Journal of Children and Media* 1 (1):15–24.

Budig, Michelle J. 2002. "Male Advantage and the Gender Composition of Jobs: Who Rides the Glass Escalator?" *Social Problems* 49 (2):258–277.

Bullard, Robert D. 1993. *Dumping in Dixie: Race, Class, and Environmental Quality*. 2nd ed. Boulder, CO: Westview Press.

———, and Beverly Wright. 2009. *Race, Place, and Environmental Justice after Hurricane Katrina*. Boulder, CO: Westview Press.

Burawoy, Michael. 2005. "For Public Sociology." *American Sociological Review* 70 (February):4–28.

Bureau of Justice Statistics. 2010. "Key Facts at a Glance." Accessible at http://bjs.ojp.usdoj.gov/content/glance/incrt.cfm.

Bureau of Labor Statistics. 2003. "Women at Work: A Visual Essay." *Monthly Labor Review* (October):45–50.

———. 2008a. "Economic News Release: Number of Jobs Held." Accessible at www.bls.gov/news.release/nlsoy.nr0.htm.

———. 2008b. "Spotlight on Statistics: Older Workers." Accessible at http://www.bls.gov/spotlight/2008/older_workers.

———. 2009. "Characteristics of Minimum Wage Workers: 2007." Accessed January 29 (www.bls.gov/cps/minwage2007.htm).

———. 2010. "Record Unemployment among Older Workers Does Not Keep Them Out of the Job Market." *Issues in Labor Statistics* (Summary 10-04, March 2010).

———. 2011. "Union Members—2010." News Release, January 21. Accessible at http://www.bls.gov/news.release/pdf/union2.pdf.

Bureau of the Census. 1975. *Historical Statistics of the United States, Colonial Times to 1970*. Washington, DC: U.S. Government Printing Office.

———. 1994. *Statistical Abstract of the United States, 1994*. Washington, DC: U.S. Government Printing Office.

———. 2003. *Meeting 21st Century Demographic Data Needs—Implementing the American Community Survey*. Washington, DC: U.S. Government Printing Office.

———. 2004a. *Statistical Abstract of the United States, 2004–2005*. Washington, DC: U.S. Government Printing Office.

———. 2004b. "Census 2000 Final Response Rates." Accessed January 16, 2010 (www.census.gov/dmd/www/response/2000response.html).

———. 2005a. *Florida, California and Texas Future Population Growth*, Census Bureau Reports, CB05-52. Washington, DC: U.S. Government Printing Office.

———. 2005b. "American Fact Finder: Places with United States." Accessed December 12 (http://factfinder.census.gov).

———. 2006a. *Statistical Abstract of the United States 2007*. Washington, DC: U.S. Government Printing Office.

———. 2008a. *Statistical Abstract of the United States, 2008*. Washington, DC: U.S. Government Printing Office.

———. 2008b. "Total Midyear Population for the World:1900–2050." (Data updated 3/27/2008.) Accessed April 9 (www.census.gov).

———. 2008c. "America's Families and Living Arrangements 2008." Accessed at www.census.gov/population/www/socdemo/hh-fam/cps2008.html.

———. 2009a. *Statistical Abstract of the United States 2010*. Washington, DC: U.S. Government Printing Office.

———. 2009b. Population Analysis. Accessed at www.census.gov.

———. 2009c. "Historical Tables on Income Inequality." Accessed February 20, 2010 (www.census.gov/hhes/www/income/incomestats.html#incomeineq).

———. 2010a. *Statistical Abstract of the United States 2011*. Washington, DC: U.S. Government Printing Office.

———. 2010b. "America's Families and Living Arrangements: 2010." Released January. Accessible at www.census.gov/population/www/socdemo/hh-fam/cps2010.html.

———. 2010c. "Total Midyear Population for the World: 1950–2050." Updated March 10. Accessed April 20 (www.census.gov/ipc/www/idb/worldpop.php).

———. 2010d. "Historical Income Tables." Accessed April 29, 2011 (http://www.census.gov/hhes/www/income/data/historical/index.html).

———. 2011a. *Statistical Abstract of the United States 2012*. Washington, DC: U.S. Government Printing Office.

———. 2011b. International Data Base (IDB). Accessible at http://www.census.gov/ipc/www/idb/informationGateway.php.

Bures, Frank. 2011. "Can You Hear Us Now?" *Utne Reader* (March–April):8–9, 11.

Burgdorf, Robert L., Jr. 2005. "Americans with Disabilities Act of 1990 (United States)." Pp. 93–101 in *Encyclopedia of Disability*, edited by Gary Albrecht. Thousand Oaks, CA: Sage.

Burger, Jerry M. 2009. "Replicating Milgram: Would People Still Obey Today?" *American Psychologist* 64 (January):1–11.

Burger King. 2009. "Whopper Sacrifice." Accessed February 4 (www.whoppersacrifice.com/).

Burgess, Ernest W. 1925. "The Growth of the City." Pp. 47–62 in *The City*, edited by Robert E. Park, Ernest W. Burgess, and Roderick D. McKenzie. Chicago: University of Chicago Press.

Burns, Melinda. 2010. "Workfare and the Low-Wage Woman." *Miller-McClune* (November–December):76–81.

Butler, Daniel Allen. 1998. *"Unsinkable": The Full Story*. Mechanicsburg, PA: Stackpole Books.

Butler, Robert N. 1990. "A Disease Called Ageism." *Journal of American Geriatrics Society* 38 (February):178–180.

Byrd-Bredbenner, Carol, and Jessica Murray. 2003. "Comparison of the Anthropometric Measurements of Idealized Female Body Images in Media Directed to Men, Women, and Mixed Gender Audiences." *Topics in Clinical Nutrition* 18 (2):117–129.

Bystydzienski, Jill M., and Joti Sekhon. 1999. *Democratization and Women's Grassroots Movements*. Bloomington: Indiana University Press.

C

Calhoun, Craig. 1998. "Community without Propinquity Revisited." *Sociological Inquiry* 68 (Summer):373–397.

———. 2003. "Belonging in the Cosmopolitan Imaginary." *Ethnicities* 3 (December):531–553.

Call, V. R., and Teachman, J. D. 1991. "Military Service and Stability in the Family Life Course." *Military Psychology* 3:233–250.

Cameron, Deborah. 2007. *The Myth of Mars and Venus*. Oxford: Oxford University Press.

Campbell, Mary, Robert Haveman, Gary Sandefur, and Barbara Wolte. 2005. "Economic Inequality and Educational Attainment across a Generation." *Focus* 23 (Spring):11–15.

Cañas, Jesus, Roberto Coronado, and Robert W. Gilman. 2007. "Southwest Economy." March/April. Accessed April 18 (http://dallasfed.org/research/swe/2007/swe0702b.cfm).

Cantril, Hadley. 1940. *The Invasion from Mars: A Study in the Psychology of Panic*. Princeton, NJ: Princeton University Press.

Cantzler, Julia Miller. 2008. "Indian, Child Welfare Act of 1978." Pp. 714–716, vol. 2, in *Encyclopedia of Race, Ethnicity, and Society*, edited by Richard T. Schaefer. Thousand Oaks, CA: Sage.

Caplan, Ronald L. 1989. "The Commodification of American Health Care." *Social Science and Medicine* 28 (11):1139–1148.

Caplow, Theodore, and Louis Hicks. 2002. *Systems of War and Peace*. 2nd ed. Lanham, MD: University Press of America.

Capriccioso, Rob. 2010. "Obama Mentions Tribes as Part of Oil Spill Restoration; Chief Testifies on Mess." *Indian Country Today*, June 23, pp. 1, 2.

Carbon Trust. 2010. "About the Carbon Trust." Accessed April 27 (www.carbontrust.co.uk/about-carbon-trust/pages/default.aspx).

Carey, Anne R., and Karl Gelles. 2010. "What Viewers Enjoy Most about Watching the Super Bowl on TV." *USA Today*, February 5, p. A1; *Gallup Poll* (May):3.

Carlton-Ford, Steve. 2010. "Major Armed Conflicts, Militarization, and Life Chances." *Armed Forces and Society* 36 (October):864–899.

Carr, Nicholas. 2008a. *The Big Switch: Rewiring the World: From Edison to Google*. New York: Norton.

———. 2008b. "Is Google Making Us Stoopid?" *Atlantic* (July/August):56–58, 60, 62–63.

———. 2010. "Tracking Is an Assault on Liberty, with Real Dangers." *Wall Street Journal*, August 7, pp. W1, W2.

Carr, Patrick J., and Maria J. Kefalas. 2009. "The Rural Brain Drain." *Chronicle of Higher Education* (September 25):B7–B9.

Carroll, Joseph. 2006. "Public National Anthem Should Be Sung in English." *Gallup Poll* (May):3.

———. 2007. "Public Divide Over Moral Acceptability of Doctor-Assisted Suicide." Accessed June 18, 2009 (www.galluppoll.com).

Carroll, Rory, and Jonathan Franklin. 2010. "Chile Miners: Rescued Foreman Luis Urzúa's First Interview." *The Guardian*, October 14.

Caruso, Eugene M., Dobromir A. Rahnev, and Mahzarin R. Banaji. 2009. "Using Conjoint Analysis to Detect Discrimination: Revealing Covert Preferences from Overt Choices." *Social Cognition* 27 (1):128–137.

Castañeda, Jorge G. 1995. "Ferocious Differences." *Atlantic Monthly* 276 (July):68–69, 71–76.

Castells, Manuel. 2001. *The Internet Galaxy: Reflections on the Internet, Business, and Society.* New York: Oxford University Press.

———. 2010a. *The Rise of the Network Society.* 2nd ed. With a new preface. Malden, MA: Wiley-Blackwell.

———. 2010b. *The Power of Identity.* 2nd ed. With a new preface. Malden, MA: Wiley-Blackwell.

———. 2010c. *End of Millennium.* 2nd ed. With a new preface. Malden, MA: Wiley-Blackwell.

Cauchon, Dennis. 2009. "Women Gain in Historic Job Shift." *USA Today,* September 3, p. A1.

CBS News. 1979. Transcript of *Sixty Minutes* segment, "I Was Only Following Orders." March 31, pp. 2–8.

Center for Academic Integrity. 2006. *CAI Research.* Accessed January 10 (www.academicintegrity.org).

Center for American Women and Politics. 2010. *Fact Sheet: Women in the U.S. Congress 2010 and Statewide Elective Women 2010.* Rutgers, NJ: CAWP.

Center for Community College Student Engagement. 2009. *Making Connections: Dimensions of Student Engagement* (2009 CCSS Findings). Austin: University of Texas at Austin, Community College Leadership Program. Accessible at www.ccsse.org/publications/national_report_2009/ccsse09_nationalreport.pdf.

Center for Research on Education Outcomes. 2009. *Multiple Choice: Charter School Performances in 16 States.* Palo Alto, CA: CREDO, Stanford University. Accessible at http://credo.stanford.edu.

Center for Responsive Politics. 2010a. "Banking on Becoming President." Accessed April 13 (www.opensecrets.org/pres08/index.php).

———. 2010b. "Banking on Becoming President" and "The Money Behind the Elections." Accessed April 13 (www.opensecrets.org).

Centers for Disease Control and Prevention. 2010. "Binge Drinking among High School Students and Adults—United States, 2009." Washington, DC: CDC. Accessible at http://www.cdc.gov/mmwr/preview/mmwrhtml/mm5939a4.htm?s_cid=mm5939a4_w.

———. 2011a. *HIV in the United States.* Accessed May 24 (www.cdc.gov).

———. 2011b. *Health Disparities and Inequalities Report—United States, 2011.*

Centers for Medicare and Medicaid Services. 2010. "NHE Projections 2009–2019." Accessed April 18 (www.cms.hhs.gov).

Cerulo, Karen A., Janet M. Ruane, and Mary Chagko. 1992. "Technological Ties That Bind: Media Generated Primary Groups." *Communication Research* 19:109–129.

Chalfant, H. Paul, Robert E. Beckley, and C. Eddie Palmer. 1994. *Religion in Contemporary Society.* 3rd ed. Itasca, IL: F. E. Peacock.

Chambliss, William. 1973. "The Saints and the Roughnecks." *Society* 11 (November–December): 24–31.

Chan, Sewell. 2009. "City Unveils Facebook Page to Encourage Condom Use." *New York Times,* February 12, p. A32.

Charles, Susan T., and Laura L. Carstensen. 2009. "Social and Emotional Aging." *Annual Review of Psychology* 61:383–409.

Charness, Gary, and Marie-Claire Villeval. 2009. "Cooperation and Competition in International Experiments in the Field and the Laboratory." *American Economic Review* 99 (3):956–978.

Charter, David, and Jill Sherman. 1996. "Schools Must Teach New Code of Values." *London Times,* January 15, p. 1.

Chase, Randall. 2010. "O'Donnell: 'I'm Not a Witch.'" *Washington Times,* October 4. Accessed March 23 (http://www.washingtontimes.com/news/2010/oct/4/odonnell-im-not-witch/?page=2).

Chase-Dunn, Christopher, and Peter Grimes. 1995. "World-Systems Analysis." Pp. 387–417 in *Annual Review of Sociology,* 1995, edited by John Hagan. Palo Alto, CA: Annual Reviews.

———, Yukio Kawano, and Benjamin D. Brewer. 2000. "Trade Globalization Since 1795: Waves of Integration in the World System." *American Sociological Review* 65 (February):77–95.

Cheng, Shu-Ju Ada. 2003. "Rethinking the Globalization of Domestic Service." *Gender and Society* 17 (2):166–186.

Cherlin, Andrew J. 2003. "Should the Government Promote Marriage?" *Contexts* 2 (Fall):22–29.

———. 2006. On Single Mothers "Doing" Family. *Journal of Marriage and Family* 68 (November):800–803.

———. 2009. *The Marriage-Go-Round: The State of Marriage and the Family in America Today.* New York: Knopf.

———. 2010. *Public and Private Families: An Introduction.* 6th ed. New York: McGraw-Hill.

Chicago Tribune. 1997. "In London, Prince Meets a Pauper, an Ex-Classmate." December 5, p. 19.

Chin, Kolin. 1996. *Chinatown Gangs: Extortion, Enterprise, and Ethnicity.* New York: Oxford University Press.

Choi, Yoonsun, and Benjamin B. Lahey. 2006. "Testing the Model Minority Stereotype: Youth Behaviors across Racial and Ethnic Groups." *Social Science Review* (September):419–452.

Christakis, Nicholas A., and James H. Fowler. 2007. "The Spread of Obesity in a Large Social Network over 32 Years." *New England Journal of Medicine* 357 (July 26):370–379.

———, and James Fowler. 2009. *Connected: The Amazing Power of Social Networks and How They Shape Our Lives.* New York: Harper.

Chronic Poverty Research Centre. 2009. *The Chronic Poverty Report 2008–09: Escaping Poverty Traps.* Geneva: Chronic Poverty Research Centre.

Chu, Henry. 2005. "Tractors Crush Heart of a Nation." *Los Angeles Times,* July 10, p. A9.

Chu, Kathy. 2010. "Vietnam's Market Grows Up." *USA Today,* August 23, p. B3.

Chubb, Catherine, Simone Melis, Louisa Potter, and Raymond Storry. 2008. *The Global Gender Pay Gap.* London: Incomes Data Services.

Chung, Esther K., Leny Mathew, Amy C. Rothkopt, Irma T. Elo, James C. Cayne, and Jennifer F. Culhane. 2009. "Parenting Attitudes and Infant Spanking: The Influence of Childhood Experiences." *Pediatrics* 124 (August):278–286.

Clabaugh, Riche. 2010. "Gay Marriage in the States." *Christian Science Monitor,* January 24, p. 19.

Clark, Burton, and Martin Trow. 1966. "The Organizational Context." Pp. 17–70 in *The Study of College Peer Groups,* edited by Theodore M. Newcomb and Everett K. Wilson. Chicago: Aldine.

Clark, Candace. 1983. "Sickness and Social Control." Pp. 346–365 in *Social Interaction: Readings in Sociology,* 2nd ed., edited by Howard Robboy and Candace Clark. New York: St. Martin's Press.

Clark, Kim. 2010. "Can School Reform Even Really Work?" *US News and World Report* (January):23–26, 30–31.

Clarke, Adele E., Janet K. Shim, Laura Maro, Jennifer Ruth Fusket, and Jennifer R. Fishman. 2003. "Bio Medicalization: Technoscientific Transformations of Health, Illness, and U.S. Biomedicine." *American Sociological Review* 68 (April):161–194.

Clarke, Lee. 2002. "Panic: Myth or Reality?" *Contexts* 1 (Fall):21–26.

Clayton, Mark. 2011. "The New Cyber Arms Race." *Christian Science Monitor,* March 7, pp. 26–71.

Clemmitt, Marcia. 2005. "Intelligent Design." *CQ Researcher* 15 (July 29):637–660.

Clifford, Stephanie. 2008. "Billboards That Look Back." *New York Times,* May 31.

———. 2009a. "Teaching Teenagers about Harassment." *New York Times,* January 27, p. B1.

———. 2009b. "Online 'A Reason to Keep On Going.'" *New York Times,* June 2, pp. D5–D6.

Clinard, Marshall B., and Robert F. Miller. 1998. *Sociology of Deviant Behavior.* 10th ed. Fort Worth, TX: Harcourt Brace.

Clymer, Adam. 2000. "College Students Not Drawn to Voting or Politics, Poll Shows." *New York Times,* January 2, p. A14.

Coates, Rodney. 2008. "Covert Racism in the USA and Globally." *Sociology Compass* 2:208–231.

Cockerham, William C. 2009. *Medical Sociology.* 11th ed. Upper Saddle River, NJ: Prentice Hall.

Cole, Elizabeth S. 1985. "Adoption, History, Policy, and Program." Pp. 638–666 in *A Handbook of Child Welfare,* edited by John Laird and Ann Hartman. New York: Free Press.

Cole, Mike. 1988. *Bowles and Gintis Revisited: Correspondence and Contradiction in Educational Theory.* Philadelphia: Falmer.

Coleman, Isobel. 2004. "The Payoff from Women's Rights." *Foreign Affairs* 83 (May–June):80–95.

Coleman, James William. 2006. *The Criminal Elite: Understanding White-Collar Crime.* 6th ed. New York: Worth.

———, and Donald R. Cressey. 1980. *Social Problems.* New York: Harper and Row.

College Board. 2009. *Trends in College Pricing.* New York: College Board.

Collier, Paul. 2007. *The Bottom Billion.* Oxford: Oxford University Press.

Collins, Daryl, Jonathan Morduch, Stuart Rutherford, and Orlanda Ruthgen. 2009. *Portfolios of the Poor: How the World's Poor Live on $2 a Day.* Princeton, NJ: Princeton University Press.

Collins, Patricia Hill. 2000. *Black Feminist Thought: Knowledge, Consciousness, and the Politics of Empowerment.* Revised 10th anniv. 2nd ed. New York: Routledge.

Collins, Randall. 1975. *Conflict Sociology: Toward an Explanatory Sociology.* New York: Academic Press.

———. 1980. "Weber's Last Theory of Capitalism: A Systematization." *American Sociological Review* 45 (December):925–942.

———. 1986. *Weberian Sociological Theory.* New York: Cambridge University Press.

———. 1995. "Prediction in Macrosociology: The Case of the Soviet Collapse." *American Journal of Sociology* 100 (May):1552–1593.

Colucci, Jim. 2008. "All the World's a Screen." *Watch!* (June):50–53.

Commission on Civil Rights. 1976. *A Guide to Federal Laws and Regulations Prohibiting Sex Discrimination.* Washington, DC: U.S. Government Printing Office.

———. 1981. *Affirmative Action in the 1980s: Dismantling the Process of Discrimination.* Washington, DC: U.S. Government Printing Office.

Commoner, Barry. 1971. *The Closing Circle.* New York: Knopf.

———. 1990. *Making Peace with the Planet.* New York: Pantheon.

———. 2007. "At 90, an Environmentalist from the 70's Still Has Hope." *New York Times,* June 19, p. D2.

Congressional Oversight Panel. 2011. "February Oversight Report: Executive Compensation Restrictions in the Troubled Asset Relief Program." Washington, DC: COP.

Conley, Dalton. 2010. *Being Black, Living in the Red.* 10th anniversary edition. Berkeley: University of California Press.

Connell, R. W. 1987. *Gendered Power: Society, the Person, and Sexual Politics.* Stanford, CA: Stanford University Press.

———. 2002. *Gender.* Cambridge, UK: Polity Press.

———. 2005. *Masculinities.* 2nd ed. Berkeley: University of California Press.

Connelly, Marjorie. 2008. "Dissecting the Changing Electorate." *New York Times,* November 8, sec. WK.

Conner, Thaddieus, and William A. Taggart. 2009. "The Impact of Gaming on the Indian Nations in New Mexico." *Social Science Quarterly* 90 (March):52–70.

Conrad, Peter, ed. 2009a. *The Medicalization of Society: On the Transformation of Human Conditions into Treatable Disorders.* 11th ed. Baltimore, MD: Johns Hopkins University.

———. 2009b. *The Sociology of Health and Illness: Cultural Perspectives.* 8th ed. New York: Worth.

Conrad, Peter, and Kristin K. Barker. 2010. "The Social Construction of Illness: Key Insights and Policy Implications." *Journal of Health and Social Behavior* 51 (5):567–579.

Cooley, Charles. H. 1902. *Human Nature and the Social Order.* New York: Scribner.

Coontz, Stephanie. 2006. "A Pop Quiz on Marriage." *New York Times,* February 19, p. 12.

Cooper, Jeremy. 2005. "Disability Law: Europe." Pp. 444–449 in *Encyclopedia of Disability,* edited by Gary Albrecht. Thousand Oaks, CA: Sage.

Cooper, K., S. Day, A. Green, and H. Ward. 2007. "Maids, Migrants and Occupational Health in the London Sex Industry. *Anthropology and Medicine* 14 (April):41–53.

Corbett, Christianne, Catherine Hill, and Andresse St. Rose. 2008. *Where the Girls Are: The Facts about Gender Equity in Education.* Washington, DC: American Association of University Women.

Cornwell, Benjamin, Edward O. Laumann, and L. Phip Schumm. 2008. "The Social Connectedness of Older Adults: A National Profile." *American Sociological Review* 73 (April):185–203.

Coser, Lewis A. 1977. *Masters of Sociological Thought: Ideas in Historical and Social Context.* 2nd ed. New York: Harcourt, Brace and Jovanovich.

Coser, Rose Laub. 1984. "American Medicine's Ambiguous Progress." *Contemporary Sociology* 13 (January):9–13.

Côté, James E. 2000. *Arrested Adulthood: The Changing Nature of Identity and Maturity in the Late World.* New York: New York University.

Couch, Carl J. 1968. "Collective Behavior: An Examination of Some Stereotypes." *Social Problems* 15:310–322.

———. 1996. *Information Technologies and Social Orders.* Edited with an introduction by David R. Maines and Shing-Ling Chien. New York: Aldine de Gruyter.

Council on Ethical and Judicial Affairs, American Medical Association. 1992. "Decisions Near the End of Life." *Journal of the American Medical Association* 267 (April 22–29):2229–2333.

Counts, D. A. 1977. "The Good Death in Kaliai: Preparation for Death in Western New Britain." *Omega* 7:367–372.

Cox, Gerry R. 2010. *Death and the American Indian.* Omaha, NE: Grief Illustrated Press.

Cox, Oliver C. 1948. *Caste, Class, and Race: A Study in Social Dynamics.* Detroit: Wayne State University Press.

Cox, Rachel S. 2003. "Home Schooling Debate." *CQ Researcher* 13 (January 17):25–48.

Crabtree, Steve. 2010. *Religiosity Highest in World's Poorest Nations.* August 31. Accessible at www.gallup.com.

Cross, Simon, and Barbara Bagilhole. 2002. "Girls' Jobs for the Boys? Men, Masculinity and Non-Traditional Occupations." *Gender, Work, and Organization* 9 (April):204–226.

Croteau, David, and William Hoynes. 2003. *Media/Society: Industries, Images, and Audiences.* 3rd ed. Thousand Oaks, CA: Pine Forge Press.

———, and ———. 2006. *The Business of the Media: Corporate Media and the Public Interest.* 2nd ed. Thousand Oaks, CA: Pine Forge Press.

Croucher, Sheila L. 2004. *Globalization and Belonging: The Politics of Identity in a Changing World.* Lanham, MD: Rowman and Littlefield.

Crouse, Kelly. 1999. "Sociology of the *Titanic.*" *Teaching Sociology Listserv.* May 24.

Crowe, Jerry, and Valli Herman. 2005. "NBA Lists Fashion Do's and Don'ts." *Los Angeles Times,* October 19, pp. A1, A23.

Crumley, Bruce. 2010. "Boardroom Revolution." *Time,* April 26, Global section, pp. 1–2.

Cuff, E. C., W. W. Sharrock, and D. W. Francis, eds. 1990. *Perspectives in Sociology.* 3rd ed. Boston: Unwin Hyman.

Cumming, Elaine, and William E. Henry. 1961. *Growing Old: The Process of Disengagement.* New York: Basic Books.

Currie, Elliot. 1985. *Confronting Crime: An American Challenge.* New York: Pantheon.

———. 1998. *Crime and Punishment in America.* New York: Metropolis Books.

Curry, Timothy Jon. 1993. "A Little Pain Never Hurt Anyone: Athletic Career Socialization and the Normalization of Sports Injury." *Symbolic Interaction* 26 (Fall):273–290.

Curtiss, Susan. 1977. *Genie: A Psycholinguistic Study of a Modern Day "Wild Child."* New York: Academic Press.

———. 1985. "The Development of Human Cerebral Lateralization." Pp. 97–116 in *The Dual Brain,* edited by D. Frank Benson and Eran Zaidel. New York: Guilford Press.

Cushing-Daniels, Brenda, and Sheila R. Zedlewski. 2008. "Tax and Spending Policy and Economic Mobility." Washington, DC: Economic Mobility Project. Also accessible at www.economic-mobility.org/reports_and_research/literature_reviews?id=0004.

D

Dahl, Robert A. 1961. *Who Governs?* New Haven, CT: Yale University Press.

Dahrendorf, Ralf. 1958. "Toward a Theory of Social Conflict." *Journal of Conflict Resolution* 2 (June):170–183.

———. 1959. *Class and Class Conflict in Industrial Sociology.* Stanford, CA: Stanford University Press.

Daley-Harris, Sam, ed. 2002. *Pathways out of Poverty: Innovations in Microfinance for the Poorest Families.* Bloomfield, CT: Komarian Press.

Dalla, Rochelle L., and Wendy C. Gamble. 2001. "Teenage Mothering and the Navajo Reservation: An Examination of Intergovernmental Perceptions and Beliefs." *American Indian Culture and Research Journal* 25 (1):1–19.

Daniel, G. Reginald. 2006. *Race and Multiraciality in Brazil and the United States: Converging Paths?* University Park: Pennsylvania State University Press.

Daniszewski, John. 2003. "Al-Jazeera TV Draws Flak Outside—and Inside—the Arab World." *Los Angeles Times,* January 5, pp. A1, A5.

Danziger, Sandra K. 2010. "The Decline of Cash Welfare and Implications for Social Policy and Poverty." *Annual Review of Sociology* 36:523–545.

Darlin, Damon. 2006. "It's O.K to Fall Behind the Technology Curve." *New York Times,* December 30, p. B6.

Darwin, Charles. 1859. *On the Origin of Species.* London: John Murray.

David, Gary. 2004. "Scholarship on Arab Americans Distorted Past 9/11." *Al Jadid* (Winter–Spring):26–27.

———. 2008. "Arab Americans." Pp. 84–87, vol. 1, in *Encyclopedia of Race, Ethnicity, and Society,* edited by Richard T. Schaefer. Thousand Oaks, CA: Sage.

Davidson, James D., and Ralph E. Pyle. 2011. *Ranking Faiths: Religious Stratification in America.* Lanham, MD: Rowman and Littlefield.

Davies, Christie. 1989. "Goffman's Concept of the Total Institution: Criticisms and Revisions." *Human Studies* 12 (June):77–95.

Davies, Lizzy. 2010. "Sarkozy Admits Rwanda Genocide 'Flaws.'" *Guardian Weekly,* May 3, p. 12.

Davis, Darren W., and Brian D. Silver. 2003. "Stereotype Threat and Race of Interviewer Knowledge." *American Journal of Political Science* 47 (January):33–45.

Davis, Gerald. 2003. *America's Corporate Banks Are Separated by Just Four Handshakes.* Accessed March 7 (www.bus.umich.edu/research/davis.html).

———. 2004. "American Cronyism: How Executive Networks Inflated the Corporate Bubble." *Contexts* (Summer):34–40.

Davis, James A., Tom W. Smith, and Peter V. Marsden. 2009. *General Social Surveys, 1972–2008:*

Cumulative Codebook. Chicago: National Opinion Research Center.

Davis, Kingsley. 1940. "Extreme Social Isolation of a Child." *American Journal of Sociology* 45 (January):554–565.

———. 1947. "A Final Note on a Case of Extreme Isolation." *American Journal of Sociology* 52 (March):432–437.

———. [1949] 1995. *Human Society.* Reprint. New York: Macmillan.

———, and Wilbert E. Moore. 1945. "Some Principles of Stratification." *American Sociological Review* 10 (April):242–249.

Davis, Martha F. 2010. "Abortion Access in the Global Marketplace." *North Carolina Law Review* 88:1657–1685.

Davis, Mike. 2005. *Planet of Slums.* London: Verso.

Davis, Paul K., and Kim Cragin, eds. 2009. *Social Science for Counterterrorism: Putting the Pieces Together.* Santa Monica, CA: RAND.

De Anda, Roberto M. 2004. *Chicanas and Chicanos in Contemporary Society.* 2nd ed. Lanham, MD: Rowman and Littlefield.

Death Penalty Information Center. 2011. "Facts about the Death Penalty." Accessible at www.deathpenaltyinfo.org.

Deegan, Mary Jo, ed. 1991. *Women in Sociology: A Bio-Biographical Sourcebook.* Westport, CT: Greenwood.

———. 2003. "Textbooks, the History of Sociology, and the Sociological Stock of Knowledge." *Sociological Theory* 21 (November):298–305.

Deflem, Mathieu. 2005. "'Wild Beasts without Nationality': The Uncertain Origins of Interpol, 1898–1910." Pp. 275–285 in *Handbook of Transnational Crime and Justice,* edited by Philip Rerchel. Thousand Oaks, CA: Sage.

Deibert, Ronald J., John Palfrey, Rafal Rohozinski, and Jonathan Zittrain. 2008. *Access Denied: The Practice and Policy of Global Internet Filtering.* Cambridge, MA: MIT Press.

Delaney, Kevin J. 2005. "Big Mother Is Watching." *Wall Street Journal,* November 26, pp. A1, A6.

Della Porta, Donatella, and Sidney Tarrow, eds. 2005. *Transnational Protest and Global Activism.* Lanham, MD: Rowman and Littlefield.

DeNavas-Walt, Carmen, Bernadette D. Proctor, and Jessica C. Smith. 2010. "Income, Poverty, and Health Insurance Coverage in the United States: 2009." P60-238 in *Current Population Survey.* Washington, DC: U.S. Government Printing Office.

Denny, Charlotte. 2004. "Migration Myths Hold No Fears." *Guardian Weekly,* February 26, p. 12.

Denzin, Norman K. 2004. "Postmodernism." Pp. 581–583 in *Encyclopedia of Social Theory,* edited by George Ritzer. Thousand Oaks, CA: Sage.

DeParle, Jason. 2009. "The 'W' Word, Re-Engaged." *New York Times,* February 8, Week in Review, p. 1.

Department of Commerce. 2010. "Observations from the Interagency Technical Working Group on Developing a Supplemental Poverty Measure." Accessible at www.census.gov/hhes/www/povmeas/SPM_TWGobservations.pdf.

———. 2011. *NTIA Launches National Broadband Map.* Washington, DC: Department of Commerce.

Department of Education. 2006. *Integrated Postsecondary Education Data Systems, Completions, 1995–2004.* Washington, DC: NCES.

Department of Health and Human Services. 2011a. "TANF: Total Number of Families." As of 1/3/2011. Accessible at www.acf.hhs.gov/programs/ofa/data-reports/caseload/2010/2010_family_tan.htm.

———. 2011b. "AFCARS, Report." Accessed April 6 (www.acf.hhs.gov/programs/cb/stats_research/afcars/tar/report17.htm).

Department of Homeland Security. 2008. "Immigration Enforcement Actions: 2007." In *Annual Report December 2008.* Washington, DC: Department of Homeland Security.

———. 2010. *Haiti Social Media: Disaster Monitoring Initiative.* January 21. Washington, DC: U.S. Department of Homeland Security.

Department of Justice. 2000. *The Civil Liberties Act of 1988: Redress for Japanese Americans.* Accessed June 29 (www.usdoj.gov/crt/ora/main.html).

———. 2008. "Hate Crime Statistics, 2007." Accessible at www.Fbi.gov/ucr/ucr.htm.

———. 2009. *2008 Crime in the United States.* (Uniform Crime Report). Accessible at http://www.fbi.gov/ucr/cius2008/index.html.

———. 2010. "Hate Crime Statistics." Accessed November 28 (http://www2.fbi.gov/ucr/hc2009/data/table_01.html).

Department of Labor. 1995a. *Good for Business: Making Full Use of the Nation's Capital.* Washington, DC: U.S. Government Printing Office.

———. 1995b. *A Solid Investment: Making Full Use of the Nation's Human Capital.* Washington, DC: U.S. Government Printing Office.

———. 2011. "Labor Force Statistics: Table 3." Accessed March 21, 2011 (www.bls.gov/cps/tables.htm).

Department of State. 2010a. "Total Adoptions to the United States." Accessed March 31 (http://adoption.state.gov/news/total_chart.html?css=print).

———. 2010b. "Trafficking in Persons: Tier Placements." Accessed March 5, 2011 (http://www.state.gov/g/tip/rls/tiprpt/2010/142755/htm).

Desai, Manisha. 1996. "If Peasants Build Their Own Dams, What Would the State Have Left to Do?" Pp. 209–224, vol. 19, in *Research in Social Movements, Conflicts and Change,* edited by Michael Dobkowski and Isidor Wallimann. Greenwich, CT: JAI Press.

Desai, Rani A., Suchitra Krishnan-Sarin, Dana Cavallo, and Marc N. Potenza. 2010. "Video-Gaming among High School Students: Health Correlates, Gender Differences, and Problematic Gaming." *Pediatrics* 126 (November 15):1414–1424.

Deutsch, Francine M. 2007. "Undoing Gender." *Gender and Society* 21 (February):106–127.

Devitt, James. 1999. *Framing Gender on the Campaign Trail: Women's Executive Leadership and the Press.* New York: Women's Leadership Conference.

Dewan, Shaila. 2010. "To Court Blacks, Foes of Abortion Make Racial Case." *New York Times,* February 27, pp. A1, A13.

Diamond, Jared. 2003. "Globalization, Then." *Los Angeles Times,* September 14, pp. M1, M3.

Diamond, Shari Seidman, and Mary R. Rose. 2005. "Real Juries." Pp. 255–284 in *Annual Review of Law and Social Science 2005.* Palo Alto, CA: Annual Reviews.

Diefenbach, Donald L., and Mark D. West. 2007. "Television and Attitudes toward Mental Health Issues: Cultivation Analysis and the Third Person Effect." *Journal of Community Psychology* 35 (2):181–195.

Diehl, William C., and Esther Prins. 2008. "Unintentional Outcomes in Second Life: Intercultural Literacy and Cultural Identity in a Virtual World." *Language and Intercultural Communication* 8(2):101–116.

DiFonzo, Nicholas, and Prashant Bordia. 2007. *Rumor Psychology: Social and Organizational Approaches.* Washington, DC: American Psychological Association.

Dillon, Sam. 2004. "Education Can Be Long, Hard Haul for Nation's Rural Kids." *Chicago Tribune,* May 28, p. 13.

———. 2009. "As More Charter Schools Unionize, Educators Debate the Effect." *New York Times,* July 27, pp. A1, A14.

DiMaggio, Paul, Eszter Hargittai, W. Russell Neuman, and John P. Robinson. 2001. "Social Implications of the Internet." Pp. 307–336 in *Annual Review of Sociology, 2001,* edited by Karen S. Cook and John Hogan. Palo Alto, CA: Annual Reviews.

DiPrete, Thomas A., Gregory M. Eirich, and Matthew Pittinsky. 2010. "Compensation Benchmarking, Leapfrogs, and the Surge in Executive Pay." *American Journal of Sociology* 115 (May):1671–1712.

Disaster Research Center. 2011. "About the DRC." Accessed April 25 (www.udel.edu/DRC/aboutus/about.html).

Dobbin, Frank, and Jiwook Jung. 2010. "Corporate Board Gender Diversity and Stock Performance: The Competence Gap on Institutional Investor Bias?" *North Carolina Law Review* 89.

Dodds, Klaus. 2000. *Geopolitics in a Changing World.* Harlow, UK: Pearson Education.

Domhoff, G. William. 1978. *Who Really Rules? New Haven and Community Power Reexamined.* New Brunswick, NJ: Transaction.

———. 2010. *Who Rules America?* 6th ed. New York: McGraw-Hill.

Dominick, Joseph R. 2009. *The Dynamics of Mass Communication: Media in the Digital Age.* 10th ed. New York: McGraw-Hill.

Donadio, Rachel. 2009. "Facebook 'Fans' of the Mafia May Be More, Authorities Say." *New York Times,* January 20, pp. A1, A8.

Donnelly, Sally B. 2007. "Growing Younger." *Time* (January bonus section):A13–A14.

Doress, Irwin, and Jack Nusan Porter. 1977. *Kids in Cults: Why They Join, Why They Stay, Why They Leave.* Brookline, MA: Reconciliation Associates.

Dotson, Floyd. 1991. "Community." P. 55 in *Encyclopedic Dictionary of Sociology.* 4th ed. Guilford, CT: Dushkin.

Dougherty, Conor. 2011. "Population Leaves Heartland Behind." *Wall Street Journal,* April 11, p. A6.

Dougherty, Kevin, and Floyd M. Hammack. 1992. "Education Organization." Pp. 535–541 in *Encyclopedia of Sociology,* vol. 2, edited by Edgar F. Borgatta and Marie L. Borgatta. New York: Macmillan.

Downey, Liam, and Brian Hawkins. 2008. "Race, Income, and Environmental Inequality in the United States." *Sociological Perspectives* 50 (4):759–781.

Dreifus, Claudia. 2003. "A Conversation with Lee Clarke." *New York Times,* May 20, Science Times section, p. 2.

———. 2004. "A Sociologist with an Advanced Degree in Calamity." *New York Times,* September 7, p. D2.

———. 2005. "A Sociologist Confronts 'the Messy Stuff' of Race, Genes and Disease." *New York Times,* October 18.

DuBois, W. E. B. [1899] 1995. *The Philadelphia Negro: A Social Study.* Philadelphia: University of Pennsylvania Press.

———. [1900] 1969. "To the Nations of the World." Pp. 19–23 in *An ABC of Color,* edited by W. E. B. DuBois. New York: International Publishers.

———. [1903] 1961. *The Souls of Black Folks: Essays and Sketches.* New York: Fawcett.

———. [1903] 2003. *The Negro Church.* Walnut Creek, CA: AltaMira Press.

———. [1909] 1970. *The Negro American Family.* Atlanta University. Reprinted 1970. Cambridge, MA: MIT Press.

———. [1935] 1962. *Black Reconstruction in America 1860–1880.* New York: Athenaeum.

———. [1940] 1968. *Dusk of Dawn.* New York: Harcourt, Brace. Reprint. New York: Schocken Books.

Dukić, Vanja, Hedibert F. Lopes, and Nicholas G. Polson. 2011. "Tracking Flu Epidemics Using Google Flu Trends and Particle Learning." Accessible at http://faculty.chicagobooth.edu/nicholas.polson/research/papers/Track.pdf.

Dundas, Susan, and Miriam Kaufman. 2000. "The Toronto Lesbian Family Study." *Journal of Homosexuality* 40 (20):65–79.

Duneier, Mitchell. 1994a. "On the Job, but Behind the Scenes." *Chicago Tribune,* December 26, pp. 1, 24.

———. 1994b. "Battling for Control." *Chicago Tribune,* December 28, pp. 1, 8.

Dunlap, Riley E. 2010. "At 40, Environmental Movement Endures with Less Consensus." April 22. Accessed April 27 (www.gallup.com/poll/127487/Environmental-Movement-Endures-Less-Consensus.aspx?version=print).

———, and Angela G. Mertig. 1991. "The Evolution of the U.S. Environmental Movement from 1970 to 1990: An Overview." *Society of National Resources* 4 (July–September):209–218.

Dunne, Gillian A. 2000. "Opting into Motherhood: Lesbians Blurring the Boundaries and Transforming the Meaning of Parenthood and Kinship." *Gender and Society* 14 (February):11–35.

Durden, T. Elizabeth, and Robert A. Hummer. 2006. "Access to Healthcare among Working-Aged Hispanic Adults in the United States." *Social Science Quarterly* 87 (December):1319–1343.

Durex. 2007. "The Face of Global Sex 2007—First Sex: An Opportunity of a Lifetime." Accessible at http://www.durexnetwork.org/SiteCollectionDocuments/Research%20%20Face%20of%20Global%20Sex%202007.pdf.

Durkheim, Émile. [1893] 1933. *Division of Labor in Society.* Translated by George Simpson. Reprint. New York: Free Press.

———. [1895] 1964. *The Rules of Sociological Method.* Translated by Sarah A. Solovay and John H. Mueller. Reprint. New York: Free Press.

———. [1897] 1951. *Suicide.* Translated by John A. Spaulding and George Simpson. Reprint. New York: Free Press.

———. [1912] 2001. *The Elementary Forms of Religious Life.* A new translation by Carol Cosman. New York: Oxford University Press.

Duster, Troy. 2002. "Sociological Stranger in the Land of the Human Genome Project." *Contexts* 1 (Fall):69–70.

Dutta, Soumitra, and Irene Mia. 2009. *The Global Information Technology Report 2008–2009.* New York: Palgrave Macmillan.

———, and ———. 2010. *The Global Information Technology Report 2009–2010.* Geneva: World Economic Forum and INSEAD. Accessible at http://networkedreadiness.com/gitr/main/fullreport/index.html.

Dwyer, Jim. 2011. "Dizzying Price for Seeking Death Penalty." *New York Times,* June 3, p. A15.

Dzidzienyo, Anani. 1987. "Brazil." In *International Handbook on Race and Race Relations,* edited by Jay A. Sigler. New York: Greenwood Press.

F

Eaton, Leslie. 2007. "Urban to Care, Storm Evacuees Give Farm a Try." *New York Times,* April 28, pp. A1, A9.

Ebaugh, Helen Rose Fuchs. 1988. *Becoming an Ex: The Process of Role Exit.* Chicago: University of Chicago Press.

Eby, Lillian T., Charleen P. Maher, and Marcus M. Butts. 2010. "The Intersection of Work and Family Life: The Role of Affect." *Annual Review of Psychology* 61:599–622.

Eckenwiler, Mark. 1995. "In the Eyes of the Law." *Internet World* (August):74, 76–77.

Economic Mobility Project. 2009. *Findings from a National Survey and Focus Groups on Economic Mobility.* Washington, DC: Pew Charitable Trusts.

The Economist. 2003. "The One Where Pooh Goes to Sweden." (April 5):59.

———. 2004. "Battle on the Home Front." (February 21):8–10.

———. 2005a. "The Policeman's Dilemma." 377 (October 15):58–59.

———. 2005b. "We Are Tous Québécois." (January 8):39.

———. 2005c. "Behind the Digital Divide." (March 2):22–25.

———. 2008a. "A Ravenous Dragon: A Special Report on China's Quest for Resources." (March 15):1–22.

———. 2008b. "Following the Crowd." (September 6):10–11.

———. 2009a. "Burgeoning Bourgeoisie." (February 14):1–22.

———. 2009b. "Serener Streets." (August 29):28–29.

———. 2010a. "The Future Is Another Country." (July 24).

———. 2010b. "Plus One Country." (September 4):46.

———. 2010c. "The Dark Side." (September 11):15.

———. 2010d. "The Strange Death of Social-Democratic Sweden." (September 18):16–17.

———. 2011a. "The 9-Billion-People Question." (February 26):1–16.

———. 2011b. "China's Population: The Most Surprising Demographic Crisis." (May 7):43–44.

Edmans, Alex, and Xavier Gabaix. 2010. "What's Right, What's Wrong, and What's Fixable." *Pathways* (Summer):13–16.

Eggen, Dan. 2009. "AARP's Dual Role." *Washington Post National Weekly Edition* 27 (November 2):11.

Ehrenreich, Barbara. 2001. *Nickel and Dimed: On (Not)Getting By in America.* New York: Metropolitan.

———. 2009. "Is It Now a Crime to Be Poor?" *New York Times,* August 2.

Ehrlich, Paul R. 1968. *The Population Bomb.* New York: Ballantine.

———, and Anne H. Ehrlich. 1990. *The Population Explosion.* New York: Simon and Schuster.

——— and Katherine Ellison. 2002. "A Looming Threat We Won't Face." *Los Angeles Times,* January 20, p. M6.

Ellison, Brandy. 2008. "Tracking." Pp. 301–304, vol. 2, in *Encyclopedia of Race, Ethnicity, and Society,* edited by Richard T. Schaefer. Thousand Oaks, CA: Sage.

Ellison, Jesse. 2008. "A New Grip on Life." *Newsweek* 152 (December 15):64.

Ellison, Nicole, Charles Stein Field, and Cliff Lampe. 2007. "The Benefits of Facebook 'Friends': Exploring the Relationship between College Students' Use of Online Social Networks and Social Capital." *Journal of Computer-Mediated Communication* 12 (4):1143–1168.

Ellison, Ralph. 1952. *Invisible Man.* New York: Random House.

El Nasser, Haya, and Paul Overberg. 2009. "U.S. Making Sure Census Isn't Overcounted." *USA Today,* January 16.

Ely, Robin J. 1995. "The Power of Demography: Women's Social Construction of Gender Identity at Work." *Academy of Management Journal* 38 (3):589–634.

Embree, Ainslie. 2003. "Religion." Pp. 101–220 in *Understanding Contemporary India,* edited by Sumit Ganguly and Neil DeVotta. Boulder, CO: Lynne Rienner.

Engardio, Pete. 1999. "Activists without Borders." *BusinessWeek,* October 4, pp. 144–145, 148, 150.

Engels, Friedrich [1884] 1959. "The Origin of the Family, Private Property, and the State." Pp. 392–394, excerpted in *Marx and Engels: Basic Writings on Politics and Philosophy,* edited by Lewis Feuer. Garden City, NY: Anchor Books.

Ennis, Sharon R., Merarys Rios-Vargas, and Nora G. Albert. 2011. *The Hispanic Population: 2010.* 2010 Census Brief BR-04. Washington, DC: U.S. Government Printing Office.

Entine, Jon, and Martha Nichols. 1996. "Blowing the Whistle on Meaningless 'Good Intentions.'" *Chicago Tribune,* June 20, sec. 1, p. 21.

Epstein, Cynthia Fuchs. 1999. "The Major Myth of the Women's Movement." *Dissent* (Fall):83–111.

Epstein, Robert. 2005. "Psychology's Top 10 Misguided Ideas." *Psychology Today* 38 (January–February):55–58, 60.

Erikson, Kai. 1966. *Wayward Puritans: A Study in the Sociology of Deviance.* New York: Wiley.

———. 1986. "On Work and Alienation." *American Sociological Review* 51 (February):1–8.

Esbenshade, Jill. 2008. "Giving Up Against the Global Economy: New Developments in the Anti-Sweatshops Movement." *Critical Sociology* 34 (3):453–470.

Escárcega, Sylvia. 2008. "Mexico." Pp. 898–902, vol. 2, in *Encyclopedia of Race, Ethnicity, and Society,* edited by Richard T. Schaefer. Thousand Oaks, CA: Sage.

Etaugh, Claire. 2003. "Witches, Mothers and Others: Females in Children's Books." *Hilltopics* (Winter):10–13.

Etzioni, Amitai. 1964. *Modern Organization.* Englewood Cliffs, NJ: Prentice Hall.

———. 1965. *Political Unification.* New York: Holt, Rinehart and Winston.

European Metalworkers' Federation. 2010. "What Is Precious Work?" Accessed March 1, 2011 (www.emf-fem.org).

Evergeti, Venetia, and Elisabetta Zontini. 2006. "Introduction: Some Critical Reflections on Social Capital, Migration and Transnational Families." *Ethnic and Racial Studies* 29 (November):1025–1039.

F

Facebook. 2011. Statistics. Accessed January 21 (www.facebook.com/press/info.php?statistics).

Fairtrade Foundation. 2010. "Retail Products." Accessed Jan. 5 (www.fairtrade.org.uk/products/retail_products/default.aspx).

Faith, Nazila. 2005. "Iranian Cleric Turns Blogger in Campaign for Reform." *New York Times,* January 16, p. 4.

Fallows, Deborah. 2006. *Pew Internet Project Data.* Washington, DC: Pew Internet and American Life Project.

Faris, Robert, and Nart Villeneuve. 2008. "Measuring Global Internet Filtering." Pp. 5–56 in *Access Denied: The Practice and Policy of Global Internet Filtering,* edited by Ronald Deibert, John Palfrey, Rafal Rohozinski, and Jonathan Zittrain. Cambridge, MA: MIT Press.

Farley, Maggie. 2004. "U.N. Gay Policy Is Assailed." *Los Angeles Times,* April 9, p. A3.

Farley, Melissa, and Victor Malarek. 2008. "The Myth of the Victimless Crime." *New York Times,* March 12, p. A27.

Farr, Grant M. 1999. *Modern Iran.* New York: McGraw-Hill.

Farrell, Amy, and Jack McDevitt. 2010. "Identifying and Measuring Racial Profiling by the Police." *Sociology Compass* 4:77–88.

Farrell, Dan, and James C. Petersen. 2010. "The Growth of Internet Research Methods and the Reluctant Sociologist." *Alpha Kappa Delta* 80 (February):114–125.

Fausset, Richard. 2003. "Sikhs Mark New Year, Fight Post-September 11 Bias." *Los Angeles Times,* April 14, pp. B1, B7.

———. 2009. "Assisted-Suicide Debate Heats Up." *Los Angeles Times,* February 27, pp. A1, A20.

Favreault, Melissa. 2008. "Discrimination and Economic Mobility." Washington, DC: Economic Mobility Project. Also accessible at www.economicmobility.org/reports_and_research/literature_reviews?id=0004.

Feagin, Joe R. 1989. *Minority Group Issues in Higher Education: Learning from Qualitative Research.* Norman: Center for Research on Minority Education, University of Oklahoma.

———, Harnán Vera, and Nikitah Imani. 1996. *The Agony of Education: Black Students at White Colleges and Universities.* New York: Routledge.

Featherman, David L., and Robert M. Hauser. 1978. *Opportunity and Change.* New York: Aeodus.

Federal Trade Commission. 2010. "Protecting Consumer Privacy in an Era of Rapid Change: A Proposed Framework for Businesses and Policymakers." Accessible at http://www.ftc.gov/os/2010/12/101201privacyreport.pdf.

Felson, David, and Akis Kalaitzidis. 2005. "A Historical Overview of Transnational Crime."

Pp. 3–19 in *Handbook of Transnational Crime and Justice,* edited by Philip Reichel. Thousand Oaks, CA: Sage.

Feminist Majority Foundation. 2007. "Feminists Are the Majority." Accessed February 25 (www.feminist.org).

Ferber, Abby L., and Michael S. Kimmel. 2008. "The Gendered Face of Terrorism." *Sociology Compass* 2:870–887.

Ferree, Myra Marx, and David A. Merrill. 2000. "Hot Movements, Cold Cognition: Thinking about Social Movements in Gendered Frames." *Contemporary Society* 29 (May):454–462.

Feuer, Lewis S. 1989. *Marx and Engels: Basic Writings on Politics and Philosophy.* New York: Anchor Books.

Fiala, Robert. 1992. "Postindustrial Society." Pp. 1512–1522 in *Encyclopedia of Sociology,* vol. 3, edited by Edgar F. Borgatta and Marie L. Borgatta. New York: Macmillan.

Field, John. 2008. *Social Capital.* 2nd ed. London: Routledge.

Fields, Jason. 2004. "America's Families and Living Arrangements: 2003." *Current Population Reports,* ser. P-20, no. 553. Washington, DC: U.S. Government Printing Office.

Fieser, Ezra. 2009. "What Price for Good Coffee?" *Time,* October 5, pp. 61–62.

Fiji TV. 2010. Home Page. Accessed January 17 (www.fijitv.com.fj).

File, Thom, and Sarah Crissey. 2010. "Voting and Registration in the Election of November 2008." *Current Population Reports,* ser. P-20, no. 562.

Finch, Emily, and Vanessa E. Munro. 2005. "Juror Stereotypes and Blame Attribution in Rape Cases Involving Intoxicants." *British Journal of Criminology* 45 (June):25–38.

———, and ———. 2007. "The Demon Drink and the Demonized Woman: Socio-Sexual Stereotypes and Responsibility Attribution in Rape Trials Involving Intoxicants." 16 (4):591–614.

———, and ———. 2008. "Lifting the Veil: The Use of Focus Groups and Trial Simulations in Legal Research." *Journal of Law and Society* 35:30–51.

Fine, Gary Alan, and Bill Ellis. 2011. *The Global Grapevine: Why Rumors of Terrorism, Immigration, and Trade Matter.* New York: Oxford University Press.

Fine, Gary C. 2008. " Robbers Cave." Pp. 1163–1164, vol. 3, in *Encyclopedia of Race, Ethnicity, and Society,* edited by Richard T. Schaefer. Thousand Oaks, CA: Sage.

Finkel, Steven E., and James B. Rule. 1987. "Relative Deprivation and Related Psychological Theories of Civil Violence: A Critical Review." *Research in Social Movements* 9:47–69.

Finley, Nancy J. 2010. "Skating Femininity: Gender Maneuvering in Women's Roller Derby." *Journal of Contemporary Ethnography* 39 (4):359–387.

Fiola, Jan. 2008. "Brazil." Pp. 200–204, vol. 2, in *Encyclopedia of Race, Ethnicity, and Society,* edited by Richard T. Schaefer. Thousand Oaks, CA: Sage.

Fishman, Ted C. 2010a. *Shock of Gray.* New York: Scribner.

———. 2010b. "The Old World." *New York Times Magazine* (October 17):48–53.

Fiss, Peer C., and Paul M. Hirsch. 2005. "The Discourse of Globalization: Framing of an Emerging Concept." *American Sociological Review* (February):29–52.

Fitchett, George. 1980. "It's Time to Bury the Stage Theory of Death and Dying." *Oncology Nurse Exchange II* (Fall).

Fitzgerald, Kathleen J. 2008. "White Privilege." Pp. 1403–1405, vol. 3, in *Encyclopedia of Race, Ethnicity, and Society,* edited by Richard T. Schaefer. Thousand Oaks, CA: Sage.

Fitzpatrick, Maureen J., and Barbara J. McPherson. 2010. "Coloring within the Lines: Gender Stereotypes in Contemporary Coloring Books." *Sex Roles* 62:127–137.

Flacks, Richard. 1971. *Youth and Social Change.* Chicago: Markham.

Fletcher, Connie. 1995. "On the Line: Women Cops Speak Out." *Chicago Tribune Magazine,* February 19, pp. 14–19.

Flora, Cornelia Butter, and Jan L. Flora, with Susan Fey. 2004. *Rural Communities: Legacy and Change.* 2nd ed. Boulder, CO: Westview Press.

Flynn, Laurie J. 2008. "MySpace Mind-Set Finally Shows Up at the Office." *New York Times,* April 9, p. H7.

Fonseca, Felicia. 2008. "Dine College on Quest to Rename Navajo Cancer Terms." *News from Indian Country* 22 (January 7):11.

Francis, David. 2010. "Homeschoolers Seek Asylum in US." *Christian Science Monitor,* March 8, p. 12.

Frank, Robert H. 2010. "A Remedy Worse than the Disease." *Pathways* (Summer):17–21.

Franke, Richard Herbert, and James D. Kaul. 1978. "The Hawthorne Experiments: First Statistical Interpretation." *American Sociological Review* 43 (October):623–643.

Franklin, John Hope, and Evelyn Brooks Higginbotham. 2011. *From Slavery to Freedom.* 9th ed. New York: McGraw-Hill.

Franklin, Jonathan. 2010. "Chilean Miners Get Media Training to Prepare for Life above Ground." *The Guardian,* September 22.

———. 2011. *33 Men: Inside the Miraculous Survival and Dramatic Rescue of the Chilean Miners.* New York: Putnam Adult.

FreeBabarAhmad. 2011. "Home page." Accessed April 22 (www.freebabarahmad.com).

Freedom House. 2011. *Freedom in the World 2011.* Washington, DC: Freedom House.

Freeman, Jo. 1973. "The Origins of the Women's Liberation Movement." *American Journal of Sociology* 78 (January):792–811.

———. 1975. *The Politics of Women's Liberation.* New York: McKay.

Freese, Jeremy. 2008. "Genetics and the Social Science Explanation of Individual Outcomes." *American Journal of Sociology* 114 (Suppl.):51–535.

Freidson, Eliot. 1970. *Profession of Medicine.* New York: Dodd, Mead.

French, Howard W. 2000. "The Pretenders." *New York Times Magazine,* December 3, pp. 86–88.

———. 2004. "China's Textbooks Twist and Omit History." *New York Times,* December 6, p. A10.

———. 2008. "Lines of Grinding Poverty, Untouched by China's Boom." *New York Times,* January 13, p. 4.

Freudenburg, William, and Robert Gramling. 2010. *Blowout in the Gulf: The BP Oil Spill Disaster and the Future of Energy in America.* Cambridge: MIT Press.

Freudenburg, William R. 2005. "Seeing Science, Courting Conclusions: Reexamining the Intersection of Science, Corporate Cash, and the Law." *Sociological Forum* 20 (March):3–33.

Freudenheim, Milt. 2005. "Help Wanted: Oldest Workers Please Apply." *New York Times,* March 23, pp. A1, C3.

Frey, William H. 2011. *A Demographic Tipping Point among America's Three-Year-Olds.* February 7. Accessible at http://www.brookings.edu/opinions/2011/0207_population_frey.aspx?p=1.

Fridlund, Alan J., Paul Erkman, and Harriet Oster. 1987. "Facial Expressions of Emotion; Review of Literature 1970–1983." Pp. 143–224 in *Nonverbal Behavior and Communication,* 2nd ed., edited by Aron W. Seigman and Stanley Feldstein. Hillsdale, NJ: Erlbaum.

Friedan, Betty. 1963. *The Feminine Mystique.* New York: Dell.

Friedman, Louis. 2010. "NASA's Down-to-Earth Problems." *Star-Telegram* (Fort Worth), March 28. Accessible at http://www.star-telegram.com/2010/03/28/2072608/friedman-nasas-down-to-earth-problem.html.

Friends of the Congo. 2011. "Coltan: What You Should Know." Accessed May 21 (www.friendsofthecongo.org/new/coltan.php).

Fudge, Judy, and Rosemary Owens, eds. 2006. *Precarious Work, Women, and the New Economy: The Challenge to Legal Norms.* Oxford, UK: Hart.

Furstenberg, Frank F. 2007. "The Making of the Black Family: Race and Class in Qualitative Studies in the Twentieth Century." *Annual Review of Sociology* 33:429–448.

———, and Andrew Cherlin. 1991. *Divided Families: What Happens to Children When Parents Part.* Cambridge, MA: Harvard University Press.

Furstenberg, Sheela Kennedy, Jr., Vonnie C. McCloyd, Rubén G. Rumbaut, and Richard A. Setterstein, Jr. 2004. "Growing Up Is Harder to Do." *Contexts* 3:33–41.

G

Gabriel, Trip. 2010. "Despite Push, Success at Charter Schools Is Mixed." *New York Times,* May 1, pp. A1, A24–A25.

Gailey, Robert. 2007. "As History Repeats Itself, Unexpected Developments Move Us Forward." *Journal of Rehabilitation Research and Development* 44 (4):vii–xiv.

Galbraith, John Kenneth. 1977. *The Age of Uncertainty.* Boston: Houghton Mifflin.

Gale Encyclopedia of Associations: National Organizations of the U.S. 2010. Farmington Hills, MI: Gale.

Gallagher, Kevin P. 2009. "Economic Globalization and the Environment." *Annual Review of Environmental Resources* 34:279–304.

Gallup. 2009a. "Religion." Accessed April 9 (www.gallup.com).

———. 2009b. "Military and National Defense." Accessed April 17 (www.gallup.com/poll/1666/military-national-defense-aspx).

———. 2011a. *Religion.* Accessed March 27 (www.gallup.com).

———. 2011b. *Party Affiliations: 2004–2011.* Accessed April 11 (www.gallup.com/poll/15370/Party-Affiliation.aspx?version=print).

Gallup Opinion Index. 1978. "Religion in America, 1977–1978." 145 (January).

Gamson, Joshua. 1989. "Silence, Death, and the Invisible Enemy: AIDS Activism and Social Movement 'Newness.'" *Social Problems* 36 (October):351–367.

Gans, Herbert J. 1991. *People, Plans, and Policies: Essays on Poverty, Racism, and Other National Urban Problems.* New York: Columbia University Press and Russell Sage Foundation.

———.1995. *The War against the Poor: The Underclass and Antipoverty Policy.* New York: Basic Books.

Garcia-Moreno, Claudia, Henrica A. F. M. Jansen, Mary Ellsberg, Lori Heise, and Charlotte Watts. 2005. *WHO Multi-Country Study on Women's Health and Domestic Violence against Women.* Geneva, Switzerland: WHO.

Gardner, Gary, Erik Assadourian, and Radhika Sarin. 2004. "The State of Consumption Today." Pp. 3–21 in *State of the World 2004,* edited by Brian Halweil and Lisa Mastny. New York: Norton.

Gardner, Marilyn. 2003. "This View of Seniors Just Doesn't 'Ad' Up." *Christian Science Monitor,* January 15, p. 15.

Garfinkel, Harold. 1956. "Conditions of Successful Degradation Ceremonies." *American Journal of Sociology* 61 (March):420–424.

Garner, Roberta. 1996. *Contemporary Movements and Ideologies.* New York: McGraw-Hill.

———. 1999. "Virtual Social Movements." Presented at Zaldfest: A conference in honor of Mayer Zald. September 17, Ann Arbor, MI.

Garreau, Joel. 1991. *Edge City: Life on the New Frontier.* New York: Doubleday.

Garrett-Peters, Raymond. 2009. "'If I Don't Have to Work Anymore, Who Am I?': Job Loss and Collaborative Self-Concept Repair." *Journal of Contemporary Ethnography* 38 (5):547–583.

Gaudin, Sharon. 2009. "Facebook Has Whopper of a Problem with Burger King Campaign." *Computerworld,* January 15.

Gauthier-Billars, David, and Charles Forelle. 2010. "Burqa Is Banned in France." *Wall Street Journal,* September 15, pp. A1, A12.

Gay, Lesbian and Straight Education Network. 2010. "About GLSEN." Accessed April 11 (www.glsen.org).

Gecas, Viktor. 2004. "Socialization, Sociology of." Pp. 14525–14530 in *International Encyclopedia of the Social and Behavioral Sciences,* edited by Neil J. Smelser and Paul B. Baltes. Cambridge, MA: Elsevier.

Gentile, Carmen. 2009. "Student Fights Record of 'Cyberbullying.'" *New York Times,* February 8, p. 20.

Gentleman, Amelia. 2006. "Bollywood Captivated by the Call Centre Culture." *Guardian Weekly,* June 2, p. 17.

———. 2007. "Young Sikh Men Get Haircuts, Annoying Their Elders." *New York Times,* March 29, p. A3.

Gerson, Kathleen, and Jerry A. Jacobs. 2004. "The Work-Home Crunch." *Contexts* 3 (Fall):29–37.

Gerth, H. H., and C. Wright Mills. 1958. *From Max Weber: Essays in Sociology.* New York: Galaxy.

Gertner, Jon. 2005. "Our Ratings, Ourselves." *New York Times Magazine,* April 10, pp. 34–41, 56, 58, 64–65.

Gibbs, Deborah A., Sandra L. Mortin, Lawrence L. Kupper, and Ruby E. Johnson. 2007. "Child Maltreatment in Enlisted Soldiers' Families during Combat-Related Deployments." *Journal of the American Medical Association* 298 (5):528–535.

Gibbs, Nancy. 1993. "Rx for Death." *Time,* May 31, pp. 34–39.

——— 2009. "What Women Want Now." *Time* 174 (16):24–33.

Giddens, Anthony. 1991. *Modernity and Self-Identity: Self and Society in the Late Modern Age.* Cambridge, UK: Polity.

Giddings, Paul J. 2008. *Ida: A Sword among Lions.* New York: Amistad.

Gilley, Brian Joseph. 2006. *Becoming Two-Spirit: Gay Identity and Social Acceptance in Indian Country.* Lincoln: University of Nebraska Press.

Gilsdorf, Ethan. 2010. "A Virtual World That Breaks Real Barriers." *Christian Science Monitor,* September 6, pp. 36–37.

Giordano, Peggy C. 2003. "Relationships in Adolescence." Pp. 257–281 in *Annual Review of Sociology, 2003,* edited by Karen S. Cook and John Hagan. Palo Alto, CA: Annual Reviews.

———, Stephen A. Cernkovich, and Alfred DeMaris. 1993. "The Family and Peer Relations of Black Adolescents." *Journal of Marriage and Family* 55 (May): 277–287.

Giroux, Henry A. 1988. *Schooling and the Struggle for Public Life: Critical Pedagogy in the Modern Age.* Minneapolis: University of Minnesota Press.

Gitlin, Todd. 2002. *Media Unlimited: How the Torrent of Images and Sounds Overwhelms Our Lives.* New York: Henry Holt.

Glascock, Anthony P. 1990. "By Any Other Name, It Is Still Killing: A Comparison of the Treatment of the Elderly in American and Other Societies." Pp. 44–56 in *The Cultural Context of Aging: Worldwide Perspective,* edited by Jay Sokolovsky. New York: Bergen and Garvey.

Glater, Jonathan D. 2003. "Legal Research? Get Me Sushi with Footnotes." *New York Times,* October 22, p. A1.

Glazer, Susan. 2010. "Evaluating Microfinance." *LQ Global Research* 4 (April).

Glenn, David. 2007. "Anthropologists in a War Zone: Scholars Debate Their Role." *Chronicle of Higher Education* 54 (September 30):A1, A10–A12.

Global Alliance for Workers and Communities. 2003. *About Us.* Accessed April 28 (www.theglobalalliance.org).

Goering, Laurie. 2008a. "Women Urge Larger Role in Easing World's Ills." *Chicago Tribune,* March 11, p. 11.

———. 2008b. "Outsourced to India: Stress." *Chicago Tribune,* April 20, pp. 1, 18.

Goffman, Erving. 1959. *The Presentation of Self in Everyday Life.* New York: Doubleday.

———. 1961. *Asylums: Essays on the Social Situation of Mental Patients and Other Inmates.* Garden City, NY: Doubleday.

———. 1963. *Stigma: Notes on Management of Spoiled Identity.* Englewood Cliffs, NJ: Prentice Hall.

Goldstein, Greg. 1998. "World Health Organization and Housing." Pp. 636–637 in *The Encyclopedia of Housing,* edited by Willem van Vliet. Thousand Oaks, CA: Sage.

Goldstein, Melvyn C., and Cynthia M. Beall. 1981. "Modernization and Aging in the Third and Fourth World: Views from the Rural Hinterland in Nepal." *Human Organization* 40 (Spring):48–55.

Goldstone, Jack. 2010. "The New Population Bomb: The Four Megatrends That Will Change the World." *Foreign Affairs* (January/February): 31–43.

Gonzalez, David. 2003. "Latin Sweatshops Pressed by U.S. Campus Power." *New York Times,* April 4, p. A3.

Gooding, Caroline. 1994. *Disability Laws, Enabling Acts: Disability Rights in Britain and America.* Boulder, CO: Westview Press.

Goodstein, Laurie. 2008. "India, Exporter of Priests, May Keep Them Home." *New York Times,* December 30, p. A1.

Google. 2010. "Explore Flu Trends and the World." Accessible at google.org/Flutrends.

Gottdiener, Mark, and Joe R. Feagin. 1988. "The Paradigm Shift in Urban Sociology." *Urban Affairs Quarterly* 24 (December):163–187.

———, and Ray Hutchison. 2011. *The New Urban Sociology.* 4th ed. Boulder, CO: Westview Press.

Gottfredson, Michael, and Travis Hirschi. 1990. *A General Theory of Crime.* Palo Alto, CA: Stanford University Press.

Gottlieb, Lori. 2006. "How Do I Love Thee?" *Atlantic Monthly* (March):58, 60, 62–68, 70.

Gould, Elise. 2007. "The Health-Finance Debate Reaches a Fever Pitch." *Chronicle of Higher Education,* April 13, pp. B14, B15.

Gould, Larry A. 2002. "Indigenous People Policing Indigenous People: The Potential Psychological and Cultural Costs." *Social Science Journal* 39:171–188.

Government Accountability Office. 2003. "Women's Earnings: Work Patterns Partially Explain Difference between Men's and Women's Earnings." Washington, DC: U.S. Government. Printing Office.

Grady, Sarah, Stacy Bielick, and Susan Aud. 2010. *Trends in the Use of School Choice: 1993 to 2010.* Washington, DC: U.S. Government Printing Office.

Gramsci, Antonio. 1929. *Selections from the Prison Notebooks.* Edited and translated by Quintin Hoare and Geoffrey Nowell Smith. London: Lawrence and Wishort.

Grazian, David. 2010. *Mix It Up: Popular Culture, Mass Media, and Society.* New York: Norton.

Greeley, Andrew M. 1989. "Protestant and Catholic: Is the Analogical Imagination Extinct?" *American Sociological Review* 54 (August):485–502.

Greenemeier, Larry. 2010. "Gulf Spillover: Will BP's Deepwater Disaster Change the Oil Industry?" *Scientific American* (June 7). Accessible at http://www.scientificamerican.com/article.cfm?id=molotch-deepwater-environmental-sociology.

Greenhalgh, Susan. 2008. *Just One Child: Science and Policy in Deng's China.* Berkeley: University of California Press.

Greenhouse, Linda. 2008. "D.C. Ban Rejected. Landmark Decision on Covert Meaning of 2nd Amendment." *New York Times,* June 27, pp. A1, A12.

Greenhouse, Steven. 2008a. "Unions Look for New Life in the World of Obama." *New York Times,* December 29, p. B6.

———. 2008b. "Millions of Jobs of a Different Collar." *New York Times,* March 26.

———. 2009. "In America, Labor Has an Unusually Long Fuse." *New York Times,* April 5, Week in Review News, p. 3.

Groening, Chad. 2007. "Media Coverage of Virginia Tech Massacre Shows Anti-Gun Bias, Says Watchdog." Accessed May 16 (www.onenewsnow.com).

Groza, Victor, Daniela F. Ileana, and Ivor Irwin. 1999. *A Peacock or a Crow: Stories, Interviews, and Commentaries on Romanian Adoptions.* Euclid, OH: Williams Custom Publishing.

Grusky, David, and Christopher Wimer. 2010. "Editor's Note." *Pathways* (Summer):2.

Guarino, Mark. 2009. "New Orleans' 'Katrina Generation' Struggles with Drugs and Depression." *Christian Science Monitor,* May 13.

———. 2010. "Poverty's New Face: Suburbs." *Christian Science Monitor,* February 14, p. 18.

Guest, Robert. 2011. "Tribes Still Matter." *The Economist* (January 22):17–18.

Guo, Guang, Michael E. Roettger, and Tianji Cai. 2008. "The Integration of Genetic Propensities into Social-Control Models of Delinquency and Violence among Male Youths." *American Sociological Review* 73 (August):543–568.

Gurbuz, Mustafa, and Gulsum Gurbuz-Kucuksari. 2009. "Between Sacred Codes and Secular Consumer Society: The Practice of Headscarf Adoption among American College Girls." *Journal of Muslim Minority Affairs* 29 (September):387–399.

Gutiérrez, Gustavo. 1990. "Theology and the Social Sciences." Pp. 214–225 in *Liberation Theology at the Crossroads: Democracy or Revolution?* edited by Paul E. Sigmund. New York: Oxford University Press.

Guttmacher Institute. 2008. *Facts on Induced Abortion Worldwide.* New York: Guttmacher.

H

Haas, Steven A., David R. Schaefer, and Olga Kornienko. 2010. "Health and the Structure of Adolescent Social Networks." *Journal of Health and Social Behavior* 5 (4):424–439.

Hacker, Andrew. 1964. "Power to Do What?" Pp. 134–146 in *The New Sociology,* edited by Irving Louis Horowitz. New York: Oxford University Press.

Hacker, Helen Mayer. 1951. "Women as a Minority Group." *Social Forces* 30 (October):60–69.

———. 1974. "Women as a Minority Group, Twenty Years Later." Pp. 124–134 in *Who Discriminates against Women?* edited by Florence Denmark. Beverly Hills, CA: Sage.

Hall, Matthew, and Barrett Lee. 2010. "How Diverse Are US Suburbs?" *Urban Studies* 47 (January):3–28.

Hall, Mimi. 2005. "Senators 'to Demand Answers' on Slow Action." *USA Today,* September 6, p. 4A.

Hall-Jones, Peter. 2010. Unionism and Economic Performance. Accessed January 25 (www.newunionism.net/library/member%20contributions/news/unionism%20and%20economic%20performance.htm).

Hallinan, Maureen T. 1997. "The Sociological Study of Social Change." *American Sociological Review* 62 (February):1–11.

Halualani, Rona Tamiko. 2002. *In the Name of Hawaiians: Native Identities and Cultural Politics.* Minneapolis: University of Minnesota Press.

Hamilton, Darrick, and Willam Darity, Jr. 2009. "Race, Wealth, and Intergenerational Poverty." *America Prospect* (September):A10–A11.

Hamm, Steve. 2007. "Children of the Web." *BusinessWeek,* July 2, pp. 50–56, 58.

Hank, Karsten. 2001. "Changes in Child Care Could Reduce Job Options for Eastern German Mothers." *Population Today* 29 (April):3, 6.

Hanson, Ralph E. 2005. *Mass Communication: Living in a Media World.* New York: McGraw-Hill.

Haq, Husna. 2009. "An American Hijabi's View." *Christian Science Monitor,* December 13, pp. 16–17.

———. 2011. "How Marriage Is Faring." *Christian Science Monitor,* February 14, p. 21.

Harding, David J. 2009. "Violence, Older Peers, and the Socialization of Adolescent Boys in Disadvantaged Neighborhoods." *American Sociological Review* 74 (June):445–464.

Harlow, Harry F. 1971. *Learning to Love.* New York: Ballantine.

Harman, Donna. 2009. "Dubai's Glitz Lost in Grim Life." *Christian Science Monitor,* May 3, p. 8.

Harrington, Michael. 1980. "The New Class and the Left." Pp. 123–138 in *The New Class,* edited by B. Bruce Briggs. Brunswick, NJ: Transaction.

Harris, Chauncy D., and Edward Ullman. 1945. "The Nature of Cities." *Annals of the American Academy of Political and Social Science* 242 (November):7–17.

Harrisinteractive. 2008. "Cell Phone Usage Continues to Increase." Accessed January 13 (www.harrisinteractive.com).

Hartmann, Heidi, Ashley English, and Jeffrey Hayes. 2010. *Women and Men's Employment and Unemployment in the Great Recession.* Washington, DC: IWPR.

Hasen, Richard L. 2010. "What the Court Did—and Why." *The American Interest* (July–August): 49–55.

Haub, Carl. 2010. "2010 World Population Data Sheet." Washington, DC: Population Reference Bureau.

Haviland, William A., Harald E. L. Prins, Dana Walrath, and Bunny McBride. 2008. *Cultural Anthropology—The Human Challenge.* 12th ed. Belmont, CA: Wadsworth.

Hay, Andrew. 2009. "Spain's New Middle Classes Slip into Poverty." *Reuters.* April 8. Accessed May 11, 2011 (http://uk.reuters.com/article/email/ioUKTRE537029200904).

Hayden, H. Thomas. 2004. "What Happened at Abu Ghraib." Accessed August 7 (www.military.com).

He, Wan, Manisha Sengupta, Victoria A. Velkoff, and Kimberly A. DeBarros. 2005. "65 + in the United States: 2005." *Current Population Reports,* ser. P-23, no. 209. Washington, DC: U.S. Government Printing Office.

Health Care Financing Administration. 2001. *National Health Care Expenditures Projections.* Accessed August 10 (www.hcfa.gov/stats/NHE-proj/).

Hebel, Sara. 2006. "In Rural America, Few People Harvest 4-Year Degrees." *Chronicle of Higher Education* 53 (November 3):A21–A24.

Heckert, Druann, and Amy Best. 1997. "Ugly Duckling to Swan: Labeling Theory and the Stigmatization of Red Hair." *Symbolic Interaction* 20 (4):365–384.

Hedley, R. Alan. 1992. "Industrialization in Less Developed Countries." Pp. 914–920, vol. 2, in *Encyclopedia of Sociology,* edited by Edgar F. Borgatta and Marie L. Borgatta. New York: Macmillan.

Heilman, Madeline E. 2001. "Description and Prescription: How Gender Stereotypes Prevent Women's Ascent up the Organizational Ladder." *Journal of Social Issues* 57 (4):657–674.

Heisig, Jan Paul. 2011. "Who Does More Housework: Rich or Poor? A Comparison of 33 Countries." *American Sociological Review* 76 (1):74–99.

Hellmich, Nanci. 2001. "TV's Reality: No Vast American Waistlines." *USA Today,* October 8, p. D7.

Helvarg, David. 1994. *The War against Greens: The "Wise Use" Movement, the New Right and Anti-Environmental Violence.* San Francisco: Sierra Club Books.

Hendershott, Ann. 2002. *The Politics of Deviance.* San Francisco: Encounter Books.

Herman, William F. 2009. Comment on *Harvard Business Review* blog. October 6. Accessed April 11, 2010 (http://blogs.hbr.org/npr/

how-to-fix-executive-pay/2009/06/why-high-ceo-pay-is-bad-business.html).

Hertz, Rosanna. 2006. *Single by Chance. Mothers by Choice.* New York: Oxford University Press.

Hewlett, Sylvia Ann, and Carolyn Buck Luce. 2005. "Off-Ramps and On-Ramps: Keeping Talented Women on the Road to Success." *Harvard Business Review* (March):43–53.

Hickman, Jonathan. 2002. "America's 50 Best Corporations for Minorities." *Fortune* 146 (July 8):110–120.

Higgins, Chris A., Linda E. Duxbury, and Sean T. Lyons. 2010. "Coping with Overload in Stress: Men and Women in Dual-Earner Families." *Journal of Marriage and Family* 72 (August):847–859.

Higher Education Research Institute. 2004. *Trends in Political Attitudes and Voting Behavior among College Freshmen and Early Career College Graduates: What Issues Could Drive This Election?* Los Angeles: HERI, University of California, Los Angeles.

Hill, Michael R., and Susan Hoecker-Drysdale, eds. 2001. *Harriet Martineau: Theoretical and Methodological Perspectives.* New York: Routledge.

Hillery, George A. 1955. "Definitions of Community: Areas of Agreement." *Rural Sociology* (2):111–123.

Himes, Christine L. 2001. "Elderly Americans." *Population Bulletin* 56 (December).

Hira, Ron. 2008. "An Overview of the Offshoring of U.S. Jobs." Pp. 14–15 in Marlene A. Lee and Mark Mather. "U.S. Labor Force Trends." *Population Bulletin* 63 (June).

Hirschi, Travis. 1969. *Causes of Delinquency.* Berkeley: University of California Press.

Hirst, Paul, and Grahame Thompson. 1996. *Globalization in Question: The International Economy and the Possibilities of Governance.* Cambridge, UK: Polity Press.

Hitlin, Steven, and Jane Allyn Piliavin. 2004. "Values: Reviving a Dormant Concept." Pp. 359–393 in *Annual Review of Sociology, 2004,* edited by Karen S. Cook and John Hagan. Palo Alto, CA: Annual Reviews.

Hochschild, Arlie Russell. 1990. "The Second Shift: Employed Women Are Putting in Another Day of Work at Home." *Utne Reader* 38 (March–April):66–73.

———. 2005. *The Commercialization of Intimate Life: Notes from Home and Work.* Berkeley: University of California Press.

———, with Anne Machung. 1989. *The Second Shift: Working Parents and the Revolution at Home.* New York: Viking Penguin.

Hodson, Randy, and Teresa A. Sullivan. 1995. *The Social Organization of Work.* 2nd ed. Belmont, CA: Wadsworth.

Hoffman, Lois Wladis. 1985. "The Changing Genetics/Socialization Balance." *Journal of Social Issues* 41 (Spring):127–148.

Holden, Constance. 1980. "Identical Twins Reared Apart." *Science* 207 (March 21):1323–1328.

———. 1987. "The Genetics of Personality." *Science* 257 (August 7):598–601.

Holder, Kelly. 2006. "Voting and Registration in the Election of November 2004." *Current Population Reports,* ser. P-20, no. 556. Washington, DC: U.S. Government Printing Office.

Hollingshead, August B. 1975. *Elmtown's Youth and Elmtown Revisited.* New York: Wiley.

Holmes, Mary. 2009. "Commuter Couples and Distance Relationships: Living Apart Together."

Sloan Work and Family Research Network. Accessible at http://wfnetwork.bc.edu/encyclopedia_entry.php?id=15551&area=all.

Homans, George C. 1979. "Nature versus Nurture: A False Dichotomy." *Contemporary Sociology* 8 (May):345–348.

Home School Legal Defense Association. 2005. "State Laws" and "Academic Statistics on Homeschooling." Accessed May 12 (www.hslda.org).

Hondagneu-Sotelo, Pierrette, ed. 2003. *Gender and U.S. Immigration: Contemporary Trends.* Berkeley: University of California Press.

hooks, bell. 1994. *Feminist Theory: From Margin to Center.* 2nd ed. Boston: South End Press.

Horgan, John. 1993. "Eugenics Revisited." *Scientific American* 268 (June):122–128, 130–133.

Horkheimer, Max, and Theodore Adorno. [1944] 2002. *Dialectic of Enlightenment.* Palo Alto, CA: Stanford University Press.

Horowitz, Helen Lefkowitz. 1987. *Campus Life.* Chicago: University of Chicago Press.

Horrigan, John B. 2007. *A Typology of Information and Communication Technology Users.* Washington, DC: Pew Internet and American Life Project.

Horwitz, Allan V. 2002. *Creating Mental Illness.* Chicago: University of Chicago Press.

Hosokawa, William K. 1969. *Nisei: The Quiet Americans.* New York: Morrow.

Hospice Association of America. 2008. *Hospice Facts and Statistics.* Washington, DC: Hospice Association of America.

Houseman, John. 1972. *Run Through.* New York: Simon and Schuster.

Houser, Trevor, Shashank Mohamad, and Robert Heilmayer. 2009. *A Green Global Recovery? Assessing U.S. Economic Stimulus and the Prospects for International Coordination.* Washington, DC: World Resources Institute of Peterson Institute for International Economics.

Housing and Urban Development. 2010. *The Annual Homeless Assessment Report to Congress.* Washington, DC: U.S. Government Printing Office.

Howard, Alex. 2011. "For Election Info, the Internet a New High-Water Mark." Accessed April 11 (http://radar.oreilly.com/print/2011/03/pew-internet-election-2010.html).

Howard, Judith A. 1999. "Border Crossings between Women's Studies and Sociology." *Contemporary Sociology* 28 (September):525–528.

———, and Jocelyn Hollander. 1997. *Gendered Situations, Gendered Selves.* Thousand Oaks, CA: Sage.

Howard, Michael. 2009. *Modern Wicca: A History from Gerald Gardner to the Present.* St. Paul, MN: Llewellyn Books.

Howard, Michael C. 1989. *Contemporary Cultural Anthropology.* 3rd ed. Glenview, IL: Scott, Foresman.

Howard, Russell D., and Reid L. Sawyer. 2003. *Terrorism and Counterterrorism: Understanding the New Security Environment.* Guilford, CT: McGraw-Hill/Dushkin.

Howden, Lindsay M., and Julie A. Meyer. 2011. *Age and Sex Composition: 2010.* May 2011. 2010 Census Brief BR-03.

Hu, Winnie. 2010. "In a New Role, Teachers Move to Run Schools." *New York Times,* September 7, pp. A1, A20.

Huang, Gary. 1988. "Daily Addressing Ritual: A Cross-Cultural Study." Presented at the annual meeting of the American Sociological Association, Atlanta.

Huff, Charlotte. 2007. "Survival of the Fittest." *American Way,* May 1, pp. 30–35.

Hughes, Everett. 1945. "Dilemmas and Contradictions of Status." *American Journal of Sociology* 50 (March):353–359.

Hughlett, Mike. 2008. "Sitting Pretty." *Chicago Tribune,* September 14, sec. 5, pp. 1, 7.

Human Genome Project. 2010. "Human Genome Project Information." Accessed April 21 (www.ornl.gov/sci/techresources/human_genome/home.shtml).

———. 2011. "Human Genome Project Information." Accessed April 25 (www.ornl.gov).

Human Rights Campaign. 2010. *Equity from State to State 2010.* Washington, DC: Human Rights Foundation.

———. "State Laws." Accessed August 5 at http://www.hrc.org/laws_and_elections/state.asp.

Human Terrain System. 2010. "Welcome to the HTS Home Page." Accessed January 6, 2011 (http://humanterrainsystem.army.mil).

Humes, Karen R., Nicholas A. Jones, and Roberto R. Ramirez. 2011. *Overview of Race and Hispanic Origin: 2010.* 2010 Census Brief BR-02. Accessible at http://www.census.gov/prod/cen2010/briefs/c2010br-02.pdf.

Hundley, Tom, and Margaret Ramirez. 2008. "Young Muslims Put Faith in Facebook." *Chicago Tribune,* February 10, p. 12.

Hunt, Darnell. 1997. *Screening the Los Angeles "Riots": Race, Seeing, and Resistance.* New York: Cambridge University Press.

Hunter, Herbert M., ed. 2000. *The Sociology of Oliver C. Cox: New Perspectives: Research in Race and Ethnic Relations,* vol. 2. Stamford, CT: JAI Press.

Hunter, James Davison. 1991. *Culture Wars: The Struggle to Define America.* New York: Basic Books.

Huntington, Samuel P. 1993. "The Clash of Civilizations?" *Foreign Affairs* 72 (Summer):22–49.

Hurn, Christopher J. 1985. *The Limits and Possibilities of Schooling.* 2nd ed. Boston: Allyn and Bacon.

Hussar, William J., and Tabitha M. Bailey. 2011. *Projections of Education Statistics to 2019.* Washington, DC: National Center for Education Statistics.

Hyde, Janet Shibley. 2005. "The Gender Similarities Hypothesis." *American Psychologist* 60 (6):581–592.

Hymowitz, Carol, and Rachel Emma Silverman. 2001. "Can Work Place Stress Get Worse?" *Wall Street Monitor,* January 16, pp. B1, B4.

Igo, Sarah E. 2007. *The Average American: Surveys, Citizens, and the Making of a Mass Public.* Cambridge, MA: Harvard University Press.

Immervoll, Herwig, and David Barber. 2005. *Can Parents Afford to Work? Childcare Costs, Tax-Benefit Policies and Work Incentives.* Paris: Organisation for Economic Co-operation and Development.

Inglehart, Ronald, and Wayne E. Baker. 2000. "Modernization, Cultural Change, and the Persistence of Traditional Values." *American Sociological Review* 65 (February):19–51.

Innocence Project. 2011. *Facts on Post-Conviction DNA Exonerations.* Accessed March 14 (http://www.innocenceproject.org/Content/351PRINT.php).

Institute for Economics and Peace. 2010. "Global Peace Index." Accessible June 29 (www.visionofhumanity.org/gpi/results/world-map.php).

Institute for Women's Policy Research. 2009. *The Gender Wage Gap: 2008.* Washington, DC: IWPR.

Institute of International Education. 2010. "Open Doors 2010 'Fast Facts.'" Accessed at www.ies.org.

Interbrand. 2010. "Best Global Brands: 2009 Rankings." Accessible at www.interband.com/best_global_brands.aspx.

International Centre for Prison Studies. 2010. "Prison Brief—Highest to Lowest Rates." Accessed February 10 (www.kcl.ac.uk/depsta/law/research/icps/worldbrief/wpb.stats.php?area=all&category=wb_poprate).

Interface Group Report (Virginia Tech). 2007. *Presidential Internal Review.* Blacksburg, Virginia Polytechnic Institute and State University.

International Crime Victim Survey. 2004. *Nationwide Surveys in the Industrialized Countries.* Accessed February 20 (www.ruljis.leidenuniv.nl/group/jfcr/www/icvs).

International Gay and Lesbian Human Rights Commission. 2010. Home Page. Accessed February 11 (www.iglhrc.org).

International Institute for Democracy and Electoral Assistance. 2011. "Voter Turnout Database—Custom Query." Accessed April 11 (http://www/idea.int/vt/viewdata.cfm#).

International Monetary Fund. 2000. *World Economic Outlook: Asset Prices and the Business Cycle.* Washington, DC: International Monetary Fund.

International Organization for Migration. 2011. "Facts and Figures." Accessed April 25 (www.iom.int/jahia/jahia/about.migration/lang/en).

International Trade Union Confederation. 2009. "Davos: World Unions Call for Action Against Corporate Grand Theft." Accessed January 31 (www.ituc-csi.org/spip.php?article2736).

Internet Crime Complaint Center. 2009. "IC3 Annual Report on Internet Crime." Released March 31. (www.ic3.gov/media/annualreport/2008_IC3Report.pdf).

Internet World Stats. 2011. "Usage and Population Statistics" and "Internet World Users by Language." Updated on April 25, 2011. Accessed April 25 (www.internetworldstats.com).

Inter-Parliamentary Union. 2011. *Women in National Parliaments.* March 31. Accessed April 23 (www.ipu.org).

InTouch Health. 2010. "About Us." Accessed April 18 (www.intouchhealth.com).

Isaacs, Julia B. 2007a. *Economic Mobility of Families across Generations.* Washington, DC: Economic Mobility Project, Pew Charitable Trusts.

———. 2007b. *Economic Mobility of Men and Women.* Washington, DC: Economic Mobility Project.

———, Isabel V. Sawhill, and Ron Haskins. 2008. *Getting Ahead or Losing Ground: Economic Mobility in America.* Washington, DC: Pew Charitable Trusts.

Issa, Philip, and Sheila R. Zedlewski. 2011. *Poverty among Older Americans, 2009.* Washington, DC: Urban Institute. Accessible at http://www.retirementpolicy.org.

ITOPF. 2006. "Statistics: International Tanker Owners Pollution Federation Limited." Accessed May 2 (www.itopf.com/stats.html).

J

Jackson, Philip W. 1968. *Life in Classrooms.* New York: Holt.

Jacobs, Andres. 2010. "As China's Economy Grows, Pollution Worsens Despite New Efforts to Control It." *New York Times,* July 29, p. A4.

Jacobs, Jerry. 2003. "Detours on the Road to Equality: Women, Work and Higher Education." *Contexts* (Winter):32–41.

Jacobs, Tom. 2009. "Hot Men of the Links." *Miller-McCune* (May–June):79.

Jacobsen, Linda A., May Kent, Marlene Lee, and Mark Mather. 2011. "America's Aging Population." *Population Bulletin* 66 (February).

Jaffee, Daniel. 2007. *Brewing Justice: Fair Trade Coffee, Sustainability, and Survival.* Berkeley: University of California Press.

Jain, Saranga, and Kathleen Kurz. 2007. *New Insights on Preventing Child Marriage: A Global Analysis of Factors and Programs.* Washington, DC: International Center for Research on Women.

Janis, Irving. 1967. *Victims of Groupthink.* Boston: Houghton Mifflin.

Jäntti, Markus. 2009. "Mobility in the United States in Comparative Perspectives." *Focus* 26 (Fall).

Jargowsky, Paul A., and Rebecca Yang. 2006. "The 'Underclass' Revisited: A Social Problem in Decline." *Journal of Urban Affairs* 28 (1):55–70.

Jasper, James M. 1997. *The Art of Moral Protest: Culture, Biography, and Creativity in Social Movements.* Chicago: University of Chicago Press.

Jayson, Sharon. 2009. "Holding Up the Value of Marriage." *USA Today,* February 18, pp. D1, D2.

Jenkins, Henry. 2006. *Convergence Culture: Where Old and New Media Collide.* New York: New York University Press.

Jenkins, Matt. 2008. "A Really Inconvenient Truth." *Miller-McCure* 1 (March–April):38–41.

Jenkins, Richard. 1991. "Disability and Social Stratification." *British Journal of Sociology* 42 (December):557–580.

Jensen, Gary F. 2005. "Social Organization Theory." In *Encyclopedia of Criminology,* edited by Richard A. Wright and J. Mitchell Miller. Chicago: Fitzrog Dearborn.

Jervis, Rick. 2008. "New Orleans Homicides up 30% over 2006 Level." *USA Today,* January 3, p. 3A.

Jesella, Kara. 2008. "Blogging's Glass Ceiling." *New York Times,* July 27, Style section, pp. 1, 2.

Jimenez, Maria. 2009. *Humanitarian Crisis: Migrant Deaths at the U.S.–Mexico Border.* San Diego: ACLU of San Diego and Imperial Counties.

Joas, Hans, and Wolfgang Knöbl. 2009. *Social Theory: Twenty Introductory Lectures.* Cambridge: Cambridge University Press.

Johnson, Benton. 1975. *Functionalism in Modern Sociology: Understanding Talcott Parsons.* Morristown, NJ: General Learning.

Johnson, David. 2010. "Progress toward Improving the U.S. Poverty Measure: Developing the New Supplemental Poverty Measure." *Focus* 27 (Winter):1–3.

Johnson, Richard A. 1985. *American Fads.* New York: Beech Tree.

Johnson, Will. 2009. "Genie: The Wild Child." Accessed August 4, 2010 (http://knol.google.com/k/genie-the-wild-child-chapter-2#).

Jones, Del, and Barbara Hansen. 2009. "CEO Pay Packages Sink with Economy." *USA Today,* May 4, pp. B1–B2.

Jones, Jeffrey M. 2011. "Americans Increasingly Prioritize Economy over Environment" March 17. Accessed May 25 (http://www.gallup.com/poll/146681/Americans-Increasingly-Prioritize-Economy-Environment.aspx).

Jones, Jo. 2009. "Who Adopts? Characteristics of Women and Men Who Have Adopted Children." *NCHS Data Brief* (12).

Jopling, John, and Reilly Morse. 2010. "The BP Oil Disaster and Its Disproportionate Impacts on Minorities and Communities of Color." *Focus* 36 (October–November):12–14.

Jordan, Miriam. 2009. "As U.S. Job Opportunities Fade, More Mexicans Look Homeward." *Wall Street Journal,* February 13, p. A14.

Joseph, Jay. 2004. *The Gene Illusion: Genetic Research in Psychiatry and Psychology under the Microscope.* New York: Algora Books.

Jost, Kenneth. 2005. "Right to Die." *CQ Researcher,* May 13.

———. 2008. "Women in Politics." *CQ Researcher* 18 (March 21).

Juhasz, Anne McCreary. 1989. "Black Adolescents' Significant Others." *Social Behavior and Personality* 17 (2):211–214.

K

Kahn, Joseph. 2003. "Made in China, Bought in China." *New York Times,* January 5, sec. 3, pp. 1, 10.

———. 2006. "Where's Mao? Chinese Revise History Books." *New York Times,* September 1, pp. A1, A6.

Kahn, Scott D. 2011. "On the Future of Genomic Data." *Science* (February 11):728–729.

Kaiser Family Foundation. 2005. *Sex on TV4.* Santa Barbara, CA: Kaiser Family Foundation.

———. 2007. "Parents Say They're Getting Control of Their Children's Exposure to Sex and Violence in the Media—Even Online." Accessed January 2, 2008 (www.kff.org/entmedia/entmedia061907nr.cfm).

Kalleberg, Arne L. 2009. "Precarious Work, Insecure Workers: Employment Relations in Transition." *American Sociological Review* 74 (February):1–22.

Kalmijn, Matthijs. 1998. "Intermarriage and Homogamy: Causes, Patterns, Trends." *Annual Review of Sociology* 24:395–421.

Kambayashi, Takehiko. 2008. "Japanese Men Shout the Oft-Unsaid 'I love you.'" *Christian Science Monitor,* February 13.

Kamenetz, Anya. 2006. *Generation Debt.* New York: Riverhead.

Kandel, William. 2005. "Rural Hispanics at a Glance." *Economic Information Bulletin* (December).

Kang, K. Connie. 1996. "Filipinos Happy with Life in U.S. but Lack United Voice." *Los Angeles Times,* January 26, pp. A1, A20.

Karides, Marina. 2010. "Theorizing the Rise of Microenterprise Development in Caribbean Context." *Journal of World-Systems Research* 16 (2):192–216.

Karney, Benjamin R., and John S. Crown. 2007. "Families under Stress: An Assessment of Data, Theory, and Research on Marriage and Divorce in the Military." Santa Monica, CA: RAND.

Kasarda, John D. 2011. Aerotropolis.com. Accessed May 28.

——— and Greg Lindsay. 2011. *Aerotropolis: The Way We'll Live Next.* New York: Farrar, Straus and Giroux.

Katovich, Michael A. 1987. Correspondence. June 1.

Katz, Michael. 1971. *Class, Bureaucracy, and the Schools: The Illusion of Educational Change in America.* New York: Praeger.

References

Lopez, Mark Hugo. 2010. *The Latino Vote in the 2010 Elections.* Washington, DC: Pew Hispanic Center.

Lorber, Judith. 2005. *Breaking the Bowls: Degendering and Feminist Change.* New York: Norton.

Lublin, Joann S. 2010. "The Corner Office, and a Family." *Wall Street Journal,* October 18, p. B9.

Lucas, Edward. 2008. "The Electronic Bureaucrat." *The Economist* 186 (February 16, special report).

Ludwig, Jens, and Isabell Sawhill. 2007. *Success by Ten: Interviewing Early, Often, and Efficiently in the Education of Young Children.* Washington, DC: Brookings Institution.

Lukacs, Georg. 1923. *History and Class Consciousness.* London: Merlin.

Lundquist, Jennifer Hickes. 2006. "Choosing Single Motherhood." *Contexts* 5 (Fall):64–67.

Luo, Michael. 2008. "What Happens to Public Financing, When Obama Thrived without It?" *New York Times,* November 3, p. A17.

Luster, Tom, Kelly Rhoades, and Bruce Haas. 1989. "The Relation between Parental Values and Parenting Behavior: A Test of the Kohn Hypothesis." *Journal of Marriage and the Family* 51 (February):139–147.

Luttinger, Nina, and Gregory Dicum. 2006. *The Coffee Book: Anatomy of an Industry from Crop to the Last Drop.* Revised and updated. New York: New Press.

Lyall, Sarah. 2002. "For Europeans, Love, Yes; Marriage, Maybe." *New York Times,* March 24, pp. 1–8.

Lynas, Mark. 2008. *Six Degrees: Our Future on a Hotter Planet.* Washington, DC: National Geographic.

Lynn, Barry C. 2003. "Trading with a Low-Wage Tiger." *American Prospect* 14 (February):10–12.

M

MacDonald, G. Jeffrey. 2007. "Go in Search of a Church by Way of the Web." *USA Today,* October 17, p. D8.

MacDorman, Marian F., and T. J. Mathews. 2009. *Behind International Rankings of Infant Mortality: How the United States Compares with Europe.* NCHS Date Brief (No. 23, November).

MacFarquhar, Neil. 2008. "Resolute or Fearful, Many Muslims Turn to Home Schooling." *New York Times,* March 26, p. A1.

Mach, Annie, and Laura Blumenthal. 2010. "Health Insurance Coverage of Children under 19: 2008 and 2009." 2009–2011 Census Brief BR-09-11. Accessible at http://www.census.gov/prod/2010pubs/acsbr09-11.pdf.

Machalek, Richard, and Michael W. Martin. 2010. "Evolution, Biology and Society: A Conversation for the 21st-Century Sociology Classroom." *Teaching Sociology* 38 (1):35–45.

Mack, Mick G. 2003. "Does Exercise Status Influence the Impressions Formed by College Students?" *College Student Journal* 37 (December).

Mack, Raymond W., and Calvin P. Bradford. 1979. *Transforming America: Patterns of Social Change.* 2nd ed. New York: Random House.

Mackey, John. 2009. "Why Sky-High CEO Pay Is Bad Business." *Harvard Business Review* blog, June 17. Accessed April 11, 2010 (http://blogs.hbr.org/hbr/how-to-fix-executive-pay/2009/06/why-high-ceo-pay-is-bad-business.html).

Mackun, Paul, and Steven Wilson. 2011. *Population Distribution and Change: 2000 to 2010.* March 2011. 2010 Census Brief BR-01.

MacLeod, Calum. 2010. "Chinese Use Internet to Show Dissent." *USA Today,* December 29, p. 31.

MacLeod, Scott, and Vivienne Walt. 2005. "Live from Qatar." *Time,* bonus section, June, pp. A6–A8.

Maestretti, Danielle. 2009. "Information Overload." *Utne Reader* (July–August):22–23.

Magga, Ole Henrik. 2006. "Diversity in Sami Terminology for Reindeer, Snow, and Ice." *International Social Science Journal* 58 (March):25–34.

Magnier, Mark. 2004. "China Clamps Down on Web News Discussion." *Los Angeles Times,* February 26, p. A4.

Mahbub ul Haq Human Development Centre. 2000. *Human Development in South Asia 2000.* Oxford, UK: Oxford University Press for Mahbub ul Haq Human Development Centre.

Malaby, Thomas M. 2009. *Making Virtual Worlds: Linden Lab and Second Life.* Ithaca, NY: Cornell University.

Malcolm, Andrew H. 1974. "The 'Shortage' of Bathroom Tissue: A Classic Study in Rumor." *New York Times,* February 3, p. 29.

Malcolm X, with Alex Haley. [1964] 1999. *The Autobiography of Malcolm X.* Revised with Epilogue by Alex Haley and Afterword by Ossie Davis. New York: One World, Ballantine Books.

Males, Mike, and Meda-Chesney Lind. 2010. "The Myth of Mean Girls." *New York Times,* April 2, p. A21.

Malhotra, Neil, and Yotam Margalit. 2009. "State of the Nation: Anti-Semitism and the Economic Crisis." *Boston Review* (May–June). Accessible at http://bostonreview.net/BR34.3/malhotra_margalit.php.

Malthus, Thomas Robert, Julian Huxley, and Frederick Osborn. [1824] 1960. *Three Essays on Population.* Reprint. New York: New American Library.

Margolis, Mac. 2009. "The Land of Less Contrast: How Brazil Reined in Inequality. *Newsweek,* November 28.

Mark, Gloria, Victor M. Gonzalez, and Justin Harris. 2005. "No Task Left Behind? Examining the Nature of Fragmented Work." Paper presented at CHI 2005, Portland, Oregon.

Markson, Elizabeth W. 1992. "Moral Dilemmas." *Society* 29 (July–August):4–6.

Marosi, Richard. 2007. "The Nation: A Once-Porous Border Is a Turning-Back Point." *Los Angeles Times,* March 21, pp. A1, A20.

Marquis, Julie, and Dan Morain. 1999. "A Tortuous Path for the Mentally Ill." *Los Angeles Times,* November 21, pp. A1, A22, A23.

Marr, Phebe. 2003. "Civics 101, Taught by Saddam Hussein: First, Join the Paramilitary." *New York Times,* April 20.

Marshall, Brent K., and J. Steven Picou. 2008. "Postnormal Science, Precautionary Principle, and Worst Cases: The Challenge of Twenty-First-Century Catastrophes." *Sociological Inquiry* 78 (May):230–247.

Martin, Dominique, Jean-Luc Metzger, and Philippe Pierre. 2006. "The Sociology of Globalization: Theoretical and Methodological Reflections." *International Sociology* 21 (July):499–521.

Martin, Joyce A., Brady E. Hamilton, Paul D. Sutton, Stephanie J. Ventura, Fay Menacker, Sharon Kirmeyer, and T. J. Mathews. 2009. "Births: Final Data for 2006." *National Vital Statistics Reports* 57 (January 7).

Martin, Karin A. 2009. "Normalizing Heterosexuality: Mothers' Assumptions, Talk, and Strategies with Young Children." *American Sociological Review* 74 (April):190–207.

Martin, Marvin. 1996. "Sociology Adapting to Changes." *Chicago Tribune,* July 21, sec. 18, p. 20.

Martin, Susan E. 1994. "Outsider within the Station House: The Impact of Race and Gender on Black Women Politics." *Social Problems* 41 (August):383–400.

Martineau, Harriet. [1837] 1962. *Society in America.* Edited, abridged, with an introductory essay by Seymour Martin Lipset. Reprint. Garden City, NY: Doubleday.

———. [1838] 1989. *How to Observe Morals and Manners.* Philadelphia: Leal and Blanchard. Sesquentennial edition, edited by M. R. Hill, Transaction Books.

Martinez, Elizabeth. 1993. "Going Gentle into That Good Night: Is a Rightful Death a Feminist Issue?" *Ms.* 4 (July–August):65–69.

Marubbio, M. Elise. 2006. *Killing the Indian Maiden: Images of Native American Women in Film.* Lexington: University Press of Kentucky.

Marx, Earl. 2009. "How Will Fair Fare?" *Christian Science Monitor,* April 19, pp. 30–31.

Marx, Karl. [1844] 1964. "Contribution to the Critique of Hegel's Philosophy of Right." In *On Religion,* Karl Marx and Friedrich Engels. New York: Schocker Books.

———, and Friedrich Engels. [1847] 1955. *Selected Work in Two Volumes.* Reprint. Moscow: Foreign Languages Publishing House.

Maryanski, Alexandra R. 2004. "Evaluation Theory." Pp. 257–263 in *Encyclopedia of Social Theory,* edited by George Ritzer. Thousand Oaks, CA: Sage.

Mason, J. W. 1998. "The Buses Don't Stop Here Anymore." *American Prospect* 37 (March):56–62.

Massey, Douglas S. 1998. "March of Folly: U.S. Immigration Policy after NAFTA." *American Prospect* (March–April):22–23.

———. 2007. *Categorically Unequal: The American Stratification System.* New York: Russell Sage Foundation.

———. 2008. "A Mexican Apartheid." Pp. 55–57, vol. 2, in *Encyclopedia of Race, Ethnicity, and Society,* edited by Richard T. Schaefer. Thousand Oaks CA: Sage.

———, and Nancy A. Denton. 1993. *American Apartheid: Segregation and the Making of the Underclass.* Cambridge, MA: Harvard University Press.

———, and Margarita Mooney. 2007. "The Effects of America's Three Affirmative Action Programs on Academic Performance." *Social Problems* 54 (1):99–117.

Masuda, Takahiko, Phoebe C. Ellsworth, Batja Mesquita, Janxin Leu, Shigehito Tanida, and Ellen Van de Veerdonk. 2008. "Attitudes and Social Cognition: Placing the Face in Context: Cultural Differences in the Perception of Facial Emotion." *Journal of Personality and Social Psychology* 94 (3):365–381.

Masud-Piloto, Felix. 2008. "Cuban Americans." Pp. 357–359, vol. 1, in *Encyclopedia of Race, Ethnicity, and Society,* edited by Richard T. Schaefer. Thousand Oaks, CA: Sage.

Mathews, T. J., and Marian MacDorman. 2011. "Infant Mortality Statistics." *National Vital Statistics Reports* 59 (6).

Maynard, Micheline. 2010. "At Toyota, a Cultural Shift." *New York Times,* June 3, pp. B1, B6.

Mazumder, Bhashkar. 2008. *Upward Intergenerational Economic Mobility in the United States.* Washington, DC: Economic Mobility Project.

McChesney, Robert W. 2008. *The Political Economy of Media: Enduring Issues, Emerging Dilemmas.* New York: Monthly Review Press.

McCormack, Mark. 2010. "Changing Masculinities in Youth Cultures." *Qualitative Sociology* 33:111–115.

McDonald, Michael P. 2008. "The Return of the Voter: Voter Turnout in the 2008 Presidential Election." *Forum* 6(4): Article 4.

———. 2009a. "Voter Turnout." Accessed April 8 (http://elections.gmu.edu/voter_turnout.htm).

———. 2009b. "2008 Current Population Survey Voting and Registration Supplement." Accessed April 16 (http://elections.gmu.edu/CPS_2008.html).

McDowell, Linda, Adina Batnitzky, and Sarah Dyer. 2009. "Precarious Work and Economic Migration: Emerging Immigrant Divisions of Labor in Greater London's Service Sector." *International Journal of Urban and Regional Research* 31 (March):3–25.

McFalls, Joseph A., Jr. 2007. *"Population: A Lively Introduction."* 5th ed. Washington, DC: Population Reference Bureau.

McFarland, Andrew S. 2007. "Neopluralism." *Annual Review of Political Science* 10:45–66.

McGirk, Tim. 2009. "Postcard: Dubai." *Time,* October 19, p. 6.

McGlynn, Clare, and Vanessa E. Munro, eds. 2010. *Rethinking Rape Law: International and Comparative Perspectives.* London: Routledge-Cavendish.

McGue, Matt, and Thomas J. Bouchard, Jr. 1998. "Genetic and Environmental Influence on Human Behavioral Differences." Pp. 1–24 in *Annual Review of Neurosciences.* Palo Alto, CA: Annual Reviews.

McGuire, Thomas G., and Jeanne Miranda. 2008. "New Evidence Regarding Racial and Ethnic Disparities in Mental Health: Policy Implications." *Health Affairs* 27 (2):393–403.

McGurty, Eileen Maura. 2000. "Warren County, NC, and the Emergence of the Environmental Justice Movement: Unlikely Coalitions and Shared Meanings in Local Collective Action." *Society and Natural Resources* 13:373–387.

McIntosh, Peggy. 1988. "White Privilege and Male Privilege: A Personal Account of Coming to See Correspondence through Work and Women's Studies." Working Paper No. 189, Wellesley College Center for Research on Women, Wellesley, MA.

McKinlay, John B., and Sonja M. McKinlay. 1977. "The Questionable Contribution of Medical Measures to the Decline of Mortality in the United States in the Twentieth Century." *Milbank Memorial Fund Quarterly* 55 (Summer):405–428.

McLanahan, Sara, and Christine Percheski. 2008. "Family Structure and the Reproduction of Inequalities." *Annual Review of Sociology* 38:257–276.

McLuhan, Marshall. 1964. *Understanding Media: The Extensions of Man.* New York: New American Library.

———. 1967. *The Medium Is the Message: An Inventory of Effects.* New York: Bantam Books.

McNeil, Donald G., Jr. 2002. "W.H.O. Moves to Make AIDS Drugs More Accessible to Poor Worldwide." *New York Times,* August 23, p. D7.

———. 2004. "When Real Food Isn't an Option." *New York Times,* September 3, pp. A1, A5.

McPhail, Clark. 1991. *The Myth of the Madding Crowd.* New York: De Gruyter.

———. 1994. "The Dark Side of Purpose in Riots: Individual and Collective Violence." *Sociological Quarterly* 35 (January):i–xx.

———. 2006. "The Crowd and Collective Behavior: Bringing Symbolic Interaction Back In." *Symbolic Interaction* 29 (Issue 4):433–464.

———, and David Miller. 1973. "The Assembling Process: A Theoretical Empirical Examination." *American Sociological Review* 38 (December):721–735.

———. 2008. "Crowd." *Contexts* (Spring):78–79.

Mead, George H. 1934. In *Mind, Self and Society,* edited by Charles W. Morris. Chicago: University of Chicago Press.

———. 1964a. In *On Social Psychology,* edited by Anselm Strauss. Chicago: University of Chicago Press.

———. 1964b. "The Genesis of the Self and Social Control." Pp. 267–293 in *Selected Writings: George Herbert Mead,* edited by Andrew J. Reck. Indianapolis: Bobbs-Merrill.

Mead, Margaret. [1935] 2001. *Sex and Temperament in Three Primitive Societies.* New York: Perennial, HarperCollins.

Mehl, Matthias R., Simine Vazire, Nairán Ramírez-Esparza, Richard B. Slatcher, and James W. Pennebacker. 2007. "Are Women Really More Talkative than Men?" *Science* 317 (July 6):82.

Meichtry, Stacy. 2011. "Italian Mammas Put Meals on Wheels, Say 'Mangia!' to Faraway Offspring." *Wall Street Journal,* March 31, pp. A1, A14.

Mendes, Elizabeth. 2010. "New High of 46% of Americans Support Legalizing Marijuana." October 28. Accessible at http://www.gallup.com/poll/144086/New-High-Americans-Support-Legalizing-Marijuana.aspx?version=print.

Mendez, Jennifer Bickman. 1998. "Of Mops and Maids: Contradictions and Continuities in Bureaucratized Domestic Work." *Social Problems* 45 (February):114–135.

Merton, Robert. 1948. "The Bearing of Empirical Research upon the Development of Social Theory." *American Sociological Review* 13 (October):505–515.

———. 1968. *Social Theory and Social Structure.* New York Free Press.

———, and Alice S. Kitt. 1950. "Contributions to the Theory of Reference Group Behavior." Pp. 40–105 in *Continuities in Social Research: Studies in the Scope and Methods of the American Soldier,* edited by Robert K. Merton and Paul L. Lazarsfeld. New York: Free Press.

Merton, Robert K., and Patricia L. Kendall. 1946. "The Focused Interview." *American Journal of Sociology* 51 (May):541–557.

Messner, Michael A. 2002. "Gender Equity in College Sports: 6 Views." *Chronicle of Higher Education* 49 (December 6):B9–B10.

———, and Cheryl Cooky. 2010. *Gender in Televised Sports: News and Highlights Shows, 1989–2009.* Los Angeles: Center for Feminist Research, University of Southern California.

———, Margaret Carlisle Duncan, and Nicole Williams. 2006. "This Revolution Is Not Being Televised." *Contexts* 5 (Summer):34–38.

Meston, Cindy M., and David M. Buss. 2007. "Why Humanoids Have Sex." *Archives of Sexual Behavior* 36 (August).

Meyer, Karen. 2011. "Match the Disability." June 22. Unpublished paper. Chicago: DePaul University.

———. 2008. "Americans with Disabilities Act." In *Encyclopedia of Race, Ethnicity, and Society,* edited by Richard T. Schaefer. Thousand Oaks, CA: Sage.

Michals, Jennifer M. 2003. "The Price We Pay to Get Richer: A Look at Student Indebtedness." Unpublished M.A. paper, DePaul University, Chicago, IL.

Michels, Robert. 1915. *Political Parties.* Glencoe, IL: Free Press (reprinted 1949).

Microfinance Information Exchange. 2011. "MIX Market." Accessed May 24 (www.themix.org).

Miles, James. 2009. "A Wary Repeat: A Special Report on China and America." *The Economist* (October 24):1–16.

Milgram, Stanley. 1963. "Behavioral Study of Obedience." *Journal of Abnormal and Social Psychology* 67 (October):371–378.

———. 1975. *Obedience to Authority: An Experimental View.* New York: Harper and Row.

Miller, Dan E. 2006. "Rumor: An Examination of Some Stereotypes." *Symbolic Interaction* 28 (4):505–519.

Miller, David L. 2000. *Introduction to Collective Behavior and Collective Action.* 2nd ed. Prospect Heights, IL: Waveland Press.

———, and JoAnne DeRoven Darlington. 2002. "Fearing for the Safety of Others: Disasters and the Small World Problem." Paper presented at Midwest Sociological Society, Milwaukee, WI.

Miller, Jacqueline W., Timothy S. Naimi, Robert D. Brewer, and Sherry Everett Jones. 2007. "Binge Drinking and Associated Health Risk Behaviors among High School Students." *Pediatrics* 119 (January):76–85.

Miller, Laura. 2008. "The Rise of the Superclass." Accessed in *Salon* May 2 (www.salon.com/books/review/2008/03/14/superclass/print.html).

Miller, Reuben. 1988. "The Literature of Terrorism." *Terrorism* 11 (1):63–87.

Mills, C. Wright. [1959] 2000a. *The Sociological Imagination.* 40th anniversary edition. New Afterword by Todd Gitlin. New York: Oxford University Press.

———. [1956] 2000b. *The Power Elite.* New edition. Afterword by Alan Wolfe. New York: Oxford University Press.

Miner, Horace. 1956. "Body Ritual among the Nacirema." *American Anthropologist* 58 (June):503–507.

Minnesota Center for Twin and Family Research. 2010. "Research at the MCTFR." Accessed January 24 (http://mctfr.psych.umn.edu/research/).

Minyard, Jeremy, and Tim Ortyl. 2009. "Reflected Appraisals." *Context* 8 (November):6–7.

Miyata, Kakuko, and Tetsuro Kobayashi. 2008. "Causal Relationship between Internet Use and Social Capital in Japan." *Asian Journal of Social Psychology* 11:42–52.

Mizruchi, Mark S. 1996. "What Do Interlocks Do? An Analysis, Critique, and Assessment of Research on Interlocking Directorates." Pp. 271–298 in *Annual*

Review of Sociology, 1996, edited by John Hagan and Karen Cook. Palo Alto, CA: Annual Reviews.

Moeller, Philip. 2009. "Unique Havens for an Aging America." *US News and World Report* (October):62–68.

Moeller, Susan D. 1999. *Compassion Fatigue.* London: Routledge.

Mogelonsky, Marcia. 1996. "The Rocky Road to Adulthood." *American Demographics* 18 (May):26–29, 32–35, 56.

Mohai, Paul, David Pellow, and J. Timmons Roberts. 2009. "Environmental Justice." *Annual Review of Environmental Research* 34:405–430.

———, and Robin Saha. 2007. "Racial Inequality in the Distribution of Hazardous Waste: A National-Level Reassessment." *Social Problems* 54 (3):343–370.

Mol, A. J. 2010. "Ecological Modernization as a Social Theory of Environmental Reform." Pp. 63–71 in *The International Handbook of Environmental Sociology,* 2nd ed., edited by Michael R. Redcraft and Graham Woodgate. Cheltenham, UK: Edward Elgar.

———, and D. A. Sonnenfeld, eds. 2000. *Ecological Modernization around the World.* Portland, OR: Frank Cass.

———, ———, and G. Spaargaren, eds. 2009. *The Ecological Modernization Reader.* London: Routledge.

Molotch, Harvey. 1970. "Oil in Santa Barbara and Power in America." *Sociological Inquiry* 40 (Winter):131–144.

Mollen, Milton. 1992. *"A Failure of Responsibility": Report to Mayor David N. Dinkins on the December 28, 1991, Tragedy at City College of New York.* New York: Office of the Deputy Mayor for Public Safety.

Momigliana, Anna. 2010. "Italy: Over 30 and Still Living with Mom." *Christian Science Monitor,* January 27. Accessible at www.csmonitor.com/layout/set/print/content/view/print/275435.

Monaghan, Peter. 1993. "Sociologist Jailed Because He 'Wouldn't Snitch' Ponders the Way Research Ought to Be Done." *Chronicle of Higher Education* 40 (September 1):A8, A9.

Moncarz, Roger J., Michael G. Wolf, and Benjamin Wright. 2008. "Service-Providing Occupations, Offshoring, and the Labor Market." *Monthly Labor Review* (December):71–86.

Money. 1987. "A Short History of Shortages." 16 (Fall, special issue):42.

Montgomery, Marilyn J., and Gwendolyn T. Sorell. 1997. "Differences in Love Attitudes across Family Life Stages." *Family Relations* 46:55–61.

Moore, Molly. 2006. "Romance, but Not Marriage." *Washington Post National Weekly Edition,* November 27, p. 18.

Moore, Wilbert E. 1967. *Order and Change: Essays in Comparative Sociology.* New York: Wiley.

Morin, Rich. 2009. "Most Middle-Aged Adults Are Rethinking Retirement Plans." May 28. Accessed January 26, 2010 (http://pewresearch.org/pubs/1234/the-threshold-generation).

Morris, Aldon. 2000. "Reflections on Social Movement Theory: Criticisms and Proposals." *Contemporary Sociology* 29 (May):445–454.

Morrison, Denton E. 1971. "Some Notes toward Theory on Relative Deprivation, Social Movements, and Social Change." *American Behavioral Scientist* 14 (May–June):675–690.

Morrison, Peter A., and Thomas M. Bryan. 2010. "Targeting Spatial Centers of Elderly Consumers in the U.S.A." *Population Research Policy Review* 29:33–46.

Morse, Arthur D. 1967. *While Six Million Died: A Chronicle of American Apathy.* New York: Ace.

Moskos, Peter. 2008. *Cop in the Hood: My Year Policing Baltimore's Eastern District.* Princeton NJ: Princeton University Press.

Mosley, J., and E. Thomson. 1995. Pp. 148–165 in *Fatherhood: Contemporary Theory, Research and Social Policy,* edited by W. Marsiglo. Thousand Oaks, CA: Sage.

Mueller, G. O. 2001. "Transnational Crime: Definitions and Concepts." Pp. 13–21 in *Combating Transnational Crime: Concepts, Activities, and Responses,* edited by P. Williams and D. Vlassis. London: Franklin Cass.

Mufson, Steven. 2007. "Turning Down the Heat." *Washington Post National Weekly Edition* 24 (July):6–8.

Muñoz, José A. 2008. "Protest and Human Rights Networks: The Case of the Zapatista Movement." *Sociology Compass* (April):1045–1058.

Murdock, George P. 1945. "The Common Denominator of Cultures." Pp. 123–142 in *The Science of Man in the World Crisis,* edited by Ralph Linton. New York: Columbia University Press.

———. 1949. *Social Structure.* New York: Macmillan.

———. 1957. "World Ethnographic Sample." *American Anthropologist* 59 (August):664–687.

Murphy, Caryle. 2009. "Behind the Veil." *Christian Science Monitor,* December 13, pp. 12–15.

Murphy, Dean E. 1997. "A Victim of Sweden's Pursuit of Perfection." *Los Angeles Times,* September 2, pp. A1, A8.

Murray, Velma McBride, Amanda Willert, and Diane P. Stephens. 2001. "The Half-Full Glass: Resilient African American Single Mothers and Their Children." *Family Focus* (June):F4–F5.

N

NAACP. 2008. *Out of Focus—Out of Sync Take 4.* Baltimore: NAACP.

NACCRRA (National Association of Child Care Resource and Referral Agencies). 2010. "Parents and the High Cost of Child Care: 2010 Update." Accessible at http://www.naccrra.org/docs/Cost_Report_073010-final.pdf.

Nakao, Keiko, and Judith Treas. 1994. "Updating Occupational Prestige and Socioeconomic Scores: How the New Measures Measure Up." *Sociological Methodology* 24:1–72.

NARAL Pro-Choice America. 2011. "Who Decides? Restrictions on Low-Income Women's Access to Abortion." Accessed March 17 (www.prochoiceamerica.org/what-is-choice/maps-and-charts/map.jsp?mapID=4).

Nash, Manning. 1962. "Race and the Ideology of Race." *Current Anthropology* 3 (June):285–288.

National Advisory Commission on Criminal Justice. 1976. *Organized Crime.* Washington, DC: U.S. Government Printing Office.

National Alliance for Caregiving. 2009. *Caregiving in the U.S.: Executive Summary.* Washington, DC: NAC and AARP.

National Alliance for Public Charter Schools. 2010. *Measuring Charter Performance: A Review of Public Charter School Achievement Studies.* 6th ed. Washington, DC: NAPCS.

———. 2011. Number of Charter Schools 2009–2010 and 2010–2011. Communication to Schaefer from NAPCS. June 30.

National Alliance on Mental Illness. 2008. "What Is Mental Illness?" Accessed May 24, 2011 (www.nami.org).

National Alliance to End Homelessness. 2011. "Total Homelessness by State—State of Homelessness 2011." Accessible at http://www.endhomelessness.org/content/article/detail/3656.

National Center for Education Statistics. 2009. *Homeschooled Students.* Accessed May 31 (http://nces.ed.gov/programs/coe/2009/section1/indicator06.asp).

———. 2010. *Digest of Education Statistics 2009.* Accessible at http://nces.ed.gov/pubs2010/2010013.pdf.

———. 2011. *Average Undergraduate Tuition and Fees.* Accessed March 29 (http://nces.ed.gov/programs/digest/d09/tables/dt09_335.asp).

National Center on Addiction and Substance Abuse at Columbia University. 2007. *Wasting the Best and the Brightest: Substance Abuse at America's Colleges and Universities.* New York: NCASA at Columbia University.

National Conference of State Legislatures. 2011. "Same-Sex Marriage, Civil Unions and Domestic Partnerships" and "Civil Unions & Domestic Partnership Statutes." Accessed March 21 (http://www.ncsl.org).

National Council on Disability. 2004. *Righting the ADA.* Washington, DC: NCD.

National Education Association. 2009. *Rankings and Estimates: Rankings of the States 2009 and Estimates of School Statistics 2010.* Accessible at http://www.nea.org.assets/docs/010rankings.pdf.

National Gay and Lesbian Task Force. 2008. "Anti-Adoption Laws in the U.S. (as of November 4)." Accessed March 21, 2011 (www.theTaskForce.org).

National Geographic. 2005. *Atlas of the World.* 8th ed. Washington, DC: National Geographic.

National Indian Child Welfare Association. 2010. "ICWA Online Training Course." Accessed January 15 (www.nicwa.org/ica_course).

National Institute of Justice. 2005. *Sexual Assault on Campus: What Colleges and Universities Are Doing about It.* Washington, DC: National Institute of Justice.

National Institute on Aging. 1999. *Early Retirement in the United States.* Washington, DC: U.S. Government Printing Office.

National Law Center on Homelessness and Poverty. 2009a. "Homes Not Handcuffs: The Criminalization of Homelessness in U.S. Cities." Accessible at www.nationalhomeless.org.

———. 2009b. "Maryland 1st to Protect Homeless from Hate Crimes." Accessed May 8 (www.nlchp.org/news.cfm?id=98).

National Organization for Men Against Sexism. 2011. Home Page. Accessed March 17 (www.nomas.org).

National Organization of Mothers of Twins Clubs. 2010. Home Page. Accessed January 24 (www.nomotc.org).

National Vital Statistics Reports. 2010. "Births, Marriages, Divorces, and Deaths: Provisional Data for March 26, 2010." *National Vital Statistics Reports* 58 (March 26).

Navarro, Mireya. 2005. "When You Contain Multitudes." *New York Times,* April 24, pp. 1, 2.

———. 2009. "In Environmental Push, Looking to Add Diversity." *New York Times,* March 10, p. A13.

Nelson, Emily. 2004. "Goodbye, 'Friends'; Hello, New Reality." *Wall Street Journal,* February 9, pp. B6, B10.

Neuman, Lawrence W. 2009. *Understanding Research.* Boston: Allyn and Bacon.

Neuwirth, Robert. 2004. *Shadow Cities: A Billion Squatters, a New Urban World.* New York: Routledge.

Newman, William M. 1973. *American Pluralism: A Study of Minority Groups and Social Theory.* New York: Harper and Row.

Newport, Frank. 2009. *On Darwin's Birthday, Only 4 in 10 Believe in Evolution.* February 11. Accessible at www.gallup.com.

———. 2010a. *In U.S., 64% Support Death Penalty in Cases of Murder.* November 8. Accessible at http://www.gallup.com/poll/144284/Support-Death-Penalty-Cases-Murder.aspx.

———. 2010b. *In U.S., Increasing Number Have No Religious Identity.* Accessed March 28, 2011 (www.gallup.com).

———. 2010c. "Americans' Global Warming Concerns Continue to Drop." March 11. Accessed April 27 (www.gallup.com/poll/126560/Americans-global-warming-concerns-continue-drop.aspx).

———, and Lydia Saad. 2011. *Gallup Review: Public Opinion Context of Tucson Shootings.* January 10. Accessed April 25 (http://www.gallup.com/poll/145526/Gallup-Review-Public-Opinion-Context-Tucson-Shootings.aspx?version=print).

Newsday. 1997. "Japan Sterilized 16,000 Women." September 18, p. A19.

New Unionism Network. 2011. "State of the Unions." Accessed February 10 (http://www.newunionism.net/State_of_the_Unions.htm).

New York Times. 2007. "University Officials Accused of Hiding Campus Homicide." June 24, p. 19.

———. 2008. "Law and Order." January 6, pp. 10–11.

NICHD. 2007. "Children Who Complete Intensive Early Childhood Program Show Gains in Adulthood: Greater College Attendance, Lower Crime and Depression." Accessed January 7, 2008 (www.nichd.nih.gov/news.releases/early_interventions_082107.cfm).

Nielsen Company. 2009. "The Nielsen Company's Guide to Super Bowl XLIII." Accessed February 7, 2010 (http://en-us.nielsen.com/main/news/news_releases/2009/january/the_nielsen_company0).

Nielsen, Joyce McCarl, Glenda Walden, and Charlotte A. Kunkel. 2000. "Gendered Heteronormativity: Empirical Illustrations in Everyday Life." *Sociological Quarterly* 41 (2):283–296.

Niemi, Richard G., and Michael J. Hanmer. 2010. "Voter Turnout among College Students: New Data and a Rethinking of Traditional Theories." *Social Science Quarterly* 91 (June):301–323.

Niesse, Mark. 2008. "Hawaiian Sovereignty Seekers Take Over Historic Iolani Palace in Honolulu." *News from Indian Country* (May 12):3.

———. 2011. "Native Hawaiian Self-Government May Be Set Up by State." *News from Indian Country* (March):3.

Niezen, Ronald. 2005. "Digital Identity: The Construction of Virtual Selfhood in the Indigenous Peoples' Movement." *Comparative Studies in Society and History* 47 (3):532–551.

Nixon, Darren. 2009. "'I Can't Put a Smiley Face On': Working-Class Masculinity, Emotional Labor and Service Work in the 'New Economy.'" *Gender, Work and Organization* 16 (3):300–322.

Nixon, Howard L., II. 1979. *The Small Group.* Englewood Cliffs, NJ: Prentice Hall.

Noam, Eli. 2009. *Media Ownership and Concentration in America.* Cambridge, MA: Oxford University Press.

Nolan, Patrick, and Gerhard Lenski. 2009. *Human Societies: An Introduction to Macrosociology.* 11th ed. Boulder, CO: Paradigm.

Noonan, Rita K. 1995. "Women against the State: Political Opportunities and Collective Action Frames in Chile's Transition to Democracy." *Sociological Forum* 10:81–111.

NORC. 2010. "General Social Surveys, 1972–2008. Number of Memberships." Accessed February 6 (www.norc.org/GSS+Website/Browse+GSS+Variables/Mbemonic+Index/).

Nordhaus, Ted, and Michael Shellenberger. 2007. *Break Through: From the Death of Environmentalism to the Politics of Possibility.* Boston: Houghton Mifflin.

Nordholt, Eric Schulte, Marijke Hartgers, and Rita Gircour, eds. 2004. "The Dutch Virtual Census of 2001." *Analysis and Methodology.* Voorburg: Statistics Netherlands.

NORML. 2010. "Active State Medical Marijuana Programs." Accessed December 9 (http://norml.org/index.cfm?Group_ID=3391).

Norris, Poppa, and Ronald Inglehart. 2004. *Sacred and Secular: Religion and Politics Worldwide.* Cambridge: Cambridge University Press.

North Carolina Department of Environmental and Natural Resources. 2008. "Warren County PCB Landfill Fact Sheet." Accessed April 9 (www.wastenotnc.org/WarrenCo_Fact_Sheet.htm).

NPD Group. 2008. "Wired Baby Boomers Going Digital, Visiting Social Networks and Watching Videos on the Web." Accessed March 18 (www.npd.com/press/releases/press_080909.html).

Nussbaum, Bruce. 2006. "Can Wal-Mart Make It in India?" November 28. Accessed January 23, 2007 (www.businessweek.com).

O

Oberschall, Anthony. 1973. *Social Conflict and Social Movements.* Englewood Cliffs, NJ: Prentice Hall.

O'Connor, Anne-Marie. 2004. "Time of Blogs and Bombs." *Los Angeles Times,* December 27, pp. E1, E14–E15.

O'Donnell, Mike. 1992. *A New Introduction to Sociology.* Walton-on-Thames, UK: Thomas Nelson and Sons.

Office of Immigration Statistics. 2008. "2007 Yearbook of Immigration Statistics." Washington, DC: U.S. Department of Homeland Security.

Ogburn, William F. 1922. *Social Change with Respect to Culture and Original Nature.* New York: Huebsch (reprinted 1966, New York: Dell).

———, and Clark Tibbits. 1934. "The Family and Its Functions." Pp. 661–708 in *Recent Social Trends in the United States,* edited by Research Committee on Social Trends. New York: McGraw-Hill.

O'Hare, William P., and Brenda Curry-White. 1992. "Is There a Rural Underclass?" *Population Today* 20 (March):6–8.

O'Harrow, Jr., Robert. 2005. "Mining Personal Data." *Washington Post National Weekly Edition,* February 6, pp. 8–10.

Okano, Kaori, and Motonori Tsuchiya. 1999. *Education in Contemporary Japan: Inequality and Diversity.* Cambridge: Cambridge University Press.

Oliver, Melvin L., and Thomas M. Shapiro. 2006. *Black Wealth/White Wealth: New Perspectives on Racial Inequality.* 2nd ed. New York: Routledge.

Omi, Michael, and Howard Winant. 1994. *Racial Formation in the United States.* 2nd ed. New York: Routledge.

Onishi, Norimitso. 2003. "Divorce in South Korea: Striking a New Attitude." *New York Times,* September 21, p. 19.

OpenNet Initiative. 2011. Home Page. Accessed April 11 (http://opennet.net).

Orfield, Gary, and Chungmei Lee. 2007. *Historic Reversals, Accelerating Resegregation, and the Need for New Integration Strategies.* Los Angeles: Civil Rights Project, UCLA.

Organisation for Economic Co-operation and Development. 2008. *Growing Unequal? Income Distribution and Poverty in OECD Countries.* Geneva: OECD.

———. 2009a. *OECD Factbook.* Paris: OECD. Accessed February 20, 2010 (http://titania.sourceoecd.org/pdf/factbook2009/3020090 11e-12-02-02.pdf).

———. 2009b. "Green at Fifteen? How 15-Year-Olds Perform in Environmental Sciences and Geosciences in PISA 2006." PISA, OECD Publishing. Accessible at http://dx.doi.org/10.1787/9789264063600-en.

———. 2011. *Statistics on Resource Flows to Developing Countries.* Geneva: OECD. Accessible at http://www.oecd.org/dataoecd/53/43/47137659.pdf.

Ormond, James. 2005. "The McDonaldization of Football." Accessed January 23, 2006 (http://courses.essex.ac.uk/sc/sc111).

Orum, Anthony M., and John G. Dale. 2009. *Political Sociology: Power and Participation in the Modern World.* 3rd ed. New York: Oxford University Press.

Outside the Classroom. 2009. "College Students Spend More Time Drinking than Studying." Accessed March 11 (www.outsidetheclassroom.com).

Oxford Poverty and Human Development Initiative. 2011. "Multidimensional Poverty Index." Accessed March 15 (www.ophi.org.uk).

P

Pace, Richard. 1993. "First-Time Televiewing in Amazonia: Television Acculturation in Gurupa, Brazil. *Ethnology* 32:187–205.

———. 1998. "The Struggle for Amazon Town." Boulder, CO: Lynne Rienner.

Pacific Institute. 2010a. *Cleaning the Waters: A Focus on Water Quality Solutions.* Nairobi, Kenya: Pacific Institute.

———. 2010b. "Water Conflict Chronology." Accessed April 19 (www.worldwater.org/chronology.html).

Padilla, Efren N. 2008. "Filipino Americans." Pp. 493–497 in vol. 1, *Encyclopedia of Race,*

Ethnicity, and Society, edited by Richard T. Schaefer. Thousand Oaks, CA: Sage.

Page, Charles H. 1946. "Bureaucracy's Other Face." *Social Forces* 25 (October):89–94.

Page, Jeremy. 2011. "China's One-Child Plan Faces New Fire." *New York Times,* April 29, pp. A1, A12.

Pager, Devah. 2007. *Marked: Race, Crime, and Funding Work in an Era of Mass Incarceration.* Chicago: University of Chicago Press.

———, Bruce Weston, and Bart Bonikowski. 2009. "Discrimination in a Low-Wage Labor Market: A Field Experiment." *American Sociological Review* 74 (October):777–799.

Pampel, Fred C., Patrick M. Krueger, and Justin T. Denney. 2010. "Socioeconomic Disparities in Health Behaviors." *Annual Review of Sociology* 36:349–370.

Park, Robert E. 1916. "The City: Suggestions for the Investigation of Human Behavior in the Urban Environment." *American Journal of Sociology* 20 (March):577–612.

———. 1922. *The Immigrant Press and Its Control.* New York: Harper.

———. 1936. "Succession, an Ecological Concept." *American Sociological Review* 1 (April):171–179.

Parker, Ashley. 2010. "Where Parties Look for an Audience." *New York Times,* October 30.

Parker, Suzi. 2010. "A Famous Case, DNA Evidence, and New Security." *Christian Science Monitor,* November 22, p. 19.

Parsons, Talcott. 1951. *The Social System.* New York: Free Press.

———. 1966. *Societies: Evolutionary and Comparative Perspectives.* Englewood Cliffs, NJ: Prentice Hall.

———. 1975. "The Sick Role and the Role of the Physician Reconsidered." *Milbank Medical Fund Quarterly Health and Society* 53 (Summer):257–278.

———, and Robert Bales. 1955. *Family: Socialization and Interaction Process.* Glencoe, IL: Free Press.

Passel, Jeffrey S., and D'Vera Cohn. 2011. "Unauthorized Immigrant Population National and State Trends, 2010." Washington, DC: Pew Research Center.

Passero, Kathy. 2002. "Global Travel Expert Roger Axtell Explains Why." *Biography* (July):70–73, 97–98.

Patterson, Thomas E. 2005. "Young Voters and the 2004 Election." Cambridge, MA: Vanishing Voter Project, Harvard University.

Pattillo-McCoy, Mary. 1999. *Black Picket Fences: Privilege and Peril among the Black Middle Class.* Chicago: University of Chicago Press.

Pear, Robert. 1997. "Now, the Archenemies Need Each Other." *New York Times,* June 22, sec. 4, pp. 1, 4.

———. 2009. "Congress Relaxes Rules on Suits over Pay Inequity." *New York Times,* January 28, p. A14.

Pendergrast, Mark. 1999. *Uncommon Grounds: The History of Coffee and How It Transformed Our World.* New York: Basic Books.

Pennington, Bill. 2008. "College Athletic Scholarships: Expectations Lose Out to Reality." *New York Times,* March 10, pp. A1, A15.

Perez, Evan. 2010. "Violent Crime Falls Sharply." *Wall Street Journal,* May 25, p. A23.

Perlman, Janice. 2010. *Favela: Four Decades of Living on the Edge in Rio de Janeiro.* London: Oxford University Press.

Perry, Tony. 2007. "Study: Deployment Does Not Increase Divorce." *Los Angeles Times,* April 16.

Peter, Laurence J., and Raymond Hull. 1969. *The Peter Principle.* New York: Morrow.

Petersen, John L. 2009. "How 'Wild Cards' May Reshape Our Future." *Futurist* (May–June):19–20.

Petersen, William. 1979. *Malthus.* Cambridge, MA: Harvard University Press.

Peterson, Karen S. 2003. "Unmarried with Children: For Better or Worse." *USA Today,* August 18, pp. 1A, 8A.

Petrášová, Alexandra. 2006. *Social Protection in the European Union.* Brussels: European Union.

Pew Forum on Religion and Public Life. 2008. *U.S. Religious Landscape Survey.* Washington, DC: Author.

———. 2010a. *U.S. Religious Knowledge Survey.* Washington, DC: Pew Forum. Accessible at http://pewforum.org.

———. 2010b. *Religious Knowledge Query.* Accessed March 23, 2011 (http://pewforum.org/Uploaded-Files/Topics/Belief-and-practices/religious-knowledge-quiz-handout.pdf).

Pew Global Attitudes Project. 2007. *Global Unease with Major World Powers.* Washington, DC: Pew Global.

Pew Internet and American Life Project. 2009. *Barriers to Broadband Adoption.* Accessed July 7 (http://www.pewinternet.org/Reports/2009/10-Home-Broadband-Adoption-2009/5-Barriers-to-broadband-adoption.aspx).

Pew Internet Project. 2009. "Demographics of Internet Users." Accessed February 4 (www.pewinternet.org/trends/User_Demo_Jan_2009.htm).

———. 2010. "Demographics of Internet Users." November 16. Accessible at www.pewinternet.org/Static-Pages/Trend-Data/Whos-Online.aspx.

Pew Research Center. 2009. "Americans Now Divided Over Both Issues: Public Takes Conservative Turn on Gun Control, Abortion." News release. Washington, DC: Pew Research Center.

———. 2010. *Marrying Out.* Washington, DC: PRC.

Pfeifer, Mark. 2008. "Vietnamese Americans" Pp. 1365–1368, vol. 3, in *Encyclopedia of Race, Ethnicity, and Society,* edited by Richard T. Schaefer. Thousand Oaks, CA: Sage.

Phelan, Jo C., Bruce G. Lint, and Parisha Tehranifar. 2010. "Social Conditions as Fundamental Causes of Health Inequalities: Theory, Evidence, and Policy Implications." *Journal of Health and Social Behavior* 51 (5):528–540.

Phillips, E. Barbara. 1996. *City Lights: Urban–Suburban Life in the Global Society.* New York: Oxford University Press.

Phillips, Susan A. 1999. *Wallbangin': Graffiti and Gangs in L.A.* Chicago: University of Chicago Press.

Piaget, Jean. 1954. *Construction of Reality in the Child.* Translated by Margaret Cook. New York: Basic Books.

Picca, Leslie Houts, and Joe R. Feagin. 2007. *Two-Faced Racism: Whites in Backstage and Frontstage.* New York: Routledge.

Pickert, Kate. 2009. "Getting Well While You Shop." *Time,* June 22, pp. 68–70.

Pincus, Fred L. 2003. *Reverse Discrimination: Dismantling the Myth.* Boulder, CO: Lynne Rienner.

———. 2008. "Reverse Discrimination." Pp. 1159–1161, vol. 3, in *Encyclopedia of Race, Ethnicity, and Society,* edited by Richard T. Schaefer. Thousand Oaks, CA: Sage.

Pinderhughes, Dianne. 1987. *Race and Ethnicity in Chicago Politics: A Reexamination of Pluralist Theory.* Urbana: University of Illinois Press.

Pinderhughes, Raquel. 2008. "Green Collar Jobs." Accessed June 29 (www.urbanhabitat.org/node/528).

Piven, Frances Fox, and Richard A. Cloward. 1996. "Welfare Reform and the New Class War." Pp. 72–86 in *Myths about the Powerless: Contesting Social Inequalities,* edited by M. Brinton Lykes, Ali Banuazizi, Ramsay Liem, and Michael Morris. Philadelphia: Temple University Press.

Plomin, Robert. 1989. "Determinants of Behavior." *American Psychologist* 44 (February):105–111.

Plüss, Caroline. 2005. "Constructing Globalized Ethnicity." *International Sociology* 20 (June):201–224.

Pogash, Carol. 2008. "Poor Students in High School Suffer Stigma from Lunch Aid." *New York Times,* March 1, pp. A1, A14.

Polletta, Francesca, and James M. Jasper. 2001. "Collective Identity and Social Movements." Pp. 283–305 in *Annual Review of Sociology, 2001,* edited by Karen S. Cook and Leslie Hogan. Palo Alto, CA: Annual Reviews.

Pontin, Jason. 2007. "First, Cure Malaria. Next, Global Warming." *New York Times,* June 3, p. 3.

Popenoe, David, and Barbara Dafoe Whitehead. 1999. *Should We Live Together? What Young Adults Need to Know about Cohabitation before Marriage.* Rutgers, NJ: The National Marriage Project.

Population Reference Bureau. 1996. "Speaking Graphically." *Population Today* 24 (June/July).

Portes, Alejandro, Cristina Escobar, and Renelinda Arana. 2008. "Bridging the Gap: Transnational and Ethnic Organizations in the Political Incorporation of Immigrants in the United States." *Ethnic and Racial Studies* 31 (September 6):1056–1090.

Powell, Brian, Catherine Bolzendahl, Claudia Geist, and Lola Carr Steelman. 2010. *Counted Out. Same-Sex Relationships and Americans' Definitions of Family.* New York: Russell Sage Foundation.

Powell, Gary N. 2010. *Women and Men in Management.* 4th ed. Thousand Oaks, CA: Sage.

Prehn, John W. 1991. "Migration." Pp. 190–191 in *Encyclopedia of Sociology,* 4th ed. Guilford, CT: Dushkin.

Preston, Jennifer, and Brian Stelter. 2011. "Cellphone Cameras Become World's Eyes and Ears on Protests across the Middle East." *New York Times,* February 19, p. A7.

Priest, Dana. 2008. "Soldiers on the Edge." *Washington Post National Weekly Edition* 25 (February 4):8–9.

Prince, Martin, Vikram Patel, Shekhar Saxena, Mario Maj, Johanna Maselko, Michael Phillips, and Atif Rahman. 2007. "No Health without Mental Health." *The Lancet* 370 (September 8):859–877.

Proulx, Nichole, Sanfra L. Caron, and Mary Ellin Logue. 2006. "A Look at the Implications of Age Differences in Marriage." *Journal of Couple and Relationship Therapy* 5 (October):43–64.

Provasnik, Stephen, and Michael Planty. 2008. *Community Colleges: Special Supplement to the Condition of Education 2008.* Washington, DC: U.S. Government Printing Office.

Pryor, John H., Sylvia Hurtado, Victor B. Saenz, José Luis Santos, and William S. Korn. 2007. *The American Freshman: Forty Year Trends.* Los Angeles: Higher Education Research Institute, UCLA.

———, ———, Linda DeAngelo, Laura Palucki Blake, and Serge Tran. 2010. *The American Freshman: National Norms Fall 2010.* Los Angeles: Higher Education Research Institute, UCLA.

Quadagno, Jill. 2008. *Aging and the Life Course: An Introduction to Social Gerontology.* 4th ed. New York: McGraw-Hill.

———. 2011. *Aging and the Life Course: An Introduction to Social Gerontology.* 5th ed. New York: McGraw-Hill.

Quarantelli, Enrico L. 1957. "The Behavior of Panic Participants." *Sociology and Social Research* 41 (January):187–194.

———, and Russell R. Dynes. 1970. "Property Norms and Looting: Their Patterns in Continuity Crises." *Phylon* (Summer):168–182.

———, and James R. Hundley, Jr. 1975. "A Test of Some Propositions about Crowd Formation and Behavior." Pp. 538–554 in *Readings in Collective Behavior,* edited by Robert R. Evans. Chicago: Rand McNally.

Quillian, Lincoln. 2006. "New Approaches to Understanding Racial Prejudice and Discrimination." *Annual Review of Sociology* 32:299–328.

Quinney, Richard. 1970. *The Social Reality of Crime.* Boston: Little, Brown.

———. 1974. *Criminal Justice in America.* Boston: Little, Brown.

———. 1979. *Criminology.* 2nd ed. Boston: Little, Brown.

———. 1980. *Class, State and Crime.* 2nd ed. New York: Longman.

Rabikovitch, Shelley, and James Lewis, eds. 2004. *The Encyclopedia of Modern Witchcraft and New Paganism.* New York: Citadel Press.

Rainie, Lee. 2005. *Sports Fantasy Leagues Online.* Washington, DC: Pew Internet and American Life Project.

Rajan, Gita, and Shailja Sharma. 2006. *New Cosmopolitanisms: South Asians in the US.* Stanford, CA: Stanford University Press.

Ramet, Sabrina. 1991. *Social Currents in Eastern Europe: The Source and Meaning of the Great Transformation.* Durham, NC: Duke University Press.

Rampell, Catherine. 2010. "The Growing Underclass: Jobs Gone Forever." *New York Times Online.* Accessed March 5, 2011 (http://economix.blogs.nytimes.com/2010/01/28/the-growing-underclass-jobs-gone-forever/?pagemode=print).

Ramirez, Eddy. 2002. "Ageism in the Media Is Seen as Harmful to Health of the Elderly." *Los Angeles Times,* September 5, p. A20.

RAND. 2007. "RAND Study Finds Divorce among Soldiers Has Not Spiked Higher Despite Stress Created by Battlefield Deployments." News release. April 12 (www.rand.org).

———. 2010. "Retail Medical Clinics Perform Well Relative to Other Medical Settings." *RAND Review* (Winter 2009–2010). Accessed January 25 (www.rand.org/publications/randreview/issues/winter2009/news.html#medclinics).

Rangaswamy, Padma. 2005. "Asian Indians in Chicago." In *The New Chicago,* edited by John Koval et al. Philadelphia: Temple University Press.

Ratha, Dilip, Sanket Mohaptra, and Ani Silwat. 2010. "Outlook for Remittance Flows 2010–2011." *Migration and Development Brief, World Bank.*

Ravitch, Diane. 2010. *The Death and Life of the Great American School System: How Testing and Choice Are Undermining Education.* New York: Basic Books.

Rawlinson, Linnie, and Nick Hunt. 2009. "Jackson Dies, Almost Takes Internet with Him." Accessed July 1 (www.cnn.com/2009/TECH/06/26/michael.jackson.internet/).

Ray, Raka. 1999. *Fields of Protest: Women's Movement in India.* Minneapolis: University of Minnesota Press.

Raybon, Patricia. 1989. "A Case for 'Severe Bias.'" *Newsweek* 114 (October 2):11.

Reinharz, Shulamit. 1992. *Feminist Methods in Social Research.* New York: Oxford University Press.

Reitzes, Donald C., and Elizabeth J. Mutran. 2006. "Lingering Identities in Retirement." *Sociological Quarterly* 47:333–359.

Religion News Service. 2003. "New U.S. Guidelines on Prayer in Schools Get Mixed Reaction." *Los Angeles Times,* February 15, p. B24.

Religion Watch. 2006. "Hinduism Shaping India's Pragmatic Use of Biotechnology." April.

Rennison, Callie. 2002. *Criminal Victimization 2001. Changes 2000–01 with Trends 1993–2001.* Washington, DC: U.S. Government Printing Office.

Renzulli, Linda A., and Vincent J. Roscigno. 2007. "Charter Schools and Public Good." *Contexts* 6 (Winter):31–36.

Reschovsky, Clara. 2004. *Journey to Work: 2000.* Census 2000 Brief C2KBR-23. Washington, DC: U.S. Government Printing Office.

Reuters. 2009. "Terrorism Suspect Wins Police Brutality Claim." Accessed May 18 (http://uk.reuters.com).

———. 2010. "Geoghegan Replaces Feinberg as Pay Czar." September 10. Accessed March 5, 2011 (http://www.reuters.com/assets/print?aid=USTRE6894ZH20100910).

Revkin, Andrew C. 2007. "Wealth and Poverty, Drought and Flood: Report from Four Fronts in the War on Warming." *New York Times,* April 3, pp. D4–D5.

Rice, Ronald E. 2008. *Media Ownership: Research and Regulation.* Cresskill, NJ: Hampton Press.

Rideout, Victoria K., Ulla G. Foehr, and Donald F. Roberts. 2010. Generation M: Media in the Lives of 8–18 Year-Olds. Kaiser Family Foundation. Accessible at www.kff.org/entmedia/mh012010pkg.cfm.

Riding, Alan. 1998. "Why 'Titanic' Conquered the World." *New York Times,* April 26, sec. 2, pp. 1, 28, 29.

———. 2005. "Unesco Adopts New Plan against Cultural Invasion." *New York Times,* October 21, p. B3.

Rieker, Patricia R., and Chloe E. Bird. 2000. "Sociological Explanations of Gender Differences in Mental and Physical Health." Pp. 98–113 in *Handbook of Medical Sociology,* edited by Chloe Bird, Peter Conrad, and Allan Fremont. New York: Prentice Hall.

Rifkin, Jeremy. 1995. *The End of Work; The Decline of the Global Labor Force and the Dawn of the Post-Market Era.* New York: Tarcher/Putnam.

———. 1996. "Civil Society in the Information Age." *The Nation* 262 (February 26):11–12, 14–16.

Riley, Matilda White, Robert L. Kahn, and Anne Foner. 1994a. *Age and Structural Lag.* New York: Wiley InterScience.

———, Robert L. Kahn, and Anne Foner, in association with Karin A. Mock. 1994b. "Introduction: The Mismatch between People and Structures." Pp. 1–36 in *Age and Structural Lag,* edited by Matilda White Riley, Robert L. Kahn, and Anne Foner. New York: Wiley InterScience.

Rimer, Sara. 1998. "As Centenarians Thrive, 'Old' Is Redefined." *New York Times,* June 22, pp. A1, A14.

Ritzer, George. 1977. *Working: Conflict and Change.* 2nd ed. Englewood Cliffs, NJ: Prentice Hall.

———. 2000. *The McDonaldization of Society.* New Century Edition. Thousand Oaks, CA: Pine Forge Press.

———. 2002. *McDonaldization: The Reader.* Thousand Oaks, CA: Pine Forge Press.

———. 2004. *The Globalization of Nothing.* Thousand Oaks, CA: Pine Forge Press.

———. 2008. *The McDonaldization of Society 5.* Thousand Oaks, CA: Sage.

———. 2011. *McDonaldization of Society 6.* Thousand Oaks, CA: Sage.

Robelon, Erik W. 2007. "'Moment-of-Silence' Generates Loud Debate in Illinois." *Education Week,* October 24.

Roberts, J. Timmons, Peter E. Grines, and Jodie L. Mańale. 2003. "Social Roots of Global Environmental Change: A World-Systems Analysis of Carbon Dioxide Emissions." *Journal of World-Systems Research* 9 (Summer):277–315.

Roberts, Sam. 2010. "Extended Family Households Are on the Rise, Census Finds." *New York Times,* March 19.

Robertson, Roland. 1988. "The Sociological Significance of Culture: Some General Considerations." *Theory, Culture, and Society* 5 (February):3–23.

Robinson, Kristopher, and Edward M. Crenshaw. 2010. "Reevaluating the Global Digital Divide: Socio-Demographic and Conflict Barriers to the Internet Revolution." *Sociological Inquiry* 80 (February):34–62

Robison, Jennifer. 2002. "Feminism—What's in a Name?" Accessed February 25, 2007 (www.galluppoll.com).

Rodman, George. 2011. *Mass Media in a Changing World.* 3rd ed. New York: McGraw-Hill.

Rogan, Eugene. 2009. "Sand, Sea and Shopping." *Guardian Weekly,* October 16, pp. 38–39.

Roman, John, Aaron Chalfin, Aaron Sundquist, Carly Knight, and Askar Darmenov. 2008. *The Cost of the Death Penalty in Maryland.* Washington, DC: Urban Institute.

Rootes, Christopher. 2007. "Environmental Movements." Pp. 608–640 in *The Blackwell Companion to Social Movements,* edited by David A. Snow, Sarah A. Sovle, and Hanspeter Kriesi. Malden, MA: Blackwell.

Roscigno, Vincent J. 2010. "Ageism in the American Workplace." *Contexts* (Winter):15–21.

Rose, Arnold. 1951. *The Roots of Prejudice.* Paris: UNESCO.

Rose, Peter I., Myron Glazer, and Penina Migdal Glazer. 1979. "In Controlled Environments: Four Cases of Intense Resocialization." Pp. 320–338 in *Socialization and the Life Cycle,* edited by Peter I. Rose. New York: St. Martin's Press.

Rosen, Eva, and Sudhir Alladi Venkatesh. 2008. "A Perversion of Choice: Sex Work Offers Just Enough in Chicago's Urban Ghetto." *Journal of Contemporary Ethnography* (August):417–441.

Rosenberg, Douglas H. 1991. "Capitalism." Pp. 33–34 in *Encyclopedic Dictionary of Sociology,* 4th ed., edited by Dushkin Publishing Group. Guilford, CT: Dushkin.

Rosenberg, Howard. 2003. "Snippets of the 'Unique' Al Jazeera." *Los Angeles Times,* April 4, pp. E1, E37.

Rosenfeld, Jake. 2010. "Little Labor." *Pathways* (Summer):4–6.

Rosenfeld, Michael J. 2010. "Meeting Online: The Rise of the Internet as a Social Intermediary." Accessed April 2 (www.stanford.edu/~mrosenfe/Rosenfeld_How_Couples_Meet_PAA_updated.pdf).

Rosenthal, Robert, and Lenore Jacobson. 1968. *Pygmalion in the Classroom.* New York: Holt.

———. 1992. *Pygmalion in the Classroom: Teacher Expectations and Pupils' Intellectual Development.* Newly expanded edition. Bancyfelin, UK: Crown House.

Ross, John. 1996. "To Die in the Street: Mexico City's Homeless Population Booms as Economic Crisis Shakes Social Protections." *SSSP Newsletter* 27 (Summer):14–15.

Rossi, Alice S. 1968. "Transition to Parenthood." *Journal of Marriage and the Family* 30 (February):26–39.

———. 1984. "Gender and Parenthood." *American Sociological Review* 49 (February):1–19.

Rossi, Peter H. 1987. "No Good Applied Social Research Goes Unpunished." *Society* 25 (November–December):73–79.

Rossides, Daniel W. 1997. *Social Stratification: The Interplay of Class, Race, and Gender.* 2nd ed. Upper Saddle River, NJ: Prentice Hall.

Roszak, Theodore. 1969. *The Making of a Counterculture.* Garden City, NY: Doubleday.

Rothkopf, David. 2008. *Superclass: The Global Power Elite and the World They Are Making.* New York: Farrar, Straus and Giroux.

Roy, Donald F. 1959. "'Banana Time': Job Satisfaction and Informal Interaction." *Human Organization* 18 (Winter):158–168.

Rubin, Alissa J. 2003. "Pat-Down on the Way to Prayer." *Los Angeles Times,* November 25, pp. A1, A5.

———, and Sam Dagher. 2009. "Election Quotas for Iraqi Women Are Weakened, Provoking Anger as Vote Nears." *New York Times,* January 14, p. A13.

Ruebain, David. 2005. "Disability Discrimination Act of 1995 (United Kingdom)." Pp. 420–422 in *Encyclopedia of Disability,* edited by Gary Albrecht. Thousand Oaks, CA: Sage.

Ryan, William. 1976. *Blaming the Victim.* Rev. ed. New York: Random House.

Rymer, Russ. 1993. *Genie: An Abused Child's Flight from Science.* New York: HarperCollins.

Saad, Lydia. 2004. "Divorce Doesn't Last." *Gallup Poll Tuesday Briefing.* March 30. Accessible at www.gallup.com.

———. 2010a. "Public Agrees with Court: Campaign Money Is 'Free Speech.'" January 22. Accessed April 13 (www.gallup.com).

———. 2010b. "Parties Even in Congressional Midterm Preferences." April 7. Accessed April 16 (www.gallup.com).

———. 2010c. "Americans Firm in Prioritizing Economy over Environment." March 18. Accessible at www.gallup.com.

———. 2011. "Americans' Worries about Economy, Budget Top Other Issues." March 21. Accessible at www.gallup.com.

Sabol, William J., Heather C. West, and Matthew Cooper. 2009. "Prisoners in 2008." *Bureau of Justice Statistics Bulletin* (December).

Sachs, Jeffrey D. 2005. *The End of Poverty: Economic Possibilities for Our Time.* New York: Penguin.

Sacks, Peter. 2007. *Tearing Down the Gates: Confronting the Class Divide in American Education.* Berkeley: University of California Press.

Sagarin, Edward, and Jose Sanchez. 1988. "Ideology and Deviance: The Case of the Debate over the Biological Factor." *Deviant Behavior* 9 (1):87–99.

Saguy, Abigail, and Rene Almeling. 2008. "Fat in the Fire? Science, the News Media, and the 'Obesity Epidemic.'" *Sociological Forum* 23 (March):53–83.

Said, Edward W. 2001. "The Clash of Ignorance." *Nation,* October 22.

Sale, Kirkpatrick. 1996. *Rebels against the Future: The Luddites and Their War on the Industrial Revolution* (with a new preface by the author). Reading, MA: Addison-Wesley.

Salem, Richard, and Stanislaus Grabarek. 1986. "Sociology B.A.s in a Corporate Setting: How Can They Get There and of What Value Are They?" *Teaching Sociology* 14 (October):273–275.

Sampson, Robert J., and W. Byron Graves. 1989. "Community Structure and Crime: Testing Social-Disorganization Theory." *American Journal of Sociology* 94 (January):774–802.

Samuels, Robert. 2010. "A Suicide Reminds Gulf Coast of Oil Spill." *Miami Herald,* June 28. Accessible at http://www.mcclatchydc.com/2010/06/28/96665/a-suicide-reminds-gulf-coast-of.html.

Samuelson, Paul A., and William D. Nordhaus. 2010. *Economics.* 19th ed. New York: McGraw-Hill.

Sanday, Peggy Reeves. 2002. *Women at the Center: Life in a Modern Matriarchy.* Ithaca, NY: Cornell University Press.

———. 2008. Home Page. Accessed March 15 (www.sas.upenn.edu/psanday/).

Sandefur, Rebecca L. 2008. "Access to Civil Justice and Race, Class, and Gender Inequality." *Annual Review of Sociology* 34:339–358.

Sanders, Edmund. 2004. "Coming of Age in Iraq." *Los Angeles Times,* August 14, pp. A1, A5.

Sanderson, Warren, and Sergei Scherbov. 2008. "Rethinking Age and Aging." *Population Bulletin* 63 (December).

Santos, José Alcides Figueiredo. 2006. "Class Effects on Racial Inequality in Brazil." *Dados* 2:1–35.

Sanua, Marianne R. 2007. "AJC and Intermarriage: The Complexities of Jewish Continuity, 1960–2006." Pp. 3–32 in *American Jewish Yearbook 2007,* edited by David Singer and Lawrence Grossman. New York: American Jewish Committee.

Sanyal, Paromita. 2009. "From Credit to Collective Action: The Role of Microfinance in Promoting Women's Social Capital and Normative Influence." *American Sociological Review* 74 (August):529–550.

Sapir, Edward. 1929. "The State of Linguistics as a Science." *Language* 5 (4):207–214.

Saporito, Bill. 2007. "Restoring Wal-Mart." *Time* 170 (November 12):46–48, 50, 52.

Sassen, Saskia. 2005. "New Global Classes: Implications for Politics." Pp. 143–170 in *The New Egalitarianism,* edited by Anthony Giddens and Patrick Diamond. Cambridge: Polity.

Sawhill, Isabel, and Ron Haskins. 2009. "If You Can Make It Here . . ." *Washington Post National Weekly Edition,* November 9, p. 27.

———, and John E. Morton. 2007. *Economic Mobility: Is the American Dream Alive and Well?* Washington, DC: Economic Mobility Project, Pew Charitable Trusts.

Sayer, Liana C., Suzanne M. Bianchi, and John P. Robinson. 2004. "Are Parents Investing Less in Children? Trends in Mothers' and Fathers' Time with Children." *American Journal of Sociology* 110 (July):1–43.

Scarce, Rik. 2005. "A Law to Protect Scholars." *Chronicle of Higher Education,* August 12, p. 324.

Schadler, Ted. 2009. *US Telecommuting Forecast, 2009–2016.* Accessible at www.forester.com.

Schaefer, Peter. 2008. "Digital Divide." Pp. 388–389, vol. 1, in *Encyclopedia of Race, Ethnicity, and Society in the United States,* edited by Richard T. Schaefer. Thousand Oaks, CA: Sage.

Schaefer, Richard T. 1998. "Differential Racial Mortality and the 1995 Chicago Heat Wave." Presentation at the annual meeting of the American Sociological Association, August, San Francisco.

———. 2008a. "Australia, Indigenous People." Pp. 115–119, vol. 1, in *Encyclopedia of Race, Ethnicity, and Society,* edited by Richard T. Schaefer. Thousand Oaks, CA: Sage.

———. 2008b. "'Power' and 'Power Elite.'" In *Encyclopedia of Social Problems,* edited by Vincent Parrillo. Thousand Oaks, CA: Sage.

———. 2011. *Race and Ethnicity in the United States.* 12th ed. Census Update. Upper Saddle River, NJ: Prentice Hall.

———. 2012. *Racial and Ethnic Groups.* 13th ed. Upper Saddle River, NJ: Pearson.

———, and William Zellner. 2011. *Extraordinary Groups.* 9th ed. New York: Worth.

Scharnberg, Kirsten. 2007. "Black Market for Midwives Defies Bans." *Chicago Tribune,* November 25, pp. 1, 10.

Scherer, Ron. 2009. "Job Migration to Suburbs: An Unstoppable Flow?" *New York Times,* April 6.

———. 2010a. "A Long Struggle to Find Jobs." *Christian Science Monitor,* January 31, pp. 18–19.

———. 2010b. "For Jobless, Online Friends Can Be Lifelines." *Christian Science Monitor,* March 25, p. 21.

Scherer/Owings, Michael. 2010. "The Permanent Campaign." *Time* 173:48.

Schleifer, Yigal. 2009. "In Turkey, Surfing for Brides." *Christian Science Monitor,* July 5, p. 14.

Schlesinger, Traci. 2011. "The Failure of Race-Neutral Policies: How Mandatory Terms and Sentencing Enhancements Increased Racial Disparities in Prison Admission Rates." *Crime & Delinquency* 57 (January):56–81. Published online 2008 (http://cad.sagepub.com/pap.dtl).

Schmeeckle, Maria. 2007. "Gender Dynamics in Stepfamilies: Adult Stepchildren's

Views." *Journal of Marriage and Family* 69 (February):174–189.

———, Roseann Giarrusso, Du Feng, and Vern L. Bengtson. 2006. "What Makes Someone Family? Adult Children's Perceptions of Current and Former Stepparents." *Journal of Marriage and Family* 68 (August):595–610.

Schnaiberg, Allan. 1994. *Environment and Society: The Enduring Conflict.* New York: St. Martin's Press.

Schneider, Friedrich. 2010. "Dues and Don'ts." *The Economist* (August 14):62.

Schonfeld, Erick. 2010. "Costolo: Twitter Now Has 190 Million Users Tweeting 65 Million Times a Day." Accessible at TechCrunch at http://techcrunch.com/2010/06/08/twitter-190-million-users/.

Schram, Sangord F., Ruhard C. Fording, Joe Soss, and Linda Houser. 2009. "Deciding to Discipline: Race, Choice and Punishment at the Frontlines of Welfare Reform." *American Sociological Review* 74 (June):398–422.

Schull, Natasha Dow. 2005. "Digital Gambling: The Coincidence of Desire and Design." *Annals of the American Academy of Political and Social Science* 597 (1):65–81.

Schulman, Gary I. 1974. "Race, Sex, and Violence: A Laboratory Test of the Sexual Threat of the Black Male Hypothesis." *American Journal of Sociology* 79 (March):1260–1272.

Schur, Edwin M. 1965. *Crimes without Victims: Deviant Behavior and Public Policy.* Englewood Cliffs, NJ: Prentice Hall.

———. 1968. *Law and Society: A Sociological View.* New York: Random House.

———. 1985. "'Crimes without Victims': A 20-Year Reassessment." Paper presented at the annual meeting of the Society for the Study of Social Problems.

Schwartz, Howard D., ed. 1994. *Dominant Issues in Medical Sociology.* 3rd ed. New York: McGraw-Hill.

Schwartz, Mattathias. 2006. "The Hold-'Em Holdup." *New York Times Magazine,* June 11.

Schwartz, Shalom H., and Anat Bardi. 2001. "Value Hierarchies across Cultures: Taking a Similarities Perspective." *Journal of Cross-Cultural Perspective* 32 (May):268–290.

Schwartzman, Paul. 2009. "Nowhere to Go but Down." *Washington Post National Weekly Edition,* August 10, pp. 13–14.

Scotch, Richard. 1989. "Politics and Policy in the History of the Disability Rights Movement." *The Milbank Quarterly* 67 (Suppl. 2):380–400.

———. 2001. *From Good Will to Civil Rights: Transforming Federal Disability Policy.* 2nd ed. Philadelphia: Temple University Press.

Scott, Alan. 1990. *Ideology and the New Social Movements.* London: Unwin Hyman.

Scott, Gregory. 2001. "Broken Windows behind Bars: Eradicating Prison Gangs through Ecological Hardening and Symbolic Cleansing." *Corrections Management Quarterly* 5 (Winter):23–36.

Scott, W. Richard, and Gerald F. Davis. 2007. *Organizations and Organizing: Rational, Natural and Open Systems Perspectives.* New York: Pearson.

Search Engine Watch. 2011. "comScore: Bing Grows for Sixth Straight Year." March 16. Accessible at http://searchenginewatch.com/3642049.

Seccombe, Karen. 2011. "So You Think I Drive a Cadillac?" Boston: Allyn and Bacon.

Secretan, Thierry. 1995. *Going into Darkness: Fantastic Coffins from Africa.* London: Thames and Hudson.

Security on Campus. 2008. "Complying with the Jeanne Clery Act." Accessed January 13 (www.securityoncampus.org/crimestats/index.html).

Seidman, Steven. 1994. "Heterosexism in America: Prejudice against Gay Men and Lesbians." Pp. 578–593 in *Introduction to Social Problems,* edited by Craig Calhoun and George Ritzer. New York: McGraw-Hill.

Sellers, Frances Stead. 2004. "Voter Globalization." *Washington Post National Weekly Edition,* November 29, p. 22.

Selod, Saher Farooq. 2008a. "Muslim Americans." Pp. 920–923, vol. 2, in *Encyclopedia of Race, Ethnicity, and Society,* edited by Richard T. Schaefer. Thousand Oaks, CA: Sage.

———. 2008b. "Veil." Pp. 1359–1360, vol. 3, in *Encyclopedia of Race, Ethnicity, and Society,* edited by Richard T. Schaefer. Thousand Oaks, CA: Sage.

Sengupta, Somini. 2004. "For Iraqi Girls, Changing Land Narrows Lines." *New York Times,* June 27, pp. A1, A11.

———. 2006. "Report Shows Muslims Near Bottom of Social Ladder." *New York Times,* November 29, p. A4.

———. 2009. "An Empire for Poor Working Women, Guided by a Gandhian Approach." *New York Times,* March 7, p. A6.

Senior Action in a Gay Environment. 2010. Home Page. Accessed March 21 (www.sageusa.org).

Sernau, Scott. 2001. *Worlds Apart: Social Inequalities in a New Century.* Thousand Oaks, CA: Pine Forge Press.

Settersten, Richard, and Barbara Ray. 2011. *Not Quite Adults: Why 20-Somethings Are Choosing a Slower Path to Adulthood, and Why It's Good for Everyone.* New York: Bantam.

Shachtman, Tom. 2006. *Rumspringa: To Be or Not to Be Amish.* New York: North Point Press.

Shah, Anup. 2009. "Climate Justice and Equity." October 4. Accessed December 12 (www.globalissues.org/print/articles/231).

Shane, Scott. 2010. "Wars Fought and Wars Googled." *New York Times,* June 27, pp. PWK1–5.

Shapiro, Joseph P. 1993. *No Pity: People with Disabilities Forging a New Civil Rights Movement.* New York: Times Books.

Shapiro, Thomas M., Tatjana Meschede, and Laura Sullivan. 2010. "The Racial Wealth Gap Increases Fourfold." Research and Policy Brief, Institute on Assets and Social Policy, Brandeis University.

Shapley, Dan. 2010. "4 Dirty Secrets of the Exxon Valdez Oil Spill." Accessed May 3 (www.thedailygreen.com).

Sharkey, Patrick. 2009. *Neighbors and the Black-White Mobility Gap.* Washington, DC: Economic Mobility Project.

Sharma, Hari M., and Gerard C. Bodeker. 1998. "Alternative Medicine." Pp. 228–229 in *Britannica Book of the Year 1998.* Chicago: Encyclopaedia Britannica.

Sharp, Jeff S., and Jill K. Clark. 2008. "Between the Country and the Concrete: Rediscovering the Rural-Urban Fringe." *City and Community* 7 (March):61–77.

Shaw, Claude, and Henry D. McKay. 1942. *Juvenile Delinquency and Urban Areas.* Chicago: University of Chicago Press.

Sheehan, Charles. 2005. "Poor Seniors Take On Plans of Condo Giant." *Chicago Tribune,* March 22, pp. 1, 9.

Sherman, Arloc. 2007. *Income Inequality Hits Record Levels, New CBO Data Show.* Washington, DC: Center on Budget and Policy Priorities.

Shibutani, Tamotshu. 1966. *Improvised News: A Sociological Study of Rumor.* Indianapolis: Bobbs-Merrill.

Shin, Hyon B., and Rosalind Bruno. 2003. "Language Use and English-Speaking Ability: 2000." *Census 2000 Brief,* C2KBR-29. Washington, DC: U.S. Government Printing Office.

Shogren, Elizabeth. 1994. "Treatment against Their Will." *Los Angeles Times,* August 18, pp. A1, A14–A15.

Shostak, Arthur B. 2002. "Clinical Sociology and the Art of Peace Promotion: Earning a World without War." Pp. 325–345 in *Using Sociology: An Introduction from the Applied and Clinical Perspectives,* edited by Roger A. Straus. Lanham, MD: Rowman and Littlefield.

Sicular, Terry, Ximing Yue, Bjorn Gustafsson, and Shi Li. 2006. "The Urban-Rural Income Gap and Inequality in China." Research Paper No. 2006/135, United Nations University—World Institute for Development Economic Research.

Sieber, Renée E., Daniel Spitzberg, Hannah Muffatt, Kristen Brewer, Blanka Füleki, and Naomi Arbit. 2006. *Influencing Climate Change Policy: Environmental Non-Governmental Organizations (ENGOs) Using Virtual and Physical Activism.* Montreal: McGill University.

Siegel, Paul, Elizabeth Martin, and Rusalind Bruno. 2001. "Language Use and Linguistic Isolation: Historical Data and Methodological Issues." Paper presented at the Statistical Policy Seminar, Bethesda, MD.

Silver, Ira. 1996. "Role Transitions, Objects, and Identity." *Symbolic Interaction* 10 (1):1–20.

Silverman, Rachel Emma. 2009. "As Jobs Grow Scarce, Commuter Marriages Rise." Accessed March 31, 2010 (http://blogs.wsj.com/juggle/2009/01/16/as-jobs-grow-scarce-commuter-marriages-rise/).

Silverstein, Ken. 2010. "Shopping for Sweat: The Human Cost of a Two-Dollar T-shirt." *Harpers* 320 (January):36–44.

Simmel, Georg. [1917] 1950. *Sociology of Georg Simmel.* Translated by K. Wolff. Glencoe, IL: Free Press (originally written in 1902–1917).

Simmons, Tavia, and Martin O'Connell. 2003. "Married-Couple and Unmarried-Partner Households: 2000." *Census 2000 Special Reports,* CENBR-5. Washington, DC: U.S. Government Printing Office.

Simon, Stephanie. 2007. "It's Easter; Shall We Gather at the Desktops?" *Los Angeles Times,* April 8, p. A13.

Sisson, Carmen K. 2007. "The Virtual War Family." *Christian Science Monitor,* May 29.

Sjoberg, Gideon. 1960. *The Preindustrial City: Past and Present.* Glencoe, IL: Free Press.

Skinner, E. Benjamin. 2008. "People for Sale." *Foreign Policy* (March–April).

Slack, Jennifer Daryl, and J. Macgregor Wise. 2007. *Culture + Technology.* New York: Peter Lang.

Slackman, Michael. 2008. "9/11 Rumors That Harden into Conventional Wisdom." *New York Times,* September 9, p. A16.

Slavin, Barbara. 2007. "Child Marriage Rife in Nations Getting U.S. Aid." *USA Today,* July 17, p. 6A.

Slavin, Robert E., and A. Cheung. 2003. *Effective Reading Programs for English Language Learners: A Best-Evidence Synthesis.* Baltimore: Johns Hopkins University, Center for Research on the Education of Students Placed at Risk.

Sloan, Allan. 2009. "What's Still Wrong with Wall Street." *Time,* November 9, pp. 24–29.

Slug-Lines.com. 2008. "A Unique Commuter Solution." Accessed January 9, 2009 (www.slug-lines.com).

Smart, Barry. 1990. "Modernity, Postmodernity, and the Present." Pp. 14–30 in *Theories of Modernity and Postmodernity,* edited by Bryan S. Turner. Newbury Park, CA: Sage.

Smeeding, Timothy M. 2008. "Poorer by Comparison: "Poverty, Work, and Public Policy in Comparative Perspective." *Pathways* (Winter):3–5.

Smelser, Neil. 1962. *Theory of Collective Behavior.* New York: Free Press.

———. 1963. *The Sociology of Economic Life.* Englewood Cliffs, NJ: Prentice Hall.

———. 1981. *Sociology.* Englewood Cliffs, NJ: Prentice Hall.

Smith, Aaron. 2009. *The Internet's Role in Campaign 2000.* Washington, DC: Pew Internet and American Life Project.

Smith, Christian. 1991. *The Emergence of Liberation Theology: Radical Religion and Social Movement Theory.* Chicago: University of Chicago Press.

———. 2007. "Getting a Life: The Challenge of Emerging Adulthood." *Books and Culture: A Christian Review* (November–December).

———. 2008. "Future Directions of the Sociology of Religion." *Social Forces* 86 (June): 1564–1589.

Smith, Craig S. 2006. "Romania's Orphans Face Widespread Abuse, Group Says." *New York Times,* May 10, p. A3.

Smith, Dan. 1999. *The State of the World Atlas.* 6th ed. London: Penguin.

Smith, David A. 1995. "The New Urban Sociology Meets the Old: Rereading Some Classical Human Ecology." *Urban Affairs Review* 20 (January):432–457.

———, and Michael Timberlake. 1993. "World Cities: A Political Economy/Global Network Approach." Pp. 181–207 in *Urban Sociology in Transition,* edited by Ray Hutchison. Greenwich, CT: JAI Press.

Smith, David M., and Gary J. Gates. 2001. *Gay and Lesbian Families in the United States: Same-Sex Unmarried Partner Households.* Washington, DC: Human Rights Campaign.

Smith, Denise, and Hava Tillipman. 2000. "The Older Population in the United States." *Current Population Reports,* ser. P-20, no. 532. Washington, DC: U.S. Government Printing Office.

Smith, Michael Peter. 1988. *City, State, and Market.* New York: Basil Blackwell.

Smith, Peter. 2008. "Going Global: The Transnational Politics of the Debt Movement." *Globalizations* 5 (March):13–33.

Smith, Tom W. 2003. *Coming of Age in 21st Century America: Public Attitudes toward the Importance and Timing of Transition to Adulthood.* Chicago: National Opinion Research Center.

———. 2009. *Religious Change around the World.* Chicago: NORC/University of Chicago.

Snow, David A., Louis A. Zurcher, Jr., and Robert Peters. 1981. "Victory Celebrations as Theater: A Dramaturgical Approach to Crowd Behavior." *Symbolic Interaction* 4:21–42.

Snyder, Thomas D. 1996. *Digest of Education Statistics 1996.* Washington, DC: U.S. Government Printing Office.

Somavia, Juan. 2008. "The ILO at 90 Working for Social Justice." *World of Work* 64 (December):4–5.

Sorokin, Pitirim A. [1927] 1959. *Social and Cultural Mobility.* New York: Free Press.

Southern Poverty Law Center. 2010. "Active 'Patriot' Groups in the United States in 2009." Accessed November 5 (www.splcenter.org/patriot).

Spalter-Roth, Roberta, and Nicole Van Vooren. 2008a. "What Are They Doing with a Bachelor's Degree in Sociology?" Washington, DC: American Sociological Association. Accessible at http://asanet.org/galleries/research/ASAresearchbrief_corrections.pdf.

———. 2008b. "Skills, Reasons and Jobs. What Happened to the Class of 2005." Washington, DC: American Sociological Association. Accessible at http://asanet.org.

———. 2010. *Mixed Success: Four Years of Experiences of 2005 Sociology Graduates.* Washington, DC: American Sociology Association.

Speak, Suzanne, and Graham Tipple. 2006. "Perceptions, Persecution and Pity: The Limitations of Interventions for Homelessness in Developing Countries." *International Journal of Urban and Regional Research* 30 (March):172–188.

Spencer, Nancy. 2008. "Title IX." Pp. 1308–1310, vol. 3, in *Encyclopedia of Race, Ethnicity, and Society,* edited by Richard T. Schaefer. Thousand Oaks, CA: Sage.

Spitzer, Steven. 1975. "Toward a Marxian Theory of Deviance." *Social Problems* 22 (June):641–651.

Sprague, Joey. 2005. *Feminist Methodologies for Critical Research: Bridging Differences.* Lanham, MD: AltaMira Press.

Squires, Gregory D., ed. 2002. *Urban Sprawl: Causes, Consequences and Policy Responses.* Washington, DC: Urban Institute.

Stahler-Sholk, Richard. 2008. "Zapatista Rebellion." Pp. 1423–1424, vol. 3, in *Encyclopedia of Race, Ethnicity, and Society,* edited by Richard T. Schaefer. Thousand Oaks, CA: Sage.

Stanley, Alessandra. 2007. "Deadly Rampage and No Loss for Words." *New York Times,* April 17.

Stark, Andrew. 2011. "The Price of Moral Purity." *Wall Street Journal,* February 4.

Stark, Rodney. 2004. *Exploring the Religious Life.* Baltimore: Johns Hopkins University Press.

———, and William Sims Bainbridge. 1979. "Of Churches, Sects, and Cults: Preliminary Concepts for a Theory of Religious Movements." *Journal for the Scientific Study of Religion* 18 (June):117–131.

———, and ———. 1985. *The Future of Religion.* Berkeley: University of California Press.

Starr, Paul. 2010. "The Next Health-Reform Campaign." *American Prospect* (September):A3, A5–A7.

Staton, Ron. 2004. "Still Fighting for National Hawaiian Recognition." *Asian Week,* January 22, p. 8.

Steel, Emily. 2010. "Some Data-Miners Ready to Reveal What They Know. *Wall Street Journal,* December 3, pp. B1, B2.

Steffen, Alex, ed. 2008. *World Changing: A User's Guide for the 21st Century.* New York: Harry N. Abrams.

Stein, Leonard I. 1967. "The Doctor-Nurse Game." *Archives of General Psychology* 16:699–703.

Stenning, Derrick J. 1958. "Household Viability among the Pastoral Fulani." Pp. 92–119 in *The Developmental Cycle in Domestic Groups,* edited by John R. Goody. Cambridge, UK: Cambridge University Press.

Stevick, Richard A. 2007. *Growing Up Amish: The Teenage Years.* Baltimore: Johns Hopkins University Press.

Stewart, Robb M. 2010. "Wal-Mart Sets African Offer." *Wall Street Journal,* November 30, p. B2.

Stockard, Janice E. 2002. *Marriage in Culture.* Belmont, CA: Thomson Wadsworth.

Stolberg, Sheryl Gay. 1995. "Affirmative Action Gains Often Come at a High Cost." *Los Angeles Times,* March 29, pp. A1, A13–A16.

———. 2008. "Richest Nations Pledge to Halve Greenhouse Gas." *New York Times,* July 9, pp. A1, A13.

Stone, Andrea, and Marisol Bello. 2009. "Mom's Plight Shows Army Strain." *USA Today,* March 4, p. 3A.

Stoner, Madeleine R. 2008. "Homelessness." pp. 641–644, vol. 2, in *Encyclopedia of Race, Ethnicity, and Society,* edited by Richard T. Schaefer. Thousand Oaks, CA: Sage.

Strassman, W. Paul. 1998. "Third World Housing." Pp. 589–592 in *The Encyclopedia of Housing,* edited by Willem van Vliet. Thousand Oaks, CA: Sage.

Strauss, Gary. 2002. "'Good Old Boys' Network Still Rules Corporate Boards." *USA Today,* November 1, pp. B1, B2.

———. 2011. "$228, 000 for a Part-Time Job? Apparently, That's Not Enough." *USA Today,* March 4, p. A1.

Street, Marc D. 1997. "Groupthink: An Examination of Theoretical Issues, Implications, and Future Research Systems." *Small Group Research* 28 (February):72–93.

Subramaniam, Mangala. 2006. *The Power of Women's Organization: Gender, Caste, and Class in India.* Lanham, MD: Lexington Books.

Suitor, J. Jill, Staci A. Minyard, and Rebecca S. Carter. 2001. "'Did You See What I Saw?' Gender Differences in Perceptions of Avenues to Prestige among Adolescents." *Sociological Inquiry* 71 (Fall):437–454.

Sullivan, Harry Stack. [1953] 1968. *The Interpersonal Theory of Psychiatry.* Edited by Helen Swick Perry and Mary Ladd Gawel. New York: Norton.

Sullivan, Kevin. 2006. "Bridging the Digital Divide." *Washington Post National Weekly Edition* 25 (July 17):11–12.

Sum, Andrew, Paul Harrington, and Ishwar Khatiwada. 2006. *The Impact of New Immigrants on Young Native-Born Workers, 2000–2005.* Washington, DC: Center for Immigration Studies.

Sumner, William G. 1906. *Folkways.* New York: Ginn.

Sunstein, Cass. 2002. *Republic.com.* Rutgers, NJ: Princeton University Press.

SustainAbility. 2006. *Brazil—Country of Diversities and Inequalities.* London: SustainAbility.

Sutch, Richard, and Susan B. Carter. 2006. *Historical Statutes of US: Earliest Time to the Present.* Cambridge: Cambridge University Press.

Sutcliffe, Bob. 2002. *100 Ways of Seeing an Unequal World.* London: Zed Books.

Sutherland, Edwin H. 1937. *The Professional Thief.* Chicago: University of Chicago Press.

———. 1940. "White-Collar Criminality." *American Sociological Review* 5 (February):1–11.

———. 1949. *White Collar Crime.* New York: Dryden.

———. 1983. *White Collar Crime: The Uncut Version.* New Haven, CT: Yale University Press.

———, Donald R. Cressey, and David F. Luckenbill. 1992. *Principles of Criminology.* 11th ed. New York: Rowman and Littlefield.

Swatos, William H., Jr., ed. 1998. *Encyclopedia of Religion and Society.* Lanham, MD: AltaMira.

Sweet, Kimberly. 2001. "Sex Sells a Second Time." *Chicago Journal* 93 (April):12–13.

Swidler, Ann. 1986. "Culture in Action: Symbols and Strategies." *American Sociological Review* 51 (April): 273–286.

Swift, Mike. 2011. "Facebook Gaining Overseas as Growth in U.S. Users Slows." *Chicago Tribune,* January 24, p. 19.

Szasz, Andrew. 2007. *Shopping Our Way to Safety: How We Changed from Protecting the Environment to Protecting Ourselves.* Minneapolis: University of Minnesota Press.

Szasz, Thomas. 2010. *The Myth of Mental Illness: Foundations of a Theory of Personal Conduct.* 50th Anniversary Edition. New York: Harper Perennial.

T

Tabuchi, Hiroko. 2010. "For Some of Japan's Jobless, New Homes Just 5 Feet Wide." *New York Times,* January 2, pp. A1, A3.

Tanielian, Terri. 2009. "Assessing Combat Exposure and Post-Traumatic Stress Disorder in Troops and Estimating the Costs to Society." Testimony presented before the House Veterans' Affairs Committee, Subcommittee on Disability Assistance and Memorial Affairs, March 24.

Tannen, Deborah. 1990. *You Just Don't Understand: Women and Men in Conversation.* New York: Ballantine.

Tatchell, Jo. 2009. *A Diamond in the Desert: Behind the Scenes in the World's Richest City.* London: Hodder and Stoughton.

Taylor, Verta. 1999. "Gender and Social Movements: Gender Processes in Women's Self-Help Movements." *Gender and Society* 13:8–33.

———. 2004. "Social Movements and Gender." Pp. 14348–14352 in *International Encyclopedia of the Social and Behavioral Sciences,* edited by Neil J. Smelser and Paul B. Baltes. New York: Elsevier.

———, Leila J. Rupp, and Nancy Whittier. 2009. *Feminist Frontiers.* 8th ed. New York: McGraw-Hill.

Tedeschi, Bob. 2006. "Those Born to Shop Can Now Use Cellphones." *New York Times,* January 2.

Telles, Edward E. 2004. *Race in America: The Significance of Skin Color in Brazil.* Princeton, NJ: Princeton University Press.

Therborn, Göran. 2010. Review of "Unveiling Inequality." *Contemporary Sociology* 39 (5):585–586.

Third World Institute. 2007. *The World Guide.* 11th ed. Oxford: New Internationalist Publications.

Thomas, Evan, and Pat Wingert. 2010. "Understanding Charter Schools." *Newsweek* 155 (June 21):46.

Thomas, Gordon, and Max Morgan Witts. 1974. *Voyage of the Damned.* Greenwich, CT: Fawcett Crest.

Thomas, R. Murray. 2003. "New Frontiers in Cheating." In *Encyclopaedia Britannica 2003 Book of the Year.* Chicago: Encyclopaedia Britannica.

Thomas, William I. 1923. *The Unadjusted Girl.* Boston: Little, Brown.

Thomasrobb.com. 2007. "WhitePride TV." Accessed May 7 (http://thomasrobb.com).

Thompson, Clive. 2005. "Meet the Life Hackers." *New York Times Magazine,* October 16, pp. 40–45.

Thompson, Ginger. 2001. "Why Peace Eludes Mexico's Indians." *New York Times,* March 11, sec. WK, p. 16.

Thompson, Neil B. 1972. "The Mysterious Fall of the Nacirema." *Natural History* (December).

Thompson, Tony. 2005. "Romanians Are Being Paid to Play Computer Games for Westerners." *Guardian Weekly,* March 25, p. 17.

Threadcraft, Shatema. 2008. "Welfare Queen." In *Encyclopedia of Race, Ethnicity and Society,* edited by Richard T. Schaefer. Thousand Oaks, CA: Sage.

Thurm, Scott. 2010. "Oracle's Ellison: Pay King." *Wall Street Journal,* July 27, pp. A1, A16.

Thurow, Lester. 1984. "The Disappearance of the Middle Class." *New York Times,* February 5, sec. 5, p. 2.

Tibbles, Kevin. 2007. "Web Sites Encourage Eating Disorders." *Today,* February 18. Accessed May 7 (www.msabc.msn.com).

Tierney, John. 1990. "Betting the Planet." *New York Times Magazine,* December 2, pp. 52–53, 71, 74, 76, 78, 80–81.

Tierney, Kathleen J. 2007. "From the Margins to the Mainstream? Disaster Research at the Crossroads." *Annual Review of Sociology* 33:503–525.

———. 1980. "Emergent Norm Theory as 'Theory': An Analysis and Critique of Turner's Formulation." Pp. 42–53 in *Collective Behavior: A Source Book,* edited by Meredith David Pugh. St. Paul, MN: West.

Tierney, William G., and Karri A. Holley. 2008. "Intelligent Design and the Attack on Scientific Inquiry." *Cultural Studies Critical Methodologies* 8 (February): 39–49.

Tigay, Chanan. 2011. "Women and Sports." *CQ Researcher* 21 (March 25).

Tilly, Charles. 1964. *The Vendée.* Cambridge, MA: Harvard University Press.

———. 1993. *Popular Contention in Great Britain 1758–1834.* Cambridge, MA: Harvard University Press.

———. 2003. *The Politics of Collective Violence.* New York: Cambridge University Press.

———. 2004. *Social Movements, 1768–2004.* Boulder, CO: Paradigm.

———. 2007. "Trust Networks in Transnational Migration." *Sociological Forum* 22 (March):3–24.

Timmerman, Kelsey. 2009. *Where Am I Wearing?* Hoboken NJ: Wiley.

Toensing, Gale Country. 2009. "Akaka Bill Gets Obama Approval." *Indian Country Today* (August 19):1, 2.

Tonkinson, Robert. 1978. *The Mardudjara Aborigines.* New York: Holt.

Tönnies, Ferdinand. [1887] 1988. *Community and Society.* Rutgers, NJ: Transaction.

Toossi, Mitra. 2009. "Employment Outlook: 2008–2018." *Monthly Labor Review* (November):30–51.

Toppo, Greg. 2011. "The Search for a New Way to Test Schoolkids." *USA Today,* March 18, p. A4.

Toro, Paul A. 2007. "Toward an International Understanding of Homelessness." *Journal of Social Issues* 63 (3):461–481.

Torres, Lourdes. 2008. "Puerto Rican Americans" and "Puerto Rico." Pp. 1082–1089, vol. 3, in *Encyclopedia of Race, Ethnicity, and Society,* edited by Richard T. Schaefer. Thousand Oaks, CA: Sage.

Touraine, Alain. 1974. *The Academic System in American Society.* New York: McGraw-Hill.

Transactional Records Access Clearinghouse. 2009. "TRAC Monthly Bulletins by Topic, September 2009." Accessed February 11, 2010 (www.trac.syr.edu/tracreports/bulletins/white_collar_crime/monthly_sep09/fil).

Traynor, Ian. 2008. "Europe Expects a Flood of Climate Refugees." *Guardian Weekly,* March 14, p. 1–2.

Trotter III, Robert T., and Juan Antonio Chavira. 1997. *Curanderismo: Mexican American Folk Healing.* Athens: University of Georgia Press.

Truman, Jennifer L., and Michael R. Rand. 2010. "Criminal Victimization, 2009." Bureau of Justice Statistics Bulletin (October).

Trumbull, Mark. 2006. "America's Younger Workers Losing Ground on Income." *Christian Science Monitor,* February 27.

Tschorn, Adam. 2010. "Parkour Ready to Launch." *Chicago Tribune,* July 25, sec. 6, pp. 20–21.

Tuchman, Gaye. 1992. "Feminist Theory." Pp. 695–704 in *Encyclopedia of Sociology,* vol. 2, edited by Edgar F. Borgatta and Marie L. Borgatta. New York: Macmillan.

Tucker, Robert C. (ed.) 1978. *The Marx-Engels Reader.* 2nd ed. New York: Norton.

Ture, Kwame, and Charles Hamilton. 1992. *Black Power: The Politics of Liberation.* With new Afterword by authors. New York: Vintage Books.

Turkle, Sherry. 2004. "How Computers Change the Way We Think." *Chronicle of Higher Education* 50 (January 30):B26–B28.

———. 2011. *Alone Together: Why We Expect More from Technology and Less from Each Other.* New York: Basic Books.

Turner, Bryan S., ed. 1990. *Theories of Modernity and Postmodernity.* Newbury Park, CA: Sage.

Turner, Ralph, and Lewis M. Killian. 1987. *Collective Behavior.* 3rd ed. Englewood Cliffs, NJ: Prentice Hall.

Turner, S. Derek, and Mark Cooper. 2006. *Out of the Picture: Minority and Female TV Station Ownership in the United States.* Washington, DC: Free Press.

U

UNAIDS. 2010. *Global Report: UNAIDS Report on the Global AIDS Epidemic 2010.* Geneva: UNAIDS.

UNHCR. 2010. *UNHCR Statistical Yearbook 2009.* Geneva: UNHCR.

UNICEF. 2010. "Child Marriage." Accessed January 15 (www.unicef.org/progressfprchildren/2007n6/index_41848.htm?q=printme).

United Nations. 2005. *The Millennium Development Goals Report.* Washington, DC: United Nations.

532

———. 2009. *International Migration Report 2006: A Global Assessment.* New York: United Nations, Economic and Social Affairs.

United Nations Development Fund for Women. 2009. *Who Answers to Women?* New York: UNIFEM.

United Nations Development Programme. 1995. *Human Development Report 1995.* New York: Oxford University Press.

———. 2000. *Poverty Report 2000: Overcoming Human Poverty.* Washington, DC: UNDP.

———. 2009. *Overcoming Barriers: Human Mobility and Development.* New York: Palgrave Macmillan.

United Nations Economic and Social Council. 2010. "Review of the Implementation of the Beijing Declaration." New York: Economic and Social Council.

United Nations Framework Convention on Climate Change. 2010. Home Page. Accessed April 19 (http://unfcc.int).

United Nations Office on Drugs and Crime. 2005. "The United Nations Convention against Transnational Organized Crime and Its Protocols." Accessed March 18 (www.unodc.org).

United Nations Population Division. 2007. *World Abortion Policies 2007.* New York: UNPD.

United Nations Statistics Division. 2008. "Singulate Mean Age at Marriage." Accessed March 1, 2009 (http://data.un.org/search.aspx?q=marriage).

———. 2009. *Demographic Yearbook 2007.* Accessed April 1, 2010 (http://unstats.un.org/unsd/demographic/products/dyb/dyb2.htm).

United Way of King County. 2010. "Community Assessment." Accessed January 18 (www.uwkc/printver.asp?ref=kcca/data/languages/isolation.asp).

University of Michigan. 2003. *Information on Admissions Lawsuits.* Accessed August 8 (www.umich.edu/urel/admissions).

Urban Dictionary. 2010. "Urban Amish." Accessed April 28 (www.urbandictionary.com/define.php?term=urban%20amish).

Urbina, Ian. 2002. "Al Jazeera: Hits, Misses and Ricochets." *Asia Times,* December 25.

U.S. English. 2010. "Making English the Official Language." Accessed January 17 (www.us-english.org/inc/).

U.S. Surgeon General. 1999. *Surgeon General's Report on Mental Health.* Washington, DC: U.S. Government Printing Office.

U.S. Trade Representative. 2007. "Trade Promotion Authority Delivers Jobs, Growth, Prosperity, and Security at Home." January 31 Fact Sheet. Accessed February 19 (www.ustr.gov).

V

Vaidhyanathan, Siva. 2008. "Generational Myth: Not All Young People Are Tech-Savvy." *Chronicle of Higher Education,* September 19, pp. B7–B9.

Vamosi, Robert, Mary Monahan, and Rachel Kim. 2010. *2010 Identity Fraud Survey Report.* Pleasanton, CA: Javelin Strategy.

van den Berghe, Pierre. 1978. *Race and Racism: A Comparative Perspective.* 2nd ed. New York: Wiley.

Van Gennep, Arnold. [1909] 1960. *The Rites of Passage.* Translated by Monika B. Vizedom and Gabrielle L. Caffee. Chicago: University of Chicago Press.

van Vucht Tijssen, Lieteke. 1990. "Women between Modernity and Postmodernity." Pp. 147–163 in *Theories of Modernity and Postmodernity,* edited by Bryan S. Turner. London: Sage.

Vargas, Jose Antonio. 2007. "YouTube Gets Serious with Links to Candidates." *Washington Post,* March 2, p. C1.

Vasagar, Jeeran. 2005. "'At Last Rwanda Is Known for Something Positive." *Guardian Weekly,* July 22, p. 18.

Vaughan, R. M. 2007. "Cairo's Man Show." *Utne Reader* (March–April):94–95.

Veblen, Thorstein. [1899] 1964. *Theory of the Leisure Class.* New York: Macmillan. New York: Penguin.

———. 1919. *The Vested Interests and the State of the Industrial Arts.* New York: Huebsch.

Velásquez, Carmen, and P. Rafael Hernández-Arias. 2009. *Voices from the Communities: Community Health Assets and Needs Assessment.* Chicago: Alivio Medical Center and Stearns Center for Community-Based Service Learning.

Velasquez-Manoff, Moises. 2009. "Could Water Scarcity Cause International Conflict?" *Christian Science Monitor,* October 26.

Venkatesh, Sudhir Alladi. 2006. *Off the Books: The Underground Economy of the Urban Poor.* Cambridge, MA: Harvard University Press.

———. 2008. *Gang Leader for a Day: A Rogue Sociologist Takes to the Streets.* New York: Penguin Press.

Vernon, Glenn. 1962. *Sociology and Religion.* New York: McGraw-Hill.

Villarreal, Andrés. 2004. "The Social Ecology of Rural Violence: Land Scarcity, the Organization of Agricultural Production, and the Presence of the State." *American Journal of Sociology* 110 (September):313–348.

Vincent, Grayson, and Victoria A. Velkoff. 2010. "The Next Four Decades." *Current Population Reports,* ser. P-25, no. 138. Washington, DC: U.S. Government Printing Office.

Viramontes, Helena Maria. 2007. "Loyalty Spoken Here." *Los Angeles Times,* September 23, p. R7.

Visitability. 2009. "Visitability: Becoming a National Trend." Accessed May 5 (www.visitability.org).

Visser, Jelle. 2006. "Union Membership Statistics in 24 Countries." *Monthly Labor Review* (January):38–49.

W

Wachtendorf, Tricia. 2002. "A Changing Risk Environment: Lessons Learned from the 9/11 World Trade Center Disaster." Presentation at the Sociological Perspectives on Disasters, Mt. Macedon, Australia, July.

Waelde, Lynn C., Madeline Uddo, Renee Marquett, Melanie Ropelato, Sharifa Freightman, Adit Pardo, and Jacqueline Salazar. 2008. "A Pilot Study of Meditation for Mental Health Workers Following Hurricane Katrina." *Journal of Traumatic Stress* 21 (5):497–500.

Wages for Housework Campaign. 1999. *Wages for Housework Campaign.* Circular. Los Angeles.

Wagley, Charles, and Marvin Harris. 1958. *Minorities in the New World: Six Case Studies.* New York: Columbia University Press.

Waite, Linda. 2000. "The Family as a Social Organization: Key Ideas for the Twenty-First Century." *Contemporary Sociology* 29 (May):463–469.

Waitzkin, Howard. 1986. *The Second Sickness: Contradictions of Capitalist Health Care.* Chicago: University of Chicago Press.

Walder, Andrew. G. 2009. "Political Sociology and Social Movements." *Annual Review of Sociology* 35:393–412.

———, and Giang Hoang Nguyen. 2008. "Ownership, Organization, and Income Inequality: Market Transition in Rural Vietnam." *American Sociological Review* 73 (April):251–269.

Waldman, Amy. 2004a. "India Takes Economic Spotlight, and Critics Are Unkind." *New York Times,* March 7, p. 3.

———. 2004b. "Low-Tech or High, Jobs Are Scarce in India's Boon." *New York Times,* May 6, p. A3.

———. 2004c. "What India's Upset Vote Reveals: The High Tech Is Skin Deep." *New York Times,* May 15, p. A5.

Walker, Andrea C., and David E. Balk. 2007. "Bereavement Rituals in the Muscogee Creek Tribe." *Death Studies* 31:633–652.

Walker, Edward. 2010. "Activism Industry-Driven." *Contexts* (Spring):43–49.

Walker, Marcus, and Roger Thurow. 2009. U.S., Europe Are Ocean Apart on Human Toll of Joblessness. *Wall Street Journal,* May 7, pp. A1, A14.

Wallace, Nicole. 2010. "Gifts for Oil Spill Total $4 Million, but More Is Needed." *The Chronicle of Philanthropy* 24 (14):1.

Wallace, Ruth A., and Alison Wolf. 1980. *Contemporary Sociological Theory.* Englewood Cliffs, NJ: Prentice Hall.

Wallerstein, Immanuel. 1974. *The Modern World System.* New York: Academic Press.

———. 1979a. *Capitalist World Economy.* Cambridge: Cambridge University Press.

———. 1979b. *The End of the World as We Know It: Social Science for the Twenty-First Century.* Minneapolis: University of Minnesota Press.

———. 2000. *The Essential Wallerstein.* New York: New Press.

Wallis, Claudia. 2008. "How to Make Great Teachers." *Time* 171 (February 25):28–34.

Walmart. 2010. "The Ten-foot Attitude." Accessed January 17 (www.wal-martchina.com/english/walmart/rule/10.htm).

Wang, Feng. 2011. "The Future of a Demographic Overachiever: Long-Term Implications of the Demographic Transition in China." *Population and Development Review* 37 (Suppl.):173–190.

———. and Cai Yong. 2011. "China's One-Child Policy at 39." May 31. Washington, DC: Brooking Institution.

Wang, Meiyan, and Fand Cai. 2006. "Gender Wage Differentials in China's Urban Labor Market." Research Paper No. 2006/141. United Nations University World Institute for Development Economics Research.

Watson, Paul. 2005. "Defying Tradition." *Los Angeles Times,* April 24, p. 56.

Wattenberg, Martin P. 2008. *Is Voting for Young People?* New York: Pearson Longman.

Weber, Max. [1904] 1949. Methodology of the Social Sciences. Translated by Edward A. Shils and Henry A. Finch. Glencoe, IL: Free Press.

———. [1913–1922] 1947. *The Theory of Social and Economic Organization.* Translated by A. Henderson and T. Parsons. New York: Free Press.

———. [1916] 1958. *The Religion of India: The Sociology of Hinduism and Buddhism.* New York: Free Press.

Wechsler, Henry, J. E. Lee, M. Kuo, M. Seibring, T. F. Nelson, and H. Lee. 2002. "Trends in College Binge Drinking during a Period of Increased Prevention Efforts: Findings from Four Harvard School of Public Health College Alcohol Surveys: 1993–2001." *Journal of American College Health* 50 (5):203–217.

———, Mark Seibring, I-Chao Liu, and Marilyn Ahl. 2004. "Colleges Respond to Student Binge Drinking: Reducing Student Demand or Limiting Access." *Journal of American College Health* 52 (4):159–168.

The Week. 2009. "First Assisted-Suicide Death." (June 5):7.

———. 2010a. "The Mystery of Falling Crime Rates." (July 16):13.

———. 2010b. "They're Watching You." (September 17):15

———. 2011. "Fighting over Food." (March 4):15.

Weeks, John R. 2008. *Population: An Introduction to Concepts and Issues.* 10th ed. Belmont, CA: Wadsworth.

———. 2012. *Population: An Introduction to Concepts and Issues.* 11th ed. Belmont, CA: Cengage.

Weinberg, Daniel H. 2004. *Evidence from Census 2000 About Earnings by Detailed Occupation for Men and Women.* CENSR-15. Washington, DC: U.S. Government Printing Office.

———, 2007. "Earnings by Gender: Evidence from Census 2000." *Monthly Labor Review* (July–August):26–34.

Weinraub, Bernard. 2004. "UPN Show Is Called Insensitive to Amish." *New York Times,* March 4, pp. B1, B8.

Weinstein, Henry. 2002. "Airport Screener Curb Is Regretful." *Los Angeles Times,* November 16, pp. B1, B14.

Weitz, Rose. 2007. *The Sociology of Health, Illness, and Heath Care.* 4th ed. Belmont, CA: Thomson.

Welch, William M. 2011. "More Hawaii Residents Identify as Mixed Race." *USA Today,* February 28.

Wells-Barnett, Ida B. 1970. *Crusade for Justice: The Autobiography of Ida B. Wells.* Edited by Alfreda M. Duster. Chicago: University of Chicago Press.

Wentling, Tre, Elroi Windsor, Kristin Schilt, and Betsy Lucal. 2008. "Teaching Transgender." *Teaching Sociology* 36 (January):49–57.

Wentz, Laurel, and Claire Atkinson. 2005. "'Apprentice' Translators Hope for Hits All Over Globe." *Advertising Age,* February 14, pp. 3, 73.

West, Candace, and Don H. Zimmerman. 1987. "Doing Gender." *Gender and Society* 1 (June):125–151.

Westergaard-Nielsen, Niels. 2008. *Low-Wage Work in Denmark.* New York: Russell Sage Foundation.

Wheller, Kellie. 2009. "After Listening to This Story." Accessed August 20 (www.npr.org/templates/story/story.php?storyId=1119880383).

White, David Manning. 1950. "'The Gatekeeper': A Case Study in the Selection of News." *Journalism Quarterly* 27 (Fall):383–390.

White House. 2011. "Faith-Based Office Convening on Global Hunger Gets Glowing Reviews from National Leaders." Accessed March 28 (http://www.whitehouse.gov/blog/2011/01/21/ faith-based-office-convening-global-hunger-gets-glowing-reviews-national-leaders).

Whitlock, Craig. 2005. "The Internet as Bully Pulpit." *Washington Post National Weekly Edition* 22 (August 22):9.

Whittaker, Stephanie. 2006. "Who Would You Prefer to Work For?" *Gazette* (Montreal), November 4, p. 1.

Whyte, William Foote. 1981. *Street Corner Society: Social Structure of an Italian Slum.* 3rd ed. Chicago: University of Chicago Press.

Whyte, William H., Jr. 1952. "Groupthink." *Fortune* (March):114–117, 142, 146.

Wilford, John Noble. 1997. "New Clues Show Where People Made the Great Leap to Agriculture." *New York Times,* November 18, pp. B9, B12.

Wilgoren, Jodi. 2005. "In Kansas, Darwinism Goes on Trial Once More." *New York Times,* May 6, p. A14.

Wilkes, Rima, and John Iceland. 2004. "Hypersegregation in the Twenty-First Century." *Demography* 41 (February):23–36.

Williams, Carol J. 1995. "Taking an Eager Step Back." *Los Angeles Times,* June 3, pp. A1, A14.

Williams, Christine L. 1992. "The Glass Escalator: Hidden Advantages for Men in the 'Female' Professions." *Social Problems* 39 (3):253–267.

———. 1995. *Still a Man's World: Men Who Do Women's Work.* Berkeley: University of California Press.

Williams, David R., and Chiquita Collins. 2004. "Reparations." *American Behavioral Scientist* 47 (March):977–1000.

Williams, Kristine N., Ruth Herman, Byron Gajewski, and Kristel Wilson. 2009. "Elderspeak Communication: Impact on Dementia Care." *American Journal of Alzheimer's Disease and Other Dementias* 24 (March):11–20.

Williams, Robin M., Jr. 1970. *American Society.* 3rd ed. New York: Knopf.

———, with John P. Dean and Edward A. Suchman. 1964. *Strangers Next Door: Ethnic Relations in American Communities.* Englewood Cliffs, NJ: Prentice Hall.

Wills, Jeremiah B., and Barbara J. Risman. 2006. "The Visibility of Feminist Thought in Family Studies." *Journal of Marriage and Family* 68 (August):690–700.

Wilson, Edward O. 1975. *Sociobiology: The New Synthesis.* Cambridge, MA: Harvard University Press.

———. 1978. *On Human Nature.* Cambridge, MA: Harvard University Press.

———. 2000. *Sociobiology: The New Synthesis.* Cambridge, MA: Belknap Press, Harvard University Press.

Wilson, John. 1973. *Introduction to Social Movements.* New York: Basic Books.

Wilson, William Julius. 1980. *The Declining Significance of Race: Blacks and Changing American Institutions.* 2nd ed. Chicago: University of Chicago Press.

———. 1987. *The Truly Disadvantaged: The Inner City, the Underclass and Public Policy.* Chicago: University of Chicago Press.

———. 1996. *When Work Disappears: The World of the New Urban Poor.* New York: Knopf.

———. 1999. *The Bridge over the Racial Divide: Rising Inequality and Coalition Politics.* Berkeley: University of California Press.

———. 2009. *More Than Just Race: Being Black and Poor in the Inner City.* New York: Norton.

———, J. M. Quane, and B. H. Rankin. 2004. "Underclass." In *International Encyclopedia of Social and Behavioral Sciences.* New York: Elsevier.

———, and Richard P. Taub in collaboration with Reuben A. Buford May and Mary Pattillo. 2006. "Groveland: A Stable African American Community." Pp. 128–160 in *There Goes the Neighborhood* by William Julius Wilson and Richard P. Taub. New York: Knopf.

Winant, Howard B. 1994. *Racial Conditions: Politics, Theory, Comparisons.* Minneapolis: University of Minnesota Press.

———. 2006. "Race and Racism: Towards a Global Future." *Ethnic and Racial Studies* 29 (September):986–1003.

Wines, Michael. 2005. "Same-Sex Unions to Become Legal in South Africa." *USA Today,* December 2, p. A6.

Winickoff, Jonathan P., Joan Friebely, Susanne E. Tanski, Cheryl Sherrod, George E. Matt, Mebourne F. Hovell, and Robert C. McMillen. 2009. "Beliefs about the Health Effects of 'Third-hand' Smoke and Home Smoking Bans." *Pediatrics* 123 (January):74–79.

Winter, J. Allen. 2008. "Symbolic Ethnicity." Pp. 1288–1290, vol. 3, in *Encyclopedia of Race, Ethnicity, and Society,* edited by Richard T. Schaefer. Thousand Oaks, CA: Sage.

Wirth, Louis. 1928. *The Ghetto.* Chicago: University of Chicago Press.

———. 1931. "Clinical Sociology." *American Journal of Sociology* 37 (July):49–60.

———. 1938. "Urbanism as a Way of Life." *American Journal of Sociology* 44 (July):1–24.

Wolf, Naomi. 1992. *The Beauty Myth: How Images of Beauty Are Used against Women.* New York: Anchor Books.

Wolfe, Alan. 2008. "Pew in the Pews." *Chronicle of Higher Education,* March 21, pp. B5–B6.

Women's Flat Track Derby Association. 2011. "Women's Flat Track Derby Association." Accessible at http://www.wftda.com/about.html.

Women's Sports Foundation. 2011. *Title IX.* Accessed March 29 (http://www.womenssportsfoundation.org/Issues-And-Research/Title-IX.aspx).

Wong, Morrison G. 2006. "Chinese Americans." Pp. 110–145 in *Asian Americans: Contemporary Trends and Issues,* 2nd ed., edited by Pyong Gap Min. Thousand Oaks, CA: Sage.

Working Women's Forum. 2010. Home Page. Accessed April 28 (www.workingwomensforum.org).

Workman, Thomas A. 2008. "The Real Impact of Virtual Worlds." *Chronicle of Higher Education,* September 19, pp. B12–B13.

World Bank. 2001. *World Development Report 2002. Building Instructions for Markets.* New York: Oxford University Press.

———. 2003. *World Development Report 2003: Sustainable Development in a Dynamic World.* Washington, DC: World Bank.

———. 2007. *World Development Indicators 2007.* Washington, DC: World Bank.

———. 2009. *World Development Indicators 2009.* Washington, DC: World Bank.

———. 2010a. *World Development Indicators 2010.* Washington, DC: World Bank.

———. 2010b. *World Development Report 2010: Development and Climate Change.* Washington, DC: World Bank.

———. 2011. *Development Indicators 2011.* Washington, DC: World Bank.

World Development Forum. 1990. "The Danger of Television." 8 (July 15):4.

World Economic Forum. 2010. "The Global Competitiveness Report 2010–2011." Geneva: WEF. Accessible at http://www.weforum.org/en/initiatives/gcp/Global%20Competitiveness%20Report/index.htm.

World Health Organization. 2000. *The World Health Report 2000. Health Systems: Improving Performance.* Geneva: WHO.

———. 2009. "Biotechnology (GM Foods)." Accessed May 11 (www.who.int/foodsafety/biotech/en/).

———. 2010. "Suicide Prevention." Accessed October 31 (http://www.who.int/mental_health/prevention/en/).

World Public Opinion. 2008. "World Publics Reject Torture." Accessed January 18, 2010 (www.worldpublicopinion.org/pipa/articles/btjustice-human_rightsra/496.php?nid=&id=&pnt=496).

Worth, Robert F. 2008. "As Taboos Ease, Saudi Girl Group Dares to Rock." *New York Times,* November 24, pp. A1, A9.

Wortham, Robert A. 2008. "DuBois, William Edward Burghardt." Pp. 423–427, vol. 1, in *Encyclopedia of Race, Ethnicity, and Society,* edited by Richard T. Schaefer. Thousand Oaks CA: Sage.

Wray, Matt, Matthew Miller, Jill Gurvey, Joanna Carroll, and Ichiro Kawachi. 2008. "Leaving Las Vegas: Exposure to Las Vegas and Risk of Suicide." *Social Science and Medicine* 67:1882–1888.

Wright, Charles R. 1986. *Mass Communication: A Sociological Perspective.* 3rd ed. New York: Random House.

Wright, Erik Olin, David Hachen, Cynthia Costello, and Joy Sprague. 1982. "The American Class Structure." *American Sociological Review* 47 (December):709–726.

Wright, Eric R., William P. Gronfein, and Timothy J. Owens. 2000. "Deinstitutionalization, Social Rejection, and the Self-Esteem of Former Mental Patients." *Journal of Health and Social Behavior* (March).

Wu, Tim. 2010. *The Master Switch.* New York: Knopf.

Wyatt, Edward. 2009. "No Smooth Ride on TV Networks' Road to Diversity." *New York Times,* March 18, pp. 1, 5.

Yamagata, Hisashi, Kuang S. Yeh, Shelby Stewman, and Hiroko Dodge. 1997. "Sex Segregation and Glass Ceilings: A Comparative Statistics Model of Women's Career Opportunities in the Federal Government over a Quarter Century." *American Journal of Sociology* 103 (November):566–632.

Yap, Kioe Sheng. 1998. "Squatter Settlements." Pp. 554–556 in *The Encyclopedia of Housing,* edited by Willem van Vliet. Thousand Oaks, CA: Sage.

Yardley, William. 2009. "A 2nd State Lets Doctors Lend Help in Suicide." *New York Times,* March 5, p. A15.

Yinger, J. Milton. 1970. *The Scientific Study of Religion.* New York: Macmillan.

York, Richard, Eugene A. Rosa, and Thomas Dietz. 2010. "Ecological Modernization Theory: Theoretical and Empirical Challenges." Pp. 77–90 in *The International Handbook and Environmental Sociology,* 2nd ed., edited by Michael R. Redclift and Graham Woodgate. Cheltenham, UK: Edward Elgar.

Yunus, Muhammad. 2010. *Building Social Business.* New York: Perseus.

Zang, Xiaowei. 2002. "Labor Market Segmentation and Income Inequality in Urban China." *Sociological Quarterly* 43 (1):27–44.

Zarembo, Alan. 2004a. "A Theater of Inquiry and Evil." *Los Angeles Times,* July 15, pp. A1, A24, A25.

———. 2004b. "Physician, Remake Thyself: Lured by Higher Pay and Heavy Recruiting, Philippine Doctors Are Getting Additional Degrees and Starting Over in the U.S. as Nurses." *Los Angeles Times,* January 10, pp. A1, A10.

Zeitzen, Miriam Koktvedgaard. 2008. *Polygamy: A Cross-Cultural Analysis.* Oxford, UK: Berg.

Zellner, William M. 1995. *Counter Cultures: A Sociological Analysis.* New York: St. Martin's Press.

Zernike, Kate. 2002. "With Student Cheating on the Rise, More Colleges Are Turning to Honor Codes." *New York Times,* November 2, p. A10.

Zhang, Xiaodan. 2009. "Trade Unions Under the Modernization of Paternalists Rule in China." *Journal of Labor and Society* 12 (June):193–218.

Zi, Jui-Chung Allen. 2007. *The Kids Are OK: Divorce and Children's Behavior Problems.* Santa Monica, CA: RAND.

Zia, Helen. 2000. *Asian American Dreams: The Emergence of an American People.* New York: Farrar, Straus and Giroux.

Zimbardo, Philip G., 2004. "Power Turns Good Soldiers into 'Bad Apples.'" *Boston Globe,* May 9. Also accessible at www.prisonexp.org.

———. 2007a. "Revisiting the Stanford Prison Experiment: A Lesson in the Power of the Situation." *Chronicle of Higher Education* 53 (March 20):B6, B7.

———. 2007b. *The Lucifer Effect: Understanding How Good People Turn Evil.* New York: Random House.

———, Robert L. Johnson, and Vivian McCann. 2009. *Psychology: Core Concepts.* 6th ed. Boston: Allyn and Bacon.

Zimmerman, Ann, and Emily Nelson. 2006. "With Profits Elusive, Wal-Mart to Exit Germany." *Wall Street Journal,* July 29, pp. A1, A6.

Zimmerman, Seth. 2008a. "Globalization and Economic Mobility." Washington, DC: Economic Mobility Project. Also accessible at www.economicmobility.org/reports_and_research/literature_reviews?id=0004.

———. 2008b. *Labor Market Institutions and Economic Mobility.* Washington, DC: Pew Charitable Trusts.

Zipp, Yvonne. 2009. Courts Divided on Police Use of GPS Tracking. *Christian Science Monitor,* May 15.

Zittrain, Jonathan, and John Palfrey. 2008. "Reluctant Gatekeepers: Corporate Ethics on a Filtered Internet." Pp. 103–122 in *Access Denied,* edited by Ronald Deibert, John Palfrey, Rafal Rohozinski, and Jonathan Zittrain. Cambridge, MA: MIT Press.

Zogby. 2010. "Zogby Interactive: 54% Support Ethnic & Religious Profiling; 71% Favor Full-Body Scans." February 4. Accessed July 2, 2011 (http://www.zogby.com/news/2010/02/04/zogby-interactive-54-support-ethnic-religious-profiling-71-favor-full-body-scans/).

Zola, Irving K. 1972. "Medicine as an Institution of Social Control." *Sociological Review* 20 (November):487–504.

———. 1983. *Socio-Medical Inquiries.* Philadelphia: Temple University Press.

Zoroya, Gregg. 2009. "Military Divorces Edge Up as War Takes Its Toll." *USA Today,* November 11.

Zweigenhaft, Richard L., and G. William Domhoff. 2006. *Diversity in the Power Elite: How It Happened, Why It Matters.* 2nd ed. New York: Rowman and Littlefield.

Zywica, Jolene, and James Danowski. 2008. "The Faces of Facebookers: Investigating Social Enhancement and Social Compensation Hypotheses; Predicting Facebook and Offline Popularity from Sociability and Self-Esteem, and Mapping the Meanings of Popularity with Semantic Networks." *Journal of Computer-Mediated Communication* 14:1–34.

acknowledgments

Chapter 1

page 4: Quotation from Kelsey Timmerman. 2009. *Where Am I Wearing? A Global Tour to the Countries, Factories, and People that Make Our Clothes.* © 2009. Reproduced with permission of John Wiley & Sons, Inc.

page 19: Cartoon by Jim Morin, Miami Herald, Cartoon Arts International Inc.

Chapter 2

page 28: Quotation from Patricia A. Adler and Peter Adler. 2007. "The Demedicalization of Self-Injury: From Psychopathology to Sociological Deviance," *Journal of Contemporary Ethnography* 36, Issue 5, (October 2007):537–570. Copyright © 2007. Reprinted by permission of SAGE Publications.

page 33: Figure 2-4 from Author's analysis of *2009 General Social Survey* in DeNavas-Walt et al. 2009. National Opinion Research Center.

page 34: *Doonesbury* © 1989 G. B. Trudeau. Reprinted with permission of Universal Uclick. All rights reserved.

page 36: Cartoon by F MINUS © 2007 Tony Carrillo. Reprinted by Universal Uclick for UFS. All rights reserved.

page 38: Figure from BabyNameWizard.com, used by permission.

page 42: Figure 2-5 from Henry J. Kaiser Family Foundation. November 2005. Sex on TV 4, Executive Summary; a Biennial Report of the Kaiser Family Foundation (#7399). This information was reprinted with permission from the Henry J. Kaiser Family Foundation. The Kaiser Family Foundation is a non-profit private operating foundation, based in Menlo Park, California, dedicated to producing and communicating the best possible analysis and information on health issues.

page 44: Figure 2-7 from The Gallup poll, October 28, 2010, "New High of 46% of Americans Support Legalizing Marijuana," by Elizabeth Mendes. Copyright © 2010 Gallup, Princeton, NJ. All rights reserved. Reprinted with permission.

page 44: Figure 2-8 from The Gallup poll, October 28, 2010, "New High of 46% of Americans Support Legalizing Marijuana," by Elizabeth Mendes. Copyright © 2010 Gallup, Princeton, NJ. All rights reserved. Reprinted with permission.

Chapter 3

page 52: Quotation from Horace Miner. 1956. "Body Ritual among the Nacirema." *American Anthropologist*, vol. 58 (3), 1956: pp. 503–504. © 1956 American Anthropological Association.

page 56: Figure 3-1 adapted in part from "The State of the World's Children 2009," UNICEF, and in part from "Progress for Children: A World Fit for Children Statistical Review," Number 6, December 2007, UNICEF global databases, UNICEF, NY.

page 65: Figure 3-2 from John H. Pryor, Sylvia Hurtado, Linda DeAngelo, Laura Palucki Blake, and Serge Tran. 2010. *The American Freshman: National Norms for Fall 2007, 2010.* UCLA Higher Education Research Institute. © 2010 The Regents of the University of California. All rights reserved.

page 67: Figure 3-3 adapted from Views on Torture, "World Public Opinion on Torture," June 24, 2008. Reprinted by permission.

Chapter 4

page 76: Quotation from Mary Pattillo-McCoy. 1999. *Black Picket Fences: Privilege and Peril among the Black Middle Class*: 100–102. Copyright 1999. Reprinted by permission of University of Chicago Press.

page 78: Figure 4-1 from Susan Curtiss. 1977. *Genie: A Psycholinguistic Study of a Modern-Day "Wild Child,"* p. 275. Copyright Academic Press 1977. Reprinted with permission of Elsevier.

page 82: Quotation from Daniel Albas and Cheryl Albas. 1988. "Aces and Bombers: The Post-Exam Impression Management Strategies of Students." *Symbolic Interaction,* University of California Press–Journals. Reproduced by permission of the authors.

page 82: Cartoon by Scott Arthur Masear. Reprinted by permission of www.CartoonStock.com.

page 86: Table 4-3 adapted from Jill Suitor, Staci A. Minyard, and Rebecca S. Carter. 2001. "Did You See What I Saw? Gender Difference in Perceptions of Avenues to Prestige among Adolescents," *Sociological Inquiry* 71 (Fall 2001):445, Table 2. University of Texas Press. Wiley-Blackwell Publishing Ltd.

page 87: Cartoon by STAHLER © 2010 Jeff Stahler. Reprinted by Universal Uclick for UFS. All rights reserved.

page 87: Figure 4-2 from Henry J. Kaiser Family Foundation. 2010. Victoria J. Rideout et al., "Generation M^2: Media in the Lives of 8- to 18-Year-Olds," January 2010 (#8010). This information was reprinted with permission from the Henry J. Kaiser Family Foundation. The Kaiser Family Foundation is a non-profit private operating foundation, based in Menlo Park, California, dedicated to producing and communicating the best possible analysis and information on health issues.

page 90: Table 4-4 from Tom Smith. 2003. "Coming of Age in 21st Century America: Public Attitudes Toward the Importance and Timing of Transition to Adulthood." Based on the 2002 General Social Survey of 1,398 people. Used by permission of National Opinion Research Center.

Chapter 5

page 98: Quotation from Philip G. Zimbardo. 2007. *The Lucifer Effect: Understanding How Good People Turn Evil.* Copyright © 2007 by Philip G. Zimbardo, Inc. Used by permission of Random House, Inc. and by the Random House Group Ltd.

page 107: Screen shot from Second Life. Second Life® is a trademark of Linden Research, Inc. Certain materials have been reproduced with the permission of Linden Research, Inc.

page 108: © Dean Vietor/The New Yorker Collection/www.cartoonbank.com.

page 112: Cartoon by Daryl Cagle. © 2004 Daryl Cagle, MSNBC, and Political-Cartoons.com.

Chapter 6

page 118: Quotation from George Ritzer. 2010. *The McDonaldization of Society 6.* Copyright © 2010 by Sage Publications, Inc. Books. Reproduced with permission of Pine Forge Press, a Division of Sage Publications, Inc. via Copyright Clearance Center.

page 120: © Robert Weber/The New Yorker Collection/www.cartoonbank.com.

Chapter 7

page 136: Quotation from David Grazian. 2010. *Mix It Up: Popular Culture, Mass Media, and Society.* Copyright © 2010 by W. W. Norton & Company, Inc. Used by permission of W. W. Norton & Company, Inc.

page 138: Table 7-1 adapted from John B. Horrigan, *A Typology of Information and Communication Technology Users,* May 7, 2007, p. 5–11, www.pewinternet.org/Reports/2007/A-Typology-of-Information-and-Communication-Technology-Users.aspx. Pew Internet & American Life Project.

page 138: Logo used by permission of New York City Department of Health and Mental Hygiene.

page 142: Cartoon by Dana Summers. © Tribune Media Services, Inc. All Rights Reserved. Reprinted with permission.

page 145: Table from World Economic Forum. 2010. *The Global Competitiveness Report 2010–2011.* World Economic Forum, Switzerland. Copyright © 2010 by the World Economic Forum.

page 146: Figure 7-2 adapted from Michael A. Messner, Margaret Carlisle Duncan, and Nicole William. 2006. "The Revolution Is Not Being Televised," *Contexts*, vol. 5, no. 3 (Summer 2006), p. 35. American Sociological Association. © 2006 by SAGE Publications. Reprinted by permission of SAGE Publications.

page 148: Figure 7-4 adapted from Demographics of Internet Users. Based on a November–December 2009 national survey released January 6, 2009, accessed February 7, 2010 at www.pewinternet.org/static-pages/trend-data/whos-online.aspx. Pew Internet & American Life Project.

page 153 :Cartoon by Harley Schwadron. Reprinted with permission.

Chapter 8

page 158: Quotation from Peter Moskos. 2008. *Cop in the Hood: My Year Policing Baltimore's Eastern District.* © 2008 by Princeton University Press. Reprinted by permission of Princeton University Press.

536

Acknowledgments

page 164: Figure from Henry Wechsler et al. 2002. "Trends in College Binge Drinking During a Period of Increased Prevention Efforts," *Journal of American College Health,* 2002, vol. 50(5). Reprinted by permission of the publisher, Taylor & Francis Ltd. http://www.tandf.co.uk/journals.

page 166: Figure 8-1 adapted from NORML 2010. Used by permission of the National Organization for the Reform of Marijuana Laws (NORML).

page 167: Table 8-1 from Robert K. Merton. 1968. *Social Theory and Social Structure,* Revised and Enlarged Edition. Adapted by permission of The Free Press, a Division of Simon & Schuster, Inc. Copyright © 1967, 1968 by Robert K. Merton. Copyright renewed 1985 by Robert K. Merton. All rights reserved.

page 174: Cartoon by Sidney Harris. © ScienceCartoonsPlus.com.

Chapter 9

page 186: Quotation from Barbara Ehrenreich. 2009. "Is It Now a Crime to Be Poor?" *New York Times,* August 9, 2009. From *The New York Times,* © 2009 The New York Times All rights reserved. Used by permission and protected by the Copyright Laws of the U.S. The printing, copying, redistribution, or retransmission of this Content without express written permission is prohibited. And reprinted by permission of International Creative Management, Inc. Copyright © 2009 by Barbara Ehrenreich.

page 191: Cartoon © 2008 Pat Bagley, The Salt Lake Tribune, and Political Cartoons.com.

page 196: Table 9-3 from James. A. Davis and Tom W. Smith. 2009. *General Social Surveys, 1972–2008.* Used by permission of the National Opinion Research Center.

page 204: Cartoon by Matt Davies. © Tribune Media Services, Inc. All Rights Reserved. Reprinted with permission.

page 205: Figure 9-5 from Bhashkar Mazumder. 2008. *Upward Intergenerational Economic Mobility in the United States.* Washington, DC: Economic Mobility Project, An initiative of the Pew Charitable Trusts. Used by permission of Dr. Bhashkar Mazumder.

page 207: Nick Anderson Editorial Cartoon used with the permission of Nick Anderson, the Washington Post Writers Group and the Cartoonist Group. All rights reserved.

Chapter 10

page 214: Quotation from Paul Collier. 2007. *The Bottom Billion: Why the Poorest Countries Are Failing and What Can Be Done About It.* © 2007 Paul Collier. Used with permission of Oxford University Press, UK.

page 215: Figure 10-1 adapted from Bob Sutcliffe. 2002. *100 Ways of Seeing an Unequal World,* Fig 1, p. 18. London: Zed Books. Reprinted by permission.

page 217: Figure 10-2 adapted in part from John R. Weeks. 2012. *Population* 11e. © 2012 Wadsworth, a part of Cengage Learning Inc. Reproduced by permission of www.cengage.com/permissions. And adapted in part from Carl Haub. 2010. *2010 World Population Data Sheet.* Used by permission of Population Reference Bureau.

page 220: Figure 10-4 adapted from World Development Indicators 2010 by the World Bank 2010. Copyright 2010. Used by permission of the International Bank for Reconstruction and Development/World Bank via Copyright Clearance Center.

page 221: Figure 10-5 from Chronic Poverty Research Centre. 2009. Administered by Institute for Development Policy and Management, School of Environment and Development, University of Manchester, UK. Used by permission.

page 222: Figure 10-6 OECD Statistics on Resource Flows to Developing Countries (Feb 2011), Table 1, p. 2. www.oecd.org/dataoecd/53/43/47137659.pdf.

page 224: Figure adapted from Edward Telles. 2004:108. *Race in Another America: The Significance of Skin Color.* Princeton University Press. Reprinted by permission of Princeton University Press.

page 225: Figure 10-7 World Bank. 2010. W*orld Development Indicators 2010.* Copyright 2010. Used by permission of the International Bank for Reconstruction and Development/World Bank via Copyright Clearance Center.

Chapter 11

page 236: Quotation from Helen Zia. 2000. *Asian American Dreams: The Emergence of an American People.* Copyright © 2000 Helen Zia. of Published by Farrar, Straus & Giroux, LLC.

page 240: Nick Anderson Editorial Cartoon used with the permission of Nick Anderson, the Washington Post Writers Group and the Cartoonist Group. All rights reserved.

page 255: Figure 11-6 © 2010 Arab American Institute.

page 260: Cartoon by STEIN © 2006. Reprinted with permission by UNIVERSAL UCLICK for UFS. All rights reserved.

Chapter 12

page 266: Quotation from Nancy J. Finley. 2010. "Skating Femininity: Gender Maneuvering in Women's Roller Derby," *Journal of Contemporary Ethnography,* 39(4):359-360, 371–372, 377. Reprinted by permission of SAGE Publications.

page 268: Table 12-1 from Joyce McCarl Nielsen, et al. 2000. "Gendered Heteronormativity: Empirical Illustrations in Everyday Life," *Sociological Quarterly* 41 (no. 2):287. © 2000. Blackwell Publishing. Reprinted by permission.

page 280: Figure 12-5 from NARAL Pro-Choice America Foundation 2011. Used by permission of NARAL, Washington, DC.

Chapter 13

page 288: Quotation from Ted C. Fishman. 2010. Reprinted with the permission of Scribner, a Division of Simon & Schuster, Inc., from *Shock Of Gray: The Aging Of The World's Population And How It Pits Young against Old, Child against Parent, Worker against Boss, Company against Rival, and Nation against Nation* by Ted C. Fishman. Copyright © 2010 by Ted C. Fishman. All rights reserved.

page 294: © Barbara Smaller/The New Yorker Collection/www.cartoonbank.com.

page 294: Figure 13-2 © AARP. 2006. *Attitudes Toward Work and Job Security.* Washington, DC: AARP, 2006.

page 297: Figure 13-3 from Linda Jacobsen, Mary Kent, Marlene Lee, and Mark Mather, America's Aging Population," *Population Bulletin* 66 (Feb):3. Used by permission of Population Reference Bureau.

Chapter 14

page 306: Quotation from Andrew J. Cherlin. 2009. *The Marriage-Go-Round: The State of Marriage and the Family in America Today.* Copyright © 2009 by Andrew J. Cherlin. Used by permission of Alfred A. Knopf, a division of Random House, Inc.

page 319: Signe Wilkinson Editorial Cartoon used with the permission of Signe Wilkinson, the Washington Post Writers Group and the Cartoonist Group. All rights reserved.

page 323: Cartoon by Harley Schwadron. Reprinted with permission.

Chapter 15

page 330: Quotation from Nikki Bado-Fralick and Rebecca Sachs Norris. 2010. *Toying with God: The World of Religious Games and Dolls,* pp. 7–8, 29–30. © 2010. Reprinted by permission of Baylor University Press.

page 333: Figure 15-1 from The Pew Forum on Religion and Public Life, Religious Knowledge Quiz, September 28, 2010, http://features.pewforum.org/quiz/us-religious-knowledge. Pew Internet & American Life Project.

page 337 Cartoon © 2007 Riber Hansson, www.PoliticalCartoons.com.

page 344: Cartoon © 2005 Sandy Huffaker, www.PoliticalCartoons.com.

Chapter 16

page 350: Quotation from Diane Ravitch. 2010. *The Death and Life of the Great American School System: How Testing and Choice are Undermining Education.* Copyright © 2010 Diane Ravitch. Reprinted by permission of Basic Books, a member of the Perseus Books Group.

page 352: Google logo © Google Inc.

page 354: Cartoon by Kirk Anderson. Used by permission of Kirk Anderson, www.kirktoons.com.

page 364: Figure 16-7 from National Alliance for Public Charter Schools. (2011). *The Public Charter Schools Dashboard.* Washington, DC: NAPCS.

Chapter 17

page 370: Quotation from Martin P. Wattenberg. 2008. *Is Voting for Young People?* pp. 1–2, 3. Copyright © 2008 by Pearson Education, Inc. Reprinted by permission. Users may not reproduce copies without permission of Pearson Education.

page 372: Figure 17-1 adapted from OpenNet Initiative 2011. Copyright © The OpenNet Initiative 2011. All rights reserved.

page 378: Figure 17-3 adapted from Inter-Parliamentary Union (IPU), 2011, Women in National Parliaments, www.ipu.org/wmn-e/classif.htm. Used by permission.

page 379: Figure 17-4 (right) from G. William Domhoff. 2010. *Who Rules America*, 6e. © 2010 by The McGraw-Hill Companies, Inc. Reproduced by permission.

page 382: Figure 17-5 Military and National Defense from The Gallup Poll. Copyright © 2009 The Gallup Organization, Princeton, NJ. All rights reserved. Reprinted with permission.

page 383: Figure 17-6, 2010 Global Peace Index, Institute for Economics and Peace.

page 386: Cartoon by STEIN © 2010 Ed Stein. Reprinted with permission by UNIVERSAL UCLICK for UFS. All rights reserved.

Chapter 18

page 392: Quotation from John Bowes (ed.). 2011. *The Fair Trade Revolution,* pp. ix, 2–3, 231–232, Pluto Press. Reprinted by permission of Pluto Press.

page 396: Figure from S. Acharya. 2000. In Mahbub ul Haq Human Development Centre, *Human Development in South Asia 2000: The Gender Question,* p. 54. Oxford University Press, Karachi.

page 398: Cartoon by Mike Thompson, Detroit Free Press.

page 401: Quotation from Sheryl Stolberg. 1995. "Affirmative Action Gains Often Come at a High Cost," *Los Angeles Times,* March 29, 1995:A14. Copyright © 1995 Los Angeles Times. Reprinted by permission.

page 401: Cartoon © 2003 Mike Keefe, The Denver Post, www.PoliticalCartoons.com.

Chapter 19

page 410: Quotation from Andrew Szasz. 2007. *Shopping Our Way to Safety.* University of Minnesota Press. Copyright 2007 by the Regents of the University of Minnesota.

page 412: Figure 19-1 from Carl Haub. 2010. *World Population Data Sheet 2010.* Used by permission of Population Reference Bureau.

page 416: Figure 19-2 from UNAIDS. 2010. Adapted from Global report: UNAIDS report on the global AIDS Epidemic 2010. Copyright © 2010 Joint UN Program on HIV/AIDS (UNAIDS). All rights reserved. Courtesy UNAIDS, Geneva, Switzerland.

page 419: © Michael Maslin/The New Yorker Collection/www.cartoonbank.com.

page 426: Signe Wilkinson Editorial Cartoon used with the permission of Signe Wilkinson, the Washington Post Writers Group and the Cartoonist Group. All rights reserved.

page 427: Quotation from Neil B. Thompson. 1972. Reprinted from *Natural History,* December 1972; copyright © Natural History Magazine, Inc. 1972.

page 428: Cartoon by Joseph Farris. Reprinted by permission of Miller-McCune and Joseph Farris. www.josephfarris.com.

page 429: Figure 19-6 from the Washington Post © 2007 The Washington Post. All rights reserved. Used by permission and protected by the Copyright Laws of the U.S. The printing, copying, redistribution, or retransmission of the Material without express written permission is prohibited. http://www.washingtonpost.com.

page 431: Figure 19-7 from Jeffrey M. Jones. 2011. "Americans Increasingly Prioritize Economy Over Environment," March 17, 2011, from The Gallup Poll. Copyright © 2011 The Gallup Organization, Princeton, NJ. All rights reserved. Reprinted with permission.

page 431: Figure 19-8 Adapted from OECD. 2009. "Green at Fifteen?: How 15-Year-Olds Perform in Environmental Science and Geoscience in PISA 2006," p. 40, www.oecd.org/pisa.

Chapter 20

page 438: Quotation from John D. Kasarda and Greg Lindsay. 2010. *Aerotropolis: The Way We'll Live Next.* New York: Farrar, Straus & Giroux.

page 440: Cartoon by Manny Francisco © 2008 www.PoliticalCartoons.com.

page 448: Table 20-2 Based on Gideon Sjoberg. 1960. *The Preindustrial City: Past and Present*:323–328. Adapted with permission of The Free Press, a Division of Simon & Schuster Adult Publishing Group. Copyright © 1960 by The Free Press. Copyright © renewed 1968 by Gideon Sjoberg. All rights reserved. And based on E. Barbara Phillips. 1996. *City Lights: Urban-Suburban Life in the Global Society*, 2/e. Copyright © 1981 by E. Barbara Phillips and Richard T. LeGates, 1996 by E. Barbara Phillips. Oxford University Press. Used by permission.

page 449: Figure 20-4 adapted from *National Geographic Atlas of the World,* 8e. National Geographic Society, 2005. National Geographic Society, 2005. NG Maps/National Geographic Stock.

page 449: Figure 20-5 adapted from Chauncy Harris and Edward Ullmann. 1945. "The Nature of Cities," *Annals of the American Academy of Political and Social Science,* 242 (November):13. Reprinted by permission of American Academy of Political and Social Science, Philadelphia.

Chapter 21

page 462: Quotation from Gary Alan Fine and Bill Ellis. 2011. *The Global Grapevine: Why Rumors of Terrorism, Immigrations, and Trade Matter,* Oxford University Press. © 2011 Gary Alan Fine and Bill Ellis. Used with permission of Oxford University Press, UK.

page 472: Illustration reprinted by permission of the publisher from John B. Christiansen and Sharon N. Barnartt, *Deaf President Now! The 1988 Revolution at Gallaudet University* (Washington, DC: Gallaudet University Press, 1995), p. 22. Copyright 1995 by Gallaudet University.

page 477: Table 21-3 adapted from Karen Meyer, "Match the Disability." April 30, 2007. Chicago: DePaul University. Reproduced with permission.

Chapter 22

page 484: Quotation from Nick Bilton. 2010. *I Live in the Future & Here's How It Works: Why Your World, Work, and Brain are Being Creatively Disrupted.* Copyright © 2010 by Nick Bilton. Used by permission of Crown Business, a division of Random House, Inc.

page 491: Cartoon by Baloo, from *The Wall Street Journal,* permission Cartoon Features Syndicate.

page 496: Figure 22-1 adapted from *National Geographic Atlas of the World,* 8e. National Geographic Society, 2005. National Geographic Society, 2005. NG Maps/National Geographic Stock.

Trendspotting

Chapter 2, page 33: Bureau of the Census 2004b; El Nasser and Overburg 2009; Nordholt et al. 2004. Chapter 3, page 61: American Community Survey 2010, Table 1602; Link et al. 2006; Siegal et al. 2001; United Way of King County 2010. Chapter 4, page 79: Knopmen et al 2010; Martin et al. 2009; National Organization of Mothers of Twins Clubs 2010. Chapter 5, page 106: Economist 2010a; Facebook 2011; Haub 2010; Schonfeld 2010. Chapter 6, page 125: Bonikowski and McPherson 2006; NORC 2010. Chapter 7, page 147: Rainie et al. 2003; Pew Internet and American Life Project 2009. Chapter 8, page 165: Bureau of Justice Statistics 2010; International Centre for Prison Studies 2010; Sabol et al. 2009. Chapter 9, page 198: Cauchon 2009; Hartmann et al. 2010; Institute for Women's Policy Research 2009. Chapter 10, page 216: Bureau of the Census 2008b; *The Economist* 2011a; *The Week* 2011. Chapter 11, page 242: Alliance for Board Diversity 2008. Chapter 12, page 278: Bureau of the Census 2009a:378. Chapter 13, page 299: Bureau of Labor Statistics 2008b, 2010, Toossi 2009. Chapter 14, page 312: Kershaw 2009; Minyard and Ortyl 2010; Proulx et al. 2006. Chapter 15, page 332: Baker and Smith 2009; Kosmin et al. 2009; Lalli 2009. Chapter 16, page 355: Aud et al. 2010. Chapter 17, p. 374: Freedom House 2011. Chapter 18, page 393: Bureau of Labor Statistics 2009. Chapter 19, page 420: InTouch Health 2010; Laermer 2002:191–195. Chapter 20, page 452: J. Goldstone 2010. Chapter 21, page 469: Newport and Saad 2011. Chapter 22, page 488: Arias 2010: Table 12; Bureau of the Census 2010a: Table 102.

photo credits

name index

THE WORLD AS A VILLAGE

Imagine that the Earth is a village of only 1,000 people rather than a world with over 6.7 billion inhabitants. Though it would not be easy to walk the Earth and get a sense of its many cultures and societies, you could walk through a village of 1,000 people and get a feeling for the diversity there.

Here Is What You Would See:

280 people under the age of 15, **70** people over the age of 65

140 with no access to improved water supplies

470 people living on less than $2 a day, **140** of whom live on less than a $1 a day

496 people who are female, **504** people who are male

333 Christians (**170** of them Roman Catholic), **210** Muslims, **132** Hindus, **63** Buddhists, **112** followers of other faiths, **117** nonreligious, **23** atheists

134 people speaking Mandarin, **62** people speaking Hindi, **50** people speaking Spanish, **48** people speaking English, **29** people speaking Arabic, **27** people speaking Portuguese, **26** people speaking Russian, **26** people speaking Bengali, **598** people speaking other languages as their first language

122 illiterate adults (out of a total of **720** adults)

1 physician and **3** hospital beds

540 with no access to improved sanitation facilities

118 automobiles, **890** televisions, **200** telephones, **510** cellular phones, **150** personal computers, **105** different newspapers, **23** iPods

And if you came back in a year there would be **1,012** people in the village.

See Acknowledgments for source information.

Applications of *Sociology's* Major Theoretical Approaches

Sociology provides comprehensive coverage of the major sociological perspectives. This summary table includes a sample of the topics in the text that have been explored using the major approaches. The numbers in parentheses indicate the pertinent chapters.

FUNCTIONALIST PERSPECTIVE

Defined and explained (1)
Adoption (14)
AIDS epidemic (19)
Anomie theory of deviance (8)
Bilingualism (3)
Bureaucratization of schools (16)
Campaign financing (17)
Charter schools (16)
Cow worship in India (1)
Culture (3, 16)
Davis and Moore's view of stratification (9)
Death penalty (8)
Disengagement theory of aging (13)
Dominant ideology (3)
Durkheim's view of deviance (8)
Dysfunctions of racism (11)
Ethnocentrism (3)
Family (14)
Formal organizations (6)
Functions of dying (13)
Functions of racism (11)
Gans's functions of poverty (9)
Gay marriage (14)
Gender stratification (12)
Global immigration (11)
Gulf Coast oil spill (1)
Health and illness (19)
Human ecology (19, 20)
In-groups and out-groups (6)
Inauguration of President Barack Obama (5)
Integrative function of religion (15)
Media and social norms (7)
Media and socialization (7)
Media and status conferral (7)
Media concentration (7)
Media promotion of consumption (7)
Modernization theory (10)
Multinational corporations (10)
Narcotizing effect of the media (7)
Racial prejudice and discrimination (11)
Rumors (21)
Social change (16, 22)
Social control (8, 16)
Social institutions (5)
Socialization function of religion (15)
Socialization in schools (4, 16)
Subcultures (3)
Transnationals (22)
Urban ecology (20)

CONFLICT PERSPECTIVE

Defined and explained (1)
Abortion (12)
Access to health care (19)
Access to technology (22)
Affirmative action (18)
Age stratification (13)
AIDS epidemic (19)
Bilingualism (3)
Bureaucratization of schools (16)
Campaign financing (17)
Capitalism (15, 18)
Charter schools (16)
Corporate welfare (9)
Correspondence principle (16)
Credentialism (16)
Culture (3)
Day care funding (4)
Death penalty (8)
Deviance (8)
Disability as a master status (5)
Disability rights (21)
Dominant ideology (3, 7, 9)
Downsizing (18)
Elite model of the U.S. power structure (17)
Environmental issues (19)
Environmentalism (19)
Exploitation theory of discrimination (11)
Family (14)
Gay marriage (14)
Gender equity in education (16)
Gender stratification (12)
Global immigration (11)
Gulf Coast oil spill (1)
Hidden curriculum (16)
Iron Law of Oligarchy (6)
Labor unions (6)
Marx's view of stratification (9)
Matrix of domination (12)
Media concentration (7)
Media gatekeeping (7)
Media stereotypes (7)
Medicalization of society (19)
Microfinancing (18)
Model minority (11)
Multinational corporations (10)
New urban sociology (20)
Poverty (9)
Privacy and technology (22)
Racism and health (19)
Religion and social control (15)
Religion as a source of social support (15)
Right to die (13)
School violence (16)
Social change (22)
Social control (8)
Social institutions (5)
Socialization in schools (4)
Subcultures (3)
Tracking (16)
Transnationals (22)
Victimless crimes (8)
White-collar crime (8)
World systems analysis (10, 20, 22)

INTERACTIONIST PERSPECTIVE

Defined and explained (1)
Activity theory of aging (13)
Adoption (14)
Affirmative action (18)
AIDS epidemic (19)
Campaign financing (17)
Charismatic authority (17)
Commuter behavior (1)
Conspicuous consumption (9)
Contact hypothesis (11)
Culture (3)
Differential association (8)
Disability rights (21)
Dramaturgical approach (4, 17)
Electronic communication (7)
Family (14)
Gay marriage (14)
Gender stratification (12)
Gulf Coast oil spill (1)
Health and illness (19)
Human relations approach (6)

Influence of social media sites on politics (17)
Media concentration (7)
Microfinancing (18)
Obedience (8)
Presentation of the self (4)
Routine activities theory (8)
Small groups (6)
Social disorganization theory (8)
Social institutions (5)
Tattoo symbols of 9/11 (1)
Teacher-expectancy effect (16)
Teenage pregnancy (14)
Transnationals (22)
Unions (6)
Vested interests in NASA's Constellation Project (22)

FEMINIST PERSPECTIVE

Defined and explained (1)
Day care funding (4)
Deviance (8)
Dominant ideology (3)
Ethnographic research (2)
Family (14)
Gender gap in education (16)
Gender stratification (12)
Gulf Coast oil spill (1)
Language (3)
Matrix of domination (12)
Media stereotypes (7)
Microfinancing (18)
Pornography (7)
Rape (8)
Religion and social control (15)
Research methodology (2)
School violence (16)
Victimless crimes (8)
Women's movement (12)

LABELING THEORY

Defined and explained (8)
AIDS epidemic (19)
Disabilities and labeling (5)
Disability rights (21)
Health and illness (19)
Mental illness (19)
Profiling at airports (11)
Racial profiling (8)
Sexual deviance (8)
Societal reaction approach (8)
Teacher-expectancy effect (16)
Victimless crimes (8)

Coverage of Race and Ethnicity, Gender, and Social Class

Sociology provides comprehensive coverage of race and ethnicity, gender, and social class and of the intersection of those variables. This summary table includes a sample of the related topics in the text. The dots that precede the entries indicate the type of coverage:

- RACE AND ETHNICITY
- GENDER
- SOCIAL CLASS

CHAPTER 1
- Class conflict
- Community health care
- Elijah Anderson
- Gender and talkativeness
- Gender and the 2004 tsunami
- Haiti earthquake
- Hurricane Katrina
- Ida Wells-Barnett
- W. E. B. DuBois
- Working poor

CHAPTER 2
- Gender and sexually explicit language
- Gender stereotyping in children's books
- Sexual behavior in China
- Televised sports coverage

CHAPTER 3
- Culture and values
- Cultural genocide
- Culture and food
- Ethnicity and language
- Ethnicity and nonverbal communication
- Ethnocentrism in education
- Gender and language
- Indian call center subculture
- Indigenous peoples of Brazil
- Linguistic isolation among immigrants
- Race and language
- Walmart in Germany

CHAPTER 4
- Black middle class
- Gender roles
- Race and socialization
- Rites of passage
- Socialization of Amish children

CHAPTER 5
- Cultural differences in social interaction
- Ethnicity and role strain
- Gender and social institutions
- Navajo justice
- Race and social institutions
- Race as a master status

CHAPTER 6
- Gender and formal organizations
- Marx and alienation
- Social policy and unions

CHAPTER 7
- Al Jazeera
- Coverage of women's sports
- Digital divide
- Ethnic stereotypes
- Gender and online gaming
- Gender stereotypes
- Pornography
- Race and audience perceptions
- Racial minorities in reality TV
- Social media use during Arab Spring

CHAPTER 8
- Differential justice
- Ethnicity and deviance
- Gender and deviance
- Race and the death penalty
- Race in Milgram's obedience experiment
- Racial profiling
- Social class and deviant identity
- White-collar crime

CHAPTER 9
- Entire chapter
- Caste system in India
- Ethnicity and wealth
- Feminization of poverty
- Gender and income
- Gender and social class
- Gender and social mobility
- Hurricane Katrina aftermath
- Poverty in U.S. and Congo
- Race and poverty
- Race and social mobility
- Race and wealth
- Shrinking middle class
- Social class and financial aid

CHAPTER 10
- Ethnic cleansing
- Ethnicity, wealth, and poverty
- Gender and social mobility
- Multinational corporations
- Race and social class in Mexico
- Stratification in Mexico

CHAPTER 11
- Entire chapter
- Aboriginal people of Australia
- Affirmative action
- Asian Indians
- Central and South Americans
- Economic status of racial/ethnic groups
- Ethnic inequality
- Expulsion of ethnic Roma from France
- Global immigration
- Latino voting patterns
- Multiple racial/ethnic identities
- Race relations as a zero sum game
- White privilege

CHAPTER 12
- Entire chapter
- Attitudes toward a female boss
- Bias against female board members
- Cross-cultural perspective on gender
- Gender and human sexuality
- Gender inequality in housework
- Iraqi girls
- Matrix of domination
- Muslim women
- Sex discrimination
- Symbolic meaning of Muslim headscarf

CHAPTER 13
- Fulani and aging
- Native Americans and death
- Race and aging
- Sherpas and aging
- Social class and aging

CHAPTER 14
- Arranged marriage
- Divorce in South Korea
- Ethnic differences in family life
- Gay marriage
- Households in which women earn more than their husbands
- Interracial marriage
- Male dominance of family
- Navajo family
- Polygamy among the Nyinba
- Racial differences in family life
- Single fathers
- Single-parent families by racial/ethnic group
- Social class differences in family life

CHAPTER 15
- Islam in the United States
- Muslim hajj
- Religion and economic progress
- Religion and social change
- Religion and social class
- Religion in India

CHAPTER 16
- Black students at White universities
- *Brown v. Board of Education* legacy
- College enrollment among racial minorities and women
- Educational inequality
- Gender equity in education
- Gender gap in education
- Schooling of girls in developing nations
- Title IX

CHAPTER 17
- Gender quotas
- Native Hawaiian sovereignty movement
- Power elite
- Race and gender in politics
- Women in politics
- Women in uniform

CHAPTER 18
- Affirmative action
- Capitalism in China
- Informal economy
- Microfinancing
- Racial/ethnic composition of labor force
- Worker alienation
- Working women in China and Nepal

CHAPTER 19
- Cultural beliefs of immigrants
- Doctor-nurse relationship
- Environmental justice
- Folk remedies
- Gender and health
- Navajo medicine
- Racial/ethnic population and hazardous waste sites
- Racism and health
- Social class and health